The Study of Economics

Principles, Concepts & Applications

Sixth Edition

authors

Turley Mings
Dr. Turley Mings received his undergraduate degree in economics from Occidental College and his Ph.D. in economics from the University of California at Berkeley. He is Professor Emeritus of economics at San Jose State University where he taught the introductory course for 30 years. He served as director of the Center for Economic Education for 20 years, developing strategies for teaching economics and conducting in-service workshops at all levels.

Matthew Marlin
Dr. Matthew Marlin received his Ph.D. in economics from Florida State University. He is a professor of economics at Duquesne University in Pittsburgh, where he has taught since 1987. He has served as the associate director of Duquesne's Center for Economic Education and is the founder and director of the School of Business Study Abroad program. During his almost 20 years in academia he has published a number of articles in the areas of economic development and municipal bond markets. His current interests include forensic economics, foreign economies, and a good game of chess.

*For Kurt Rethwisch, who completed
my education in economics*

The Study of
Economics

Principles, Concepts & Applications

Sixth Edition

CONNECT**TEXT**

Turley Mings

Matthew Marlin

Dushkin/McGraw-Hill

A Division of The **McGraw-Hill** Companies

Dushkin/McGraw-Hill

A Division of The **McGraw·Hill** *Companies*

THE STUDY OF ECONOMICS: PRINCIPLES, CONCEPTS & APPLICATIONS

This book is printed on acid-free paper.

ISBN 0–07–366242–9

Vice President and Publisher *Jeffrey L. Hahn*
Editors *Theodore Knight, Ava Suntoke*
Production Manager *Brenda S. Filley*
Director of Technology *Jonathan Stowe*
Technology Development Editor *Marcuss Oslander*
Web Developer *Shawn Callahan*
Design and Production *Karen Slaght & Associates*
Permissions Editor *Rose Gleich*

Manufactured in compliance with NASTA specifications.
Compositor: *Shepherd Inc.*
Typeface: *10/12 Galliard*
Printer: *Quebecor, Dubuque, IA*
Cover design: *Rokusek Design*

Library of Congress Catalog Card Number: 98-74979

Printed in the United States of America

2 3 4 5 6 QBCQBC 4 3 2 1 0

http://www.mhhe.com

preface

In some ways, the sixth edition of *The Study of Economics* is very similar to prior editions, and in some ways it is very different. The book retains the basic features that have characterized it since the first edition: the presentation of economic concepts within the context of articles dealing with the real world that begin every chapter, the use of case applications to further enhance real world applicability, and the consistent grouping of concepts in three or four sections in each chapter. There are, of course, new topics in these articles and case applications, including the Southeast Asian financial crisis, Islamic economics, the tobacco settlement, the transition of the former communist countries, privatization of Social Security, the economic impact of the Internet, the euro, intellectual property rights, and an overall increased emphasis on global issues.

ConnecText

The biggest difference between this and prior editions is the incorporation of interactive exercises through the ConnectText Web site accompanying this text. Relevant activities are marked with a "Webby mouse" icon. No matter how current the information in a textbook is when it is written, there is no way that some of it can escape being out of date by the time it reaches the student's hands. The Internet allows us to overcome this problem by enabling us to provide extensions to the cases and articles, to update the data presented in the text's graphs and tables, and to present new cases and analyses as our fast changing world evolves. For example, the opening article to chapter 8 discusses the potential role to be played by the telephone, cable, and Internet companies in providing information on the "Superhighway." It was current when written, but since that time the merger between AT&T and TCI has shaken things up. Through the Internet, we can extend the article and update the saga as it develops.

The capabilities of Internet technology also permit interaction between students and instructors. The instructor can design interactive exercises and assign homework problems that can be submitted via e-mail. Despite being in its infancy, the Internet is already changing the delivery format of instructional materials. How it will change in the years between this and the seventh edition is anybody's guess. To confront this unknown, our Web site will be continually updated between now and the publication of that seventh edition—not only in terms of the content, but also in the technology with which it is delivered.

User-Friendly Approach

A basic principle of learning theory is that the learner needs familiar intellectual pegs on which to hang unfamiliar ideas. This is important in a field like economics where abstraction and confusing graphs often lead to the student missing the forest because of all the effort required to learn the trees. The use of familiar topics in the opening articles and case applications is one way in which we do this. For example, the concepts of specialization and the gains from trade are introduced in chapter 3 through a discussion of the evolution of the electric guitar and amplified music. Whenever possible, the topics are those that are of interest to high school seniors and college students—hamburgers, music, bikes, cars, and computers.

A second way that we have made the material more "user friendly" is by avoiding excessive graphical analysis. It is often alleged that economics is the only discipline in which we have tried to teach everything we know about the subject in the beginning course. The rule in this text has been to include only those tools of economic analysis that will be useful to students in understanding the world around them. The book avoids purely technical devices that are relevant for business or economics majors but have no immediate value to beginning students or nonmajors. When a simple model serves as well to explain a set of relationships, it has been used in place of a more complicated model. An example is the use of the GDP tank model in chapter 12 rather than the abstract Keynesian cross diagram. Also missing from this edition are the discussion of marginal utility and a presentation of the Viner cost curves. While the former is essential for understanding advanced economic analysis, it is not necessary at this level. Likewise, the average, marginal, and total cost curves are not really needed to understand the basic idea that price minus cost equals profit.

The only "traditional" economic graphs that remain in the text are the circular flow model, and of course, supply and demand. Removing other graphs does not reduce the rigor of the text. If the student can leave the course understanding the significance of market allocation through reliance on supply and demand, they will have learned a great deal. To that end, those graphs that remain are emphasized not only in the text, but in the Web site as well.

Although the text makes extensive use of the case applications, it would be a mistake to categorize *The Study of Economics* as a casebook. It presents economic theory in as systematic a framework of organization as more traditional texts. Each of the major areas of economics is discussed thoroughly, starting with economic methods and fundamental choices about the use of scarce resources (chapters 1–4). It then moves on to deal with the microeconomic topics of markets, consumers, businesses, industrial organization and performance, the role of government in influencing resource allocation, and the distribution of income in chapters 5–9. Macroeconomics—money, public finance, national income, inflation, unemployment, and stabilization policies are covered in chapters 10–14. Global economic issues such as international trade, the balance of payments, exchange rates, the transition from communism to capitalism, and the problems of the less developed countries are discussed in the final four chapters. While microeconomics is presented first in the text's organization, macroeconomics can just as easily be covered before microeconomics without any loss in student comprehension.

◤ Case Applications

In this edition, 14 case applications have been labeled "comparative" and consider foreign economies and international issues in whole or in part.

The questions following each case application and the study questions at the end of each chapter are designed to be useful for class discussion, either as a whole class with the teacher leading the discussion, or in small discussion groups. Although every question cannot be addressed, the authors can contribute to the discussion via e-mail on the Web site.

There is a consistent pattern for the questions that follow each case application. The first question of the three is one that a student who has read the material should not have too much difficulty in answering. Taxonomically, the first question is a concept recognition/simple application question. The second question is generally more difficult, requiring analytical thinking. It is a complex application/analysis type question. The third question is an open-ended question involving the student's own personal belief system and attitudes as well as the concepts presented in the text. These questions are of the integrative/valuation type. Most of the case applications also have an Internet-based question that will involve the student in doing his or her own current research into the issue. The instructor might ask the students to complete this research before having them answer the more opinion-laden third question. Doing so helps to develop the scientific link between hypotheses and conclusions.

◤ Ancillary Materials

In addition to the Web site, supplementary materials include an instructor's guide (*Teaching and Testing from The Study of Economics*), a student workbook (*Working with The Study of Economics*), a test-generating program, and a PowerPoint presentation. The instructor's guide includes an additional discussion of the text presentation, teaching strategies, suggested answers to all the analysis and study questions at the end of each chapter of the text, and schematic outlines for each chapter. The student workbook contains review exercises, additional case applications, with questions for each section of each chapter, self-test multiple-choice questions, and schematic outlines of every chapter section.

As a total package, *The Study of Economics* and the supplementary materials that accompany it achieves two interrelated objectives: it makes learning economics interesting and easy for the student, and it makes teaching economics much easier for the instructor.

Turley Mings
Matthew Marlin

contents in brief

CONNECTEXT

Please visit the Web site of
The Study of Economics
Principles, Concepts & Applications, Sixth Edition, at

http://www.dushkin.com/connectext/econ/

to access the Web connections
that complement the text.

contents

Unit One

Foundations   2

Unit Two

Microeconomics 118

Unit Three

Macroeconomics   256

Unit Four

World Economics   410

Welcome to the study of economics. We hope that you will find it interesting and worthwhile; we have done our best to make it so. Interest in economics is higher today than it has ever been, at least since the Depression era of the 1930s. Today's daily newspapers, weekly newsmagazines, nightly newscasts, and the World Wide Web are full of reporting on the latest domestic and world economic developments and what these developments mean for us.

In order to help you gain an economic understanding of current events and problems, we have incorporated many applications of economic concepts in the text. The applications are continuously interwoven with the explanations of economic principles to make it easier for you to see the relevance of these ideas and to make it more interesting. Economics sometimes has the reputation of being a difficult, dull, and abstract subject. We hope that this book will convince you that this doesn't have to be the case. Certainly economics is complicated, but by taking it one step at a time and being clear on just what each idea means and how it is used, you can enjoy it, master it, and find it useful.

What is economics? One definition is, "Economics is the social science concerned with how resources are used to satisfy people's wants." The subject matter of economics is divided into two major fields. One deals with the individual units in an economy, the individual businesses, workers, consumers, and so forth. This is called **microeconomics** because it takes a detailed look at the economic decisions made by individuals, businesses, and governments, and how these decisions influence prices, output, and the efficient use of a country's resources. The other major area is **macroeconomics,** which deals with the broad measurements of economic activity such as the average price level, employment, and total output. *The Study of Economics* is divided into 4 parts. The first part consists of 4 chapters on the fundamentals of economics. This is fol-lowed by 5 chapters on microeconomics, 5 chapters on macroeconomics, and 4 chapters on the world economy.

The organization of each chapter of the text follows a consistent pattern, and each part of the chapter has a specific function. New to this edition, there are Web icons through-out the text that correspond to pages on the text's accompanying Web site. These pages provide a variety of different activities related to the material presented in that portion of the text. Some activities are designed to update cases and data, some to provide interactive exercises to help you master certain concepts, some to find out *your* opinion on controversial economic issues. The Web site also contains practice quizzes, useful links, and other materials to help you in your study of economics. It also gives us a means to keep economic data up to date. An economic analysis of current events is a weekly feature.

Each chapter opens with an interactive *Web survey*—questions designed to make you think about some of the things we are going to talk about. The introductory article features an event or problem related to the economic topics covered in the chapter. Chapter 3, for example, which deals with specialization and economic systems, begins with an article about how specialization has changed the way guitars are made, and how technology is changing the entire music industry. The economic concepts that explain how specialization leads to an increased output of goods and services in an economy are introduced. The introductory articles conclude with a preview of the content of the chapter and a set of learning objectives that give you an idea of the main ideas in the chapter. After reading each article, you can go to the chapter's *Article Extension* on the Web site and find out more, or updated, information about the article's topic. For example, the Article Extension for chapter 3 discusses the impact of MP3s on the recording industry. This probably will change over time as we keep you up to date on the economics of technology in the music industry. The next feature of the chapters is one that we hope you will enjoy. These pointed (and, we hope, amusing) cartoons relate the topic of the introductory article to the economic content of the body of the chapter.

The economic topics of the chapter are broken down into 3 or 4 *analysis sections,* each headed by an organizing question, such as *Why are economic systems needed?* Each of these sections is further subdivided into discussions of the individual concepts that are relevant to answering the organizing question. The contents explained under the above question are *specialization, comparative advantage,* and *interdependence.* Each analysis section also has an Internet site, *EconExplorer.* EconExplorer is where you will find exercises, updates, and links that make the concepts in that section more alive for you. When new concepts and unfamiliar terms are introduced, they are put in **bold face** type in the text, as microeconomics and macroeconomics are above, and defined in the *in-text glossary.* There is also an *end-of-the-book glossary,* keyed to the text pages and arranged alphabetically, incorporating all of these terms. For your fun and convenience the Web site has this glosssary in an interactive form.

Each analysis concludes with a short case that illustrates the application of the concepts covered in the section. Recognizing the increased importance of the world economy to our own, many of the case applications in this edition are *comparative cases* that compare the United States to foreign countries or an international issue. And again, we will take advantage of the Internet to update cases, provide you with sources for further research, and get your opinion about some very controversial issues.

Following each case application are 3 questions that ask you to apply the economic concepts in the preceding section to the case application. The first of the 3 questions should be fairly easy for you to answer if you have read the section carefully. The second question will usually be somewhat more difficult, requiring you to employ your reasoning powers in applying economic concepts. Question 3 calls for your opinion based on your own attitudes and judgments, as well as what you have learned about the topic. We hope you'll take the time to share your opinions with us via the Internet, and we in turn, will provide you with survey results which will allow you to compare your answers with those of other students.

There is a *Putting It Together* summary of the chapter's principal economic ideas at the end of each chapter. There is also an essay on some *perspective* of the topic covered in the chapter from the viewpoint of an influential economist or from a relevant historical event that has shaped our view. The chapters then conclude with the *For Further Study and Analysis* section that includes study questions, analytical exercises, and references to books and Web sites for pursuing the material in more depth. The study questions are not review questions as such, but are intended to expand and reinforce your understanding of the material and, where appropriate, to give you a chance to apply it in your own locality.

Also available is a student study guide, *Working with the Study of Economics,* that contains review exercises, additional applications, practice questions, and a schematic outline of each section of the chapters. To get the most out of reading the text, it is recommended that you look over the schematic outline of a chapter section before you read it and then review the outline when you have finished reading the section.

The introductory articles and the case applications in the chapters are similar to those reported on in the news media. They have been selected with two things in mind: their interest and relevance and their suitability for applying the economic concepts in the chapter. In some cases, the names of the people and their experiences are composites of the experiences of different individuals and do not refer to an actual person.

We hope that you will look for opportunities to apply the economic understandings you gain from this book to stories currently in the news. There is a valuable collection of analytical tools in the intellectual toolbox of economics that, once you have learned how to use them, can be applied to the understanding of new problems as they arise. The trick is to recognize which tools of analysis are useful for a particular problem. The knowledge and practice that you get from this book should enable you to do that.

Unit One

Foundations

The foundations of economics are the ideas that form the basis of the discipline. They are fundamental to the different areas of economic applications.

chapter one
Economic Methods

Economics is a social science that is concerned with how resources are used to satisfy people's wants. By use of the scientific method and economic reasoning, economics enables us to understand and deal with problems that arise. The economics discipline has a set of factual and theoretical tools to apply to the solution of those problems. Descriptive charts and analytical diagrams are particularly useful tools in economics.

chapter two
Economic Choices

Scarcity of resources relative to our needs and wants requires that we make choices about the alternative uses of those resources. In allocating resources, an economy must resolve the basic economic questions of what, how, and for whom to produce. Societies make choices in accordance with certain economic and socioeconomic goals.

chapter three
The Economic System

Societies need a system to organize and coordinate economic activities in an efficient way. This makes the different elements in an economy interdependent. There are three principal types of economic systems, but modern economies are a mixture. The U.S. economy is predominantly market-directed.

chapter four
Market Pricing

In a market system, prices are determined by the demand for and the supply of goods and services. At the equilibrium price there is no shortage or surplus. If the conditions that determine demand or supply change, the equilibrium price and the quantity bought and sold will change.

chapter one

Economic Methods

The study of economics involves a special way of looking at the world around us and the way things work. This approach has been described as "the economic way of thinking." Once learned, it comes in handy in dealing with many types of situations, even some that are not necessarily thought of as being "economics." On the face of it, the subject of the introductory article for this first chapter might include some things that seem to be noneconomic in nature, such as the issues of water pollution and insecticides. But, as we shall see, such issues are as much in the realm of economics as is the question of whether to grow grapes or to raise fish.

▶ An Apple a Day

When Richard Hernandez and his wife, Maria, step out of their Northern California home each morning, they are greeted by the sight of their 250 acres of apple trees. It is only May, but the apples are beginning to form on the trees, and they must begin to plan the harvest that will occur sometime in September or October, depending on the weather.

If all goes well, Richard and Maria hope to harvest and sell about 1,000 tons of Granny Smith apples. This will earn them enough income to pay the mortgage on their orchard, make the payments on their truck and tractor, pay for fertilizer and insecticides, and hire enough workers to help them pick the apples once they are ripe. In addition, the tractor is 7 years old, and they realize that because it will not last forever, they must put away some money each year to pay for repairs and eventually buy a new tractor. Any money left over is theirs to keep to pay for their living expenses. The size of the harvest and the price that they get for their apples will determine if there is enough for a new car or television, or if the old car and TV will have to last another year.

In addition to their apples, Richard and Maria raise bees. Not only do they earn some extra income selling honey, but the bees' diet consists of apple blossom nectar. This saves the expense of providing food for the bees, and in addition, the bees provide a valuable service by pollinating the apple blossoms. If not for the bees, they would need to pay to artificially pollinate the apple blossoms in order for the trees to produce apples.

The selling price of their apples will depend on a number of different things. If other U.S. growers have good years, they know that it will push down the price of apples. With the passage of the North American Free Trade Agreement (NAFTA), a lot of Canadian and Mexican apples are reaching U.S. markets, and this puts further downward pressure on apple prices. Because they use top quality fertilizers, modern equipment, and improved high-yield apple trees, however, Richard and Maria get more apples per tree than their foreign competitors and can therefore compete with the imports. Also, because of a major advertising campaign, Canadian and Mexican consumers are becoming more familiar with their bright green Granny Smith apples, and exports to these countries have increased in the past couple of years. These new and expanding markets should help keep the prices stable or even allow them to increase a little.

Consumers are fussy about the apples that they buy. They like their apples uniformly green (or red) and they do not like bruises or worm holes. Although such apples can be sold to juice or applesauce processors, they bring a much lower price (about $175 per ton compared to over $400 per ton for unblemished apples). Consequently, Richard and Maria must use insecticides to combat red banded leaf rollers, coddling moths, lesser apple worms, and tufted apple bud moths. Unfortunately, some of these insecticides are harmful to consumers, so the U.S. Environmental Protection Agency (EPA) has banned the use of many of the low-cost, highly effective insecticides that were previously used to control these pests. This makes the apples safer for consumers, but more expensive to produce, and therefore more expensive in the stores (Figure 1).

This is not the only area of their business that concerns the EPA. Some of the fertilizer that Maria and Richard use washes into local streams and lakes after heavy rainfalls. Once in the streams, the organic wastes contained in the fertilizer increase the growth of water plants and algae. These plants compete with fish populations for available oxygen and harm the local fish population. In addition, the organic matter can kill helpful bacteria found in the streams, causing the water to change color and smell bad. One or two small apple orchards in the area do not use enough fertilizer to cause problems, but after Richard and Maria and others in the area started new

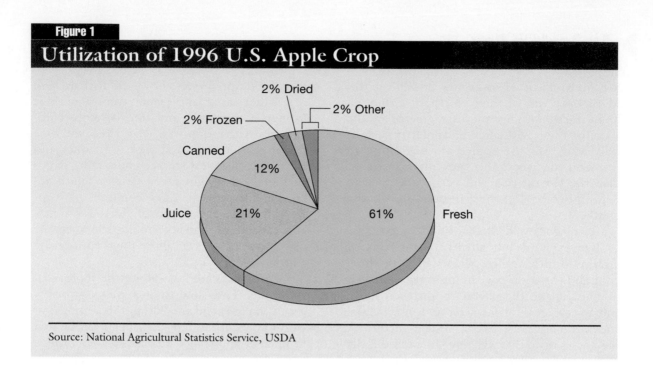

Figure 1

Utilization of 1996 U.S. Apple Crop

2% Dried

2% Frozen

2% Other

Canned

12%

Juice 21%

61% Fresh

Source: National Agricultural Statistics Service, USDA

orchards and expanded old ones, the local fishermen began to notice a significant decrease in the number of fish in the local streams and lakes. Maria likes to go fishing, and the fact that there are fewer fish in the streams upsets her. On the other hand, Richard wants a new television set this year, and although less fertilizer means more fish, it also means fewer apples, less income, and perhaps no new TV.

The new markets that are opening up because of NAFTA have made Maria and Richard think about some different products that they might grow. Their honey business has been successful, but Richard has read that the price of grapes has been increasing over the past few years, and neither Canada nor Mexico have suitable climates for growing grapes. One of their neighbors owns about 25 acres of sunny hillside property that is not good for apple trees, but might be very productive for either new bee hives or growing grapes. Maria and Richard have a good credit history, and they could borrow the money to buy the land from their neighbor, but they must be able to earn enough from either the grape harvest or the honey production to pay

the bank both the money they borrow plus the interest that the bank will charge on the loan. Interest rates have been pretty low, and the price their neighbor is asking for the property is reasonable, but one or two bad years would make it difficult to repay the loan. On the other hand, one or two good years will earn them enough income to pay back the loan and put aside savings for their retirement.

As another alternative, the shortage of fish in the local streams and lakes has made Maria think that they could instead borrow the money to buy a small pond on the other side of their property to raise trout. After all, as people become more conscious of their diets, the demand for fish has been increasing, and aquaculture seems to be a potentially profitable business. This winter they will study these two conflicting options and try to determine which one makes the most sense.

Once upon a time it was much easier to grow apples (and other agricultural products). According to legend, in the early 1800s, Johnny Appleseed was able to travel across this country spreading appleseeds that grew into trees, providing enough apples for the local community. Today, most people like nice juicy apples, but very few of us live in places where we can walk into the countryside and pick the apples that we want. Therefore some people grow apples for all the rest of us. As much as Maria and Richard would like to provide us with apples for free, they need to pay the expenses involved in growing the apples and they need to have enough income to buy all the same things that the rest of us would like to have. At the same time, they need to look to the future and adapt their production so that they are producing the things that the rest of us like to eat.

Chapter Preview

Examining the problems and decisions faced in producing apples, a relatively simple industry, provides a good illustration of economic methods. The decisions are not easy to make because of all the conflicting interests. There are the conflicting interests of apple growers and fishermen on one hand, the choice to be made between low-cost apple production and the possible danger from insecticides, and the decision of whether to expand into the grape- or fish-producing industry. We will use the example of growing apples as a reference when we ask the following questions: What is economics? What are the tools of economics? What are the uses of graphs? *The chapter is followed by an appendix on how to construct and interpret line graphs.*

Learning Objectives

After completing this chapter, you should be able to:

1. Explain scarcity as an economic term.
2. List the factors of production and give an example of each.
3. Describe the steps in the scientific method.
4. Give three definitions of economics.
5. Describe three types of factual tools used in economics.
6. Describe the theoretical tools used in economics.
7. Give four examples of different types of charts.
8. Explain what an analytical diagram is used for.
9. Draw and label an analytical diagram showing the relationship between two variables.

▶ What Is Economics?

One common definition of economics is that "economics is the social science concerned with how **resources** are used to satisfy people's wants." This section discusses the basis of economics as a science and the methods it uses.

◣ Scarcity

Deciding what to produce and how to produce it is a problem that naturally lends itself to the study of economics for a number of reasons, whether we are talking about producing apples, honey, grapes, or steel. Most importantly, such decisions involve dealing with **scarcity.** The need for a science of economics comes from scarcity. We have only a limited amount of resources to satisfy our unlimited wants for goods and services. As a result, we need to economize on the use of those resources to get the greatest benefit out of them.

Resources used to produce goods and services, called the **factors of production,** consist of **land, labor,** and **capital.** Land includes all

resources the inputs that are used in production. They include natural resources (minerals, timber, rivers), labor (blue collar, white collar), and capital (machinery, buildings).

scarcity the limited resources for production relative to the demand for goods and services.

factors of production another name for the productive resources of land, labor, and capital.

land all natural resources, including fields, forests, mineral deposits, the sea, and other gifts of nature.

labor all human resources, including manual, clerical, technical, professional, and managerial labor.

capital the means of production, including computers, buildings, machinery, and tools; alternatively, it can mean financial capital, the money used to acquire the factors of production.

Figure 2

Size of U.S. Labor Force, 1950–1996

Labor is the most important factor of production. The United States added over twice as many workers to the labor force in the last 2 decades as it did in the previous 2 decades.

U.S. Department of Commerce, Bureau of Labor Statistics, *Employment and Earnings.*

natural resources: the minerals under the surface, the forests on it, and even the air above it. Labor refers to all types of human resources, managers and professionals as well as manual and clerical workers. **Entrepreneurs** are a particular type of human resource. They are individuals who see the possibility of profitable production and organize the resources to produce a good or service. Richard and Maria are providing their own labor when they work in their business every day. In addition, they act as entrepreneurs when they make decisions about what to produce and how best to produce it (Figure 2).

Capital refers to the machinery, factories, and office buildings used in production, for example, the trucks and tractors used in running an orchard (Figure 3). **Technology** and information, both of which have increasing importance in today's economy, are also classified as capital resources. In the case of the former, new technology is generally introduced as improvements in existing capital resources. It also refers to the use of new and improved fertilizers, pesticides, and high-yield trees that permit greater apple production per tree. **Financial capital** is not a real resource like the factors of production, but it enables entrepreneurs and managers

to purchase any of the factors of production. The bank loan that Richard and Maria are considering is an example of financial capital.

Even in such a wealthy country as the United States, we do not have enough of these resources to satisfy all of our wants. How does resource scarcity apply to the case of growing apples? If there is one thing that you would think there is enough of, it is land. However, a sunny hillside used to grow grapes cannot at the same time be used to produce honey, and a bank loan used to buy a piece of land cannot be used to buy a small pond.

The above example also allows us to introduce another definition of economics. Economics

entrepreneur a business innovator who sees the opportunity to make a profit from a new product, new process, or unexploited raw material and then brings together the land, labor, and capital to exploit the opportunity.

technology the body of skills and knowledge that comprises the processes used in production.

financial capital the money to acquire the factors of production.

Figure 3

Business Capital Stock, 1970–1994 (1987 dollars)

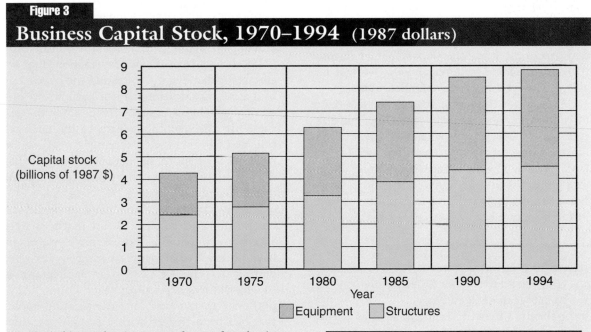

Capital is another important factor of production. The amount of real capital has more than doubled since 1970. The stock of equipment has increased faster than structures.

Source: U.S. Bureau of Economic Analysis, *Survey of Current Business.*

There must be a demand for an item in order for it to be scarce in the economic sense. These one-clawed lobsters are rarer than lobsters with two claws, but because there is no great demand for them, they are not considered scarce.

is often defined as "the science of choice" because scarcity forces us to make choices about what we will do with our scarce resources. The consequences of these choices are also an important part of the study of economics. If we choose to use our scarce resources wisely, we will be able to satisfy more of our unlimited wants.

We cannot emphasize enough the fact that, in economics, scarcity is not the same thing as rarity. We have plenty of land in the United States, but because of competing uses for it, land is scarce. On the other hand, a thing could be rare; but if no one wants it, it is not scarce. For example, radioactive waste and one-clawed lobsters are rare but not scarce.

scientific method a procedure used by scientists to develop explanations for events and test the validity of those explanations.

hypothesis a tentative explanation of an event; used as a basis for further research.

The Scientific Method

Economics, like other sciences, makes use of the **scientific method.** This consists of (1) observing an event under certain conditions, (2) devising a **hypothesis** (explanation) that accounts for that event, (3) testing the hypothesis by gathering additional information and observing whether a repeat of the conditions assumed by the hypothesis leads to the same result, and (4) tentatively accepting, revising, or rejecting the hypothesis, depending on whether it correctly predicts a repetition of the event under those conditions.

Many examples of possible uses of the scientific method can be found in the article about growing apples. For example, we might have observed that people eating apples were getting sick and we needed an explanation as to why this was happening. We then might hypothesize that it was caused by eating apples that had been treated with a certain pesticide. The scientific method would call for testing this hypothesis under the same conditions that

Table 1   The Scientific Method

Procedure	Example
1. Observe an event.	1. Observe a reduced number of fish in local streams.
2. Make a hypothesis to explain the event.	2. Fertilizer runoff from farms and orchards reduces the number of fish in streams.
3. Test the hypothesis by performing experiments under the same conditions (if that is possible), gathering additional evidence on the relationship between the effects and the assumed cause.	3. Count the number of fish in a body of water similar to that near the observed stream (if that is possible). Replicate the observed fertilizer runoff, and observe whether or not the number of fish is reduced.
4. Tentatively accept, revise, or reject the hypothesis, depending on whether it explains the event. Predict future events on the basis of the test results, and observe whether or not the predictions are accurate.	4. The hypothesis explaining the reduced number of fish is tentatively accepted because the predictions were accurate. In the future, use less fertilizer to produce higher yields of fish.

The scientific method of investigation can be applied to the specific case of water pollution.

existed with the apples that caused the sickness. A possible test of the hypothesis might be to give one group of people apples that had been treated with the pesticide and another group apples that had not been treated. If members of the group that eat the treated the apples get sick and members of the other group do not, then the hypothesis would be tentatively accepted.

If the evidence did not support the hypothesis (if the people who ate the treated apples did not get sick) then the hypothesis would be rejected. In this case, it would be necessary to formulate and test new hypotheses until one is accepted. Of course, researchers would not be likely to experiment with human subjects. This points out a very important difficulty when using the scientific method. To be precise as possible in our tests, we would like to use the same conditions and subjects as we originally observed. This is not always possible.

Another example of the use of the scientific method is shown in Table 1. This example shows how the scientific method could be used to understand the reason for the reduced number of fish in the local stream. Although conducting the test using fish in an aquarium might be easier, it is important to replicate the original conditions as closely as possible (Step 3).

Economics makes use of the scientific method, but it differs from some of the other sciences—laboratory sciences such as chemistry—because it is a social science. Economists usually are not able to conduct controlled experiments (experiments that replicate the observed event) in order to test hypotheses. They must depend on the observation of real-world events, which seldom occur under exactly the same conditions from one time to the next. For example, the amount of fish people want to buy may change because of changing consumer preferences or income. Economics is not, therefore, an exact science.

Economic Reasoning

Still another definition of economics is that economics is the way an economist thinks. The science of economics is characterized by a particular way of analyzing problems. It is called the economic way of thinking or **economic reasoning.** Whatever their personal and political views, economists have a similar approach to examining the way the world works. They make use of a common set of tools of economic

economic reasoning the application of theoretical and factual tools of economic analysis to explaining economic developments or solving economic problems.

analysis. (We will discuss what these tools are in the next section.)

The case of water pollution provides an illustration of what is unique about the economic way of thinking. Water pollution has reached serious levels because individuals, businesses, and frequently even governments treat water as a **free good.** Since it does not have a direct cost, as do **economic goods,** water is freely used to dispose of fertilizer runoff and other harmful products, without regard to its scarcity. According to the economic way of thinking, on the other hand, all costs should be included as costs of production, whether they are paid by the producer or not. For example, Richard and Maria Hernandez should include the cost of a polluted stream along with their cost of labor, bank loans, and their tractor when determining whether they should grow apples, produce honey, or grow grapes.

The economic way of thinking would generally prefer policies that force producers to bear all of the costs of production, both costs they incur when running their business as well as the costs to society created when their fertilizer washes into streams or the pesticides they use cause people to get sick. To most economists, that would be a better policy than one that imposes an outright ban on using fertilizer or pesticides (policies that deal with such issues are discussed in chapter 8, "Government and Business.")

In poor countries, the need to use forests for firewood often outweighs the economic—and environmental—consequences. Economic policies must take such value judgments into consideration.

What Is Economics?

EconExplorer

free good a production or consumption good that does not have a direct cost.

economic good any good or service that sells for a price; that is, a good that is not free.

Since economics is not an exact science, economists depend to a great extent on logical analysis, making use of the principles of economics. These principles include assumptions about how people, businesses, and governments behave. On the basis of these assumptions, economists predict the results of particular events or policies; for example, what the results of banning fertilizers would be. Is the reduced production of apples worth more or less than the lost fish? Economic reasoning consists of applying economic principles to explain events, predict outcomes, and recommend policies.

Because of differences in individual preferences and belief systems, economics must also take value judgments into account. A policy that makes sense economically may not be acceptable if it violates people's sense of what is right or just. For example, a number of the

(Continued on page 14)

Case Application

Who Needs the Rain Forests?

Who needs the rain forests? In the United States, the remaining rain forests have, for the most part, become tourist attractions. But in other parts of the world—Central and South America, Southeast Asia, West Africa—the rain forests are a vital part of the environment and economy. There are many competing uses for the rain forests, not only by people who live there, but also by people who live in other parts of the world. (To see a map of the world's rain forests, visit www.richmond.edu/~ed344/97/biomes/rainforest.html.)

At the subsistence level, people who live in the tropical rain forests use the wood from felled trees as fuel for heating and cooking as they are generally too poor to afford other types of fuel such as kerosene, gasoline, or natural gas. As their economies and populations grow, they also need new land on which to grow their crops and graze their livestock. To do this they clear the rain forest land of trees and underbrush, often by burning. (In 1997, such burning in the Indonesian rain forests produced so much smoke that many people died from inhaling it in cities miles and miles away from the forests!) Despite the lush foliage and giant trees, however, the land in most rain forests is usually of low quality; most nutrients and minerals are in the foliage, not in soil. Crops can be grown on the newly cleared land for only a few years, and then it loses its fertility, and more land must be cleared.

The logging industry also uses the rain forests to acquire timber for the world's construction and furniture industries. In Malaysia, the world's leading producer of sawed logs, the rain forests are being depleted of their trees so rapidly that many Malaysian companies are moving into the Central and South American rain forests where trees are more plentiful and government regulations protecting the forests are not so strict.

Other people who need the rain forests are medical and scientific researchers. Rain forests are the only source of a variety of rare plants that have medicinal properties. Pharmacy shelves in the United States already contain numerous drugs that have been developed from rain forest plants. They include treatments for heart disease, inflammation, and malaria. Of the estimated 250,000 known plants in the world, only about 5,000 have been tested for their possible medicinal use. Yet already U.S. consumers are spending more than $6 billion per year on pharmaceuticals that are derived from rain forest plants.

Rain forest plants have already yielded compounds being used to treat AIDS and cancer. Bristol-Myers has screened and tested the extracts from almost 400 plants from Surinam alone for use in combating these diseases. Finding the plants with these properties is just the first step, however. Next the active chemical compound needs to be isolated and tested first on animals and then on human beings. After that it needs to be tested and approved for use by the Food and Drug Administration, often a very expensive and time-consuming process. Finally, the compound must either be reproduced in a laboratory or, if that cannot be done, plants need to be cultivated in greenhouses in sufficient quantities to satisfy the demand for them. (The plants are usually too rare or too hard to find in the rain forests to make that a reliable source.)

Rain forests also provide recreation for tourists and travelers who are looking for something new and different to do on their vacations. Tourism is one of the world's largest industries, with more than $3.5 trillion spent each year by tourists. Ecotourism is a fast-growing segment of this industry, and increasing numbers of people are spending their vacations exploring the fauna and flora of the world's rain forests. Conservation International, an organization that promotes ecological awareness, reports that a recent survey showed that about 67 percent of travelers are interested in vacations that are oriented toward ecology and conservation.

The beauty and variety of bird species are a source of delight to bird-watchers worldwide. Ecological imbalances resulting from tropical deforestation threaten and sometimes destroy the habitats of birds. This is a major concern of ecologists and environmental groups, particularly in the economically developed countries.

(Continued from page 12)

poorer developing countries, like Mexico, have resisted international agreements to reduce the use of certain pesticides. They argue that the developed countries grew wealthy by using the least expensive and most effective production methods, regardless of their impacts on the environment. It was not until after these countries became rich that they began to become concerned about environmental problems. The developing countries feel that improving their economies and feeding their people is more important than long-term negative effects on their environments.

Economic reasoning is similar to the process of critical thinking. You will have a chance to practice critical thinking skills frequently as you go through this book. For example, the Economic Reasoning questions following the Case Applications at the end of each chapter section call for critical thinking. The first question in each set of three is a comprehension question. The second question involves economic analysis and critical thinking skills. The third question calls for you to apply your own value judgments, along with economic reasoning, in arriving at an answer.

Not only people, but a large number of animal and bird species need the rain forests, many of them for their very survival. Several varieties of birds found in North America—warblers, thrushes, swifts, tanagers, and flycatchers—migrate each year to forests in Central and South America for the winter. Loss of habitat due to deforestation is the principal cause of the decline or actual extinction of endangered species, from tigers in Sumatra to orangutans in Indonesia.

Finally, we are becoming increasingly aware that everybody in the world needs the rain forests to stabilize and clean Earth's environment. The rain forests absorb large quantities of the world's carbon dioxide emissions and thereby help in limiting the problem of global warming.

Despite the needs of local inhabitants, loggers, researchers, patients with certain diseases, tourists, endangered species, and the world at large, the rain forests are rapidly disappearing. Estimates range from 27 to 50 million acres being destroyed every year by loggers, miners, farmers, and ranchers. This is an area equal in size to half the land mass of Japan! Conservation International estimates that an acre of the Brazilian rain forest, the world's largest, is destroyed every nine seconds. And the trend toward deforestation is increasing; the United Nations reports that it has accelerated by 50% during the 1990s.

Economic Reasoning

1. Rain forests are considered which factor of production?

2. Use the scientific method to develop a hypothesis about the relationship between the rain forests and global warming, endangered species, or the development of new medicines. How would you go about testing the hypothesis?

3. Do you think that the industrialized countries should contribute money to save the remaining rain forests in the less developed parts of the world? Why or why not?

Who Needs the Rain Forests?

Use the World Wide Web to visit Conservation International (www.conservation.org/), the United Nations environmental site (www.unep.org/), or the Environmental Organization WebDirectory at http://www.webdirectory.com/ and follow the links to forests and then rain forests. Should any of the facts reported in this article be revised? Are the rain forests still being depleted rapidly, or is the world acting to save them?

▶ What Are the Tools of Economics?

Important in the economic way of thinking are the factual and theoretical tools of economics. Many of them are useful in analyzing the problems of production and environmental trade-offs.

◤ Factual Tools

The factual tools used by economists are **statistics,** history, and how **institutions** operate. The term "statistics" has a couple of meanings. First, statistics are the data (numbers) that economists use in various economic measurements, such as production, prices, or interest rates. Second, statistics can refer to the methods employed in

statistics the data that describe economic variables; also the techniques of analyzing, interpreting, and presenting data.

institutions decision-making units, established practices, or laws.

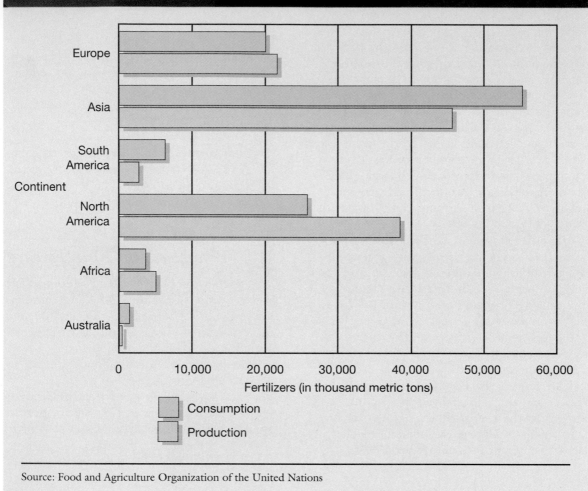

Figure 4

Consumption and Production of Fertilizers by Continent, 1993–1994

Source: Food and Agriculture Organization of the United Nations

studying the data, such as finding an average. Statistics are often essential to understanding a problem and determining what to do about it. For example, data collected on the effect of pesticides have caused increasing concern about the safety of agricultural products imported from Mexico.

What Are the Tools of Economics?

EconExplorer

History, especially economic history, is another useful tool in helping economists understand what is going on and how to deal with current problems. The experience of the industrial countries of North America and Western Europe has been that their economic growth was accompanied by greatly increased use of pesticides and fertilizer to expand their economies. If the developing countries of Asia, Africa, and Latin America follow the same path to economic growth, their aquatic resources will be damaged and there may also be long-term health risks associated with unsafe pesticides. Figure 4 shows that the use of fertilizers is much lower in Africa and South America than in other parts of the

State capitol buildings, like this one in Connecticut, symbolize an important legislative institution in the United States.

world. If people in these parts of the world are to catch up in food production, they will need to make much more intensive use of this factor of production. On the other hand, this might bring about increased damage to aquatic resources.

Institutions are important organizations, customs, or patterns of behavior in a society. In economics institutions can be a wide variety of things. They may vary from the banking system to labor unions, from the legal principle of private property ownership to the federal bureaucracy. They include the military, the media, accounting practices, and the zero population movement.

The institution of private property has permitted owners of land to use their property in order to produce those products that they believe customers want. Unfortunately, such use may also damage the environment as well as customers. To reduce these problems the institution of private property is now being modified. Owners are being restricted from using their property without regard to how the environment is affected.

◪ Theoretical Tools

The principal theoretical tools that are used in economics are concepts and models. **Economic concepts** are ideas. They are words or phrases that convey a specific meaning in economics. The subsections in the chapters of this book are organized by major concepts that are *preceded by the color bar* ◪.

Other concepts are shown in **bold type** and defined in the marginal glossary, especially if their meaning in economics is different or more precise than the meaning of the word in general. Usually a concept means the same in economics as it does in ordinary usage. But sometimes it has a particular meaning. In economics, for instance, the concept of scarcity does not indicate that there is necessarily only a small amount of something. Instead, it takes

economic concept a word or phrase that conveys an economic idea.

into account the amount available relative to the amount desired.

The most important theoretical tools of economists are **economic models,** which are simplified representations of the real world. Models are abstractions, reflecting only the most important aspects of a situation. A model

---

economic model a simplified representation of the cause-and-effect relationships in a particular situation. Models may be in verbal, graphic, or equation form.

variable a quantity—such as number of workers, amount of carbon dioxide, or interest rate—whose value changes in relationship to changes in the values of other associated items.

---

of apple production would show the predictable relationship between the amounts of fertilizer, pesticides, capital, and labor and the number of apples produced. It would not include other factors that might cause apple output to vary from one year to the next, such as hailstorms, drought, and so forth. Random events are excluded from models in order to reveal the systematic relationships between the important **variables.**

Models can be stated in words, or as mathematical equations. (Although we will not use mathematical models in this text, economists use them widely to test their hypotheses.)

Alternatively, models can be shown visually as graphs. The graphic model is the most common and useful form in studying economics. We will examine different types of graphs and how they are used in the next section.

Owners of private property are being restricted from using it without regard to how the environment is affected. This North Carolina farmer is not free to spray his corn with whatever pesticide he chooses.

Case Application

Something in the Air

There is something in the air all around us, and we may not like what it is. It is also in our water and in our land. It is pollution, the unwanted, and sometimes dangerous, side effect of economic production. Burning fossil fuels to produce electricity or power our trucks and cars releases sulfur and carbon dioxide into the atmosphere, and these lead to global warming (the *greenhouse effect*) and respiratory diseases. Putting fertilizer on our crops and processing lumber into paper result in our streams and lakes being polluted and the loss of clean, safe water and aquatic life. Manufacturing steel and chemicals sometimes leads to dangerous compounds being left in the ground, contaminating our groundwater. Using nuclear fuels results in radioactive waste products that can be deadly for thousands of years.

Some amount of pollution can be absorbed and cleaned by the earth's natural cleansing and diluting properties, but when it is excessive, we all suffer the consequences. According to the data in Table 2, air pollution alone is responsible for 2.7 million deaths

The great global challenge of the next century is the environment. We need to cooperate to preserve planet Earth for future generations.

every year. Most air pollution currently comes from the world's industrialized countries where there is much more industrial activity and many more cars than in the less developed parts of the world. These countries, however, are less densely populated and have better medical care, so the number of deaths caused by the pollution is much lower than in the less developed countries. While it may be good news that the less developed countries are growing and expanding their economic activity, the bad news is that increased pollution is accompanying that growth. Asia is currently the source of only 17% of the world's greenhouse gases but, because of its growth, its contribution to air pollution is growing at four times the world average. Some forms of air pollution threaten the very future of planet Earth.

The water in most Asian countries is almost as deadly as the air, and hundreds of thousands of people die every year from drinking polluted water. In addition to industrial pollutants, most Asian rivers contain 50 times more sewage than the World Health Organization deems safe. In the Chinese village of Badui one-third of the population is seriously ill or mentally retarded, many children's growth is stunted, and even the livestock is often sick and blind. The cause? Most blame this tragedy on the Liujiaxia fertilizer factory upstream that dumps its waste products directly into the river.

The dangers from pollution present a serious problem, which is difficult to deal with. On the one hand, countries that are developing are more concerned about feeding, clothing, and housing their people than about such things as the ozone layer and the greenhouse effect. In reply to the requests by the industrialized countries to reduce their pollution, they point out that pollution abatement is an expensive luxury that they cannot afford. They also add that the industrialized countries industrialized and damaged the environment first and then, when they could afford to, they instituted strict pollution control laws. At a 1997 global summit on the environment in Kyoto, Japan, one of the major points of debate was how much the developed and undeveloped countries should contribute to the reduction of harmful air pollutants.

Economic Reasoning

1. What factual tools of economic reasoning do you find in this case application?

2. What theoretical tools of economic reasoning do you find in this case application?

3. Do you think that the less developed countries of the world should be required to produce their goods and services in a way that minimizes pollution?

 ### Something in the Air

Visit http://www.webdirectory.com/ and click on Pollution. Find out what is being done to improve pollution control in less developed countries.

Table 2	Deaths from Air Pollution
Region	**Total Deaths**
India	673,000
Sub-Saharan Africa	522,000
China	443,000
Other Asian Countries	443,000
Latin America	406,000
Former USSR and Eastern Europe	100,000
Advanced Industrial Economies	79,000
Middle East	57,000
TOTAL	**2,723,000**

Source: *New York Times,* November 29, 1997, pages A1 and A7.

What Are the Uses of Graphs?

It is increasingly important to be able to read and use graphs. Besides being important in studying economics, it helps you to understand a great deal of what appears in the news media. It also is becoming more necessary in many of today's occupations.

◢ Descriptive Charts

Charts are widely used to present information, such as statistical data, visually. One type of chart commonly seen is the pie chart. Pie charts are used to show the relative size of the components (parts) of a whole. An example is Figure 1, which shows the different uses for apples. Another example is shown in Figure 5, where a pie chart is used to show the distribution of U.S. employment in different industries.

The graph showing the size of the U.S. labor force, reproduced as Figure 6, represents another type of chart. It is a *line graph* that shows how the number of workers in the labor force has changed over the years. The number of workers is a variable with the quantity measured on the vertical axis of the graph. The years are shown on the horizontal axis. This special type of line graph, with the values of the variable measured on the vertical axis and the years shown on the horizontal axis, is called a **time series.**

Another commonly seen graph is the column chart. It is useful in comparing the value of one variable with another or comparing the values of a variable over a period of time. An example of a column chart is Figure 3 on page 9. This is a stacked column chart that

---

chart a graphical representation of statistical data or other information.

time series the changes in the values of a variable over time; a chart in which time—generally years—is one of the variables.

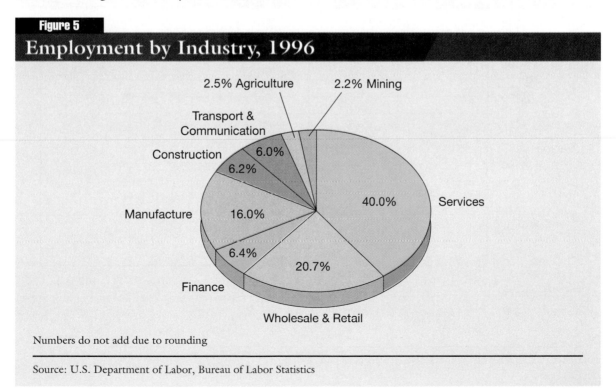

Figure 5
Employment by Industry, 1996

- 2.5% Agriculture
- 2.2% Mining
- Transport & Communication 6.0%
- Construction 6.2%
- Manufacture 16.0%
- 40.0% Services
- 6.4%
- 20.7%
- Finance
- Wholesale & Retail

Numbers do not add due to rounding

Source: U.S. Department of Labor, Bureau of Labor Statistics

Figure 6

Line Graph

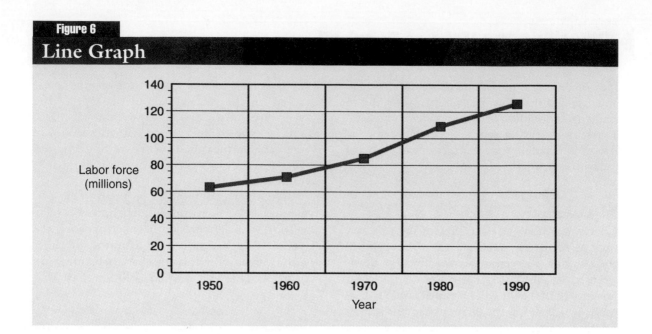

Figure 7

Labor Force by Gender, 1970–1995

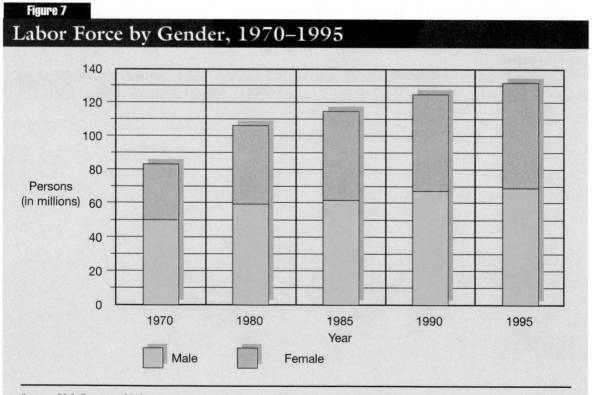

Source: U.S. Bureau of Labor Statistics, Employment and Earnings

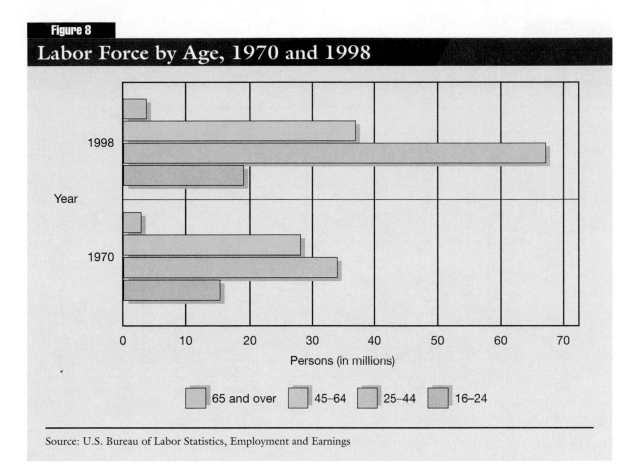

Figure 8

Labor Force by Age, 1970 and 1998

Year

1998

1970

Persons (in millions)

0   10   20   30   40   50   60   70

■ 65 and over   □ 45–64   ▨ 25–44   ▨ 16–24

Source: U.S. Bureau of Labor Statistics, Employment and Earnings

shows how the quantity of capital used by industries has increased over time. It also shows how much of the capital consists of machinery and equipment relative to factory buildings and other business structures. Similarly, the stacked column chart shown in Figure 7 shows how the size of the U.S. labor force has increased over time. It also shows how the number of men and women in the U.S. labor force has changed over time.

Bar charts are like column charts turned on their side. Figure 8 is similar to the bar chart in Figure 4 shown on page 16. Instead of showing the use of fertilizers and pesticides, it shows another aspect of the U.S. labor force: its composition according to the age of the workers who make it up.

An *area chart* is particularly suited to demonstrating how the relative importance of different components of a variable change over

time. The chart on page 294 is an area chart showing how the composition of total unemployment has changed. There are additional types of charts—scatter charts, range charts, three-dimensional charts—but the ones described above are those most commonly encountered.

◪ Analytical Diagrams

Economic **diagrams** are visual models. They resemble line charts, but instead of showing how

---

diagram a graph that shows the relationship between two or more variables that may or may not have values that can actually be measured; a graphical model.

Hypothetical Relationship between Annual Earnings and Education Level

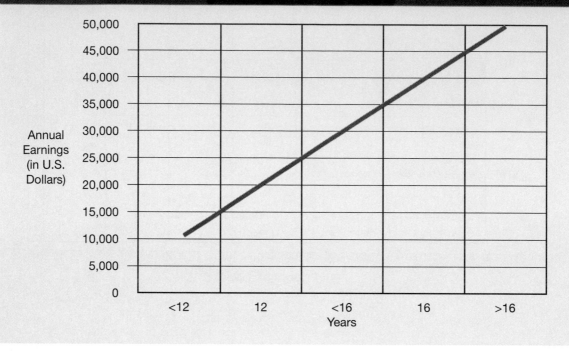

Annual Earnings (in U.S. Dollars) vs. Years

a variable changes over time or with respect to a country, industry, or other category, a diagram shows how two or more variables relate to each other. They are graphic models based on observation and economic reasoning.

What Are the Uses of Graphs?

EconExplorer

direct relationship a relationship between two variables in which their values increase and decrease together.

As an example of such a model, let us take the relationship between years of school and earnings. In Figure 9a, we measure the number of years of school on the horizontal axis and the wage or salary level on the vertical axis. The measurements of the number of years of school and earnings both begin at 0 in the lower left corner of the diagram. The amount of school increases to the right on the horizontal axis and the level of earnings increases as we move up the vertical axis. The purpose of the diagram is to show the interaction between education and earnings. The *upward* sloping line in the diagram shows us that as years of school *increase*, earnings also *increase*. The type of relationship between these two variables is said to be a **direct relationship;** as the amount of one increases, the amount of the other also increases.

Hypothetical Relationship between National Income and the Percentage of Agricultural Workers

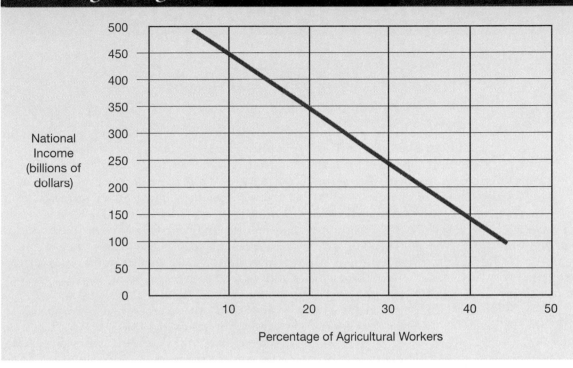

National Income (billions of dollars) — vertical axis

Percentage of Agricultural Workers — horizontal axis

Figure 9b is constructed in a similar manner, except in this diagram the horizontal axis measures the percentage of a country's population that is employed in agriculture, and the vertical axis shows the average level of income in that country. The *downward* sloping line in this diagram shows us that as the percentage of the labor force in agriculture *decreases,* the average income of the population *increases.* This type of relationship is said to be an **inverse relationship;** as the amount of one variable increases the other decreases. We will make more use of this type of model in the next chapter.

Diagrams are used a great deal in studying economics to illustrate economic principles and relationships. If you are not experienced with diagrams, you should read the appendix to this chapter and practice drawing diagrams to become familiar with them.

inverse relationship a relationship between two variables in which the value of one decreases as the value of the other increases.

Comparative
Case Application

The Energy Gluttons

The United States has the biggest economy in the world, producing over one-fifth of all the world's goods and services. Our high level of production means that we are also the world's biggest user of energy. In 1996 this country was responsible for over one-quarter of the world's energy consumption. Not only did we use the energy to produce goods and services, we also used it for transportation. About two-thirds of the petroleum we use powers cars and trucks. In contrast, Western Europe used about 44% of its energy for transportation and Japan, about 35%.

One of the reasons for this is that our country is bigger than other countries and we travel longer distances. More important, however, is America's long love affair with the automobile. Our cars are bigger and less fuel efficient, and we rely on them more than people in other countries who depend on mass transit for work, school, shopping, and recreation.

Public policy in the United States has reinforced and encouraged our consumption of gasoline. While gasoline taxes in Western Europe and Japan can be as high as $2 to $3 per gallon, U.S. taxes are about 40 cents per gallon (combined state and federal taxes). As a consequence, a gallon of gasoline that in the United States costs as little as $1.15 at the beginning of 1998 costs well over $3.00 in most foreign countries. At those prices, is it any wonder that the Europeans and Japanese have a preference for smaller cars?

Because of the oil crisis of the 1970s, the price of a barrel of crude petroleum increased from around $3 in 1973 to almost $40 in 1980, and the average price of a gallon of gasoline in the United States increased from under 40 cents to about $1.20. As a result, imports of small, fuel-efficient automobiles increased and U.S. car makers began to design and produce smaller, more efficient cars in order to save Americans money and compete with the flood of imports. Between 1973 and 1991, the average fuel mileage of cars and light trucks in the United States increased from 13.3 to 20.1 miles per gallon. As you can see from the table on page 27, the higher prices of petroleum caused Americans to reduce their consumption of oil relative to the rest of the world.

Over time, however, we seem to have forgotten our lesson. As of January, 1998, oil prices had dropped to $16.35 per barrel, and after adjusting for inflation, gasoline prices were much lower than they were in 1973. As a result of cheaper gasoline, U.S. auto makers and U.S. car buyers are switching more and more to gas-guzzling sport utility vehicles that get very poor gas mileage. Sport utility vehicles (SUV) sales in the United States exceeded 2 million in 1997, a 250% increase from the number sold in 1991. This trend is expected to continue, with sales increases of between 20 and 40% by 2001.

One of the side effects of our tremendous use of energy is that the United States is also the world's biggest producer of carbon

Table 3   Percentages of World Energy Consumption by Region, 1960–1996

Year	United States	Europe	Soviet Union*	Asia	Other
1960	37	27	15	13	8
1970	34	27	16	14	9
1980	28	25	17	19	11
1991	24	21	16	26	13
1996	25	21	11	27	13

The U.S. share of world energy consumption is down from earlier years.

*In 1991 the Soviet Union dissolved; 11 of the 15 former Soviet republics joined to form the Commonwealth of Independent States.

Source: Statistical Office of the United Nations, *Energy Statistics Yearbook,* annual; and British Petroleum at www.bp.com/bpstats/index.html.

dioxide, a by-product of the burning of fossil fuels for transportation and other energy uses. With only about 5% of the world's population, we nonetheless produce about 20% of the world's carbon dioxide, and thus contribute much more than our fair share to global warming and the greenhouse effect.

Economic Reasoning

1. Which type of graph would be best suited to show the relationship between gasoline prices and the amount of gasoline that people want to buy? Use some hypothetical data to draw the graph and label it.

2. Which type of graph would be best suited to showing the information provided in the table above? Draw the graph and label it.

3. Are you in favor of raising the federal gasoline tax from 18 cents to $1? What are some of the arguments for and against such a tax increase?

The Energy Gluttons

Visit www.bp.com/bpstats/index.html on the Internet and update the table above. Has the small increase in the U.S. share in 1996 continued? For more information about energy use and prices, visit the U.S. Energy Information Administration at www.eia.doe.gov/. For example, trace what has happened to the price of a barrel of petroleum from 1997 to today.

▶ Putting It Together

Economics is the social science concerned with how resources are used to satisfy people's wants. The science of economics arises from the need to overcome *scarcity*. The *resources* available for production are not sufficient to satisfy all our wants. We need therefore to use them in such a way as to maximize output. These *factors of production* are *land* (all natural resources), *labor* (including managerial and professional), and *capital* (machinery, buildings, technology, and information). *Financial capital* is used by *entrepreneurs* and managers to purchase the factors of production.

The *scientific method* is a process of observing events, forming hypotheses concerning their causes, testing the hypotheses, and rejecting, revising, or tentatively accepting them. Economics makes use of the scientific method, but it is a social science, not a laboratory science, and cannot do controlled experiments. It applies logical analysis based on economic principles to explain events, predict outcomes, and recommend policies. Economic policies must take into account an individual's and a society's value judgments as well.

Economic reasoning is based on the application of economic principles and the use of a common set of tools of economic analysis. *Free goods* do not have a direct cost, while *economic goods* do.

Economics makes use of factual and theoretical tools. The factual tools are *statistics*, history, and the functioning of *institutions*. The theoretical tools are *economic concepts*, words that may have a more specialized meaning in economics than they do in general use, and *economic models* simplified representations of the real world. Models may be in verbal, mathematical, or visual form.

The use of capital equipment makes farmers more productive so they can produce more apples at a lower cost.

Graphs may be charts that visually present statistical information, or they may be diagrams that show the relationship of *variables* to each other in an economic model. It depends on the nature of the information to be shown. Charts may take the form of pie charts, line charts, columnar charts, bar charts, or others. Charts that show the values of a variable over a succession of years are called *time series*.

Diagrams are visual models based on observation and economic reasoning. In the case of agricultural employment and average income, the two variables have an *inverse* rather than a *direct relationship*.

$\$$ Perspective $\$$

The Master Model Builder

Paul Anthony Samuelson (born 1915) Born in Gary, Indiana, Samuelson attended the University of Chicago, the temple of conservative economics. He studied under a number of the leading economists of the time, some with well-deserved reputations as tyrants in their classes. The young Samuelson had the guts and the knowledge to challenge them when he thought they had made a mistake—and get away with it.

He graduated in 1935 and would have been happy to pursue a doctoral degree at Chicago. But the scholarship that he received required him to change schools, so he went to Harvard, where he received his Ph.D. in 1941. Since 1940 he has been on the faculty of the Massachusetts Institute of Technology.

In 1947, at the age of 32, he published *Foundations of Modern Economics*. Milton Friedman, himself a University of Chicago product and quite conservative (see Perspective, p. 383), wrote that *Foundations* "immediately established his [Samuelson's] reputation as a brilliant and original mathematical economist" (*Newsweek*, November 9, 1970, p. 80).

Samuelson's introductory economics text was published a year later. It was subsequently translated into other languages and published in a number of countries. In 1958, in collaboration with two coauthors, he published *Linear Programming and Economic Analysis*.

In 1970, the second year that the Nobel Prize in economics was awarded, it went to an American, Paul Samuelson. It was in recognition of his outstanding work in constructing economic models. According to the Nobel Prize citation: "By his many contributions, Samuelson has done more than any other contemporary economist to raise the level of scientific analysis in economic theory."

Samuelson got off to a fast start in becoming the first American to win a Nobel Prize in economics. As an undergraduate student at the University of Chicago, he was allowed to attend graduate economics classes. Some leading economists today, who were then graduate students in those classes, report that they were intimidated by his intellectual ability. Remembering the "shock" of encountering Samuelson as a competitor in class, one of those graduate students, Martin Bronfenbrenner, now a renowned economist

himself, has said of the course instructor, "I shall always be grateful for [the professor's] kindly assurances that one need not really be another Samuelson to pass muster as an economist" (Feiwel, p. 349. See Further Reading). Before he finished graduate school, Samuelson had published two papers that set forth models that were major contributions to economic theory. His subsequent articles fill the four large volumes of *The Collected Scientific Papers of Paul Samuelson*.

The mathematical models in those papers are not easy reading, even for other economists. But Samuelson proved his versatility by writing an introductory textbook that was the most successful economics text of all time. *Economics: An Introductory Analysis* (1948) was the leading introductory economics text for 2 decades, selling over 3 million copies.

In addition to his activities as a researcher and textbook writer, Samuelson has been a columnist for *Newsweek* magazine and was an adviser to the government during the Kennedy administration. He has been a teacher most of his life and an occasional speculator in the commodities market. The success of his textbook and commodities speculation made Samuelson a millionaire. By excelling in the world of finance as well as scholarship, he joins another great economist of the past, John Maynard Keynes, who is the subject of the Perspective in chapter 12.

Samuelson the scientist and capitalist is also Samuelson the social critic who believes that government economic activities have been too much "suppressed—so that we have public squalor along with private, really decadent, opulence" (*Science News,* Oct. 31, 1970, p. 348).

For Further Study and Analysis

Study Questions

1. Give all the examples of scarcity that you can find in the introductory article on the Hernandez orchard.
2. Name something in addition to radioactive waste that is rare but not scarce.
3. What factors of production are used in your school? Do any of them appear to be more scarce than others? Which ones?
4. Give all the examples of the different factors of production that you can find in the introductory article about the Hernandez orchard.
5. Use the three different definitions of economics to "economically" describe the Hernandez orchard.
6. Air is sometimes considered to be a "free good." Does excessive use of that good lead to problems in the quality of the air? Is clean air scarce?
7. What example of each of the three factual tools used in economics do you find in the case application entitled The Energy Gluttons? (p. 26)
8. Do you find any economic concepts or models in that application? What are they?
9. What type of chart would be most appropriate for showing how your time is allocated during a weekday between the following categories: attending school, traveling, eating, studying, engaging in leisure activities, sleeping, and other? Draw such a graph in its basic form and label it.
10. What variables are involved in the case application entitled Who Needs the Rain Forests? (p. 13)? Pick two of those variables that have an inverse relationship and draw a diagram that shows the inverse relationship.

Exercises in Analysis

1. Visit a local business and gather information on the factors of production used in that business. Ask the manager if there have been any recent technological improvements in the operations of the business. Write a short paper describing what resources are used in the business.
2. Visit a public park and a neighborhood street in your town. How clean and well maintained are they in comparison to your home? Use the economic concept of private property to explain why there is a difference.
3. Prepare a short paper describing the school that you attend using the factual tools of economic analysis. Make at least two graphs to help show the composition of the students at your school.

4. Find examples in newspapers or magazines of the following types of graphs: pie charts, line charts, column charts, and bar charts. For each type, identify what the variable is that is being measured and what it is being measured with respect to (time, industries, states, and so forth).

Further Reading/Research

Web Sites for Economic Data and Reports

The Federal Reserve Bank of St. Louis: http://www.stls.frb.org/fred/

The U.S. Department of Commerce, Bureau of Economic Analysis: http://www.bea.doc.gov/beahome.html

For access to the Economic Report of the President, the Statistical Abstract of the United States, and the U.S. Budget: http://www.census.gov/statab/

Brown, E. Cary, and Robert M. Solow, eds. *Paul Samuelson and Modern Economic Theory.* New York: McGraw-Hill, 1983. This book is a *Festschrift,* a collection of articles published to honor a scholar, which the Feiwel book (see below) claims not to be. The lead monograph is by Samuelson himself and provides an insight into his personality.

Collins, Mark, ed. *The Last Rain Forests: A World Conservation Atlas.* New York: Oxford University Press, 1990. Discusses what rain forests are, how they work, the pressures on them, and why we need them. Describes the people of the rain forests and the challenge of conservation.

The Encyclopedic Dictionary of Economics. 4th ed. Guilford, Conn.: Dushkin Publishing Group, 1991. Explanations of economic terms, theories, and institutions, organized alphabetically.

Feiwel, George R., ed. *Samuelson and Neoclassical Economics.* Boston: Kluwer-Nijhoff Publishing, 1982. A varied selection of monographs by representative scholars of widely divergent perceptions discussing, sometimes critically, Samuelson's "history-making contributions to and impact on the economics of our age."

Flavin, Christopher. "Slowing Global Warming" in *Worldwatch Institute Report: State of the World—1990.* New York: W. W. Norton, 1990. The Worldwatch Institute publishes an annual report on "progress toward a sustainable society," which surveys the status of environmental and food conditions in the world. This article describes the causes of the greenhouse effect and alternative strategies for lessening its impact.

Gore, Albert. *Earth in the Balance: Ecology and the Human Spirit.* Boston: Houghton Mifflin, 1992. The vice president covers the concerns about environmental degradation in the context of human ecology. He discusses the environmental policies needed to ensure protection for the environment.

Park, Chris C. *Tropical Rain Forests.* New York: Routledge, 1992. Examines the human ecology of the rain forests. Describes the deforestation of the rain forests that has taken place and conservation measures that could be taken in managing the remaining rain forests.

Peltz, Liz. *Take the Heat Off the Planet: How You Can Really Stop the Climate Change.* London: Friends of the Earth, 1993. A program of energy conservation to reduce emission of the gases that can cause global warming.

Wyman, Richard, ed. *Global Climate Change and Life on Earth.* New York: Routledge, 1991. Covers the environmental aspects of global warming. Examines the conservation of biological diversity, the role of forests in affecting greenhouse gas composition of the atmosphere, and the impact of climate-induced rise in the sea level in coastal areas.

a p p e n d i x

Constructing and Reading Diagrams

Here is how the points on a diagram are constructed. Let us take a noneconomic example that is familiar—an automobile trip. Our destination is 200 miles away. We are interested in how long it will take us to get there and where we will be at different times along the way.

In order to show this information graphically, let us draw a diagram that measures the driving time in hours on the horizontal axis and the distance covered in miles on the vertical

axis. The axes with their appropriate scales are shown in Figure A.

How far we travel in a given amount of time depends, of course, on our driving speed. If we drive at a constant 40 miles per hour, at the end of the first hour we will have covered 40 miles, at the end of the second hour 80 miles, and so forth. The relationship between time and distance traveled is plotted in Figure B. At the 1-hour mark on the horizontal axis, a vertical line

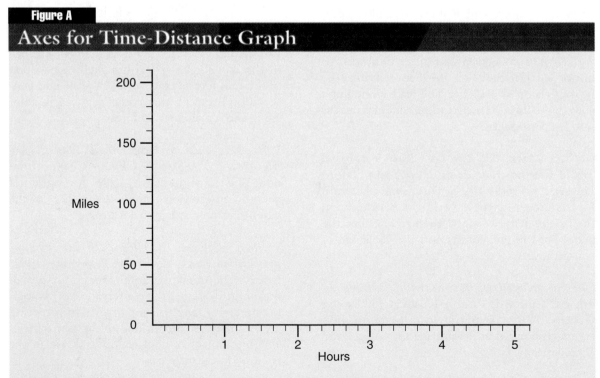

Figure A

Axes for Time-Distance Graph

Measurement scales for the items being compared are put on the horizontal and vertical axes of the diagram.

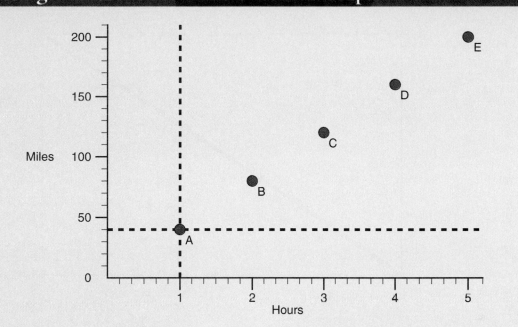

Figure B
Plotting Points on the Time-Distance Graph

Points are plotted on the diagram showing the distance traveled each hour at a speed of 40 miles per hour.

is drawn—referred to as a perpendicular. At the 40-mile mark on the vertical axis, an intersecting line is drawn—also called a perpendicular because it is perpendicular to that axis. Where the two lines cross at point A is the first point plotted on the time-distance diagram.

If we plot the additional distances traveled at the end of each subsequent hour of driving time in the same fashion, we find points B, C, D, and E. At the end of 5 hours, we will reach our destination 200 miles away.

The dots in Figure B show how far we have gone at the end of each hour. Since we are traveling at a constant rate of speed, a line connecting the dots would show the distance traveled at any point in time. Such a line showing the relationship between two variables—here time and distance—is generally referred to as a curve, even when it is a straight line, as it would be in this case. The line in Figure C we can label the 40-mph Travel Curve.

To find how far we have traveled at any particular time, we draw a perpendicular from the horizontal axis to the travel curve and locate the

corresponding point on the vertical axis. If we want to know how far we will have traveled in 3½ hours, we draw a perpendicular from the 3½-hour point on the horizontal axis to the travel curve in Figure D. This gives point X on the curve. From point X we draw a perpendicular across to the vertical axis. The perpendicular intersects the vertical axis at 140 miles.

From the graph we could similarly find how long it would take to reach any particular place along the way. If we wished to know when we would pass through a town 100 miles from home, we draw a perpendicular in Figure D from the vertical axis at 100 miles to the travel curve. It intersects the travel curve at point Y. From that point we drop a perpendicular to the horizontal axis. It shows that we would pass through the town 2½ hours after we leave home.

If we wish to make the trip in less time, we can increase our speed. Figure E shows the travel curve for a speed of 50 miles an hour. Because more distance is covered each hour, the new travel curve rises more steeply than the previous one. It shows that we would reach our

Figure C

40-mph Travel Curve

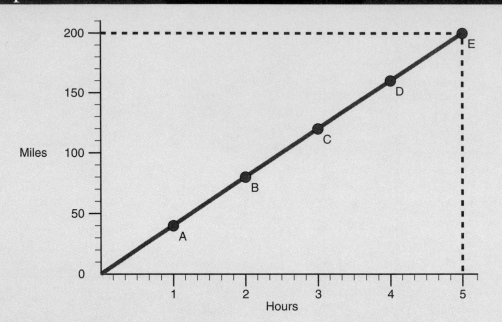

A line on a diagram showing the relationship of the variables is referred to as a curve, even when it is a straight line.

Using Travel-Curve Diagram

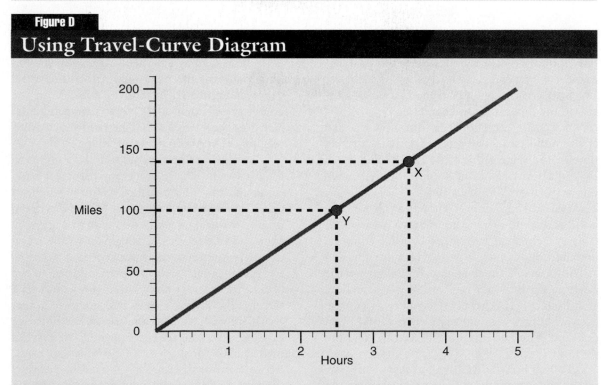

Information is obtained from a diagram by finding corresponding points on the axes with the use of perpendiculars.

50-mph Travel Curve

The travel curve relating the distance covered to the driving time is steeper for a speed of 50 miles per hour than for a speed of 40 miles per hour.

destination in 4 hours instead of 5. It also shows that we would pass through the town 100 miles from home in 2 hours.

In these diagrams we have assumed a constant rate of speed during the whole trip, so the travel curve rises at a constant slope. What will happen if the rate of speed changes during the trip? Let us say that the first two hours we can drive only 40 miles per hour because of congested traffic, but the third hour we can drive 50 and after that 65 miles an hour. The travel curve based on those speeds is shown in Figure F. As speed increases, the slope of the curve becomes steeper. To find the time required to reach the destination, we draw a perpendicular from the 200-mile mark on the vertical axis to the travel curve. From that point we draw a perpendicular down to the horizontal axis where it intersects the time scale at 4 hours and 5 minutes.

The relationship of time to distance in the travel curve is positive (or direct). As one increases, so does the other. Therefore, the curve slopes upward to the right. The relationship of

other variables may be negative (or inverse). As one increases, the other decreases. For example, the distance driven and the amount of gas remaining in the tank are inversely related. In Figure G the miles driven are shown on the horizontal axis and the amount of gasoline in the tank on the vertical axis. Assuming that the car has a 15-gallon tank and gets 25 miles to a gallon, the amount of gas remaining at any point on the trip can be determined from the curve. If we wish to find the amount of gasoline remaining in the tank after 300 miles, we draw a perpendicular from the 300-mile mark on the horizontal axis up to the intersection with the curve and from that point draw a perpendicular across to the vertical axis. It shows that we have 3 gallons left and had better start looking for a filling station.

Because the relationship between miles driven and the amount of gas left in the tank is negative—as one increases the other decreases—the curve slopes downward to the right. The curve ends at the horizontal axis because you cannot have less than zero gas in the tank.

Travel Curve with Increasing Speeds

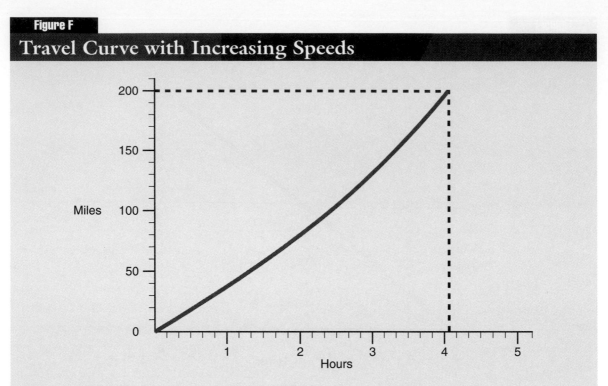

As the driving speed increases over time, the travel curve becomes steeper.

Gasoline-Distance Graph

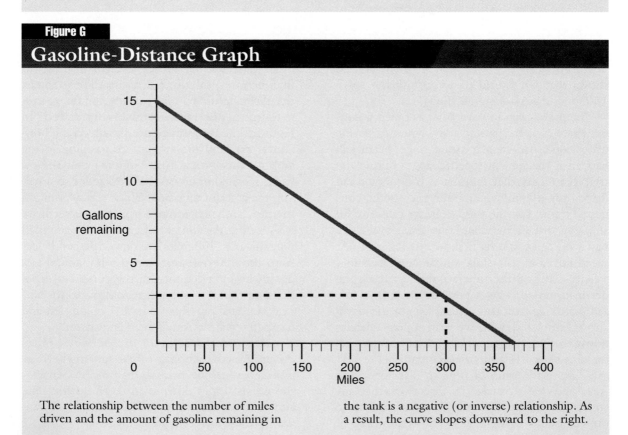

The relationship between the number of miles driven and the amount of gasoline remaining in the tank is a negative (or inverse) relationship. As a result, the curve slopes downward to the right.

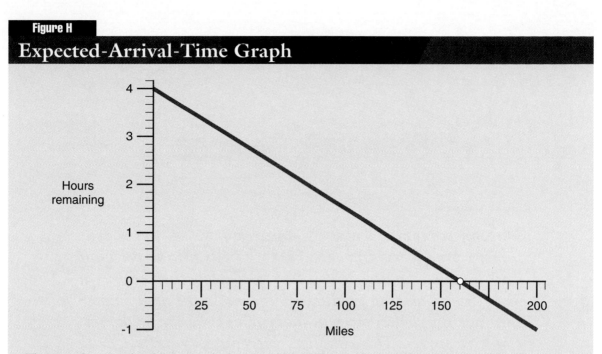

Figure H

Expected-Arrival-Time Graph

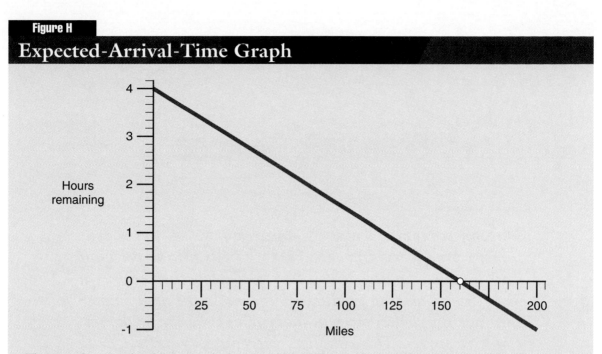

The part of a curve that falls below the horizontal axis indicates negative values of the variable measured on the vertical axis.

However, there are some variables that can have negative values—become less than zero. Let us suppose that this trip we have been discussing is to visit some friends and we have notified them that we expect to arrive at 4 P.M. We plan on leaving at noon and driving at a speed of 50 miles per hour. However, we encounter bad weather and are able to average only 40 miles an hour. The vertical axis in Figure H shows the amount of time remaining before our anticipated arrival. The distance driven is shown on the horizontal axis. We expected to cover the 200 miles in 4 hours, but due to the weather delay we cover only 160 miles at the end of 4 hours. The amount of time by which we are late in arriving is shown below the horizontal axis where the values are negative. We arrive at our destination an hour later than expected.

In becoming better acquainted with graphs and how to use them, it is helpful to draw diagrams yourself. You will be given the opportunity to do this in some of the Economic Reasoning questions following the Case Applications.

Here is a suggestion for a diagram that you could practice on now. Draw a graph showing the relationship of the number of weeks in your economics course and the number of chapters that you are going to cover in the text. Put the number of weeks on the horizontal axis scale and the number of chapters on the vertical axis scale. Draw a curve showing the relationship between the number of weeks and the number of chapters if you were to cover the chapters at a constant rate. Draw another curve on the same diagram showing the relationship between the number of weeks and the number of chapters covered if you instead spend more time on the early chapters and less time on later chapters. (For the second curve don't bother to plot specific points; just make a freehand drawing of the curve showing its general shape and location in relation to the first curve.)

Practice using the diagram by locating, with the use of perpendiculars, in which weeks you will complete the first third of the chapters under each of the two assumptions—a constant rate of covering the material and an increasing rate.

chapter two

Economic Choices

Making economic choices is something we all do as consumers, producers, and members of society. Many personal and business choices are important—whether to buy a house, what goods to produce—but among the most important are the choices citizens make about the use of the nation's resources. This chapter's introductory article deals with some of the choices we make when we produce steel.

► Steeling Away 🕸

Well, we're living here in Allentown

And they're tearing all the factories down.

Billy Joel, "Allentown"

In Pittsburgh, on the western side of the state of Pennsylvania, they have been tearing all the factories down since the late 1970s. The latest round occurred in 1997 as the LTV Steel Company shut down its Hazelton coke processing plant early in 1998. In the first place, the demand for coke, a material processed from coal and used to heat steel mill blast furnaces, has decreased with the fall in world demand for basic steel. Second, processing coal into coke is a dirty business, creating unpleasant fumes and filling the air with harmful pollutants such as sulfur dioxide and carbon dioxide. The U.S. Environmental Protection Agency (EPA) has ruled that American steel producers must reduce the pollutants they emit if they wish to continue making coke. But to do so would require the installation of expensive pollution control equipment and LTV had to decide whether it was worth undergoing this expense. To make the decision, the company projected the future demand for and price of steel and compared it to the costs of buying and installing the equipment. Unfortunately for the hundreds of workers who will lose their jobs, LTV decided that it would not be profitable to produce coke in Pittsburgh in an environmentally sound manner.

It was not always hard times in the Pittsburgh steel industry. During the first decades of the twentieth century the city boomed, as the world needed more and more steel for railroads, skyscrapers, the fledgling auto industry, and armaments to fight World War I. Companies such as U.S. Steel, Bethlehem Steel, and Jones and Laughlin grew large and rich as they sold their product throughout the United States and the world. Pittsburgh became the world's leading producer of steel.

Why did Pittsburgh become the steel-producing capital of the world? The manufacture of steel requires two key inputs: coal and iron ore. Both are heavy and expensive to transport and so minimizing transportation costs was important. Regions that specialized in making steel therefore were close to either the coal or iron ore deposits, and Pittsburgh is situated on one of the world's largest and most accessible deposits of coal. Iron ore from Minnesota and other areas could be shipped across the Great Lakes and down the Mississippi and Ohio Rivers until it reached Pittsburgh. The finished product could then be transported on either the same rivers or on rail lines that crisscrossed the region. (Two other major U.S. steel production centers, Gary, Indiana, and Mobile, Alabama, are also located so as to minimize transportation costs.)

The production of steel requires lots of capital and lots of labor. Producing steel traditionally required giant blast furnaces and rolling mills that stretched along the local riverbanks for mile after mile. The money to finance the construction and expansion of these mills came from individuals and businesses, who saved some of their money and either lent it to the steel companies for the promise of being paid interest, or became part owners of the companies through buying shares of their stock. There was great demand for labor in the early 1900s, and local communities were not large enough to provide the mills with all the workers that they needed. To remedy the situation, workers who could not find good jobs in their home countries came from all parts of the world to live and work in Pittsburgh. In its heyday, Pittsburgh was a mighty industrial town with furnaces burning 24 hours a day, tended by thousands of workers speaking Italian, Polish, Hungarian, and many other languages.

Pittsburgh was also a very dirty city. For those 24 hours a day that the steel mills operated, they belched and hurled thick greasy smoke, soot, and ashes into the air. As the coal was poured down the nearby hillsides into the mills it covered the city in a thick layer of fine black dust that stained the buildings black and coated the people's lungs. The smoke, soot, and dust were so dense that often street lights had to be turned on in the middle of the day because the sun could not penetrate the dark clouds that covered the city. The smokestacks that rose from the 3,000 degree coke-burning furnaces shot flames high into the air, and the slag heaps where the molten waste products were dumped glowed for days. One observer of the city commented that, when viewed from the surrounding hills, Pittsburgh looked like "hell with the lid taken off."

Steel production and consumption peaked in the United States in 1973 with the production of almost 151 million tons of steel and the domestic consumption of almost 123 million tons. The difference between production and domestic consumption consisted of exports and waste—an average of 26% of all production became waste products. In total, U.S. steel mills employed about 509,000 workers.

By 1990, the picture was entirely different. Production and consumption were both down to less than 90 million tons, and employment was down to 252,000. In Pittsburgh, the mills that had produced most of the world's steel for nearly a century were silent and deserted. Along the rivers were mile after mile of huge, rusted buildings. The small towns surrounding the mills were almost as silent and many of the houses and stores were boarded up and abandoned. Although some steel was still being made in Pittsburgh, much more was being made in other states. What happened to cause the change? Four things: the demand for steel

had fallen, steel mills in foreign countries were taking away a lot of business from American steel companies, the American people decided that they preferred clean air to more steel, and finally, technological improvements changed the way steel is made.

First, as our economy became more technological than industrial in the 1970s and 1980s, it put increasing emphasis on providing services and products such as television sets, telecommunications, and computers, which use very little steel. Further aggravating the problems faced by steel companies, Americans and the rest of the world became more energy conscious because of the dramatic increase in oil prices in the 1970s. The auto industry, one of the biggest users of steel, needed to develop more fuel-efficient cars. One way of doing this was to make cars lighter by using less steel.

Second, not only is the world using less steel, but countries other than the United States are producing more to meet their domestic consumption and exporting it to other countries, including the United States. This competition has caused many American firms to get out of the steel business and into other, more technologically advanced types of business. As shown in Figure 1, in 1996, the United States, which once led the world in steel production is now third, behind China and Japan.

Third, in addition to the hardships caused by reduced demand and foreign competition, in 1972 the U.S. government passed our first Clean Air and Clean Water bills. This legislation essentially required all businesses to take responsibility for reducing air and water pollution. This did not present a hardship for some businesses such as law firms and retailers, but it did impose a tremendous burden on the steel industry. Companies in the industry had traditionally been able to use the surrounding air and water as an inexpensive place to dump their waste products. New requirements prohibiting such practices meant that they would need to install expensive equipment to control pollution and, in the future,

Figure 1

World Steel Production, 1996

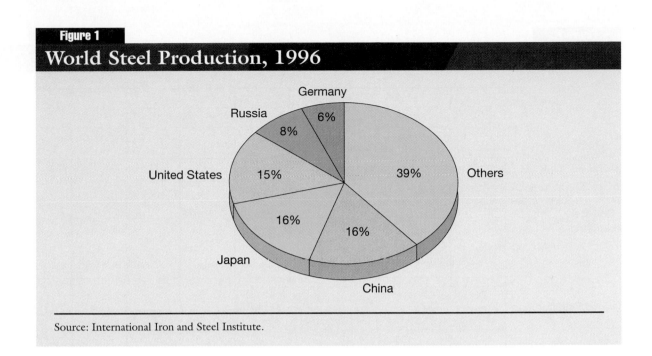

Source: International Iron and Steel Institute.

any new steel-making equipment would need to be redesigned to limit the pollution it generated. The legislation has led to a much cleaner environment in the United States, but it also raised production costs in the domestic steel industry.

Fourth, although the giant, smoke-belching steel mills are indeed a thing of the past, high-tech mini-mills that make basic steel and specialized steel products are thriving and successfully competing in markets all over the globe. They are doing so by using new technologies, such as recycling scrap, new automated continuous casting processes, and electric furnaces that do not require the use of environmentally hazardous coal and coke. They have also reduced the wasted portion of produced steel from 26% down to 14%. An important side effect of these technologies is that steel mills need much less coal and iron ore and are not therefore restricted to locations adjacent to coal and/or iron mines. As a consequence, Pittsburgh has lost its importance as the leading steel-producing region of the country.

Someone who had lived in Pittsburgh during the heyday of the steel industry would hardly recognize the city today. Its downtown is a financial center with gleaming office buildings, it is one of the world's leading centers for the development of robotics technology and software engineering, and its health care industry is among the world's leaders in organ transplant research and technology. There are also a number of firms that produce pollution control equipment. Most of the children of the men and women who worked in the steel industry no longer labor in the mills. Although a few still work in the handful of new mini-mills in the region, many more are accountants, financiers, medical technicians, computer designers, and engineers. Figure 2 shows how the nature of Pennsylvania's workforce has changed from 1974 to 1994. Similar to the rest of the United States, the local labor force employed in manufacturing is decreasing while employment in services and high-tech industries expands.

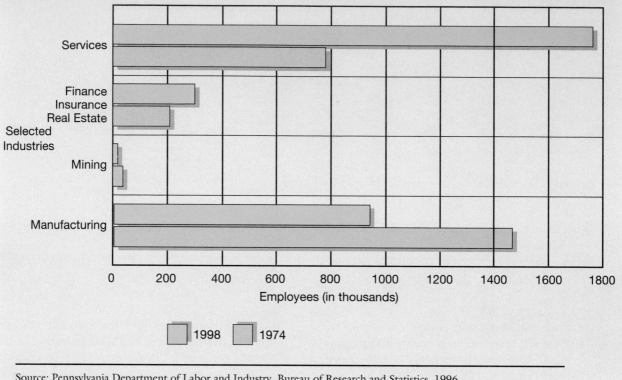

Figure 2

Civilian Labor Force, Pennsylvania, 1974 and 1998

Employees (in thousands)

Selected Industries: Services, Finance Insurance Real Estate, Mining, Manufacturing

■ 1998   ■ 1974

Source: Pennsylvania Department of Labor and Industry, Bureau of Research and Statistics, 1996.

Chapter Preview

Households, businesses, and governments must continually make decisions about how best to spend the limited amount of money that they have. In the same way, societies must continually make decisions about the best way to use their scarce resources to make the different things that people want. How successful we are at choosing the best use of these resources determines how well we can achieve our economic goals. This chapter will help you understand these issues better by examining the questions, What are the consequences of economic choices? What are the basic economic questions? What are society's economic goals?

Learning Objectives

After completing this chapter, you should be able to:

1. Define and give examples of economic trade-offs.
2. Apply the concept of opportunity cost to any economic choice.
3. Use a production possibility frontier to demonstrate increasing costs, trade-offs, opportunity cost, and economic growth.
4. Give examples of the three basic economic questions.
5. Understand the four primary economic goals of society.
6. Explain the effect on output of increasing employment to full employment.
7. Explain the effect on output of improving economic efficiency.
8. Explain the effect on economic growth of producing and using technologically sophisticated capital goods.
9. Give examples of trade-offs between economic and socioeconomic goals.
10. Understand the connection between choices in consumption and choices in production.

▶ What Are the Consequences of Economic Choices?

An abundant supply of everything relative to the demand for it would mean that individuals and society could be as wasteful as they pleased and not have to consider making choices. But because of scarcity, we must make choices, and choices involve **trade-offs.** In turn, because we must make trade-offs, we must endure opportunity costs.

◼ Trade-offs

As individuals our financial resources are limited. This means that if you spend $40 on a concert ticket, you cannot use that $40 to buy some new clothes. In economics we refer to this as a trade-off; to get one thing you need to sacrifice something else. Similarly, because resources are scarce in relation to the demand for them, using them to produce one thing means that others will not be produced. A choice to use our bricks, lumber, architects, and electricians to build steel mills means that we cannot use these resources to build pollution control equipment. While we might gain in terms of the amount of steel that we have, we must trade-off some clean air to obtain it.

Although trade-off decisions are made by individual consumers, producers, and the government, in our economy most are made by consumers. And, every time that people go to the store to shop, they affect the decisions

trade-off   the choice between alternative uses for a given quantity of a resource.

The production of any commodity represents an economic choice. Factors such as climate and profitability play a part in a farmer's decision to produce grapes rather than honey.

coated cereals, resources will be allocated to raising honey bees. True, boxes used to carry grapes and raisins cannot take the place of glass jars for storing honey, but the land, labor, and capital used to produce one can be transferred, or reallocated, into the production of the other.

Similarly, if as a society, we decide to "consume" cleaner air, fewer resources will be allocated to producing polluting industries and more will be allocated to producing pollution-control equipment. When consumers or societies make trade-offs in what they consume, producers must make trade-offs in the allocation of resources.

Opportunity Costs

To make the best possible use of our limited resources, we need to compare the trade-off possibilities to find out what is gained and what is lost. The value of the sacrificed alternative is called the **opportunity cost** of whatever is produced or consumed. Opportunity cost is measured by the benefit that must be sacrificed in order to gain something. For a consumer, the opportunity cost of buying a steel-belted radial tire might be the sacrificed benefit of going to a concert. For a steel producer, the opportunity cost of installing pollution-control equipment might be the benefits that would result from installing a new electric furnace and hiring new workers. For a society, the opportunity cost of clean air might be fewer steel-belted tires (and other things).

The often-heard economic expression "There is no such thing as a free lunch" refers to the concept of opportunity cost. Opportunity cost applies not only to economic decisions, but to everything that you do. That "free" hour you spend working on your jump shot costs you an hour that you could have spent roller-blading, working at a part-time job, doing homework, or working on your inside game. Because time is the ultimate scarce resource, everything that you do has a very real opportunity cost in terms of time.

Production Possibilities Frontier

Trade-offs and opportunity costs can be shown in a special type of analytical diagram called a **production possibilities frontier (PPF)**.

about how resources are allocated. For example, if people buy raisin bran cereal, resources will need to be **allocated** to the production of grapes and raisins. If instead they buy honey-

allocation the different uses to which resources are put in order to produce different goods and services. The manner in which a society allocates its scarce resources determines what it produces.

opportunity cost real economic cost of a good or service produced measured by the value of the sacrificed alternative.

production possibility frontier (PPF) the line on a graph showing the different maximum output combinations of goods or services that can be obtained from a fixed amount of resources.

The opportunity cost of something is the value of the sacrificed alternative. The opportunity cost of going to a concert might be a new compact disc.

Figure 3 shows the trade-off between steel and oranges. The diagram shows the different amounts of the two goods that can be produced with a *fixed amount of resources*. It allows us to compare the opportunity costs of our alternative choices by showing the amount of one good that must be sacrificed in order to obtain some of the other.

Tons of oranges are measured from left to right along the horizontal axis and tons of steel are measured from bottom to top on the vertical axis. Suppose that if all of the country's available resources were put into producing steel, the country could produce 50 million tons of it. If, instead, all of those same resources were put into producing oranges, we could produce 100 million tons of them. If we allocate part of our resources to make steel and the other part for oranges, and if we assume that the trade-off between the two outputs is constant, the line marked PPF shows the different combinations of steel and oranges that can be produced. It represents the maximum combinations of the two outputs that can be produced with the available resources. The distance of the PPF from the origin indicates the total level of output. PPFs

Figure 3

Trade-off between Production of Steel and Oranges

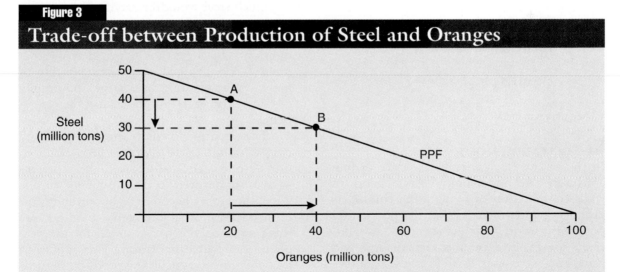

Moving from point A to point B on the production possibility frontier results in an increase in production of oranges of 20 million tons, with an opportunity cost of 10 million tons reduction in steel production.

farther from the origin indicate a greater output of both goods. Combinations of goods that lie outside the PPF are unattainable with existing resources and technology.

If the nation chose to allocate its resources to produce the combination shown at point A, it could produce 20 million tons of oranges and 40 million tons of steel. If it reallocated its resources to produce at point B, it could produce 40 million tons of oranges and 30 million tons of steel. The opportunity cost of changing the composition of output from A to B, of increasing orange production by 20 million tons (from 20 to 40), is reducing steel production by 10 million tons (from 40 to 30). Similarly, if we go from B to A, the opportunity cost of increasing steel production by 10 million tons is decreasing orange production by 20 million tons. The opportunity costs would be the same wherever we moved along the PPF because we assumed that the trade-off ratio was constant at 2:1. Each ton of steel costs us 2 tons of oranges, and each ton of oranges costs us 0.5 tons of steel. Notice that the PPF cannot tell us if one combination of steel and oranges is better than another, it can only show us the different combinations that are available to us.

What Are the Consequences of Economic Choices?

EconExplorer

▶ Increasing Costs

In the real world, trade-off ratios are seldom constant. The opportunity costs depend on what combination of outputs the country is producing and where it is on the production possibility frontier. If our resources are allocated somewhat evenly between oranges and steel, then it is easy to shift a few resources from one to the other without significantly affecting the trade-off ratio. If the economy increases its production of oranges at the expense of steel, however, more and more resources suitable to making steel will be shifted into orange production. At the extreme, we would be tearing down steel mills and growing oranges in Pittsburgh. This could be done using greenhouses, but it would be very costly in terms of the forgone steel, which is easier to produce in Pittsburgh. At the other extreme, if resources are increasingly allocated to producing steel, we eventually would be tearing out orange trees in Florida to make room for steel mills, which would require that coal and iron ore be transported all the way to Florida.

This situation is pictured in Figure 4 on page 48. Here the trade-offs are not constant. Still using the same amount of resources, the opportunity costs of steel and oranges vary, depending on where you are on the production possibility frontier. The more of one good that you produce, the more costly it is to produce increasingly more of it. If the country were devoting *all* its resources to steel and nothing to oranges (point A), it would only need to sacrifice a small amount of steel (m) to get a big increase in orange production (n) if it moved to point B. It might, for example, plant orange trees outside Orlando on what had been a steel mill. While not much steel would be sacrificed because it is not a very productive location for a mill, it would result in a large increase in orange production. On the other hand, if it were at point C and changed output composition to point D, there would be a large opportunity cost in lost steel (o) to get a small increase in oranges (p).

The situation of increasing opportunity costs as resources are allocated increasingly to one output is the usual case. The more resources are devoted to the production of one good, the higher becomes its opportunity cost in the sacrifice of an alternative good because some resources are better suited for the production of that other good. This applies to everything from agricultural products to manufactured goods to the provision of different kinds of services.

Case Application

Tough Choices

Imagine being in a major shopping mall with $25 in your pocket. Think of all the things that you would like to buy, and think of all the options you are facing. CDs? A new shirt? A video game? Well, if you think that you have tough choices to make, think about the choices that the U.S. government has to make about how to spend its money. Of course it has almost $1.6 trillion dollars to spend, but there are about 260 million people to spend it on. And unlike your situation, where only one person has to decide, U.S. spending plans have to be agreed on by 435 congressional representatives and 100 senators!

As the United States heads for the twenty-first century, we are in the unusual position of having a government *budget surplus*—an excess of tax revenues over expenditures. The 1998 budget of the U.S. federal government forecasts a surplus of $22 billion, and it forecasts increased surpluses through the year 2010. The last time the government had a budget surplus was in 1969. In each year since, the federal government has spent more than it took in, leaving it with a *budget deficit*. The shortfall in revenues was made up for by borrowing. In 1992 the government borrowed a record $290 billion dollars. When you add up all the annual deficits that have occurred through the years, the total national debt is now over $5 trillion!

There are many different opinions about what to spend the government's money on. During the cold war, a big part of our spending was for our armed forces. In 1990 defense spending accounted for the largest part of the federal budget: about 24% of total spending. By 1997, defense spending (17% of the budget) had fallen to second behind Social Security (23%). The third biggest part of the budget (15%) went to pay interest on that $5 trillion dollars worth of outstanding debt, and the fourth largest share (13%) was used to fund Medicare, a program to help provide health care for retirees. The remainder of the budget had to be stretched to pay for roads and highways, the space program, foreign aid, maintaining our national parks, environmental protection, help for the needy, housing, and everything else that the federal government helps to pay for.

Our projected budget surpluses not only come from reduced military spending. The biggest reason for the surplus is the fact the U.S. economy has been growing steadily since 1991. When the economy grows, people earn more money and they pay more taxes. In addition, since more people have jobs, less money needs to be spent on social programs to help the poor. (Of course, should economic growth slow and the country enter a *recession*, those planned surpluses may disappear quite quickly!)

The fact that we are planning to have budget surpluses for the next few years has a lot of people interested in how to spend this extra money. Some think that the surplus should be returned to the taxpayers in the form of a tax cut; others think that it should be used to make some extra payment on that national debt; and others think that it should be used to expand federal assistance for child care, health insurance, and education. One alternative that is receiving more and more attention is to maintain this surplus to help pay for the increased Social Security and Medicare benefits that are going to occur in the next several years. People used to receive these benefits when they turned 65. To save money, Congress has recently increased the qualifying age to 67. Still, the record number of baby boomers (people born between 1945 and 1955) who will begin collecting benefits in 2010 are going to put a huge strain on the system.

Economic Reasoning

1. What is an example of a trade-off in this case application? What is the opportunity cost associated with the trade-off?

2. What are some of the opportunity costs of using the projected budget surplus to reduce taxes? What are some of the opportunity costs of not cutting taxes?

3. What do you think should be done with the projected budget surplus?

Tough Choices

Use the Web to visit the Congressional Budget Office Web site at w.cbo.gov/ and click on The Economic and Budget Outlook and then on The Budget Outlook. How big is the current "baseline" budget deficit (or surplus), and what is it projected to be during the next 3 years?

(Continued from page 46)

Figure 4

Production Possibility Frontier with Increasing Costs

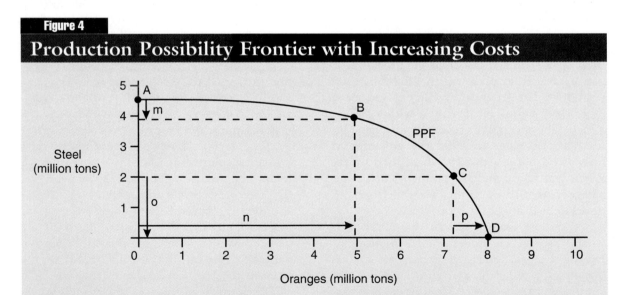

With increasing costs, which is the usual case, if a country were devoting all its resources to the production of steel (point A), it could have a great increase in orange production (n) by sacrificing a small amount of steel output (m). On the other hand, if it were already producing mostly oranges (point C) and moved to total production of oranges (point D), the increased amount of oranges (p) would be small in comparison to the reduced steel production (o).

What Are the Basic Economic Questions?

In allocating resources, there are three basic economic questions that must be resolved by every society. Given its scarce resources, it must decide what to produce, how to produce it, and once produced, who gets it. To a large extent, the kind of economic system that a society adopts determines how it resolves these questions. This chapter will introduce these questions and the next chapter will continue to explore how they are answered by different economic systems.

What to Produce?

Because of the scarcity of resources, a society cannot produce everything it wants. Therefore, the economy must continually decide what mix of goods and services it is going to produce with its limited resources. Is it going to produce steel or CDs? Basketballs or shoes? Health care or military armaments? Somehow it must determine an answer to this **"what" question.**

In the United States, how consumers, businesses, and governments allocate their spending among different uses determines what gets produced. If consumers decide that they like ski boats more than they like cars, more resources will be allocated to fiberglass and less to steel. If they decide that they prefer to spend less and save more, more money will be available for businesses to borrow and invest in new capital. This will mean more resources used in producing equipment, factories, and office buildings. There will also be more home construction and automobile production because there will be more money for lending to finance these purchases.

Government choices also influence what gets produced. When the cold war ended the government reduced military spending from $304 billion in 1989 to $272 in 1997, and it faced numerous choices about what to do with the tax revenues it had been spending on national defense. One option was to reduce taxes and thereby increase consumers' after-tax incomes. This would have directed resources into the production of consumer goods and services. Consumers would have been able to buy more electronic goods, restaurant meals, and vacations. Alternatively, it could have kept the tax revenue and spent it to finance other programs, for instance, new roads and bridges. In this case, the steel and highway construction industries would have expanded. As it turned out, much of the "extra" money has been used to fund the increased health care costs for older Americans and the poor (see chapter 9).

What Are the Basic Economic Questions?

EconExplorer

How to Produce?

Once an economy determines the mix of goods and services to which it is going to allocate its resources it must determine what production methods are going to be used. The resolution of the **"how" question** depends on resources available to an economy. If a country has a lot of unemployed or **underemployed** labor, it will use labor-intensive production techniques. If it has a lot of capital equipment relative to the amount of available labor, it will use capital-intensive production techniques.

"what" question the question concerning the decisions made by an economy about what (and how much of) particular goods and services to produce with its limited resources.

"how" question the question concerning the decisions made by an economy about the technology used to produce goods and services.

underemployed resources resources that are not used to their fullest potential.

Figure 5

Production Possibilities for Consumer and Capital Goods

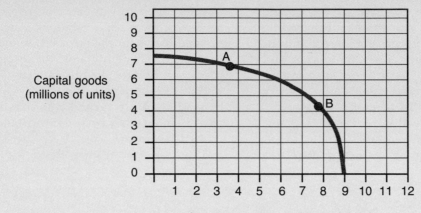

Capital goods
(millions of units)

Consumer goods (millions of units)

The resources that are made available by a decrease in consumer goods can be used to produce capital goods. A point such as B may satisfy more of our current wants, but a point such as A will lead to greater satisfaction of future wants.

Whether we choose to spend our money or save it will not only affect what gets produced, it will also affect production methods in the economy. If we save, and our resources go into private investment, production will become more capital intensive. In all sectors of the economy, there will be more capital used in production relative to the amount of labor, and this leads to increased *future* output. In the case of government spending, there will also be more real capital if the spending goes toward better highways, bridges, airports, and public transportation facilities—the **infrastructure** (or public capital) of the economy. This will similarly make the economy more productive.

infrastructure an economy's stock of capital—much of it publicly owned—that provides basic services to producers and consumers. Includes such facilities as highways, electric power, water supplies, educational institutions, and health services.

Similar to its use in showing the trade-off between two specific goods, the PPF can be used to show the trade-off between abstract types of goods such as the consumer goods and capital goods discussed above. Such a PPF is shown in Figure 5. At point B, the economy is producing 8 hypothetical units of consumer goods and 4 hypothetical units of capital goods. As explained above, choosing to produce more units of capital will make the economy more productive. To do so by moving to point A, however, where it is producing 7 units of capital, requires the sacrifice of 4 units of consumer goods.

Answering the "how" question also involves technology. Developing new technologies and using them in new equipment (capital) or production processes will enable us to produce more output from our available resources. For example, in 1920 it took 2.1 tons of coal and 1.6 tons of iron ore to make one ton of steel. Today, improved technology permits us to make one ton of steel from only 0.5 tons of coal and 1.2 tons of ore. Similarly, the use of high-efficiency appliances enables us to stretch our energy resources farther, and the use of computers allows a law office to

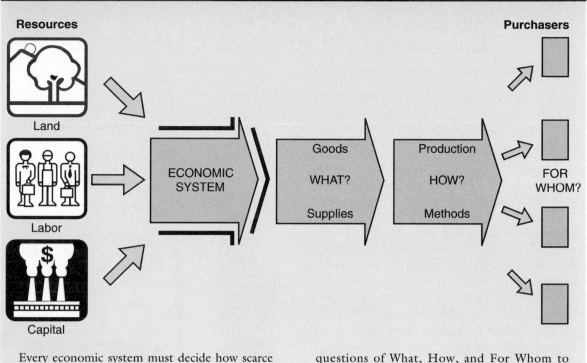

Figure 6

The Economic System

Resources

Land

Labor

Capital

ECONOMIC SYSTEM

Goods

WHAT?

Supplies

Production

HOW?

Methods

Purchasers

FOR WHOM?

Every economic system must decide how scarce resources will be used to answer the three basic questions of What, How, and For Whom to produce.

handle more cases. How we produce therefore reflects the available technology that we develop and choose to adopt. Just like the absolute amount of capital influences how much we can produce, so does the *technological quality* of the capital.

▶ For Whom to Produce?

The third basic economic decision every economic system must make is how to allocate finished goods and services among its population. The resolution of the **"for whom" question** determines who gets how much of what is produced. Because the economy cannot produce as much of everything as we would like it to produce, the output must be rationed in some fashion.

The "for whom" question does not imply that a particular item is produced for a particular consumer, but rather that different groups

will benefit from the different ways that we choose to spend our money. If we want more and bigger cars, auto and steel workers will receive more income and will get an increased share of our total production. If we choose to save our money, people who make investment goods will receive an increased share. If we choose to devote more resources to social programs, the less fortunate will receive an increased share.

"for whom" question the question concerning the decisions made by an economy about income distribution—who gets how much of the goods and services produced.

Comparative Case Application

To Nuclear or Not to Nuclear

Electricity is a vital input for a modern industrial economy. Factories, retail stores, businesses, and households could not function without it. The production of electricity therefore becomes one of the most important industries in any economy. Since the time of the Industrial Revolution (see chapter 3 Perspective), the world's more developed economies have produced most of their electricity by burning fossil fuels (coal, petroleum, and natural gas). There are, however, two significant problems with this strategy. First, fossil fuels are nonrenewable, and we will run out of them some day. Second, the burning of fossil fuels pollutes our atmosphere and contributes to the problem of global warming. What are we going to do?

In the 1960s, it appeared that the answer would be nuclear power. Having learned how to harness atomic energy to produce electricity, the world anticipated an energy source that could provide an almost unlimited supply of electricity at costs so low that it would be unnecessary to even monitor the amounts used. Three decades later, after the United States spent $112 billion constructing over 100 nuclear power plants, and another $25 billion on over 100 that were never completed, we hit a wall of cost overruns and accidents that stopped the nuclear energy movement nearly dead in its tracks. We have not started a new nuclear power plant in the United States since 1978.

One of the major reasons for the slowdown was that the cost per kilowatt of electricity produced in a nuclear plant rose from approximately the same as it was for a coal-fired plant in the early 1970s, to twice as much as the coal burner by the mid-1980s. For example, the Marble Hill nuclear power station in

Pilgrim Station nuclear power plant, Plymouth, Massachusetts.

Indiana had been projected to cost $1.4 billion when construction began in 1978. By the time work was abandoned on the half-finished plant in 1983, some $2.5 billion had already been spent. The estimated final cost would have been $7.7 billion, or more. To cover these losses, the utility company that was building the plant increased the rates it charged on electricity from its other plants and reduced the profits paid to its stockholders by 67 percent.

Just as important as the higher costs was the growing concern over the safety of nuclear power. There had been a few serious accidents in the 1970s, but the real turning point was the 1979 accident at the Three Mile Island nuclear plant near Harrisburg, Pennsylvania, which very nearly approached the ultimate disaster—a meltdown of the radioactive core. Confidence in the safety of nuclear power was further shaken by an accident at Chernobyl, Ukraine,

A youngster swallows an antiradiation solution in a Warsaw clinic in March 1986 as part of a precaution against fallout from the Chernobyl nuclear power plant accident in the neighboring Soviet Union.

in the former Soviet Union. In 1986, there was an explosion and fire in one of the Chernobyl nuclear reactors. The short-term consequences were the deaths of 30 people immediately following the accident, but no one can say what the long-term consequences may be. Some 100,000 people had to be evacuated from the immediate vicinity, and for miles the land surrounding the plant has become uninhabitable because of the high levels of radiation. Radioactive fallout from the plant drifted across borders, forcing the destruction of crops and livestock in a number of neighboring European countries.

Despite the costs and fears, the world, especially the developing countries of South and East Asia, need energy. Solar, thermal, and hydroelectric power are potential alternatives, but they will not be able to provide sufficient energy in the foreseeable future. The consequences of burning fossil fuels to produce the needed power are a more rapid depletion of our fixed supplies and increased environmental problems such as pollution and global warming. Nuclear power therefore remains a very promising alternative.

As of May 1997, there were 444 nuclear power plants in operation throughout the world, with the greatest number (110) being in the United States. Other countries that are very dependent on nuclear power include France (58 plants), Japan (53 plants), and Great Britain (35 plants). These countries, especially Japan, are highly industrialized and need a lot of energy, but do not have abundant supplies of fossil fuels.

Even though the construction of nuclear plants in the United States has stopped, as of May 1997 there were 35 under construction in other parts of the world. Eleven of these are in the developing countries of South and East Asia (China, Korea, India, and Pakistan), and 15 are in former communist countries (Czech Republic, Romania, Slovenia, Ukraine, and other countries in the former Soviet Union).

Economic Reasoning

1. Which of the basic economic questions are involved in this case? In what way?

2. In what way does resource availability affect the resolution of the "how" question with respect to electric power generation in the United States and Japan?

3. Who should make the determination about which is the safest and most efficient way to produce electricity: burning fossil fuels or splitting atoms? Should it be the electric power industry, citizens, or the government? Should there be international rules governing the use of nuclear power?

To Nuclear or Not to Nuclear

Use the Internet to visit the International Atomic Energy Commission at www.iaea. or.at/worldatom/ and see how many nuclear plants are currently operating worldwide. Have there been any major safety issues raised in the past year?

▶ What Are Society's Economic Goals?

We make economic choices in the light of certain goals. There are four goals that societies aim to achieve that are principally economic in nature. In addition to these economic goals, there are social goals with important economic dimensions. This section examines the goals that often underlie decisions as to what trade-offs a society will make and what opportunity costs it will bear in resolving the three basic economic questions.

◢ Growth

Economic growth means a continuing increase in the capacity of an economy to produce goods and services. To most economists, this is

---

economic growth an increase in the production capacity of the economy.

---

the most important economic goal. If the main purpose of an economy is to satisfy consumer wants with its scarce resources, then the economy must strive to produce as much output as possible and to keep increasing that output. This will enable people to have more steel, a cleaner environment, better health care and education, more museums and libraries, or whatever it is that the people in that society want. In short, the greater the economic growth, the greater a society's material standard of living.

As suggested above, one way to increase economic growth is to defer current consumption and put more resources into producing capital goods. Figure 7 illustrates that how we allocate our resources will affect the rate of growth. If most of them are used to produce consumer goods, (point B), this would give us a lower rate of growth, shown by the

Investment in technologically advanced equipment like robotics increases economic efficiency and growth. Although some workers might lose assembly line jobs, others will find new jobs making robots.

Figure 7

Growth of the Economy with Different Current Allocations of Resources between Capital Goods and Consumption Goods

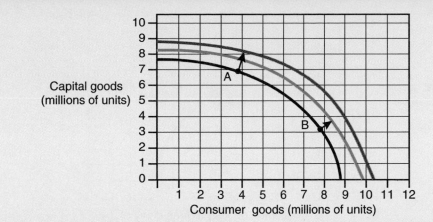

If most of the resources went into the production of consumer goods, as shown by point B, we would have a higher current standard of living; but economic growth during the next few years would only expand to the green line. If the resources were allocated as shown by point A, however, the economy would expand to the brown line, making even higher future living standards possible.

outward shift of the PPF curve only as far as the green line. On the other hand, if we allocate more resources to capital goods, a larger amount of investment would occur (point A). This larger investment would give us a higher growth rate, as shown by the outward shift of the PPF curve to the brown line. At any point on the brown line, the PPF shows us that we can have more of both capital *and* consumer goods. This is the essence of economic growth.

▨ Efficiency

Given that scarcity means that we cannot have everything we would like to have, it makes sense that we should try to get as much as possible from the resources that we have at our disposal. This means efficiently allocating resources to where they are the most productive. Land in Florida should be allocated to growing oranges and land in Pennsylvania should be used for making steel. The same holds true for all our scarce resources. We are better off if Mark Mc Gwire hits baseballs and your instructor teaches economics than we would be if they switched jobs. The efficient allocation of resources is important to ensure maximum economic growth.

As mentioned, one of the most important ways we achieve increased **efficiency** is by improving the technology of production. The steel industry employs a lot of highly skilled labor in research and development (R&D). These scientists, engineers, technical personnel, and their technological discoveries have enabled us continually to find cleaner and better ways to make steel using less coal, ore, and energy.

We can use the production possibilities frontier shown in Figure 8 to illustrate the concept of efficiency. The PPF shows us the maximum amount of two goods that we can obtain from given resources. However, we can obtain this maximum only if we allocate our resources to their most productive uses. For example, point A in the figure indicates what will happen if we use our resources inefficiently. In this case

efficiency maximizing the amount of output obtained from a given amount of resources or minimizing the amount of resources used for a given amount of output.

Figure 8

Production with Unemployed Resources Compared to Full Employment Production

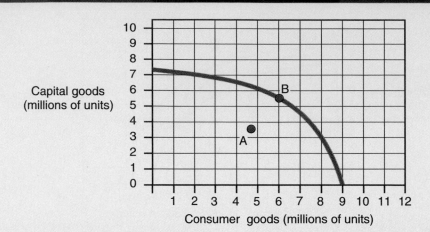

Production at less than full employment is represented by point A, which lies inside the production possibilities curve. Point B on the PPF is full employment, with more output of consumer goods and capital goods. Maintaining full employment in a rapidly changing economy is easier if the economy is healthy to begin with.

we are only obtaining 4 units of capital and 5 units of consumer goods. Point B shows that with efficient resource use we can have 6 units of capital goods and 6 units of consumer goods. Since most people prefer to have more goods rather than fewer goods, the efficient use of our resources is an economic goal as it increases our output by 2 units of capital and 1 unit of consumer goods.

◥ Full Employment

In order to achieve the greatest possible output and achieve economic growth, an economy must also attain **full employment.** This means that nearly everyone who wants to work can find a job. Full employment is an important economic goal for two reasons: because jobs are the main source of most people's incomes, and because full employment is necessary for an

full employment employment of nearly everyone who desires to work. In practice, an unemployment level of not more than 4–5% is considered full employment.

economy to fully utilize its limited resources. Labor is a resource, and unemployed labor means loss of production from a resource that can never be recovered.

Similar to the case of inefficiency, unemployment can be shown in the PPF diagram in Figure 8. If unemployment exists, the economy will be operating at a point inside the production possibility frontier. Point A represents less than full employment output. Moving to point B on the curve gives us full employment and increased production of both capital goods and consumer goods.

In a rapidly changing world, where new goods and services are constantly being put on the market and technology is changing rapidly, it is sometimes difficult to reallocate labor from one type of job to another. This is easier if the economy is healthy to begin with or if the reallocation is spread out over a number of years. This is not always the case, however, and it is sometimes difficult for an economy to maintain full employment. The steel industry provides a good example of this. With the closing of mills, many workers were unemployed for a long period of time before they could retrain for jobs in new, emerging businesses.

The Social Security Administration helps to ensure that Americans have financial security in their retirement years.

Price Stability

Another economic goal is to maintain **price stability.** Price stability is the avoidance of rapid changes in the general price level of goods and services. Prices of individual goods and services go up and down in response to changes in the costs of producing them and the demand for them. When there is **inflation,** however, the prices of most things rising rapidly at the same time can disrupt the economy in many ways. Not only can inflation impose financial burdens on some members of the economy, it can also make it difficult for people to make well-informed choices about what to buy or whether or not to invest in new capital. As a consequence, like inefficiency and unemployment, unstable prices can prevent an economy from reaching its maximum production possibilities.

Socioeconomic Goals

There is not much disagreement over the desirability of the four primarily economic goals discussed above (although there is a great deal of debate over how best to achieve them). There are some additional goals of society that are to a lesser degree economic in

price stability a constant average level of prices for all goods and services.
inflation a continuously rising general price level, resulting in a reduction in the purchasing power of money.

Case Application

The Computer Craze

It was only about 18 years ago, in 1981, that IBM introduced its first desktop personal computer (PC), the 5150. This marvel of technology had one 5¼ inch disk drive (160KB capacity), no hard drive, and it cost about $3000. Fully loaded with graphics capabilities and a color monitor it cost $6,000. (In today's dollars that would be over $10,000!) A standard word processing package required the user to insert different disks to check spelling or to use a dictionary. Compare that to the features on today's PCs that cost half as much!

Computers have taken over the workplace and made many workplace products obsolete. Typewriters are a thing of the past as are standard cash registers. Now we type using computers and our grocery store purchases are scanned, priced, and recorded by computers. The same holds true for just about every business in the United States, from auto repair shops to information booths at the city zoo. Our cars have computers to monitor climate and gas mileage and computerized robots and

In the split second it takes the checkout clerk to flick an item across the scanner, many functions take place. The item and its price are recorded on the receipt, the store inventory is updated, and this may trigger a reorder of the item in the supplier's computer.

nature—what we might term **socioeconomic goals**—about which there is less universal agreement. An examination of public policies indicates that the following might be included among socioeconomic goals: protection of the environment from pollution, financial security for individuals, economic equity, just treatment for all individuals in economic matters, and freedom to carry out economic choices.

 What Are Society's Economic Goals?

EconExplorer

control systems do the work that people used to do not so many years ago.

People once had fears of being "replaced by a button"—losing their jobs to computers that could do the same work more efficiently and cheaper. Has that been the case? Not really. Although it is true that many jobs once done by people are being performed by computers, many more jobs have been created for chip manufacturers, PC makers, programmers, systems analysts, and so forth. (Keep in mind that many people had the same fears at the turn of the last century when the introduction of automobiles put a lot of blacksmiths and horse stables out of business.)

Computers also help us make more and better products than we ever could before, and they enable us to produce them cheaper. Computer-aided design helps us make more fuel-efficient cars and safer airplanes. They allow musicians to create new sounds and movie makers to create wonderful special effects. They help to reduce the time a lawyer must spend to help a client, and they even allow students to learn more by doing research on the Internet, and to type their papers faster with no spelling mistakes!

Economic Reasoning

1. Which primary economic goals are advanced through the use of computers? How?

2. Does the use of computers involve a trade-off among different economic and socioeconomic goals? Which goals?

3. Do you favor or oppose the increased use of computers to replace people in the workplace?

The Computer Craze

This manuscript is being produced on a state-of-the-art 333 megahertz Pentium II processor, with 128 SDRAM, 8.4 GB hard drive and a 19-inch monitor PC that sold for $2,600 at the beginning of 1998. Use the Internet to find out what a state-of-the-art PC currently costs, and compare the RAM and megahertz. (To learn about the history of personal computers, start at http://www1.islandnet.com/~kpolsson/and go to the Microcomputers link.)

Very often the attainment of socioeconomic goals involves a trade-off with the attainment of economic goals. For example, maximizing economic growth and maintaining full employment often conflict with our desire for clean air and water. Financial security and economic equity often conflict with the goal of economic efficiency. When such conflicts occur, it is often the role of society to resolve them, usually by having our governments make decisions about the relative importance of economic and socioeconomic goals. We will return to some of these conflicts and their resolution in later chapters.

socioeconomic goal the type of social goal that has important economic dimensions.

▶ Putting It Together

Because resources are insufficient to produce all the things we want, we have to choose how best to use those resources. In deciding how to use our limited resources, certain *trade-offs* are necessary.

The value of what we give up when resources are used to produce one thing rather than another is the *opportunity cost* of what is produced. In order to get the greatest benefits from our limited resources, we should use them for the outputs that best serve our needs. If we do not, then the opportunity costs of what we produce will be too high.

A *production possibility frontier (PPF)* shows the trade-off between two alternative uses of a resource. The PPF shows the opportunity cost of producing more of one good by showing the amount of the alternative good that is sacrificed. Production possibility frontiers generally curve outward because of *increasing opportunity costs* incurred as more of

one good is produced. Production possibility frontiers are economic tools helpful in analyzing the opportunity costs of trade-offs.

All economic systems must resolve three basic economic questions: *what to produce; how to produce; for whom to produce.* Scarcity cannot efficiently be dealt with unless the economy *allocates* its resources to producing the goods and services most needed and desired. An economic system needs also to utilize the most efficient production methods with the resources available. Finally, an economic system must determine who gets how much of what is produced.

There are four principally economic goals by which the effectiveness of an economy can be judged: *efficiency, price stability, full employment,* and *growth.* Some *socioeconomic goals* of our society are protection of the environment, financial security, equity, justice, and freedom in economic matters.

$ Perspective $

The Affluent Society

John Kenneth Galbraith (born 1908) Galbraith is a lofty economist in more than one sense. At 6' 8" he towers over colleagues and debate opponents. Born on a farm in Ontario, Canada, he graduated from an agricultural college in the depths of the Depression in the 1930s. He came to the United States for graduate study and remained to teach at the University of California–Berkeley, at Princeton, and, most notably, at Harvard, retiring in 1973. He gave up the Harvard classroom to embark on a 3½-year project that took him to many locations around the world narrating a television series *The Age of Uncertainty*, which he wrote. *The Age of Uncertainty* was a broad, sweeping overview of the history of economic ideas.

Of the 20-some books he has written, *The Affluent Society* and two others form an important triad on the functioning of our capitalist economy. The second book in the triad is *The New Industrial State* (1967), which examines the way decisions are made in modern corporations, their relationship to government, and the consequences for society. The third book is *Economics and the Public Purpose* (1973), in which Galbraith argues the necessity for government to act as a "countervailing power" against the economic and political power of big business and labor.

John Kenneth Galbraith, one of the most provocative modern economists, wrote a book in 1958 entitled *The Affluent Society*. In it he argued that the problem that had traditionally been of primary concern to economists, how to increase production, was no longer the most important problem in industrially advanced countries like the United States. He maintained that the problem of production had been so well solved that all citizens could have enough to satisfy their needs if output were distributed more equally. Furthermore, he said, a lot of what we produced was intentional waste, such as oversized cars. He noted that most of us eat too much, not too little.

Other social scientists have made the same point. Vance Packard maintained in *The Waste Makers* that the American economy has come to depend on consumption for the sake of consumption, planned obsolescence, and "progress through the throwaway spirit."

In the 1970s, the energy crunch, the decline in productivity and income growth, the shift to smaller cars, and the increased emphasis on conservation led to talk about "an age of limits" and cast doubt on the affluent society thesis. But these developments did not convince Galbraith to change his view that total output is not the main concern. Of more importance is the uses to which output is allocated. Poverty and hunger continue to persist in an economy of abundance. Public squalor in the streets of our cities contrasts with the opulence of the offices in the skyscrapers above. Many types of jobs are unnecessarily arduous, boring, or dangerous, for the sake of maximizing total output.

Galbraith's thesis is contrary to the current movement in economic policy—the emphasis on increasing productivity and total output, the reduction of government spending in favor of private spending, the cutbacks in Occupational Safety and Health

Agency activities, and the truce in the war on poverty, both at home and abroad. Being out of step with the popular parade is not unusual for Galbraith. He notes in his introduction to *The Affluent Society*, "I have read on occasion that I find perverse pleasure in attacking the conventional myth. I do not, and on the contrary, it is very hard work. Some day for recreation I intend to write a book affirming fully all the unquestioned economic truths."

For Further Study and Analysis

Study Questions

1. Why are trade-offs necessary in any economic system?
2. Give an example of a personal economic choice you have made recently. What was the constraint that you faced and what was the opportunity cost?
3. Give an example of an economic choice made by society as a whole. How was the choice made and what were some possible opportunity costs?
4. What are three examples of differences in the resolution of the "what" question in the United States today compared to five years ago?
5. How has the increased use of technology affected the resolution of the "how" question in the steel industry?
6. What determines how much of the nation's output of goods and services is allocated to you?
7. Points on a production possibility frontier, such as points A and B in Figure 4, show the different combinations of two goods that could be produced with the available resources. Would it be possible to produce at a point outside the PPF curve? What would such a point mean and how can an economy reach such a point?
8. Some economic and socioeconomic goals are complementary; achieving one goal helps to achieve another goal. What is one example where economic and socioeconomic goals are complementary? What is one example of where economic and socioeconomic goals conflict?
9. In other cases, there are conflicts between different economic goals: efforts to achieve one make it more difficult to achieve another. What is an example of a conflict between economic goals?
10. Give an example of the connection between choices in consumption and choices in production.
11. What goals does Galbraith consider the most important in the United States today?

Exercises in Analysis

1. Prepare an analysis of the alternative uses of any selected natural resource (coal, for example) by considering the following questions: (a) What are three alternative uses of this resource? (b) What are the trade-offs for any one of the three uses you have selected? (c) What is the opportunity cost of using the natural resource for any one of the three uses you chose?
2. Select a local business and discuss how it resolves the "what," "how," and "for whom" questions. Has it changed the way that it resolves these questions over time?

3. Reread the opening article for chapter 1, An Apple a Day, and find all the examples of trade-offs and opportunity cost.

4. Prepare a list of government policy measures that promote our social goals of full employment, economic growth, protection of the environment, or financial security.

5. Construct a production possibilities frontier that shows the trade-off between steel production and clean air. Explain why increasing opportunity costs will exist.

Further Reading

Ayres, Robert U., and Steven M. Miller. *Robotics: Applications and Social Implications.* Cambridge, Mass.: Ballinger, 1983. Discusses the technology and the costs and benefits of robots. Examines also the impact of robotization on employment and productivity and its policy implications.

Burnham, James B. *Changes and Challenges: The Transformation of the U.S. Steel Industry.* St. Louis, MO: Center for the Study of American Business, Washington University, 1993. Gives a good account of the technological changes that have occurred in the U.S. steel industry since 1960.

Cohen, Bernard Leonard. *The Nuclear Energy Option: An Alternative for the 90s.* New York: Plenum Press, 1990. An analysis of energy needs and comparison of nuclear energy with other energy sources in satisfying these needs.

Cole, Don, ed. *Annual Editions: Microeconomics.* Guilford, CT: Dushkin/McGraw-Hill, various years. This annual publication always includes a number of articles (with commentary) that provide real-world examples of opportunity cost.

Gold, David. *The Impact of Defense Spending on Investment, Productivity and Economic Growth.* Washington, D. C.: Center for Budget and Policy Priorities, 1990. A study of how much defense expenditures affect the civilian sectors of the economy.

Hoerr, John P. *And the Wolf Finally Came.* Pittsburgh, University of Pittsburgh Press, 1988. An excellent description of the collapse of the Pittsburgh steel industry.

Johnson, David B. *Public Choice: An Introduction to the New Political Economy.* Mountain View, CA: Bristlecone Books, 1991. Chapter 2 provides an excellent, if somewhat advanced, description of the importance of choice in a market economy.

Medvedev, Grigorii. *No Breathing Room: The Aftermath of Chernobyl.* New York: Basic Books, 1993. A first-person account of the Chernobyl accident and what followed by a department chief in the Directorate for Nuclear Energy in the former Soviet Union.

Pligt, J. van der. *Nuclear Energy and the Public.* Cambridge, Mass.: Blackwell, 1992. Examines public opinion concerning the nuclear industry and the effects of accidents at nuclear plants.

Ross, Alastair. *Dynamic Factory Automation: Creating Flexible Work Systems for Competitive Manufacturing.* New York: McGraw-Hill, 1992. An examination of modern robots in industry and the use of automation to be competitive in the world marketplace.

Thompson, Donald B. "The Human Trauma of Steel's Decline." *Industry Week,* September 2, 1985., pp. 38–44. Discusses the hardships faced by communities and the unemployed in the aftermath of the closing of many steel mills.

chapter three

Economic Systems

Every society, from the most primitive to the most advanced, must find a way to answer the basic economic questions of "what, how, and who." The institutional arrangement that a society uses to answer the questions is called an economic system. Although societies evolve over time due to social and technological change, there are basic identifiable characteristics of different types of economic systems that remain consistent over long periods of time.

That Old Time Rock and Roll

In 1833 a German immigrant named Christian Frederick Martin established a small shop on Hudson Street in New York City that made some of the world's finest acoustic guitars. Working with about 20 skilled craftsmen, Martin could produce about 125 high-quality guitars every year. Unlike today, there were very few stores that specialized in selling musical instruments. This was primarily because so few instruments were made. Martin's guitars were sold to music teachers, who would then resell them to their students.

Making guitars in the early nineteenth century required a great deal of skill and a few simple tools. A master and his fellow craftsmen would carefully select a few materials to construct the instrument. The rosewood back and sides needed to be meticulously shaped, finished, and attached to each other. They were then attached to a top that was just as carefully fashioned out of spruce. The neck was made from finely finished mahogany with an ebony fingerboard and bridge. Although commonly referred to as "catgut," the guitar strings were actually made from sheep's intestines.

The guitars made by Martin, and others, could be heard in homes, music halls, concert halls, at weddings, parties, dances, and all those places where people gathered to play and listen to music. At a minimum, all that was needed was a single guitar player and his or her guitar and a room, and even the room was unnecessary if the weather was nice. Throw in a fiddle, bass, and banjo, and there would be music and dancing as long as the musicians could keep on playing. Without amplification, however, the size the audience was limited because the sound could only be heard for a short distance. The introduction of separate microphones in the early 1900s solved this problem, but it really did not influence the way that the music was made or heard.

Like everything else, the guitar industry changed with the times. Although Martin was still in business and still making some of the world's finest acoustic guitars in the late 1940s, other guitar makers began to electrify the sound. In an attempt to deal with the problem of amplification, guitar companies such as Gibson and Fender had flirted with the use of microphones attached to the inside of hollow-body guitars for years. The resulting vibrations, however, limited the ability to really crank up the volume. In 1948 the guitar world changed dramatically when Leo Fender introduced the first solid-body electric guitar: the *Broadcaster*. Renamed the *Telecaster* in 1951, it evolved into the famous Fender *Stratocaster* played by George Harrison and John Lennon of the Beatles, and then by Jimi Hendrix, Eric Clapton, Jeff Beck, Bonnie Raitt, Stevie Ray Vaughn, and Mark Knopfler. The Gibson Company followed with their own soon-to-be-legend, the Gibson *Les Paul*, in 1952. Variations on this model have been played by Duane Allman, Keith Richards, and, most notably, Jimmy Page in *Stairway to Heaven*.

The introduction of the solid-body electric guitar changed the way we play and listen to guitar music. With an amplified electric guitar one musician could achieve the volume of an entire brass band or a 1940s big band. In the 1950s and early 1960s the technology was relatively simple: the guitarist plugged his or her guitar (and microphone if there were vocals) into an amplifier, plugged the amp into an electric socket, then began to play. Throw in another guitar, an electric bass, and a drummer, and the Beatles had the technology to revolutionize music with a four-piece combo.

If you go to a concert today, you will be amazed to find out how much even this has changed. When Bonnie Raitt straps on her guitar, the only thing it is plugged into is a wireless transmitter worn on the back of her belt. This gives her the freedom to move around the stage without tripping over wires. The transmitter sends electronic signals to a stomp box, which she can work with her feet to modify the sound, and to rack-mounted digital-effects machines.

Making music today often requires more than just a guitar. The inputs of electronics, sound, and computer specialists allow recorded music to be heard by millions of people.

The sound is then transmitted to an amplifier and a microphone, both of which are connected by cable to a giant mixing board at the back of the auditorium, concert hall, or stadium. The music goes next to a power amplifier and then to the speakers, which finally send it out to the audience at 125 decibels. As one guitar historian put it, "Today we're listening to amplified electric signals, not musical instruments."

We also listen to music differently than we did in the past, and it is not just the concert experience that has changed. Today we can listen to music on home or automobile sound systems that contain tuners, tape decks, and compact disc (CD) players. We can listen to CDs and tapes on portable systems while we roller blade, walk along a beach, or through a park. When we go to the movies, we hear a digitally produced soundtrack that is played through surround-sound audio systems, which can shake the theater. We can go to karaoke bars and sing along with the music from the lyrics that flash across a screen. We can even go home, flip on the television and watch and hear our music on MTV or VH1.

The way we make guitars has also changed. Where Martin could produce about 125 guitars a year with 20 craftsmen in 1833, today Fender and Gibson can turn out thousands of guitars every year. Of course to do so requires the inputs of literally millions of people all over the world, even though Gibson and Fender may directly employ only a few hundred workers. For example, a *Les Paul Classic* is not only built out of wood (maple, mahogany, and rosewood), but it also has nickel hardware, a ceramic humbucker (a sound pickup device), steel strings, and any number of electronic components fashioned out of copper, silver, and plastic. Electric guitar manufacturers cannot make all their parts the way Martin did in the 1830s. They need to rely on any number of suppliers, who, in turn, rely on their suppliers.

To achieve the sound we want to hear in a concert hall, architects have to design the hall, and manufacturers have to build amps, speakers, cables, mixing boards, computers, and wireless transmitters—not to mention the steel, concrete, wiring, and plumbing necessary to build the hall! To achieve the sound we want when we turn on our CD players also requires all the things that go into making and running a sound studio, physically making a CD, putting the sound onto the CD, and getting that CD to a store near you.

Although we may have lost some of the human touch that was involved with making music in years gone by, today music can reach millions of people whom it could not reach then. We have more guitars, more CDs, and more places and ways to listen to them. To get this increase in the production of music, however, we need to depend on people as diverse as loggers in Malaysia, miners in Bolivia, computer chip makers in Japan, programmers in California, steel makers in Pennsylvania, and, of course, a guitar player in Nashville who knows how to make his Gibson or Fender wail.

Chapter Preview
The way that music is played and heard has changed over the past two hundred years in an effort to better satisfy the economic goals of growth and efficiency. The manner in which society organizes production to deal with the problem of scarcity and make the things we want is continually evolving. In some countries it has evolved in different directions than in others. But every society still has to resolve the same basic economic questions of "what, how, and who." This chapter will examine the way economies are organized to deal with scarcity by asking the following questions: Why are economic systems needed? What are the principal types of economic systems? How does a market system resolve the three basic economic questions?

Learning Objectives
After completing this chapter, you should be able to:
1. Distinguish between absolute and comparative advantage.
2. Explain why specialization based on comparative advantage results in greater economic growth and interdependence.
3. Explain why specialization creates the coordination problem.
4. Identify the three major types of economic systems, and explain how they differ.
5. Explain how a market system resolves the three basic economic questions.
6. Distinguish between goods and services sold in product markets and those sold in factor markets.
7. Understand the two complementary flows in the circular flow diagram of a market economy.

Why Are Economic Systems Needed?

Back in 1833, Christian Martin and his craftsmen were largely on their own when they designed and built a guitar. Today, Fender and Gibson depend on many different people and companies to help them make a guitar and all the necessary additional accessories that are needed to play it. They depend on steel and nickel makers, computer and amplifier companies, and the electric company that provides the energy to power their factory and their guitars. In many ways these companies are much like the economy as a whole. In achieving greater efficiency in production, we have become more dependent on others, thereby increasing the need for an economic system to organize and coordinate the diverse economic activities of our society.

Specialization

In the early nineteenth century, many Americans were very much self-sufficient. They could raise their own food, make their own clothes, build their own houses, and even make some of their own musical instruments. Although many of the products made this way were beautiful and remain highly prized, they were very simple and now most of us would be very dissatisfied if these were the only products that we had. The kinds of things that we produce today are so sophisticated that no one person or small group of people could possibly produce them. No one person could make an electric guitar, a television, or a compact disc. Instead, we rely on one person (or firm) to produce lumber, another to make transistors, another to make ceramics, another to make plastic, another to make metals, and so on.

In the production of most products there is a division of labor into specialized tasks that results in greater efficiency and lower production costs. One reason why this division of labor results in greater efficiency and lower costs is that **specialization** enables a producer to concentrate on only one job. We can have more and better electric guitars if Fender and Gibson concentrate on making the guitars while they let someone else concentrate on making steel guitar strings and someone else concentrate on making the electricity that powers the guitars.

Adam Smith noted the production gains that come from specialization over two hundred years ago. In *The Wealth of Nations* he described how the production of a simple pin required a piece of wire to be heated, stretched, cut, sharpened, attached to a pinhead, and then stuck into a piece of paper (pins used to be sold in sheets of paper that had a given number of pins stuck into them). He noticed that one person working alone could produce only about 20 pins in one day. However, if labor were divided into separate tasks—one person stretching the wire, a second cutting it, and so on—then ten people working together could produce thousands of pins in a day. In the twentieth century, Henry Ford used this same principle when he produced automobiles on an assembly line composed of many workers, each doing a specialized task. By doing so, Ford was able to produce enough cars at a low enough cost to make them affordable to most people.

The important point to understand about specialization is that it enables us to produce a lot more pins, cars, and guitars than we could if we were not so specialized. It enables us to use our scarce resources more efficiently to produce more and better quality goods—the basic essence of economic growth.

specialization concentrating the activity of a unit of a production resource–especially labor–on a single task or production operation. Also applies to the specialization of nations in producing those goods and services that their resources are best suited to produce.

Why Are Economic Systems Needed?

EconExplorer

Pittsburgh obviously lacks the climate for growing oranges that exists in Florida and California, and thus these warmer states have a comparative advantage in growing citrus fruits. Pittsburgh, however, has a comparative advantage in making steel because of the nearby coal and ore deposits.

Absolute and Comparative Advantage

Specialization will lead to increased production, but to take advantage of it, economies need to decide who should specialize in doing what. Let us take the example of Angela and Harry. She is the town's best certified public accountant, and she put herself through college by painting houses. Not only can she do a simple tax return in one hour, but her experience painting houses also made her the best house painter in town; she paints an average house in 20 hours. Harry is a professional house painter who can paint a house in 40 hours, but he gets confused by government tax forms and it takes him 5 hours to do his tax return.

Suppose Angela charges $100 per hour to do tax returns and Harry charges $25 per hour to paint houses. If Angela painted her own house, her opportunity cost would be $2,000 in lost tax preparation earnings (20 hours times $100 per hour). It is less costly to hire Harry and pay him $1,000 to paint her house (40 hours times $25). On the other hand, it would cost Harry $125 in lost earnings to prepare his own tax return (5 hours times $25) while he could have it prepared by Angela for only $100. It makes sense, therefore, for Angela to prepare both tax returns while Harry paints both houses.

The above example points out the important distinction between **absolute advantage** and **comparative advantage.** Angela has an

absolute advantage a producer has an absolute advantage relative to another producer if he or she can produce more of a good or service than the other with the same amount of resources.

comparative advantage a producer has a comparative advantage relative to another producer if he or she can produce a good or service at a lower opportunity cost than the other.

absolute advantage in painting and preparing taxes because she can do both of them better than Harry. On the other hand, Harry has a comparative advantage in painting houses because his opportunity cost of painting is lower than Angela's. In the same manner, Angela has a comparative advantage in preparing taxes because that is the job where her opportunity cost is lower. When two people have comparative advantages in producing different things, both can gain by specializing in what they do relatively best, and then trading with the other person. It does not matter if one person has an absolute advantage relative to someone else; the gains from specialization and trade come from comparative, not absolute, advantages.

The principle of comparative advantage also exists for regions and countries. If you think back to the example of orange trees and steel mills in chapter 2, you should recognize that Pittsburgh has a comparative advantage in making steel and Orlando a comparative advantage in growing oranges. People in both regions can have more steel and oranges if the regions specialize in what they do best (specialize where they have a comparative advantage) and trade. The Hernandez example in chapter 1 also illustrates comparative advantage. In a very real way, their decision to grow apples, grapes, or fish will depend on where they decide their comparative advantage lies.

Comparative advantage is also the basis for international trade among countries. Even though the United States may have an absolute advantage in the production of toys and textiles compared to China (the United States can pro-

duce more toys and textiles than China if it chooses to), the Chinese have a comparative advantage in making these items. Their opportunity costs are lower because toy and textile manufacturing can be very labor intensive, and China has a very large unskilled labor force. The United States has a comparative advantage in making computers, so the United States specializes in making PCs and Macs, and then trades them to the Chinese for toys and textiles.

To summarize, individuals, regions within a country, and nations all tend to specialize in the production of those things in which they have a comparative advantage. By doing so, the total output available from our given resources can be maximized.

◆ Interdependence

Specialization results in **interdependence**—the reliance of different individuals and businesses on each other. Guitar makers cannot specialize in what they do best without the help and cooperation of others. They depend on loggers and sawmills for their wood and steel companies for their strings. They depend on electricians and computer experts to design and make the amps and other components, so that Bonnie Raitt and Stevie Ray Vaughn can play their guitars for audiences worldwide.

This interdependence requires an economic system to coordinate everyone's various activities. As the degree of specialization and interdependence has increased over the years, so has the complexity of the **coordination problem.** It was a relatively simple task for Christian Martin to acquire the needed resources and supervise his craftsmen in the making of guitars, but how can today's guitar makers be sure that someone is making the right steel strings and electronic components that they need? How can Harry the painter be sure that the local hardware store will have the brushes and scrapers that he needs, and how can Angela the accountant be sure that the local office supply store will have the computer disks that she needs? And how can you be sure that when you go to the store, they have the toothpaste, apples, and *Stratocasters* that you are looking for?

interdependence the relationships between individuals and institutions in a country or between countries that arises because of specialization of production.

coordination problem the problem of how we make sure that all the specialized activities of people will be brought together by an economic system to answer the basic economic questions.

Case Application

The Efficiencyburger

In 1948 the McDonald brothers opened a small restaurant in San Bernadino, California, specializing in the production of hamburgers. They developed a method of producing hamburgers so easily and inexpensively that they could be sold profitably at 15 cents each.

Today the McDonald's hamburger chain (the original McDonald brothers are no longer associated with it) sells more hamburgers than anyone in the world. The key to McDonald's method of low-cost production is specialization. The menu at McDonald's is limited to a select number of items. This cuts food waste to a minimum and eliminates much of the expense associated with an extensive menu.

For the sake of efficiency, each job at McDonald's has been refined and simplified. Like workers on an assembly line, workers have one specialty, although they have the skills to perform other jobs. A typical restaurant has a fry specialist, a grill specialist, a shake specialist, and a cash register operator, all coordinated by a production control specialist. To learn the system, owners and franchise operators attend McDonald's "Hamburger University" in Elk Grove, Illinois, where they take a 19-day course in that leads to a "Bachelor of Hamburgerology with a minor in French Fries."

The McDonald's operation is dedicated to speed. A burger, fries, and shake can be turned out in 50 seconds. Production is tightly controlled in an effort to maintain freshness. Unsold burgers are destroyed if not sold in 10 minutes, french fries are destroyed after 7 minutes.

Everything is done the same way at every McDonald's restaurant—the way the hamburgers are made, the napkins used, and even the greetings used by the salespeople. Because of this, your food will taste the same and the restaurant will look the same whether you are in Chicago, Paris, or Tokyo.

This consistency has proven to be a formula for success throughout the world. At the end of 1997, the chain had more than 22,000 restaurants in 106 countries (107 by 1998 with the opening of the first McDonald's in Lebanon). The company added 1,224 restaurants in the first 9 months of 1997, or one every five hours. About 85% of these new restaurants were outside the United States, and majority of the company's earnings are now made in foreign countries.

Consistency, however, is not always the key to success, and even McDonald's has learned to adapt its products for some foreign markets. Out of respect for the people of India who do not eat beef, McDonald's restaurants in New Delhi and Mumbai serve both vegetarian burgers and nuggets (with chili and masala dipping sauces), as well as the Maharaja Mac, made with "two all-lamb patties, special sauce, lettuce, cheese, pickles, onions, on a sesame seed bun!"

The busiest McDonald's in the world is in Moscow, Russia, and it has been since it opened in January, 1990. It seats 700 people and serves an average of 40,000 people each day. In its first 7 years of operation, it served over 40 million orders of *katoful fries* (french fries), 25 million *Beeg Maks,* and 60 million drinks. During 1997 it introduced its Chicken McNuggets, and illustrated the technique of "McNugget Dunking" in the first commercial they ever produced in Russia.

Although there is a tremendous demand for McDonald's meals in Russia, it was difficult for the company to produce up to their international standards. For example, each hamburger patty must contain between 15.8% and 16.5% fat, and each batch of apple pie filling has to contain 40% apples. Initially, nearly all of the basic ingredients were to be supplied by collectives and government-owned farms, but these suppliers proved to be undependable. Unused to the ways that businesses in market economies were forced to operate to satisfy customers, suppliers were very careless about meeting schedules and standards. To remedy the situation, McDonald's took over the supply operations and produced its own lettuce, hamburger buns, and milk.

Economic Reasoning

1. What economic principle did McDonald's adopt so successfully that it was copied by others? What are the names of some of these "others"?

2. How does the operation of the Moscow McDonald's reflect the relationship between specialization and interdependence?

3. One objective of economies is to avoid waste, but McDonald's policy is to destroy unsold hamburgers after 10 minutes. Is this a good idea? Why or why not?

The Efficiencyburger

Visit McDonald's on the Internet at www.mcdonalds.com. Update the information provided in this story. How many restaurants does McDonald's operate and in how many countries are they located?

▶ What Are the Principal Types of Economic Systems?

The greater the specialization and interdependence in economic activities, the more important is the development of an economic system to organize and coordinate production and distribution. Different types of economic systems have evolved in response to the need to coordinate activities, to respond to the questions of what to produce, how to produce it, and how to allocate what is produced. The purpose of this section is to introduce three different types of economic systems that resolve the coordination problem in different ways.

Market Economies

Allocating resources and finished products in a **market economy** requires three things. First of all, individuals (and companies) have **private property rights:** the right to own private property and use it in whatever way they think best, provided that they obey the law. Second, they must have the right to freely trade or sell their property to others. Third, a market economy will function best when everybody is allowed to pursue their self-interest. For individuals this means receiving

market economy an economic system in which the basic questions of what, how, and for whom to produce are resolved primarily by buyers and sellers interacting in markets.

private property rights the exclusive right of someone to use a scarce resource or good in whatever manner they think best.

In a free market such as the United States, the supply of a product is governed by the choices of consumers, that is, by consumer demand.

are the private property of the supplier. Once purchased, these materials become the private property of the Fender Company. The supplier is free to sell its property to Fender, or Gibson, or Martin. The guitar companies are then free to use these resources any way that they choose, and to sell their products to different music stores throughout the world. If you go shopping for a guitar, you have the right to use your money (a type of property) to buy whichever guitar you prefer. Each of these transactions involves the free and voluntary choices of people exchanging the rights to private property. In each case, the motivation to exchange the rights to the property involves the pursuit of the greatest profits or benefits.

It is important to realize that the economic power in a market economy is held by individual decision makers who are making choices about what is right for them. As discussed in chapter 2, by making these choices the decision makers are influencing where resources will be allocated. It is also important to realize that the existence of private property creates a class of "care-takers." People are more likely to take good care of a resource or good if they know that it is theirs.

What Are the Principal Types of Economic Systems?

EconExplorer

the most benefits for their dollars, and for businesses it means trying to make the greatest profits.

The Fender Company is free to negotiate with its different suppliers to buy inputs that

Market economies are often called capitalist or free enterprise economies. We will examine in more detail how such an economic system resolves the what, how, and for whom questions in the next section of this chapter and in other chapters that follow.

When sellers are not allowed to raise the price of goods that are in great demand or short supply, the goods are often rationed to those who have the most time to wait in line.

◥ Centrally Directed Economies

In **centrally directed** or **command economies,** most production is controlled by the government. The major decisions concerning what to produce, how to produce, and for whom to produce are made by centralized authoritarian agencies. Typically, a central planning commission draws up a master plan, which is then put into effect by national, regional and local government agencies. Unlike

---

centrally directed (command) economy an economic system in which the basic questions of what, how, and for whom to produce are resolved primarily by governmental authority.

---

market economies, where they are privately owned, the natural resources and capital goods are owned by the government. Workers are generally employed in government enterprises or in the government agencies that plan and administer the system.

Resources are allocated in a much different way in a centrally directed economy than they are in a market economy. In a market economy, guitar string manufacturers, responding to signals from the market for guitar strings, decide how many and what kind of strings to make. In a command economy, the central planning authority decides how many and what type of strings will be produced. The manufacturers are given production goals and permission to buy the supplies necessary to produce the number and type of strings decided upon. They may also be given directions about whom to buy their steel from, what

A hydroelectric dam is an example of the type of good produced by government in mixed economies such as the United States.

kind of steel to use, and which guitar makers and stores they must sell the strings to. Since they do not own the resources, individuals and businesses cannot make decisions about how they should be used.

Once the strings are produced, they are placed on sale in government-owned stores or sold to government-owned guitar makers. The price, rather than being determined by the interplay between sellers and buyers in the marketplace, is determined by the government. When there is an insufficient quantity available to satisfy all who would like to purchase strings at that price, they may be allocated to buyers by a formal rationing system, with some reserved for new guitars and others reserved for replacement purposes. Or they may be allocated on a first come, first served basis, resulting in lines of customers at stores when there are supplies available. The operation of centrally directed economies is covered more fully in the opening article of chapter 17.

◤ Traditional Economies

In earlier ages, and, to some extent in nonindustrialized countries today, basic economic decisions depended on tradition and not on the function of markets or the commands of a centralized authority. In **traditional economies** goods are produced and distributed

---

traditional economy an economic system in which the basic questions of what, how, and for whom to produce are resolved primarily by custom and tradition.

---

in certain ways because that is the way it has always been done.

India, with almost a billion people, provides a good example of a traditional economy in the way jobs are allocated. For centuries, India's population was divided by a caste system, a way of classifying people according to the social class, or caste, into which they were born. Regardless of comparative advantages, people born into certain castes could only do the kind of jobs that members of those castes traditionally did. Today the Indian constitution guarantees equal rights and opportunities regardless of caste and creed. But centuries of rigidity have resulted in an underutilized and inefficiently allocated labor force. Opportunities for education and advancement are scarce because of the pressures of India's huge population. It is hard to move to a different location where there may be more jobs because of poverty, lack of education, housing, transportation/travel problems, and so forth. Traditional beliefs play a part, too. People tend to believe that the life they are born into is a part of their destiny, and there is little motivation to surmount the huge difficulties and look for something different. These factors determine what kinds of occupations are open to which people, how much they earn, and, therefore, how much income they will have to purchase goods and services.

Experience has shown that tradition is still very strong in many nonindustrial nations that are trying to industrialize. Even the lure of profits, an almost irresistible force in most places, is frequently unable to overcome the force of custom in traditional societies. The nonindustrialized, or less developed countries (LDCs), are the subject of chapter 18.

Mixed Economies

The actual systems in existence throughout the world are not pure market, pure centrally directed, or pure traditional economies. They are mixtures of the three, and these **mixed economies** take many different forms. Some, such as that of the United States, are basically market economies with a mixture of government regulation and government ownership. For example, the U.S. government is not in the business of making music or guitars, but it does influence both industries. The government encourages songwriting by providing and enforcing copyright laws for songwriters. It encourages the recording industry through laws that make it illegal to record someone's performance or re-record their music and sell bootleg tapes. It protects Gibson, Fender, and Martin against other companies that might make knockoff guitars and pass them off as the real thing.

Other economies, such as that of China, are primarily centrally directed but have some private ownership and sales. The countries that were formerly part of the Soviet Union and the countries of Eastern Europe are in transition from centrally directed economies to market economies. As for India, its economy combines all three forms—market, command, and traditional—in a very mixed system.

Most of this book, with the exception of the last two chapters, describes the operation of the type of economic system found in the United States, Canada, Western Europe, Japan, and other industrialized countries. They are basically market economies in which the government plays a significant but secondary role.

mixed economy an economic system in which the basic questions of what, how, and for whom to produce are resolved by a mixture of market forces with governmental direction and/or custom and tradition.

Comparative Case Application

Islamic Economics

Many economic systems are strongly influenced by the religious beliefs of their populations. Buddhism is the most widely practiced religion in China and Japan, and in both countries one can see the Buddhist belief in hard work, savings, and a moderate lifestyle. In India the caste system imposed by the Hindu religion influences the lifestyle and employment opportunities of many people. In Western Europe and the United States the Protestant work ethic indeed reflects the values included in the philosophical beliefs of most Protestant denominations. As the world approaches the second millennium, however, probably no religion on earth is having more of an impact on the economic lives of the world's citizens than the religion of Islam.

After Christianity, Islam has the greatest following in the world. It is also the fastest growing. Islam was founded by the prophet Muhammad (A.D. 570–632) who received revelations from Allah (God) about how people should live their lives. These revelations were recorded in the sacred text the Koran, (the "bible" of Islam). Together with other statements and commentary made by Muhammad, the Koran provides the basis for the Islamic code of law, the *Shari'a*. Although there are many different interpretations of the *Shari'a*, many countries base not only their civil law on the code, but also the fundamental rules that govern their economic systems. The fact that most of the people in a country may be Muslims does not necessarily mean that the country will be run by Islamic principles. Countries that do currently base their eco-

Despite different religions and customs, most people in the world still rely on some type of business activity to make a living.

nomic laws on the *Shari'a* include Sudan, Saudi Arabia, Qatar and other states in the Persian Gulf, Iran, and Pakistan. Countries that are leaning toward adopting Islamic economic rules include Afghanistan, Nigeria, Egypt, and Malaysia.

Despite the different interpretations, the *Shari'a* includes four basic principles that most Muslims accept as fundamental to the Islamic way of doing business and organizing economic activity. First, the code demands that one must give alms, or charity, to the poor. This is known as *zakat*. Islamic governments often use this principle to justify wealth and income taxation of the rich in order to redistribute income to the poor. Other taxes may be used to finance other government activities (military, roads, and so on), but the use of taxes to redistribute income and help the poor is firmly grounded in the teachings of Muhammad.

A second Islamic economic principle that has a strong influence on economic activity is the demand that people work hard and trade fairly with one another. There are no Islamic rules against earning a lot of money and enjoying the fruits of one's labor, provided that you earn your money fairly and you do not cheat anyone. Despite the fact that governments own a great deal of the property in most Islamic countries, there are no Islamic prohibitions against owning private property and making a profit.

The third Islamic economic principle allows for businesses to share their profits with people who invest with them (*qirad*). This allows investors to provide financial capital to help entrepreneurs who might have good ideas but no money to open a business. The investors put up the money and the entrepreneurs then give them an agreed-upon percentage of any profits that are earned. This type of arrangement is known as the *mudarabah*, and it is a very important way for Islamic businesses to raise capital, because the fourth major part of the Islamic economic code prohibits the charging of interest on loans.

In most industrially advanced economies, the banking system plays the important role of accepting deposits from savers and lending these deposits to households and businesses who need to borrow. Banks attract deposits from savers by paying interest on savings accounts, and they earn profits by charging higher interest rates to those who borrow the funds. One important outcome of such an institutional arrangement is that the funds get loaned to those who have the best uses for them and therefore can pay the highest interest rates. This leads to the economy's savings ultimately being used in the most productive ways possible.

The prohibition against interest (*riba*) makes it very difficult for Islamic economies to get money from the hands of savers into the hands of those who need to borrow it to invest in new capital, equipment, or to start new businesses. It also makes it difficult to allocate the available savings to the best possible uses. Islamic banks have, however, found ingenious ways to get around the problem. For example, banks can take in deposits from savers and then lend this money to businesses that promise to pay a set percentage of their profits to the bank. The bank then distributes these profits to depositors based on their overall share of the bank's total deposits. Rather then actually loaning money to businesses, bank depositors in essence become part-owners of all businesses that the banks lend to. Alternatively, using a practice similar to the *mudarabah* discussed above, banks can purchase the goods that a business needs and then sell these goods to the business at a higher price. This higher price will be paid back to the bank at a later date. If the business fails, the bank does not get its money back. Although this may seem like charging interest, it is not because the bank is sharing the risk with business in a manner similar to profit sharing. One serious problem with this system, however, is that it may be difficult for the lenders to determine just how much profit the business is making, and this makes it easy for the businesses to sometimes defraud the lenders.

Banks that operate under Islamic principles currently exist in over 50 countries, and they are the only kind of banks that are allowed to operate in Iran, Pakistan, and Sudan. In Saudi Arabia, banks may charge interest, but the strict interpretation of the *Shari'a* by the Saudi courts make it difficult to legally collect interest from a debtor who cannot pay back his loan.

Economic Reasoning

1. What type of economic system is typified by a country that adopts Islamic laws? How are the economic outcomes similar to and different from those in the United States?

2. Explain how one goes about borrowing money to buy a car or a house in the United States, and how one would go about doing this in a country that allowed only Islamic banks.

3. Do you think it is appropriate to charge interest on loans? What would be the consequences for the economy if people were not allowed to charge or earn interest?

Islamic Economics

Use the World Wide Web to research how many Muslims there are in the world and how many countries officially have Islamic governments.

How Does a Market System Resolve the Three Basic Economic Questions?

As we have seen, there are three basic types of economic systems. The one we are most familiar with is that of the United States—the market economy. A market economy determines what to produce, how production will take place, and how output will be allocated to individuals largely on the basis of market forces. What these forces are and how they form the answers to the basic questions are surveyed here and examined more closely in the following chapters.

Markets

The word **"market"** can have a variety of meanings. Markets differ in the way they are structured and the way they operate. Some are highly organized and are found in particular locations to which the buyers and sellers come. Gibson and Fender buy wood and guitar strings in "markets" that consist of buyers and sellers negotiating over the phone, via e-mail, or in person at sawmills and steel mills. In effect, the buyers bid against each other for the products offered for sale by the sellers, and the highest bidder gets the product.

Both buyers and sellers get what they want at the best prices they are able to obtain, and the market is usually cleared of all merchandise as every seller finds a willing buyer. Consumers buy guitars in a "market" that consists of different retail stores, radio stations compete in a market for listeners, and musicians compete in a market to sell their CDs, tapes, and concert tickets.

Incentives

Why do markets function in the first place? What is it that makes them work? Although the people who own the Fender and Gibson companies may

---

marketplace (market) a network of dealings between buyers and sellers of a resource or product (good or service); the dealings may take place at a particular location, or they may take place by communication at a distance with no face-to-face contact between buyers and sellers.

---

like guitar music, that is not the reason for which they borrowed money, hired workers, bought supplies and made electric guitars. Instead, they anticipated that enough people would buy their products at a high enough price to enable them to cover their costs and have some money left over. This anticipated profit provided them with an **incentive** to make electric guitars. In a market economy the opportunity to make a profit is the usual incentive for producing a good or service. If there are people who are able and willing to pay a price high enough to cover production costs and yield some profit, an incentive exists for someone to produce the good or service.

A rise in price is generally an incentive to produce more. A decrease in price generally brings a decrease in production. For example, an increase in guitar sales and/or prices would provide an incentive for Gibson and Fender to expand their output, and it might entice new companies to enter the market. As a consequence, more guitars would be bought and sold, and more labor, wood, and steel would be allocated to making them. Similarly, a decline in guitar sales and/or prices would signal existing producers to reduce their output and perhaps, in the extreme, to get out of the business. The consequence of this would be fewer guitars

bought and sold, and some labor, wood, and steel would instead be used to produce other things. In a market economy prices and the profit incentive determine how our resources are allocated to the production of different goods and services.

◤ Product and Factor Markets

Final goods and services are sold to consumers in what economists call **product markets.** In product markets, the sellers are businesses and the buyers are individuals and **households.** The markets where land, labor, and capital resources are bought and sold are referred to as **factor markets.** In these markets the sellers are the owners of resources and the buyers are businesses. Sometimes it is easy to determine whether a good is being sold in a product market or a factor market. For example, a piece of unfinished mahogany would obviously be sold in a factor market, while a mahogany end table purchased for someone's home would be sold in a product market. At other times the distinction is not so clear. Guitar strings sold by music stores to their customers are sold in a product market. Those sold to Fender or Gibson to be put on new guitars, however, are sold in a factor market—they become a factor of production in the making of a guitar.

◤ Circular Flow of the Economy

In a market economy the factor and product markets support each other and keep the system going. Owners of resources provide the land, labor, and capital that business firms need to function, and business firms provide the finished goods and services consumers want. In a market economy the owners of resources are also the individual consumers, or households. Firms pay money to the households for the use of the factors of production. These payments are **rent** for land, **wages** and **salaries** for labor, and **interest** for the use of financial capital (borrowed money). Households, for their part, use the **factor incomes** they receive to purchase

---

incentive a motivation to undertake an action or to refrain from undertaking an action; in a market economy profits are the incentive to produce.

product market a market in which finished goods and services are exchanged.

household an economic unit consisting of an individual or a family.

factor market a market in which resources and semifinished products are exchanged.

rent a factor payment for the use of land.

wage or salary a factor payment for labor service.

interest a factor payment for the use of financial capital.

factor incomes the return to factors of production as a reward for productive activity.

A finished product is sold to a customer in a product market, as in the case of these baked goods being sold in a bakery.

the goods and services they want from the business firms. Everyone's receipts are someone else's expenditure, and money and real products circulate from households to businesses in a continual manner.

The basic functioning of a market economy can be shown as a **circular flow diagram** with two complementary circles flowing in opposite directions (Figure 1). The outer circle shows the flow of "real" inputs and outputs from firms and households.

Households provide resources to firms in the factor market, the firms use them to produce finished products, which then go to households in the product market. Some of the products are used to increase households' resources (in addition to their labor), and these then go back into the cycle. The inner circle shows the corresponding money payments made for the resources in the factor market (the rents, wages, and interest), and the money payments for the finished goods and services purchased in the product market.

circular flow diagram an analytical diagram showing the economic relationships between the major sectors of an economic system.

Figure 1.

Circular Flow Diagram

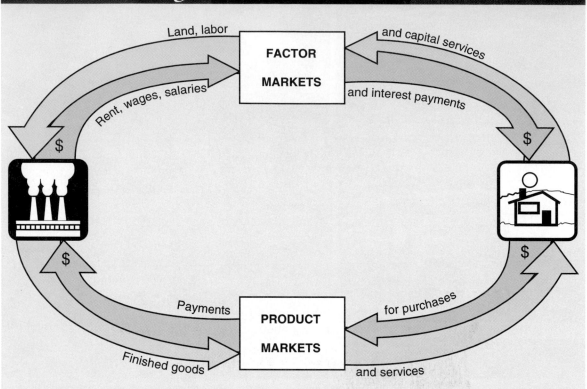

Land, labor

FACTOR MARKETS

and capital services

Rent, wages, salaries

and interest payments

Payments

PRODUCT MARKETS

for purchases

Finished goods

and services

As illustrated by this circular flow diagram, a constant exchange of goods and services and production occurs between business and individuals (households) in a self-sustaining market economy.

The model of the market system shown here is overly simplified. The transactions among different firms in the business sector are not shown in our diagram, nor are the effects of government, foreign trade, or the banking system. The diagram shows a closed, static system without growth. It is a useful model, however, for illustrating the interdependence of economic sectors and the self-sustaining operation of a market economy. We will make use of an expanded and more elaborate model for studying how the economy works in later chapters.

◣ Market System Resolution vs. Alternatives

During most of this century, from the 1920s to the late 1980s, there were two rather well-defined competing systems: free-market and centrally directed. Each had elements of the other—the government postal service and public transportation in market economies and farmers' markets for fruits and vegetables in command economies—but the basic foundations of how the systems worked were quite different. Today with the breakup of the Soviet Union and economic reforms in China, the contrast of different economic systems is less distinct.

Case Application

The Burger Wars

It seems that everybody loves the All-American fast-food combo of hamburgers, French fries and milkshakes, but many Americans, worried about their weight and health, are increasingly avoiding such junk food because of its high fat content and calories. In an effort to keep their customers, hamburger chains such as McDonald's and Burger King seem to be constantly fighting the "Burger Wars," where first one and then the other offer price reductions or special merchandise in order to lure customers into their restaurants.

What do you suppose would happen, however, if tomorrow morning a new medical study reported that burgers, fries, and shakes are actually good for you? That they reduce cholesterol, replace thinning hair, and add 5 years to your life?

Well, if you owned Belinda's Burgers, a local burger joint, the first thing you would notice would be a lot more customers crowding into your restaurant. You might not raise the price of your meals, but you certainly are going to forget about that reduced price promotion you had planned for the following month! If after a month or two of increased sales you are convinced that this is not just a passing fad, you might decide to expand your hours and your physical space. You might, for example, expand your dining area from 60 to 85 seats, and stay open until 2:00 A.M. instead of closing at midnight. Sales and profits are up, and all in all it is a great time to be in the business of selling hamburgers.

Unfortunately for someone selling tacos and burritos, the newly released medical report had absolutely nothing positive to say

Because of the competition, hamburger restaurants need to produce tasty food at competitive prices if they are to stay in business.

about Mexican-style fast food. If you happen to own a taco joint, the news is not good at all. Many of your customers who used to eat burgers half the time and tacos the other half, are now eating only burgers. Sales are down,

In the fast food industry, the interplay of consumers, producers, and various other factors of the market system results in a competitive environment.

down the block to Tony's for lunch or late night snacks. In response, she embarks on that long-delayed price-cutting promotion, offering a free small drink with every burger and fries. Tony, knowing all too well how important it is to keep his customers, drops the price on his fries, and the burger wars are back on!

What does all this mean to you as a typical customer who loves burgers and fries and was delighted to find out that you can eat them with a clear conscience? What did you want? You wanted more burgers, fries, and shakes, and you wanted them at a fair price. As described in this story, what eventually happened? Everybody ended up with more burgers, fries, and shakes being produced, and the burger wars ensured that prices could not and would not be too high.

profits are terrible, and it is doubtful that you will be able to stay in business very much longer if you don't do something soon. What can be done?

An almost obvious answer to the taco joint blues is to switch your restaurant over to making burgers! You already have a kitchen, dining area, and take-out window. With a few modifications you can be turning out burgers in no time. So, you take down the Tony's Terrific Tacos sign, replace it with one that reads Tony's Terrific Burgers, and watch the customers begin to trickle back in.

Of course, Tony's new-found success is not happy news for Belinda. After going to all that trouble to expand her space and hours, now she is seeing some of her customers going

Economic Reasoning

1. Identify all the components of a market system that you can find in the above article.

2. Describe how prices and profits helped to allocate resources to their most highly valued use.

3. Belinda and Tony need to compete for customers. What kinds of things do you think it is okay for them to do, and what kinds of things should they be prevented from doing?

The Burger Wars

Visit the Burger King and McDonald's Web pages. Do the two restaurants compete for customers who are concerned about the healthiness of the food they eat? In what ways do they compete for customers?

▶ Putting It Together

In attempting to overcome the problem of scarcity, *specialization* in production has developed in order to increase efficiency and enlarge output. Workers, regions, and nations get the largest returns for their efforts by concentrating on the economic activity that they perform most efficiently.

A producer who can produce a good or service with a smaller amount of factor inputs of land, labor, and capital than another producer has an *absolute advantage* in the production of that good or service.

If one producer has an absolute advantage in the production of two or more goods or services, it would pay for that producer to specialize in that good or service produced with the greatest efficiency relative to another producer of the same goods or services. The second producer, who is less efficient in producing both outputs, should specialize in producing that good or service which is produced with the least relative inefficiency. This is a case of *comparative advantage*.

Specialization results in *interdependence*. Workers and firms are dependent on each other and on the buyers of the finished products. This gives rise to the *coordination problem*. The more specialized and interdependent economic activities become, the greater is the importance of a smoothly functioning economic system to coordinate production and distribution.

There are three basic types of economic systems, and each resolves the "what," "how," and "for whom" questions in a different way. In a *market economy,* the interplay of buyers and sellers in many various markets determines what will be produced, how it will be produced, and for whom it will be produced. *Markets* are places or arrangements for the exchange of goods and services. In a *command economy,* a centrally directed, authoritarian agency decides what to produce, how to produce it, and for whom to produce it. *Traditional economies* use custom to resolve these basic questions. Most economic systems today are actually *mixed economies* with elements of traditional, command, and market economies.

By becoming increasingly specialized, modern economies can produce a lot more music than was possible at an old-time barn dance.

The United States has basically a market economy. Producers in this economic system react to price signals from markets and the desire to make a profit when deciding what to produce and how to produce it. It is this profit *incentive* that motivates businesses to make the things that we want.

There are basically two types of markets in a market economy: *factor markets* and *product markets.* Factor markets are where the factors of production (resources) are purchased by businesses in order to produce goods and services. The factors are purchased from the *households* that own them. Households use the income earned from selling their resources to purchase the goods and services from businesses in the product markets.

In our market economy, each person's spending is another person's income. The *rent, wages,* and *interest* paid out by business firms to households are spent by households in exchange for the goods and services produced by business firms. The flows of finished goods and services and factor inputs are paid for by the counterflows of *factor incomes* and sales revenues. Together they form a *circular flow* in our economy that is self-perpetuating.

Perspective

The Industrial Revolution

James Watt and his improved steam engine, which was perhaps the most important invention of the Industrial Revolution.

Additional information on the Industrial Revolution can be found in *The Industrial Revolution* by T. S. Ashton (New York: Oxford University Press, 1961); *The Industrial Revolution and Economic Growth* by R. M. Hartwell (Oxford: Blackwell, 1970); and *Workers in the Industrial Revolution* by P. N. Stearns (New Brunswick, NJ: Transaction Books, 1974).

The Industrial Revolution was a period of great change, during which basically agricultural countries with small, home-based "cottage industries" were transformed into industrial societies characterized by machine-dominated factory production, centered in heavily populated cities.

The Industrial Revolution first took place in Great Britain between 1750 and 1850. It did not become widely diffused in the rest of Europe and North America until the second half of the nineteenth century, and it is only now spreading to some parts of the world, as the nonindustrialized nations strive to change from agricultural economies to industrial economies.

During the century between the mid-1700s and the mid-1800s drastic changes in production methods and in the products themselves occurred. The changes were initiated by the invention of spinning and weaving equipment in the textile industry, which took textile production out of homes and put it into factories. Perhaps the most important invention was the improved steam engine developed by James Watt in 1769, because it provided an efficient motive source to power the other new inventions. It also advanced the art of machine toolmaking.

The production of textiles, metal products, and other goods with the use of power equipment instead of hand tools gave the United Kingdom (which included Great Britain, Scotland, Northern Ireland, and Wales) such a large competitive edge over other countries that it became the wealthiest and most powerful country of the nineteenth century.

The wealth created by the Industrial Revolution at first did not benefit the workers. In fact, many workers viewed the new machinery as a competitive threat to their livelihood. They feared machines would put them out of work. There were riots, and factories and machinery were destroyed. As a result, laws were passed that made the willful destruction of any building containing machinery an offense punishable by death. Working conditions were very bad; and labor, especially child labor, was grossly exploited in the early factory system of the Industrial Revolution.

In our time, we have reaped the benefits of the Industrial Revolution—high consumption levels and increased leisure time—along with its costs, such as pollution of the environment and depletion of our energy and other resources. The slowing of productivity growth in recent decades has led to calls for a "new Industrial Revolution," which might again transform not only production methods but society itself.

For Further Study and Analysis

Study Questions

1. Are the household chores in your home assigned according to absolute or comparative advantage? Can you suggest how the principle of comparative advantage could help you better reallocate those chores?
2. What is an example of a specialized job with which you are personally familiar? How is that job performed efficiently as a result of specialization?
3. Specialization and interdependence increase efficiency, but what disadvantage might result from interdependence? Give an example.
4. What instances of interdependence can you identify in the music industry?
5. To really understand the coordination problem, list as many of the different people and businesses that are necessary for you to have a cup of coffee in the morning (with milk and sugar).
6. Was Christian Martin's original shop in New York representative of a traditional economy or a market economy? Why?
7. Give an example of a factor market in which you have participated. What factor did you provide and what was the factor income called?
8. Who is your favorite guitar player? Describe how a market economy makes sure that you get to listen to him or her play.
9. Explain how an owner of a business also represents a household. Describe how this person participates in the circular flow of a market economy.
10. How did the Industrial Revolution affect the outcome of the three basic economic questions?

Exercises in Analysis

1. Visit a local fast-food restaurant and observe the job specialization in production there. Write a short paper on what you observe.
2. Prepare a short paper showing how elements of command and traditional economies can be found in the United States.
3. On the basis of what you know about different countries and using any available resource materials, make a list of countries that would be classed as basically market economies, centrally directed economies, or traditional economies.
4. Write a short essay on what influences will determine the number of electric guitars produced in the United States and the world.

Further Reading

Cole, Don, ed. *Annual Editions: Microeconomics.* Guilford, CT: Dushkin/McGraw-Hill, various years. This annual publication always includes a number of articles (with commentary) about how different types of economic systems operate.

Fishwick, Marshall, ed. *Ronald Revisited: The World of Ronald McDonald.* Bowling Green, Ohio: Bowling Green University Popular Press, 1983. A collection of essays on McDonald's and the fast-food industry.

For a lot of information about the history of guitars you can visit www.Gruhn.com/ and click on the Library link. George Gruhn is one of the world's leading experts on guitars, and owns one of the country's greatest music stores in Nashville, Tennessee.

For information about Gibson and Fender products, you can visit their Web sites at www.gibson.com and www.fender.com.

Goldman, Minton F., ed. *Global Studies: Russia, Eurasia, & Central/Eastern Europe.* Seventh edition. Guilford, CT: Dushkin/McGraw-Hill, 1998. A comprehensive volume providing a foundation of information—geographic, cultural, economic, political, and historical—allowing students to better understand the current and future problems within this region.

Johnson, David B. *Public Choice: An Introduction to the New Political Economy.* Mountain View, CA: Bristlecone Books, 1991. Chapter 3 provides an excellent, if somewhat advanced, description of the workings of a market economy.

Kohler, Heinz. *Economic Systems and Human Welfare: A Global Survey.* Cincinnati, OH: South-Western Publishing, 1997. Chapter 3 presents a good comparison of the philosophies underlying market and command economies. Chapters 7, 8, and 14 present good descriptions of the U.S., Soviet, and Indian economies, respectively.

Swartz, Thomas R. and Frank J. Bonello, eds. *Taking Sides: Clashing Views on Controversial Economic Issues, 8th Edition.* Guilford, CT, Dushkin/McGraw-Hill, 1998.

Lachmann, Ludwig M. *The Market as an Economic Process*. Oxford, U.K.: Blackwell Scientific Publications, 1986. An examination of how markets function and what they accomplish, looked at from an economic doctrines approach.

Nellis, John. *Improving the Performance of Soviet Enterprises*. Washington, D. C.: World Bank Publications, 1991. Examines the history of state enterprises and compares their productivity with that of the newer forms of business organization emerging in the former Soviet states.

Trachtenbberg, Jeffrey A. and Eben Shapiro. "Record-Store Shakeout Rocks Music Industry." *Wall Street Journal,* February 26, 1996, pp. B1 and B8. An example of how the sale of CDs and tapes had changed in the past few years. (Reprinted in Cole, Don, ed. *Annual Editions: Microeconomics 98/99*. Guilford, CT: Dushkin/McGraw-Hill, 1998).

chapter four

Market Pricing

The American economy is basically run by the market-place, with each individual helping to direct the economy by the market choices he or she makes. The marketplace, however, sets its own terms, and both consumers and producers are forced to adjust their decisions to changes in the market. This chapter's introductory article illustrates how an act of nature can alter the market and our behavior.

The Peanut Butter Crunch

Peanut butter sandwiches are almost as much a part of American food culture as apple pie. Generations of children have been raised on them. Not even the fear of peanut butter sticking to the roof of our mouth (called arachisbutyrophobia) deters us from consuming great quantities of it. In the camps set up for homeless refugees after the 1994 Los Angeles earthquake, peanut butter was the food most in demand, suggesting that it has a comforting effect. Americans consume over 800 million pounds of the gooey stuff every year at a cost of more than $1 billion.

It was therefore a blow to American families and their budgets when the great peanut butter shortage hit in 1981, emptying grocery shelves and causing prices to double in a single year. Who was responsible for this rapid rise in peanut butter prices? Was there a sinister international peanut conspiracy manipulating the market to drive prices up? No, not really. Actually, it was just nature playing tricks with agricultural production again. A summer drought in Georgia, Texas, and other peanut-growing states reduced the peanut crop by 42%. This shortage raised peanut prices from $445 a ton to as high as $2,000 a ton.

Faced with such high peanut butter prices, some buyers turned to a substitute made with cottonseeds flavored with peanut oil. While this substitute had fewer calories and was considered more nutritious than peanut butter, its best attribute was its price, which was about one-third less than peanut butter.

Those with a real passion for peanut butter, however, stuck to the high-priced original in such numbers that the shelves in many stores were cleared of it. Although there was a good deal of consumer resistance to the high price, not everyone was willing to settle for a substitute. The decline in peanut butter sales was actually proportionally smaller than the decline in the peanut harvest. This was probably because peanut butter manufacturers purchased more of the available peanuts than the customary 50% of the crop they normally used.

Good weather is not the only thing that can result in an increased crop of peanuts. Improved strains of peanut seeds and more efficient machinery also help keep supplies up and prices down.

In 1997, U.S. peanut growers produced over 3.6 billion pounds of peanuts, very close to what was expected at the beginning of the year. When the crop was reduced by the drought, as in 1981, peanut butter producers were willing to pay higher prices for peanuts in order to acquire a larger share of the smaller supply available. They were induced to do this in part because many consumers would not give up peanut butter even in the face of rising prices and in part because the cost of the peanuts is only a fraction of the total costs of producing and selling peanut butter. The demand behavior of consumers and the behavior of production costs combined to determine what quantity peanut butter companies would produce and at what price they could sell their output.

Chapter Preview

Market prices are the result of many influences, including consumer preferences, available supplies, and government policies. The prices of agricultural commodities are especially sensitive to these influences. They are affected by weather conditions, damage from insects and disease, changes in foreign demand, changes in the prices of products that can be used as substitutes, and of course, by government regulations. This chapter will explore how different influences in the marketplace interact to determine prices. We shall investigate the following questions: What forces determine prices in the marketplace? What determines demand? What determines supply? Why do prices change?

Learning Objectives

After completing this chapter, you should be able to:

1. Explain the laws of supply and demand.

2. List and understand the determinants of demand.

3. List and understand the determinants of supply.

4. Distinguish between short- and long-run supply.

5. Identify the causes of shifts in demand and explain how they affect market equilibrium.

6. Identify the causes of shifts in supply and explain how they affect market equilibrium.

7. Explain why shortages and surpluses cause prices to move toward equilibrium.

8. Distinguish between a change in demand and a change in quantity demanded.

9. Distinguish between a change in supply and a change in quantity supplied.

▶ What Forces Determine Prices in the Marketplace?

The key element in the functioning of a market economy is the allocation of resources through the voluntary exchange of goods and services. These goods and services are not directly traded for each other in our modern economy, as they would be in a primitive barter economy. Instead they are bought and sold for money in markets where each good and service has its price. This section examines how prices are determined.

◢ Demand (The Consumers' Side of the Market)

Households in the United States consume over 800 million pounds of peanut butter every year. It is a staple of the American diet. When the price of peanut butter nearly doubled, some people cut back their purchases. The **quantity demanded** decreased because of the higher price. For virtually every product or service, an increase in price results in a smaller amount demanded. This is the **law of demand:** at a given point in time, a rise in price causes a fall in the quantity demanded, whereas a decline in price causes an increase in the quantity demanded.

There are two reasons why people behave according to the law of demand. The first is that when the price of a product rises, people tend to buy less of that product and buy a cheaper substitute instead. This is the **substitution effect,** replacing a more costly item with a less costly one. The second reason is that when the price of a product goes down, people can afford to buy more of it, and when the price goes up, they can't afford to buy as much. This is the **income effect.**

Let's take a look at a hypothetical family—the Yangs—buying peanut butter at alternative prices. At $2.50 a jar, the Yangs buy three jars of peanut butter a month. If the price rises to $4.70 a jar, they cut back their purchases to two jars a month. Instead of peanut butter sandwiches, the Yang children take bologna or tuna sandwiches to school. If another year's drought causes the price to go up to $8.00 a jar, the Yangs cut down to one jar a month. At prices higher than $8.00 a jar, the Yangs give up peanut butter altogether as a luxury they can't afford.

On the other hand, if there is an especially large crop of peanuts, and the price of a jar of peanut butter falls to $1.80 a jar, the Yangs increase their consumption to four jars a month. With a further drop to $1.50 a jar, the Yangs would increase consumption to five jars a month.

The Yangs' **demand** for peanut butter is given in Table 1, which shows the number of jars they would buy each month at different possible prices. This is the Yangs' **demand schedule** for peanut butter.

A demand schedule also can be shown in the form of a diagram as in Figure 1. In this diagram of the Yangs' demand schedule for peanut butter, the alternative prices for peanut butter are shown on the vertical axis and the corresponding quantities of peanut butter that

---

quantity demanded the amount of a good or service that consumers would purchase at a particular price.

law of demand the quantity demanded of a good or service varies inversely with its price; the lower the price the larger the quantity demanded, and the higher the price the smaller the quantity demanded.

substitution effect the effect of a change in the price of a good or service on the amount purchased that results from the consumer substituting a relatively less expensive alternative.

income effect the effect of a change in the price of a good or service on the amount purchased that results from a change in purchasing power of the consumer's income due to the price change.

demand the relationship between the quantities of a good or service that consumers desire to purchase at any particular time and the various prices that can exist for the good or service.

demand schedule a table recording the number of units of a good or service demanded at various possible prices.

Figure 1

Yang Demand for Peanut Butter

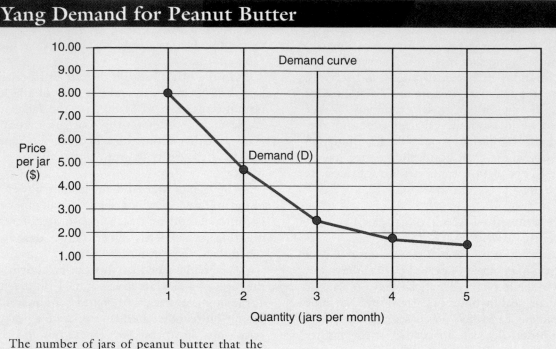

The number of jars of peanut butter that the Yang family would buy in a month depends on the price.

Table 1	Yang Demand Schedule	
Price per Jar	**Number of Jars per Month**	
$1.50	5	
1.80	4	
2.50	3	
4.70	2	
8.00	1	

they would buy on the horizontal axis. This is the customary way to diagram a market (demand and supply) situation. Prices are always on the vertical axis, and quantities are always on the horizontal axis.

demand curve a graphic representation of the relationship between price and quantity demanded.

If we locate for each price on the vertical axis the corresponding quantity demanded at that price on the horizontal axis, given in Table 1, and then draw a line connecting these points, we have a **demand curve.** (We locate points on the demand curve by drawing perpendiculars from corresponding prices and quantities, as shown in the appendix to chapter 1, page 32.). The demand curve on our chart slopes downward from upper left to lower right. Consistent with the law of demand, the lower the price, the more the Yangs would buy; the higher the price, the less the Yangs would buy.

Figure 1 shows the individual household demand for peanut butter. How about the whole market demand for peanut butter? Let us assume that in the town where the Yangs live there are 9,999 other families who have the same demand for peanut butter that the Yangs have. If we multiply the number of jars that the Yang family would buy at different prices by 10,000, we get a hypothetical

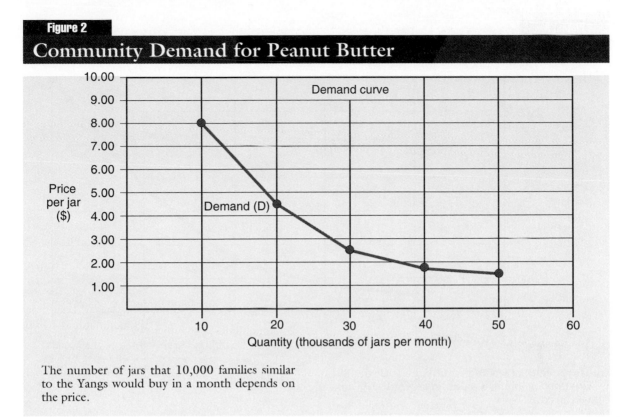

Figure 2

Community Demand for Peanut Butter

The number of jars that 10,000 families similar to the Yangs would buy in a month depends on the price.

community demand schedule for peanut butter. This is shown in Table 2. To assume that all the families have the same demand for peanut butter is, of course, a simplification. In real life, different families have different demands for peanut butter as well as for other products and services. (We will see in the next section what determines each individual's demand.) Note that the demand curves indicate only what quantities consumers would like to buy at various prices, not how much they *can* buy.

The data in Table 2 are plotted on the diagram in Figure 2. This shows how much peanut butter would be demanded at different prices ranging from $1.50 to $8.00 per jar in a community composed of 10,000 families, each with the same demand for peanut butter as the Yangs.

◤ Supply (The Sellers' Side of the Market)

Demand schedules are economic models that help us understand consumer reaction to various

Table 2 Community Demand Schedule

Price per Jar	Number of Jars per Month
$1.50	50,000
1.80	40,000
2.50	30,000
4.70	20,000
8.00	10,000

community demand schedule the sum of all the individual demand schedules in a particular market showing the total quantities demanded by the buyers in the market at each of the various possible prices.

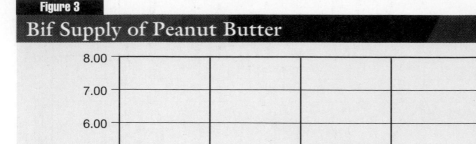

Figure 3

Bif Supply of Peanut Butter

The number of jars of peanut butter that the Bif Company would like to sell in a month depends on the price.

Table 3	Bif Supply Schedule
Price per Jar	**Number of Jars per Month**
$1.50	1,000
1.80	2,000
2.50	3,000
4.70	4,000
8.00	5,000

supply the relationship between the quantities of a good or service that sellers wish to market at any particular time and the various prices that can exist for the good or service.

supply schedule a table recording the number of units of a good or service supplied at various possible prices.

supply curve a graphic representation of the relationship between price and quantity supplied.

prices of a product. To see the behavior of **supply** on the sellers' side of the market, we make use of a **supply schedule.** Sellers have just the opposite attitude toward prices that consumers have. The higher the price of a product, the more of the product sellers are willing to offer for sale. Table 3 shows the amounts of peanut butter one hypothetical seller, Bif Peanut Butter, would have offered at different prices before the drought. At low prices, Bif is not willing to supply much peanut butter (the company will use its resources in other endeavors). At higher prices, the company has an incentive to obtain more peanuts, jars, workers, and so on, and offer more for sale. Table 3 is the supply schedule for one producer of peanut butter. (In the third section of this chapter we will examine what determines the quantities sellers are willing to offer at different prices.)

If we plot the points indicating how much peanut butter Bif will supply at different prices and then connect these points, we get the **supply curve** shown in Figure 3. Note that the

Figure 4

Market Supply of Peanut Butter

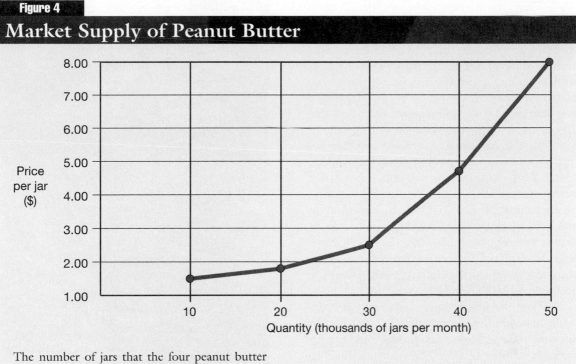

The number of jars that the four peanut butter producers would like to sell in a month depends on the price.

supply curve slopes upward to the right, indicating that higher prices are associated with larger quantities supplied. In providing more peanut butter at higher prices, Bif is complying with the **law of supply:** the higher the price of a good or service, the more will be offered for sale.

If we assume that there are 10 other peanut butter suppliers similar to Bif in the market, we create the market supply schedule shown in Table 4 and the market supply curve shown in Figure 4. Note that the supply curves indicate only what quantities sellers would like to sell at various prices, not how much they *can* sell. How much they can sell depends on the demand schedule. *It is very important to keep in mind that supply and demand schedules are determined independently by different considerations, but they jointly determine price as shown in the following section.*

Table 4	Market Supply Schedule

Price per Jar	Number of Jars per Month
$1.50	10,000
1.80	20,000
2.50	30,000
4.70	40,000
8.00	50,000

law of supply the quantity supplied of a good or service varies directly with its price; the lower the price the smaller the quantity supplied, and the higher the price the larger the quantity supplied.

◣ Equilibrium

The Yang family, along with all of the other potential peanut butter customers in their community, determines the demand by their willingness to buy a certain number of jars at any particular price. It may not be until they see what the price is on the supermarket shelf that they decide how many jars they are going to buy. But the community demand schedule accurately describes their behavior on the average. If the Yang family does not buy any peanut butter one month because they are on vacation, another family is just as likely to buy twice as much because they are having a picnic. With demand curves, as with many economic variables, individual variations from the average tend to cancel each other out when you are dealing with large numbers.

Bif and the other peanut butter suppliers determine what the supply will be at different prices by their willingness to produce and market a certain number of jars. The sellers are likely to plan in advance how much they will offer for sale depending upon the price they can get. The market supply schedule gives the total amounts they will offer to sell at different prices.

The actual market price is determined when the two sides of the market, the buyers and the sellers, come together. Out of all the possible prices, only one price can exist in a market at a given time. Normally, that is the price that "clears the market"—the price at which the amount the buyers are willing to purchase just equals the amount the sellers are willing to supply. That price is called the **equilibrium price**.

Market equilibrium is shown when we put the demand curve and the supply curve on the same diagram. The point at which they intersect

Hot dogs are one of the more popular meats for sandwiches. An affordable price keeps the quantity demanded high.

shows the price that clears the market. The equilibrium price for peanut butter in our example is $2.50, as shown in Figure 5.

🕸🖱 What Forces Determine Prices in the Marketplace?

EconExplorer

---

equilibrium price the price at which the quantity of a good or service offered by suppliers is exactly equal to the quantity that is demanded by purchasers in a particular period of time.

At a price of $2.50 per jar, the families in the community wanted to buy 30,000 jars of peanut butter a month, which the suppliers were willing to sell. If the market price had been less than $2.50, the buyers would have wanted more, but the suppliers would not have

Figure 5

Market Price

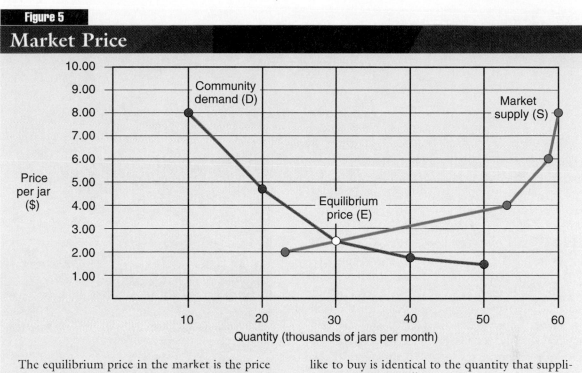

The equilibrium price in the market is the price at which the quantity that consumers would like to buy is identical to the quantity that suppliers would like to sell.

been willing to sell as much. As a result, a **shortage** would have developed. Whenever there is a shortage, the price will eventually go up. Buyers, in effect, would have been bidding against one another for the short supply. This would have raised the price to the equilibrium level.

If the market price had been higher than $2.50, there would have been a **surplus** of peanut butter and the higher price would not have been maintained. Competition among sellers to get rid of their overstock would have driven the price down to $2.50. Whenever there is a surplus, the price goes down. Freely competitive markets are self-equilibrating, with the price always adjusting to the level that clears the market over a period of time. If the price is below equilibrium, a shortage will develop and drive the price up. If the price is above equilibrium, a surplus will

develop and drive the price down. In our economy, however, we sometimes find markets that are not freely competitive, as in the case of government-regulated prices. In such noncompetitive markets, surpluses or shortages can persist for a long time.

shortage   an excess of quantity demanded over quantity supplied that occurs when a price is below the equilibrium price. Shortages cause prices to increase.

surplus   an excess of quantity supplied over quantity demanded that occurs when a price is above the equilibrium price. Surpluses cause prices to decrease.

Case Application

Price-Gouging

Hurricane Fran ripped through the Carolinas in September 1996, causing $9 billion in damage, 7 years after Hurricane Hugo devastated the region in 1989. People say that natural disasters bring out the best in people, but many in the Carolinas would tell you that these hurricanes brought out the worst in some contractors, carpenters, hardware stores, lumber, and tree removal services. These businesses are in greatest demand after a natural disaster rips roofs off houses, disrupts water and electric service, and leaves people with freezers full of food threatening to spoil. In especially high demand at such a time are gasoline-powered electric generators.

After the hurricanes hit, the prices of these goods and services increased dramatically. With demand outstripping the available supply, people waited in lines, spent hours searching for goods, and paid a premium price for them when they found them. Enterprising individuals took their trucks and drove hours to distant cities where the needed supplies were available, and brought them back to Charlotte and Charleston, where they sold them for a profit. Skilled tradesmen left their jobs in undamaged cities and drove hours to the stricken areas to offer their services for a premium price. National and regional hardware stores that sold chain saws and generators diverted their stocks from other cities to the Carolinas as quickly as possible to increase available supplies. Eventually, these increased supplies coming from other areas pushed prices back down to normal levels.

Many people saw these actions as "price-gouging." The governor of North Carolina, James B. Hunt Jr., and his attorney general, Michael F. Easley, criticized those who—by their depiction—made a fast buck off the mis-

Natural disasters create an increased and immediate demand for building materials and electric generators.

ery of others. They, and other government leaders, made impassioned appeals to people not to "unfairly" raise prices and to report price-gougers. Some local governments passed ordinances forbidding such price increases.

Other people saw what happened as the result of a more powerful law, the law of supply and demand. The increased demand that occurs after such disasters is going to result in shortages of many goods and services, and there needs to be a way to allocate the available products among buyers. If prices are controlled, vendors will not increase the quantities they are supplying to the market during a period of time. Nor will additional supplies be so quick to flow to the distressed areas. Those who are first in line will get what is available, others will have to wait until demand decreases or supplies increase to get their roofs fixed and uprooted trees removed.

On the other hand, if price increases are permitted, vendors will increase the quantities of goods and services provided. At the higher prices, some people who do not desperately need repairs right away will decide to wait for prices to come back down. Others—those with the most to lose or the most pressing need for immediate repairs—will go ahead and pay the higher price instead of waiting.

Forcing vendors to keep their prices low benefits those who have the time to wait in line or those who get to the stores first—it discriminates against those who are slow or live far away from the stores. Allowing prices to rise discriminates against those with less money than time. The benefit of allowing prices to rise, however, is that it increases the options available to people; they still have the choice of waiting, but, if they choose, they can elect to pay the higher price and have their repairs done immediately.

▶ What Determines Demand?

We have seen that there is a predictable relationship between the price of a good or service and the quantity demanded—the lower the price, the larger the quantity. But what determines how much demand there will be for a good or service at any particular price? Or, for that matter, whether there will be any demand at all? This analysis section examines the determinants of demand.

◤ Tastes and Preferences

Consumer tastes and preferences are particularly important determinants of demand. Eating peanut butter is a taste that many people acquire when they are young and retain to a greater or lesser extent throughout their lives.

The fact that people like or dislike peanut butter is the first thing that determines their demand for the product. As they grow older, their tastes may change, and they may not want as much peanut butter as before.

◤ Income

In order for demand to exist for a product, the desire for the product must be backed up by

---

consumer tastes and preferences individual liking or partiality for specific goods or services.

In the cereal aisle of the supermarket, consumers have an array of choices. Their preferences, and therefore demand, may be dictated by price, taste, packaging, and other factors.

Substitutes and Complements

A third determinant of demand for a particular product is the availability and price of **substitutes** and **complements.** A substitute is a product that can be used in place of another product. For example, there are some close substitutes for peanut butter that are made from nuts, such as almonds, or from cottonseeds or sunflower seeds. More general substitutes—not in looks or taste, but in function—are cheese, bologna, and tuna fish. With these substitutes available, many families might not be willing to pay higher prices for peanut butter, at least not for as many jars of peanut butter as they had been purchasing.

Complements are goods that are used together. Among the products that are complements to peanut butter, a favorite one is jelly. Another might be marshmallow cream. A rise in the price of jelly would result in less peanut butter being demanded, since peanut butter and jelly are used together so often. While a rise in the price of a substitute, cheese for example, generally results in an increase in the demand for a product like peanut butter, a rise in the price of a complement, such as jelly, results in a decrease in the demand for the product. Conversely, a drop in the price of cheese would cause the demand for peanut butter to go down, while a fall in jelly prices would cause it to go up.

the ability to pay for it. This is sometimes called effective demand. Without the ability to pay for a product, demand for that product does not exist. Our income determines how much money we have to spend; therefore, a person's income plays an important role in determining that person's demand for a product. Increases in income enable people to purchase more goods and services, including more peanut butter, if that is what they choose to spend part of their increased income for. In short, if incomes increase, demand generally increases as well.

What Determines Demand?

EconExplorer

substitute a product that is interchangeable in use with another product.

complement a product that is employed jointly in conjunction with another product.

Population

Finally, the demand for a product depends on the number of people in the market area. Since peanut butter is eaten in every part of the United States and is an easily transported, nonperishable item, the potential domestic market population is over 250 million. Increases in population result in greater demand for virtually everything that is produced. Selling in other countries also results in larger demand for the domestically produced product.

Case Application

Pedal Power

In the 1970s and 1980s, the baby boom generation became interested in fitness and exercise, and recreational jogging became one of the country's most popular pastimes. Unfortunately, jogging takes a tremendous toll on knees and other joints. The introduction of bicycling as an Olympic event in 1984 gave the boomers increased exposure to an alternative, less damaging, recreational sport and elevated their interest. As a result, the boomers and their children (the baby boom "echo") have taken up bicycling in a big way. Bicycling is now the third most popular recreational sports activity in the United States, after swimming and exercise walking; about 53 million Americans ride a bicycle at least once each year.

The great strength of bicycling is its diversity. People of all ages and in all places can enjoy the sport, and, like golf, another popular pursuit, it is a healthy activity that people can enjoy for a lifetime. To accommodate cyclists, a growing number of tour companies organize bicycle vacations for riders through the canyons of Arizona and Utah, along the Pacific Coast in Oregon, and through the Appalachian Mountains. The "Rails to Trails" program that is converting unused railroad beds to bike trails offers bikers a safe, well-maintained place to spend a day by themselves or with family and friends.

There are about 6,800 bicycle shops in the United States (California, New York, and Florida have the most), and about half their revenues are earned by selling bikes. About 70% of these are family-oriented shops that sell a wide range of products. The rest are primarily "pro shops" that deal in top-of-the-line bicycles that are usually imported from other countries. The most rapidly growing part of the market, however, is not the bikes themselves but the accessories, especially cycle clothing. Sales of eye-catching outfits, shoes, and headgear grew at 25% a year during the early 1990s. The popularity of hip-hugging spandex shorts and flashy jerseys was such that stores selling only cycling-style clothing, but not bicycles, sprang up. As with participants in other activities like golf, jogging, skiing, and aerobics, cyclists not only want to enjoy their sport, but they want to look good while doing it.

The popularity of biking has been influenced by manufacturers who are designing bikes to meet the needs and wants of the population. In addition to mountain and hybrid bikes that allow riders more freedom to ride off-road, manufacturers are making bikes more comfortable, more reliable, and are outfitting them with gears that are easier to operate, and other features. Mountain bikes have made up about 60% of total sales in the past few years, but new designs and ideas include electric-assist bicycles, recumbent bicycles, and "comfort bicycles" designed for older riders.

U.S. bicycle sales peaked at 15 million in 1973 when 10-speed, drop-handlebar racing bikes were a major fad. The fad passed because the look and design of these bikes did not really suit the type of activity that people wanted to pursue. The recession of the early 1990s also hurt the sales of high-end recreational goods. When workers either lost their jobs or feared that they might do so, high-priced bicycles and cycle clothing became luxuries that were dispensable. With the development of the mountain bike in the late 1980s, interest again picked up and annual bike sales increased steadily from 9.9 million in 1988 to 13 million in 1993. Since then, they have leveled off between 10 and 11 million bikes per year.

In addition to being a great recreational item, statistics show that over 5% of bike use is for commuting, and that this is a growing part of the market. Cycling not only saves on the costs of gas, automobile maintenance, and parking, but it is much friendlier to the environment. Bicycles are becoming a legitimate part of the nation's transportation mix, and this justifies increased support for cycling-friendly roads and trails.

Economic Reasoning

1. Which of the determinants of demand were responsible for expanding the market for bicycles and accessories? What caused a slowdown in sales of high-end bikes and accessories?

2. If lower import taxes were to reduce the prices of bicycles, what impact would they have on the demand for cycle clothing? Why?

3. Do you think that governments should spend more on developing and building bike lanes along roads and bike trails along unused rail lines? Why or why not?

Pedal Power

You can find out just about anything you ever wanted to know about the bicycle industry at the National Bicycle Dealers' Association's home page, http://NBDA.com. Use their Business Files and Bicycle Sales Statistics links to prepare a report on current sales and developments in the bicycle industry.

▶ What Determines Supply?

The determinants of supply are totally different from the determinants of demand. As we noted above, demand does not determine supply, and vice versa. Of course if there is no demand for a product, it will not be produced. But the amounts that producers are willing to offer for sale at different prices are not the same as the amounts that are demanded at those prices. The supply schedule, as we have seen, is independent of the demand schedule. This makes sense since demand is determined by buyers and supply by a totally different group—sellers.

The most important determinant of supply is the cost of production. In the peanut butter industry, the price of peanuts, the wages of factory workers, and the price of jars, as well as how efficiently these factors are used in production, are among the things that determine production cost.

The expansion of a plant can increase product output in the long run.

◤ Prices of Resources

The price of necessary inputs in the production process will affect the amount of a product that a seller is willing to put on the market at different prices. If resource prices, such as wages, peanuts, or energy costs increase, producers will be willing to supply less peanut butter at any given price—supply will decrease. Alternatively, if the price of these resources decreases, the supply will increase.

What Determines Supply?

EconExplorer

◤ Technology

As we saw in chapter 1, technology describes the manner in which our resources are combined to produce products. Technological improvements allow us to get more output from a given amount of resources, or the same amount of output from fewer resources. As a consequence, improvements in technology allow producers to supply increased amounts of a product at any given price. Technological advances have been a primary reason behind the increased supplies of most manufactured products in the world today.

◤ Short Run

How supply behaves also depends on the time period under consideration. At any given time, peanut butter producers can adjust their output only over a limited range. They have only so many ovens for roasting peanuts, just so much factory space for processing them, and only so

Jojoba: A Desert Weed That Smells Like Money

Before sperm whales came under the protection of international whaling agreements, millions of pounds of whale oil were used in the production of leather, textiles, pharmaceuticals, and polishes. The oil was also highly prized as a lubricant because it prevented corrosion in transmissions, gears, and machine parts. There was no close substitute, and sperm whale oil was considered so vital that it was stockpiled in case of emergency shortages. In the early 1970s, however, the United States, Canada, and many other countries banned the use of all whale products because sperm whales were in danger of extinction. Efforts to produce synthetic substitutes proved unsuccessful, and a search for a viable substitute for whale oil began.

As it turns out, a desert bush called jojoba (pronounced "ho-´ho-ba" and scientifically known as *Simmondsia chinensis*) provides an excellent substitute for whale oil. Native to Mexico and the southwestern United States, the jojoba plant produces peanut-sized seeds that are half filled with a colorless liquid wax with properties very similar to whale oil. Even

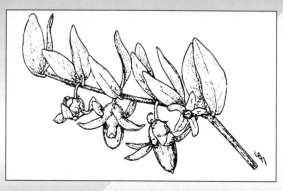

Seeds of the jojoba bush produce a wax used in commercial lubricants, cosmetics, and hair products.

better, jojoba oil is much purer than whale oil, it is odorless, it never gets rancid, and it does not deteriorate even after long periods of high-pressure or high-temperature use. Ancestors of Native Americans in the region used jojoba wax as a hair conditioner, and many modern cosmetic manufacturers use jojoba as an important ingredient in hair-care and skin-care products.

many machines for filling jars. In the **short run** they can vary their output only within the limits of their existing plant and equipment. They can increase production by purchasing more peanuts and jars and hiring more workers. They can put on a night shift of workers to increase

output. But in the short run, they cannot add to their existing plant and equipment to increase the amount of output.

Increasing the output in the short run generally increases the cost of producing each unit. More workers in the plant means that each one has a smaller amount of capital equipment to work with, so average labor output falls. In addition, adding night shifts or asking workers to work longer hours requires overtime pay. Consequently, producers will have to get higher prices to induce them to expand production.

short run a period of time so short that the amount of some factor inputs cannot be varied.

Sometimes called coffee berry or goat nut, jojoba is a renewable resource. Each bush lives for 100 to 200 years and apparently is not subject to serious insect damage or disease. The only downside seems to be that it takes a new plant about 5 years to produce a harvestable quantity of seeds. The supply of wild seeds was so limited that, when their commercial properties were first discovered, the price of jojoba oil increased in 1 year from $40 to over $200 a gallon!

Now, however, the commercial growing of jojoba on plantations, which began in earnest in 1978, has brought the price down substantially (the first commercial production was in Israel). Newly designed harvesting machines shake the seeds off the plant and onto a conveyer belt where a blower removes the chaff and the seeds are bagged for transport. Rising supply is matching demand as more and more uses are found for this amazing plant.

Finally, if you ever go off-road biking in the Southwest, you might be interested to know that jojoba bushes have a high Crash Factor Index (10). If you have to crash into something, well, jojobas are spineless, nontoxic, and tough enough to catch you as you hurtle over your handlebars, yet resilient enough so that there's no way the crunch is going to kill the plant! (A barrel cactus, which can kill *you*, has a Crash Factor Index of 0.)

Economic Reasoning

1. What period of time is the long run for increasing jojoba production?

2. Why was jojoba so expensive in the short run? Why did it become cheaper in the long run?

3. Investment in jojoba in the United States was encouraged by special government subsidies to help start jojoba plantations. Should jojoba growers be given special treatment by the government? Why or why not?

Jojoba: A Desert Weed That Smells Like Money

Search the Web for jojoba sites and see how many different benefits are claimed for products containing jojoba oil. The J & J Jojoba Newsletter at http://www.ultranet.com/~adamo/CA_Gold/news.htm#1_2 is a good starting point.

Long Run

Production in the **long run** differs from short-run production costs in that the size of the plant and the amounts and types of equipment can be altered. If market conditions justify it, a producer can expand output in the long run by building larger production facilities. Additional outputs can then be produced more efficiently in the long run than they can in the short run.

The exact time period that divides the short run from the long run varies from industry to industry. A copy firm that duplicates printed materials for customers may have a long run of a few weeks—only as long as it takes to rent additional floor space and install some more copying machines. For an electric power company, however, the long run is a matter of years. Building an additional electric power plant takes a long time.

---

long run a period of time sufficiently long that the amount of all factor inputs can be varied.

► Why Do Prices Change?

Prices generally do not remain constant for very long in our economy. They are always changing because the factors determining demand change, or the factors determining supply change, or both do. *Changes in demand and supply cause prices to change, and not the other way around.* In this section of the chapter we will examine why prices change.

◤ Shifts in Demand

If there is a change in any of the four determinants of demand for a good or service—tastes,

shift in demand a change in the quantity of a good or service that would be purchased at each possible price.

incomes, the prices and availability of substitutes and complements, or population size—there will be a **shift in the demand** schedule. More or less of the item will be demanded at each and every price.

Assume, for example, that research were to show peanut butter was a major cause of baldness. Publication of this news would probably result in a significant decline in the quantity of peanut butter demanded at every price (because there was a change in people's tastes). Such a demand shift is shown in Figure 6. The original equilibrium price of a jar of peanut butter, as reflected in Figure 5, was $2.50. Let us assume the news story causes the demand to fall by 5,000 jars per month. This is reflected by a shift of the demand schedule from D_1 to D_2. As a result of this shift, the price of a jar of peanut butter drops to $2.32 and the number of jars purchased falls to 27,500.

Figure 6
Shift in Demand

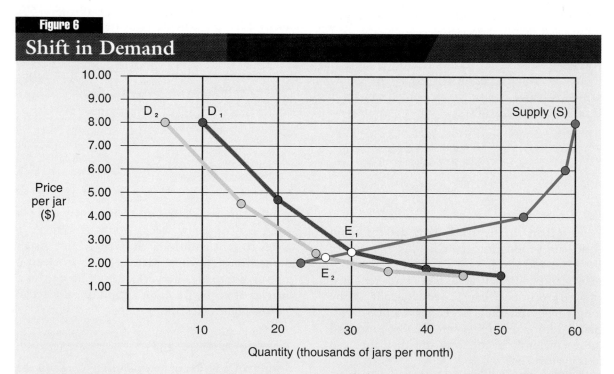

A report that peanut butter is related to baldness causes the demand to shift from D_1 to D_2 and the equilibrium price to fall from $2.50 to $2.32.

Prices of agricultural products are affected by shifts in the demand schedule.

Notice that the decrease in quantity purchased is less than the decrease in demand. The news story caused demand to decrease by 5,000 jars at a price of $2.50. At that, or any given price, the consumers wanted 5,000 fewer jars than before (check this out yourself by comparing the amounts demanded at different prices along the two demand curves). The quantity purchased fell from 30,000 to 27,500, however, a decline of only 2,500 jars. The reason that the decrease in the quantity purchased was not as great as the decrease in demand is because of the price reduction. Decreasing demand causes suppliers to cut their prices. This is shown in Figure 6 by the movement down the supply curve (which has not changed) from E_1 to E_2. Suppliers cut their price because with smaller output their short-run production costs are lower.

In summary, the news story about the alleged relationship between peanut butter and baldness caused a downward shift in demand from D_1 to D_2, a reduction of 5,000 jars. This fall in demand caused a reduction of the price of a jar of peanut butter from $2.50 to $2.32. At this new equilibrium price the quantity demanded and supplied is 27,500 jars. The demand shift caused a reduction in the quantity supplied of 2,500 jars. Note that there has been no change in the supply schedule. At any given price, suppliers would be willing to sell as much as before the demand shift. Also note that the reduction in price to $2.32 did *not* cause demand to increase. Demand only changes when one of the four determinants of demand changes.

Shifts in Supply

The rise in the cost of peanuts because of the drought caused a **shift in the supply** schedule for peanut butter. In Figure 7, the original hypothetical supply of peanut butter is represented by S_1. The rise in production costs because of higher peanut prices in the drought resulted in a fall in the peanut butter supply to S_2. At each price, sellers were offering a smaller quantity for sale than the year before. (Check this out yourself by comparing the different amounts offered at different prices along the two supply curves.)

As a result, the market equilibrium as shown in Figure 7 moved from E_1 to E_2. The jump in price from $2.50 to $4.70 a jar caused families to cut back on their peanut butter consumption. This did not represent a shift in demand, but rather a movement back along the existing demand curve to a smaller quantity at the higher price. The quantity demanded decreased because of the change in supply, not because of any change in demand (shift in the demand schedule).

It is easy to confuse the causes of market changes between those changes that are the result of changed demand and those that are the result of changed supply. If peanut prices

shift in supply a change in the quantity of a good or service that would be offered for sale at each possible price.

Figure 7

Shift in Supply

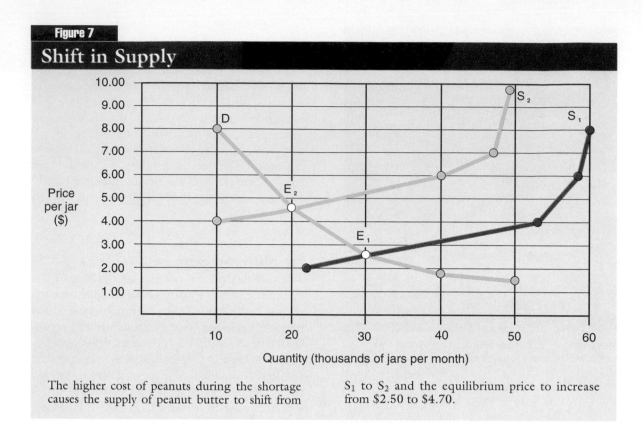

Quantity (thousands of jars per month)

The higher cost of peanuts during the shortage causes the supply of peanut butter to shift from S_1 to S_2 and the equilibrium price to increase from $2.50 to $4.70.

were to decline because of improved technology or resource prices, and as a result families began consuming more peanut butter, people might refer to this increased consumption as an increase in demand. The real reason for the changed consumption, however, would be the increase in supply. An increase in supply, by reducing the market price, causes an increase in the *quantity demanded*—represented by a movement downward to the right on the existing demand curve. This is different from an increase in *demand*—represented by a shift upward to the right of the whole demand curve. Likewise, an increase in demand resulting from a change in income, for example, would lead to an increase in the *quantity supplied* represented by an upward movement along the existing supply curve.

 Why Do Prices Change?

EconExplorer

To determine whether a market change is the result of a change in demand or a change in supply, look at the cause of the change. If it is due to a change in tastes, incomes, the availability or prices of substitutes and complements, or population size, the cause is a change in demand. If the market change is due to a change in production costs, the cause is a change in supply.

Comparative Case Application

Oiled and Ready

The world's demand for oil is steadily increasing. Americans, the world's biggest consumers of petroleum products, are switching to gas-guzzling sport utility vehicles and light trucks. The economies of East and Southeast Asia are using more petroleum to fuel their economic growth, and 75% of the families in China (the world's most populous country) are hoping to buy their first automobiles within the next 5 years. You would think that this increase in demand would be pushing oil prices through the roof. In fact, after adjusting for inflation, at $14 to $15 per barrel in early 1998, oil prices were about one-half of what they were at their peak in 1980–81. What's happening here?

Many economists and petroleum experts are as surprised as the rest of us. Based on assumptions of soaring demand and limited supply, forecasts made in 1980 predicted that by 1997 oil would cost $98 a barrel, and in 1991 forecasters were still predicting the price would be around $45. How could they be so wrong? Well, they might have been correct about the anticipated increases in demand, but they missed the oil well with their forecasts about supply (Figure 8).

Actually, soaring demand in the 1980s did lead to skyrocketing oil prices in the short run as producers tried to meet demand by running their existing facilities to the limit. But these prices also resulted in long-run changes. Enticed by the higher prices, oil companies expanded their exploration for new fields and invested in new technologies for finding oil and getting it out of the ground. What is happening then, is that as fast as the demand for petroleum has grown, the supply of petroleum has been growing even faster. And the key to this increase in supply is technology.

Oil does not always exist in nice, big, easy-to-access pools just below the earth's surface. When it does, it is easy to drill for and extract. Pools such as these were therefore tapped, and sometimes drained, many years ago. A large portion of the world's *proven oil reserves,* oil that we know exists but have not yet extracted, lies deep under the ocean floor or in endless, narrow, underground cracks that stretch for mile upon mile. Getting this oil to the surface used to be extremely costly, thus making the cost of producing a barrel very high.

Modern technology has been conquering such problems at an amazing rate. For example, in 1994 Shell Oil spent $1.2 billion for a floating oil platform that could produce less than 50,000 barrels per day. In 1998, a British Petroleum platform costing just $85 million will be pumping 35,000 barrels per day in a similar location. Or consider that just a few years ago, only about 35% of the oil in a typical oil field could be extracted. New technologies that force air down into the well can drain 70% of that oil at no increase in cost. Finally, consider that at one time oil drills moved in only one direction, straight down or at an angle. New, "geosteering" drill bits guided by computers go down, left, right, and

Advanced technology for oil exploration has resulted in new sources of oil. With increased supplies, the price of oil has been kept under control.

even up again, to follow seams of oil for miles along narrow cracks that are deep below the earth's surface. In fact, the costs of finding and extracting a barrel of oil from the ground have dropped about 60% in the past 10 years.[1]

One result of these technological advances is that more companies can produce more oil at lower costs, resulting in lower prices per barrel and cheaper gasoline prices at the fuel pump (see the Case Application on The Energy Gluttons, page 26). Another result of technological advance is that we know much more about how much oil actually exists under the ground and under the ocean. Instead of running out of petroleum as many doomsayers predicted, proven reserves have actually *increased* by 60% between 1980 and 1997.

1. "The New Economics of Oil." *BusinessWeek*, November 3, 1997, pp. 140–148.

Figure 8

Prices of Petroleum per Barrel

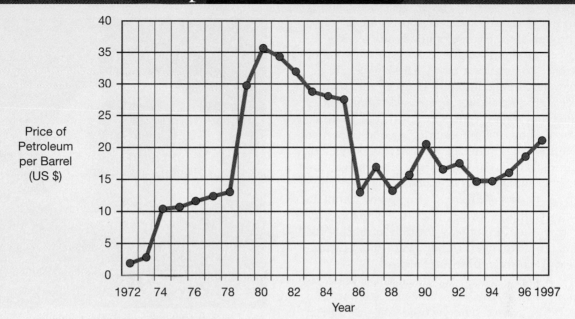

Price of Petroleum per Barrel (US $)

Year

Economic Reasoning

1. What has been happening to the demand for and supply of oil in the past few years? What determinants of demand and supply have caused these changes?
2. Draw a supply-demand graph and use it to show what has happened in the petroleum market over the past decade. If prices have fallen, which has increased more, supply or demand?
3. Burning petroleum pollutes the environment, and cheaper oil encourages us to burn more and pollute more. Do you think that we should tax oil to encourage people to burn less of it? Why or why not?

Oiled and Ready

Visit the British Petroleum Web site at http://www.bp.com/bpstats/index.html. While you are there, check out the geographic distribution of the world's proven oil reserves. Why would a war in the Middle East have an impact on oil prices?

For more information about petroleum, visit the Energy Source Network at or the Energy Information Administration at http://www.eia.doe.gov/

▶ Putting It Together

In our economic system resources are allocated through the exchange of goods and services between producers and consumers. Each good or service commands a price. These prices are determined by the interplay between the *demand* for a product and its *supply*. A *demand schedule* and its graphic representation, the *demand curve,* show the amounts of a good or service buyers would purchase at different prices. For almost any item, the higher the price, the smaller the *quantity demanded*. This is referred to as the *law of demand*. People buy less of an item at higher prices because of the *income effect*—they cannot afford to buy as much—and because of the *substitution effect*—they buy relatively less costly substitutes instead.

A *supply schedule* and its graphic representation, the *supply curve,* show the amounts of a good or service sellers would offer for sale at different prices. For virtually any good or service, the higher the price, the larger the quantity that will be offered for sale. This is referred to as the *law of supply*.

When buyers and sellers come together in the market, an *equilibrium price* is established where the quantity demanded equals the quantity supplied. This is the market-clearing price at which there are no *shortages* and no *surpluses*. In competitive markets, prices cannot stay above or below the equilibrium point for very long. Competitive pressures push prices back down or up to the equilibrium point.

The determinants of demand are *consumer tastes and preferences,* income levels, the availability and prices of substitutes and *complements,* and the population size of the market.

Supply is determined by production costs. The *short-run* situation assumes that plant size, equipment, resource prices, and technology do not change; the *long-run* situation assumes that production capacity and technology can change.

Agricultural products like peanut butter are particularly sensitive to the influences that cause shifts in demand and supply.

A change in demand or supply is reflected by changes along the entire demand or supply schedule. This causes the schedule to shift left or right. *Shifts in demand* and *shifts in supply* cause equilibrium prices to change in the marketplace. In contrast to shifts in the whole schedule, changes in the quantity demanded or the quantity supplied reflect movements by sellers or buyers along existing demand or supply curves. These changes in quantity demanded or supplied are the result of price changes.

An increase in demand will raise prices and cause suppliers to offer more for sale in the short run. If they expect the increased demand to be permanent, they will invest in new plant and equipment and thereby increase production capacity and long-run supply.

Perspective

Adam Smith's Marketplace

Adam Smith (1723–1790) Adam Smith was born in Scotland. At the age of 3, he was kidnapped by gypsies but soon rescued. A sickly child, he was in the habit of talking to himself when alone and remained absentminded throughout his life, although he had an extraordinary memory. At the age of 28, he became professor of moral philosophy at the University of Glasgow in Scotland. He was a popular lecturer, and his classes were very well attended. At the age of 40, after the publication of his first book, *The Theory of Moral Sentiments,* he accepted an appointment as traveling tutor to the young duke of Buccleuch. He accompanied the duke to France and became acquainted with the intellectual leaders of the country, including a number of Physiocrats. When he returned to England, Smith worked on his masterpiece, *The Wealth of Nations,* for a decade before its publication in 1776. Two years later he was appointed commissioner of customs in Scotland. Not long before his death in 1790, he expressed the regret that he had "done so little" in his lifetime.

Adam Smith is considered the father of economics. Before him, economics was studied either as a branch of politics called political economy or as an area of philosophy. Economics was born as a distinct discipline with the publication of Smith's *The Wealth of Nations* in 1776. It was a remarkable book setting forth expositions of basic economic ideas, which hold up very well today, along with a mind-boggling amount of factual data.

Among the most important and enduring contributions to economic thought was Smith's explanation of the beneficial workings of the free marketplace. He explained market equilibrium as follows:

> The quantity of every commodity brought to market naturally suits itself to the effectual demand. It is the interest of all those who employ their land, labour, or stock [capital] in bringing any commodity to market, that the quantity never should exceed the effectual demand; and it is the interest of all other people that it never should fall short of that demand.

A major thrust of *The Wealth of Nations* was that market prices and quantities should be permitted to adjust to their equilibrium levels without any interference from the government.

Smith was arguing in opposition to the system of mercantilism under which the government exercised a great deal of control over economic life. The government regulated production and trade with the objective of bringing gold and silver into the coffers of the state.

Smith contended that a nation's real wealth would be maximized by allowing individuals to make economic decisions based on the forces of the marketplace, unhindered by government regulations. He maintained that in pursuing their own self-interest, people would be guided by an *invisible hand* to maximize their personal contribution to the economy. Smith's views had been greatly influenced by the 3 years he spent in France associating with the French Physiocrats. The Physiocrats promoted a policy of *laissez-faire,* which called for the government to keep its hands off trade and allow prices to seek their natural levels.

Because of his *laissez-faire* doctrine, Adam Smith is greatly admired by economic conservatives today. But Smith was anything but a conservative in his day. He was, in fact, someone that we might today call a consumer advocate, protesting the special interests backed by governments that profited at the expense of the general public.

Study Questions

1. "Retail Stores Increase Sales of Computer Games." Does this headline reflect a change in the demand for computer games? Explain.

2. "British Cattle Discovered to Have Mad Cow Disease." How would this affect the demand for beef in the United States?

3. "Manufacturer Introduces Home CD Recorder." Explain how this would affect the demand for prerecorded CDs.

4. Despite the fact that the demand for CD players increased tremendously during the 1990s, the price of CD players continued to decline during the decade. Does this contradict the laws of supply and demand? Explain.

5. "Steel Mills Required to Install New Pollution Control Equipment." How would this regulation affect the supply of steel?

6. The North American Free Trade Agreement (NAFTA) allows American producers to ship their goods to Canada and Mexico without paying any tariffs. How will this affect the demand for U.S. goods?

7. The stated price on a Super Bowl ticket might be $250, but scalpers can sell a ticket for $1,000. Is $250 above or below the equilibrium price? At $250, is there a surplus or shortage of tickets?

8. Use a supply and demand graph to explain what would happen to the equilibrium price and output for BeeBop athletic shoes in each of the following scenarios:
   a. Everybody decides that wearing athletic shoes is totally not cool.
   b. The price of rival Neki athletic shoes decreases substantially.
   c. New laws force BeeBop to close the low-wage Asian "sweatshops" where it manufactures many of its shoes.
   d. The world price of rubber decreases due to the financial crisis in Southeast Asia.
   e. The number of people in the 12- to 15-year-old age group increases.
   f. The cost of participating in athletic activities increases, so students are discouraged from running around and spend more time doing their homework.

9. Look back at the case application The Efficiencyburger in chapter 3. Draw the supply and demand curves for hamburgers before the medical study showing the benefits of burgers is released. Show what happens to demand in the short run and supply in the long run. Explain where there was a change in demand, a change in supply, a change in quantity demanded, and a change in quantity supplied.

10. What would happen if the government determined that peanut butter is vital to the public interest and put a price control into effect that would not let the price of peanut butter increase after the 1981 drought?

Exercises in Analysis

1. Make a table of the number of times each month you would attend a movie at different possible admission prices from $1 to $10 in steps of $1. Then draw a diagram of your demand for going to the movies. Total the demand schedules for a group of seven students to obtain a community demand schedule; then draw the demand curve. Save the results for use in an exercise at the end of chapter 5.

2. Take a tape or audio CD of your favorite group to school and ask a sample of 10 students how much they would pay for it at a record store. Assuming that each student in the sample represents one-tenth of the total number of students at your school, use the data to draw a community demand curve for the tape or CD. What would cause the demand curve to change?

3. Visit the BP Statistical Review of World Energy 1997 Web site at http://www.bp.com/bpstats/index.html and find the current world price for a barrel of petroleum. What has caused the price to change since 1990? Diagram the change in market conditions that led to the price change.
4. Look up "capitalists" in the encyclopedia. Write an explanation of what a capitalist is in your own words.
5. Visit Peanut Links at http://nespal.cpes.peachnet.edu/peanut/ and get a recipe for peanut butter pie or cookies, and send the output to me or give it to your teacher. Visit the Peanut Butter site at http://www.peanutbutterlovers.com/home.html and play the peanut butter trivia game.

Further Reading

Deutschman, Alan. *Winning Money for College.* 3rd ed. Princeton, NJ: Peterson's Guides, 1992. This is a "how-to" book on the strategies for winning college scholarships. For each scholarship program, it gives the rules and procedures, helpful hints, program deadlines, and where to obtain more information.

Haase, Edward F., and William G. McGinnies, eds. *Jojoba and Its Uses.* Tucson: University of Arizona Press, 1972. An examination of the various types of applications that jojoba can substitute for other products and in what ways it is superior.

Horsnell, Paul, and Robert Mobra. *Oil Markets and Prices.* Oxford: Oxford University Press, 1993. A more technical treatise on the setting of prices in the petroleum market.

Leider, Robert, and Anna Leider. *Leider's Lecture: A Complete Course in Understanding Financial Aid.* Alexandria, VA: Octameron Press, 1992. A handbook of sources of student aid and how to go about applying for scholarships.

Linam, Del. *Jojoba Fever: A Survey of a New Agricultural Industry.* Burbank, CA: Burbank Books, 1981. A look at the emergence of jojoba growing as an industry.

Seymour, Adam. *The Oil Price and Non-OPEC Supplies.* Oxford: Oxford Institute for Energy Studies, 1990. Examines how new petroleum supplies coming on line from other areas have weakened the power of OPEC to control world oil prices.

Tempest, Paul, ed. *The Politics of Middle East Oil.* London: Graham & Trotman, 1993. A study of the political aspects of the petroleum industry and trade in oil.

Verleger, Philip K., Jr. *Adjusting to Volatile Energy Prices.* Washington, DC: Institute for International Economics, 1994. Covers the pricing of petroleum products, the industry's structure, and the market behavior.

Unit Two

Microeconomics

The field of economics is divided into two major areas, microeconomics and macroeconomics. Microeconomics includes the topics that have to do with the individual units of the economy, the households and the firms, and with the way markets for products and resources behave.

chapter eight
Government and Business

The government intervenes in business in various ways, regulating industries and sometimes producing goods and services. There are a variety of government agencies that enforce laws and regulations to protect consumers, workers, and the environment.

chapter five
Earning and Spending: The Consumer

In a market economy, consumers dictate what is produced by their spending decisions. They make their spending and saving decisions in the way that obtains the most satisfaction from their incomes, based on the information available.

chapter nine
Government and Households

Free-market economies do not always result in outcomes that are consistent with the country's social goals. Sometimes it is necessary for the government to intervene in the economy in order to alleviate poverty, ensure pensions and medical care for retirees, make sure that workplaces are safe for employees, and protect consumers from potentially unsafe products.

chapter six
The Business Firm and Market Structure

In a market economy, the private business firm is the principal supplier of goods and services. Consumers express their will in the marketplace, and it is up to the individual enterprises to put together the labor, capital, and natural resources to satisfy these consumer demands. The degree to which consumers are satisfied often depends upon the market structure of the industry the firms are in.

chapter seven
Industrial Performance

The performance of industries is measured by their productivity, the quality of their product, their responsiveness to the market, and their responsiveness to social concerns. There are various ways that American industries can improve their performance. The amount of industry concentration affects performance.

chapter five

Earning and Spending: The Consumer

A major portion of what economics is about is how people earn their incomes and how they spend them. The end result of nearly all economic activity is consumption. In the United States, the consumer is said to be king or queen—consumer demand dictates what will be produced.

▶ Blowing Smoke Rings 🕸

Sweet Virginia cigarette

Burning in my hand,

Well, you used to be a friend of mine,

But now I understand.

You've been eating up inside me for some time,

But I know your gonna get me

Somewhere along the line.

—*Billy Joel, "Somewhere Along the Line"*

In 1964 the surgeon general of the United States published a report on medical findings indicating that cigarette smoking is linked to lung cancer. Additional research since then has implicated cigarettes in heart disease, emphysema, and other health problems. A RAND Corporation study estimates that for each pack of cigarettes smoked, a person's life expectancy is reduced by more than 2 hours.

According to the U.S. Centers for Disease Control and Prevention, tobacco use causes the deaths of about 390,000 people a year. Nonsmokers subjected to long-term exposure to secondhand smoke, especially children, are also at significant risk for smoking-related diseases. Secondhand smoke kills an estimated 9,000 nonsmokers a year and aggravates asthma and other health problems for others. As the public has become aware of the dangers of cigarette smoking, consumption has declined. The proportion of the U.S. population who smokes, which amounted to 40% at the time of the surgeon general's report, is only just about 20% today (50 million Americans are smokers, 36 million have quit the habit).

The tobacco industry is also coming under increased pressure from government agencies that have spent an estimated $53 billion per year to provide health care to people with smoking-related diseases. Governments are successfully suing to require the tobacco companies to reimburse them for these costs. Both state governments and the federal government have charged that tobacco companies had information about the dangers of smoking and about how addictive nicotine is, yet they intentionally kept this information secret. Texas, Florida, and Mississippi each settled suits that together totaled nearly $30 billion, and 40 other states are negotiating an agreement that will cost the industry $368.5 billion if the proposed settlement is accepted.

The wholesale value of cigarette sales is over $27 billion a year, and, despite the industry's recent setbacks, cigarette makers are still among the most profitable companies in the nation. If another product had experienced the bad press that cigarettes have had in the last 3 decades, we would expect the producers to be in big trouble financially. How is it, then, that the cigarette companies are doing so well?

One important reason is that their customers have a particular type of loyalty not found in most products: namely, addiction. This has helped make tobacco a very profitable industry in the face of a shrinking market. Even with a decline in the number of packs sold due to a tenfold increase in cigarette prices since the surgeon general's report, the operating profits of the tobacco companies have nevertheless remained high. Whether measured as a percentage of sales or as a percentage of the amount invested in the companies, the profits of cigarette manufacturers have always been, and still continue to be, among the highest for any industry.

One way the tobacco companies have ensured that profits continue to roll in is by spending hundreds of millions of dollars advertising and promoting their products. Philip Morris got to be the world leader with successful advertising campaigns that created images of the macho, tattooed Marlboro man and the liberated Virginia Slims woman. Ironically, the original model for the Marlboro man died in 1987 of emphysema, a lung disease caused by smoking.

Another advertising campaign that has drawn heated criticism from health officials and antismoking groups is the Old Joe Camel character promoted by R. J. Reynolds Tobacco Company, the number two producer. Old Joe is a cartoon character that has served as a mascot for Camel cigarettes, and, to the dismay of many, this ad campaign was targeted directly at younger people. According to critics, backed by studies showing the popularity of the character among children as young as 6 years, Old Joe has contributed to the increase in smoking by children. Association does not necessarily mean causation, but what is troubling to many is that about 1 million teenagers take up smoking each year. Children, young women, and African Americans are the only groups that have shown a rise in the rate of smoking since the surgeon general's report.

The combination of physical and psychological addiction to smoking plus heavy advertising promotion enables the tobacco companies to remain profitable, even in the face of the negative health reports. Cigarettes are one of the highest taxed products in the United States—federal taxes are 24 cents per pack (1998) and state taxes range from 2.5 cents in Virginia to 82.5 cents in Washington. Despite the higher prices resulting from these taxes, producers are still able to sell billions of cigarettes. With cigarettes, price is not as important as addiction and image in purchasing decisions.

Chapter Preview

The money that people receive as income comes from a variety of sources. After they earn their incomes, they must make decisions about how much of their money they want to spend and how much to save. Most of our incomes are used for what economists call consumption spending, and when functioning as consumers, people are faced with a multitude of decisions. Just as the economy does not have enough resources to produce everything that is desired, people do not have enough income to buy everything they want. The decisions that they make reflect their priorities and the information that is available to them. In this chapter we will examine how people earn their incomes and how they spend them. The questions to be discussed are: What determines incomes? What choices do consumers make? How can consumers make better choices?

Learning Objectives

After completing this chapter, you should be able to:

1. Define and describe the different income sources that make up the functional distribution of income.
2. Explain how the use of capital influences the demand for labor.
3. Understand the special characteristics of rent and its relationship to limited supply.
4. Understand the concept of elasticity of demand.
5. Differentiate among perfectly elastic, relatively elastic, unitary elastic, relatively inelastic, and perfectly inelastic demand.
6. Compute a demand elasticity ratio.
7. Define consumer sovereignty and explain how it is related to the allocation of resources.
8. Define average propensity to consume and average propensity to save.
9. Explain how consumers get information about the products that they buy.
10. Explain how information influences consumer choices.

▶ What Determines Incomes?

Where do consumers get the money that they spend and save? As shown in the Circular Flow Diagram (page 82), people earn their incomes by providing privately owned resources (the factors of production) to businesses. The most important resource that people own is their labor, and, consequently, most income in the United States is labor income—wages and salaries. People have other assets, however, which they provide to businesses in return for income. In this section we shall look at the different ways that people earn the income that they spend and save.

◪ Functional Income Distribution

Household incomes are received in a variety of ways—as wages and salaries, rent, interest, and profits. The **functional distribution of income**

---

functional income distribution the shares of total income distributed according to the type of factor service for which they are paid, that is, rent as a payment for land, wages for labor, and interest for capital.

Figure 1

Functional Distribution of Income, 1997

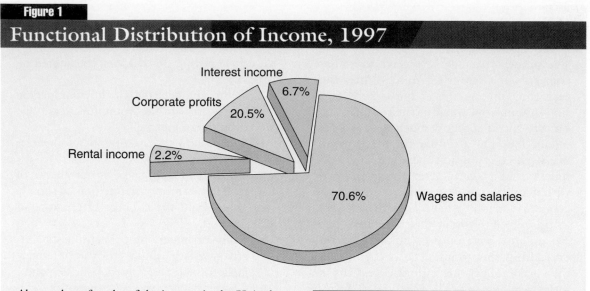

Almost three-fourths of the income in the United States is from wages and salaries. The remainder is in the form of proprietors' income, rent, corporate profits, and interest.

Source: U.S. Department of Commerce, Bureau of Economic Analysis.

shows the source of people's incomes by these four categories. Figure 1 shows this distribution in the United States. In 1997, about 70% of total national income came from wages and salaries, followed in importance by profits, interest, and rent. As will be explained below, the name *functional* comes from the fact that each type of income reflects the function of resource used to earn it.

▼ Wages and Salaries

Wages and salaries are the price of labor services, and like other prices, they are determined by the interaction of supply and demand. All else the same, the greater the demand for, or the smaller the supply of, a particular type of labor, the more that type of labor will earn.

The demand for labor is a **derived demand** because it is derived from (depends on)

derived demand the demand for a factor of production that comes from the demand for the goods or services that the factor produces.

the demand for the goods and services that labor produces. For example, the demand for stage designers depends on consumer demand for theatrical shows and the demand for surgeons depends on the demand for medical operations.

The amount of capital used by a business affects the demand for labor. If labor and capital are substitutes, then increasing the amount of capital will decrease the demand for labor. This often occurs when capital is cheaper than labor. An example would be when a person is replaced by a machine, such as a factory worker by a robot, or a person at an information booth by an interactive computer screen. More often, though, labor and capital are complements, and an increase in the amount of capital requires an increase in the demand for labor. For example, a software development company that buys six new PCs will need six new programmers. Although we are not used to thinking of labor and capital as being complements, if you think about it, the number of jobs in the United States has grown fairly steadily over the years, right along with steady increases in the country's stock of capital goods.

Figure 2

Net Effect on Wages of an Increase in Labor Supply and Demand

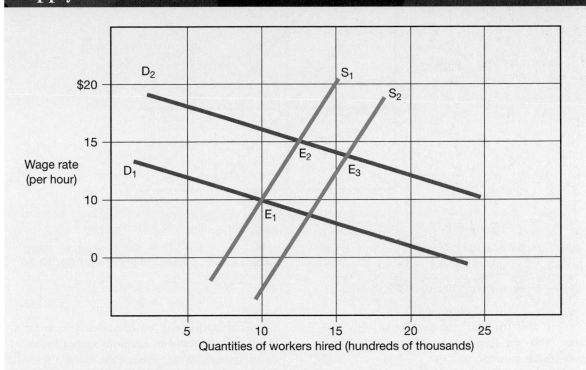

An increased demand for programmers from D_1 to D_2 will cause their wages to increase from $10 to $15 per hour. These higher wages, though, will induce more people to become programmers, thus causing the supply to increase from S_1 to S_2 and pushing wages back down a little.

What Determines Incomes?

EconExplorer

The supply of labor reflects the number of people who have the needed skills and are seeking employment in different occupations. In the short run, higher wages in an occupation will result in workers with these skills offering more hours to employers; the supply curve for labor slopes up and to the right. In the long run, these higher wages will create an incentive for more people to get the needed skills and enter that occupation. As the demand for computers increases, the derived demand for programmers increases and results in higher wages for people with these skills. As a result of these higher wages, more people have learned to be programmers, and the resulting increased supply of programmers has brought their earnings back down a little.

In Figure 2, the original wage for programmers is determined by the interaction of demand (D_1) and supply (S_1). As demand increased to D_2, wages increased from $10 per hour ($E_1$) to $15 per hour ($E_2$). New entrants to the labor force and people willing to switch jobs noted these rising wages and studied to be programmers, resulting in an increase in supply (S_2) and a decrease in wages to $13 per hour

Figure 3

Factor Market Adjustments to an Increase in Demand

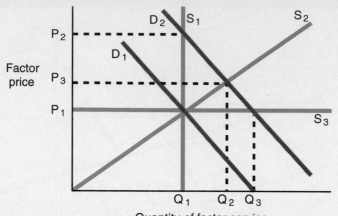

An increase in demand for a factor from D_1 to D_2 will have more of an effect on price or on quantity depending on whether the factor supply is perfectly inelastic, like S_1, which represents land, more elastic, like S_2, which might be skilled labor, or perfectly elastic, like S_3, which might be unskilled labor.

(E_3). In this manner, the market system allocates labor to those occupations where it is most highly valued.

✖ Rent

Rent received by persons (not including rent receipts of businesses) is the smallest of the income shares, accounting for only a little over 2% of national income.

In economic analysis, rent is the payment made for the use of land. Because land is pretty much fixed (unchanging) in supply, the level of rent depends almost entirely on the demand for the resource. A big demand results in a very high rent, and a small demand results in a low rent. This is so because the supply is fixed and cannot expand or contract in response to price changes. The effect of an increase in demand on rent is compared with the effect of an increase in demand on the prices of other types of resources in Figure 3.

The supply schedule for land is shown by S_1. It is vertical because the quantity of land is fixed and does not change with changes in the price of using it (rent). If the demand for land increases from D_1 to D_2, the rent on land will increase from P_1 to P_2, but the quantity rented stays at Q_1. With land, the whole adjustment to an increase in demand is accommodated by an increase in rent. At the other extreme, if a resource has a perfectly elastic supply such as S_3, the increase in demand results in no change in the price. The increased demand instead is accommodated entirely by an increase in the quantity supplied, reflected in the move from Q_1 to Q_3. Most factor inputs fall between these two extremes. An increase in demand is partly accommodated by an increase in price and partly accommodated by an increase in the quantity supplied. If the factor has a supply schedule such as S_2, an increase in demand from D_1 to D_2 results in some increase in price from P_1 to P_3 and some increase in the quantity supplied from Q_1 to Q_2.

Although rents are just the smallest share of income receipts, rent-type earnings are frequently found in wages and salaries. This helps to explain why such large differences can exist in how much different people earn. The $11 million salary paid to Albert Bell by the Chicago White Sox in 1998 is more like a rent than a salary. The same is true of the incomes of movie and pop music stars.

(Continued on page 128)

Case Application

Five Strikes and You're Out

Everybody knows that in baseball it is three strikes and you're out. Not anymore. So far there have been five strikes by ball players unhappy with free agency compensation, proposed salary caps, pension arrangements, and arbitration rules. The first two strikes, at the start of the 1972 season and during the 1980 exhibition season, were short-lived. Strike three came in the middle of the 1981 season and lasted 50 days, causing a loss of 712 games. The fourth strike, in 1985, lasted only two days. The fifth one, which began in 1994, however, lasted 232 days, and 921 regular season games and the World Series were cancelled. It even carried over into the 1995 exhibition season, when the major league teams filled their line-ups with "replacement players." Although the strike ended in time for the 1995 regular season, many fans figured that five strikes were enough, and interest and attendance began to decline.

The 1994–95 strike was particularly maddening to the fans. The main issue over which the strike was called was a salary cap proposed by the owners. Here were two groups of millionaires fighting over money. On one side were the owners whose franchises were going way up in value. For example, in 1979, the Baltimore Orioles were purchased for $11 million, in 1988 they were sold for $70 million, and in 1993, the same team sold for $173 million. On the other were the "workers" whose salaries averaged about $1 million per year in 1994. Fans making 25,000 or so per year did not feel a lot of empathy for the striking ballplayers, and many were actually hoping that the replacement players would get a chance to play in big league stadiums.

Two major issues are confronting major league baseball franchises. First, the owners of some teams want new ball parks with high-

The home run race in 1998 reignited fan interest in the American Pastime.

profit luxury boxes, and they want the local taxpayers to pay for them! They threaten to move their teams or sell them to new owners in other cities if their current home cities do not pay up. A major league franchise is not all that important to a city's economy (a large supermarket generates as much income for the city), but losing a team would result in losses for local bars, concessionaires, parking lots, hotels, restaurants, and so on. In addition, the local fans will feel a very real psychological loss.

Second, many baseball teams that operate in smaller cities such as Milwaukee, Pittsburgh, and Seattle cannot afford to pay the high salaries that the star players are able to get from the richer, big-city markets. About 44% of teams' revenues come from ticket sales, and most of the rest comes from selling spots on national and local cable television. These teams cannot remain competitive unless the owners and players agree to either salary caps or revenue sharing among the teams.

Economic Reasoning

1. According to the functional distribution of income, what types of income would be affected by baseball strikes and teams changing cities?

2. Why do baseball players earn so much money?

3. Are the high salaries paid to professional athletes justified? Why or why not?

Five Strikes and You're Out

Browse the Web and prepare a report on the salaries in different professional sports.

For most occupations, an increase in demand only raises wages by a small amount. The increase in the supply of workers attracted by higher wages accommodates the balance of the increased demand. But when there is a unique talent involved and the supply cannot be increased, the wage may go very high as demand increases. The market adjustment to an increase in the demand for a scarce or unusual talent such as hitting 40 home runs a year, or being a box office draw like Arnold Schwartzenegger is shown by the S_1 outcome in Figure 3. By comparison, the adjustment to an increase in the demand for unskilled labor would be more like that for S_3, while an increase in the demand for a skilled occupation would lie in between, as in the S_2 case.

Interest

Interest income accounted for a little under 7% of total income in 1997. Interest is the factor payment for the use of financial capital. On the one hand it can be thought of as the price of borrowing money, on the other it is the amount of income people can earn by saving and lending their money instead of spending it on consumption goods. The more that people save and the higher that interest rates are, the more interest income people will earn.

Like other economic prices, interest rates are determined through the interaction of supply and demand. The supply of financial capital comes mainly from household and business sav-

ings. Generally, a rise in the interest rate should make more savings available by making it more profitable for people to save, rather than spend, a larger percentage of their income. As explained earlier, however, other factors have a big impact on how much people desire to save. As a result, the effect of a change in the interest rate on the supply of savings is not predictable.

On the other hand, the demand for financial capital tends to behave like the demand for other goods and services—more is borrowed at lower interest rates and less is borrowed when interest rates increase. Ultimately, the interest rate depends on the amount of financial capital available relative to the demand for borrowing to finance business investment, household purchases, and government deficits.

Profits

Profits are often the least understood type of income. It is clear what the other factor payments are for: wages are the payment for labor services, rents for the use of land, and interest for the use of financial capital. But for what factor service are profits paid? Profits are sometimes said to be the payment to entrepreneurs for perceiving a need for a new or better good or service, organizing the factors of production to satisfy that need, and taking the necessary financial risks. More will be said about profits in chapter 6 when our discussion turns from the consumer to businesses.

What Choices Do Consumers Make?

The interplay between demand and supply in a market economy determines the prices of goods and services. Prices, in turn, influence consumer choices between different goods and services. They also affect consumer decisions about how much to save rather than spend.

Spending Choices

People are faced with spending, or **consumption,** choices every day. Such decisions depend on personal preferences and the prices of different goods and services in the marketplace. Given people's preferences, the law of demand tells us that at lower prices people buy more of a good and at higher prices they buy less, but it does not tell us anything about *how much* more or less they buy. Depending on the good in question, consumers react differently to price changes. Sometimes price changes result in large changes in the quantity demanded and sometimes there is hardly any effect. Econo-

mists use the concept **price elasticity of demand** (or simply "elasticity of demand") to describe how much the quantity demanded changes when the price of a good changes.

What Choices Do Consumers Make?

EconExplorer

---

consumption the use of income to buy consumer goods and services instead of saving. According to economic jargon, after-tax income can be used for only two things—consumption or saving.

price elasticity of demand the relative size of the change in the quantity demanded of a good or service as a result of a small change in its price.

Americans require more income each year to buy the necessities of life. The growth of home entertainment, such as these stereo systems, however, demonstrates that the demand for recreational products remains high.

Price elasticity of demand is an important characteristic of consumer behavior. It is vital to understanding spending decisions by consumers and pricing decisions by producers. If the quantity demanded of a good or service changes a lot when the price changes, then the demand for that good or service is said to be **elastic**—it is very responsive to price changes. Sellers would need to be very careful about rising prices because they would lose a lot of sales. Alternatively, if the quantity demanded changes very little when the price changes, then the demand for that good or service is **inelastic,** or unresponsive to price changes. In this instance, sellers could raise prices without losing a lot of customers.

Because of its importance, it is useful to have a measurement of elasticity. Demand is said to be elastic if a change in price is met with a greater percentage change in quantity demanded. For example, if price increases or decreases by 10%, the quantity demanded will decrease or increase by *more than* 10%. If, on the other hand, a price changes by 10% and the quantity demanded changes by *less than* 10%, then the demand is inelastic. If we know how much quantity demanded changes when a good's price changes, we can

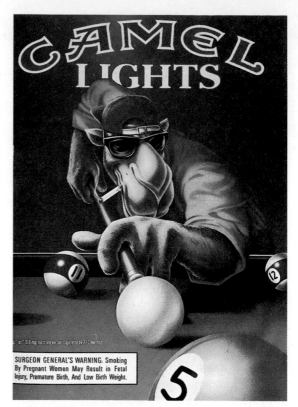

Once a person is addicted to nicotine, his or her demand for cigarettes becomes inelastic. Advertising is therefore used in order to induce new smokers into the habit.

elastic a demand condition in which the relative size of the change in quantity demanded is greater than the size of the price change.

inelastic a demand condition in which the relative size of the change in the quantity demanded is less than the size of the price change.

elasticity ratio a measurement of the degree of the response of a change in quantity demanded to a change in price.

unitary elasticity a demand condition in which the relative change in the quantity demanded is the same as the size of the price change.

calculate the demand elasticity by dividing the percentage change in the quantity demanded by the percentage change in price. This is the **elasticity ratio:**

$$\text{Elasticity Ratio} = \frac{\text{\% change in Q (quantity demanded)}}{\text{\% change in P (price)}}$$

From this equation it can be seen that if the percentage change in quantity demanded is greater than the percentage change in price, the elasticity ratio will be greater than 1. If the elasticity ratio is greater than 1, demand is elastic. If it is less than 1 because quantity demanded changes less than price, demand is inelastic. If the ratio is exactly 1, the demand elasticity is unitary. **Unitary elasticity** exists when the

Figure 4

Types of Demand Elasticity

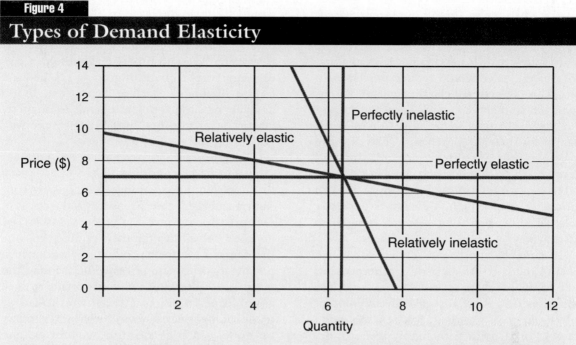

The degree of elasticity of demand for a good or service can range from perfectly elastic (horizontal demand curve) to perfectly inelastic (vertical demand curve). The elasticity of demand is usually somewhere in between these extremes.

change in quantity is identical to the relative change in price, when demand is neither elastic nor inelastic but right in between.

Because of their addictive nature, the demand for cigarettes is inelastic once a person is hooked. According to a study by the National Bureau of Economic Research, younger smokers, who are not as hooked on smoking, have a more elastic demand for cigarettes. Smokers between the ages of 12 and 17 have a demand elasticity for cigarettes equal to 1.40. This means that if cigarette prices increased by 10% from $2.00 a pack to $2.20 a pack, a smoker in this age group would purchase 14% fewer cigarettes.

$$\text{Elasticity Ratio} = \frac{\% \text{ change in Q}}{\% \text{ change in P}} = \frac{14\%}{10\%} = 1.40$$

Because the ratio is greater than 1, the demand is elastic.

Older, more established, smokers have a more inelastic demand for cigarettes. The elasticity ratio for those in the 20- to 25-year-old range is 0.9, and for even older smokers the ratio falls to 0.1—a 10% increase in price leads to only a 1% reduction in cigarette purchases! The government is well aware of this fact, and it knows that raising the tax on cigarettes will not cause established smokers to reduce their consumption by very much. Its campaign to reduce teen smoking by increasing the tax on cigarettes, however, is based on the knowledge that the demand by younger smokers is much more price elastic.

In general, the slope of a demand curve indicates how elastic or inelastic the demand for a product is. The various degrees of elasticity are represented in Figure 4. An elastic demand curve tends to be somewhat horizontal. It shows that small changes in price result in large changes in the amounts purchased. The demand for cigarettes by young smokers might have a slope like this. At the extreme, an absolutely flat demand curve indicates that a rise in the price would reduce purchases to zero. This is **perfectly elastic** demand. An inelastic demand curve is more vertical, showing that large changes in price result in small changes in quantity purchased. This is more descriptive of an older smokers' demand curve. At the extreme, if changes in price resulted in no change whatsoever in the amounts purchased, the demand is **perfectly inelastic,** shown by a curve that is straight up and down.

In general, goods and services for which demand tends to be inelastic are **necessities,** those for which there are either no or few close substitutes, and those that take an insignificant part of our total spending. Salt is a very good example of an item with highly inelastic demand. It has few close substitutes, and the amount we pay for salt is an insignificant part of our total spending. If the price of salt were to increase from 50¢ to $1.00 per box, there

would be little decrease in the quantity demanded. Those goods and services that tend to have an elastic demand are **luxuries,** those that have many close substitutes, and those that cost us a significant amount of money. The demand for specific brands, such as Pepsi-Cola, Exxon gasoline, or Crest toothpaste tends to be pretty elastic because other brands represent very good substitutes.

Price elasticity of demand is an important characteristic of consumer behavior. It is vital to understanding spending decisions by consumers and pricing decisions by producers. Producers try to convince consumers that there are no good substitutes for their product, making the demand for their product inelastic, which permits them to raise prices without losing too many sales. Elasticity is also important to such governmental decisions as what fares to charge on public transit systems and what taxes to levy on goods, such as gasoline, cigarettes, and liquor. If the demand for bus tickets is elastic, then fares that are too high will result in fewer riders. If taxes are placed on goods with elastic demands, the resulting higher prices will result in far fewer sales and tax revenues will be pretty skimpy.

perfectly elastic a demand condition in which the quantity demanded varies from zero to infinity when there is a change in the price.

perfectly inelastic a demand condition in which there is no change in the quantity demanded when price changes.

necessity a good or service which is considered essential to a person's well-being.

luxury a good or service which increases satisfaction but is not considered essential to well-being.

consumer sovereignty the condition in a market economy by which consumer decisions about which goods and services to purchase determine what is produced.

Consumer Sovereignty

Consumer spending decisions are crucial in the functioning of a market economy because they are the most important determinant of the allocation of resources. These decisions are the basis of resolving the "what to produce" question. Producers generally provide goods and services for which there is sufficient consumer demand and stop producing goods and services for which demand is insufficient. In this way producers reflect the will of the consumer. **Consumer sovereignty** exists when the choices of consumers in the market determine what producers make.

When the news about the effects of cigarette smoking on health first appeared, many concerned smokers switched to cigarettes with less tar and nicotine, the suspected causes of

Buying stocks or bonds are only two of a wide range of alternative ways for households to save.

damage. Encouraged by cigarette company advertisements, they thought that by switching to reduced-tar brands they could have their cigarettes and their health, too. As a result, the manufacturers increased production of reduced-tar cigarettes until they constituted well over half of the total amount produced. As it turned out, a lot of those who switched found that they were smoking more of the less flavorful brands, thus defeating the purpose, and went back to the stronger cigarettes. Even though consumers sometimes are not always sure of *what* they want, consumer sovereignty determines what is produced.

◢ Savings Choices

Consumers have two alternatives for their after-tax income: they can spend it, or they can save it. On the average, we in the United States currently spend about **95%** of our after-tax (disposable) income on goods and services. This is the **average propensity to consume.** Propensity means inclination. In this case, we are inclined to spend 95 cents of every after-tax dollar we receive. We put the remaining 5 cents of each dollar of after-tax income into savings. Our **average propensity to save** is 5%.

Economists consider any use of money other than consumption spending to be savings. In addition to traditional savings accounts at local banks, savings includes purchases of stocks and bonds, money market or mutual funds, life insurance policies, or real estate. Savers try to find the best way to save in order to get the largest returns from their savings for the amount of risk they are willing to take. At one time people often kept their savings in cookie jars or under mattresses, and maybe there are some who still do. But this is an inefficient way to save, because the savings earn no returns as they would if they were put into a savings account or used to buy stocks. For most people, the largest amount of savings they have is the **equity** in their house. Equity is the money value of a property less the value of outstanding mortgages.

Deciding how to save is important to the individual and to the economy as a whole because savings provide the funds that other individuals use to buy houses and that business firms borrow to begin or expand production. Savings are channeled by banks, brokerage firms, pension funds, and insurance companies into productive investments. Therefore, individual consumer decisions on saving can have a significant impact on the entire economy.

average propensity to consume the percentage of after-tax income which, on the average, consumers spend on goods and services.

average propensity to save the percentage of after-tax income which, on the average, consumers save.

equity the owner's share of the value of property or other assets, net of mortgages or other liabilities.

Case Application

The Channel Race

According to the research firm of Veronis, Suhler & Associates, Americans spend an average of 9½ hours per day on entertainment: watching television or rented videos, going to the movies, reading books and magazines, or surfing the Web. This creates a giant market for the entertainment industry, and entertainment firms from television and movie studios to Internet providers are aggressively competing to keep or increase their share of the market.

In the 1980s cable television was a relatively new technology, and for the first time consumers could choose among dozens of cable television channels instead of the three major networks. The industry exploded in the 1990s, and by using satellite systems, consumers were able to access literally hundreds of different channels. Entertainment firms attempted to lure more and more viewers by offering increasingly specialized options from cartoon, golf, and shopping channels to subscription "tickets" to watch specific sports teams. Whatever interest a group of people might have, the industry sought to satisfy with increased programming.

In the next few years, who knows what kind of entertainment options we will have as televisions are increasingly linked to computers and the Internet. Perhaps we'll be playing interactive virtual reality games from our living rooms on our high-definition digital televisions. Maybe we'll be changing the cast, script, language, and camera angles in a movie we're watching on a rented computer disk. Whatever it is, we can be sure that businesses will be trying to determine what we want so that they can provide it for us.

Satellite systems are a high-tech innovation that bring almost unlimited entertainment options to U.S. homes today and hold promise for much more in the future.

Economic Reasoning

1. What role does consumer sovereignty play in the entertainment options that are available to us?
2. How does consumer sovereignty affect the allocation of resources in the entertainment industry?
3. What effect has the introduction of satellite systems had on the elasticity of demand for cable television service?
4. Do you think that the entertainment industry should keep adding new and different TV channels? Why or why not?

How Can Consumers Make Better Choices?

Consumers try to get the most they can out of the dollars they spend or save. Obtaining the maximum **utility** from our income, however, is not always easy. This section examines under what conditions consumers can make better consumption and savings decisions.

Information

An essential requirement for making wise consumer spending and saving decisions is to have sufficient and accurate information about your choices. For product information, the consumer should know what goods and services are available, where they can be obtained, what prices they are selling for, their quality and serviceability, and their distinctive characteristics.

But there is a cost to obtaining information—the opportunity cost of the time involved in seeking the information. If you were in the market for an automobile, it would be wise to visit a number of dealers, get comparative prices, read consumer magazines and test reports on the characteristics and quality of the different makes, and talk to car owners. On the other hand, if you are buying a can of tomatoes, it doesn't pay to put that much time into deciding which brand to buy and where to buy it.

A problem faced by consumers is that there is no way that they can obtain all the product information they need to make informed decisions. Sometimes we rely on the reputation of a particular producer—indicated through the use of brand names—for quality information. In other instances, especially when foods and drugs are concerned, we depend on government-imposed standards and testing. The government requires firms in certain industries to make information available about their products, such as the fat and caloric content of packaged foods, the energy efficiency of home appliances, and the gas mileage of different car makes. Cigarette manufacturers must print warnings about the health dangers of their products on the packages and in their advertisements. The government also requires lending institutions to inform borrowers in writing of the actual rates of interest they will be paying and the other conditions of a loan. A major purpose of these government requirements is to reduce information costs for consumers and enable them to obtain greater utility from their income.

Similarly, in making savings decisions, consumers need to know how safe their savings are against being reduced in value (the risk factor), how easily they can be turned into cash (their liquidity), and how much the earnings on their savings will be. The availability of financial information on the Internet gives savers a wealth of up-to-date information about stock prices and interest rates around the world. Government regulations are still needed, however, to ensure that such information is accurate.

With respect to cigarettes, an important piece of information consumers did not have prior to the surgeon general's report concerned the effects of smoking on health. Smokers who died of lung cancer or other smoking-related diseases were not able to make informed decisions about the allocation of their spending in the absence of information concerning the relationship between cigarette consumption and health. With that

---

utility the amount of satisfaction a consumer derives from consumption of a good or service.

Information, such as an automobile's gas mileage, is an essential requirement for making wise consumer spending decisions.

information, they might have decided to continue smoking, to cut down on the amount, to switch to lower-tar cigarettes, or to quit smoking. The fact that cigarette manufacturers had this information but hid it from consumers forms the basis for many of the current lawsuits. Whatever their choice, it would be a more efficient allocation of income if based on full knowledge about the product.

◆ Advertising

The most prevalent source of information about products and services is advertising. There is a good deal of dispute over the merits of advertising. Some of advertising's benefits are that it informs consumers of what is available, where it can be purchased, and at what price. Advertisements also present the distinguishing characteristics of different products and services. This is essential information in making consumer choices. By identifying producers through the use of brand names, it may encourage them to maintain the quality of and service for their products.

 How Can Consumers Make Better Choices?

EconExplorer

On the negative side, advertising (which includes fancy packaging) generally adds to the cost of products and thus reduces consumers' purchasing power. Advertising may help eliminate all but the biggest firms—the ones that can afford the high advertising costs in certain industries—from the market. It also helps create wants and fads and thereby affects consumer sovereignty. If the advertising is false or misleading, it will reduce consumer satisfaction.

The heavy advertising by cigarette companies is credited for maintaining a large market for their product in the face of information about its detrimental effects on health. The image created by advertising that smoking is sophisticated, sexy, macho, or whatever the advertising firms think people might identify with, has been effective in offsetting the health warnings, especially in inducing those who have not yet developed the habit to begin smoking.

Comparative Case Application

Intellectual Property Rights

It is easy to enforce property rights with products such as cars and earrings, or pieces of land. But what about with ideas: intellectual property? Making bootleg tapes or copying software is stealing someone's intellectual property just like taking someone's car or earrings is stealing their physical property. It is, however, much more difficult to protect intellectual property.

In the United States, *intellectual property rights (IPRs)* are protected through the use of patents (for inventions), copyrights (for artistic and written materials), and trademarks. A problem arises because other countries either do not have such protection, or even if they do, the laws are not always strictly enforced. In some instances, producers in other countries make counterfeit copies of movie videos, music CDs, and computer software for sale and use in their country because they simply cannot afford the price of legitimate copies. China, for example, is jokingly referred to as a "one-copy country," because one copy is all they need to make enough copies for all that can afford the product. In other instances, counterfeit goods are exported back to the United States and to other countries.

The purpose of IPRs is to give producers an incentive to invest their time and scarce resources in inventing and creating new products. This is especially true for pharmaceutical manufacturers who spend millions of dollars to develop new drugs in an effort to defeat cancer, AIDS, and other diseases. Once developed, the cost of mass producing a new drug is relatively inexpensive. Drug companies, however, must be able to charge a high enough price to recoup their R&D costs, or they will not be able to fund the research that may lead to important

medical breakthroughs. If another company—domestic or foreign—copies their product and sells it less expensively, the original company will not be able to recapture their research costs, and there will be no incentive to do the research. Patent protection gives individuals and companies a financial incentive to develop new products by granting the exclusive right to produce, license, and sell a product for 17 years.

In a similar way, copyrights give programmers, artists, writers, songwriters, and movie producers an incentive to create software, books, plays, songs, and movies. You cannot, for example, copy or record, and then sell a Billy Joel song without his permission. In an extreme case, Jimmy Buffet sued the owner of a hamburger chain for naming his restaurants Cheeseburger in Paradise—the title of one of Buffet's early songs.

Examples of trademark violations abound. When you buy a shirt with an American manufacturer's insignia on the front, it may not have been made by that firm. Counterfeit copies of clothes with well-known trademark symbols have been produced in foreign countries and sold in regular retail outlets as the legitimate article.

Other favorites of the counterfeiters have been Rolex watches, Gucci leather goods, Levi's jeans, Spalding sporting goods, Apple computers, Nike shoes and apparel, industrial parts, and electronic components. The merchandise counterfeiters are taking advantage of the reputation and market success of name brand producers. The public's familiarity with manufacturers' trademarks was built up by a great amount of promotional advertising, as well as by the quality of the products themselves. The prices of the legitimate products include those advertising costs. Thus, even if the imitation products were of as high a quality as the originals, they could be sold at lower prices because they do not have to cover the promotional costs.

What is worse, you could be driving your car after having the brakes relined and have an accident because the brake linings that were installed were inferior imitations of a name brand. Automobile parts have long been a favorite target of counterfeit manufacturers. A car company executive collected over 225 different parts that were sold with Ford company markings but were not legitimate Ford products.

Since the fake products generally do not meet the quality standards of the originals, there are potential health and safety problems. Counterfeit birth control pills labeled as G. D. Searle brand were delivered to pharmacists, forcing the company to recall more than 1 million pills to find the bogus ones. The cause of a helicopter crash and the death of its pilot have been traced to a defective counterfeit part in the rotor assembly. The country of Kenya lost nearly a quarter of its coffee crop because its farmers used ineffective, counterfeit fungicides.

Most of these imitation goods are produced by countries in the Far East. One of the major trade issues between the United States and China has been the latter's reluctance to enforce the IPRs of American producers. (The 1998 blockbuster movie, *Titanic,* was available on video in China before it opened in American theaters!) Because the per capita income in China is less than $1,000 per year, the Chinese cannot afford to pay a price that includes all the development costs of a product. The only way they can see a Disney movie, listen to an Eric Clapton tape, or run Windows on their PCs is by buying pirated copies.

Passing international laws protecting IPRs has been one of the primary aims of the General Agreement on Tariffs and Trade (GATT), a global conference of more than 100 countries that establishes rules for international trade.

The laws in this country have also been strengthened. In 1984 Congress passed legislation bolstering the trademark laws and giving customs agents more powers to search out and confiscate imitation products coming into the country. With the customs service concentrating on narcotics smuggling, however, only a small fraction of the counterfeit imports are caught.

An important IPR issue involves people in countries who cannot afford the "full" price of life-saving drugs. Providing medicines to these countries at prices lower than those charged in the developed countries is not a solution because the medicines can be bought cheaply in those countries and then resold at a profit in the developed countries. It might be stealing, and the counterfeit drugs may not be as effective as the real thing, but what are the choices?

Economic Reasoning

1. What consumer information is conveyed by a trademark?

2. How do violations of intellectual property rights destroy incentives for companies to engage in research and creative activities?

3. Would you knowingly buy an imitation Apple computer made in China if you could get it at a greatly discounted price, say one-half the price of a legitimate Apple, if you lived in the United States? What if you lived in China?

Intellectual Property Rights

Visit the International Anticounterfeiting Coalition at http://www.ari.net/iacc/home.html and click on Museum of Fakes. Could you, or anyone you know, have perhaps used one of these counterfeit products?

▶ Putting It Together

The prices of productive inputs are determined by supply and demand just like the prices of finished goods and services. The demand for productive resources, including labor, is a *derived demand*, meaning that it depends on the demand for the products that consumers want to buy. The demand for labor is also influenced by the amount of physical capital each worker has to work with.

The functional income distribution reflects the way income is earned by labor, land, capital, and entrepreneurship. Each of these resources serves a functional purpose in production, and is paid in a different way. Wages and salaries are paid for labor, rent is paid for the use of land, and interest is paid for the use of financial capital. The income from entrepreneurship is profit. In addition to being the source of people's income, factor payments allocate productive resources to their most productive uses and serve as an incentive to produce.

Consumers dictate what will be produced in a market economy. They express their wants through their purchases of the goods and services they desire at the prices they are willing to pay. This is *consumer sovereignty*. Some goods such as food, housing, clothing, and medical care are *necessities* for all consumers. Other goods and services, on which we may choose to spend our incomes, are *luxuries*.

If we do not change the amount we buy of something by very much when its price changes, it has an *inelastic demand*. If the amount demanded varies a great deal with changes in the price, the item has an *elastic demand*. The *elasticity ratio* is measured by dividing the percentage change in the quantity demanded of a good or service by the percentage change in its price. If the elasticity ratio is less than 1, demand is inelastic. If the elasticity ratio is greater than 1, demand is elastic. If the elasticity ratio is exactly 1, demand elasticity is *unitary*.

The decision to smoke or not to smoke is an economic as well as a health choice, involving such concepts as trade-offs and utility.

The percentage of our total disposable income that we spend on goods and services is our *average propensity to consume*. The percentage that we put into savings is our *average propensity to save*. Saving takes many forms: savings accounts, stocks, bonds, real estate, etc. The *equity* in their homes represents the greatest amount of savings for most households.

In order to obtain the maximum benefit or *utility* from our spending and saving, we need full and accurate information on which to base our decisions. Commercial advertising is one source of product information, and to the extent that it provides useful information, it is helpful in making consumer choices. It may add to the cost of products, however, and when it does not provide accurate, useful information, it is wasteful at best and sometimes misleading.

$ Perspective $

Conspicuous Consumption

Thorstein Veblen (1857–1929) Of Norwegian parentage, Veblen was raised in a Wisconsin farm community. He was educated at some of the country's best universities (Johns Hopkins, Yale, and Cornell), but his agricultural background gave him an appreciation for the realities of life that shaped his thinking about economics. He mistrusted the theoretical formulations of the marginalist school of economists, who held that the economy worked according to certain economic "laws" and automatically made adjustments "at the margin" to give the optimum outcome. Instead, Veblen emphasized the importance of the way a society's culture and institutions dictate economic outcomes, and he is credited with being the founder of the institutionalist school of economics.

In addition to *The Theory of the Leisure Class* (1899), Veblen's books on economics include *The Theory of Business Enterprise* (1904), *The Engineers and the Price System* (1921), and *Absentee Ownership and Business Enterprise* (1923). He also wrote on other subjects, such as the way universities are run, the subject of *The Higher Learning in America* (1918), and published articles on sociology and anthropology, as well as a translation of ancient Nordic sagas, *The Laxdoela Saga* (1925).

Consumers are supposed to be calculating buyers, spending their limited income to get the most utility. But are they? Why do they spend $100 for a pair of designer jeans with a particular label on the back or $50 for a knit shirt with a trademark insignia on the pocket when for about half the price they could buy very similar items without the identifying trademarks? How can shops on exclusive Rodeo Drive in Beverly Hills charge so much more for merchandise than stores do only a few blocks away on Wilshire Boulevard in West Los Angeles?

These phenomena were explained as far back as 1899 by an American economist, Thorstein Veblen. In his best-known work, *The Theory of the Leisure Class,* Veblen pointed out that people at the high end of the income ladder, whom he referred to as the "leisure class," set the consumption standards that other income classes try to emulate. "Conspicuous consumption of valuable goods is a means of reputability to the gen-

tleman of leisure," Veblen said, and "members of each [social] stratum accept as their ideal of decency the scheme of life in vogue in the next higher stratum, and bend their energies to live up to that ideal." In other words, people try to copy the lifestyle of those above them on the income ladder, and the ones at the top display their purchasing power by *conspicuous consumption* of expensive things. Purchasing things because they are expensively chic has been termed "the Veblen effect."

A similar but somewhat different consumption behavior is "the snob effect." The snob effect depends on the consumption of a good being confined to a very limited number of people. Buying a Mercedes automobile might be an example of the Veblen effect at work, while buying a gold-plated Mercedes would be an example of the snob effect.

We have another type of consumer motivation at work at the other extreme, "the bandwagon effect." The bandwagon effect arises when people purchase a good because "everyone else has one." An example of the bandwagon effect is the popularity of high-tech sneakers.

Do the various psychological motivations that drive people to buy certain goods undermine the idea of maximizing total utility? Not at all. Utility comes from psychological satisfaction as well as from satisfaction in use. In the words of Veblen, we derive satisfaction from "the utility of consumption as an evidence of wealth."

For Further Study and Analysis

Study Questions

1. How would the increase in the demand for a product affect the wages of workers in that industry? Why?
2. How can increased investment in capital equipment sometimes result in less demand for labor and sometimes result in more demand for labor?
3. In what way are the enormous salaries earned by professional athletes and movie stars similar to rent?
4. Indicate whether the demand for the following goods is price elastic or price inelastic, and explain why.
   a. gasoline
   b. Exxon gasoline
   c. toothpicks
   d. insulin (for a diabetic)
   e. backpacks
   f. CD players
   g. in-line skates
   h. Coca-Cola
5. What goods do you think would have a higher price elasticity of demand than others? Give three examples and explain why you think they would have a high elasticity.
6. Besides salt and drinking water, what other items that you use regularly have an inelastic demand? Pick one of those items and explain why if its price went up 10% you would reduce your consumption of the item by less than 10%.
7. If you were the owner of a business and trying to decide what price to charge for your product or service, why would the elasticity of demand be an important consideration?
8. A hamburger stand raised the price of its hamburgers from $2.00 to $2.50. As a result, its sales of hamburgers fell from 200 per day to 180 per day. Was the demand for its hamburgers elastic or inelastic? How can you tell?
9. Why would something that has many close substitutes tend to have an elastic demand?
10. If the average propensity to consume was 90% of after-tax income, what would the average propensity to save be?
11. How does advertising affect the elasticity of demand for a product?
12. How will NAFTA affect the elasticity of demand for the products of U.S. producers?
13. Chemically, all aspirin is the same, but some brands of aspirin sell for much more than other brands. Why do consumers often purchase the higher-priced aspirin when all aspirin is chemically the same?
14. What are examples of purchases you have made because of the Veblen effect, the snob effect, and the bandwagon effect?

Exercises in Analysis

1. Go to your library and look at the classified want ads that your local newspaper was running 10 years ago. Then look at the ads this week. Prepare a report describing how the demand for labor has changed and how this demand has been influenced by the way that product demand has changed during this time.

2. In the first exercise at the end of chapter 4, you constructed the demand schedule of a group of students for movie theater tickets. Using the data from that demand schedule, calculate the elasticity of demand for movie theater tickets when the price falls from $7 to $6. Then calculate the elasticity of demand when the price is reduced from $3 to $2. How do the two elasticity ratios compare? Can you draw any generalizations from these comparisons about the behavior of elasticity of demand at high prices compared to low prices? Save the results of this exercise for use in an exercise at the end of chapter 6.

3. Make a list of the goods on which the federal government or your state government levies an excise tax (a tax placed on a specific good like cigarettes). Do you think that the demand for these goods is elastic or inelastic? Explain what effect this will have on tax revenues.

4. The theory of consumer sovereignty holds that only those goods and services consumers want are produced. Prepare a report showing the principle of consumer sovereignty at work in the personal computer industry in recent years.

5. Write a paper comparing the advertising in a section of your Sunday newspaper with the advertising in an hour of prime-time television. Which has the most useful information for the consumer? Which has the most uninformative, repetitive, and/or misleading advertising?

Further Reading

Bradbury, David E. *A Uses and Gratification Study of Three Audiences: Cable Decliners, Basic Cable Subscribers, and Pay Cable Subscribers.* Philadelphia: Temple University thesis, 1990. Research into what motivates people to subscribe to multiple cable channels.

Chollat-Traquet, Claire. *Women and Tobacco.* Geneva: World Health Organization, 1992. An examination of the rising incidence of use of tobacco among the female population.

Earl, Peter. *Lifestyle Economics.* New York: St. Martin's Press, 1986. Analyzes the processes of consumer choice making.

Heilbroner, Robert L. "The Savage Society of Thornstein Veblen," in *The Worldly Philosophers* 4th Edition. New York: Simon & Schuster, 1972.

Morrow, David J. "Why You Can't Tell What Things Cost." *New York Times,* March 2, 1997. P. E5. Reprinted in *Annual Editions: Microeconomics 98/99.* Guilford, CT: Dushkin/McGraw-Hill, 1998.

Napier, Christine, ed. *Issues in Tobacco.* New York: American Council on Science and Health, 1992. A study of the toxological effects of tobacco and the health aspects of smoking.

O'Shaughnessy, John. *Why People Buy.* New York: Oxford University Press, 1987. The author examines consumer behavior with respect to what motivates people to buy specific products and brands. He makes use of a social science survey approach, based on buyers' statements.

Otnes, Per, ed. *The Sociology of Consumption.* Atlantic Highlands, NJ: Humanities Press International, 1988. A study of consumer behavior from the standpoint of economic and sociological doctrines.

Penz, G. Peter. *Consumer Sovereignty and Human Interests.* Cambridge: Cambridge University Press, 1986. A view of the operation of consumer sovereignty with respect to private-want satisfaction, social wants, and human interests and deprivation.

_____. *Strategies to Control Tobacco Use in the United States: A Blueprint for Public Health Action in the 1990s.* Bethesda, MD: National Cancer Institute, 1991. Smoking prevention and control.

White, Larry C. *Merchants of Death: The American Tobacco Industry.* New York: William Morrow, 1988. This book attacks "the big lie" put forth by the cigarette companies that there is no proof that smoking kills. It investigates the role of advertising in promoting and romanticizing smoking.

Whitman, M. J. *Tobacco through the Smokescreen.* New York: M. J. Whitman, 1993. The author explores product liability in the tobacco industry.

chapter six

The Business Firm and Market Structure

In the American economy, decisions about what, how, and for whom to produce are made primarily by private business firms. Their decisions are dictated by the marketplace, but for some products the market is more dictatorial than others. For farmers the market is often fickle, as the following article shows.

▶ Farm Aid

Each year since 1985, rock stars John Mellencamp, Neil Young, and Willie Nelson have organized Farm Aid concerts to help America's small farmers. The 1997 concert was in Tinley Park, Illinois. In addition to these stars, the concert also featured Hootie and the Blowfish and the Allman Brothers band. Since 1985, Farm Aid concerts have raised over $11 million to help small farmers. Why do America's small farmers need the help?

To begin with, we were once a nation of small farmers. In 1935, the peak year, 22 million Americans lived on 6.8 million farms. Today, less than 5 million Americans live on the nation's 1.9 million farms. Agriculture in the United States has become big business, and, although most farms are still small and individually owned, over the last 60 years an increasing share of income has been earned by large farming operations. The reason behind these developments is technology.

America's grain is harvested by giant combines, its cows are milked by computerized milking machines, and satellites developed by the Defense Department for military purposes are now being used by its farmers to monitor and fine tune the fertilizer and pesticide needs of their farms. Farmers use computers to check the global market prices of their crops, to check weather reports, and to analyze the weight gain of their livestock. Bioengineered seeds lead to vastly increased yields per acre of land, and genetically tailored products such as square tomatoes and thick skinned oranges (both easier to ship) reduce waste. Although highly controversial, genetic tinkering, synthetic hormones, and chemical additives result in livestock that grows bigger and faster with less food. Computerized henhouses use automated systems to feed a million chickens and collect their eggs with a minimum of labor.

All these technological advances lead to huge gains in productivity, but they cannot be used on small farms; the expense of these kinds of operations needs to be spread out over lots and lots of acres or livestock in order for them to be economically feasible. In addition, the cost of many of these inputs is beyond the reach of most small farmers. To raise the money necessary for such investment, they would need to find financial partners, or they would need to incorporate their farms and sell shares of stock to investors they do not know. The only alternatives are to get another job in addition to running the farm, or to get out of the business altogether. Many have chosen the latter alternative; hence the decline in the number of small farms.

Many small farmers cannot support themselves through farming alone. The average small farmer in the United States earned only about 10% of his or her income from the sale of farm products. The majority of them earn most of their income by working in jobs unrelated to their farms. Although most farms are still owned by individuals, in 1995 the average sales volume or revenue *(not profits)* for individually owned farms was only $54,300. Farms that were owned by partnerships averaged sales of $218,800, and corporate farms averaged sales of almost $577,000 per farm.

Hastening the decline in the number of farmers in the United States was a series of bad business decisions in the 1980s. With rising food prices, many farmers extended themselves too far by buying too much land and equipment on credit. When interest rates rose and food prices fell, they were unable to cover their debts. In the 1980s, some 400,000 farmers either went into bankruptcy or quit before their creditors took over. The farm population fell by 14% during the decade. The Great Flood of 1993 dealt Midwestern farmers another major blow when 354 counties in 9 states were flooded and most of their crops were lost.

It is not all gloom and doom for the nation's remaining farmers, however. Those who weathered the storm saw increased profits from the late 1980s through 1994, when total farm

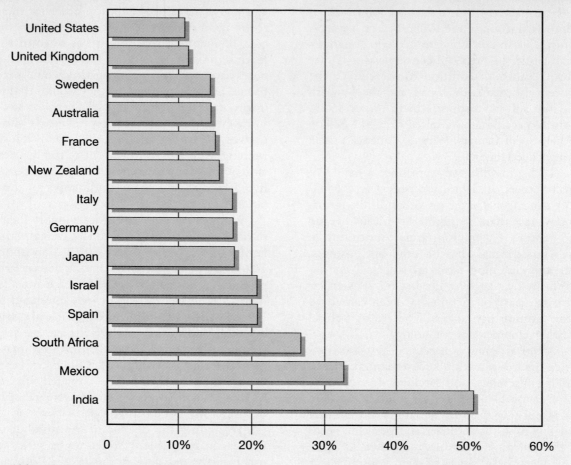

Figure 1

Percentage of Income Spent on Food in 1996

Although Americans eat very well and eat more than most people in the world, we spend less of our incomes on food than anyone else. This is because the tremendous productivity of American farmers keeps supplies plentiful and prices low.

revenues were $197.8 billion and profits equaled $50.5 billion. In 1995, although total revenues increased to $203.8 billion, profits dipped to $48.8 billion. The reason that profits dropped even though sales increased was that production costs increased more rapidly than revenues.

The outlook for American farmers is pretty good. Given that America is the world's most efficient food producer, new trade agreements with other nations such as the General Agreement on Tariffs and Trade (GATT) and the North American Free Trade Agreement (NAFTA) should open up new and expanding markets for America's farmers. In addition, because of their productivity, we spend less of our income on food than any other nation in the world and still eat much better than most.

Chapter Preview

Farmers traditionally represent the epitome of free enterprise in action. In a market economy, the private business firm is the principal supplier of goods and services. Consumers express their will in the marketplace, and it is up to the individual enterprises to put together the labor, capital, and natural resources to satisfy these consumer demands.

This chapter will explain how the business sector of the economy works and how the market structure of an industry determines the quantity of goods and services produced and prices charged. These matters will be explored by asking these questions: What are the forms and economic functions of business firms? What determines a firm's profits? How does industry markct structurc affcct price and output decisions?

Learning Objectives

After completing this chapter, you should be able to:

1. List the three main forms of business organization and cite the advantages and disadvantages of each.
2. Describe the four functions of business firms.
3. Distinguish between fixed costs and variable costs.
4. Show the relationship between total cost and total revenue to profit.
5. Distinguish between a normal rate of return and economic profit.
6. List the characteristics of a purely competitive industry.
7. Explain why consumers benefit when industries are purely competitive.
8. Explain why purely competitive firms cannot make economic profits in the long run.
9. Explain how differentiated competition, monopoly, and shared monopoly differ from pure competition in terms of number of firms, barriers to entry, homogeneous products, and long-term profits.

What Are the Forms and Economic Functions of Business Firms?

The three basic allocation questions that an economic system must resolve were described in chapter 2 as the "what to produce," "how to produce," and "for whom to produce" questions. In a market economy, how well these questions are answered may be influenced by the way businesses are organized and how well they perform certain necessary functions.

Forms of Business Organization

By far the overwhelming majority of farms and other businesses are individual **proprietorships,** owned and operated by one individual or one family. This type of business organization accounts for some 87% of the total number of farms and 70% of farm real assets (value of land and buildings). About 10% of farms are **partnerships,** which own 16% of farm real assets. Only 3% are **corporations,** but they have over 11% of the real assets. (The remaining 3% of farm assets are owned by agricultural **cooperatives.**)

There is a trend in the United States toward fewer and larger farms. This has led to concerns about the consequences if family farms (proprietorships) are allowed to go under and be replaced by corporate farming. Since food is a necessity of life, what would be the results if all agriculture fell into the hands of a few giant corporations? Could this happen? And would these corporations then raise food prices to levels people could not afford? Will the agricultural industry end up like the automobile industry, with just a handful of giant producers?

The economic organization of agriculture differs from the economic organization of other types of industries. In nonfarm industries taken together, 73% of the firms are proprietorships, but those proprietorships account for only 6% of total industry sales, while corporations account for 90%. Although larger farms are replacing smaller ones, at present the corporate form of business does not dominate in agriculture as it does in manufacturing. Whether it will in the future depends on the relative production costs of the different types of business organization in agriculture.

Proprietorships, partnerships, and corporations each have their advantages and disadvantages. One of the advantages of a proprietorship is that, depending on the type of business, it can be relatively inexpensive to start. Over one-fourth of all farms are less than 50 acres in size. The average investment in land and buildings for a family farm is less than $300,000—not a big investment compared to a manufacturing plant. Another advantage of proprietorships is that the owner-operator makes all of the decisions and keeps all of the profits, on which only personal income taxes are paid.

On the other side, a major disadvantage of a proprietorship business is that the owner is personally responsible for the debts of the business if it goes bankrupt. The owner may be forced to sell his or her house and other personal property in order to pay creditors if the business fails. Some of the other disadvantages are that the business is legally terminated when the owner dies, and a single owner often does not have access to enough investment funds (financial capital) to make the business succeed.

Sometimes people will pool their resources and talents and start a business as partners. There are only 15% as many partnerships as

---

proprietorship a business enterprise with a single private owner.

partnership a nonincorporated business enterprise with two or more owners.

corporation a business enterprise that is owned by stockholders and is chartered by the state or federal government to do business as a legal entity.

cooperatives producer and worker cooperatives are associations in which the members join in production and marketing and share the profits. Consumer cooperatives are associations of consumers engaged in retail trade, sharing the profits as a dividend among the members.

Figure 2

Types of Business Organization
Nonfarm and Farm

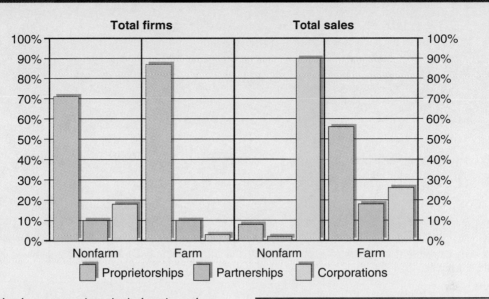

Total sales by corporations in industries other than agriculture are many times the sales of proprietorships, even though the number of corporations is only about one-fourth the number of proprietorships. In farming, however, proprietorships dominate the industry in sales as well as in numbers.

Sources: Nonfarm: U.S. Internal Revenue Service, *Statistics of Income.* Farm: U.S. Bureau of the Census, *1987 Census of Agriculture,* vol. 1.

there are individual proprietorships; but since partnerships tend to be larger in size, their total sales are over half of the total sales of proprietorships. The principal advantage of partnerships over proprietorships is that two or more people have more assets and capital than an individual—two heads and checkbooks are better than one. A disadvantage is that each individual is personally liable for all decisions made and for all financial obligations of the company. Another drawback of the partnership form of business organization is that if one of the partners dies, the business is dissolved in the eyes of the law, just as a proprietorship is when the owner dies.

The corporate form of business is one in which owners buy shares in the enterprise through stock purchases. Instead of borrowing money to start or enlarge a business, a corporation issues stock certificates that represent part ownership in the company. Large corporations often issue millions of shares of stock selling for as little as $10 per share. By buying some of these stocks, small savers can be part owners of billion dollar corporations. The corporation is therefore owned by its stockholders, but it is a legal entity separate from its owners, that is, for legal purposes the government treats corporations as if they are individuals.

The corporation has the advantage of **limited liability** for the stockholders. Unlike

limited liability a legal provision that protects individual stockholders of a corporation from being sued by creditors of the corporation to collect unpaid debts of the firm.

The sprawling Chrysler headquarters and plant illustrate the large amount of capital and labor involved in a major corporate enterprise.

proprietorships and partnerships, the owners of a corporation are normally not personally liable for debts of the company. The corporation is legally treated as an individual and is responsible for its financial obligations. If it fails, its stockholders can only lose the amount they have invested in their stock. Furthermore, when ownership of a corporation changes through the sale of shares in the company, the corporate firm is not legally dissolved.

The corporate form of business organization has some specific disadvantages: corporations are more regulated by the government than other businesses, they must pay corporate income taxes on their earnings, there are state and legal fees charged for incorporation, and the ownership is obviously very dispersed. Instead of keeping a close watch over the business, the owners (stockholders) must trust hired managers and CEOs to take care of their interests. Corporations must be chartered by the state in which they are legally headquartered or, in some cases, by the federal government. The costs of incorporation and the difficulty in finding someone to buy their stock tend to discourage small firms from incorporating. There are some small corporations, including professionals such as doctors, who incorpo-

rate, but the typical corporation is quite large. Although only 20% of the nation's nonfarm businesses are corporations, they account for 90% of total business receipts.

Proprietorships, partnerships, and corporations allow individuals with ideas, talent, and a willingness to work the opportunity to take a risk on their abilities. If they succeed, they reap the financial and personal rewards of their efforts, and the economy benefits from the availability of a product or service at a price people are willing to pay. If they fail, they suffer the brunt of the failure. It is a ruthless process because the overwhelming majority of new businesses do fail, but it serves an economizing function. Businesses normally do not continue in operation when they do not satisfy consumer demand efficiently.

The Four Functions of Business

The first function of any type of business firm is to determine what will be produced by *identifying what consumers want* and will pay for. Farmers have a particularly difficult time predicting this because they must make their production decisions at planting time on the basis of what they think the market will be the following year at harvest time. And because American farmers are so dependent on foreign markets to dispose of a large part of their output, their decision about what to produce is complicated by the need to know what world demand will be as well as what domestic demand will be. Will the rest of the world follow the health-conscious fads of Americans, or will they continue to want American beef and tobacco?

At least farmers are producing necessities that are always in demand—food and fibers. But America's taste in food is constantly changing. During the past 25 years, our red meat and egg consumption dropped by 13% and 24%, respectively, as we became more conscious of the dangers of high-fat and high-cholesterol diets. At the same time, our consumption of fruits and vegetables rose 22% and our poultry consumption rose by a whopping 86%.

Producers in other industries have different problems in identifying consumer wants. For example, when should television manufacturers switch to making high-definition TVs and when should music stores switch to selling over the Internet instead of in traditional retail stores? How will we listen to music and watch movies 5 years from now? What will we want to wear? Identifying what new products consumers will buy and how they will shop for them is the first task of the entrepreneur.

After figuring out what consumers want, business firms must decide how the wanted good or service is going to be made. What mix of the factors of production—land, labor, and capital—will best produce the desired output? The second function of businesses therefore is *to organize production* to resolve the "how" question. It is the most complex function of business firms. How effectively they perform it usually determines whether they succeed or fail.

Real capital investment is important in resolving the "how" question. It may be possible to change production methods to increase efficiency without new capital investment, perhaps by organizing workers into production teams and giving the teams broad decision-making authority. But most changes in production methods are associated with the installation of new, more technologically advanced, machinery and equipment.

Attempting to expand the size of their operations, many small farmers invested too heavily in farm equipment in the 1970s and too

heavily in land in the 1980s, and found themselves in financial trouble when markets weakened and land prices fell. They had so much invested in expensive equipment and land that they could not meet their current bills. Farmers who had invested less in land and capital equipment, renting the large machinery when it was needed, and depending more on their labor for cultivating and harvesting, fared better. Corporate farms, on the other hand, were able to make efficient use of capital equipment because with their large size they could employ it more continuously; the machinery was not idle as much of the time as it was on a small farm.

As we suggested, answering the "how" question is difficult: farmers need to invest and expand to take advantage of new technologies. If they don't invest in new capital their productivity will lag, but if they overinvest they might not be able to pay their bills. It takes a talented entrepreneur to run a successful business in a market economy!

Businesses decide not only what will be produced and how, but they also decide *how purchasing power is allocated*. This is their third function. In resolving the "for whom" question, they do not decide who will purchase their products; rather consumers decide for themselves what they will purchase under the principle of consumer sovereignty. But businesses do determine how much will be paid to the different suppliers of different inputs and therefore how much purchasing power each supplier has. As part of the circular flow of economic activity, businesses allocate the revenue they receive from sales to pay their employees, suppliers, investors, and creditors. This allocation reflects decisions made when businesses determine "how" they are going to produce their output; when they select their desired mix of land, labor, and capital, they necessarily allocate revenues to rent, wages, and interest.

The income received by the firm's employees and other factor inputs is spent, in turn, on other goods and services, or it is saved. In a freely functioning market economy, it is purchasing power that determines the answer to the "for whom" question. When businesses are in an economic squeeze, it spreads to their suppliers.

(Continued on page 154)

Case Application

Running with the Bulls

A stock market (or stock exchange) is a vitally important institution in any modern economy. As explained in the text, corporations are owned by stockholders who buy part ownership of a company by buying shares of its stock. A stock market is where these stocks are bought and sold. The three largest stock markets in the United States are the New York Stock Exchange (NYSE), the American Stock Exchange (AMEX) and the Nasdaq (National Association of Securities Dealers Automated Quotation) Stock Exchange. The stock of larger corporations will be bought and sold ("listed") in one of these markets or in one of a handful of small, regional stock markets. Brokerage houses (Merrill Lynch, Dean Witter, and many others) are companies that are permitted to actually buy and sell stocks in these exchanges. If someone wishes to make a transaction, he or she must do it through a stockbroker who charges a fee for this service. There are also tens of thousands of small, publicly traded corporations whose stock is not sold or listed on these exchanges because of the expense involved. Instead, it is sold by brokers "over the counter."

When companies incorporate or increase the amount of stock in their company, the new shares are initially sold to investment banks that then sell them to stockbrokers. The brokers will in turn resell the stock to individuals or institutional investors, such as pension funds and life insurance companies, which have contributions and premiums that they need to invest. After the initial stock offering, shares can be bought and sold simply by phoning a broker or by making trades through the broker over the Internet.

When a corporation earns a profit, it either pays the profit to shareholders or it retains the earnings and puts them back into the company in the form of new capital investment. In the former case, shareholders are paid a dividend for each share of stock they own. In the latter, the market value of the stock increases because it now represents ownership of more capital. The owner can then sell the stock and make a type of profit referred to as a *capital gain* because the owner's gain came from the increased capital value of the company.

The price of a share of stock depends on the future earnings of a corporation. If profits increase, the value of the shares will increase because owners will either earn a larger dividend or the value of the share itself will increase. Because no one knows for sure what future profits will be, stock buyers must speculate on what the future holds. If they are optimistic they will buy shares in the company and the increased demand will cause the price per share to increase, sometimes even if actual profits do not increase. This will result in an increased price to earnings (P-E) ratio. If they think the earnings outlook is poor, they will sell their shares and cause the price to decrease. Those who are optimistic about the market are called *bulls* and those who are pessimistic are called *bears*.

There exist a number of indices that are designed to give investors a picture of how the overall stock market is performing. The best known of these, the Dow Jones industrial average, is an index of only 30 of the largest industrial companies traded on the NYSE. A broader index is the Standard and Poor's index (the S&P 500) of the 500 biggest companies traded on the NYSE. The AMEX and Nasdaq also have indices that reflect the average value and change in value of the stocks traded in their markets. In general, all of these indices tend to move up and down together. When these indices rise over an extended period of time, it is referred to as a *bull market,* and when they fall it is called a *bear market*. With one or two

Table 2 — How to Read the Daily Stock Market Report for the Gap (Market Symbol GPS on the NYSE) March 23, 1998

High 47¹³⁄₁₆	Low 19⅞	Stock GPS	Div 0.20	Yld % 0.44	P-E Ratio 35	Sales (000s) 753	High 44⅞	Low 45⅝	Close 45⅛	Change ⅝
The highest price of GAP shares in current year.			Annual dividend per share in dollars to stock- holders	Yield = Div. × 100 ÷ closing price	Price-earnings ratio: the number of times the current market value of the company exceeds its annual profits.	Number of shares that changed hands (753,000).	In day			Net price change from previous day's closing price (expressed as a fraction of a dollar).

setbacks, the bulls have been running strong in the United States for the past several years. The Dow Jones average was around 2000 in 1988 and over 9000 in early 1999. Although the numbers themselves mean little, they do show that the value of these 30 stocks has increased by 4½ times in just 10 years!

How do investors know whether a stock will increase or decrease in value? There is no shortage of "experts" who profess to know the answer—and are willing to sell it for a price. However, examinations of the predictions of stock market analysts suggest that one can do just as well by consulting the stars, the length of women's skirts, or which football conference won the Super Bowl. Although it is purely co-incidence, all of these have been better indicators of the overall direction of stock prices than many of the experts. A famous experiment a few years ago pitted five professional stock market experts against a chimpanzee who picked her stocks by throwing darts at a printout of the NYSE stocks. Sure enough, Ola the chimp's stocks did better on average than the experts'.

In their ability to pick individual stocks, market analysts have difficulty doing better than random chance because stocks are traded in a "perfect market," a market where information is freely available to everyone and everyone has the same information about the company. As a result, the price of a stock reflects any good or bad news that is likely to affect future earnings, or what people expect them to be. The current market price of a stock is therefore the best estimate of what it is worth.

The only advantage anyone can have in the stock market is to know something about the company that others do not know. For example, if someone knew that Company A was about to buy or merge with Company B by buying all of B's stock at a price higher than the current market price, the person could buy stock in B and then sell it at a profit after the merger. The use of such "insider information" is both unethical and illegal. The Securities and Exchange Commission (SEC), the government agency that monitors stock and bond markets, investigates and prosecutes those who engage in insider trading.

Just about all financial experts advise people not to put all of their eggs into one basket by buying stock in just one or two companies. But because of brokers' fees, it is not economical for small investors to buy a few shares in one company and a few shares in another. A solution to this problem lies in the use of stock mutual funds. Mutual funds are formed when many different investors pool their funds and a professional fund manager selects and invests their money in a number of different stocks. The fund investors therefore are able to easily diversify their stock holdings in different companies simply by buying shares in a mutual fund. Different mutual funds have different objectives: some invest in large, stable, "blue chip" companies, others in stocks that are riskier but may offer higher returns, and others specialize in specific industries like medical equipment, leisure products, or metals. A recent area of mutual fund growth has been in funds that specialize in foreign stocks or stocks from one specific foreign country. Still other mutual funds simply buy equal proportions of all the companies included in the S&P 500 or some other index so that the return to fund owners simply reflects the overall movement of the NYSE. These funds are called "index funds."

Stock exchanges are important because they allow firms to raise investment capital and they allow investors to put their savings in different companies. In this manner, stock exchanges are one of the primary ways in which a free market economy goes about allocating scarce financial capital to competing uses.

Economic Reasoning

1. Is the ownership of most business organizations traded in the stock market? Ownership in what type of business organizations is traded in the stock market?

2. Which functions of business firms are most affected by the stock market? How?

3. Would the returns to owners of index funds be better or worse than the returns to owners of mutual funds that have their stocks selected by professional fund managers? Why or why not?

4. Examine the mutual fund listings in your local paper. How many specialized funds (international, specific industries, and so on) can you identify?

Running with the Bulls

Visit Yahoo! Finance at http://quote.yahoo.com/. Use the "symbol look up" function to find the symbol for a company of your choosing and replicate the stock report for the GAP shown in this case. Click on the Major U.S. Indices link and trace the Dow Jones industrial average for the past year.

(Continued from page 151)

When farmers were losing money in the 1980s, it also affected farm equipment dealers, fertilizer and pesticide companies, and the banks that lent them money. All too frequently whole communities suffered with the farmers.

The fourth function of business firms is *real capital investment*. One of the most important roles played by businesses is to use the country's savings to increase the economy's stock of **real capital**—the barns, factories, office buildings, machinery, tools, computers, and other equipment used to produce goods and services. This investment in real capital is an important economic function because it makes possible the expansion and modernization of production. Such investment has made it possible for fewer and fewer farmers to produce ever-increasing amounts of food, and it has made American agriculture the most productive in the world. Although this has not always benefited farmers, it has been very good for consumers.

What Are the Forms and Economic Functions of Business Firms?

EconExplorer

Saving and investment are also an aspect of the resolution of the "what" question because if all resources were allocated to the production of consumption goods and none for capital goods, the economy would not grow. By investing in real capital, business firms shift some resources from production for present consumption to production for increasing future consumption. This is sometimes referred to as the "when to consume" question.

real capital the buildings, machinery, tools, and equipment used in production.

What Determines a Firm's Profits?

The objective of producers in all types of business organizations is to make the largest possible profit. Profit is the difference between the revenue a firm takes in and the costs it incurs. Like other producers, farmers try to maximize profits or minimize losses. This is accomplished by producing the most profitable quantity of output with the resources available. We will use a farm operation to illustrate how costs and revenue are determined and how they determine profits.

Costs

To illustrate how a firm's costs affect production decisions, we will use the example of a chicken farm. We will assume that the farm has 300,000 laying hens, three employees, and an owner-manager. The farm also has capital costs. Modern chicken farms keep the hens in environmentally controlled cages, with feeding equipment and egg collection both automated. The hens will have to be replaced each year because hens have a limited time of productivity. In contrast to farms that grow crops, chicken farms do not need much land, just a few acres. During its productive span, a hen will lay, on the average, about 250 eggs a year, so we will also assume that the farm produces 75 million eggs per year, or about 520,000 dozen eggs per month (75 million eggs divided by 12 months equals 6.25 million eggs per month, or 520,933 dozen eggs per month).

Like other businesses, chicken farms have two categories of costs: fixed and variable. **Fixed costs** are those that do not change with changes in the quantity of goods or services produced. The principal fixed costs of a business are the costs of its buildings, equipment, and land, that is, the real capital invested. When a building is constructed and machinery and equipment purchased, they are expected to have specified lifetimes before needing replacement. If a building is expected to have a useful lifetime of 40 years, one-fortieth of the cost of the building is charged as a fixed cost of the business each year. This is called **depreciation.** If a piece of equipment is expected to have a productive life of 10 years, one-tenth of the cost of the equipment is

Despite the fact that the expression "chicken feed" usually implies something does not cost much, chicken feed is a major variable cost of producing eggs.

charged as a fixed cost for depreciation for each year of its expected productive life. Businesses, including farms, usually borrow the money to pay for their buildings and equipment, and pay it back to the lender over a period of time equal to their productive lives. For example, if a tractor will last 10 years, it will be paid for by making monthly payments over a 10-year period.

The productive life of machinery and equipment usually depends more on the rate of technological advances in an industry than it does on actual physical wear and tear. If an industry is undergoing rapid technological change, the capital goods used in the industry usually become obsolete and inefficient and have to be replaced long before they wear out.

The fixed costs of a chicken farm include the monthly payments for the buildings and

---

fixed costs production costs that do not change with changes in the quantity of output.

depreciation the costs of buildings, machinery, tools, and equipment that are allocated to output during a given production period.

---

equipment and replacement of the hen flock. Unlike machinery, laying hens do not become obsolete, but they do wear out and have to be replaced—a sort of "hen depreciation."

Suppose that the chicken farm has monthly debt payments of $48,000 for its capital, and that the price of a laying hen is $1.20. On a monthly basis, each hen costs $0.10, and if there are 300,000 hens, the monthly fixed costs for hens is $30,000. The total fixed costs are then equal to $78,000 per month ($48,000 + $30,000). It is important to recognize that these fixed costs must be paid whether the farm (or any business) is operating or not operating (see Table 1, page 158).

The **variable costs** of a business are those costs that increase with each additional unit that is produced. Variable costs include the labor, raw materials, and other costs that depend upon the quantity of goods produced and sold. Unlike fixed costs, when output equals zero, variable costs are also equal to zero.

The largest cost item in producing eggs is feed, which amounts to about 80% of the variable cost. Other variable costs include labor, energy for lighting and temperature control of the henhouses, medication, litter, and other supplies.

Suppose the variable costs per dozen eggs are as follows:

Feed	$0.28
Labor	$0.05
Energy and Miscellaneous	$0.02
Variable costs per dozen eggs	$0.35

When the farm is producing 520,000 dozen eggs per month, its monthly variable costs will be equal to 520,000 × $0.35 or $182,000 per month.

Total costs are the fixed costs plus the variable costs for a particular level of output. At zero output, total costs equal fixed costs. Total costs rise with output by the amount of additional variable costs. An equation measuring total costs would be:

$$\text{Total Costs (TC)} = \text{Fixed Costs (FC)} + \text{Variable Costs (VC)}$$

The total monthly costs of the chicken farm when it is producing 520,000 dozen eggs per month are:

$$TC = \$78,000 + \$182,000 = \$260,000$$

The total costs of the chicken farm are $260,000. Its **average cost** (AC) per dozen eggs is the total costs divided by the output (Q).

$$AC = TC/Q = \$260,000/520,000 \text{ doz.} = \$0.50/\text{doz.}$$

The farm could produce less or more than 520,000 dozen eggs per month by adding or culling (that is, disposing of) some hens, changing the amount or mixture of feed, or altering the length of time the henhouses are lit each day (light makes the hens lay more eggs). For a farm with existing buildings and equipment, however, there is one and only one level of egg production that will be most efficient. Any other level of production—either larger or smaller—would raise the average cost of producing a dozen eggs and make it difficult for the farm to sell its eggs in competition with other egg producers.

At lower output levels average costs might be higher because the fixed costs are spread out over fewer hens. At greater output levels, **diminishing returns** will eventually occur. When one factor of production is fixed, for example, land or buildings in the short run, it requires successively larger amounts of the other inputs to increase another unit of output. Because of diminishing returns, the short-run cost of producing successive units of output will eventually in-

variable costs production costs that change with changes in the quantity of output.

total costs the sum of fixed costs and variable costs.

average costs total costs divided by the number of units produced.

diminishing returns the common condition in which additional inputs produce successively smaller increments of output.

crease. On a farm, too many chickens in a hen-house might cause the hens to reduce their egg production, they might need more medication, or more workers might be needed. Although farmers and other entrepreneurs are never really 100% sure that they are producing the most efficient level of output, we'll suppose that this farmer is pretty sure that the average cost is minimized at 520,000 dozen eggs per month.

◆ Revenue

The money that a firm receives from the sale of its products or services is the company's revenue. **Total revenue** is the price of the product times the number of units sold.

$$\text{Total Revenue (TR)} = \text{Price (P)} \times \text{Quantity (Q)}$$

For an egg farm, the monthly revenue is the price it receives for a dozen eggs times the number of dozen sold in the month. Because there are a number of farms trying to sell their eggs to the same buyers and eggs are a standardized commodity, the egg producer (the farm owner, that is, not the hen) has little control over the price. The producer must sell eggs of a given size and type at the going market price, whatever the price is and however small or large the farm's egg production.

If the average wholesale market price for eggs is $0.60 a dozen and the farm produces and sells 520,000 dozen eggs per month, the farm's total revenue per month is:

$$TR = P \times Q$$
$$TR = \$0.60 \times 520{,}000 \text{ doz.} = \$312{,}000$$

◆ Profits

Profits are determined by subtracting total costs from total revenue.

$$\text{Profit (Pf)} = \text{Total Revenue (TR)} - \text{Total Cost (TC)}$$

The egg farm we have been looking at would appear to have profits of $52,000 a month:

$$Pf = TR - TC$$
$$Pf = \$312{,}000 - \$260{,}000 - \$52{,}000[1]$$

However this "accounting" profit figure does not take into account some **implicit costs** to the owner of operating the farm. It does not, for instance, take into account the managerial costs of running the farm. Since the owner is the manager, unless he or she pays him- or herself a salary, the accounting profit figure overstates the actual profitability of the business. Part of that $52,000 is really compensation to the owner for performing the managerial functions of running the farm. If we assume that the value of the management service provided by the owner—the salary and benefits that would have to be paid to someone else to manage the operation, or the amount the owner could earn managing some other egg farm—is $6,000 a month, the profit figure is reduced to $46,000.

Another cost not included in computing the farm's profits is a fair return on the money the owner has invested in the business. If the investment in land, buildings, equipment, and hens were financed with borrowed money, the principal and interest on the loan would appear as a fixed cost along with depreciation. But if the investment is the owner's own capital, which is the case here, there is no actual

---

total revenue the sum of receipts from all of the units sold; price × quantity.

profits the net return after subtracting total costs from total revenue. If costs are greater than revenue, profits are negative.

implicit costs the opportunity costs of using one's own labor and/or capital resources in a business. Although there are no direct monetary payments associated with implicit costs, they are real costs of doing business.

---

[1]Note that the profit could also be calculated by realizing that the farm makes a ten cent profit on each dozen eggs—the average cost of producing a dozen eggs is $0.50 and the dozen eggs sells for $0.60. Ten cents profit per dozen times 520,000 dozen equals $52,000.

Table 1 — Summary of Egg Farm Revenues, Costs, and Profit (Monthly)

Total Revenue (TR) $0.60 × 520,000 doz. eggs		$312,000
Fixed Costs Borrowed Capital Hens Total Fixed Costs (FC)	$48,000 $30,000 $78,000	
Variable Costs (VC) $0.35 × 520,000 doz eggs	$182,000	
Total Costs (TC = FC + VC)		$260,000
"Accounting" Profits (TR – TC)		$52,000
Implicit Costs Owner's Labor and Management Invested Equity Capital Total Implicit Costs	$6,000 $40,000	$46,000
Economic Profits		$6,000

interest payment. Nevertheless, there is a cost to the owner of the capital tied up in the business—an opportunity cost of the money, which could otherwise be earning a return on loan to another business or in some other investment.

The return calculated on the owner's invested capital should be what the capital would earn on the average if put into some other investment having the same degree of risk. This expected return on the capital invested in the business is the **normal rate of return** (or **normal profit**) and is included as a cost when determining the firm's **economic profits.**

normal rate of return (normal profit) the rate of earnings on invested capital that is normal for a given degree of risk.

economic profits earnings on invested capital that are in excess of the normal rate of return.

What Determines a Firm's Profits?

EconExplorer

Suppose the chicken farmer has invested $3,200,000 of personal, partners', or stockholders' money (this is an example of owners' equity). If the normal rate of return on investments with a similar amount of risk is 15%, the annual cost to the owner of having this capital tied up in the chicken farm is ($3,200,000 × .15) = $480,000. On a monthly basis, this is equal to $40,000. When this is added to the other costs of the business, profits are reduced to $6,000 per month.

Sometimes, after subtracting the value of the owner-manager's time and the opportunity cost of the owner's capital, economic profits are negative, that is, total cost exceeds total revenue. In such instances, the owner is subsidizing the business with his or her labor and the use of his or her capital. This is not unusual

(Continued on page 160)

Case Application

Aging Rockers Hit the Road One More Time

Over two decades after they rode the wave of rock and roll to the top of the charts, aging rock stars such as the Who, the Rolling Stones, Starship, Billy Joel, Eric Clapton, and Paul McCartney are cashing in on the nostalgia of the 1960s generation and the curiosity of that generation's children. The sixties-era parents and their children sometimes attend the concerts together as a sharing experience (although some parents use protective earplugs). Other families prefer to share the experience separately.

Whether it's together or separately, the two generations have been buying enough tickets to support the concerts of the superstars of the past. They and a few, but not most, of the more transient current rock-and-roll groups can still sell out performances. But many concert promoters have discovered that lesser-known groups don't draw well enough to cover expenses. Costs have greatly increased. The cost of liability insurance, for example, has multiplied many times over. If promoters have to guarantee the performers $80,000, lay out another $20,000 for rental of the arena, purchase liability insurance, rent sound and lighting systems, and pay for radio and newspaper advertisements, they face at least a $140,000 outlay before they even start to sell tickets. Performance costs such as hiring ushers, security guards, and the many ticket checkers needed to counter widespread counterfeiting of concert tickets add to promoters' expenses. They also have to pay the ticket agencies a percentage of each ticket sold and pay state taxes on the tickets.

Table 2	Costs of a Rock Concert
Expense	**Cost**
Performers	$80,000
Arena rental	20,000
Insurance	14,600
Sound system	5,700
Lighting system	3,200
Radio advertising	9,800
Newspaper advertising	6,700
Personnel (ushers, etc.)	2.70 per ticket sold
Ticket agency	1.50 per ticket sold
State taxes	1.80 per ticket sold

The costs for a medium-size rock concert are shown in Table 2. With these high costs for a less established group that may or may not draw a capacity crowd, it is not surprising that promoters turn to the '60s rock stars who can draw on two generations of fans to fill the arenas.

Economic Reasoning

1. What are the fixed costs shown for a rock concert? What are the variable costs?
2. How many tickets would the promoter have to sell at $26.00 per ticket to cover the above costs of a concert?
3. If the promoter could count on selling only enough tickets to cover those costs, do you think it would be a good idea to go ahead and put on the concert? Why or why not?

where proprietorships are concerned. Small business owners frequently pay a price for being their own boss. In such instances, the owner-manager will continue to operate at a loss or they will leave the business.

When total revenue is exactly equal to total cost, including all opportunity costs, economic profits are equal to zero and the firm is earning the normal rate of return—just as much as the owner could earn in any alternative business that has similar risk. A normal rate of return is just enough to keep someone in a business—they cannot make any more in alternative businesses, so there is no incentive to exit this industry and enter another. Nor is there an incentive for others to enter this particular industry. On the other hand, when earnings are greater than the normal rate of return—when an economic profit is being earned—other investors will have an incentive to enter this busi-

ness. In this manner, economic profits guide scarce resources to their highest valued uses.

As with other branches of farming, the egg business is undergoing consolidation. In 1975 there were about 10,000 commercial egg producers in the United States. In 1996 there were less than 1,000, but the average farm had close to 300,000 hens. As with other types of farms, smaller farmers are experiencing negative economic profits and many are leaving the business. The industry is becoming dominated by corporate firms such as Cargill, the nation's largest egg company, with a flock under contract of about 9 million birds, as well as Rose Acre Farms and Michael Foods. Cargill achieved its dominant position in part because it is an integrated company, producing the chicken feed purchased by its own and other growers and marketing its eggs under the Sunny Fresh label.

How Does Industry Market Structure Affect Price and Output Decisions?

An industry is defined as a collection of firms that produce similar products. It can be characterized according to the number of firms in the

industry market structure a classification system that describes industries according to the number of firms in the industry, the ease of entry, and the standardization of industry products. The four usual classifications are pure competition, differentiated competition, oligopoly, and monopoly.

pure competition a condition prevailing in an industry in which there are such a large number of firms producing a standardized product that no single firm can noticeably affect the market price by changing its output; also an industry in which firms can easily enter or leave.

barriers to entry or exit legal or institutional factors that prevent a firm from entering or leaving an industry. For example, licenses, patents, or one firm's control of a necessary input.

industry, whether the products are standardized or not, and how difficult it is for new firms to enter the industry. There are many firms that produce eggs, the product is pretty standardized, and, provided one has or can raise the necessary financial capital, there is nothing to stop a new firm from entering the industry. Other industries, however, have different market characteristics from those of farming. There are four types of **industry market structure** and, although firms in each of the four types attempt to maximize their profits, the results are different in the four different types of industries.

◢ Pure Competition

Agriculture represents an industry that is as close to **pure competition** as one can find. Purely competitive industries are those in which there are a large number of relatively small producers supplying a standardized or homogeneous product, and in which there are no **barriers to entry or exit**. Firms in such industries do not have any choice about what price they charge—they are often referred to as price-takers—because none of them are large enough relative to the market to influence market supply or price. If a wheat farmer tries to charge more for wheat than the going price in the wheat market, there won't be any buyers. Nor would it pay wheat farmers to set their price below the market price because they can sell all of their wheat at that price. Wheat farmers, therefore, because they sell a standardized product in competition with many other suppliers, have no control over price. The only economic choice they have is how much wheat to sell at the going price.

There are two important outcomes that result from pure competition. First, because there are no barriers to entry, if firms in the industry are making more than the going rate of return (an economic profit), then, in the long run, other firms will enter this business because it offers profits in excess of those that can be made elsewhere. Purely competitive firms, like all firms, are motivated to maximize their profits. Unfortunately for such firms, however, although economic profits can exist in the short run, long-run profits cannot remain. Profits in purely competitive industries will tend to move toward the going rate of return—a normal profit. Second, because other firms can enter the industry and offer customers a standardized product, firms in the industry are forced to produce at a minimum cost and sell at the lowest possible price or they will lose sales to competitors.

The overall outcome of pure competition is one that is beneficial to consumers and society in general. Firms will use scarce resources to produce and sell goods at the lowest possible prices. They will earn enough in the long run—a normal profit—to keep them in business providing goods that consumers want.

◤ Differentiated Competition

An industry with **differentiated competition**, sometimes called monopolistic competition, is like pure competition except that it produces **differentiated products** instead of homogeneous ones. Each firm differentiates its product to make it unique and to appeal to customers. The fast-food industry is a good example of differentiated competition. The Big Mac, the

McDonald's used to package their hamburgers in distinctive styrofoam containers. Now, bowing to concern about the environment, the company has changed its packaging to biodegradable paper.

Whopper, and Wendy's Big Deluxe are all hamburgers that the producers attempt to differentiate from the competition. Other examples include consumer goods like toothpaste, shampoo, shoes, apparel, soft drinks, and restaurants. In fact, most consumer goods in the United States are produced in industries with this kind of market structure.

As a result of the relative ease of entry into differentiated competition industries, economic profits tend not to last in the long run. Firms in these industries spend a lot of money on advertising and packaging in order to differentiate their product and convince customers that there are no good substitutes for their product. But other firms in the industry are doing the same thing, and since the products are similar,

differentiated competition an industry without entry barriers in which there are a large number of firms producing similar but not identical products; sometimes called monopolistic competition.
differentiated products similar but not identical products produced by different firms.

Figure 3

Diamond Monopoly

When market demand for diamonds shifted from D₁ to D₂, De Beers reduced the supply from S₁ to S₂ in order to keep the equilibrium price from falling to P₃.

---

price competition also exists. As a result profits tend to fall to the normal rate of return and, similar to pure competition, economic profits disappear over time.

◆ Pure Monopoly

At the opposite end of the spectrum from pure competition is the industry with only one firm that sells a product with no close substitutes, **pure monopoly.** Except for **public utilities**—industries such as electricity, gas, and water transmission, and local telephone service—there are not many examples of pure monopolies. One of the reasons for a firm becoming and maintaining a monopoly position is that such industries are usually characterized by significant barriers to entry. Because of these barriers, the monopoly firm has the potential to earn and keep economic profits in the long run.

One industry that is a virtual monopoly is the diamond industry. De Beers Consolidated Mines, a South African company, controls over 80% of the world's wholesale diamond business. As a result, it has been able to manipulate prices by controlling the supply ever since 1934. Unlike competitive firms that are too small relative to the entire industry to influence the market price, De Beers can cause prices to

pure monopoly an industry in which there is only one firm.

public utility an industry that produces an essential public service such as electricity, gas, water, and telephone service; normally, a single firm is granted a local monopoly to provide the service.

increase or decrease because it controls the market supply.

In the early 1980s, there was a break in the diamond market because of a sharp drop in the demand for diamonds by investors. In just one year, diamond prices fell by one-third. The price of a flawless one-carat diamond dropped from $63,000 to $40,000. To stop the slide in prices, De Beers cut back sales of diamonds to dealers. The changes in the diamond market are shown in Figure 3. Because of the lessened demand for diamonds by investors and speculators, the market demand fell from D_1 to D_2. To stop the price decline, De Beers reduced the supply of uncut diamonds offered to dealers from S_1 to S_2. De Beers might have attempted to raise the price back to P_1 by reducing the supply even further. But they felt that the March 1980 price, inflated by speculation, was too high to maintain a healthy diamond market and maximize profits. To get the price of a flawless one-carat diamond back up to $60,000, they would have to have cut production by more than 60%.

There are few pure monopolies—even De Beers' control over diamond prices is threatened by the possibility of increased supplies from Russia and Angola—but most industries have some degree of monopolistic pricing. Unlike producers in a purely competitive industry, who have to sell their product at the prevailing market price, firms in monopolistic industries can raise or lower their prices to maximize their profits. If they lower prices, they will sell more. If they raise prices, they will sell less but receive more per unit sold.

Monopolists are subject to the law of demand; they cannot arbitrarily raise their prices as high as they might like. Although a monopoly is defined as producing a good for which there is no good substitute, if prices rise too much, companies will produce and consumers will find substitutes. For example, for years cable companies thought they had a monopoly on multichannel television services. As prices and technology both increased, this monopoly was undercut and challenged by satellite systems. The same holds true for cellular telephone service that has entered into competition with local telephone companies.

Shared Monopoly

Single-firm monopolies like De Beers are rare, but there are many industries in which the market is controlled by only a few firms. According to the most common measurement, any industry in which four firms or fewer account for over 50% of industry sales is considered a **shared monopoly.** If there is a formal agreement among the firms regarding pricing and/or dividing up the market, the group of firms is called a **cartel.** The Organization of Petroleum Exporting Countries (OPEC) is a prominent example of a cartel, but in general, cartels are illegal in the United States. If there is no formal agreement among the firms, the industry is called an **oligopoly.** Oligopolies are characterized by substantial barriers to entry and can have either homogeneous or differentiated products. Many industries in the United States, including the steel, aluminum, cigarette, metal can, breakfast cereal, and automobile industries, are oligopolistic. The steel, can, and aluminum industries produce homogeneous products, while the cigarette, cereal, and automobile industries produce differentiated products.

As in pure monopolies, above-normal profits in shared monopoly industries can be maintained over the long run by restricting output.

---

shared monopoly an industry in which there are only a few firms; more specifically, an industry in which four or fewer firms account for more than 50% of industry sales.

cartel an industry in which the firms have an agreement to set prices and/or divide the market among members of the cartel.

oligopoly a shared monopoly in which there is no explicit agreement among the firms.

Case Application

Crashing the PC Market

During the early to mid-1990s, the percentage of American homes with a personal home computer stayed fairly constant at around 40%. In 1997, the percentage inched up to 43% as computer prices dropped 30% and broke through the $1,000 barrier for the first time. At this price, it is expected that the median income of households buying PCs will fall from the current $50,000 to under $30,000. The home computer will no longer be something limited to upper-income, white-collar families, but will become as common as telephones and televisions in the typical American home. Just as Henry Ford revolutionized the auto industry by making a car for the masses—the Model T—today's PC manufacturers are looking to sell PCs for around $600 by Christmas 1998.

A problem being faced by both manufacturers and vendors is the shrinking profit margin on PCs. A typical computer superstore like CompUSA makes about a $175 margin on an $1,800 PC, and nets a $75 profit after selling costs are deducted. At $1,000, the margin is practically zero, and the only way for either manufacturers or retailers to stay in business is going to be by selling increased volumes. Despite the growing market, many market analysts think that these increased volumes are going to come either by mergers or by the bigger firms swallowing up the smaller ones. Some of this has already begun, as Compaq has recently acquired Digital Equipment Corporation (DEC).

The price reductions are occurring for two reasons. First, the prices of inputs are falling. A 166 megahertz MMX processor that cost $255 in mid-1997 costs only $89 in 1998. Sixteen megabytes of RAM that cost $320 in 1994 cost $39 four years later. These cost reductions are due not only to improved technology, but also to increased competition among chip makers. For example, Intel, the industry leader, is under increased pressure from Cyrix Corporation and Advanced Micro Devices. Second, because of the similarities among PCs made by different companies, cutthroat competition in the industry has led to a price war where the prize is market share.

Worldwide PC sales reached 80 million in 1997, and are expected to top 100 million in 1999. Manufacturers are scrambling to increase their market shares to take advantage of

Because of barriers to entry, it is difficult or impossible for new competitors to enter the industry, increase supply, and cause prices to decrease. Long-run economic profits are possible, and, the smaller the number of firms in the industry, the easier it is for them to maintain maximum profits.

It benefits the firms in a shared monopoly to cooperate and so produce the quantity and charge the price that a pure monopolist would. But where there is no formal agreement among the firms in the industry, and sometimes even when there is, this cooperation is difficult to sustain because of the desire of each firm to get a larger share of the market. In addition, formal agreements among firms to fix prices are against the law in the United States (see chapter 8). The danger of a price war among the

Table 3 — Market Share in U.S. Retail Stores (January 1998)

Company	Market Share
Compaq	36%
Packard Bell NEC	21%
Hewlett-Packard	14%
IBM	14%
Sony	5%
CTX	3%
Total	**93%**

Source: Computer Intelligence

this growing market. Currently, the top six producers account for about 93% of sales in U.S. retail stores, with the balance being made up by numerous small firms that buy components and sell "clones" at discounted prices.

The figures in Table 3 represent sales at U.S. retail stores only. When sales made over the telephone or through the Internet are included, the market shares of these firms drop because of companies like Dell and Gateway that sell most of their machines by mail order. In 1996, retail stores accounted for 81% of all sales, but this number is falling because of the lower overhead (fixed costs) of vendors who do not need to pay for retail space.

Industry analysts believe that 1998 will be a year of transition for PC makers. Manufacturers are going to need to increase their sales volumes to offset lower prices, Internet sales will be increasing, and a lot of small producers and vendors are going to be bought by others or go out of business.

Economic Reasoning

1. In what type of market structure have the PC makers been operating? How can you tell?

2. What do you think will happen to long-run profits in the PC industry? Why? Will the amount of consolidation through mergers make a difference?

3. Do you think that Internet sales of PCs will have an impact on traditional retail store profits? Why or why not?

4. Do you think it is beneficial to have PC makers merge or acquire other firms that make PCs? Why or why not?

Crashing the PC Market

For more information about the PC market, visit the Computer Intelligence home page at http://www.ci.zd.com/.

different firms is a threat to profits in a shared monopoly. As a result, we frequently see a practice of **price leadership** in this type of industry. One firm, usually the most powerful, takes the lead in setting the price. The other firms follow its price leadership and avoid price competition. Price leadership is most likely to be found in industries with a standardized product such as steel.

price leadership a common practice in shared monopoly industries by which one of the firms in the industry, normally one of the largest, changes its prices, and the other firms follow its lead.

▶ Putting It Together

Businesses may be organized as individual *proprietorships*, *partnerships*, or *corporations*. Some other small businesses are organized as *cooperatives*. Proprietorships are the most numerous, but because they are typically small, they account for only a minor percentage of total business sales. Partnerships make possible the pooling of the capital and/or abilities of two or more people. The advantages of proprietorships and partnerships are that they are easily and inexpensively started; the owners are responsible for success or failure of the business; and they reap the rewards or suffer the losses. The disadvantages of proprietorships and partnerships include the following: owners are personally responsible for

the debts of the business if it goes bankrupt; the business legally terminates if an owner dies or withdraws; and owners may not have sufficient capital to enable the business to succeed.

The corporate form of business organization is one in which the ownership is represented by stock. Corporations, although fewer in number than proprietorships, do most of the nation's business because of their large size. Stockholders are only subject to *limited liability*, they are not personally responsible for actions of the firm or for its indebtedness. The selling of stock makes it possible for corporations to pool large amounts of capital. Change of ownership does not terminate the life of the

firm, since a corporation is a legal entity (or "person"). The disadvantages of the corporate form are as follows: it costs money to get a corporate charter; corporations are more regulated than other businesses, especially in that they must publicly disclose information about themselves; corporations must pay corporate taxes on their earnings; and the ownership control is diluted among many owners.

The economic functions of business firms are to identify needs (what to produce), organize production (how to produce), allocate revenues (for whom to produce), and invest in *real capital* (plant and equipment).

The costs of production are divided into *fixed costs* and *variable costs.* Fixed costs are those that are paid regardless of the level of output. Even if the firm stops production altogether, fixed costs continue in the short run. In general, fixed costs are the costs of *depreciation* on plant and equipment and interest charges on borrowed funds. In economic analysis, fixed costs also include the *implicit cost* of the owners' time and capital invested in the business. Variable costs are the costs that increase with each additional unit produced. They are generally the costs of labor and raw materials. *Total costs* are the fixed costs plus the variable costs for a particular level of output. At zero output, total costs are the amount of fixed costs. As output increases, total costs rise by the amount of additional variable costs. A business that earns enough revenue to just cover its total costs is earning the *normal rate of return* or a *normal profit.*

In agriculture—in fact in industries in general—firms encounter *diminishing returns* with expanding output. In the short run, with fixed size of plant and equipment, adding variable inputs results in smaller and smaller additions to output. These diminishing returns cause costs to rise at an increasing rate for a firm.

Total revenue is the price of the product multiplied by the number of units sold. If the firm can sell more without lowering its price, as is the case with a firm in a purely competitive industry, total revenue rises at a constant rate with increasing output. *Profits* are total revenue minus total cost.

Economists classify industries according to their *industrial market structure. Purely competitive* industries are those in which there are a large number of firms producing a *homogeneous product.* Each firm in the industry produces such a small part of the total industry output that it cannot noticeably affect the market price. Purely competitive firms can earn *economic profits* in the short run. But the lack of *barriers to entry* to new firms trying to enter the industry will result in an increased supply. Prices drop, and profits will fall to the normal rate of return in the long run. Because of competition, purely competitive firms must operate at their most efficient level of output, which is also where they earn a normal rate of return.

An industry with *differentiated competition* has many firms producing a similar but not identical product. These are referred to as *differentiated products.* Promotional costs tend to be high in these industries, while profits tend to be low in the long run because of competition.

A *pure monopoly* is an industry in which there is only one firm producing a product, and the product has no close substitutes. Monopolistic firms, unlike purely competitive firms, can adjust the supply price to obtain maximum profits. They produce the quantity of output that provides the greatest difference between total revenue and total cost. Because of barriers to entry, they can protect their profits from potential new entrants. With the exception of *public utilities,* there are few pure monopolies in the United States.

A *shared monopoly* is an industry in which there are only a few firms that account for the majority of industry sales. They may produce a homogeneous product such as aluminum or a differentiated product such as automobiles. Firms in these industries tend to avoid price competition. They may establish a *cartel* with a formal agreement, like OPEC, or they may be an *oligopoly* and follow a practice of *price leadership.*

$ Perspective $

The Evolution of the Modern Corporation

A Dutch East India Company seashore market in Batavia (about 1682) represents the activities of one of the world's earliest corporations.

Additional information about the evolution of corporations can be found in *The Modern Corporation* and *Private Property* by Adolf A. Berle and Gardner Means (Buffalo, NY: W. S. Hein, 1982 [reprint of 1933 edition]); *Essays in the Earlier History of American Corporations* by Joseph S. Davis (Cambridge, MA: Harvard University Press, 1917); *Great Enterprise: Growth and Behavior of the Big Corporation* by Herrymon Maurer (New York: Macmillan, 1955); and *The Corporation in the Emergent American Society* by William L. Warner (New York: Harper & Row, 1962).

Technological changes in production techniques associated with the Industrial Revolution (see Perspective in chapter 3) are generally credited with establishing the nature of our present economy. But changes in business organization and management have also played a crucial role. If it were not for a parallel revolution in business organization, the mass production methods of the Industrial Revolution could not have been as extensively implemented as they were.

The most important aspect of this business revolution was the development of the modern corporation. The corporate form of business organization actually existed in Roman times, although it was not well evolved. It first achieved some importance as the form of organization for trading companies of the sixteenth and seventeenth centuries.

The Dutch East India Company, chartered in 1602, used the capital of its investors to finance voyages to procure spices and other exotic merchandise from Asia for sale in Europe. The British government chartered private trading companies, such as the Hudson's Bay Company (chartered in 1670), to develop trade and settlements in the New World in order to secure its colonization. Until well into the nineteenth century, corporate charters in Europe were granted by the king or parliament only for special purposes. In 1800, England and France together had only a few dozen such corporations.

It was in the United States that the corporate form of business first obtained widespread importance. By 1800 there were already some 300 private business corporations. At first, state legislatures, like the kings and parliaments of Europe, granted individual corporate charters. But in 1811 New York enacted a general incorporation law providing for corporate charters to be issued by New York's secretary of state. Today state governments grant most corporate charters, but the federal government also charters firms in some fields such as banking (federal savings and loan banks), transportation (railroads), and communications (Comsat).

Today there are over 2 million corporations in the United States. About 100 of them own one-half of the total corporate wealth, and the trend is continuing toward fewer and larger corporations.

For Further Study and Analysis

Study Questions

1. Why isn't it a good idea to join in a partnership if you do not know the other partners very well? Does the same consideration apply to buying shares in a corporation?
2. Review the introductory article in chapter 1, "An Apple a Day." List the fixed and variable costs on the Hernandez farm.
3. Why would the capital equipment of a firm in a dynamic industry such as electronics depreciate more rapidly than in an industry such as textile manufacturing?
4. What is the difference between a normal profit and an economic profit?
5. Why is a firm more likely to encounter diminishing returns in the short run than in the long run?
6. Why do economic profits tend to disappear in pure competition in the long run?
7. Why do purely competitive firms in the long run have to operate at the level of output that minimizes their average cost while monopolists do not?
8. Why would oligopolistic firms producing homogeneous goods have an easier time forming a cartel than firms producing differentiated goods?
9. What are examples of firms in your area that represent each of the four types of industry structure? If there are no firms that correspond exactly to one or more of the four types, what firm comes closest to the industry type?
10. What are three examples of industries in which advertising expenditures appear to be especially large? Are these industries purely competitive, monopolies, shared monopolies with standardized products or with differentiated products, or differentiated competition industries?
11. List at least three firms that are monopolies or close to being monopolies. What are the barriers that keep competition out?
12. Explain why as a consumer you would prefer to buy from firms in competitive industries, but as a seller you would rather be in noncompetitive (monopoly or shared monopoly) industry.

Exercises in Analysis

1. Select a corporation, and find a copy of its annual report on the Web. Using the report as a source, write a short paper on the operations of the company, including such information as the amount of capital investment, annual sales, fixed and variable costs, and profits.
2. Interview the owner of a business in your area. Find out what type of industry the business is in, whether it is purely competitive, monopolistic, shared monopoly, or differentiated competition. Find out how the business decides what price to charge. Ask the owner if he or she experiments with different prices to see the effect on total revenue and profits. Write a report on the interview.
3. Visit a grocery store and examine the breakfast cereal aisle. How many different kinds of cereal can you find? Examine the labels and determine how many different companies actually make breakfast cereal. Is there much variation in price? What type of market structure would you say best describes the breakfast cereal industry?
4. In Exercise 2 at the end of chapter 5, you calculated the elasticity of demand of your group for movie theater tickets for price

changes from $7 to $6 and from $3 to $2. Calculate the effect of these same price changes on total revenue. Compare the results for your group with the results found by other groups in the class. From this information, can you make any generalizations about the relationship between elasticity of demand and the effect of price changes on total revenue?

Further Reading

To learn more about American agriculture, visit the U.S. Department of Agriculture National Agricultural Statistics Service at http://www.usda.gov/nass/. To learn about the egg industry, visit the American Egg Board at http://www.aeb.org/.

Caves, Richard. *American Industry: Structure, Conduct, Performance.* 6th ed. Englewood Cliffs, NJ: Prentice Hall, 1987. A short book on the economics of industrial organization.

Davidson, Osha Gray. *Broken Heartland: The Rise of America's Rural Ghetto.* New York: Free Press, 1990. Traces rural conditions and the situation of the rural poor in the United States. Describes the social conditions affecting farmers.

Dunnan, Nancy. *The Stock Market.* Englewood Cliffs, NJ: Silver Burdett Press, 1990. A simplified description of what stocks are, how they are bought and sold, and the functions and operations of stock exchanges.

Giles, A. K. *Getting Out of Farming?* Reading, U.K.: University of Reading, 1991. An examination of the management of agricultural resources.

Goering, Peter. *From the Ground Up: Rethinking Industrial Agriculture.* Berkeley, CA: International Society for Ecology and Agriculture, 1993. A study of the economic and ecological aspects of agriculture. It looks at what is necessary for sustainable agriculture and the effects of agricultural innovations.

Hamlin, Christopher, and Philip T. Shepard. *Deep Disagreement in U.S. Agriculture: Making Sense of Policy Conflict.* Boulder, CO: Westview Press, 1992. An inquiry into U.S. agricultural policies and their consequences.

Hirt, Geoffrey A., and Stanley B. Block. *Fundamentals of Investment Management,* 5th Ed. Chicago: Irwin, 1996. Chapters 2 and 3 provide background information on the hows and whys of stock markets.

Malkiel, Burton G. *A Random Walk Down Wall Street.* 4th ed. New York: W. W. Norton, 1985. "Taken to its logical extreme, [the random walk principle] means that a blindfolded monkey throwing darts at a newspaper's financial pages could select a portfolio that would do just as well as one carefully selected by the experts" (p. 16).

Mamis, Justine. *The Nature of Risk: Stock Market Survival and the Meaning of Life.* Reading, MA: Addison-Wesley, 1991. The nature of risk and the psychology of risk taking as applied to speculation in stocks.

Mayer, Martin. *Stealing the Market: How the Giant Brokerage Firms, with Help from the SEC, Stole the Stock Market from Investors.* New York: Basic Books, 1992. Examines the changes in the dynamics of the stock market and the role played by the Securities and Exchange Commission.

Rogers, Kenny, and Len Epand. *Making It with Music: Kenny Rogers' Guide to the Music Business*. New York: Harper & Row, 1978. An examination of the economic aspects of the music business from the standpoint of the performer.

Shapiro, Carl, and Hal Varian. *Information Rules*, Boston: Harvard University Press, 1999. An excellent explanation of how fundamental economic principles still apply in the age of e-commerce and electronic information.

Shover, John. *First Majority—Last Minority: The Transforming of Rural Life in America*. De Kalb, IL: Northern Illinois University Press, 1976. Traces the revolution in American agriculture that has transformed a one-time majority of the population into a vanishing minority—the parts played by technology, agribusiness, and the federal government.

Thompson, Paul B., Robert J. Mathews, and Eileen D. van Ravenswaay. *Ethics, Public Policy and Agriculture*. New York: Macmillan, 1994. An examination of the moral and ethical aspects of the treatment of the agricultural sector. The role of the federal government in agriculture.

Tweeten, Luther. *Causes and Consequences of Structural Change in the Farming Industry*. Washington, DC: National Planning Association, 1984. Discusses farm size and technology with respect to the causes and consequences of structural change in agriculture.

World Wide Web. www.quicken.excite.com/dir is a site that has an entry for everything you want to know about investing.

World Wide Web. www/quicken.excite.com/dir/p-intuit/investments/stocks/exchanges provides links to the world's stock exchange home pages.

chapter seven

Industrial Performance

As the 1990s opened, U.S. industry was on the ropes, seemingly near death. Productivity was down; many industries were losing out to foreign competitors; some of the largest, most powerful corporations were in financial difficulty; and the economy was heading into recession. But as the decade heads toward a close, U.S. industry is making a remarkable comeback. The recovery of U.S. industry has led to one of the longest peacetime economic expansions in our history. The story of this decline and recovery is the topic of this chapter's introductory article.

The Industrial Phoenix

Resembling the phoenix of Egyptian mythology, U.S. industry has been reborn from the ashes of its funeral pyre. Like that legendary bird, it has exhibited the power of self-regeneration.

Between 1978 and 1988, the U.S. share of world automobile production fell from 29% to 18%. Its share of world machine tools production declined by half, from 14% to 7%. In the new high-tech industries, mostly pioneered by U.S. firms, the losses were even more striking. U.S. production of DRAMs (dynamic random-access memory chips) fell from 73% of the world supply to 17%, and its output of floppy disks for computers dropped from 66% to just 4%.

For two decades, in fact, the world's most powerful economy lost ground to its foreign competitors. Most of the losses by American firms went to Japanese industries. From 1971 to 1991, the Japanese economy grew at nearly twice the rate of the American economy. Total real output growth in the United States during those years averaged 2.5%, while Japanese growth averaged 4.4%.

Ironically, the success of Japanese industry was due in no small way to the part played by American tutors. During the occupation of Japan by the U.S. Army following World War II, General Douglas MacArthur sent for a U.S. electronics engineer to restart the Japanese radio industry. The occupation authorities needed to be able to communicate with the Japanese people. The engineer, Homer Sarasohn, found that of the first batch of radio vacuum tubes produced by the Japanese factories, 99% were defective. "The idea of quality they did not understand," he said. Discovering that the Japanese lacked any knowledge of modern business practices, he and a colleague, with MacArthur's blessing, set up a course of instruction for Japanese managers. Among the principles taught in the course were that a company must have a concise and complete statement of the purpose of the company, providing direction for the efforts of management and labor; that quality is the first consideration and profits follow; and that every employee deserves the same respect accorded to managers, since democratic management is good management.

Out of the course came the future leaders of some of Japan's most successful companies: Sony, Matsushita, and Mitsubishi, among others. The course was still being taught to Japanese executives 25 years after Sarasohn departed.

Today the Japanese continue to put to use the principles taught in the course. Meanwhile, during the 1970s and 1980s, American businesses were turning their attention from a focus on production to a focus on finance and marketing. Increasingly, top management in U.S. industry came from the accounting or sales departments of a company rather than from the production side.

Japanese managers were more alert than Americans in taking advantage of technological advances. In one case, an American firm invented a major consumer electronics product, the home videotape recorder, only to forfeit its production to Japan. The original patents for videotape recording machines were held by Ampex Corporation of Redwood City, California. In the 1960s Ampex produced videotape equipment for the broadcast industry and attempted to develop a model for the consumer market. Due to inadequate engineering know-how and managerial indecision, it failed to mass-produce its videotape recorder design successfully.

Even though Ampex put $90 million into the VCR venture, the company failed to produce a machine that was small enough, reliable enough, and cheap enough to sell in the consumer market. Other U.S. companies, such as RCA and Cartrivision, also attempted to develop home VCRs. Cartrivision even got as far as marketing a model in 1972, but it was unsuccessful.

Meanwhile, Sony and other Japanese companies were working to improve the design and simplify the production process in order to make videotape recorders acceptable and affordable to consumers. In 1975, when Sony put its first Betamax on the market, Japan was on its way to adding the videotape recorder industry to its trophy case of consumer electronics industries, along with stereos, audio cassettes, television sets, calculators, and digital watches.

But because of the American automobile industry's great importance in the economy,

Japanese market incursion had the greatest impact there. By itself, the auto industry accounts for 3.7% of total U.S. GDP, and more if you include related industries. By 1997 Japanese producers had captured 37% of the American market, not counting Japanese cars sold by U.S. companies under their brand names.

As U.S. automakers lost market share to the Japanese, they saw their profits evaporate. General Motors suffered financial losses of $38 billion in its North American auto market between 1990 and 1993. It was forced to shut down dozens of plants and lay off some 200,000 workers. GM paid a dear price for poor labor relations management in 1997 when a 17-day strike cost the company $900 million in after-tax profits, and again in 1998 when workers struck for a total of 54 days. According to a study conducted in June 1997, GM has the lowest productivity of any auto company in North America. GM has announced that over the next few years it will further cut over 50,000 jobs in a bid to become more efficient.

The striking successes of the Japanese in one industry after another in taking market share away from American firms shook the U.S. business community, especially Detroit, out of its complacency. American firms began to study and adopt Japanese business practices. In some cases they formed joint ventures with Japanese companies to facilitate the transfer of management and operations know-how.

Belatedly getting themselves in competitive fighting trim, the U.S. automakers began to regain market share. First, in 1992 the Ford Taurus won the title of best-selling car away from the previous favorite, the Honda Accord. Then Chrysler's Stratus and Cirrus took more market share away from Honda. Even General Motors broke into the black in 1993, although it was its foreign car manufacturing divisions and other subsidiaries that provided the profit margin; U.S. car sales were still in the red.

By the end of 1993, the U.S. auto industry had turned the corner on market share. Increased auto sales accounted for nearly half of the rise in the nation's output in the fourth quarter of the year. In January 1994, the Japanese share was down to 28.7%. Other U.S. industries were also fighting back, some even more successfully. These included laptop computer makers, the semiconductor industry, and even the steel industry, which many observers had written off two decades ago. The semiconductor industry, which had lost its leading position as world supplier of electronic chips to the Japanese in 1985, regained that distinction in 1992 and has maintained its supremacy into 1998. The American semiconductor industry will receive a further boost in sales and profits from the unification of Europe and the revival of the Asian economies.

The U.S. auto industry has not fully recovered from the beating it received in the 80s and early 90s. As the next millennium approaches, critics agree that the auto industry is poised to repeat the mistakes of the 70s. Although GM, Ford, and Chrysler have attempted to adopt the Japanese auto makers' approach, they have failed in instituting a corporate culture that is labor friendly. Furthermore, American automakers have failed to incorporate flexibility into their manufacturing plants. Japanese auto manufacturers have been successful at transforming a plant that produced cars into one that produces trucks in a short time, in response to changes in consumer demand. American automakers, on the other hand, spend billions of dollars constructing new plants for new lines of cars or trucks.

The successful turnaround of American industries has been accompanied by problems cropping up for the Japanese economy: rising interest rates, scandals in government and finance, wild movements on the stock market, declines in asset values, bank failures, and a prolonged recession. There are also sectors of the Japanese economy that are quite unproductive. This is especially true of their agricultural industry and distribution systems. Japanese laws protect uneconomical small farms and mom-and-pop retail stores to keep them in business. As a result, the Japanese pay up to 3 times as much as Americans for food and staples. Rice in Japan costs 10 times the world price because of government subsidies to the politically powerful farm bloc. A multilayered, high-cost distribution system adds as much as 60% to the price of Japanese products. The outcome is that a third of the country's export industry goods cost more in Japan than in the United States. A camera that cost $380 in New York City, for example, was priced at $539 in Tokyo.

As a consequence of such large markups and the inflated price of land in Japan, where it takes a family an average of 17 years before they can afford to buy their own home, the costs of living in Japan are very high. The desire for a better standard of living makes Japanese workers put in an average of 300 more hours on the job per year than workers in the United States. This includes a great deal of overtime. There are recent indications that the Japanese are beginning to rebel against the austerity of high living costs and long work hours. As for the United States, Japanese competition actually did us a favor by forcing U.S. industries to refocus on quality and productivity. With the increasing interdependence of world markets, the competitive stimulus and lessons learned from Japanese producers in the 1980s proved invaluable to American industries in the 1990s.

Chapter Preview
The comeback of American industry was due to a number of transformations in such areas as the firm's improved productivity, its quicker response to changes in consumer preferences, and its industrial market structure. We will examine how these have affected industry performance through asking the following: What determines industry performance? How can industry performance be improved? What are the effects of market structure on industry performance?

Learning Objectives
After completing this chapter, you should be able to:

1. Describe four factors that determine industry performance. Define productivity and describe how it is measured.
2. Explain why product quality is important and how it can be improved.
3. Describe why and how businesses respond to social concerns.
4. Explain the importance of investment in capital equipment.
5. Explain why capital investment is so low in the United States and how it can be increased.
6. Understand the importance of research and development.
7. Describe employee involvement and explain how it improves productivity.
8. List and give examples of three kinds of employee involvement teams.
9. Describe market concentration and explain how it is measured by the concentration ratio.
10. Explain the difference between market and aggregate concentration.
11. Explain the consequences of high market concentration.

What Determines Industry Performance?

In chapter 2 we noted that one of the principal goals of an economic system is satisfying consumer wants efficiently. We evaluated industrial performance by examining how efficient an industry is in producing high quality goods that meet the needs and wants of consumers and society. Why did the Japanese and other producers appear to be outdistancing the United States in industrial performance and what have we done to catch up? Exploring these issues is the object of this section.

✖ Productivity

Overall U.S. industrial **productivity** has been stagnating since 1973. During the 15 years up to 1973, output per labor hour grew at an average of 2.5% a year. Increases have averaged 2% a year from the very beginning of the century. But from 1974 to 1997, productivity rose on the average less than 1% per year.

While the difference between 1% and 2% per year may not sound like much, it has a great impact over a period of time. With annual increases in productivity of 2%, output per person doubles every 35 years due to compounding. At 1% productivity growth, it takes twice as long, 70 years, to get the same increase in output.

Overall, the United States still leads Japan and other countries in productivity, resulting from the advantages of a large integrated market, wealth of resources, free international trade, and the encouragement of competition and prohibition of anticompetitive practices (see chapter 8, p. 205). But a study by McKinsey Global Institute spanning the years 1987–1990 showed that in five of the nine industries covered in the study, the Japanese

labor force was more productive than American workers. The industries in which Japanese productivity excelled were carmaking, car parts, consumer electronics, metalworking, and steel. Overall Japanese productivity is dragged down by low worker productivity in the food industry, where the United States is much more efficient.

Measures of U.S. productivity have varied a great deal in recent years. In 1993, productivity in U.S. manufacturing accelerated—a customary occurrence during the recovery from a recession—but then it slowed down again to much less than 1.0% in 1994 and 1995. It then rebounded to nearly 2.0% in 1996 and 1.7% in 1997. Much of this variation can be explained by the fact that the statistics may not be accurately catching what is going on. We know how to measure manufacturing output per hour, but we are not yet skilled in how to measure output in a high-tech service economy where the output of Internet services has to be included along with the output of widgets. When we do, we might find that U.S. productivity is doing quite well, owing to our more intensive use of computers than our global rivals (Figure 1).

What Determines Industry Performance?

EconExplorer

✖ Quality

In addition to the problem of lagging productivity in the 1980s, American industry suffered in comparison with other producers in the area of quality. This was especially obvious in the case of U.S. automobiles compared to Japanese. The number of defects per vehicle built by U.S. automakers averaged 1.7 per vehicle in 1990, while the number of defects of Japanese cars sold in the United States averaged 1.2, a 30% lower level. But by 1998, domestic cars—Ford, Chrysler, and GM products—were fast

---

productivity a ratio of the amount of output per unit of input; it denotes the efficiency with which resources (people, tools, knowledge, and energy) are used to produce goods and services; usually measured as output per hour of labor.

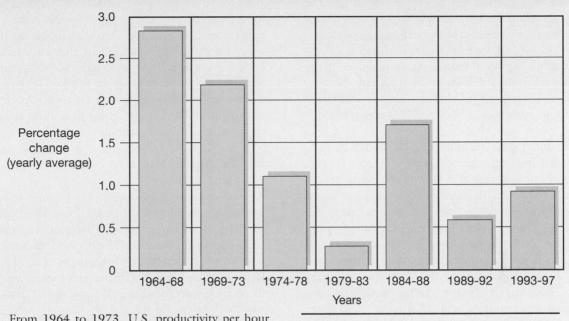

Figure 1

Rates of Increase in Productivity per Hour of Labor in the U.S. Nonfarm Business Sector, 1964–1997

From 1964 to 1973, U.S. productivity per hour of labor rose an average of 2.5% a year. Since then, productivity gains have averaged less than 1% a year.

Source: U.S. Department of Labor, Bureau of Labor Statistics.

becoming the quality equals of their Japanese counterparts, according to the 1998 J. D. Power Initial Quality Survey. For example, albeit designed in conjunction with Japanese partners, GM's Saturn rated a tie for first in Power's consumer satisfaction survey in that year; GM's 3.8 liter V-6 engine is considered among the world's best by most experts; and Chrysler's "cab-forward" designs are being copied by foreign rivals. Even *Consumer Reports,* best known for criticizing domestic auto quality, is beginning to have positive things to say about some home-bred models.

The concern with quality starts with the parts purchased from suppliers. The U.S. suppliers of parts for cars produced by Nissan in this country averaged 2 defects per 1,000 parts compared to only 1 defect per 1,000 parts from its Japanese suppliers. Japanese manufacturers are more demanding of quality from suppliers

than their American counterparts. Honda examined over 250 potential suppliers of metal stampings before choosing 6. Mazda was in contact with 1,000 U.S. suppliers when setting up its manufacturing facilities in this country but found only 65 that satisfied its standards.

After Japanese firms choose a supplier, they work closely with the supplier to reduce the defect rate even further. The practice of American producers, on the other hand, has in the past been to maintain a distance from their suppliers, constantly bidding them against competing firms to get the lowest possible prices. Chrysler was the first U.S. automaker to switch to the Japanese system of "presourcing" parts. For its new Chrysler Cirrus and Dodge Stratus, 95% of the parts were from suppliers chosen before the parts were designed, eliminating competitive bidding.

In order to promote attention to quality by American firms, Congress established the

Malcolm Baldridge National Quality Award, given annually. Of the tens of thousands of firms eligible to compete for the award, only 106 applied in the first 2 years. Those that entered, and even some who did not yet feel ready, found that the standards for the competition brought an urgency to the firm's concern with quality improvements.

Motorola, one of the first American firms to adopt Japanese management practices and a Baldridge award winner in the first year, insisted that all of its eligible suppliers also prepare to compete. It dropped 200 who refused.

◪ Responsiveness to the Market

Producing a quality product efficiently is not good enough unless it is a product that people want to buy. What features does a customer want in a product? When does the customer need delivery? What level of support, including maintenance, does the customer require after delivery? Firms that respond quickly to such questions are more likely to be successful. Japanese producers take pains to satisfy their clients, possibly because Japanese customers in their domestic market are very particular. They demand not only high-quality products, but good service to back them up. If the car of a Japanese customer breaks down, the dealer will often pick it up, repair it promptly, and return it free of charge. A few American auto companies have adopted the Japanese service approach by offering prompt roadside assistance for mechanical problems on new cars.

Japanese manufacturers have responded to changes in market preferences more quickly than U.S. firms. The lead time for producing a new model automobile from design to production was only 3 to 4 years for Japanese car companies. By comparison, it took 5 years for American manufacturers to get a new model in production. This gave the Japanese greater flexibility in responding to changing consumer tastes and introducing advanced engineering and styling features.

This situation changed in the early 1990s. In the 20 years up to 1992, Chrysler introduced only three basic chassis designs. Between 1992 and 1994 alone, it introduced five new chassis designs. Ford and General Motors also began to introduce new models at record rates. Their willingness to introduce new products helped domestic automakers get a big jump on international rivals in the production of sport utility vehicles.

More and more products are being targeted at specific market niches. Producers in the United States have traditionally planned for long production runs in order to reduce the average cost of a product. Japanese firms, on the other hand, build flexible plants that can readily be shifted between the production of differentiated products according to market demand. This enables them to satisfy customer preferences quickly and at the same time hold down the costs of inventory storage.

◪ Responsiveness to Social Concerns

Another measure of industry performance today is the responsibility shown by firms with respect to such social concerns as environmental protection, resource conservation, product safety, and equal opportunity for employees. To a large extent, these concerns are forced upon firms by government regulations, about which more will be said in the next chapter.

Public opinion and liability suits are also causing businesses to clean up their acts. Polls show that 83% of the American public is concerned about the environment and only 36% think that industry is doing an adequate job of protecting it. The rising voice of concern by the citizenry over air and water pollution, accumulation of garbage—especially nonbiodegradable plastics—and waste of natural resources has led to changes in corporate behavior.

In the past, businesses tended to ignore environmental problems and oppose environmental protection laws because of the costs involved. But in the face of aroused public opinion and legal pressures, corporations are showing more environmental awareness. Some are even taking a leading role. As stated by Elliot Hoffman, president of Just Desserts, Inc., "Once content to focus solely on the bottom line and leave other issues to government, business has become a proactive force on the front lines of social change. This phenomenon is called social responsibility, a term increasingly heard in boardrooms across America as companies—some gladly, some kicking and screaming—take a hard look at themselves and their practices."

One important example of a company responding to the pressure for environmental responsibility occurred in 1990. Under threat of a consumer **boycott** of all of its products, the H. J. Heinz Company announced that its StarKist cannery would no longer buy tuna from fishing boats using gill nets. Such gill nets killed thousands of dolphins each year. Other tuna canners immediately followed suit, and in early 1998, a dozen tuna-fishing nations, including the United States reached a historic agreement to protect dolphins. In other industries, electronics firms have stopped using CFCs (chlorofluorocarbons) chemicals that destroy the ozone layer and contribute to global warming—and the American Paper Institute, an industry association, says that 45% of all paper used in 1995 was recaptured for recycling, thereby saving millions of trees. Another area of interest to many people is how companies such as Nike and Kathie Lee Gifford's fashion company react to consumer concerns about their footwear and fashions being produced in unsafe sweatshops by poorly paid foreign workers. One way that the U.S. investment community has responded to these concerns has been by selling stock mutual funds that invest only in firms that practice social responsibility.

 ## What Determines Industry Performance?

EconExplorer

Social responsibility is one area of industry performance in which the Japanese have lagged behind. The United Nations Environmental Program has ranked Japan last in overall environmental concern and awareness among 14 industrialized countries surveyed. It was one of the last countries to stop slaughtering whales and continues to be one of the worst offenders in the illicit marketing of endangered wildlife. It gives little attention to recycling, and the Japanese landscape is littered with solid waste. Stung by world environmentalist accusations of irresponsibility, however, the Japanese government has embarked on an effort to turn the country around on environmental concerns.

Responsiveness to social concerns is another measure of industry performance. Businesses such as StarKist often find that it makes economic sense to pay attention to public opinion on issues like environmental protection, rather than risk being boycotted.

As far as American firms are concerned, does their improved social behavior represent a basic attitude change by business or only a temporary accommodation to the pressures? A survey of MBA candidates at the nation's business schools found 89% of them saying that corporations should become more directly involved in solving the country's major social problems. By comparison, only 69% of current business executives believe that. Many business schools have introduced mandatory ethics courses into the curriculum. They have been encouraged to do this by those in the corporate community who see an urgent need to prepare future business leaders to deal with complex ethical questions. There are those, however, including some teachers who have taught such courses, who are skeptical about whether ethics can be instilled by a course in school.

boycott refusal by consumers to buy the products or services of a firm.

Comparative Case Application

Eyes Too Big in a Tantalizing Market

With the global scope of markets and the liberalization of market restrictions in emerging economies in the 1990s, auto producers began salivating over the vast number of potential customers in Asia, Latin America, and Eastern Europe. While the auto markets in the United States, Europe, and Japan were relatively saturated, with one car for every 1.7 persons in the United States, one for every 2.5 persons in Europe, and one for every 3 in Japan, there was only one car per 680 persons in China, per 70 persons in Thailand, per 14 in Brazil, per 12.5 in Mexico, and per 6 in Poland.

The most enticing market of all was Asia, one of the fastest growing regions in the world in the early to mid-1990s. Car sales in the growing economies of Southeast Asia reached 1.6 million units in 1995, and projections made in early 1997 were that sales would reach 3 million units by 2000. In just four countries, the Philippines, Thailand, Malaysia and Indonesia, sales grew from about 250,000 in 1985 to over 1.1 million in 1995. A rule of thumb in the auto industry is that car sales will take off in a country when the average per-capita income reaches $3,000. The above countries have, or have just about reached this mark. Although not there yet, the populations of China and India are so enormous (2 billion plus people) that only a tiny percentage of the people in these countries need to have the income to buy a car to make them extremely lucrative markets.

The cars being built for the Asian market had to be different than those the established companies were selling in the developed economies of Japan, Europe, and North America. According to *Asiaweek,* the ideal Asian car would have an undercarriage one foot off the ground; a tailpipe that would be higher than local flood waters; a suspension as tough as any sport utility vehicle (SUV); powerful headlights for rural areas; bumpers strong enough to ward off trucks, water buffalo, and city traffic that is among the worst in the world; and it would be nonpolluting because of the densely populated metropolitan areas. The car also had to be inexpensive, durable, and easy to repair. While no one car could meet all these criteria, the world's biggest auto makers all went to Asia to give it a try.

To avoid paying high tariffs and to keep transportation costs down, Japanese, Korean, U.S., and European car makers spent millions of dollars building auto plants in Southeast Asia to make these specialized cars. Toyota began to make its Soluna model in a $100 million factory in Thailand, and Honda built a $120 million factory in the same country to make its City sedan. Although produced at home, South Korea's Kia was introduced with the Asian market in mind, and Samsung, another giant Korean conglomerate, entered the auto industry and produced its first car in late 1997. Japan has long been the clear leader in the region, and U.S. firms were late arrivals, but arrive they did, along with VW, Fiat, and other European manufacturers.

In addition to well-known makes and models, Indonesia partnered with Kia to make its own auto, the Timor, and Malaysia partnered with Mitsubishi to start its own auto company, Proton. Proton became so successful that not only did it produce the most popular car in Malaysia (64% of sales in 1997), but the company bought control of the Britain's super-high end Lotus and produced its first Lotus in Kuala Lumpur in 1997.

Besides producing cars for unfamiliar markets, the auto companies had to manufacture the cars under unfamiliar production conditions. Infrastructure facilities such as transportation, power, and water were often undependable. Governed by local-content rules that required them to acquire a certain percentage of their components from local suppliers, foreign producers encountered delivery and quality problems. A VW plant in Shanghai, for example, had to test all of the dome light switches it received because one-fifth of them did not work. Supply bottlenecks, traffic congestion, and cultural dictates regarding labor played havoc with production schedules.

So after all was said and done, millions of dollars were invested in East and Southeast Asia to establish a regional auto industry to supply the demand of fast-growing economies. And then what happened? The bottom fell out of the region's economies. The Southeast Asian regional financial crisis of late 1997 is expected to cause 1998 car sales to plummet over 50% in Thailand, Malaysia, and Indonesia, and around 20% in the Philippines and South Korea. In an industry with high fixed costs, where firms need to produce at near maximum capacity to cover their costs, the Asian auto industry was running at 30% capacity at the start of 1998, and carmakers were losing, instead of making, millions. When the crisis ends and the regional car market does turn around, the companies still in business should do well—experts think that the region will account for about 40% of the growth in global auto demand from 1998 to 2002. It will be interesting to see which companies are left standing to satisfy that demand.

Economic Reasoning

1. In what respects do automobile producers have to respond to market needs in the emerging economies? Give examples.

2. Would you expect the productivity of U.S. auto plants in developing countries to compare favorably with productivity in domestic plants? Why or why not?

3. Do you think it was a good idea for the world's major auto companies (and new companies in other countries) to go to Asia to try to build the "Asian" car? Why or why not?

Eyes Too Big in a Tantalizing Market

Visit Autofacts at www.autofacts.com and see how the Asian auto industry is faring these days.

▶ How Can Industry Performance Be Improved?

Faced with increasing threat of competition from Japanese and other foreign producers, American industries are being forced to get back into shape in order to ward off the challenges. They need to improve productivity, reduce delivery times, better manage their inventory, and, overall, do a better job satisfying their customers. In this section we will investigate the factors that increase productivity and improve other aspects of industry performance.

capital equipment the machinery and tools used to produce goods and services.

real investment the purchase of business structures and capital equipment; measured in dollars of constant value to adjust for inflation.

▨ Investment in Capital Equipment

Although productivity is commonly measured as output per hour of labor, the quantity of output depends greatly on the amount of investment in **capital equipment.** This includes machine tools, robots, computers, and the like that labor works with. Fixed private investment decreased during the recession in 1990–91, but has increased steadily since. This increase was a major reason for the country's continued economic expansion during this period (Figure 2).

Real investment in buildings and equipment falls during periods of slow economic

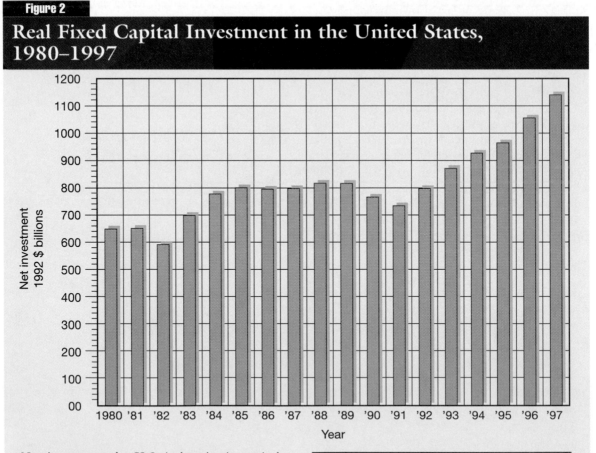

Figure 2

Real Fixed Capital Investment in the United States, 1980–1997

Net investment by U.S. industries in capital equipment declines during periods of slow business activity and low sales volume. A smaller capital stock results in lower productivity of labor.

Source: Federal Reserve Bank of St. Louis.

activity and rises when economic activity is expanding. In order to increase productivity, new investment in producers' durable equipment must exceed the rate of increase in the size of the labor force—this increases the amount of capital that each worker has to work with. Although the U.S. labor force has been growing at a faster rate than that of Japan, fixed capital formation in this country as a percentage of total output has been only half the Japanese rate in recent years (Figure 3).

One area where U.S. firms have been leaders in investment is computer technology. Although computer hardware has always been considered as a part of a firm's investment in real capital, we are coming to realize that the purchase and installation of advanced software also is a significant form of capital investment that enhances productivity. The **automation** of production with the use of computer-controlled equipment has revolutionized manufacturing. Computers are used to design new products, and to develop three-dimensional models on computer screens that can be tested for stress and aerodynamics and linked to machine tools, to aid in the actual fabrication of an object (see the case application, The New Industrial Revolution on page 190).

Enterprise-application software, such as Oracle and SAP, is increasingly being used by

---

automation production techniques that adjust automatically to the needs of the processing operation by the use of control devices.

Figure 3

Ratio of Gross Domestic Capital Formation to Total Output, 1970–1996

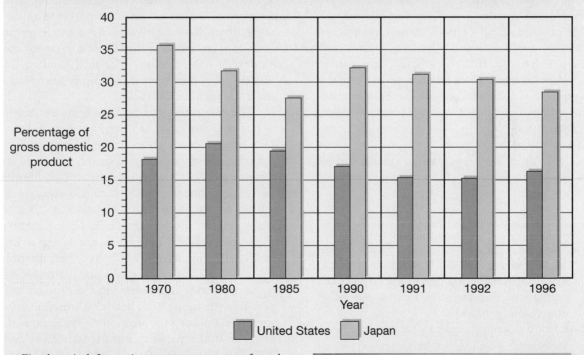

Fixed capital formation as a percentage of total output is only half as large in the United States as in Japan, although the U.S. labor force is growing at a faster rate than the Japanese labor force. As a result, productivity in the United States has suffered by comparison.

Source: U.S. Department of Commerce, International Trade Administration.

companies to link all their operations, from sales to inventory adjustment to delivery. Using such software, a company can, for example, coordinate the sale of 2,000 cases of baby food in Brazil with the nearest warehouses and delivery trucks, assess its inventory in South America, instruct a regional manufacturing plant to replace the 2,000 cases, order more inputs, notify its accountants of the income, and report the sales to the marketing staff.

Enterprise-application software can also monitor the flow of **just-in-time** manufacturing methods to ensure that companies do not have too many or too few necessary inputs for production needs. Under this system, raw materials and subassemblies from suppliers are delivered to the plant at the time they are needed. This eliminates investment in inventories, and it reduces warehouse and distribution costs. Incoming supplies can often be delivered directly to their processing area. Many U.S. firms have implemented just-in-time methods in recent years. Some Japanese voices, however, have been raised in criticism of the just-in-time system because of all of the delivery trucks running around Tokyo and other major cities contributing to traffic congestion and smog. Another problem arises when a critical supplier cannot provide needed inputs. Recently, a company supplying a brake part to Toyota in Japan burned down, leaving Toyota with only a few days worth of brake parts. Because of the small available inventory, Toyota had to suspend all its operations for a few days until supplies could be resumed.

---

just-in-time a system that provides for raw materials and subassemblies to be delivered by suppliers to the location where they will be processed at the time they are needed rather than being stored in inventories.

junk bonds bonds that pay higher than normal interest rates because they have a greater risk of default.

One of the reasons for the low investment rate in the United States in the 1980s was the high cost of financial capital—the high interest rate for borrowed money. A study by B. Douglas Bernheim of Northwestern University and John B. Shoven of Stanford University showed that U.S. firms incurred the highest after-tax costs of capital—over 5%—among all of the leading industrialized nations. At the same time, capital cost Japanese firms less than 3%, while the cost to British and West German companies was in between.

Financial capital is cheaper in Japan largely because of their high savings rate. Savings are the major source of funds for investment, and the savings rate in the United States, both private and public, reached historic lows in the decade of the 80s. (Public savings, the difference between government revenues and government spending, are covered in chapter 13.)

Another reason for the low rate of real capital investment in the 1980s was the diversion of financial capital from the purchase of new plants and equipment into the purchase of existing firms. These buyouts, financed in great measure by **junk bonds** (see Corporate Raiders, LBOs, and the Feeding Frenzy, on p. 195), drove interest rates higher and made real investment less attractive.

The investment rate by U.S. firms also tends to be lower than that of their Japanese counterparts because of the shorter time horizon of corporation objectives in this country. If American corporate executives do not see the likelihood that an investment in new plant and equipment will pay for itself and return a profit in a very few years, they will not undertake it. Japanese business leaders, on the other hand, are willing to invest for the long term. They believe that increasing their companies' market share by reducing production costs and improving the product will pay off in the future. The heads of American corporations are not in a position to be as patient. They are under pressure from stockholders and Wall Street analysts to show good earnings reports every quarter. If they do not, the value of the company's stock may fall and the president may be ousted, or at the least not given the customary year-end bonus.

Some of the ways that real capital investment can be increased, thus raising productivity and lowering production costs, are

1. to lower interest rates by increasing private and public savings,
2. to redirect capital from financial speculation to new investment, and
3. to shift the pressures on corporate executives from short-term to long-term performance objectives.

Investment in Human Capital

Another lesson that American industry learned from the Japanese is the value of investing in its workers. The investment in productive equipment must be accompanied by the training of workers to use the equipment. Studies have shown that investment in **human capital** is actually more effective in raising productivity than investment in physical facilities. According to *Training*, a human resources magazine, American firms spent $58.6 billion on employee training in 1997, a 30% increase over the amount they spent in 1992. Although most of this training was in-house, the market for companies that specialize in worker training grew to nearly $3.8 billion in 1997 and is expected to reach $4.7 billion in 1998. Instructor-led training still makes up about 80% of the business, but technology-based training via satellite and computer links is the fastest growing part of the market.

Investment in human capital is an important way of improving industry performance. Training programs help workers learn critical, technical, and interpersonal skills.

How Can Industry Performance Be Improved?

EconExplorer

Studies of increasing labor productivity in specific firms have shown the existence of a **learning curve.** A plant with new equipment and new technology will achieve increasing labor productivity for a period of time as the total number of units produced increases. However, the successive increases of output per worker will be greater at first and then gradually diminish as the learning curve flattens out. The steeper the initial slope of the learning curve, the faster costs of production will drop and the more profitable the investment will be. One reason that Japanese firms are able to be so competitive in world markets is that the learning curve in Japanese industries appears to be steeper than it is in American industries, as the hypothetical learning curves in Figure 4

human capital labor that is literate, skilled, trained, healthy, and economically motivated.

learning curve a diagram showing how labor productivity increases as the total number of units produced by a new plant (or with new technology) increases over time.

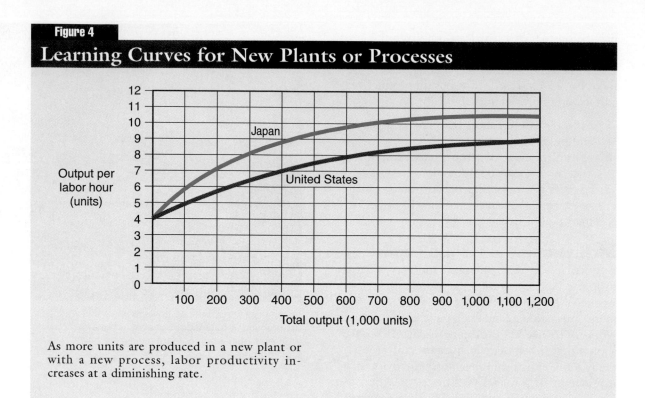

Figure 4

Learning Curves for New Plants or Processes

Output per labor hour (units)

Japan

United States

Total output (1,000 units)

As more units are produced in a new plant or with a new process, labor productivity increases at a diminishing rate.

illustrate. The steepness of the learning curve depends upon the amount and quality of the training given to workers, attitudes of workers toward their jobs and the employer, and the degree of flexibility of work rules.

One of the first companies to get the message on the importance of worker training was Motorola. In order to compete with global challengers to its electronics business, it invested heavily in computer-controlled robots in its factories. To operate the high-tech equipment, it needed workers with higher skill levels than those of its existing workforce. The company determined that employees should have at least fifth-grade math skills and seventh-grade reading skills to work in its plants. It discovered, however, that fully half of its workers needed remedial training to reach this level. To retrain its existing workforce and train new employees, it established a $10 million center for training and education where workers attended classes 5 hours a day for 4 months. To upgrade performance on a continuing basis, the company has set a goal that every employee from janitor up to the president of the company receive 40 hours of training each year. In keeping with its emphasis on the importance of training, Motorola has established Motorola University, an in-house program to update its employees on the latest developments in management theory.

Some companies have adopted the Japanese practice of **cross-training** workers for different jobs. This provides a more flexible workforce that can switch from one operation to another as production demands require, detect flaws in each other's work, and jointly solve production problems. It also has the side benefit of reducing worker boredom, a problem on traditional assembly lines where the worker does one repetitive job all day long, day after day.

cross-training giving workers training in performing more than one task.

Employee Involvement

The real secret of Japanese industry success may lie in their belief in **employee involvement (EI).** As indicated above, training and education (investment in human capital) seem to be the most critical elements of a productive workforce. Second to training, most companies are stressing the importance of involving all employees in decision-making processes that can reduce costs, improve productivity and quality, and satisfy the demands of customers. For example, industry studies show that as much as 75% of all manufacturing costs are locked in by the product design. In Japanese firms, the product design engineers work closely with the manufacturing departments to avoid designs that will present manufacturing problems or be costly to make. In the United States, conversely, it has been traditional for the white-collar design people to have little contact with the blue-collar manufacturing people, and this often causes problems when designs are not easily adapted to the workers' production techniques.

There has been in the past a basic difference in philosophy about the use of labor in Japanese and U.S. companies. Japanese companies view their workers as valuable assets whose use should be maximized. Management in this country, on the other hand, has tended to view workers as expensive inputs whose cost should be minimized. The nature of relationships within a company is also different in the two countries. U.S. companies have vertical lines of authority like the military. Communications between different departments in a company go up a chain of command to a high level and back down another chain of command. In Japanese companies there are continual communications between members of different departments at the same level and levels above and below as well. This is a flatter system of organization than that of U.S. businesses.

This is changing as more and more American companies realize the importance of **employee empowerment:** allowing their employees to make decisions about how things are done on the shop floor and throughout the company. Employee involvement can take dif-

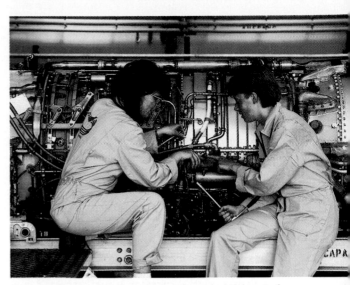
Ensuring the quality of products is an essential part of total quality management (TQM).

ferent forms, from self-contained teams of workers that operate without direct supervision to worker participation in such managerial decisions as what types of investment to undertake. There are three basic types of EI teams:

1. Self-managing teams. These are customarily made up of 5 to 15 employees, who produce an entire product rather than make subunits. Team members learn all jobs and rotate from job to job. They take on such managerial functions as work and vacation scheduling and materials ordering. The Volvo auto company in Sweden led in the

employee involvement (EI) various programs for incorporating hourly-wage workers in decision making; may involve decisions on production methods, work scheduling, and purchase of capital equipment.

employee empowerment giving workers the ability and responsibility to make decisions about how their work should best be done.

use of this type of EI team. Example: Teams at a General Mills cereal plant in Lodi, California, operate production and maintain the machinery so effectively that the factory runs with no managers present during the night shift.

2. Problem-solving teams. These consist of hourly and salaried volunteers, generally 5 to 12, from different areas of a department. They meet one or two hours a week to discuss ways of improving quality, efficiency, and work environment. Known as "quality circles," this type of EI team was developed and used widely in Japan. Now the system is in use in thousands of American companies. Example: A team of Federal Express clerks, meeting weekly, spotted and solved a billing problem that was costing the company $2.1 million a year.

3. Special-purpose teams. These teams are made up of workers and managers who undertake such tasks as designing and introducing work reforms and new technology, meeting with suppliers and customers, or linking separate functions within the plant. This type of team is more common in the United States than in Japan. Example: A team of Chaparral Steel mill workers examined new production machinery in other countries before selecting and installing

machines that helped make their mill one of the world's most efficient.

After employee involvement and teamwork, businesses cite **total quality management (TQM)** or **business process reengineering (BPR)** as the next most important way that employees can contribute to company success. Both of these related concepts simply refer to the fact that employees who are involved in what they are doing, and who take pride and care to continuously reduce defects, increase productivity, improve their product, and above all, satisfy their customers, will contribute immensely to a successful business enterprise. Although these ideas may seem obvious, it is sometimes difficult for management to put aside their old attitudes that management always knows what is best and that workers are simply there to do what they are told.

Employee involvement programs have been very helpful to some U.S. companies in increasing productivity and improving quality. A study of over 2,700 manufacturing companies by *IndustryWeek* found that the companies using the above, and other employee involvement practices, outscored those that had no such programs on nearly every performance measure.

Opposition to EI has come from labor unions and from middle management. Some labor leaders see EI as just a cover for management to get more work out of its employees for the same wages—a new version of the old work speed-up routine. The president of a paperworkers' union local was quoted as saying:

> What the company wants is for us to work like the Japanese. Everybody go out and do jumping jacks in the morning and kiss each other when they go home at night. You work as a team, rat on each other, and lose control of your destiny. That's not going to work in this country.*

*John Brodie, president, United Paperworkers Local 448, Chester, Pennsylvania. Quoted in *BusinessWeek,* July 10, 1989, p. 56.

total quality management (TQM) a way of managing a firm that puts an emphasis on satisfying customer needs by continuous improvement in product quality, employee training, employee involvement, and the use of statistical tools to monitor the quality of output.

business process reengineering (BPR) a reorganization of a company to make use of just-in-time methods, and multidisciplinary teams of workers aimed at production in the least time with no defects.

Table 1　Factors Responsible for Production Growth in the United States, 1929–1982

Factor	% Total Growth
Labor input	32
Technology	28
Capital input	19
Education	14
Economies of scale	9
Improved resource allocation	8
Negative growth factors 　costs of pollution abatement, protecting worker 　safety and health, dishonesty and crime, etc.	–10
	100

Source: Based on data from Edward F. Denison, *Trends in American Economic Growth, 1929–1982* (Washington, DC: The Brookings Institution, 1985).

More damaging to EI programs than unions has been the opposition of middle managers and foremen. They see worker participation as a threat not only to their authority but to their jobs, and not without reason. Changing from a vertical system of management to a flatter organizational system often means that half or more of the middle management positions are eliminated through downsizing.

◪ Research and Development

A statistical analysis commissioned by *Business-Week* demonstrated beyond any doubt that the companies that were most successful in their markets were those that spent the most on research and development per dollar of sales and per employee.

But industry-funded R & D spending in the United States as a percentage of total output has lagged behind both Japan and the Federal Republic of Germany for two decades. In industries such as electrical equipment and ceramics, Japanese companies regularly spend 30% to 60% more on R & D than do their U.S. counterparts.

Investment in R & D may result in new products or in new production technologies. The importance of earlier R & D spending for new technology is demonstrated in a study by Edward F. Denison on the factors contributing to production growth in the United States from 1929 to 1982. It shows that technology made the second largest contribution to increased output. It ranked just behind the amount of labor input and ahead of both the quantity of capital and the contribution of education (Table 1).

The importance of increased private R & D spending in this country is greater as a result of declining government spending on R & D for the military. Also, a higher level of cooperation between industry and universities is necessary, particularly to stimulate more applied research. Scientific discoveries in university research are implemented too slowly in industry production.

Case Application

The New Industrial Revolution

The first Industrial Revolution (see Perspective, p. 86) was the second most important economic event in humankind's history, exceeded in significance only by the change from nomadic wandering to settled agriculture. We are now in the midst of a second Industrial Revolution, which also may have far-reaching effects. At the heart of this new revolution is a tiny piece of silicon, a "chip," less than the size of a fingernail. This chip is a microprocessor, which can do everything from controlling the shutter speed on a camera to weighing the cargo of a truck. When linked to input-output and programming units on separate chips, it forms the central processing unit (CPU) of a computer.

The public is most familiar with the uses of microprocessors in consumer goods such as pocket calculators, automobile controls, and personal computers, but it is their industrial applications that may ultimately have a greater impact on our lives. A Kansas City, Missouri, firm manufacturing air conditioning refrigeration systems for buildings formerly needed months of engineering work and production time to custom design and fabricate a system for a new building. Now it can do the job in a few weeks with only one-fourth the personnel formerly needed. It is able to do this through the use of CAD/CAM (computer-aided design/computer-aided manufacturing). CAD/CAM is to the second Industrial Revolution what the steam engine was to the first.

The first major CAD project was the development of the Boeing 777, introduced in 1994. Previously, airplanes had been designed with the aid of physical mock-ups to ensure that the millions of parts fit together. With the 777, the fit was all done by means of an electronic mock-up on the computer. Eu-

rope's Airbus has recently followed suit with the design of its new aircraft, and every major shipbuilder in the world is now using CAD/CAM to design and build the ships of tomorrow. Until now, only engineers with 10 to 15 years of expertise could design ship bodies, but three-dimensional software helps less-experienced engineers draw up a complex plan quickly. While still expensive, CAD/CAM is being used in an increasing number of industries to design everything from jewelry and Wedgwood dinnerware to the world's fastest bicycle (233 mph!). Perhaps the biggest impact has been in the auto industry where CAD/CAM has changed everything about the way a car is designed and built.

The maximum use of CAD/CAM is the factory totally automated by computer-integrated manufacturing (CIM). What effect will CIM have on workers' jobs? Is the U.S. labor force going to be thrown out of work en masse? Will we see workers riot as they did when machines were installed in factories at the beginning of the first Industrial Revolution? The answer to these questions is probably not. Just as the first Industrial Revolution was responsible for creating more jobs than the total number of workers employed when it began, this second revolution will very likely create more than enough new opportunities to offset the jobs eliminated. However, this technological revolution will radically alter the types of jobs available and most likely cause temporary dislocations. There will be jobs in the industries that produce the new equipment, jobs in operating and maintaining the equipment, and, most of all, jobs in a variety of new industries created by the reduction in costs due to CIM. The worldwide market for CAD/CAM and related computer-based engineering programs is expected to reach over $8 billion in 1997, with North America accounting for 38% of sales and Europe accounting for another 37% (Japan is lagging in this important area with an expected 17% of sales).

The transition will not occur overnight. Only about one-quarter of all industrial plants in the United States—mainly auto and auto parts, aerospace, electronics, electrical and mechanical engineering, food, and paper companies—are currently making use of CAD/CAM. The adoption of computerized automation is slow because of the high cost of the equipment. It can cost anywhere from $100,000 to $1 million for one device. The vast sums of money needed to finance the second Industrial Revolution will be difficult to find. But firms that do not make the investments will not be able to compete. CIM enables companies to produce custom-made products of the highest quality to the customer's order at the least cost. Increasingly, as time goes on, companies that do not install CIM systems will not be able to match the quality and prices of those producers that do, both domestic and foreign.

Another cost of automation is the extensive retraining of workers and managers required. Since only 30% or 40% of the costs of production have anything to do with actually producing a part, the main impact of CIM will be on planning, scheduling, and controlling the use of equipment. This change will totally transform the functions of management. In the second Industrial Revolution, the managers may resist the introduction of the new production techniques more than the workers.

Economic Reasoning

1. What is an example of investment in real capital that is improving industry performance in this case application?

2. Why does automation of production require investment in human capital?

3. Do you think EI teams of workers and managers should decide on investments in CAD/CAM, or should investment decisions be left to management and owners? Why? If such decisions do include workers, which of the three types of EI teams would be involved?

The New Industrial Revolution

Visit http://www.pcwebopaedia.com/computer_aided_manufacturing.htm for some links to the world's CAD/CAM and CIM producers. Visit Delcam at www.delcam.com and make a list of products that are being made with CAD/CAM.

What Are the Effects of Market Structure on Industry Performance?

In the last section of chapter 6, we examined the different types of industry structure, from pure competition to pure monopoly. Industry performance can be affected by how monopolistic the industry is, that is, how close it is to pure monopoly.

Market Concentration

The degree of concentration in an industry is determined by the number of firms in the industry that are competing for customers. The degree of **market concentration** ranges from pure monopoly as the most concentrated to pure competition as the least concentrated. Reduction of the number of firms in an industry increases market concentration and enables the firms in the industry to exert more control over prices.

When there are fewer firms, each firm faces a demand curve for its output that is more inelastic because there are fewer substitutes available. As a result, it can raise prices without as much loss in sales. Also, the more concentrated an industry is, the more likely it is to follow the practice of price leadership and avoid price competition.

The degree of concentration in an industry is measured by the proportion of total sales accounted for by the largest firms in that industry. The percentage of industry sales accounted for by the four largest firms is the most commonly used **concentration ratio.** Industries in which the four largest firms account for over 50% of sales can be considered shared monopolies. In the United States, these include the motor vehicle, photographic equipment, tire, aircraft, and breakfast cereal industries. When the concentration ratio is less than 25%, industries are assumed to be competitive. This is the case with such industries as printing, sawmills, fluid milk, software, plastics, and paper mills.

Approximately one-third of the sales of American industry fall into the shared monopoly category, and another third are competitive. The remaining third, those in industries with concentration ratios between 25% and 50%, are neither clearly monopolistic nor clearly competitive. The extent of monopoly power in American business as defined by the concentration ratio, however, is perhaps understated. There can be local monopolies that have as much power in their area as national monopolies do in the nation as a whole. For example, consider a campus bookstore or dining facility. Furthermore, the way industries are defined frequently masks the actual amount of monopoly that exists in the economy. For example, the largest four producers of salt account for 80% of salt sales. But in the data on which concentration ratios are based, salt producers are lumped together with firms producing other chemical compounds. As a result of this, the entire industry is classified as competitive. On the other hand, concentration ratios that only include domestic firms ignore the impact of foreign competition, and thus may overstate the degree of monopoly power.

Aggregate Concentration

If instead of market concentration we look at the **aggregate concentration** of all industries, we see that there has been a dramatic increase in the overall amount of concentration in American industry. Aggregate concentration is the percentage of total sales of all industries accounted for by the nation's largest corporations. Today, fewer than 200 corporations

---

market concentration a measure of the number of firms in an industry.

concentration ratio the percentage of total sales of an industry accounted for by the largest four firms. An alternative measure is the percentage of sales accounted for by the largest eight firms.

aggregate concentration a measure of the proportion of the total sales of all industries accounted for by the largest firms in the country. There is no common standard for measuring the aggregate concentration ratio.

control the same proportion of business assets that the 1,000 largest corporations controlled in 1941.

The idealized concept of a market economy is an unconcentrated one in which large numbers of small firms compete for customers by offering better products and lower prices. This market model does not correspond to the real world of concentrated industries.

Concentration and Industry Performance

Concentration in an industry may result from barriers to entry, **mergers,** or **predatory business practices,** including such illegal ones as **price discrimination,** sales below cost, and **kickbacks.**

In the 1980s a controversy arose among economists regarding the effects of industry concentration. Up until then there was general agreement, at least among economists in industrialized countries, that unregulated monopolies have undesirable effects on the economy and on consumer welfare. One of the most obvious effects is **monopolistic pricing.** With only a few firms in an industry, barriers to entry of new firms, and a lack of close substitutes for products sold under monopolistic conditions, firms can charge prices substantially above their costs of production and make monopoly profits. The Federal Trade Commission once estimated that eliminating concentration in industries would reduce prices by 25% or more.

Another result of concentration is **misallocation of resources.** Monopolies keep prices high by limiting the supply of the product on the market. As a result, monopolistic industries have less need for labor, raw materials, and capital equipment than they would if they were more competitive. The resources squeezed out of monopolistic industries by restricting output are diverted to other industries where they are in surplus. The surplus of these factors in the other industries lowers the incomes of the households that provide them. Too few resources are used in a particular industry when that industry is monopolistic. Our resources would be used more efficiently if industries were more competitive. One estimate is that

the misallocation of resources, resulting from monopoly pricing, costs the economy between $48 billion and $60 billion a year in lower total output.

Although large firms can have lower costs than small firms because of **economies of scale,** monopoly may instead result in higher costs. Firms in competitive industries are forced by market pressures to operate at or near their most efficient production levels. Monopolistic firms are not subject to this pressure and may therefore permit costs to rise above the lowest possible cost per unit.

One reason for higher costs in shared monopoly and differentiated competition industries is the amount of money they spend on non-price competition, especially advertising. If advertising provides useful information to buyers, it is not wasteful of resources. Advertising

merger a contractual joining of the assets of one formerly independent company with those of another; may be a horizontal merger of companies producing the same product, a vertical merger of companies producing different stages of a product in the same industry, or a conglomerate merger of companies producing in different industries.

predatory business practice any action on the part of a firm carried out solely to interfere with a competitor.

price discrimination selling a product to two different buyers at different prices where all other conditions are the same.

kickback the return of a portion of a payment or commission in accordance with a secret agreement.

monopolistic pricing setting a price above the level necessary to bring a product to market by restricting the supply of the product.

misallocation of resources not producing the mix of products and services that would maximize consumer satisfaction.

economies of scale decreasing costs per unit as plant size increases.

that describes real attributes of the product, where it can be purchased, and at what price, is a productive service that improves the operation of markets. This is the case with most newspaper advertising. But much advertising is repetitive and is purchased only for the purpose of countering a rival's advertising claims, such as in many national television ad campaigns. Competitive firms selling a standardized product do not have large advertising budgets. They do not need them because there are buyers at the market price for all that they can produce, and they cannot afford large advertising outlays because they must keep their costs down to be able to sell at the market price.

What Are the Effects of Market Structure on Industry Performance?

EconExplorer

Other forms of non-price competition that drive up costs are **product differentiation** and packaging. In differentiated competition industries, a firm will often attempt to differentiate its product in the minds of consumers from that of its competitors in order to segment the market and make the demand for its product more inelastic. Product differentiation purely for the sake of promotion is found extensively in the detergent, soft drink, and cosmetics in-

product differentiation a device used by business firms to distinguish their product from the products of other firms in the same industry.

vertical integration separate divisions of one company producing the different stages of a product and marketing their output to one another.

dustries, among others. Differentiation may take the form of "additives," product appearance, or packaging. Distinctive packaging for the sake of product differentiation adds greatly to the cost of many products. A University of California study showed that $1 of every $11 spent on products goes for packaging, and in one-fourth of the industries studied, the packaging cost more than the contents.

Industry concentration may also result in greater economic instability, due to the pricing practices in monopolistic industries. During periods of good business with booming sales, all businesses are likely to raise prices. During times of depressed business conditions, firms in competitive industries are forced by falling sales and the resulting price competition to reduce prices. This helps to maintain sales and cushion the amount of unemployment. But such is not the case in monopolistic industries. When sales decline, shared monopolies are likely to hold their prices stable or even raise them in order to increase their margin of profit on each unit sold to compensate for the reduction in sales volume.

Against this view of the drawbacks of concentration in industry, some economists now argue that the emergence of global competition has made national monopolies irrelevant. If domestic monopolies charge prices that are higher than costs of production, including a normal profit, foreign producers will enter the market and drive prices down. Furthermore, they maintain, global competition calls for companies that are very large and also for cooperation among the firms in a country's industries. Small, independent firms do not have the financial resources to develop and market products in competition with aggressive manufacturing giants outside the United States.

According to these economists, cooperation among firms plays a large part in the Japanese national competitive advantage. In the semiconductor industry, for example, such companies as Hitachi, NEC, and Fujitsu are **vertically integrated.** Individual firms are

(Continued on page 196)

Case Application

Corporate Raiders, LBOs, and the Feeding Frenzy

One way for a company to grow in size or enter new markets is simply by merging with or acquiring another company that is in the same or a different industry. In the former case, the combined firm results in increased market concentration, in the latter the result is a firm involved in increasingly diverse businesses. In both cases aggregate concentration will increase.

We are accustomed to thinking of acquisitions in terms of large, successful companies buying up small, less successful companies—big fish swallowing little fish. In the 1980s there was a lot of this going on, but more characteristic of the decade was the acquisition of one giant corporation by another—big fish swallowing other big fish. Gulf Oil, the 11th largest company in 1983, was acquired by Standard Oil of California (now Chevron), the 9th largest; General Foods, 38th on the list of the 500 largest firms in 1985, was purchased by Philip Morris, number 27, as was Kraft in 1987, when it was 31st and Philip Morris 12th; and number 54 in 1984, Nabisco, was acquired by R. J. Reynolds, number 23.

In the latter part of the decade, the feeding frenzy increased as a result of corporate raiders and leveraged buyouts (LBOs). Leading raiders such as T. Boone Pickens, Sir James Goldsmith, and Irv ("the Liquidator") Jacobs were constantly on the lookout for likely takeover targets with undervalued assets or complacent managements. Sometimes the raiders succeeded in getting control of the company's assets. Other times they arranged to be bought off by management with "greenmail," payments for the raiders' stockholdings at far above the market price for the stock.

Leveraged buyouts occur when a financier realizes that the total value of a corporation's stock is less than the value of the company's assets. The financier will then borrow enough money to buy all the stock, take over ownership of the company, and then sell the assets at a profit. Because such deals can be risky, interest rates on the borrowed funds were higher than normal. These securities acquired the name "junk bonds" because of their high risk.

As the decade of the 1980s came to a close, the acquisition feeding frenzy spent itself from its excesses. The "inventor" of junk bonds to finance LBOs, Michael Milken of the investment banking firm of Drexel Burnham Lambert, paid $600 million in fines and restitutions and went to prison for fraud. Drexel Burnham Lambert was forced to dissolve, and other aggressive acquisition financiers pulled back.

As the economy began to recover from recession, however, so did merger and acquisition fever. In 1993 there were $230 billion worth of deals initiated in the United States. By 1997 the amount had risen to $919 billion, and global activity reached $1.6 trillion (a 48% increase from 1996). Whereas the merger wave of the 1980s was brought about by innovations in finance, the factors that increased the current amount of merger and acquisition (M&A) activity are deregulation, finding strategic partners in order to compete in the global market, the end of the cold war (leading to changes in the defense industry), and the soaring value of the U.S. stock market. When a company's share prices increase, they can more easily buy another company by paying with their stock instead of cash. The shareholders of the acquired company receive shares in the acquiring company in place of their original shares.

Another difference from past merger activity is in the types of businesses being merged;

there has been a shift toward consolidation in financial services and communications. The leading industries for mergers in 1997 were telecommunications (mostly due to World-Com's $42 billion bid for MCI), commercial banks, investment banks, utilities, and credit institutions. Together, mergers in these industries accounted for 35% of 1997's M&A activity. Only two of the top ten industries—utilities and oil/gas—were in manufacturing.

Sometimes, after swallowing a meal of unrelated businesses, the acquiring company finds that it does not have the skills necessary to run a business in the subsidiary's field, and the resulting indigestion causes the company to have to "spin off" the subsidiary to concentrate on its "core" business. Some recent examples include PepsiCo shedding its restaurant operations which included Taco Bell, Pizza Hut, and KFC (Kentucky Fried Chicken); Westinghouse spinning off its industrial businesses to concentrate on broadcasting; AT&T selling Lucent Technologies; and Quaker Oats divesting itself of Fisher-Price, the toy maker.

Economic Reasoning

1. What effect did Chevron's acquisition of Gulf Oil have on market concentration in the petroleum industry?

2. How could PepsiCo's divestiture of Taco Bell, KFC, and Pizza Hut into separate companies affect the price of fast food and the allocation of resources?

3. Was the creation of the junk bond market good for American business? Why or why not?

Corporate Raiders, LBOs, and the Feeding Frenzy

Visit Yahoo!'s business site at http://quote.yahoo.com and click on My Yahoo View. Type "mergers" into the search box and see what's going on with "merger mania" these days.

(Continued from page 194)

associated with industrial groups in which they have close ties with each other, with large Tokyo banks, with their suppliers, and with the government. Industrial policies and export strategies are devised and promoted by the Ministry of International Trade and Industry (MITI). It encourages cooperation among firms to carry out the strategies.

But the idea that Japan's success in world markets is due to cartel practices in its industries, aided and abetted by MITI, is challenged by Michael Porter of the Harvard Business School in *The Competitive Advantage of Nations* (see Further Reading at the end of the chapter). Porter maintains that the success of Japanese firms is due not to their cooperation or to assistance by the government, but rather to vigorous domestic rivalry among companies in their home market. The Japanese industries in which there is the fiercest competition among the firms in the domestic market—autos, consumer electronics, televisions, and cameras—are the very ones that have been the most successful abroad. On the other hand, in those Japanese industries in which there are strong cartels and government restrictions on competition—construction, agriculture, food, paper, commodity chemicals, and fibers—costs are so high that Japan cannot compete with other countries. According to Porter, this is no accident. It is competition at home that has made Japanese companies lean and mean for kung-fu assaults on foreign markets.

▶ Putting It Together

A principal determinant of industry performance is *productivity*. Productivity is customarily measured by the amount of output per hour of labor. Productivity growth in the United States in the past two decades has been lower than in Japan and a number of other countries, although the United States is catching up. The level of industry performance also depends on the responsiveness of companies to market preferences and changes. Production is increasingly targeted at specific market niches, which necessitates flexible plants and *automated* systems and processes.

Another indication of performance is the quality of goods and services produced by industry. In order to encourage U.S. firms to devote more effort to improving quality, Congress established the Malcolm Baldridge National Quality Award in 1988.

Today, industry performance is also measured by the extent to which businesses act responsibly in environmental protection, resource conservation, product safety, and equal opportunity for employees.

One means of raising productivity is increasing the amount of *real investment* in *capital equipment*. Financial capital is more costly in the United States than in Japan because the savings rate is lower here both for households and government, because financial capital has been diverted from real investment to financial speculation through the use of *junk bonds,* for example, and because of the short time horizon of U.S. corporation executives, who are under pressure to show good profit reports every quarter.

Investment in computer systems to implement practices such as *just-in-time* manufacturing methods—a way to have raw materials and subassemblies delivered by suppliers to the location where they are needed at the time they are needed. Computers also run enterprise-application software, which is used to run all aspects of

Industry performance depends on investment in capital equipment as well as on the productivity of labor.

a business, from order-taking to inventory replenishment.

Another way of increasing productivity and also improving quality is by investment in *human capital*. When new equipment and technology are introduced in a plant, there is a *learning curve* of rising productivity. The learning curve for Japanese companies is steeper than for American companies, in part because the Japanese invest more in training their workers than do U.S. firms, but U.S. firms are quickly catching up. *Cross-training* workers provides a more flexible labor force and reduces worker boredom.

An innovation first introduced in the United States but extensively put to use in Japan is *employee involvement (EI)*. EI programs may include *empowered* self-managing teams, problem-solving teams, or special-purpose teams. EI also includes using the principles of *total quality management (TQM)* and *business process reengineering (BPR)*.

Japanese firms view their workers as valuable assets to be maximized, while U.S. firms have been inclined to view their workers as expensive inputs whose costs are to be minimized. In U.S. firms, the organization is vertical, while in Japanese firms, it is flatter, resulting in closer communications. Some labor leaders and middle managers in the United States have opposed EI programs.

Spending on research and development has in the past been an important factor responsible for growth in the U.S. economy. Private R & D spending takes on increased importance today as the government cuts back on military-related R & D, and more cooperation between industry and universities is needed.

Market concentration is determined by the number of firms in an industry. The *concentration ratio* is customarily measured by the percentage of industry sales accounted for by the four largest firms. If it is over 50%, the industry is a shared monopoly. If it is less than 25%, the industry is competitive.

Aggregate concentration is the share of total output of all industries accounted for by the nation's largest firms. Concentration may result from *mergers,* barriers to entry, or *predatory business practices* such as *price discrimination,* sales below cost, and *kickbacks.*

The consequences of high industry concentration include monopolistic pricing, *misallocation of resources* (despite *economies of scale*), uneconomical *product differentiation,* and greater economic instability.

$ Perspective $

An Imperfect World

Joan Violet Robinson (1903–1984) The daughter of a British major-general, Joan Robinson received an "upper class" education in exclusive English schools. She taught at Cambridge University for 42 years until her retirement in 1973. She visited the United States to deliver lectures to various groups, including the American Economic Association, and she spent a few months at Stanford University in 1969 as a special professor.

Referred to at times by other economists as "the magnificent queen" and "the magnificent tigress," her small stature belied the force of her presence. In face-to-face debates, the rigor of her uncompromising intellectual honesty was a match for such leading American economists as Nobel Prize–winners Paul Samuelson and Robert Solow.

In addition to her work on the structure of industry and capital theory, she wrote on such subjects as Marxian economics (*Essay on Marxian Economics*, 1942) and China (*The Cultural Revolution in China*, 1969).

Classical economists, starting with Adam Smith (1723–1790) and culminating in the neoclassical writings of Alfred Marshall (1842–1924), formulated their economic ideas around the concept of pure competition and its antithesis, pure monopoly. But the world is not composed of purely competitive and purely monopolistic markets. In the real world, industries lie somewhere between these extremes.

One of the first economists to light the way through the murky regions of imperfect competition was Joan Robinson. In her classic work, *The Economics of Imperfect Competition* (1933), she developed a model of an economy consisting of shared monopolies. Reversing the approach of earlier economists, she treated pure competition as a special case, just as it is in the real world.

In her subsequent writings, Robinson explored the relationship of the market behavior of business enterprises and labor unions to the economic growth and stability of the capitalist system. In her view, the desire of capitalists to retain as much as they can of sales revenues for reinvestment and growth is in conflict with the desire of labor unions to obtain a larger share of the proceeds for the workers.

The struggle between these two monopolistic forces, big business and big labor, creates uncertainty in the business world and causes fluctuations in economic growth. Robinson believed the efforts of businesses and unionized workers to increase their respective shares of business income also contribute to inflation.

Robinson was one of the century's leading economic theorists and was considered a prime candidate for the Nobel Prize in economics. Nonetheless, she had disdain for the abstract mathematical manipulations that are so common in modern economic theory. She described the mathematical economists' models as being "such a thin story that they have to put it into algebra."

More than most of her contemporaries, Robinson's approach to economics was strongly tied to the realities of market practices. She made significant contributions to economics by wedding the theoretical models of the neoclassical and marginalist schools of economics to the pragmatism of Veblen and the institutionalists.

For Further Study and Analysis

Study Questions

1. According to Figure 1, page 177, what was the period of highest productivity growth in the past 30 years? What was the period of lowest productivity growth? Approximately what was the difference in productivity growth rates during those two periods?

2. Why did Motorola insist that its suppliers compete for the Malcolm Baldridge Award?

3. What is a recent example of a product, domestic or imported, that was targeted at a specific market niche?

4. If the increase and improvement in new producers' durable equipment does not keep pace with the increase in the size of the labor force, what will happen to productivity? Why?

5. Why might it be difficult to measure productivity in service industries or industries that produce computer software?

6. What sorts of worker skills are necessary in order for EI programs to work successfully? Does the use of EI programs make investment in human capital more or less important?

7. In 1992, total sales of the aerospace industry in the United States amounted to $135 billion. The largest producers were Boeing with $30 billion in sales, United Technologies with $22 billion in sales, McDonnell Douglas with $18 billion in sales, and AlliedSignal with $12 billion in sales. What was the concentration ratio in the aerospace industry? Was the industry a shared monopoly, competitive, or in between?

8. In 1997, Boeing and McDonnell Douglas merged. What impact do you think this will have on economic performance in the aerospace industry?

9. How do monopolies manage to keep prices higher than they would be in a competitive market? Why do they not raise their prices even higher?

10. What are examples of informative advertising? What are examples of non-informative advertising?

Exercises in Analysis

1. From the most recent Economic Report of the President or another source find the productivity increase for the previous year and compare it with the average for 1993–97 shown in Figure 1. (Another good source is the Bureau of Labor Statistics at http://stats.bls.gov/ashome.html)

2. Survey local industries or firms that you know about and write a paper on their worker training and/or employee involvement programs.

3. Select an industry that is important in your state or province and write a short paper on the extent to which that industry is concentrated.

4. Write a short paper describing the relative growth rates of the U.S. and Japanese economies over the past decade.

Further Reading

Craypo, Charles, and Bruce Nissen, eds. *Grand Designs: The Impact of Corporate Strategies on Workers*. Ithaca, NY: ILRPress, 1993. Examines the effects of corporate conduct such as restructuring, plant shutdowns, and relocation on workers, communities, and unemployment.

Dertouzos, Michael L., Richard K. Lester, and Robert M. Solow. *Made in America: Regaining the Productive Edge*. Cambridge, MA: MIT Press, 1989. This is a thorough examination of the performance of American industry and how it can be improved, the results of a 2-year study by the Massachusetts Institute of Technology Commission on Industrial Productivity.

Emmott, Bill. *Japanophobia: The Myth of the Invincible Japanese*. New York: Times Books, 1993. Emmott does not subscribe to the common view of Japanese economic dominance. He points to many mistakes the Japanese government and industries have made.

Fallows, James. *Looking at the Sun*. New York: Pantheon, 1994. Fallows argues that, despite

Japan's difficulties in the early 1990s, for us to write it off would be a big mistake.

Goldstein, Morris. *The Asian Financial Crisis.* Washington: Institute for International Economics, 1998. Although focusing on the 1997 "Asian Flu," it provides a good description of Japan's current economic problems and how they are adding to the difficulties of resolving the regional crisis.

Hornbeck, David M., and Lester M. Salamon, eds. *Human Capital and America's Future: An Economic Strategy for the 90s.* Baltimore: Johns Hopkins University Press, 1991. How manpower policy can solve the productivity problem and again make the United States the competitive leader worldwide.

Karier, Thomas. *Beyond Competition: The Economics of Mergers and Monopoly Power.* Armonk, NY: M. E. Sharpe, 1993. A new look at how the current movements in industry concentration affect competitive markets and economic performance.

Keller, Maryann. *Collision: GM, Toyota, Volkswagen, and the Race to Own the 21st Century.* New York: Currency Doubleday, 1993. An analyst of the automobile industry for the securities business looks at U.S., German, and Japanese car producers in their positioning to capture market share in world markets.

Kolberg, William H., and Foster C. Smith. *Rebuilding America's Workforce: Business Strategies to Close the Competitive Gap.* Homewood, IL: Business One Irwin, 1992. The authors examine the way to maximize human capital in the United States with manpower planning and occupational training.

Pine, B. Joseph. *Mass Customization: The New Frontier in Business Competition.* Boston: Harvard Business School Press, 1993. Technological innovations in production and managerial methods permit flexible manufacturing and service to meet special customer needs.

Porter, Michael. *The Competitive Advantage of Nations.* New York: The Free Press, 1990. The results of a 4-year study of the degree of success in global markets of 10 countries shows that the ability to compete internationally depends on improvements in technology and productivity that result from vigorous competition in a nation's markets.

Robinson, Stanley L. *Harnessing Technology: The Management of Technology for the Nontechnologist.* New York: Van Nostrand Reinhold, 1991. Discusses the automation of manufacturing processes as viewed by managers who are not technically trained.

Ross, Alastair. *Dynamic Factory Automation: Creating Flexible Systems for Competitive Manufacturing.* New York: McGraw-Hill, 1992. Examines the use of industrial robots to increase plant productivity from a more technical standpoint than Robinson presents in his book listed above.

Rutledge, John, and Deborah Allen. *Rust to Riches: The Coming of the Second Industrial Revolution.* New York: Harper & Row, 1989. The authors begin this book with a futuristic look backwards from the year 2041 on the reasons for the demise of General Motors. Despite this dour introduction, the book's outlook is optimistic. Its authors believe that the baby boomers will rescue the U.S. economy as they mature and shift from consumption to savings, thus providing more capital for investment.

Sazanami, Yoko, Urata Shujiro, and Hiroki Kawai. *Measuring the Costs of Protection in Japan.* Washington: Institute for International Economics, 1995. Questions the correctness of past Japanese policies and explores their impact on the welfare of the Japanese people.

Stalk, George. *Competing against Time: How Time-Based Competition Is Reshaping Global Markets.* New York: Free Press, 1990. Examines the importance of time management in production and delivery in today's highly competitive international markets. Argues that comparative advantage is now often based on timeliness.

Taninecz, George. "Best Practices and Performances." *IndustryWeek,* December 1, 1997, pp. 28–43.

World Press Review. June 1998, pp. 8–13. "Will Japan Sink the World?" A series of short articles that explore the consequences of Japan's current economic woes for the rest of the world.

chapter eight

Government and Business

We have seen major changes in the automobile industry, but they are nothing compared to the coming changes in the telecommunications industry. The telecommunications industry has historically been regulated by the government, but the pace of change in the industry is making it difficult for government regulation to keep up.

▶ Who Is Building the Information Superhighway?

In 1876, Alexander Graham Bell received patent number 174,465 for an improvement in the telegraph—the telephone. What began as a novelty—that was almost not produced because he could not find investors—eventually became a necessity of modern life. From its beginning in the last century the telephone industry was dominated by Bell's company, American Telephone and Telegraph (AT&T). AT&T's dominance was given official sanction by the Communications Act of 1934, which made it an authorized monopoly in providing local and long-distance telephone service. Because of the importance of accessible communications and because of the monopolistic nature of the industry, in the past, telecommunications were strictly regulated by government.

Regulation of the phone system by the Federal Communications Commission (FCC) involved give and take on both sides. The FCC determined prices and service areas. The opportunity to buy local service was required to be universal, and local service prices were kept down to help make phone access available to everyone. This was accomplished by charging higher prices for long-distance service, which was considered a luxury. While AT&T was allowed to keep its monopoly position in telecommunications, it was not allowed to compete in other unregulated markets.

For 50 years, until its breakup in 1984, AT&T (or Ma Bell, as it was often known) had four primary parts that operated in conjunction with one another to provide America's telephone service. First, telephone hardware was designed by AT&T's Bell Labs, one of the world's leading research institutions. Second, its unregulated subsidiary, Western Electric, manufactured equipment from phones to switchboards that was leased (never sold) to residential and business customers. Third, the company provided local (dial-tone) service to homes and businesses through its local telephone companies. Fourth, the company provided long-distance toll service that connected one local system to another over long-distance telephone lines. Although it was a monopoly, Ma Bell was never characterized by the extreme inefficiencies or poor service that many monopolies exhibit. During this time, the U.S. phone system was the envy of the world.

AT&T's monopoly position was initially due to the technical nature of the industry. Because it would be inefficient and costly to have two or more companies stringing wires between homes and businesses, there was only room for one company in the industry. As is often the case, however, technological advances change the nature of an industry and, at least technically, allow for competition. During the late 1940s, new technologies were developed that allowed telephone messages to be relayed via microwave transmission. This meant that any number of companies could build microwave relay stations and offer long-distance service that connected local companies. AT&T, however, successfully argued for years that such companies could not connect their systems to AT&T's local phones or switchboards, effectively preventing them from entering the market.

After 10 years of legal battles and $10 million in legal costs, in 1978, Microwave Communications, Inc. (MCI) was finally allowed to offer long-distance service using AT&T's local systems. (In contrast to the time and costs of the legal battles, MCI's first long-distance route cost $2 million and took 7 months to build.) The changes in technology eventually led the U.S. Justice Department to order the breakup of Ma Bell and so promote competition in the long-distance segment of the communications industry. In 1984, the telephone industry was restructured by a compromise agreement, a so-called consent decree, which settled a decade-long court suit. In the settlement AT&T was divorced from the local telephone service companies, which were reorganized into seven independent regional companies known as the "Baby Bells." AT&T was left with its long-distance services, its manufacturing subsidiary, Western Electric (WE), Bell Labs (later renamed Lucent Technologies), and the freedom to enter unregulated markets, such as computers. The Baby Bells remained the regulated segment of the market, providing local phone service while being prohibited from entering the long-distance market.

The 10 years following the breakup saw an amazing revolution in the telephone industry as the competition to provide long-distance service became fierce. AT&T is still the largest provider with a 42% share of the market, but the newly created MCI/World-Com will have a 23% share, and Sprint 9%. Perhaps even more important, MCI/World-Com will provide about 60% of all Internet connections, an increasingly important part of the market.

New technologies are diminishing the importance of the traditional telephone business and may eventually render it obsolete. The marriage of computers with new transmission paths, such as cellular phones, satellites, and fiber optics, promises to create entirely new products and markets. The day is not far off when we will have one system that will allow us to watch TV, access the Internet, work with a computer, get lessons via satellite, and make telephone calls. One of the biggest remaining questions is, who is going to provide that access?

In February 1996, President Clinton signed the Telecommunications Reform Act. The primary goal of the act is to open the entire gamut of telecommunications to competition. It does this by eventually allowing long-distance companies, the Baby Bells, cable companies, electric companies, and companies that do not yet exist to offer everything from local and long-distance telephone services to television and Internet access. No one can say which providers will eventually win the biggest market shares, but there is no doubt that consumers will be big winners as they will be offered an amazing array of services by an increased number of competitors.

Chapter Preview

In an ideal free market economy, there is only a small role for government. In reality, however, government is often needed because sometimes markets fail to allocate resources efficiently. This can happen when there is monopoly power, when there are desired goods that markets cannot produce profitably, and when the production of a good imposes unwanted costs on third parties. In this chapter we will explore such market failures by asking: How does the government limit monopoly power? Why does the government produce certain goods and services? What is the role of the government in protecting the environment?

Learning Objectives

After completing this chapter, you should be able to:

1. Explain the purposes of the Interstate Commerce Act and the Sherman, Clayton, and Celler-Kefauver Acts.
2. Explain the purpose of industry R & D consortiums and why they are exempt from the antitrust laws.
3. List the causes of natural monopoly and explain why natural monopolies often do not remain natural monopolies.
4. Explain why it is often necessary for public utility commissions to regulate natural monopolies.
5. Explain the reasons for and the consequences of deregulation.
6. Identify the kinds of goods and services that are collective goods and explain why the government often provides them.
7. Explain the concepts of external economies and external costs.
8. Explain why pollution exists.
9. Describe three alternative types of policies that the government can use to reduce pollution.

How Does the Government Limit Monopoly Power?

The last section in the preceding chapter discussed the economic consequences of monopolistic industries. The economic disadvantages of monopoly behavior were recognized by Adam Smith in *The Wealth of Nations* as early as the eighteenth century. But it wasn't until the end of the nineteenth century that the government undertook measures to curb monopolies.

Antitrust Legislation

Much as AT&T dominated the telephone industry in this century, the powerhouses of the previous century were the railroad **trusts.** They generated a great deal of public resentment because of their monopolistic behavior. Especially angry were the farmers, who were almost totally dependent on railroads to transport their crops to market. Because farmers had little choice of transportation services, the railroads serving particular farming regions could charge extremely high rates. This enabled the railroads to give rebates (partial returns of payments) to large industrial shippers as a means of attracting their business. These and other abuses led to the passage of the

trust a combination of producers in the same industry under joint direction for the purpose of exerting monopoly power.

Been Rolling a Little too High.

Policing the railroad monopoly was the first mandate of the ICC, as shown in this early cartoon.

Interstate Commerce Act by Congress in 1887. This law required that all rail rates for railroad traffic between states be fair and reasonable. The Interstate Commerce Act strictly forbade competing railroads from making arrangements for sharing traffic and earnings. It required that all rates be published and adhered to, thus limiting **rate discrimination.** To oversee the application of the Interstate Commerce Act, Congress established the Interstate Commerce Commission (ICC).

The Interstate Commerce Act was the first **antitrust legislation,** but because the railroads were not the only businesses abusing monopoly powers, a more comprehensive law soon followed. The Sherman Antitrust Act was passed in 1890 declaring illegal all contracts, combinations

rate discrimination (price discrimination) charging different customers different rates for services of equal production cost.

antitrust legislation laws that prohibit or limit monopolies or monopolistic practices.

of business firms, and conspiracies that were in restraint of interstate or foreign trade. Any person who monopolized, attempted to monopolize, or conspired with others to monopolize any part of commerce between the states or with foreign countries was guilty of a misdemeanor.

The Sherman Act formed the basic national antitrust legislation. However, lack of enforcement funding, nonaggressive attorneys general, and conservative interpretation of the law by the courts made the Sherman Act relatively ineffective in the years following its passage. In fact, many monopoly practices became more apparent after its enactment. The Clayton Antitrust Act (1914) helped to remedy this situation by putting teeth in the Sherman Act. Among other things, it prevented firms from acquiring stock in competing companies and it prohibited price discrimination if the price discrimination injured competition. Later, price discrimination that injured buyers was also outlawed unless the difference in prices charged to two buyers could be justified by actual differences in the costs of supplying the buyers.

In addition to restricting monopoly practices, the Sherman and Clayton Acts were aimed at preventing collusion among firms to raise prices and at practices that reduced competition in the marketplace—a frequent occurrence in shared monopolies. But the merger of two competing firms into a single company was not prohibited, and there were many of these following the end of World War II. As a result, the Celler-Kefauver Antimerger Act was passed in 1950 to slow down the wave of mergers. Congress was concerned about the increasing amount of concentration in American industry. The Celler-Kefauver Act forbids mergers in which a company acquires the assets of another company when this lessens competition. It has greatly reduced horizontal mergers, but not vertical and conglomerate mergers, which do not directly increase the concentration ratio.

In 1997 the Justice Department (which enforces the antitrust laws) established new guidelines that relaxed the rules regarding horizontal mergers. Mergers that result in increased market concentration may nonetheless be allowed if the companies can show that resulting cost savings, better products, or better service can offset any anticompetitive effects. Violations of the country's antitrust laws, however, can still result in serious penalties. In 1998 Ucar International, a producer of graphite electrodes, paid a record $110 million fine for price fixing. This was the largest antitrust penalty ever assessed against a firm, exceeding the fine of $100 million levied against food giant Archer-Daniels-Midland in 1996 for the same crime.

◢ Industrial Consortiums

In order to meet the challenge of global competition described in the last chapter, there has been some modification of antitrust policy. The National Co-operative Research Act of 1984 exempts companies engaged in joint R & D projects from some antitrust provisions. Its purpose was to enable firms to pool resources and expertise in order to spread the costs and risks of developing new technologies. For example, it might allow GM, Ford, and Chrysler to work together to develop more advanced braking systems. More than 300 such research agreements are now registered with the Justice Department.

The government has taken even more direct action by initiating a program to encourage collaboration among the firms in certain industries in research and development. The most important instance was in 1987 when the Commerce Department organized the leading semiconductor companies into an **industry consortium** for the development of advanced chip-making technology. The consortium, Semiconductor Manufacturing Technology (Sematech), was formed of 14 companies and funded 50% by the Pentagon. Sematech was important in helping the American semiconductor industry to recapture world leadership in chip-making from the Japanese.

In other actions to facilitate cooperative research efforts, the government has created more than 30 research centers at universities with the goal of promoting rapid application of the most recent technological discoveries to production. Since 1985 the government-funded National Science Foundation has set up 18 Engineering Research Centers at universities to encourage academic research specifically related to the needs of industry. Legislation passed in 1986 permits the government's own laboratories to collaborate with industries in turning the results of their research into useful products.

There is pressure from business to relax the antitrust laws further in order to allow for joint manufacturing and marketing activities as well as research. Some observers fear that such a liberalization of antitrust policies could result in less domestic competition, higher prices, and lower investment. As indicated in the last chapter, vigorous domestic competition among firms in an industry is the best guarantee that the industry will be competitive in the international marketplace. On the other hand, many believe that global competition reduces the need for sterner antitrust policies. First, as long as foreign competition exists, there is little need to worry about domestic monopoly power. Second, as noted above, successfully competing in global markets requires that U.S. firms be big enough and free enough to compete with firms in countries with less strict antitrust laws.

◢ Public Utility Regulation

Among major countries, a privately owned and operated telephone system serving the nation is unique to the United States. In other countries, the telephone system, like the postal system here, is a government agency. In many countries, in fact, the telephone and postal systems are operated by the same government agency. The railroad, electric power, and various other industries are also government owned in most countries, even those countries that are considered capitalist. In the United States these industries have traditionally been privately owned corporations, but they are subject to **government regulation.** As discussed below, many of these industries have been deregulated.

There are, however, some industries in which competitive conditions, having a large

---

industry consortium a combination of firms in an industry to carry out a common purpose.
government regulation government control of the prices charged and services provided by firms that produce goods that are vital to the public's well-being.

Due to economies of scale, electricity is often more efficiently provided by one utility. The utility is then considered a natural monopoly and is subject to regulation by a public utility commission.

number of firms competing in the same market, would be inefficient. These are industries where **natural monopolies** exist, industries where the market is best served when there is only one firm. Public utility companies fall into this category. Natural gas, water, cable TV, and electric service are examples of natural monopolies. It would be wasteful to duplicate the networks of pipes and wires that distribute these throughout a city.

natural monopoly an industry in which the economies of scale are so extensive that a single firm can supply the whole market more efficiently than two or more firms could; natural monopolies are generally public utilities.

public utility commission a regulatory body whose members are appointed by government to set rates and services provided by public utility firms.

Natural monopolies arise when the economies of scale in production are so great that one large utility company serving a city or region is considered more efficient than a number of smaller ones. Because of the lower costs that result when one firm supplies the whole market, the government treats public utilities differently than other industries. It either grants a franchise to a single firm and then closely regulates it or provides the service itself, as with community-owned utilities.

In order to prevent privately owned public utilities from charging monopolistic prices or providing inadequate service, **public utility commissions** are appointed in each state to regulate the companies. When the utility wants to raise its rates or change the level of its service, the commission holds public hearings at which concerned parties, including consumers, give testimony. It then approves, disapproves, or modifies the proposed changes. If a commission finds that a utility company has been overcharging customers, it can order refunds to be made.

Government regulation of public utilities faces the problem of reconciling adequate service at fair prices with a fair return to the stockholders who own the utility. This is usually done by calculating a utility's costs and then allowing it to charge customers a rate that earns a certain predetermined rate of profit. Such calculations, however, are beset with pitfalls. How does the commission decide on what constitutes a "fair" return? Should the costs of unfinished nuclear plants be passed on to rate payers or be absorbed by stockholders? (see Case Application To Nuclear or Not to Nuclear, p. 52). What are considered legitimate business costs? For example, if AT&T, which is regulated, bought equipment that was overpriced from its unregulated subsidiary Western Electric, AT&T would make more than a fair return through the high profits earned by WE. Perhaps the greatest drawback to the fair-return principle of regulation is that it discourages improvements in efficiency and innovation because any resulting increase in profits is eliminated by offsetting rate reductions. Just as bad, mismanagement and inefficient operation can lead to higher costs, but these are passed on to consumers in the form of higher rates.

Advances in technology have reduced the monopoly power of natural monopolies and have created competition where none existed before. For example, only your local phone company has a phone line strung to your house, but cellular phones currently eliminate the need for these lines and provide competition to the regional Baby Bells. Although cellular prices are still much higher, who knows what the future will bring? Cable TV companies have the technology to provide telephone service; the only thing that stands in the way of this challenge to the local phone service is government regulations, which are being phased out. Cable TV itself was once viewed as being a natural monopoly because of the need to have a cable strung to your house, but satellite TV provides unregulated competition. Even though there are no substitutes (yet?) for the wires and pipes that bring us electricity and natural gas, there are many different companies that produce the electricity and gas, leaving only the delivery of energy as a natural monopoly. While still tied to the local utility for delivery, consumers in many states are being given the opportunity to buy their energy from numerous competing producers.

How Does the Government Limit Monopoly Power?

EconExplorer

Deregulation

The difficulty of establishing rates that return no more or less than a fair profit on a regulated company's investment is only one of the problems faced by government regulation. With respect to regulated industries other than public utilities, the original purpose of government regulation was to prevent monopoly and foster competition. In many cases, however, regulation resulted in restricting competition rather than promoting it. The airline and trucking industries are examples of industries that were regulated in such a way as to prevent competition and protect the railroads.

Growing dissatisfaction with the results of regulation has led to widespread **deregulation** in recent years. Railroad regulatory reform acts in 1976 and 1980 allowed railroads to set prices, start new services, abandon old services, and sign long-term contracts without Interstate Commerce Commission approval. Under the Airline Deregulation Act of 1978, the airlines were freed to select their routes and set their prices for the first time in 40 years. The Motor Carrier Act of 1980 did the same thing for the interstate trucking industry, despite opposition by the large trucking firms and the Teamsters Union. Both feared that increased competition would reduce hauling rates, profits, and wages in the industry. Partial deregulation has also been applied to banks, savings and loan associations, and other financial services firms.

deregulation the process of eliminating government regulations and reducing the scope and power of regulatory bodies.

The breakup of the long-distance telephone service industry provides one example of the reasons for government intervention in a market economy and the problems that are involved.

In a 1993 study by Clifford Winston of the Brookings Institution, published in the *Journal of Economic Literature,* it was shown that deregulation of seven industries in the 1970s and 1980s resulted in lower prices and better services for consumers. Furthermore, the producers benefited as well in increased profits. The net gain to the economy is calculated to be between $36 and $46 billion a year.

Deregulation has not been accomplished without pain. Some older firms could not meet the new competition and failed, putting their employees out of work. Some new firms expanded too aggressively and also failed. Labor unions in industries where regulation limited competition enjoyed high wages by forcing the firms to share their monopolistic revenues. After deregulation introduced competitive pricing into such industries, many union members were forced to take pay cuts. Others lost their jobs due to cost-cutting reorganizations by the firms. Even customers sometimes suffered. Airline passengers were left stranded with useless tickets when an airline could no longer pay its bills and had to shut down. Bank depositors were hit with large increases in service charges when banks had to pay competitive interest rates and made up the revenue losses by raising their service fees. Families, whose basic telephone service had been subsidized by revenue from business long-distance calls under AT&T, found bigger telephone bills after deregulation of the industry.

Despite these numerous problems, deregulation has in general achieved its aims. It has revitalized industries, providing consumers with a wider selection of services, usually at lower prices. Where prices have gone up—local telephone service charges, for example—the increases can be attributed to the elimination of artificial pricing structures that do not reflect actual costs.

It is a basic tenet of economics that prices should be in accord with costs in order to bring about the most efficient allocation of resources. Consumer wants will not be satisfied as fully with a price system that does not reflect actual production costs, as often happens with regulation and monopoly power. Achieving a more rational allocation of our resources is one of the main objectives of deregulation.

Case Application

Air Warfare

Prior to the Airline Deregulation Act of 1978, the domestic airline industry was a government-controlled cartel. Routes between cities were allocated to specific carriers by the Civil Aeronautics Board (CAB), and competition from other airlines was not permitted. The CAB set fares according to the distance flown.

After deregulation came into effect in 1982–83, a number of new airlines entered the industry, and existing airlines expanded their services to routes that had previously been closed to them. There were constant fare wars to attract passengers to these expanded services.

Not all areas of the country benefited from more air service. Under CAB regulation, airlines had been forced to provide unprofitable service to small cities in order to be granted routes to service major markets. After deregulation, some small cities lost all airline service.

There was concern that safety would also suffer under deregulation. With cutthroat price competition and rapid expansion of routes, it was feared that airlines would skimp on equipment maintenance and allow unsafe planes to take off. These fears have proved groundless. Although the CAB was phased out of existence, the Federal Aviation Administration (FAA) has responsibility for inspecting airline equipment maintenance and safety procedures.

The safety record for air travel has actually improved significantly since deregulation. In the decade following deregulation, the average number of commercial airline accidents decreased by more than one-third compared to the decade before deregulation. Considering the great increase in the number of people flying, the safety improvement was even more striking. There was a decrease of 57% in fatal

Deregulation of the airlines provided consumers with a wider selection of services at lower prices. But when an airline went bankrupt in the competitive market, passengers were sometimes left stranded with useless tickets.

accidents per million passenger miles traveled. These safety improvements are credited to advancing technology and better understanding of dangers like wind shear rather than to deregulation, but deregulation apparently has not been detrimental to safety.

Other aspects of air travel have not fared as well under deregulation. The increased number of flights, especially during the popular morning and evening departure and arrival hours, has resulted in frequent delays. There is flagrant overbooking, causing passengers to be bumped from flights. Complaints about lost and battered luggage have increased faster than passenger traffic. And complaints about inedible airline food are louder than ever. Critics of the industry observe that the airlines ignore such complaints until they get into financial difficulties. Only when they are about to go under, as a last desperate measure, do they attempt to improve passenger comfort. By then it may be too late to save themselves.

Many airlines could not adjust to the competitive environment and failed; there have been more than 50 mergers and 150 bankruptcies since deregulation. But new start-ups and expansion by small regional carriers have taken their place. Those that have survived have apparently done well. Between 1985 and 1995, airline passenger miles increased from 382 million to 547 million, and industry profits increased from $863 million to $2,377 million.

Not all is sweetness and equality in the industry, however. The nation's two largest airlines, American and United, have had a big advantage over competing carriers because of their ownership of the two computerized reservation systems over which travel agents book flights. Although government regulations prohibit bias in the use of those systems, it is estimated that the airlines owning the systems gain an advantage of $2–$3 billion in ticket sales over competing carriers.

And savings on fares have been unequal, depending on routes. Fares are higher for those cities where one carrier dominates the market. Following deregulation, airlines adopted a route system based on hub cities. Major carriers have one or two hub cities for their fleet. They fly passengers from their point of origin to the airline's hub city, where they are consolidated into planes flying to a passenger's final destination. This is cost-effective for the airlines, though for passengers it is more time consuming than nonstop flights.

Another advantage the hub-and-spoke system gives the airlines is more control over prices. Since flights into and out of each hub city are dominated by the airline that uses that hub, it has a near monopoly on that market. A passenger can fly from a hub city on a competing airline, but then he or she usually must fly to that carrier's hub and catch a connecting flight. Although usually less expensive, the cost in terms of time is often not worth the savings on the ticket price.

At nine major airports, over 60% of all traffic is controlled by a single airline, and the numbers are increasing. The effect on prices of this lack of competition is clear. A study of airline pricing, conducted by Severin Borstein of the University of Michigan, revealed a strong link between prices and the amount of competition in a particular market. He found, for example, that USAir, whose hub is Pittsburgh, charges 20.5 cents per mile on flights to and from Pittsburgh where it has an 85% share of the market, while it charges only 15.8 cents per mile on flights to other destinations. Similar differences exist in pricing for TWA in St. Louis (83% market share), Northwest in Minneapolis (79%) and Detroit (77%), American in Dallas (63%) and Miami (62%), Delta in Atlanta (59%), and United in Denver (65%) and Chicago (51%). The General Accounting Office found that fares were 27% higher at airports dominated by one carrier than at airports with competition.

The high profits earned by hub carriers have attracted many small regional, discount carriers such as Vanguard and AirTran into these markets. The dominant hub carriers have responded by attempting to block gate access to these competitors and by matching discounted fares to the few cities where the regional carriers fly. The resulting fare wars have been a boon to travelers, but the regional carriers have complained that the dominant hub carriers are using predatory pricing to compete unfairly. Once they are driven out of the market, they claim, the hub carriers raise their rates back to the previous high levels.

Senator Mike DeWine, chairman of the Judiciary Subcommittee on Antitrust, Business Practices, and Competition is conducting an investigation of the airline industry. He states, "We need to determine whether hubs are producing the benefits of competition, or, as some argue, permitting the dominant carrier at the hub to impose monopoly prices on the public."*

Economic Reasoning

1. Is air transportation a natural monopoly? Explain.

2. What benefits resulted from deregulating the airline industry? What drawbacks?

3. Do you think airline hubs are "producing the benefits of competition," or are they imposing "monopoly prices on the public"?

———

*Quoted in the *Atlanta Journal and Constitution,* April 2, 1998.

Why Does the Government Produce Goods and Services?

In a market economy, consumer sovereignty is supposed to dictate what is produced. Consumers voting with their dollars in the marketplace decide how resources will be allocated: this product or service will be supplied because it can be sold at a profit, and that product or service will not be supplied because it cannot be sold at a profit. If that is the way the system is supposed to work, why does the government provide a variety of goods and services that do not produce profits? Why does it provide mail service, highways, bridges, dams, lighthouses, harbors, air traffic controls, national defense, and, at the local level, schools and police and fire departments? This next section examines these questions.

◢ Collective Goods

Goods like running shoes, pizza, and earrings are usually used or consumed only by the people who pay for them. They can be shared, but only with the permission of the owner. Other goods, for example, a fireworks display, lack this property. Once the fireworks are up in the air, they can be enjoyed by many people at the same time, and it is very difficult to exclude anyone from watching them. Goods with these properties are called **collective goods.** Goods such as these present a problem for the market because if no one can be excluded from consuming the good, there is an incentive for people to consume it but not to pay for it. Businesses therefore cannot make a profit selling the good and they will not produce it. If the good or service is considered of sufficient importance to society to justify its production but it cannot be sold for a price that covers its production and distribution costs, it may be supplied by the government. It pays for it both by fees for service and by tax money. Collective goods are also called public goods.

---

collective good (public good)   a good or service that can be used by many at the same time without diminishing any one person's consumption; it is difficult to exclude someone from using the good.

Some things are clearly collective goods. National defense is an obvious case. It is not feasible for individuals to purchase their own ICBMs to protect their homes against attack from foreign enemies. Public safety, a clean environment, and scientific advances are also collectively consumed. Another example is the preservation of endangered species. Everyone benefits when various birds and animals are able to survive and support a healthy ecosystem.

Some goods have many, but not all, of the attributes of collective goods. In the case of sidewalks, public parks, and local roads, it might be possible to collect user fees to pay for the service, but the collection costs would be too great to make it workable. In addition, these goods can be consumed up to a point by many people at the same time, but when congestion sets in, the goods technically no longer meet the definition of a collective good. Goods such as these are also provided by the government.

A problem with collective goods is determining how much of the goods to produce. Some people may favor heavy defense spending while others prefer less, but the government only provides a given amount. Some people might find this to be the optimal amount for them, but most will find it to be either too much or too little. Nonetheless, people must still pay their taxes to finance defense spending, whether they are happy with the amount provided or not. Contrast this with a consumer purchasing some new clothes. The consumer buys just the number of shoes and shirts that makes him or her happy. In addition, government provision is often inefficient, because like private monopolies, it often faces no competition that requires it to produce quality output at a low cost. Because of these problems, many economists believe that whenever possible, the production of goods and services should be **privatized,** instead of relying on government provision.

Why Does the Government Produce Goods and Services?

EconExplorer

External Economies

Goods and services sometimes benefit people other than the purchasers. A telephone, for instance, not only benefits the subscriber but also provides benefits to everyone who places a call to that number. The subscriber pays for the telephone and pays the monthly service charges, but all of the callers receive benefits from that telephone as well, even though they do not pay for it. Of course, most of them have telephones of their own, which they do pay for. But the more people that have telephones, the more useful a telephone is to each person. A telephone is a good that has **external economies;** it benefits not only the purchaser but other people as well.

The existence of external economies is often a reason for governments to provide goods and services, even if they could be provided by the private sector. If goods and services are supplied by private enterprises, the price must cover their costs, that is, buyers must pay for the total costs of production and distribution. But buyers only consider the benefits to themselves when making purchases.

privatization allowing the private sector to produce goods and services that once were provided by the government.

external economies benefits that accrue to parties other than the producer and purchaser of the good or service; benefits for which payment is not collected.

If others would also benefit by the good or service being produced and consumed, then leaving these goods in the realm of the market will result in less than the optimal amount being produced. There are some products for which the external economies are so significant that production of more than the market-determined quantity of them is justified.

External economies, for example, are a justification for the government to pay for education. If our country did not have a literate population, it could not operate its industries efficiently or provide the professional services needed by people. Also, the public could not effectively participate in the political process. As a result, the country would be less productive and probably less politically stable. Because of the external economies resulting from education, families are not required to pay the full costs of their children's schooling. The government pays most of the costs for public education. Public health services (especially immunizations), medical research, consumer information, and city transit systems are other instances where services benefit people other than those directly receiving the services.

Libraries, museums, and zoos are a variation of this type of good. They are considered **merit goods.** They enrich our entire culture, not just individuals, and they are so important that everyone merits access to them. Because the social value of such services is greater than the price buyers will pay, the government provides the services either for free or at less than full cost.

◤ Collective Goods and Equity

Sometimes collective goods are provided in order to meet the goal of greater equity. Public transportation, for example, is most heavily used by lower-income groups, including young people and the elderly. This is one of the justifications for government subsidies to public transit systems. It helps to achieve the socioeconomic goal of greater economic equity.

An alternate way to achieve the goal of greater equity would be direct subsidies to low-income people. In some ways, this would satisfy the goal of equity more efficiently. Income supplements might help low-income people more than subsidized bus fares because such supplements permit them to choose the best transportation means for their particular circumstances. The same reasoning has led to rent supplements for the poor as an alternative to public housing.

The argument over which is the best approach, income supplements or public services, continues. The answer may depend on whether providing a particular public service satisfies other objectives as well as equity. It is possible that direct income supplements to low-income families to help them pay for private transportation could be less expensive than maintaining public transit. But it would also result in more pollution, greater traffic and parking congestion, and more vehicle accidents. On the other hand, some argue that income supplements are not a good idea because they can be used to buy other unnecessary goods, for which the public may not be willing to provide tax dollars.

It has been proposed that collective goods be subjected to cost-benefit analyses to balance total costs against total benefits. By balancing estimated benefits against estimated costs, an outcome similar to individual decision making in the market might result. Such analyses are difficult, however, where **externalities** and equity considerations are involved.

---

merit goods goods (including services) that have a social value over and above their utility for the individual consumer.

externalities external economies or external diseconomies (external costs).

Case Application

The New War between the States

There's a new war between the states, only this time it's not between the North and the South, but among states and cities throughout the nation that are locked in a struggle for industry and jobs. Economic development has become a popular rallying cry for politicians seeking to increase jobs, incomes, and tax bases in their communities.

State and local economic development policies began in earnest in the 1960s when Sun Belt states that lacked an industrial base offered financial inducements to manufacturing firms to locate new facilities in their regions. The success of some of these programs resulted in retaliation by Rust Belt states, and the subsidy war was on. At first subsidies were used primarily to lure manufacturing facilities from one region to another, but soon they were being used as inducements to get firms to stay where they were and not move. Today, hardly any major investment project—manufacturing, commercial, or retail—is undertaken without some form of state or local government support.

The subsidies take a variety of forms and include low-interest loans, state and local tax forgiveness, infrastructure and site improvements, utility connections, road and highway construction, land grants, and worker training programs. Proponents of the programs argue that they lead to increased jobs in their jurisdictions, but critics contend that they are often simply giveaways to firms that would most likely locate or expand in the subsidized location, anyway. Many people who work for government economic development agencies admit that they are forced to offer subsidies to some firms because if they do not, some other community will.

The newest battle in the war is being fought over sports stadiums. In city after city, the owners of professional sports franchises are demanding that local governments either finance, or help finance, new facilities, or the franchise will move to another city that will. Nationwide, between 1990 and 2000, 75 new facilities have been built, are under construction, or will be started. Sixty-six percent of these are public/private partnerships, 20% are being financed completely by the public sector, and only 14% are being built entirely with private funds. In California alone the $2.1 billion being spent on sports facilities represents the largest investment in any industry in the decade.

Advocates of public funding for sports facilities believe that maintaining a professional franchise in their city is necessary in order to attract other businesses, increase jobs and incomes, and to protect the city's reputation as a major league town. Opponents argue that the costs are too high and that major league franchises add only a few jobs to the local economy. According to *USA Today,* Baltimore's Camden Yards Ballpark is costing the state $14 million a year in subsidies and the price of each job created to date is $127,000. Mark S. Rosentraub, the leading expert on stadium financing, claims that Jacobs Field in Cleveland cost the city $230,000 per job. As for the importance of franchises to the local economy, Rosentraub goes on to say that the professional sports teams in Atlanta contribute only a tenth of one percent of all the jobs in the metropolitan region.

Citizen opposition to public funding for stadiums is growing. The San Francisco Giants are building a privately funded park after voters repeatedly defeated referendums asking for tax dollar support. Voters in Pittsburgh turned down a similar ballot initiative that proposed new taxes to fund new football and baseball stadiums, but civic leaders, fearing the loss of their teams, are nonetheless going ahead with an alternative plan to use existing tax dollars to help pay for the facilities.

As long as other cities and states are offering subsidies to privately owned sports teams and other private businesses, it is difficult for a community to not offer competing subsidies if it wants to keep its businesses or teams. One proposed solution to the problem is for the National League of Cities and the U.S. Conference of Mayors to agree to end or limit all such programs, and sign a peace treaty that would end this new war between the states.

Economic Reasoning

1. What external benefits are generated by economic development programs?

2. Are sports stadiums collective goods? Do they generate external economies?

3. Do you think that public money should be used to subsidize sports facilities or private businesses? Why or why not?

▶ What Is the Role of Government in Protecting the Environment?

In 1962 Rachel Carson published the landmark book *The Silent Spring,* alerting the public to the hazards of toxic wastes that were threatening our environment. Although at first dismissed by some as a kook, she finally got her message through, and America woke up and began to deal with the problem of pollution. The Environmental Protection Agency (EPA) was formed in 1970, and since that time Congress has passed a series of increasingly tough environmental protection measures dealing with air and water pollution and toxic waste cleanup. The existence of pollution provides a good reason for government involvement in the economy.

◼ Why Pollution Exists

An Indiana steel mill in a market economy must keep its costs down if it hopes to successfully compete with other mills and make a profit. Some ways to lower costs are to dump its slag (solid metal waste) in an empty field, burn cheap high-sulfur coal in its furnaces, and dump the dirty water it uses to cool the molten steel into a nearby river. It can then sell its steel at a low enough price to compete with other mills that are doing the same thing.

The obvious problem with this is that the people who live near the mill not only suffer from increased health problems caused by toxic wastes and dirty air and water, but they also suffer the other costs associated with pollution—fewer fish and other wildlife, lost recreational sites, foul odors, and unpleasant surroundings. If the Indiana mill makes a decision to install expensive pollution control equipment and be environmentally friendly, while mills in Pittsburgh and Mobile do not, the Indiana mill will not be able to compete and will go out of business. In this case, allowing the market system to operate to satisfy steel producers and consumers results in an undesirable outcome; the system fails because it cannot achieve the socioeconomic goal of a clean environment.

The reason that the market system fails is that producers and consumers in some circumstances do not pay the full costs of what they use, including the environmental costs. Without environmental protection laws, steel buyers do not have to pay the costs of environmental damage done to the air and water. Motorists do not have to include in the cost of running their cars the health and environmental damage resulting from automobile exhaust emissions. Airlines, and their passengers, do not generally have to pay for the noise pollution that they create in the neighborhoods of airports when landing and taking off. These costs, which are not paid by the producer or user, are called **external costs** because they are imposed on other people.

External costs often arise when the environment is treated as a free good (see chapter 1, p. 12) because no one can claim ownership of the country's air or water. If a local business tries to shift its costs to you by dumping its trash on your front lawn, you can take legal measures to rectify the situation because you can show that someone is violating your property. If the business dumps its waste products in the air or water, however, there is little that you as an individual can do because you do not own the air or water.

Because no one individual can claim property rights to air and water, society, acting through government, must claim these rights. The solution is to make producers and buyers **internalize the external costs** by requiring them to shoulder the full costs of production. The government cannot directly attach price tags to air and water, but it can require firms to stop using the earth, air, and water as free garbage disposals. In the case of steel mills, this is accomplished by requiring the installation of smoke scrubbers on smoke stacks. For auto exhaust pollution, installation and proper maintenance of exhaust emission control devices and the use of lead-free gasoline are required. In the case of airport noise, the solutions are to require airlines to fly planes with quieter engines, limit their hours of takeoffs and landings, and restrict their flight patterns.

By shifting some of the costs of production to third parties, businesses lower their costs and prices and increase their output. In contrast to the case of external economies where the market system provides too little of a good or service, the existence of external costs means that too much of a good is being produced and used at too low a price. Forcing firms to internalize their externalities will result in higher costs and prices and a reduced supply of output. These are the costs of a clean environment.

The control of pollution presents an important example of a trade-off. On one hand, if we choose to have a cleaner and safer environment, the opportunity cost will be that we produce and buy less steel, pay more for our cars and get lower gas mileage, fly at less convenient hours, and so on. The effects will also be felt by many workers who will lose their jobs in some high pollution industries as output contracts. On the other hand, new jobs are being created in those industries that produce pollution control equipment and conduct environmental research, and our nation's health care costs will be reduced.

In affluent countries like the United States, the price of a clean environment is very low in terms of what we must give up—perhaps one less television set or having to drive the family car for an extra year instead of buying a new one. According to the EPA, the United States spends only 1.7% of its total income on pollution reduction, much less than the 4.2% spent on shoes and clothing or the 9.3% spent on housing. For us, a clean environment is relatively inexpensive. In less developed countries, however, the cost of pollution control might be roofs over many heads, meals on the table, or energy to keep the family warm at night. The costs of a clean environment are indeed much higher and, faced with such trade-offs, many of these countries are forced to forgo pollution control because it is too expensive.

external costs costs of the production process that are not borne by the producer or by the purchaser of the product and are therefore not taken into consideration in production and consumption decisions.

internalize external costs the process of transforming external costs into internal costs so that the producer and consumer of a good pay the full cost of its production.

◤ How Pollution Is Controlled

The above examples of direct regulation are the most common means used by government to protect the environment. For example, cars and trucks are required to reduce carbon monoxide emissions to a set level, electric utilities are required to reduce sulfur dioxide emissions to a set level, and so on. However, these **command-and-control regulations** have been criticized by economists because by themselves they do not reduce pollution in an economically efficient manner.

In order to improve economic efficiency, the comprehensive Clean Air Act that was passed in 1990 permits, among other things, the sale of emission allowances, which are granted to plants faced with heavy pollution-control costs. This policy allows the government to set a level of total allowable sulfur dioxide emissions, for example, and to provide "emission permits" that allow the holder of the permit to emit a specified amount of sulfur dioxide. Permits are distributed to existing plants based on historical emission patterns, and the firms are then allowed to buy and sell the permits at market-determined prices. The point of marketable emission permits is that they encourage firms that find emission control less costly than buying the permits to clean up. At the same time they enable other companies, for whom emission control is more costly, to purchase the right to continue polluting. In contrast to simple command-and-control regulation, the government does not determine exactly which plants reduce emissions, it just sets the overall amount of emissions that will be allowed. The following example shows how marketable emission permits can improve economic efficiency.

Suppose that two electric utilities have plants that were built in different years and have different pollution-control equipment. Each plant burns coal and emits 500 tons of sulfur dioxide per year. The cost to the older plant to reduce emissions is $250 per ton and the cost to the newer plant, because of better technology, is only $150 per ton. Using command-and-control regulations, the EPA may require each plant to reduce emissions to 300 tons per year, a reduction of 200 tons. Compliance for the older plant will cost it $50,000 ($250 a ton × 200 tons) and compliance for the newer plant will cost $30,000 ($150 × 200)—a total cost of $80,000 to reduce total emissions by 400 tons. This is not an efficient solution because 400 tons of emissions could be removed by the newer plant for only $60,000, a $20,000 saving to the economy. It would not be equitable, however, to require the newer firm to remove 400 tons from the air while the older firm is required to do nothing.

Now suppose instead that each utility was initially issued permits that allowed it to emit 300 tons of sulfur dioxide a year. Rather than pay $250 per ton to reduce its pollution to the required level, the older firm may be willing to buy 200 tons of permits from the newer firm for $200 per ton, at a total cost of $40,000. Because it now has 500 tons of permits, it does not need to reduce its emissions and this saves the older plant $10,000. Having sold 200 tons of its permits, the newer firm will only have 100 tons of permits left and it will need to reduce its emissions by 400 tons. This will cost it $60,000. It has, however, earned $40,000 from the sale of its permits, so its net cost is only $20,000, and it too saves $10,000! The new firm ends up removing all 400 tons of pollutants from the air, which makes sense because it can do so at a lower cost.

The EPA currently allows the sale of permits on the Chicago Board of Trade, where the permits are bought and sold on a daily basis at market-determined prices. Should society decide in the future that existing levels of pollution are still too high, the government can purchase existing permits and destroy them. In the meantime, environmental and other concerned groups are also free to buy the permits and destroy them. Even some companies have contributed in this manner. In 1993, Northeast

---

command-and-control regulations a system of administrative or statutory rules that requires the meeting of certain standards of performance.

Table 1   National Air Pollution Emissions, 1970–1995

(In thousands of tons except where noted)

Year	Particles*	Sulfur Dioxide	Nitrogen Dioxides	Carbon Monoxide	Lead (tons)
1970	13,044	31,161	20,625	128,079	219,471
1975	7,617	28,011	21,889	115,110	158,541
1980	7,050	25,905	23,281	115,625	74,956
1985	4,094	23,230	22,860	114,690	21,124
1990	3,195	22,433	23,038	100,650	5,666
1995	3,050	18,319	21,779	92,099	4,986

* less than 10 microns.
Source: *Statistical Abstract of the United States.*

Utilities donated a number of its permits to the American Lung Association, which then destroyed them.

What Is the Role of Government in Protecting the Environment?

EconExplorer

Another way to force an internalization of external environmental costs, used in many European countries, is to impose an emission charge on firms for the environmental damage they do. These are sometimes referred to as **eco-taxes.** The electric utility industry, for example, might be taxed $250 per ton for spewing pollutants into the air. If a firm can reduce its pollutants for less than $250 per ton, it will do so instead of paying the tax. Those firms that find it more costly to comply will pay the tax and keep on polluting. If the government decides that pollution levels are too high, it can simply raise the tax and more firms will elect to reduce their emissions. Again, the end result is that firms that can reduce their emissions at low cost do so. Whatever pollution remains comes from sources where it is most expensive to reduce it.

You should notice that none of the above policies toward pollution seek to remove pollution altogether. To do so would be too expensive and not worth the opportunity costs to society. It would not be worth it, for example, to shut down an electric plant because it emitted one-tenth of the amount of sulfur dioxide that can be absorbed by the atmosphere. What economic theory suggests is that the worst and most dangerous pollution should be cleaned up first. Successive reductions should continue so long as the benefits of removing the pollutants exceed the cost of removing them.

Have We Been Successful?

Pollution control is a growth industry in the United States. Between 1980 and 1996, industry revenues increased from $52 to $184 billion and employment increased from 462,000 to 1,305,000. Have we received anything for our money? As shown in Table 1, we have made progress in our efforts to clean up

eco-tax a fee levied by the government on each unit of environmental pollutant emitted.

(Continued on page 222)

Case Application

A Common Problem

During the sixteenth century, many English villages had commonly owned grazing grounds, referred to as *commons,* where villagers were free to graze their sheep and cattle. Every villager had an incentive to put as much of his livestock on the commons as possible, but the result was such overgrazing of the grass that the roots were often damaged and growth was reduced in following years. Since the grass was commonly owned, no one villager had an incentive to protect it and preserve it for later years.

The case of commonly owned resources presents a problem for the market system. Each individual acting to maximize his or her own well-being results in a loss to the community because common property resources will be overused and perhaps destroyed. The English eventually solved their problem by passing the Enclosure Laws that established private property. Each landowner could then determine the optimal number of animals to graze that would preserve the land for the future. Because the land was privately owned, there was now an incentive to take care of it.

The *problem of the commons,* as it has come to be known, has continued to plague economies whenever resources are jointly owned. When resources are not privately owned, they are treated as free goods by people. They will not be taken care of, and they will be overused and eventually depleted.

Ocean fishing grounds are a good example of the problem. Proper management of fishing resources would dictate that enough fish be left in an area to replenish schools for future years. Each fishing boat, however, has an incentive to catch as many fish as possible. Fish not caught by one boat will be caught by another instead of being left to spawn and maintain the size of the schools. There simply is no incentive for one boat to conserve for the future. The same problem existed with the American bison. Since no one owned the bison, no one worried about hunting them to near extinction. Actually, the only way to "own" a bison, or any other wild animal, was to kill it.

Protecting common-property resources presents a problem that the market system cannot solve unless private-property rights can be established. This just cannot be done with some resources, so the government must intervene. For example, the electromagnetic spectrum (the airwaves) is used by radio and television stations, cellular phones, pagers, garage door openers, satellite communications, and others. If everyone were allowed to broadcast or use whatever frequency they liked, the airwaves would simply get too crowded and reception would suffer. In this case, the government, through the Federal Communications Commission, took ownership of the airwaves and provides licenses for a limited amount of access.

As with the discussion of externalities in this chapter, air is a common-property resource, and consequently it gets overused because no one can claim a private property right to it. The same applies to our water resources.

There are other examples of common-property resources being overused or not cared for throughout every town and city in the country. As a taxpayer, you own your local police car fleet, but do you ever get up on a Saturday morning to wash and wax a police car? Would you wash and wax your own car? Which has more litter—a city street or a private driveway?

Common-property resources exist and often there is no way to privatize them so that they will be properly conserved. If the government does not or cannot take ownership for all of us, these resources may not be around for us to enjoy much longer.

Economic Reasoning

1. Explain why common-property resources will be overused while privately owned resources will not.

2. During the 1800s the American bison was hunted to near extinction while at the same time the number of beef cattle being raised increased exponentially. Explain why.

3. There are many ranchers who raise big game animals such as rhinoceros and lions, and charge a fee for hunters to come onto their land to hunt the animals. Do you think practices such as these help to conserve or further endanger such species?

(Continued from page 220)

the nation's air, especially in our reductions of solid particles and lead in the air. The source of most lead in the air was, at one time, auto emissions, but regulations requiring a switch to lead-free gasoline have made a very big impact. We have made less progress in reducing sulfur dioxide, 66% of which comes from electric utilities, and carbon monoxide, 69% of which comes from motor vehicles.

Although it is not as easy to measure the level of water pollution, the Sierra Club reports that as of 1997, two-thirds of the nation's lakes and rivers are safe for swimming, compared to just 36% in 1970. The Clean Water Network, however, reports that while 16% of the country's water systems are in good shape, 21% have

serious environmental problems. A major problem in reducing water pollution is that much of it comes from municipal and agricultural runoff, sources that are difficult to control.

We noted in the previous chapter that productivity in the United States has slowed considerably since the mid-1970s. Many economists argue that it is no coincidence that this productivity slowdown occurred during the same period that we made serious progress in our efforts to clean up our environment. If we put a dollar value on a healthier ecosystem and include this in measures of our nation's output, they contend that the statistics would show that our productivity has at least kept pace with prior years.

▶ Putting It Together

In the last quarter of the nineteenth century, the growth of industries in which there were a few large firms conspiring to fix prices inspired legislation to curb their monopolistic behavior. The Interstate Commerce Act of 1887 put an end to the railroad *trusts'* market-sharing agreements and *rate discrimination*. In 1890 the passage of the fundamental *antitrust legislation*, the Sherman Antitrust Act, made monopolies and attempts to monopolize illegal. The generality and vagueness of the Sherman Act made its enforcement difficult, so the Clayton Act (1914) spelled out specific anticompetitive practices that were prohibited. The wave of mergers after World War II led to the Celler-Kefauver Antimerger Act (1950), which prohibits one firm from acquiring the assets of another when this would substantially lessen competition.

To assist U.S. industry in meeting foreign competition, strict application of the antitrust laws has been modified by the National Cooperative Research Act. It permits companies to form an *industry consortium* for purposes of sharing the costs and results of R & D. Also, the government has established research centers at universities to promote rapid application of new technology in production and permits government laboratories to collaborate with industries.

Certain types of monopolies are legal. These are *natural monopolies* such as public utility companies, which, for technological reasons, are more efficiently operated as single firms. To protect consumers from monopolistic pricing, the states appoint *public utility commissions* to *regulate* utilities.

In the last decade, some regulated industries, such as railroads, trucking, airlines, petroleum, and banking, have been either partly or totally deregulated. One of the principal reasons for this *deregulation* was that the regulatory agencies were in some instances protecting and enforcing monopolization. Deregulation is aimed at increasing competition, lowering prices, and improving service in these industries.

Some types of goods and services do not lend themselves to distribution through normal market channels. National defense, highways and bridges, police and fire protection, and public transportation systems are examples of

collective goods. One reason for the government's supplying goods and services not provided by the private sector is the existence of *external economies*. *Merit goods* such as libraries and museums are provided by the government because they enrich the culture. Another justification for publicly provided goods and services is that they help achieve the goal of greater economic equity. Because the market may yield greater consumer satisfaction, many economists are in favor of *privatization* wherever it is possible.

One of the reasons for the extent of environmental pollution is that the environment is considered a free good by consumers and producers. They do not have to pay for dumping their wastes into it. Pollution can be reduced, and resources, including the environment, more efficiently used if these *external costs* are *internalized*. Forcing industries to internalize the external costs of pollution can be accomplished by regulating the amount of pollution with *command-and-control policies,* selling emission permits, or imposing *eco-taxes.* If we could somehow add our gains in reducing pollution to our measured increases in other output, many economists believe that productivity has not slowed as much as the traditional statistics would indicate.

$ Perspective $

The Interstate Highway to Serfdom

Friedrich August von Hayek (1899–1992) Friedrich Hayek, as he is known in the United States, was born in Vienna, Austria. He began his teaching career there but in 1931 went to teach at the University of London, where he stayed for nearly 2 decades. In 1950 he moved to the University of Chicago, where he was appointed Professor of Social and Moral Sciences. This impressive title reflected the expanse of Hayek's interests and writings, the scope of which includes economic theory and policy, political philosophy, legal theory, social and moral values, and experimental psychology. After 12 years at Chicago, Hayek taught for 7 years in Germany before returning to Austria to live. Some of his major publications include *Prices and Production* (1931), *The Pure Theory of Capital* (1941), *The Road to Serfdom* (1944), *Individualism and Economic Order* (1948), *The Constitution of Liberty* (1960), and *The Fatal Conceit: The Errors of Socialism* (1989).

According to an old saying, "The road to hell is paved with good intentions." According to Friedrich von Hayek, the Nobel Prize-winning economist, the road to totalitarian slavery is paved with government planning. His views have gained a wide following, and *BusinessWeek* magazine has referred to him as the intellectual godfather of today's conservative economics.

It was Hayek's work in theoretical economics dating back to the 1930s that earned him the Nobel Prize in 1974, but he is best known for his 1944 book on political philosophy, *The Road to Serfdom*. In that book he warns of the dangers of government intervention in the economy. He maintains that government planning and economic control are incompatible with competition and individualism. If the government attempts to manipulate the economy to achieve some objective such as greater equity, says Hayek, it will increasingly resort to totalitarian measures until all freedom is lost and democracy is extinguished.

In later writings, Hayek has labeled those who advocate collectivist ideas and urge government intervention in the economy as "constructivists." Constructivists are those who think that society can consciously devise policies and programs to change the way the economic system works and achieve certain goals. Constructivist programs do not work, according to Hayek, because they ignore fundamental rules of behavior that have evolved in society over a long period of time. Disregarding these rules, which have enabled existing societies to survive and prosper, will lead to social and economic decline. Hayek believes in an economic Darwinism by which the fittest have survived.

In his last book, *The Fatal Conceit: The Errors of Socialism,* published when he was 89, Hayek states that man's "fatal conceit" is his belief that he "is able to shape the world around him according to his wishes."

Hayek is not altogether dogmatic, however, in his opposition to government regulations and programs. In *The Road to Serfdom* he allows that some types of government intervention might be justified as long as they do not unduly diminish competition.

"The only question here," Hayek wrote, "is whether in the particular instance the advantages gained are greater than the social costs they impose."

In other words, Hayek would apply a type of cost-benefit analysis to any regulation.

For Further Study and Analysis

Study Questions

1. How did the monopolistic practices of the railroads in the nineteenth century frustrate the functioning of a free market?

2. How did the various laws passed by the federal government deal with the monopolistic abuses of certain industries?

3. Would you agree or disagree with the statement, "Once a natural monopoly, always a natural monopoly"? Why?

4. How are natural monopolies, such as utility companies, prevented from indulging in monopolistic practices?

5. Why should investors in utility companies be guaranteed a fair return on their investments? How would a fair return be determined?

6. Have you used any collective public goods (services) provided by the government in the past week? What are they? Could they have been produced more efficiently by the private sector?

7. Why does the government subsidize public transportation when most people do not use it?

8. Why is the use of marketable emission permits or eco-taxes more economically efficient than the simple use of command-and-control antipollution policies?

9. What are some external economies derived from goods or services that you have benefited from but have not used or paid for yourself?

10. Many of the world's nations met in Kyoto, Japan, in 1997 to agree on international standards for pollution control. Why would there be a disagreement between the more affluent and less affluent nations as to how strict these standards should be?

Exercises in Analysis

1. Both Microsoft and Barnes and Noble are involved in antitrust suits. Research one of these cases and write a report that explains which antitrust provisions are allegedly being violated. Has the case been settled? If so, what was the outcome?

2. Locate at least five business firms in your community that have had to internalize previously external costs. What effects did these newly internalized costs have on profits and on the prices charged for the companies' goods or services?

3. Use your library or the Internet to research the use of emission permits in the United States and write a report on how widely they are being used.

4. Visit the Clean Water Network at http://www.cwn.org/docs/res_f.htm and write a report about the quality of water in your state and the surrounding region.

Further Reading

Barrows, Paul. *The Economic Theory of Pollution Control*. Cambridge, MA: MIT Press, 1980. Discusses external costs, market failure, and pollution control policies.

Field, Barry. C. *Environmental Economics: An Introduction*. New York: McGraw-Hill, 1994. An explanation of how economic analysis can be used to evaluate environmental issues.

MacAvoy, Paul W. *Industry Regulation and the Performance of the American Economy*. New York: W. W. Norton, 1992. The effects of regulation and how deregulation in the 1970s and 1980s changed industry performance.

Petulla, Joseph M. *Environmental Protection in the United States.* San Francisco: San Francisco Study Center, 1987. Reviews the history of environmental protection, the roles of industry and government in environmental protection, the problems associated with it, and what can be done.

Rothman, Hal K. *The Greening of a Nation.* Fort Worth: Harcourt Brace, 1998. Reviews the history of the environmental movement in the United States since 1945.

Sigler, Jay A., and Joseph E. Murphy, eds. *Corporate Lawbreaking and Interactive Compliance: Resolving the Regulation-Deregulation Dichotomy.* New York: Quorum Books, 1991. Examines the legal and criminal aspects of corporations violating statutes and regulations, and how society is affected by such corporate behavior.

Wald, Matthew L. "Acid-Rain Pollution Credits Are Not Enticing Utilities." *New York Times,* June 5, 1995. Reprinted in *Annual Editions: Microeconomics 98/99.* Guilford, CT: Dushkin/McGraw-Hill, 1998. An argument as to why emission permits are not working as planned.

Webster, David B. "The Free Market for Clean Air." *Business and Society Review,* Summer 1994, pp. 34–37. Reprinted in *Annual Editions: Microeconomics 98/99.* Guilford, CT: Dushkin/McGraw-Hill, 1998. An argument for the use of emission permits as an efficient means of controlling air pollution.

chapter nine

Government and Households

Our government is not only involved with the business sector of the economy; it is also very involved in the day-to-day lives of the American people. While many of us complain about red tape and government interference, our lives would be much different if the government did not get involved.

▶ Cradle to Grave 🕸

The United States is one of the most market-oriented economies in the world, yet we still rely a great deal on government involvement in economic matters. In 1997, federal, state, and local government spending accounted for almost 32% of all the spending in the United States. This means that 32 cents out of every dollar spent in our country went through the government's hands to buy goods and services, to protect workers and consumers, or to redistribute income from higher- to lower-income households. While this may seem like a large percentage, the graph below shows that we are still far below the level of government involvement that occurs in most Western European countries, where in many instances government spending accounts for over half of the economic activity. And while we complain that our top income tax rate of 39.6% is too high, many European countries have top tax rates over 50%, and they exceed 60% in Denmark and the Netherlands.

The countries of Western Europe are often referred to as *welfare states*, not necessarily because everybody receives government assistance, but because they believe that an important role of government is to promote the socioeconomic goals of economic equity, financial security, and social, rather than individual, welfare. The basic European philosophy is that the market system leads to too much unfairness. While markets are relied upon to provide most goods, governments redistribute income and protect citizens from economic hardship. Rather than let important merit goods be provided through the market, the European belief is that it is better for people to pay high taxes and then have the government provide such goods for "free." The U.S. government is also involved in such activity, but often to a much lesser extent; European governments are so involved in the lives of their citizens that it is often said that they take care of their citizens from cradle to grave.

One of the most important areas of government concern is income security. In Sweden, a person under 55 who loses his or her job can receive unemployment compensation for up to 300 days, and a person over 55 can receive it for up to 450 days. The benefit is 90% of the worker's lost wages. In comparison, U.S. workers can generally get unemployment compensation of around 50% of lost wages for only 26 weeks. While Sweden offers the most generous benefits, other European countries are not that far behind. Workers' compensation—benefits paid to workers who cannot work because they were hurt on the job—is much more generous in Europe, to the point where people joke about "disability as a profession."

European labor laws are much more generous to their workers than those in the United States. Most Europeans get 6 weeks of paid vacations in addition to paid holidays. Family-leave policies are more lenient, and employers are often required to grant 6 months to 1 year of leave to mothers with newborn children. Laws in most countries make it difficult to fire a worker after they have been employed for at least a year. Funding such programs is not cheap, and much of it comes from employers who must pay high employment taxes for each worker hired. Although not a direct government expense, such policies reduce the amount of work being done and the amount of goods and services produced in order to provide social benefits for citizens.

The drawback to the generous European benefits is that many people choose not to work, and the high employment taxes levied on businesses give them less incentive to hire people. As a consequence, unemployment rates are much higher than the 5.3% rate in the United States. In February 1998, unemployment rates were 15% in Finland, 12.5% in France, 10.9% in Sweden, and 9.6% in Germany.

In order to make room in the job market for younger workers, most European countries allow people to retire with full benefits at a much younger age than in the United States. This is costly, however, because retirees will be collecting pensions for a longer period of time. European government expenses for retirement pensions are also much higher, costing an average of 10% of the GDP compared to 5% in the United States. Another way that some countries are trying to provide more jobs is by reducing the number of hours in the average work week.

Health care in most European countries is generally provided by the government. Any citizen can get their medical needs attended to at taxpayer-financed hospitals or by government-employed doctors. These systems provide medical care at a lower overall cost than in the United States, but they are not as efficient, they do not offer the range of services, and people often need to wait a long time for nonemergency care.

Similar to the United States, education through high school is publicly funded, but in Europe most universities are also taxpayer financed. All qualified students are essentially entitled to a free university education, although admission standards are much tougher than they are in the States. On average, European countries spend 5.4% of their GDP on education, compared to 5.1% in the United States.

Economists often compare the two systems to automobiles—in Europe, everyone gets to drive a small Ford. In the United States, some people drive Cadillacs while

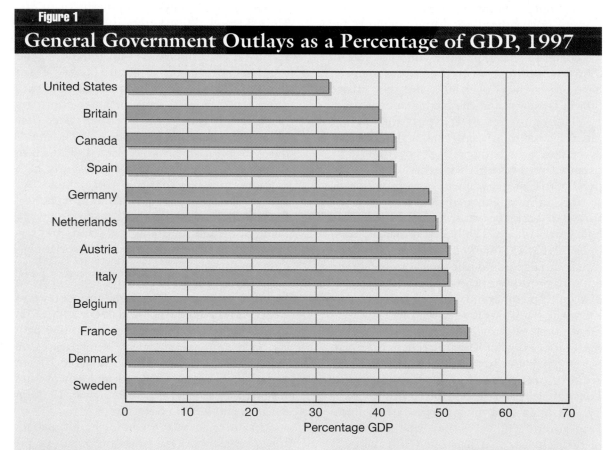

Figure 1

General Government Outlays as a Percentage of GDP, 1997

Although Americans are quick to complain about "Big Government," the size of government in the United States is significantly smaller than it is in most European countries.

Source: Economic Outlook, OECD, December 1997.

many do not have a car at all. It is a basic difference in philosophy. In the United States, the market system results in a wide disparity in income, health care, and education, but people have more opportunity to eventually own a Cadillac; in Europe, fewer people get the chance to own a Cadillac, although everybody gets to drive a car (Figure 1).

Chapter Preview

The role of government in a market economy is the subject of continuing debate. To understand the government's role in helping people, we will examine the following questions: What does the government do to reduce poverty? What does the government do to help older Americans? How does the government protect consumers and workers?

Learning Objectives

After completing this chapter, you should be able to:

1. Explain how poverty is defined.
2. Understand how income is distributed in the United States and why it is unequal.
3. Explain how rapid advances in technology can lead to a dual labor market.
4. Understand how income is distributed among people of different genders and different ethnic groups.
5. Describe different public assistance programs used to help the needy.
6. Explain the basic difference between public assistance and social insurance and the difference between public assistance and Social Security.
7. Understand the difference between Medicaid and Medicare.
8. Explain why the Social Security program is facing financial difficulties.
9. Explain how Social Security differs from private pension plans.
10. Understand how Social Security benefits are financed.
11. Understand the significance of the proposed changes to the Social Security system.
12. Understand how the government protects workers and consumers.

Table 1 — Income Distribution, 1967–1996
Money Income of Families
(Percentage distribution of total income)*

Year	Lowest Fifth	Second Fifth	Third Fifth	Fourth Fifth	Highest Fifth
1967	4.0	10.8	17.3	24.2	43.8
1970	4.1	11.1	17.5	24.4	42.8
1975	4.4	10.5	17.1	24.8	43.2
1980	4.3	10.3	16.9	24.9	43.7
1985	4.0	9.7	16.3	24.6	45.3
1990	3.9	9.6	15.9	24.0	46.6
1996	3.7	9.0	15.1	23.3	49.0
Average Class Income in 1996	$8,596	$21,097	$35,486	$54,922	$115,514

*Numbers may not add to 100% due to rounding
Source: *Statistical Abstract of the United States.*

What Does the Government Do to Reduce Poverty?

The dividing line between who is considered poor and who is not poor is called the **poverty line.** The line is defined in terms of income, and it varies depending on the number of people in a household and whether they live in a farm or nonfarm household. In 1996, the poverty line for a nonfarm family of four was an annual income of $15,911. Because poverty is defined in terms of income, it is useful to examine how income is distributed in the United States.

The Distribution of Income

One of the most important reasons that some people—the working poor—are poor is because although they work, their income is too meager to lift them out of poverty. Table 1 shows the **personal income distribution** in the United States according to five income classes for the years 1967–1996. Each class represents 20% of all income receivers, ranging from the 20% receiving the lowest incomes to the 20% receiving the highest incomes. The numbers in the table show the percentage of total income received by that group of income receivers. Comparing the percentage of total income received by the people in each fifth of the income scale, we can see the distribution of income in the United States between lower- and upper-income groups is very inequitable, and that it has become more so since 1980. (Note that the data in Table 1 refer to individual incomes while the poverty line cited above refers to a family of four, so it would not be correct to conclude that all the earners in the bottom quintile are below the poverty line.)

In 1996, the bottom 20% of income receivers earned 3.7% of total income, while the top 20% of income receivers earned 49.0% of total income. The lowest 40% of the population received 12.7% of the income, while the highest 40% received 72.3% of the income. Since 1975 the income distribution has become more unequal than at any time since the data have been published.

poverty line the family income level below which people are officially classified as poor.
personal income distribution the pattern of income distribution according to the relative size of people's income.

The highest fifth of income receivers have increased their share of income at the expense of all other families. Between 1975 and 1996 the share of total income going to the upper fifth of income receivers increased 5.8 percentage points while that going to the lowest two-fifths combined decreased 2.2 percentage points.

According to the 1997 Economic Report of the President, the most important factor contributing to inequality in earnings is technology. The reason for this is that employers in today's workplace have an increased demand for workers who understand and can work with technologically advanced machines and electronics, especially computers. As we saw in chapter 5, the wages of workers are determined by relative supply and demand. The greater the demand for certain skills and the lower the supply, the higher the income workers with that skill will command. On the other hand, workers without these skills are in much less demand, and they consequently earn much lower wages.

The differences in employee skills are largely due to differences in education, training, and ability. Workers with more of this "human capital" will be more productive, will be in greater demand, and will earn higher incomes. The falling share of income going to the bottom two-fifths of the population reflects the emergence of a **dual labor market** in the United States. A growing proportion of our population is simply being left behind without the education and skills necessary to earn a wage high enough to lift them out of poverty. For example, chapter 7 described the growing productivity of U.S. firms in the 1990s. Virtually all the gains in income associated with this productivity passed by those in the lowest income groups.

A lack of human capital may explain why the lower income groups have fallen behind since 1980, but it does not explain why the share going to the top 20% of the population increased so dramatically. The primary reason is that while there are wide differences in wages and salaries among different occupations, the greatest income variations result from differences in earnings from asset ownership—stocks, bonds, and real estate. Of those people with incomes of more than $1 million a year, the largest source of income, by far, is the **capital gains** on their assets. The second largest source of their incomes is dividends on stock. Salaries are only the third largest source of income for the nation's millionaires. The top quarter of households own over 80% of all stock, so the tremendous increase in the value of the stock market during the past decade fattened their wallets, while doing much less for those in the lower- and middle-income groups. Should the autumn 1998 stock market slide continue, many people will be hurt financially, but the biggest losses will be experienced by those who made the biggest profits.

While differences in human capital explain differences in income among various types of jobs, they do not explain disparities in income among diverse population groups. Men are not inherently more productive than women, yet according to Bureau of Labor Statistics figures for full-time workers, women earn only 75, 81, or 85 cents for every dollar paid to men, depending on whether they are Hispanic, black, or white, respectively. Nor are there any innate racial or ethnic productivity differences, but the median weekly earnings of white full-time workers in 1997 were $528, while black and Hispanic full-time workers earned only $410 and $354, respectively (Table 2).

A major objective of the Civil Rights Act of 1964, the Age Discrimination Act of 1967, and the Americans with Disabilities Act of 1990 was to remove obstacles to economic opportunity caused by racial, religious, sex,

dual labor market a labor force that is increasingly divided between high-skilled and low-skilled workers and jobs, with fewer and fewer workers or jobs in the middle.

capital gains net income realized from an increase in the market value of a real or financial asset when it is sold.

Table 2 — Differences in Opportunity and Earnings among Ethnic Groups in 1997

Ethnic Group	Percentage with 4 or More Years of College	Median Income
White	24.3%	$528
Males	26.9%	$608
Females	21.8%	$454
Black	13.6%	$410
Males	12.4%	$457
Females	14.6%	$371
Hispanic	9.3%	$354
Males	10.3%	$375
Females	8.3%	$317

Source: *Statistical Abstract of the United States.*

age, or disability discrimination. The actions of the Equal Employment Opportunity Commission (EEOC) have opened doors of increased opportunities that were previously closed to minorities, women, older people, and people with disabilities. Discriminatory attitudes and practices, however, cannot be easily reversed. Racism, sexism, and ageism have not been eliminated from society and its institutions. This is one reason for income inequality and poverty.

Lack of educational opportunities and motivations in the past is another explanation of current differences in earnings between population groups. Table 2 shows that a person's chances of having attended college depends on gender and ethnic background. White males are three times more likely to have completed college than Hispanic women. The gap is closing between males and females in educational attainment—in 1996, 36% of female high school graduates went on to college while only 33% of the male graduates did.

Perhaps the most important reason that some people are poor is that they are not able to work and earn an income. In contrast to the working poor, some people, notably female heads of households, cannot work because there simply are no decent jobs that they can fill. Even if jobs are available, the cost of child care is often out of their reach, and they cannot take jobs, even if they are available. Other people who cannot work include the homeless, older Americans, and those who are either physically or mentally disabled. Another nonworking group that is cruelly affected by poverty is our children—in 1996 one child in five in America lived in poverty.

Case Application

Created Equal, But . . .

When the 1964 Civil Rights Act made it illegal for employers to discriminate on the basis of race, religion, or sex, the focus of public attention was on the discrimination against black and other minority workers. The better-paying jobs were frequently open to white workers only. The median weekly earnings of black workers were only 70% as large as those of white workers. Since the passage of the Civil Rights Act, the income gap for black workers has been reduced from 30% less than white workers to 22% less. But the relative income of women was and still is the lowest of all; in 1997 it was only 75% that of white males.

In terms of family income rather than weekly earnings, which is a better measure of economic welfare, women are at an even greater disadvantage. Families with women as heads of the household have an average income that is only 60% as much as households headed by men. This compares with interracial and interethnic differences in family income: black families average 61% and Hispanic families 64% of the median income of white families. But the situation of women heads of households with children is the most desperate of all. Such families have a median income that is only 43% that of married-couple families with children.

The main reason for the low earnings of women is that women workers are concentrated in low-wage occupations. A study by the National Academy of Sciences has shown that the more an occupation is dominated by women, the less it tends to pay. Women constitute over 80% of the workforce in six of eight low-paying jobs: practical nurses, stitchers and sewers, child care workers, hairdressers, nurse's aides, and health care workers.

The most important reason for the slow growth of productivity in the 1980s was the low rate of productivity growth in the service industries—less than 1% a year. This was in part due to the availability of female labor to fill the low-paying jobs in that sector of the economy. Large numbers of women entered the labor force during the decade, increasing the labor force participation rate of women by 6 percentage points and adding some 15 million workers. The great majority of these new female workers went into service occupations.

The availability of this pool of cheap labor meant that service industries did not have to invest in new capital equipment to meet rising demand. In Western Europe and Japan, which did not have such a pool of cheap labor available, service companies invested heavily in new technology that resulted in productivity gains of 2% to 4% per year. The difference in productivity growth between other industrialized countries and the United States has left the United States at a disadvantage in global competition. Substandard pay for women is not only a hardship for them, but a drag on the economy as well.

Economic Reasoning

1. In which income classes of Table 1 (see p. 232) would you expect to find an unusually large proportion of women?
2. Considering the causes of income inequality, why do women predominate in six of the eight low-paying jobs?
3. Do you think that affirmative action in the hiring and promotion of women and minorities is a good idea? Why or why not?

Created Equal, But . . .

Visit the U.S. Bureau of the Census at http://www.census.gov/hhes/www/income96.html and go to the latest report on Money Income in the United States. Compare the income percentages in the latest year available to the percentages reported here. Have things become more or less equal for white, black, Hispanic, and female-headed households?

▶ What Is the Answer to Poverty?

As we have seen, an unequal distribution of income can be the result of a variety of causes. The result for those at the bottom of the income distribution ladder is poverty. Policies used to alleviate poverty include increased opportunity and transfer payments.

The antipoverty programs initiated by the Johnson administration in 1965 and expanded under following administrations reduced the absolute number of people living in poverty from 40 million in 1960 to a low of 23 million in 1973, and the percentage of the population from 22.2% in 1960 to 11.1% in 1973. This was accomplished in part by equal employment opportunities and **affirmative action programs** in government and private employment, and by government-funded jobs for the hard-core unemployed.

affirmative action program a program devised by employers to increase their hiring of women and minorities; frequently mandated by government regulations.

transfer payments expenditures for which no goods or services are exchanged. Welfare, Social Security, and unemployment compensation are government transfer payments.

Reductions in federal government funding for the antipoverty programs in the 1980s, decreases in work training opportunities, state court challenges to affirmative action programs, and elimination of day care centers, which had given mothers of young children more opportunity to work, slowed progress on increasing opportunities for economically disadvantaged groups. By 1996, the number of people below the poverty line had increased to 36.3 million, or 13.7% of the population.

What Is the Answer to Poverty?

EconExplorer

Providing increased employment and educational opportunities is one way of raising people out of poverty. But this approach misses many of those currently in need. A more direct method of assisting those living in poverty is **transfer payments.** Government transfer payments to low-income households are subsidies paid out of tax receipts to supplement the income of impoverished families. These transfers include money payments, such as **public assistance** for the poor, Social Security benefits for the aged, blind, and disabled, and unemployment compensation for those who lose their jobs. Many of these programs are referred to as **entitlement programs** because all those who meet certain income or other criteria are legally entitled to their benefits.

Up until 1997, the largest transfer program for the poor was Aid to Families with Dependent Children (AFDC). This program was developed to provide income maintenance and social services for that most needy of all groups, families below the poverty line with women heads of household. It was provided by the states, but each dollar spent by the states was matched with one to four federal dollars, depending on the wealth of the state. The Personal Responsibility and Work Opportunities Reconciliation Act of 1996 (or simply the Welfare Reform Act) replaced AFDC with **Temporary Assistance for Needy Families (TANF)**.

TANF differs from AFDC in three ways. First, unlike AFDC, which put no cap on the amount that the federal government would provide, TANF is financed with federal block grants to the states. The state can supplement the grant with its own tax revenues to provide more benefits, or it can spend less than the grant amount and use the balance for other public assistance programs. Second, there is a 5-year limit for receiving assistance, although exceptions can be made in certain cases. Third, an adult member of a family receiving TANF funds must either work or perform community service.

The TANF program is a form of what many people refer to as **workfare.** Workfare refers to programs that require public assistance recipients to "work" for the public assistance they receive. Several states adopted such programs under the AFDC program, though recipients who were unable to work or had preschool children were typically exempt from the requirements.

The idea behind workfare is to help people learn job skills and to help move people off the welfare rolls and into the workforce. Those people who cannot work because they are aged, blind, or disabled in some other

The Food Stamp Program, one of the government's largest transfer payment programs, enables low-income persons to buy more groceries.

way can qualify for **Supplementary Security Income (SSI).** Unlike TANF, which is funded through general government revenues, SSI is funded through the disability trust fund of a separate entity, the Social Security Administration.

---

public assistance government aid to needy families.

entitlement program government benefits that qualified recipients are entitled to by law, such as Social Security old-age benefits.

Temporary Assistance for Needy Families (TANF) a federally subsidized public assistance program that provides income to needy families for a limited period of eligibility.

workfare originally a program that required nonexempt welfare recipients to work at public service jobs for a given number of hours a month; now it may also include job training and wage subsidies.

Supplementary Security Income (SSI) a federal government transfer program designed especially to help poor people who are aged, blind, or otherwise disabled.

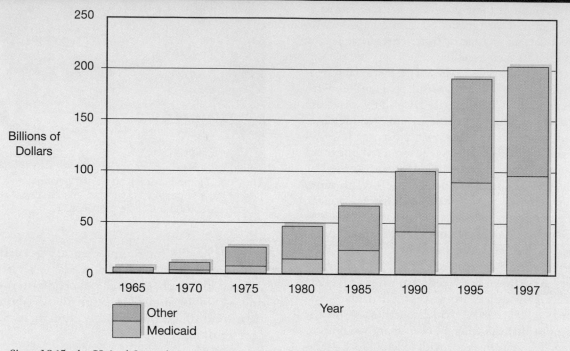

Figure 2

The Growth of Medicaid and Other Public Assistance, 1965–1997

Billions of Dollars

Other
Medicaid

Year

Since 1965, the United States has spent increasing amounts to help lift needy families out of poverty. Much of the increased cost of public assistance is due to the rising cost of health care.

Source: Congressional Budget Office.

The **earned income tax credit (EITC)** is a type of negative income tax for the working poor, who comprise 60% of all those in poverty. It was originally instituted in 1975 as a way to offset the federal tax liabilities of the poor. If a person's income is below a certain level, they receive tax credits from the government. As their incomes increase, the credits decrease until they reach a level of income where they are phased out. Succeeding tax bills have increased the maximum amount of the tax credit and provided an adjustment for inflation. As a result, many low-income families are entitled to credits that exceed their tax liabilities.

Instead of providing monetary transfers, other programs help to alleviate poverty by providing specific types of goods to supplement the cash income of the poor (Figure 2). One of the largest such programs is federally financed **food stamps.** The Food Stamp program was authorized by Congress in 1964 with the stated goal of helping low-income households obtain more balanced and nutritious diets. Stamps that can be used to purchase

earned income tax credit (EITC) a federal tax credit for poor families with earnings that offsets their tax liabilities and, for the poorest, provides an income subsidy.

food stamps certificates that can be used in place of money to purchase food items.

(Continued on page 241)

Case Application

The Rich Get Richer and the Poor Get Ketchup

Income distribution has become more unequal in the last decade, as shown in Table 1 on page 232. When we adjust for inflation, families in the lowest 20% of income receivers have virtually the same purchasing power now as they did in 1980. After adjusting for inflation, the average income in the lowest quintile increased from $8,547 in 1980 to $8,596 in 1996. A typical family in the top 20%, by contrast, has seen its real earnings rise from $87,797 to $115,514—a 32% gain.

These average figures for income classes do not show the income changes that particular subgroups have experienced, which in many cases are even more inequitable. Racial and ethnic minorities are disproportionately represented among those people below the poverty threshold. Almost 30% of the black population is classified as poor. The incidence of poverty among minorities in general is two to three times that of the white population. Families with black female householders have the highest incidence of poverty, with more than one-half of such families below the poverty level.

Because of the low average earnings of women, families exclusively dependent on the income of a female householder constitute over half of the families below the poverty line, although such families are only 10% of the population. Looked at another way, nearly a third of all female-headed households are poor. One child in five lives in poverty. Two out of every five black and Hispanic children live below the poverty level. The younger the children, the more likely they are to be poor: half of all black children under the age of 6 live in poverty. Children are now the poorest age group in the country, having displaced the elderly from this unfavorable distinction as far back as 1974,

when 15% of children were below the poverty level. Since then their economic position has deteriorated further, and now over 20% are living in poverty.

The one group that has seen significant improvement in their status is older Americans. Primarily due to increases in Social Security benefits, the percentage of the elderly that live in poverty has been reduced from about 35% in 1959 to just under 11% in 1996.

Families headed by people under 30 have been especially hard hit by the changes in income distribution. Their poverty rate has doubled in the last two decades, foreshadowing a continuation of this problem well into the future. Poverty tends to reproduce itself, creating a self-perpetuating underclass. For example, 36% of girls from welfare families end up on welfare in later years themselves, compared to 9% from nonwelfare families.

A congressional analysis of the causes of the increase in poverty found that nearly one-half of the increase was attributable to cutbacks in state and federal aid. Decreased funding for anti-poverty programs during the 1980s affected the range of antipoverty programs. Living stipends paid to welfare families with children fell 35% below the 1970 level, adjusted for inflation. A million people were eliminated from the food stamp program. Two million children were dropped from eligibility for school lunches. One cutback was reversed, however, by public reaction. There was an attempt to save money on the school lunch program by classifying ketchup as a vegetable in satisfying nutritional requirements, since ketchup was cheaper than a serving of a vegetable. The public outcry over this instance of government economizing at the expense of children's health forced a cancellation of the change.

1. What group experienced the largest increase between 1969 and 1996 in the percentage of the group living below the poverty line? Approximately how many percentage points was the increase?
2. How do government programs such as the school lunch program increase opportunities for rising out of poverty?
3. Do you think women receiving TANF should be required to participate in workfare? Why or why not?

The Rich Get Richer and the Poor Get Ketchup

Visit the U.S. Bureau of the Census Web site at http://www.census.gov/hhes/www/poverty.html and update the poverty statistics given here. Are there any other interesting facts that help you better understand the distribution of poverty in the United States?

Figure 3

The Incidence of Poverty in the United States (Selected years)

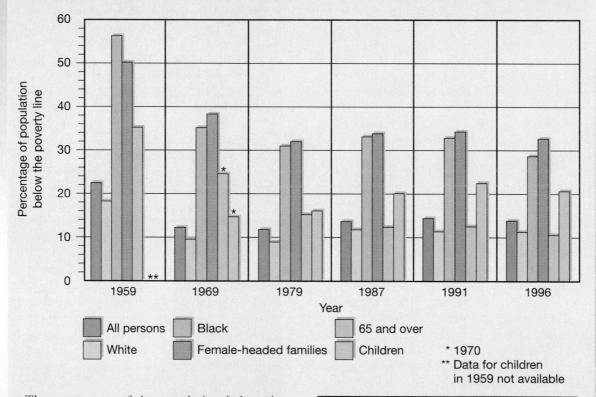

The percentage of the population below the poverty line is lower now than it was in 1959, but it has been increasing in the 1980s and 1990s. Since 1969, female-headed families have consistently been the poorest identifiable group in the United States.

Source: U.S. Bureau of the Census, *Current Population Reports.*

food vary in cost depending on the income of the recipient. For example, a person might be able to buy $100 of food stamps for $50. The program is administered by the Department of Agriculture through state and local welfare offices. Many cities also have federally funded programs that provide hot meals to the elderly each day. In order to ensure nutrition for the young, schoolchildren of low-income families are provided free or discounted lunches and, in some cases, breakfasts. Nutritional assistance for young children is also available through the Women, Infants, and Children (WIC) program.

Medicaid is a federally financed program to provide adequate health care for low-income families. With the rising cost of health care, this has been one of the fastest-growing expenditures of all federal programs. The federal government also provides housing assistance to low-income families. Some programs provide housing at subsidized rental rates in apartment buildings owned and operated by the government, and others provide rent vouchers that can be applied toward the monthly rent of a privately owned unit. Most aid for housing is funded through the U.S. Department of Housing and Urban Development (HUD).

In 1997, the federal expenditures for public assistance programs totaled $202.8 billion, or 2.5% of the nation's income. This represents a tremendous increase from 1965, when the expenditures of $5.2 billion were only 0.8% of total income. As shown in Figure 2, most of this increased spending has been for Medicaid—which now accounts for nearly half of all public assistance costs.

Transfer payments substantially reduce the portion of the nation that is poverty stricken. Without antipoverty transfer payments and nonmonetary benefits, the poverty rate would be nearly twice as high and many would be unable to obtain needed medical care. While few can dispute the necessity of transfer payments to aid the aged, blind, and disabled, poverty programs have often been criticized for creating disincentives to work and for creating a class of long-term welfare dependents. Long-term solutions to poverty such as increased education and opportunities are essential for those who are able to work. If, however, it is necessary in the short run to assist some people who can work through the use of transfers, it is also necessary to do so in a way that does not provide them with incentives to remain dependent on public assistance.

▶ What Does the Government Do to Help Older Americans?

◆ Social Security

Unlike public assistance, **Social Security** is a **social insurance** program designed to keep older Americans from falling into poverty. Is the system going broke? Will there be any money left to pay retirement benefits to the young workers who are contributing to the system now? These are troublesome but important questions because, since the passage of the Social Security Act in 1935, the Social Security system has become the cornerstone of our country's method of providing economic security to older Americans. With expenditures on retirement benefits of $362 billion in 1997, or 4.5% of the nation's total income, it also represents the largest single item in the government's budget.

Medicaid a federally subsidized, state-administered program to pay for medical and hospital costs of low-income families.

Social Security The Old Age, Survivors, Disability and Health Insurance (OASDHI) program established by the Social Security Act of 1935. Its purpose is to provide retirement and health benefits to the elderly, and public assistance to the aged, blind, and disabled poor.

social insurance government programs designed to maintain people's incomes so that they do not fall into poverty.

There are actually four separate **trust funds** under the Social Security program, which is officially known as Old Age, Survivors, Disability, and Health Insurance (OASDHI). The principal fund pays *retirement benefits* to those who are past retirement age or to their survivors, and a second fund provides *disability payments* to those who are unable to work any longer for physical or psychological reasons, although they have not reached retirement age. The other two funds are for *hospital* and *supplementary medical* care for older people—the **Medicare** program.

People qualify to collect Social Security benefits by contributing to the trust funds during their working years. OASDHI is financed by a **payroll tax.** In 1935, the tax was 2% of income on the first $3,000 earned. Today, the employee portion of the tax is 7.65% of earnings up to an income of $62,700 (although this is increased frequently). Each employer also contributes 7.65%, for a total tax of 15.3% of each dollar earned. Of this, 12.4% is used to fund old age, survivor, and disability benefits, and the balance is used to fund Medicare.

Unlike private pension plans, the Social Security system does not pay benefits out of returns on investments made with an individual's contributions to the fund. Instead, the current contributions of workers pay the benefits to present retirees. This system worked very well during the time that the labor force was expanding more rapidly than the number of people collecting benefits. But since 1950, the ratio of workers to retirees has been steadily declining, and retirees are living and collecting benefits longer. In 1950 there were 16 workers paying Social Security taxes for every person collecting retirement benefits. By 1960 the ratio had been reduced to 5 to 1. Today it is just over 3 to 1. When the baby boom generation (those born between 1946 and 1961) reaches retirement age, the ratio is expected to decline to only two workers for each retiree.

Also unlike private pension plans, Social Security is a transfer program. Instead of being directly related to contributions, the ratio of benefits to tax contributions is greater for lower-income households than for more affluent households. People who contribute more during their working lives receive more benefits than others, but the benefits are not in proportion to contributions. Conversely, those with lower lifetime earnings can expect benefits that are proportionately greater than their contributions.

In 1967, nearly a third of the country's retirees were below the poverty level and, for many, their Social Security checks were their primary source of income. By increasing benefit levels and skewing them toward those with lower incomes, the poverty rate among older Americans was cut in half. Benefits, however, which averaged about $8,000 per year in 1997, still make up 80% of household income for those in the lowest-two income quintiles of the elderly.

Due to demographics and increased benefits, the funds—especially the retirement fund—were nearing exhaustion in the early 1980s. To rescue the funds from running out of money, Congress enacted legislation in 1983 that increased Social Security revenues and reduced benefits. The bill accelerated scheduled increases in payroll taxes, raised the tax rate on the self-employed, and subjected some Social Security retirement benefits to income taxation. On the side of benefits, the most important change was to delay from 65 to 67 the age at which workers could retire with full benefits. That change will not come into effect until the year 2000, when it will be phased in gradually up to the year 2027.

Social Security Trust Funds the Social Security funds that are by law reserved for specific uses.

Medicare the health and medical care program for older Americans that is funded through one of the Social Security Trust Funds.

payroll tax a tax levied on wages and salary but not on other forms of income, such as interest, dividends, or capital gains.

Other benefit changes include a reduction in the percentage of benefits received by those who retire early, also effective at the turn of the century.

Based on the estimates at that time, those reforms were assumed to take care of the financing of the retirement fund until about the year 2020, when the large number of retiring baby boomers would necessitate additional revenue or cutbacks in benefits. They did result in the trust funds generating huge surpluses beginning in the 1990s, but the estimates were overly optimistic. More realistic data on fertility rates, life expectancies, interest rates, and the performance of the economy show that, with the present financing system, the retirement trust fund is still going to run short unless something is done. Current projections are that benefit payments will exceed contributions by 2013, and that by 2030 the accumulated surpluses in the funds will be used up.

To continue benefits at their present levels after that time might require Social Security tax rates of 35% or more. This would probably not be politically acceptable. Even now there is discussion of an emerging intergenerational conflict. An average couple retiring now at age 65 can expect cash "benefits worth over three times the amount they and their employer put in, interest included." The same couple retiring in 2025 would get only about 1.75 times the original investment. And most young people starting work now can expect to collect less than they contribute over their working lifetimes.

Medicare is in even greater financial difficulty, and its fund will be exhausted early in the twenty-first century unless action is taken. Earlier cost-containment measures imposed on hospitals and doctors and higher Medicare patient deductibles failed to stop the hemorrhaging. Medicare expenditures grew from $34 billion dollars in 1980, to $108 billion in 1990, and to $208 billion in 1997. This was one of the considerations driving the national movement for health care reform in the mid-1990s.

The idea that the Social Security trust funds are accumulating surpluses now to pay for benefits in the future is something of a fiction. The surpluses are in fact used to help the government to balance the federal budget, because the Social Security accounts are included in the government's overall budget. The government borrows from the trust funds in the same way it borrows from others—by selling them Treasury bonds. By law, the reserves of the funds can be used only to purchase U.S. government securities. The Social Security surpluses thus reduce the government's need to go into the private capital market to finance its deficit. But the government is obligated to repay the funds borrowed, and the total assets of the funds remain intact—although it will require increased future general tax revenues to pay back what the government borrowed.

The goods and services consumed by Social Security recipients are always provided from current real production, whatever the funding system. This has to be the case because every year total consumption must be equal to total production, except for inventory changes and net foreign trade. The present generation cannot produce the goods and services for its later consumption, that is, when it retires. The idea is ridiculous; there could never be enough warehouses built in which to keep the output for later consumption. Therefore, the consumption of retirees will always be provided for by the output of the current labor force. The problem is to make the financing of the transfer as equitable as possible.

◪ Social Security Reform

Every 4 years, a Social Security Advisory Council is appointed to study the Social Security system, to evaluate its financial soundness, and to recommend any changes that the committee feels are needed. The last committee report was issued in 1994, and three different proposals were offered to deal with what is believed to be a long-run funding problem for the retirement portion of the system. All would require universal participation (currently federal and many state employees are not part of the system), all would maintain the disability and transfer payment aspects of the program, and all would increase the retirement age and raise taxes on Social Security benefit checks. There are, however, significant differences in the proposals.

What Does the Government Do to Help Older Americans?

EconExplorer

The most modest suggested change is to raise payroll taxes slightly (2 percentage points) to meet future obligations. In a radical departure from the past, however, the plan recommends putting 40% of the payroll tax receipts into private capital markets—stocks and corporate bonds. Over the years, the return on stocks has exceeded the return on government bonds, and if this trend continues, the fund will earn more income with which to pay benefits.

With the first proposal, the system will remain a **defined benefits** program, and retirees will continue to receive a specified monthly amount of Social Security income each month, depending on how much they contributed to

the system and their financial situation; benefits will still be skewed toward those with lower incomes.

The second proposal is to reduce benefits by extending the retirement age and to increase revenues by increasing the payroll tax by between 1 and 2 percentage points. These extra tax revenues, however, would go into the individual's own private retirement account. The money in these accounts would be held by the Social Security Administration, but individuals would have a little discretion about where the money is invested—most likely specially approved bond and stock market funds. A minimum level of income will still be guaranteed, but total income will vary a little according to the level of private returns.

A third proposal is the most radical of all. It would reduce payroll tax contributions to the trust funds, but would require that an equal contribution be made to a private retirement account to be held and managed, within limits, by the individual in a personal security account (PSA). The PSA would be very similar to the current **individual retirement account (IRA).** There would still be a basic minimum monthly benefit paid from the now-reduced contribution to the trust fund, but most retirement income would be expected to come from individual PSAs. Such a switch would make Social Security more of a **defined contributions retirement plan.** It would also go a long way toward privatizing a large portion of Social Security.

A move toward privatizing the Social Security system, allowing participants more control over their retirement accounts, and allowing money to be invested in stocks rather than only government bonds, is a two-edged sword. On the one hand, if the stock market continues to earn more than government bonds, and people invest wisely, their retirement incomes will be greater and Social Security will not go broke trying to maintain defined benefit levels. On the other hand, if the stock market does poorly, or if people do not make wise investment choices, they may be at increased risk of falling into poverty, and all the redistribution gains made in the last 30 years will be lost.

defined benefits retirement plan a pension plan that guarantees participants a specified level of income when they retire, regardless of how much they contributed to the plan.

individual retirement account (IRA) a private savings account that is given special tax treatment as long as funds are not withdrawn before retirement.

defined contributions retirement plan a retirement plan that requires participants to contribute a specific amount of income, with retirement benefits to be determined by the amount contributed plus earnings on the contributions.

Case Application

Depending on the Next Generation

Young or old, we all need to eat, and most of us must work to earn our daily bread. Many of us, however, don't. In fact, today in the United States, 35% of the population gets to eat without working! Who are these "freeloaders"? They are the people younger than 15 and older than 65. The former group does not have to work because they are cared for by their parents or guardians. The latter group consists of retirees or pensioners, people who once worked but have retired from the workforce and receive incomes from past savings and from social insurance programs—Social Security in the United States.

The ratio of the number of people who do not work (under 16 and over 65) to the number of workers is called the *dependency ratio*, and the ratio of those over 65 to the number of workers is called the *elderly dependency ratio (EDR)*. In the United States, 22% of the population is under 15, 13% is over 65, and 65% are of working age. The dependency ratio is (22% + 13%)/65%, or 54% and the EDR is 13%/65%, or 20%.[1]

It is obvious that the greater the dependency ratio, the tougher it is for current workers to support everyone. The demographic facts are that people in the United States and Western Europe are living longer and having fewer children. This is going to lead to an increased EDR, which is the fundamental problem facing

social insurance programs. By 2030, the EDR in the United States will be around 32%. But as bad as this might be, the countries of Western Europe are going to have it worse. The 12 countries with the oldest populations in the world are all in Western Europe, and these countries also have some of the world's lowest birthrates. Current EDRs in Europe range from 21% in the Netherlands to 27% in Sweden. By 2030, demographers estimate that the EDR will reach 40% in Europe (46% in Germany)! Social insurance accounted for nearly half of all European government spending in 1998, and unless the systems are changed dramatically, this amount will necessarily increase.

The products that retirees need to live are produced by the land, labor, and capital that are in use at that time. To claim a share of the economy's output in a market economy, they therefore need to own a share of those resources. If they had saved a sufficient amount of money during their working years, then they would own a share of the economy's land or capital stock. This occurs when retirees receive their income from pension funds that are invested in corporate stocks or from real estate investments. Alternatively, had they loaned their money by buying bonds or putting their money in banks, today's retirees would be receiving the interest on the loans used to buy the land and capital.

But what if retirees did not save enough, and now own too few financial resources to support themselves? Social insurance, first established in Germany in 1891, presumes that a society is responsible for taking care of its retirees and ensuring that they receive adequate

---

[1]These figures refer only to the ages of the population, not to those who do and do not receive or pay into the Social Security system. The figures in the text differ because they refer to the actual numbers of participants.

health care and do not fall into poverty, even if they do not own enough capital (or land) resources to support themselves. If retirees cannot rely on capital resources for their income, the only alternative is to rely on labor resources. Although they cannot "own" today's workers, the government has the power through taxation to take some of these workers' earnings and use them to support the retirees. This is the basic idea behind a social insurance program funded through the use of payroll taxes.

In essence, there is a "social contract" between workers and retirees that the former will give up some of their earnings to support the latter, especially those who did not save enough to support themselves. It is scary to think how high taxes are going to have to be in order to compensate for the rising EDRs. In fact, many of the people who will be retired in 2030 are beginning to wonder if the people who are working then might just vote to cancel the contract because they find it too expensive. (You should, however, be aware of one further thing: people who are retired have a lot of time on their hands and a large percentage of them vote.)

Not so long ago, it was very common for extended families, including grandparents, to live together. The widespread adoption of the social contract implicit in social insurance in the twentieth century replaced a "family contract." In earlier years, if people survived beyond their working years, they were usually supported by their children. This was a big "if." When Bismarck established social insurance in Germany, the average life expectancy was 45 years and the qualifying retirement age was 65. Today, German life expectancy is 76 years, but the qualifying retirement age has not changed.

Most less developed countries do not have social insurance programs, and if they do, they are usually not sufficient to keep retirees out of poverty. In these countries the family contract remains the primary means of support for those who can no longer work. This is one of the reasons why these countries continue to have higher birthrates than the developed countries. Although lower birthrates and longer life expectancies might be desirable goals in these countries, they threaten the ability of those who work to support those who cannot.

Economic Reasoning

1. How are social insurance taxes affected by the elderly dependency ratio?

2. How will the amount of savings by one generation affect the productivity and earnings of the following generation?

3. Do retired citizens have a right to expect following generations to support them if they did not or were not able to save enough to support themselves in their retirement?

Depending on the Next Generation

Visit the Social Security Web site at www.ssa.gov and go to the Benefits Payments window. Click on the current year's Benefit/Tax Changes and calculate how much tax you would owe if you earned $50,000. If you earned $200,000? What percentage of your income would be paid to Social Security in each case?

What Is the Role of Government in Protecting Consumers and Workers?

Our government does not just assist and protect the poor and the elderly; it is actively involved in protecting all of us in many ways. Beginning in the 1960s, there has been a large increase in government involvement in the welfare of consumers and workers. The activities of the government in these respects are discussed in this section.

Consumer Protection

As civilized society has developed, the dangers we face have become more of our own making than from nature—poisonous chemicals, polluted air, automobile accidents, and defective products are some. And as the nature of the dangers has changed, so has the way we respond. We have increasingly looked to government to protect us from manmade dangers from which we feel incapable of protecting ourselves. Our problem is a lack of information about all the products businesses are trying to sell us, and without this information the market system fails because we will not always make well-informed decisions.

One dangerous place in modern society is the highway. Around 40,000 people are killed in automobile accidents in the United States each year. In order to reduce the death and injury rate, the Department of Transportation (DOT) has required automobile manufacturers to provide certain safety features, such as seat belts, air bags, and secure fuel tanks. The DOT conducts crash tests on new car models to determine which ones give the passengers the most protection.

One of the most important government agencies dealing with product safety is the Food and Drug Administration (FDA). If foods or medicines are found to be unsafe, the FDA has

The U.S. Department of Transportation conducts crash tests, such as this, to evaluate automobile safety, in response to increasing consumer concerns. This is one example of how consumer protection has become a function of government.

Table 3 — Selected Government Regulatory Agencies

Agency	Year Created	Regulates
Agencies that regulate specific industries:		
Interstate Commerce Commission (ICC)	1887	Railroads, trucking, pipelines, barges, express carriers
Food and Drug Administration (FDA)	1906	Food, drugs, cosmetics
Federal Reserve Board (FRB)	1913	Banks
Federal Power Commission (FPC)	1930	Public utilities
Federal Communications Commission (FCC)	1934	Radio, television, telephone, telegraph
Federal Aviation Administration (FAA)	1967	Airline safety
National Highway Traffic Safety Administration (NHTSA)	1970	Motor vehicles
Nuclear Regulatory Commission (NRC)	1975	Nuclear power plants
Agencies that regulate specific functions:		
Federal Trade Commission (FTC)	1914	Unfair business practices
Securities and Exchange Commission (SEC)	1934	Sales of securities
National Labor Relations Board (NLRB)	1935	Labor-management relations
Equal Employment Opportunity Commission (EEOC)	1964	Hiring practices
Environmental Protection Agency (EPA)	1970	Pollution of the environment
Occupational Safety and Health Administration (OSHA)	1971	Conditions in workplaces
Consumer Product Safety Commission (CPSC)	1972	Design and labeling of goods

the power to order them off the market. The agency conducts tests on prepared foods to find out if any of the ingredients are cancer-causing. No new drugs may be put on the market without the FDA's approval. It also establishes regulations regarding the production of foods to minimize the risks of consumers coming in contact with disease-causing agents such as *E. coli* and salmonella.

Another federal agency concerned with consumer safety is the Consumer Product Safety Commission (CPSC). It has issued a recall of asbestos-insulated hair dryers, put an end to the use of benzene in paint removers, banned the use of Tris (a cancer-causing flame retardant in children's clothing), and required that slats on baby cribs be set close together to prevent strangulation.

There are government agencies not only to protect our health, but to protect our pocketbooks. The Federal Trade Commission (FTC) tries to prevent deceptive advertising. It has made producers of aspirin pills, low fat and "lite" food products, toothpastes, mouthwashes, and numerous other products either prove their claims or change their advertisements.

To protect the interests of investors and provide more stability to the financial markets, the Securities and Exchange Commission (SEC) was set up in 1934 to regulate the stock market. It requires full disclosure of a company's financial condition when new stock is issued, and this has helped eliminate stock swindles.

What Is the Role of Government in Protecting Consumers and Workers?

EconExplorer

In recent years there has been legislation requiring financial institutions and companies extending credit to provide the borrower with complete information about the true interest charges and payment conditions. In some states, customers are allowed to cancel certain kinds of purchase contracts within a few days after signing them. Some of the types of contracts that

Figure 4

Death and Injury Rates on the Job, 1960–1995

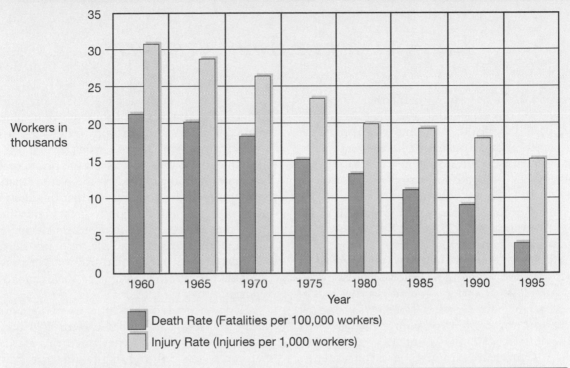

Death Rate (Fatalities per 100,000 workers)

Injury Rate (Injuries per 1,000 workers)

The rates of worker fatalities and disabling injuries have been steadily decreasing, especially since the establishment of the Occupational Safety and Health Administration in 1971.

Source: National Safety Council, *Accident Facts*.

can be canceled are land purchases in undeveloped land promotions and contracts signed with door-to-door salespeople. These laws are designed to protect consumers from being manipulated into hasty, unwise decisions by high-pressure sales techniques.

◪ Worker Protection

About 5,300 workers were killed on the job in 1995, and 3.6 million suffered disabling injuries. As high as these figures are, they are much lower than they were in the 1960s, despite a near doubling of the size of the labor force.

Improved safety on the job is credited at least in part to the establishment of the Occupational Safety and Health Administration (OSHA) in 1971. The Occupational Safety and Health Act gave OSHA, in the Department of Labor, the power and responsibility to set standards for the workplace to protect workers from work-caused injury and illness. Since 1970, the year before OSHA was established, the rate of job fatalities has been cut by more than half, and disabling injuries have declined from 26 to 15 for every thousand workers during the year. The improvement in the rates of workplace casualties is even greater than the data indicates, due to more complete reporting of casualties now than earlier (Figure 4).

OSHA regulations and plant inspections, however, have been vigorously opposed by some businesses. It has been claimed that OSHA regulations cost industry too much, that they drive some companies out of business, and that they make competition with imports difficult because

(Continued on page 251)

Case Application

Taking Cookies from Strangers

After a long day of surfing the Internet, chances are that you do not remember all the places you have been and all the Web sites you visited—but someone can. You might have given your name and e-mail address to gain access to a specific site, but did that information go to anyone else? And if it did, should you care?

Many people do care about privacy on the Net. According to a March 1998 survey by *BusinessWeek,* privacy is the most important issue that is keeping some users out of cyberspace, far ahead of other issues such as cost and complexity. Concerns include worries that others might have access to your personal information, the content of your e-mail, what sites you visit, and what purchases you make online. Cybernauts are also very concerned about the security of using their credit cards to make online purchases. According to the survey, 65% of online users are "very concerned" about giving out their credit card information over the Net, while only 56% are concerned about giving it out when catalog shopping over the telephone.

Other than the obvious fears of someone stealing and using their credit card information, why are people so concerned? One reason is familiar to anyone who goes to their mailbox and finds tons of junk mail. By knowing your e-mail address and where you go on the Net, marketers can target you with electronic junk mail advertisements that you may not want to find when you open your e-mail mailbox. America Online upset many of its subscribers when it offered information on all of them to other businesses that planned to use it for electronic telemarketing purposes. Companies such as IMGIS Inc. and Interactions Corp. are in the business of helping other companies gather and sort consumer information that they collected electronically.

Some in the industry defend the practice of using information gathered on the Net for marketing purposes by pointing out that this allows them to provide information to users about the things they are interested in, instead of sending them random advertising. True, respond users, but most say that they would like to have a say in whether or not they are put on such "e-mailing lists."

Even more troublesome to many Net users is the way that companies with Web sites use "clickstream" data that trace the places that users visit online and the ads that they "click" on. This is done through the use of "cookies," small data files that Web sites place on the *user's* hard drive the first time that the user visits a site. The cookie then collects data on the number of times that the user returns to the site and delivers it to the Web site's server. The information can then be used to target products or content to the Internet user.

To date, the Web remains one of the country's few unregulated communications networks, but this may not last much longer. The federal government is giving the Internet industry time to police itself and come up with its own voluntary system to protect user privacy, but if the Internet does not comply, the government is threatening to add cyberspace to the realm of regulated industries. The Federal Trade Commission is due to issue a report on the issue late in summer 1998. Surprisingly, since cybernauts tend to be promarket and antigovernment, 53% of those surveyed by *BusinessWeek* believed that the government should act right away to ensure Internet privacy.

One way that Web users can police themselves is to post notices at their sites that explain how personal information is used, and to give site visitors the option of having or not having this information given to others. In preparing its report, the FTC is randomly visiting 1,200 sites to see how many post privacy notices. Another way is to get a "trustmark" from TRUSTe, a nonprofit organization that makes sure that the Web site adheres to acceptable industry standards. A cybernaut visiting a Web site can see if the trustmark is displayed, and then make his or her decision about checking out the ads or buying anything at that site.

the increased costs must be reflected in higher prices. The American Textile Manufacturers Institute and 12 textile companies filed suit to overturn OSHA standards requiring mills to reduce cotton dust levels. Cotton dust causes brown lung disease among the workers. The textile firms maintained that the air filtration systems needed to meet the standards would impose unreasonable costs on the firms. But the Supreme Court rejected the arguments of the textile industry. The Court held that the law required only that the needed safety measures be "feasible," not that they meet cost-benefit criteria; and therefore the textile plants were required to install the filtration equipment.

While no one doubts that government regulations save lives, there is controversy about the cost-effectiveness of these regulations. A 1995 study by T. O. Tengs estimated the median cost per life saved by different government regulating agencies. The costs ranged from a low of $23,000 per life by the Federal Aviation Administration to $68,000 for the Consumer Product Safety Commission, to $88,000 for OSHA to $7,600,000 per life by the Environmental Protection Agency.[1] These figures suggest that while we do not abandon regulations that guard our safety, we should be trying to do so in a cost-effective manner. For example, the marketable emission permits discussed in chapter 8 represent a way to maintain our goal of a safe environment in a more economically efficient manner.

OSHA is prevented from regulating the greater part of the second most dangerous industry of all—farming—where the annual death rate is 21 per 100,000 workers, exceeded only by mining (25) and ahead of construction (15). By comparison, the death rate in manufacturing is only 3 per 100,000. More than 95% of all farms are off-limits to OSHA inspectors. Nor does the government do much to inform farmers of the dangers a farm family faces in operating machinery and using chemicals. It spends only 30 cents a year per farmer on safety education, while at the same time spending $4.48 per worker in industry and $244 per mine worker.

[1]Source: Tengs, T. O., et al., Five Hundred Life-Saving Interventions and Their Cost-Effectiveness. *Risk Analysis* (15) (1995). pp. 369–390.

◄ Putting It Together

Our government is involved in our daily lives in more ways than we often realize. It is involved in helping the poor, the elderly, and consumers and workers throughout the economy.

The most common criteria used to determine if families are poor is the *poverty line,* which varies according to family size and whether or not the family lives on a farm. Because poverty is defined in terms of income, it is helpful to analyze the *personal distribution of income* by quintiles to better understand exactly how unequal the distribution is in the United States. Since 1975, the income gap between rich and poor has grown continuously.

Rapid changes in technology and the gaps in the labor force's education levels have contributed to the emergence of a *dual labor market* where those without essential skills are being left farther and farther behind. While this might explain why the poorer segments of the population are losing ground, it does not explain why the highest income segments are increasing their share by so much. The major reason for this is that most of the wealthiest people in the country get most of their income from sources unrelated to their jobs, such as dividends, interest, and *capital gains.*

Affirmative action programs seek to achieve a long-run solution to poverty by providing equal opportunities for education and employment. In the short run, though, the government seeks to lift people out of poverty by providing *public assistance* to the poor. Public assistance is provided through *transfer payments,* which are grants of cash income, or by providing specific goods such as food and housing at subsidized prices. Many of the programs to assist the poor are referred to as *entitlement programs* because people in certain financial circumstances are legally entitled to their benefits.

For many years the primary public assistance program in the United States was Aid to Families With Dependent Children (AFDC), but this has recently been replaced by *Temporary Assistance for Needy Families (TANF),* a limited-time *workfare* program that requires most recipients to perform some kind of work

Michael Jordan's earnings reflect his unique talents, which are irreplaceable. Because the demand for these abilities is very high and the supply fixed, such earnings resemble rents rather than incomes.

in order to receive their benefits. The Social Security system provides benefits for the aged, blind, and disabled poor who cannot work through its *Supplemental Security Income (SSI)* program.

A person whose income is below a specified level is entitled to take an *earned income tax credit,* which reduces his or her federal tax liability and can even result in their receiving a check from the government instead of paying any taxes. Two of the largest public assistance programs are *food stamps,* which allow the poor to buy groceries at a subsidized price, and *Medicaid,* which provides for the health care and medical needs of those in poverty. Medicaid is the fastest-growing public assistance program in terms of expenditures.

Unlike public assistance that is designed to help the poor, *social insurance* is designed to prevent people from slipping into poverty. *Social Security,* our country's program for providing income to retired Americans, is the nation's primary social insurance program and the largest single item in the government's budget. The Social Security system comprises four trust funds; one for retirement benefits, one for disability benefits, and two for medical assistance to retired persons through the *Medicare* program.

Unlike private pension plans, Social Security does not pay benefits to each individual out of returns on his or her savings; instead benefits to retirees are paid out of the *payroll tax* on the wages and salaries of current workers. It also differs from private pensions because it redistributes income from those with high lifetime earnings to those with lower earnings.

The Social Security system is facing a financial crisis because of the large number of baby-boomers who will retire early in the twenty-first century. Some observers have proposed reforming the system to make it more of a *defined contribution* retirement program instead of a *defined benefit* program as it currently is.

Our government is active in protecting consumers from unsafe products and workers from unsafe working conditions. Agencies such as the Food and Drug Administration (FDA) and Consumer Product Safety Commission test food, drugs, and products to make sure they are not dangerous. The Federal Trade Commission makes sure that companies do not engage in false advertising, and the National Highway Safety Commission conducts safety tests and imposes regulations to protect us when we are on the road. The Occupational Safety and Health Administration (OSHA) regulates work-places to ensure worker safety, and it has been very effective in reducing the number of deaths and injuries on the job.

$ Perspective $

The New Deal

Franklin Delano Roosevelt was president of the United States from 1932 to 1944. He saw the country through the Great Depression and World War II. Although his economic policies failed to return the country to prosperity, he forever changed our thinking about the role of government in the lives of American citizens.

When Franklin Delano Roosevelt took office in 1932, the nation was in the throes of the Great Depression. Nearly 24% of the labor force was unemployed, the Dust Bowl had wiped out thousands of farms, 9,000 banks had failed, factories stood idle, and people stood in bread lines. No one knew what had caused the meltdown, and no one knew how to fix it.

FDR had promised the country a New Deal—something that would put people back to work and food back on their tables. His answer to the problem was to unleash the power of the federal government. Prior to then, economics was the province of the private sector and what public aid existed was provided by local almshouses and poor farms. In the space of a decade, the nation turned from the ideal of rugged individualism to acceptance of collective solutions to economic and social problems.

For the first time, the federal government imposed fair labor laws and the minimum wage to try to get people back to work. The National Labor Relations Board was established to allow the federal government to intervene in labor disputes, and the Civilian Conservation Corps and Works Progress Administration were founded to provide government jobs because private sector jobs did not exist. The Securities and Exchange Commission was created to regulate capital markets, the Federal Deposit Insurance Corporation was set up to protect bank deposits, and the Federal Reserve Board was granted expanded power to regulate bank loans. The Commodity Credit Corporation and the Farm Credit Administration were established to assist farmers. Not least of all, the Social Security system, requiring mandatory participation, was founded to provide a social "safety net" for the poor and elderly.

The New Deal was significant, not just because it brought the federal government into farms, factories, financial markets, and social policy, but because it changed our way of thinking about federal intervention forever. For the first time, the country accepted that the national government has a responsibility for providing economic and social security, and we have not looked back since.

For Further Study and Analysis

Study Questions

1. Why is the poverty line different for a farm family than for a nonfarm family?

2. Why has the distribution of income become more unequal during the 1990s?

3. Why do white males tend to have higher incomes than white females or members of different minority groups?

4. What is the long-term solution to poverty? Why are transfer programs considered to be short-term solutions?

5. Prior to TANF, states received anywhere from one to four dollars of federal aid for every dollar they spent on AFDC, with no cap. Given the way that TANF is financed, do you think that the states will spend more or less than they used to for public assistance?

6. Which income groups in America would prefer to keep Social Security a defined benefits program and which ones would prefer to make it a defined contributions retirement program?

7. Explain how Social Security differs from private pension plans.

8. Explain why the Social Security system is facing financial difficulties.

9. Which segments of the population would be most at risk if Social Security were to be privatized?

10. In order for the free market system to work well, why is it necessary for producers to provide consumers with the information that is required by the government?
11. Why are many economists and business people critical of OSHA policies?

Exercises in Analysis

1. Research the topic of voting patterns, and find the voting rates for people in different age groups. Does this help you understand why many politicians consider tampering with Social Security "off-limits?" (You might write your Congressman or Congresswoman and ask what their position is on reforming Social Security.)
2. Visit a grocery store in your town, read the ingredient labels on a variety of canned and packaged foods, and see how many additives you discover that you do not recognize, for example, bromelain, disodium insinate, disodium guanylate, and calcium disodium EDTA. Do you know what these things are? Do you think that the government should regulate what producers put into food products?
3. There is disagreement among people as to whether America's needy families should be helped with income transfers or with specified goods and services such as housing, food stamps, and medical care. Prepare a report that explains the pros and cons of each side.
4. Volunteer some time at a local soup kitchen, food pantry, or other agency that helps the less fortunate. Write a report on what you believe society's role should be in helping the poor.

Further Reading

Burton, C. Emory. *The Poverty Debate: Politics and the Poor in America*. New York: Greenwood Press, 1992. An examination of the social conditions of the poor in America, the situations of welfare recipients, and the role of employment.

Famighetti, Robert. *The World Almanac and Book of Facts 1997*. New York: St. Martin's Press, 1996. Provides a good summary of how Social Security benefits are determined and how the program is financed.

Hughes, Jonathan. *American Economic History*. Glenview, Ill: Scott, Foresman, 1983. Chapters 25 and 27 provide a good description of the Great Depression.

Mansfield, Edwin. *Leading Economic Controversies of 1998*. New York: W. W. Norton, 1998. Readings 1 and 2 deal with the problem of cost-of-living adjustments in the Social Security benefits, and readings 5–7 discuss the issue of income inequality.

Annual Editions: Microeconomics and *Annual Editions: Economics* series (Guilford, CT: Dushkin/McGraw-Hill, various years) always include very interesting articles about inequality and Social Security. For example, the *1998/99 Microeconomics* edition contains 7 good articles on poverty issues (Readings 41–47) and the *1998/99 Economics* edition has a lively debate about the pros and cons of privatizing Social Security (Readings 21–22). *Annual Editions: Urban Society* (1997) contains a good article about the root causes of homelessness in America (Reading 22).

Information on federal government agencies and what they do is available at their Web sites:

Consumer Product Safety Commission www.cpsc.gov

Occupational Safety and Health Administration www.osha.gov

Food and Drug Administration www.fda.gov

National Highway Traffic Safety Administration www.nhtsa.gov

Federal Aviation Administration www.faa.gov

Unit Three

Macroeconomics

Macroeconomics covers the overall aspects
of the economy. It deals with the total performance
of the economy rather than with the behavior
of individual units.

chapter ten
Money

Money comes in different forms and serves various purposes. The ways in which it is created and controlled have a major effect on the economy.

chapter eleven
Economic Instability

The two primary macroeconomic problems that societies must deal with are unemployment and inflation. Keeping both low is often difficult because there are a number of different causes of each. In addition, there often seems to be a trade-off between the two: lower inflation is often associated with rising unemployment, and vice versa.

chapter twelve
The Economy's Output

There are two different ways of measuring the total output of the economy, giving the same result. There are also two different explanations for what determines the level of total output—demand-side economics and supply-side economics—which do not come to the same conclusions.

chapter thirteen
Public Finance

Spending by the three levels of government—federal, state, and local—equals about one-third of total spending in the economy and accounts for 18% of total output. Both the type of public projects funded and the type of tax used to raise tax revenues vary with the level of government. The way in which government spending is financed affects households and the economy.

chapter fourteen
Policies for Economic Stability and Growth

The government attempts to solve the unemployment and inflation problems and simultaneously maximize total output through the use of monetary and fiscal policies. The goal of economic growth can be achieved by increasing capital investment and capital efficiency and by increases in the size and quality of the labor force.

chapter ten

Money

People often associate economics with money. As we have seen in the first half of the book, economics deals with much more than just money, but now we finally will take a look at this strange but indispensable commodity.

▶ That Curious Commodity

Money is a curious commodity. Cattle were commonly used as money in pre-Christian times, and even recently by some primitive tribes. In fact, our word *pecuniary,* which means related to money, comes from the Latin word *pecus,* meaning cattle. Cloth, corn, slaves, knives, and even beer have been used as money in different places at various times. These were types of money that had a real value. But that was not true of all forms of money used in the past. Seashells, porpoise teeth, and woodpecker scalps have little practical use; but, at one time or other, in various places, all of these items have been used as money.

Metal coins were first used as money in the seventh century B.C. in ancient Lydia, which was located in what is now Turkey. Lydian coins were stamped with the head of a lion. Coins from other places sported turtles, owls, and horses with wings. These coins were usually made from an alloy of gold and silver. The designs on coins, especially those minted by the city-states of ancient Greece, became works of art, designed by some of the greatest artists of the day. The beautiful artwork helped the coins gain recognition and acceptance.

Paper money originated with goldsmiths during the seventeenth century in London. Because the goldsmiths had safes in which to keep the precious metals that they worked with, people would bring them coins and gold and silver for safekeeping. The goldsmith gave the depositors receipts for their coins and precious metals.

It developed that these receipts would then be transferred from person to person as a means of payment. And if a wily goldsmith made out a few extra receipts and used them as a means of payment, no one would know it as long as everyone with receipts did not come to claim his or her precious metals or coins at the same time.

In the United States, after the Revolutionary War and during the next century, paper money in the form of bank notes was issued by privately owned banks. These banks were chartered by the federal government and the state governments. The state-chartered banks tended to be reckless in creating money. If someone presented a banknote for redemption, it had to be redeemed in gold or silver. Since the banks, following the example of the goldsmiths, issued more paper money than they had reserves of gold and silver, they preferred that the notes not be redeemed. Some banks made it difficult for people to find them by locating in out-of-the-way places. These hard-to-find locations were out in the wilds, and this gave rise to the term "wildcat banking."

When the Civil War broke out, the federal government put an end to the freewheeling practices of state-chartered banks. The federal government printed paper money itself— "greenbacks"—to help finance the war. But it was not until 1913, when the Federal Reserve System was established, that the federal government monopolized the issuance of bank notes.

Today, the production of currency is a big operation. There is a factory in Washington, D.C., that prints tens of millions of dollars in paper money every day. Tight security measures are used to protect this operation. Closed-circuit television cameras monitor production and inventory, and each employee must have a security clearance. This factory, the Bureau of Printing and Engraving, operates 24 hours a day, 7 days a week, including holidays.

New currency leaves the Bureau of Printing and Engraving in armored trucks for distribution to the 12 Federal Reserve banks around the country. The Federal Reserve banks act as wholesalers in passing the currency to commercial banks and other financial institutions. It is from these that the public obtains currency. Essentially, the public "buys" currency from banks with paychecks and other deposits.

If we used currency for all of our money transactions, the printing presses in the Washington printing factory could not possibly keep up with the demand. But we don't use currency for all our money transactions. In terms of the total amount paid, most of our monetary transactions are paid by check rather than currency.

The way we pay for goods and services is undergoing another change. One indication of

this change is the ever-increasing use of credit cards. When you use your credit card, the issuer of the card pays for your purchase, and you are required to pay the issuer back, with interest; basically you are taking out a high-interest loan. Fifteen percent of all purchases in the United States were made by credit cards in 1990. By 1995, the percentage had increased to 21%, and the Nilson report estimates that the percentage will increase to 33% in 2000 and 43% in 2005.

Another aspect of the changing payments mechanism is the emergent use of electronic transfers of funds to replace writing checks in making payments. Transactions at automated teller machines (ATMs) increased from an average of 373 million per month in 1988 to 915 million per month in 1997. Point of sale (POS) transfers using check (debit) cards that draw directly on the customer's checking account have also increased dramatically. Check cards were not introduced until the early 1990s. In 1993 there were an average of 59 million transactions per month. By 1997, their use had exploded to 270 million transactions per month.

These changes are altering the nature of banking. Handling currency becomes unnecessary. Dallas's Lone Star National Bank became the nation's first cashless bank in 1984. It kept no currency on hand. Among other advantages,

this eliminated any danger of robberies. On the sides of the bank were signs announcing No Cash on Premises.

The newest innovation in payments is the "smart card." An amount of purchasing power is programmed into electronic chips embedded in a plastic card that looks like a credit or check card. As the card is used to make purchases, machines at stores, restaurants, and other establishments with the necessary equipment deduct the amount of the purchase from the balance on the card until it is exhausted. The same equipment may then be used to replenish the amount of "money" in the card from the customer's bank account or from currency fed into the machine. Two popular uses of smart cards are telephone cards, and smart student ID cards that can be used to buy books, food, and vending machine items on many campuses. Some cards can even hold balances in up to five different currencies, making money changing at international borders unnecessary.

The volume of electronic payments is likely to exceed the amount paid by checks in the future. Even the paper symbols of money payments are being replaced by invisible electrical impulses. Money, that curious commodity, has come a long way from seashells and woodpecker scalps.

Chapter Preview

Although you can use a dollar bill to clean the lenses of your glasses, or a coin as an emergency screwdriver, modern money is not a very useful commodity. Its only value is that people have confidence in it and are willing to accept it in exchange for goods and services. This chapter explores the role of money in an economy by asking: What is money? What does money do? How is money created? How is the supply of money controlled?

Learning Objectives

After completing this chapter you should be able to:

1. Explain the history of money.
2. Define the M1 money supply and describe its components.
3. Explain how near money differs from money.
4. List the three functions of money.
5. Explain the characteristics that money must have in order to be functional.
6. Explain how money is created.
7. Describe the Federal Reserve System and explain what it does.
8. Explain the difference between required reserves and excess reserves.
9. Explain how changing the required reserve ratio, changing the discount rate, and open market operations can all lead to a change in the money supply.

▶ What Is Money?

As we have seen, money has taken many forms throughout the centuries. It can be anything that society generally accepts as payment for goods and services. This section will discuss what serves as money in a modern economy.

◾ Currency

In the United States today, only about 37% of our money supply is **currency.** The amount of currency in circulation increases each year by varying amounts. After regularly increasing 9–10% a year during the last half of the 1970s, the rate of growth slowed to an average of about 8% through the end of 1997.

The amount of currency in circulation depends on how much is desired by individuals and businesses. In March 1998 it totaled $432 billion. Individual and business withdrawal of currency from banks determines how much the banks will order from the **Federal Reserve System.** The government mints enough coins and prints sufficient paper money to satisfy this demand. Currency held by the government, the

Federal Reserve, or by banks is not considered part of the money supply.

At one time federal law required that the amount of currency in circulation be limited in a legally fixed ratio to the value of the banking system's gold reserves. In 1968 this requirement, known as the **gold standard,** was eliminated. The value of currency today depends

---

currency that part of the money supply consisting of coins and paper bills.

Federal Reserve System (Fed) the central bank of the United States; a system established by the Federal Reserve Act of 1913 to issue paper currency, supervise the nation's banking system, and implement monetary policy.

gold standard a method of controlling a country's money supply by tying the amount of money in circulation to the amount of gold held by the banking system.

When people withdraw cash from their checking accounts to pay for purchases, the money supply is not changed.

only on people's confidence in the stability of the U.S. economy and, as with other commodities, its supply relative to its demand.

The percentage of currency in the money supply increased gradually from 20% in 1960 to 28% in 1980 and stayed at that level until the early 1990s. Since that time, it has increased dramatically to nearly 40%. Monetary experts are not always sure why there are variations in the

demand for currency, but they do have a good idea as to why demand surged in the 1990s. One reason was the breakup of the Soviet Union (to be discussed further in chapter 17). People in the former communist countries did not believe in their domestic currency because they feared inflation would make it next to worthless. Instead, whenever they could, they converted their rubles and other currencies to U.S. dollars and saved the dollars in the belief that the dollar would keep its value over time. Another reason for the surge in the demand for our currency is that U.S. $100 bills are one of the preferred means of payment for illegal activities throughout the world.

There are also variations in the amount of currency in circulation during the year, especially around December, when it reaches a peak to accommodate the holiday buying rush. At any given time, a number of factors can affect how much of their wealth people desire to hold in the form of currency.

◤ Demand Deposits

The largest part of the money supply is not currency but **demand deposits** and **other checkable deposits**—the obligations of a financial institution that are payable whenever the depositor writes a **check** or uses a **check (debit) card.** These deposits, which may be in either commercial banks, savings banks, savings and loan associations, or credit unions, do not consist of currency. A deposit is a liability for a bank, a sum that the bank must stand ready to pay immediately upon request. A check is a written order instructing the institution to transfer funds from one account to another. In this respect, it is similar to an IOU given to a friend in exchange for a cash loan. Checks written on demand deposits differ from personal IOUs in their widespread general acceptability as money. Unlike a check written on a demand deposit, a personal IOU normally cannot be used for purchases.

Because checks drawn on deposit accounts are used to pay for goods and services, these deposits are considered money. When people use their ATM cards to make cash withdrawals from their checking accounts to pay for purchases, or when they deposit cash into their

---

demand deposits (checking accounts) liabilities of depository institutions to their customers that are payable on demand.

other checkable deposits accounts, other than demand deposit accounts in commercial banks, on which checks can be drawn, principally negotiable order of withdrawal (NOW) accounts in savings and loan banks.

check a written order to a depository institution to pay a person or institution named on it a specified sum of money.

check (debit) cards cards that can be used like Visa, MasterCard, Discover, or American Express credit cards, but instead of a loan being made to make the purchase, the purchase price is deducted from the card user's checking account balance.

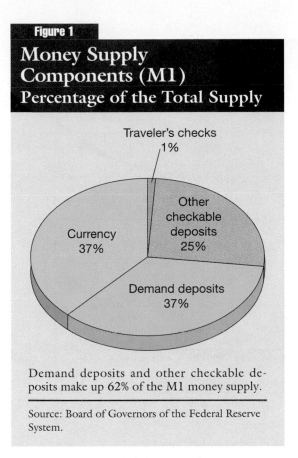

Figure 1

Money Supply Components (M1)
Percentage of the Total Supply

Traveler's checks 1%

Other checkable deposits 25%

Currency 37%

Demand deposits 37%

Demand deposits and other checkable deposits make up 62% of the M1 money supply.

Source: Board of Governors of the Federal Reserve System.

---

checking accounts, the money supply is not changed. One type of money (a checking account balance) is exchanged for another type (currency), with the total money supply remaining the same.

The most commonly used measurement of the money supply includes currency, traveler's checks, demand deposits, and other checkable deposits, such as **NOW (negotiable order of withdrawal) accounts.** This measurement of the money supply is known as **M1.** Demand and other checkable deposits constitute a little over 60% of the M1 money supply (Figure 1).

◆ Near Money

There are various types of financial assets that can be turned into money very easily. These assets are considered **near monies** (Figure 2). They include **savings deposits, certificates of deposit (CDs),** and shares in **money market**

mutual funds. The ease with which near monies can be converted into money is called their **liquidity.** Depending upon how liquid these various financial assets are, they may be included in broader definitions of the money supply referred to as **M2, M3,** and **L.**

---

negotiable order of withdrawal (NOW) accounts savings and loan bank customer accounts on which checks can be drawn.

M1 a measure of the money supply that includes currency in circulation, demand deposit accounts, negotiable order of withdrawal (NOW) accounts, automatic transfer savings (ATS) accounts, traveler's checks, and checkable money market accounts.

near money (monies) assets with a specified monetary value that are readily redeemable as money; savings accounts, certificates of deposit, and shares in money market mutual funds.

savings deposits liabilities of depository institutions to their customers that are not transferable by check and for which the institution may require advance notice before withdrawal.

certificate of deposit (CD) a deposit of a specified sum of money for a specified period of time that cannot be redeemed prior to the date specified (without penalties for early withdrawal).

money market mutual fund an investment fund that pools the assets of investors and puts the assets into debt securities that mature in less than 1 year: short-term bank CDs, corporate bonds, and 6-month Treasury bills.

liquidity the degree of ease with which an asset can be converted into money without a significant loss in value.

M2 a measure of the money supply that includes M1 plus savings deposits, small time deposits (CDs), and certain money market mutual funds.

M3 a measure of the money supply that includes M2 plus large time deposits (CDs).

L a measure of the money supply that includes M3 plus commercial paper, savings bonds, and government securities with maturities of 18 months or less.

Figure 2

The Supply of Money and Near Monies, 1980–1997

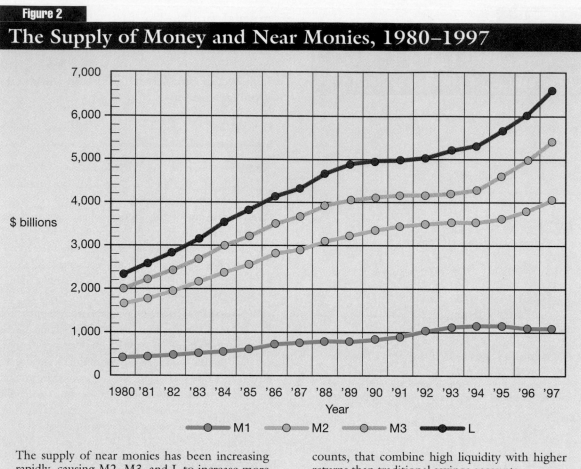

The supply of near monies has been increasing rapidly, causing M2, M3, and L to increase more rapidly than M1. This is due in large part to the growth of new money instruments, such as money market funds and money market ac-

counts, that combine high liquidity with higher returns than traditional savings accounts.

Source: Board of Governors of the Federal Reserve System.

The deregulation of the banking system in the 1980s led to the evolution of new types of financial assets, and now the line between money and near money has become blurred. Banks now provide **automatic transfer services (ATS)** from savings deposits to demand deposits. Money market funds permit investors to write checks on their fund accounts. These new types of accounts cross over the line from near money to money. Because M2 includes most types of near money, its definition is not so vague, and many economists now argue that it is a more reliable measure of the money supply than the traditional M1.

automatic transfer services (ATS) a type of account that provides for the depository institution to automatically transfer funds from the depositor's savings account to her or his checking account when it has been drawn down.

Case Application

Dealing the Cards

The stakes in the plastic card game are high and everybody wants in on the action. The average U.S. card holder now has roughly 4 bank credit cards with a total of about $4,000 in high-interest debt. Total credit card debt reached an all-time high of $455 billion in fall 1997. The market is continuing to grow, and bank card issuers are constantly filling people's mailboxes with unsolicited offers for new cards that offer everything from frequent flier airline miles to the opportunity to use a card that has your favorite sports team's logo. Although it costs the issuers anywhere from $150 to $200 to acquire a new customer, the average card holder will pay about $350 per year in interest charges. Customers are becoming wise to the marketing ploys of card issuers, and are striking back by frequently getting a new card and using it to pay off the balance on a higher-interest card that they already have.

With these universal cards—Visa, Master-Card, American Express, and Discover cards—you can buy anything from a toothbrush to an automobile. Besides the universal cards, there are also innumerable specialized credit cards issued by oil companies, department stores, airlines, hotels, and telephone companies. By the beginning of the next century, total credit card purchases will be approaching $1 trillion per year.

From the standpoint of the customer, the explosion in the popularity of credit cards is due to a number of attractions: their convenience, the chance to spread out the payments over a period of time, the reduced risk of having cash lost or stolen, and the "float" (the delay between the date of the purchase and the date when the credit card payment is due). Customers who pay off their card balances each month can use the float to get an interest-free loan for up to 60 days if they time their purchases right. For some transactions—renting a car, ordering merchandise over the phone—a credit card is a virtual necessity.

From the standpoint of the banks issuing the cards, the attraction is the high rate of interest they earn on outstanding balances. Interest charges on credit card balances are typically 18–20%, substantially higher than the 10–12% banks charge on other types of personal loans. The banks maintain that the costs of credit card fraud and defaults necessitate the high interest rates. Furthermore, they claim, cardholders are not concerned about what interest they pay, but only about the convenience of their charge cards.

The evidence suggests that banks may be right about the claim that cardholders generally are not concerned about the interest they pay. They are wrong, however, about the claim that it is economically necessary for them to charge such high rates. According to Federal Reserve data, since 1982 the profit margin on credit card business has been higher than for any other type of bank lending. Further evidence of the profitability of credit cards is the premium price paid when one bank buys the credit card business of another bank. In 10 such transactions for which the price was publicly disclosed, the accounts sold at an average premium of 17% above their value, reflecting the expected future profitability of the accounts.

Despite the high interest rates, some people are credit card junkies. Like compulsive gamblers, they are unable to control their use of the credit cards. They find themselves over their heads in debt and unable to meet their payments. About 6% of bank card balances are never paid. This often means that the cards are canceled and the cardholder gets a bad credit rating. Other people choose to make minimum use of credit cards in order to keep their spending under control. If they can pay off the balance each month, as about one-third of all cardholders do, they benefit from the convenience

Walter Cavanagh, also known as "Mr. Plastic Fantastic," displays some of his 1,356 different credit cards. Even with his record-breaking collection, however, Mr. Cavanagh possesses only 12% of the different kinds of credit cards that are available.

of credit cards but avoid the high interest charges. The issuing banks do not like this much, but they still make a profit from the annual fees paid by the cardholder plus the amounts they collect from merchants for processing charge slips.

Some credit card users elect to carry only a few cards so that in case the cards get lost or stolen it will not be difficult to notify the companies. At the other extreme are the credit card collectors. According to the *Guinness Book of World Records,* the champion cardholder is Walter Cavanagh of Santa Clara, California, who has 1,356 valid credit cards. He has the nickname of Mr. Plastic Fantastic. He keeps his credit cards in a fold-out wallet that is 250 feet long and weighs 37½ pounds. The total amount of credit available to him with the cards is over $1.6 million. However, he makes a practice of paying off all his bills each month.

Economic Reasoning

1. Is "plastic money" included in the money supply measured by M1? How can you tell whether it is?

2. Despite all the people who pay off their card balances each month, and despite all the people who default on their loans, credit card companies are still actively marketing their cards to old and new customers. Why?

3. Should the government tighten restrictions on credit card companies? What kinds of restrictions might be imposed?

► What Does Money Do?

Not only does money take different forms, it also serves various functions. In this section, we examine the different functions of money.

◣ Medium of Exchange

One function of money is that it is used as a **medium of exchange,** something that people will accept in exchange for goods or services.

The use of money to pay for things evolved as an alternative to **barter.** Using money as a medium of exchange for goods and services of all kinds is much easier than attempting to trade those goods and services directly for each other. Money generally simplifies the exchange process. There is no need in a monetary economy to waste time looking for someone who has exactly that good or service you want and who wants exactly what you have to trade. The use of money greatly simplifies exchange.

In order to serve well as a medium of exchange, whatever is used as money should be universally recognized, have an adequate but limited supply, not be easily reproduced (forged), be easily portable, and be durable. The evolution of money from seashells to bank drafts has been one long attempt to satisfy these requirements.

◣ Unit of Measurement

Some of the earlier forms of money did not serve very well as a medium of exchange. Cows, for example, are not exactly portable. They did serve another function of money, however, that of providing a **unit of measurement.** The money unit serves as a common denominator that can specify the value of something else. In societies where cattle were used for money, everyone knew pretty well the value of a cow. The value of other things could therefore be expressed in terms of how much of each was equivalent to the value of a cow.

Normally, the unit of measurement is the same as the medium of exchange, but not always. In international transactions where countries use different mediums of exchange (Japanese yen, British pounds, and so on), the American dollar is frequently used as a unit of measurement. The price of OPEC oil, for example, is quoted in U.S. dollars per barrel all over the world, and many smaller countries link ("peg") the value of their currency to the dollar.

A unit of measurement should itself be stable in value. Because of fluctuations in the value of the dollar, there have been suggestions that the world adopt a new unit of measurement. It would be based on the value of **commodities** rather than on the value of the dollar or any other currency.

◣ Store of Value

The third function of money is to serve as a **store of value,** a form in which wealth can be held. Any form of wealth may be used as a store of value, but money has the advantage of being more liquid than other forms of

---

medium of exchange a commodity accepted by common consent in payment for goods and services and as settlement of debts and contracts.

barter direct exchange of goods and services without the use of money.

unit of measurement (standard of value or unit of account) a common denominator of value in which prices are stated and accounts recorded.

commodity any economic good, but usually used to refer to basic raw materials such as oil or metals.

store of value a means of conserving purchasing power for a future time.

Figure 3

Comparisons of the Money Supply (M1) and the Purchasing Power of the Dollar, 1975–1997

(Purchasing power in 1983 dollars)

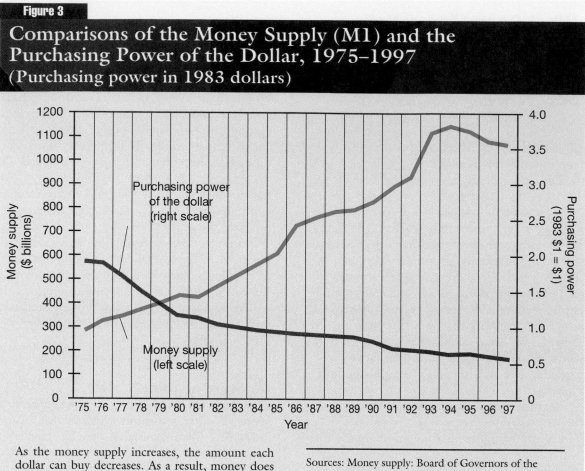

As the money supply increases, the amount each dollar can buy decreases. As a result, money does not serve very well as a store of value during inflationary times.

Sources: Money supply: Board of Governors of the Federal Reserve System.
Purchasing power of the dollar: U.S. Bureau of Labor Statistics.

wealth—money can be spent, whereas other forms of wealth cannot. Near monies are not perfectly liquid, because in order to use them for purchases you must normally convert them into currency or a demand deposit. You run the risk that converting them at a particular time may result in a loss. Holding money itself, however, results in a loss during times of rising prices. As prices rise, the real purchasing power of money declines (Figure 3). It is because the people in the former U.S.S.R.

do not believe their currency will be a good store of value that they want to hold U.S. dollars.

What Does Money Do?

EconExplorer

Case Application

POW Money

During World War II, captured servicemen in prisoner of war (POW) camps in Germany and Italy created a simple but complete economic system to serve their needs. The prisoners received Red Cross rations, which included canned milk, chocolate bars, jam, sugar, crackers, and cigarettes. Some also received gift packages from home through the mail. These rations and gifts comprised a flow of real income to the prisoners, although they had no money.

The Red Cross rations were fairly standardized, and a POW would likely find himself with a shortage of his favorite commodities and an excess of other commodities that he did not want.

The prisoners soon began to make exchanges. Out of these exchanges a market system was born. The essence of exchange is that both parties benefit. A nonsmoker gives up cigarettes he does not value for chocolate, which he does like. So the smoker gets the cigarettes and the candy lover gets the chocolate.

Exchanges at first were made through a simple barter procedure, whereby one item was swapped for another. But this process was awkward and time consuming. If one POW had some crackers and chocolate bars and wished to exchange the chocolate bars for jam to eat with the crackers, he would have to find someone else who had jam but preferred to have chocolate bars instead. Some prisoners in the camp became very good at making advantageous swaps and made a business venture of it—POW capitalists.

To get around the inconvenience of barter, a money economy gradually developed in the camps, complete with buyers, sellers, and even a merchant class. Cigarettes were used as money, and the prices of all other items were quoted in terms of how many cigarettes they were worth.

Economic Reasoning

1. Which functions of money did cigarettes perform in the POW camp?

2. Heavy air raids in the vicinity of the camp increased the consumption of cigarettes. What effect did this have on the "money supply" and the prices of things?

3. Sometimes the successful POW capitalists who profited from buying and selling things were resented by other prisoners. Was the hostility directed toward them justified? Were they providing a useful service, or were they merely leeches on the POW society?

▶ How Is Money Created?

The manner in which money is created has evolved quite a bit since the Lydians stamped out their lion-headed coins 26 centuries ago. In this section we will look at how money is created in a modern economy.

◆ Currency

As we have seen, this part of the money supply is produced by the federal government, which supplies coins and paper money in the amounts required by the public. Currency enters businesses and households through banks. An increase in the amount of currency in circulation, however, does not necessarily mean an increase in the money supply. People who need more currency "buy" it from their banks by writing checks on their deposits for the bills or coins desired. The increase in currency is offset by a decrease in demand deposits, leaving the total money supply unchanged.

It would be possible for the federal government to increase the money supply by printing more currency if it used the currency directly to pay government bills rather than selling the currency to the public through the banking system. This is not the usual practice in this country, however, and the government normally produces currency only in response to the demands from businesses and the general public.

◆ Private Borrowing

Borrowing from a bank increases the supply of money by increasing the amount of demand deposits. The borrower, in exchange for promising to repay a given sum (usually this promise is represented by a **promissory note**), receives the amount in his or her checking account. This added deposit does not reduce anyone else's deposit and, as such, represents a net increase in the supply of money. The individual is then able to use that money to purchase goods and services by writing a check on the account. The new money created by the loan is thereby transferred to someone else, who in turn may use it for other purchases.

When the borrower writes a check to repay the loan from the bank when the note comes due, his or her checking account balance is reduced and the money supply is decreased by that amount. Changes in the money supply depend on the amount of new loans relative to the amount of repayment of previous loans. When the volume of new lending by banks exceeds the repayment of previous loans, the money supply increases.

(Continued on page 271)

In a throwback to earlier forms of money, these cumbersome stones, while not easily portable, serve as a unit of measurement on the islands of Yap.

---

promissory note (IOU) a written obligation to pay a specified amount at a specified time.

Case Application

How to Create Money

One way you can create money is to print it on a printing press in your basement. But if you were to do that you could get into a lot of trouble. A perfectly legal way you can create money, however, is to take out a loan at a bank. Imagine that you have decided that you will buy a computer that costs $1,200. You go to the bank for a loan, and if the bank approves your loan for $1,200, you sign a promissory note. The banker makes out a deposit slip to be credited to your demand deposit account, and you can then write a check to pay for the computer. When the purchase is made and the computer dealer deposits your check in the bank, it is presented to your bank for payment. Your demand deposit account is decreased by the amount of the check. What has happened to your personal wealth? You now own a computer worth $1,200. You have also increased your liability by the amount of the loan ($1,200), so your personal wealth has not changed. Your assets and liabilities from this transaction are equal. But you have succeeded in increasing the money supply in the economy. That money is now in the computer dealer's checking account. When the computer dealer spends it, it will move to somcone else's account.

Economic Reasoning

1. If you borrowed the $1,200 in cash rather than having it credited to your checking account, would the effect on the money supply be the same? Why or why not?

2. When you pay off your bank loan, what happens to the money supply? Is the effect on the money supply any different depending on whether you pay the bank by check or with currency?

3. There is an old adage that bankers are only willing to loan money to people who do not need it. Those who have plenty of financial assets that can readily be turned into cash have little trouble getting a loan, whereas those who have no assets have a great deal of difficulty. Should bankers make loans only to those who have enough assets to guarantee repayment of the loan? What are the consequences of making loans to people who are not good credit risks?

 How Is Money Created?

EconExplorer

◪ Government Borrowing

When the local, state, or federal government borrows from a bank, the initial effect upon the money supply is much the same as in the case of private borrowing. New deposits are created. A government borrows by promising future repayment in return for a current deposit.

The government can then write checks on the deposit to cover its expenditures. **Treasury bills** and **bonds** are the equivalent of private promissory notes—they are the government's promises to repay its loans. The effect of federal government borrowing on the money supply is therefore really no different than the effect of private borrowing. The government gives the bank a bill or a bond that is not money and receives a checking account balance that is money. Although the value of the bank's and the government's assets does not change, the amount of money in circulation does increase.

How Is the Supply of Money Controlled?

In order for our monetary system to function successfully, people must have confidence in the value of money. This confidence can be maintained only if the quantity of money in circulation does not fluctuate excessively so that money may retain its role as a consistent measure of value. Here we will examine how the money supply is controlled to prevent excessive variations in the quantity and value of money.

◢ The Federal Reserve System

Banks in the nineteenth century engaged in unrestrained issuance of currency and imprudent lending. This caused wild fluctuations in the money supply, as excessive creation of money alternated with bank failures. Finally, after the panic of 1907, when a run on banks by people attempting to withdraw their deposits forced many banks to close, the government established a National Monetary Commission to formulate a plan for a new American banking system. The recommendations in its report led to the establishment of the Federal Reserve System in 1913. The Federal Reserve, commonly referred to as the Fed, is the **central bank** of the United States. It is an institution that acts as a banker's bank, serves the monetary needs of the federal government, and controls the monetary system.

There are 12 regional Federal Reserve banks in the country. Each one services and regulates the banks in its district. The Federal Reserve Districts are shown in Figure 4 on page 273. The system is under the overall authority of the **Fed Board of Governors** in Washington, D.C. The seven members of the board are appointed by the president of the United States and confirmed by the Senate for staggered 14-year terms. The board's chairman and vice chairman are named by the president, and confirmed by the Senate, from among the members of the board. They are appointed to serve for 4-year terms, with the possibility of reappointment so long as their board terms have not expired (Table 1, p. 274).

Only about half of the nation's commercial banks, some 7,000 banks with 39,000 branches, are members of the Federal Reserve System. These include the nation's larger, most influential banks. Nonetheless, even

Treasury bill a short-term, marketable federal government security with a maturity of 1 year or less.

bond a long-term, interest-bearing certificate issued by a business firm or government that promises to pay the bondholder a specified sum of money on a specified date.

central bank an institution that controls the issuance of currency, provides banking services to the government and to the other banks, and implements the nation's monetary policy; in the United States the Federal Reserve is the central bank.

Fed Board of Governors the governing body of the Federal Reserve System, consisting of seven members appointed by the president for 14-year terms.

Figure 4

The Federal Reserve System

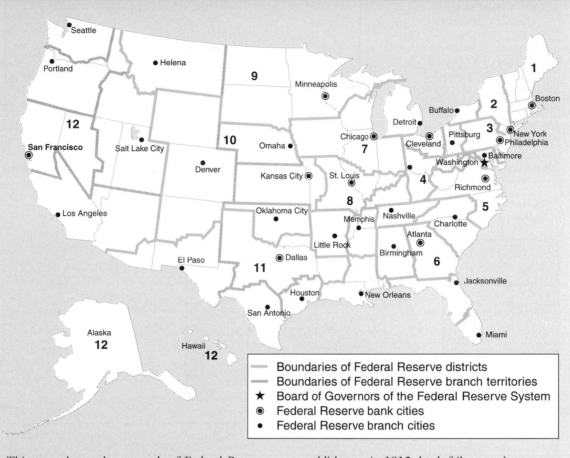

Seattle

Portland

Helena

9

Minneapolis

1

12

San Francisco

Salt Lake City

10

Omaha

Denver

Kansas City

St. Louis

Chicago

Detroit

Buffalo

Cleveland

Pittsburg

2

Boston

3

New York
Philadelphia

7

4

Washington

Baltimore

Richmond

Los Angeles

Oklahoma City

8

Memphis

Nashville

5

Charlotte

El Paso

Dallas

11

Little Rock

Atlanta

Birmingham

6

Houston

New Orleans

Jacksonville

San Antonio

Alaska

12

Hawaii

12

Miami

═══	Boundaries of Federal Reserve districts
▬▬▬	Boundaries of Federal Reserve branch territories
★	Board of Governors of the Federal Reserve System
◉	Federal Reserve bank cities
•	Federal Reserve branch cities

This map shows the network of Federal Reserve bank districts in the United States. Before the Fed's establishment in 1913, bank failures and monetary collapse threatened the economic system.

banks that are not members of the system are subject to most of the Fed's rules. The state-chartered commercial banks that are not members of the Federal Reserve System, the savings and loan banks, and the federally insured credit unions are supervised at the federal level by three other agencies: the Federal Deposit Insurance Corporation, the Office of Thrift Supervision, and the National Credit Union Administration, respectively. There are a variety of proposals before Congress to revamp the present structure of monetary supervision and control. The Fed has opposed the proposed changes because they would tend to lessen its authority and independence.

The most important function of the Federal Reserve System is to control the creation of money by **depository institutions.** There

depository institutions financial institutions that maintain deposit account obligations to their customers; includes commercial banks, savings banks, savings and loan associations, and credit unions.

Table 1 Organization of the Federal Reserve System

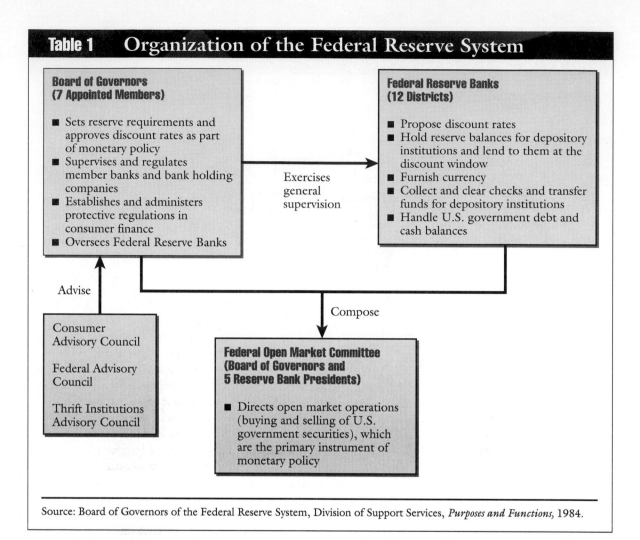

Board of Governors (7 Appointed Members)

- Sets reserve requirements and approves discount rates as part of monetary policy
- Supervises and regulates member banks and bank holding companies
- Establishes and administers protective regulations in consumer finance
- Oversees Federal Reserve Banks

Exercises general supervision

Federal Reserve Banks (12 Districts)

- Propose discount rates
- Hold reserve balances for depository institutions and lend to them at the discount window
- Furnish currency
- Collect and clear checks and transfer funds for depository institutions
- Handle U.S. government debt and cash balances

Advise

Consumer Advisory Council

Federal Advisory Council

Thrift Institutions Advisory Council

Compose

Federal Open Market Committee (Board of Governors and 5 Reserve Bank Presidents)

- Directs open market operations (buying and selling of U.S. government securities), which are the primary instrument of monetary policy

Source: Board of Governors of the Federal Reserve System, Division of Support Services, *Purposes and Functions,* 1984.

---

legal reserve requirement (required reserves) the minimum amount of money that a depository institution must have in its vault or on deposit with the Fed. The amount is a set percentage of the bank's deposits.

discount rate the interest rate charged by the Federal Reserve on loans to depository institutions.

open market operations the purchase or sale of government securities by the Federal Reserve to implement monetary policy.

required reserves see legal reserve requirement.

excess reserves reserves of depository institutions that are in excess of those required by the Federal Reserve.

are three ways by which it accomplishes this: (1) by setting **legal reserve requirements;** (2) by varying the **discount rate;** (3) by **open market operations.**

◢ Reserve Requirements

All banks are required to have a specified minimum reserve of money in their vaults or on deposit with the Federal Reserve bank in their district. These are the banks' **required reserves.** A bank's reserves may be more than the legal minimum specified, but it is not allowed to operate with less. Reserves over the legal minimum are referred to as **excess reserves.** Total reserves at a bank are therefore equal to the sum of required reserves plus excess reserves.

Table 2A	Hypothetical Bank Balance Sheet (Required reserve ratio equals 20%)		
Assets		**Liabilities**	
Total Reserves	$100 m	Demand Deposits	$100 m
Required Reserves	20 m		
Excess Reserves	80 m		
Loans	0		
Government Bonds	0		

Table 2B	Hypothetical Bank Balance Sheet (Required reserve ratio equals 20%)		
Assets		**Liabilities**	
Total Reserves	$20 m	Demand Deposits	$100 m
Required Reserves	20 m		
Excess Reserves	0		
Loans	80 m		
Government Bonds	0		

Banks in the United States can hold their assets in three different ways: reserves, bonds, and loans (promissory notes).

The Federal Reserve Board specifies the legal reserve requirements of all banks as a percentage of each bank's customer deposits—whether checking, savings, or time deposits. These reserve requirements can be varied by the Fed within statutory limits. The highest reserve requirements are imposed on checking and "checkable" savings (NOW and ATS) accounts and can vary from 8% to 14%.

Let us assume for illustration that the reserve requirement ratio is 20%. This means that the bank must have on deposit in its reserve account with the Fed at least $2 for every $10 in customer deposits on its books. If the balance sheet of the bank shows **deposit liabilities** of $100 million, the bank must have no less than $20 million in its reserve deposit. Table 2A shows such a hypothetical bank. It has a total of $100 million in demand deposits and these are all being held in reserves—$20 million in required reserves and $80 million in excess reserves. Regulations permit the bank to use the $80 million in excess reserves in only two ways: it can lend the reserves to businesses or individuals in return for promissory notes, or it can lend to the government by buying government

bonds. Of course, a third option would be to keep the money in reserves, but because reserves do not earn interest, the bank would not earn any money.

If by some chance the bank's reserves stand at less than $20 million, it must obtain additional reserves. It can do this by selling some of its financial assets, such as the government securities it owns, or by borrowing funds from the Fed or from other banks. If the bank wants to avoid these possibly costly options, it must reduce its deposit liabilities to a level that does not exceed 5 times its reserves.

Table 2B shows what the bank's balance sheet would look like if it loaned its $80 million of excess reserves to local businesses or individuals. Its excess reserves would be reduced

deposit liabilities the amount that a depository institution is obligated to pay out to its depositors, for example, the amount deposited in its checking and savings accounts.

Figure 5

Money Multiplier

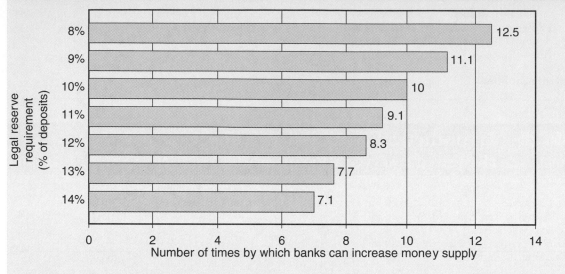

By changing the legal reserve requirement ratio, the Fed can control the supply of money. The lower the required reserve ratio, the more money banks can create by making loans.

to zero, but its total assets are still $100 million—it has $20 million in reserves (as required) and $80 million in loans or promissory notes. It has no more excess reserves. The $80 million in loans will show up as demand deposits in another bank after the borrowed money is spent. As explained above, these new demand deposits represent an increase in the money supply.

With all this in mind, let us see how the Fed controls the supply of money by altering the legal reserve requirements. Let us assume that the Fed reduces the required reserve ratio from 20% to 10%. This would mean that the bank only needs to keep $10 million in its reserve accounts, freeing it to make an additional $10 million in loans. If it did so, its total reserves would decrease to $10 million (required) while

money multiplier the ratio of the maximum increase in the money supply to an increase in bank reserves. Determined by the required reserve ratio.

its total loans would increase to $90 million. Because the total volume of loans has increased, the money supply will also increase.

Alternatively, if the Fed Board of Governors does not want banks to expand their lending because the money supply is growing too rapidly, it can prevent the bank from making new loans by keeping the reserve requirement at 20%. It then could not extend additional loans to borrowers without first increasing its reserves. Thus the money supply could be prevented from growing. It could even cause the money supply to decrease by raising the reserve requirement to 30%. This would mean that our bank must have $30 million in required reserves. If the bank had loaned out $80 million as shown in Table 2B, it would need to reduce its outstanding loans to $70 million (if its deposits do not increase). As bank loans are repaid, demand deposit balances would decrease and the money supply would decrease along with them.

The reserve requirement ratio also determines by how much the banking system can expand the money supply. The ratio of maximum money supply creation to bank-required reserves is the **money multiplier.** The total amount of money that the banking system can create is equal to

Maximum Money Supply Expansion =

$$\frac{1}{\text{Required Reserve Ratio}} \times (\text{Excess Reserves})$$

If the reserve requirement is 10%, the multiplier will equal $(1/.10)$ and the maximum expansion of the money supply is 10 times the increase in excess reserves. If the reserve requirement is 20%, the maximum expansion of the money supply is only 5 $(1/.20)$ times the amount of the increase in bank reserves. If the reserve requirement were 100%, commercial banks would be unable to expand the money supply at all. This would make it very difficult for businesses to borrow money and would seriously hamper economic activity (Figure 5).

How Is the Supply of Money Controlled?

EconExplorer

◼ Discounting

If a bank wishes to expand its lending activity but has no excess reserves, or if it finds itself below the legal reserve requirement, it may add to its reserves by borrowing from the Fed. Federal Reserve lending to commercial banks is called **discounting,** and the interest charged by the Fed for such loans is the discount rate. By increasing this rate, the Fed can discourage banks from coming to the "discount window" and asking for a loan. On the other hand, if the Fed wishes to see an expansion of the money supply, it can lower the discount rate and thereby lessen the cost of the loan. This makes borrowing additional reserves a more attractive possibility for the bank.

A bank can also supplement its reserves by borrowing the excess reserves of another bank. This type of borrowing is referred to as the **Federal Funds market.** Such interbank lending

is typically only overnight or for a few days at most to cover the bank's short-term reserve needs. The interest rate that banks charge each other for these loans is called the **Federal Funds rate.** It is one of the most closely watched interest rates because it directly influences the interest rates charged for consumer and business loans.

◼ Open Market Operations

The third way in which the Fed influences the money-creating power of banks is through open market operations. This means that the Fed purchases or sells U.S. government securities (bonds or Treasury bills) in the government securities market. The decision to buy or sell such securities is made by the **Federal Open Market Committee.** This committee is made up of the seven members of the board of governors together with the presidents of five of the Federal Reserve banks.

How Is the Supply of Money Controlled?

EconExplorer

discounting the Fed's practice of making loans to depository institutions at below-market interest rates.

Federal Funds market the market among depository institutions for temporary transfer of excess reserves from one institution to another.

Federal Funds rate the interest rate paid on Federal Funds borrowed.

Federal Open Market Committee a committee consisting of the Federal Reserve Board and the presidents of five regional Federal Reserve banks that decides on the purchase or sale of government securities by the Federal Reserve to implement monetary policy.

Figure 6

Open Market Operations

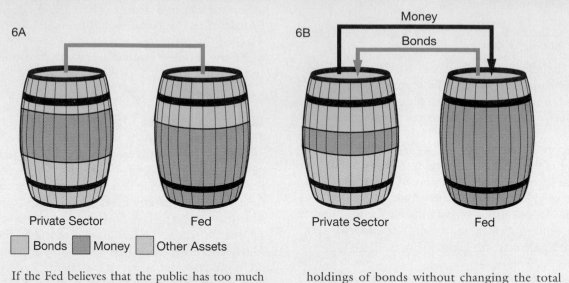

If the Fed believes that the public has too much money (6A), it will sell bonds (6B). This reduces the public's amount of money and increases its holdings of bonds without changing the total value of its assets or wealth.

When the Fed sells securities to banks, reserves flow out of the banks' reserves and Federal Reserve accounts, and the banks have fewer excess reserves left to make loans. If individuals buy the bonds that the Fed is selling, they pay with checks and this will also reduce the reserves that banks have at their disposal. Because reserves owned by the Fed are not included as a part of the money supply, the money supply will decrease. For example, suppose our hypothetical bank's balance sheet is the one depicted in Table 2A. If the Fed sells the bank $50 million worth of bonds, the bank will be left with only $30 million in excess reserves that are available for making new loans. This would slow the potential growth of the money supply. When the Fed purchases government securities, the opposite happens. The amount it pays for them ends up as new reserves for the banks. The new excess reserves in turn make it possible for these banks to create more demand deposits by making new loans.

In essence, open market operations allow the Fed to exchange money (the demand deposits that are created by new loans) for government securities that are not money. Figure 6 depicts the public's holding of money, bonds, and other assets in an "asset barrel." The Fed's assets are primarily money and bonds, and they are shown in the Fed's asset barrel. If the Fed feels that there is too much money in circulation (6A), it will exchange some of its bonds for the public's money (6B). Although the total value of assets in the public barrel has not changed, the composition of these assets has—the public now holds more bonds and less money. If the Fed wishes to increase the money supply it will do the opposite: it will buy bonds from the public and replace them with money.

In practice, open market operations is the tool most commonly used by the fed to control the money supply. The reason that this is the most popular instrument of monetary policy is that it is the most flexible. It permits the banks the greatest amount of leeway in adjusting to their individual circumstances.

Case Application

Cheap Money

Money is a real bargain in the United States. The price of money is the interest rate. But the actual cost of money is less than the quoted interest rate, the so-called "nominal rate."

One reason interest costs are less than the nominal rate is inflation. As a result of inflation, when you pay back a loan, the dollars that you use to make the payment are not worth as much as the dollars that you borrowed. The real rate of interest is the nominal rate minus the rate of inflation. If the interest rate is 10% and the inflation rate is 10%, you get the use of the money free. In this case the real rate is equal to zero.

The real interest rate is the actual cost of money to the borrower in purchasing power. Figure 7 shows the prime interest rates and the corresponding real interest rates, after

Figure 7

Prime Interest Rate, Real Interest Rate, and Tax-Adjusted Real Interest Rate, 1975–1997

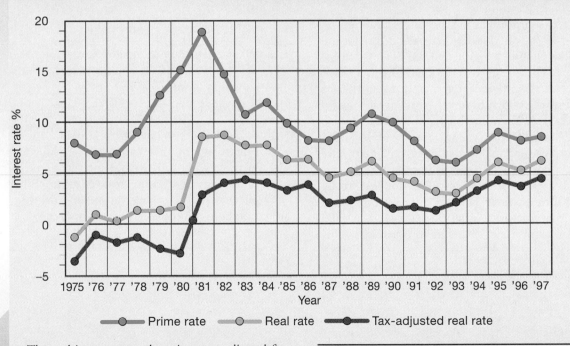

The real interest rate, the prime rate adjusted for inflation, was near or below zero in the 1970s. It increased sharply in 1994 and 1995 because of an increase in the prime rate coupled with an unexpected drop in the rate of inflation.

Source: Calculated from data from the Board of Governors of the Federal Reserve System and the Department of Labor, Bureau of Labor Statistics.

subtracting the rate of inflation, for the years 1975 to 1997. As you see, the real interest rate was less than zero in 1975. This means that lenders were subsidizing borrowers to use the lenders' money.

Of course, only the most successful, creditworthy businesses can borrow money at the prime rate. Individuals and other businesses must pay higher rates, reflecting the higher loan risks. Nonetheless, real interest rates were quite low during the 1970s.

This situation changed in the 1980s as a result of a variety of factors. One was the realization by lenders, after a succession of years of high inflation rates, that inflation was apparently going to persist and the rates they charged should take this into account. Reinforcing this movement to higher rates was the deregulation of the banking system, which eliminated interest ceilings on bank deposits. Competition for customers among banks and other financial institutions, such as money market funds, raised the cost of money to lenders, which the lenders passed on in higher interest rates charged to borrowers.

The sharp rise in the real interest rate in the mid-1990s was due to increases in the prime rate coupled with an unexpected decrease in inflation. These high real rates have been a boon to lenders, and have attracted a significant amount of money from overseas investors who want to cash in on the high real returns.

Nominal and real interest rates in some countries, Japan for example, are normally lower than in the United States. But, in this country, the real interest rate is not the "really real" interest rate. The real interest rate takes into account only inflation. It does not take into account the tax benefits to borrowers. Un-like the tax systems in other countries, our tax laws have allowed taxpayers to deduct certain interest payments from their incomes before computing their taxes.

This means that the government subsidizes borrowing. If the borrower's combined federal and state marginal income tax rate is 30%, the government picks up 30% of the nominal interest cost on eligible loans. The tax-adjusted real prime interest rates for borrowers in the 30% tax bracket are shown in Figure 7. From 1975 to 1980 they were negative. From a cost standpoint, adjusting for inflation and taxes, borrowing was cheaper than saving. By allowing deductions for interest costs and taxing interest earnings, the government discourages savings.

Economic Reasoning

1. What effect would unanticipated inflation have on the real interest rate and the amount of money that people would want to borrow? Why?

2. What effect would an increase in the Fed discount rate have on the interest rates shown in Figure 7? Why?

3. Should the tax laws stop subsidizing all borrowing by individuals? By businesses? Why or why not? Should interest earnings on savings be exempt from taxation? What effect would this have on income distribution between the wealthy and the poor?

► Putting It Together

Money can be anything that society generally accepts as payment for goods and services. What we consider money today includes not only *currency,* but also travelers' checks, *demand deposits,* and *other checkable deposits* such as *negotiable orders of withdrawal* and *ATS* accounts held at *depository institutions* such as banks, savings and loans, and credit unions. The common factor in all these accounts is that customers can access their money by either writing *checks,* or using *check (debit) cards.* This measurement of the money supply is referred to as *M1.* Currency, which consists of coins and bills not held by the banking system, constitutes almost 40% of the country's M1 money supply.

Broader measures of the money supply (*M2, M3,* and *L*) include *near monies*—other types of financial assets that are not used directly to pay for goods and services but can be turned into money quickly and easily. Near monies with a high degree of *liquidity* are *savings deposits, certificates of deposit,* and shares in *money market mutual funds.*

Money serves three distinct functions. First, it serves as a *medium of exchange* in conducting transactions. It is much more efficient in facilitating the transfer of goods and services than a *barter* system would be. The second function of money is that it serves as a *unit of measurement.* Whether or not any transactions take place, the value of goods and services is measured in units of money. The unit of measurement in international transactions is quite often the U.S. dollar. Some economists have suggested that a better unit of measurement would be obtained by basing the world's currency values on *commodity* prices. Finally, money can be used as a *store of value.* During periods of rapidly rising prices, however, it does not serve this function well.

Currency is produced by the government in response to the demand for it by businesses and the general public. The currency enters the economic system when people purchase it from banks, paying for it by check. Therefore, an increase in currency in circulation does not

increase the money supply. It is merely exchanged for a different form of money demand deposits. The money supply is increased when banks lend funds to businesses, individuals, or governments. The bank loans are in the form of new demand deposits, which borrowers can then transfer to someone else by writing checks. In return for the loan (which is part of the money supply), the borrower gives the bank a *promissory note* which is a nonmonetary asset that is equal in value to the new demand deposit. The amount borrowed continues to circulate in the banking system as additional money until the loan is repaid. Prior to 1968 the United States was on a *gold standard* and our money was backed by gold. Today our money has value only because it is accepted by others as a means of payment for goods and services.

The responsibility for controlling the money supply is in the hands of the *Federal*

Reserve System (the Fed) which is administered by the *Federal Reserve Board of Governors*. The Fed has three tools of monetary control. First, it can limit or expand the ability of banks to make loans by raising or lowering banks' reserve requirements. The *required reserves* are equal to a specified percentage of the bank's total *deposit liabilities* that must be deposited with the regional Federal Reserve bank or held in the bank's vaults. Any reserves that a bank has deposited over and above the required minimum are *excess reserves* and form the basis for an increase in loans extended by the bank to borrowers. The ratio of the maximum increase in the money supply to an increase in bank reserves is the *money multiplier*. Its size is determined by the required reserve ratio. The second instrument of the Federal Reserve monetary control is the *discount rate*. This is the interest rate that banks must pay on funds borrowed from the Fed. Lowering the discount rate encourages banks to borrow from the Federal Reserve to acquire excess reserves in order to expand loan business. Raising the discount rate discourages them from making new loans.

The third and most often employed monetary tool of the Federal Reserve is *open market operations*. This is the purchase and sale of U.S. government securities by the Fed in order to increase or decrease bank reserves. When the Fed purchases a *bond* or a *bill* in the government securities market, the amount of the check that it issues to pay for the bond becomes an addition to the reserves of the banking system, and the money supply can grow. If the Fed sells a bond, the amount that it receives from the sale diminishes bank reserves, and this slows the growth of the money supply. These operations are so important that a special committee, the *Federal Reserve Open Market Committee* was established to oversee them.

Although not a specific tool for increasing or decreasing the money supply, the Fed also sets the interest rate in the *Federal Funds market* where banks borrow each other's excess reserves for short periods of time. Changing the *Federal Funds rate* is often an indicator that the Fed is about to change the economy's available money supply.

$ Perspective $

The Big Bank Controversy

An engraving of the Bank of the United States in Philadelphia about 1799. Further information on the evolution of the nation's banking system can be found in *The Second Bank of the United States* by R. C. H. Caterall (Chicago: University of Chicago Press, 1960); *The Theory and History of Banking* by Charles Dunbar (New York: G. P. Putnam's Sons, 1917); and *Money: Whence It Came, Where It Went* by John Kenneth Galbraith (Boston: Houghton Mifflin, 1975).

From the earliest days of the American republic, there has been conflict over states' rights versus the power of the federal government. One of the first important battles in this conflict was over the control of the nation's banking system. The Federalists, led by Alexander Hamilton, wanted a strong national banking system to finance the expansion of industry. The Anti-Federalists, under the leadership of Thomas Jefferson, wanted to minimize the power of the banking system, which they did not trust to protect the predominantly agricultural interests of the country.

The initial victory went to Hamilton and the Federalists when Congress chartered the first Bank of the United States in 1791 for a period of 20 years. One-fifth of the capital needed to finance the bank was provided by the federal government and the remaining four-fifths by private investors. The national bank established branches in major cities and engaged in commercial banking activities and central bank functions. It accepted deposits from and made loans to private borrowers. It also lent money to the federal government and acted as the depository for government funds. It issued banknotes of its own and acted to curb the issuance of banknotes by state-chartered or private banks.

This latter activity generated a great deal of hostility on the part of the state banks. When the charter of the first Bank of the United States expired, it was not renewed by Congress. Freed from the restraints imposed by the national bank, state banks went on a note-issuing spree. They more than doubled their note issues in 5 years. Most of them stopped redeeming their notes for gold and silver. As a result, the notes of many banks became practically worthless. There was chaos in the banking system and numerous bank failures and alternating periods of excessive money expansion and contraction.

To end the fiscal turmoil, the second Bank of the United States was chartered in 1816. It was similar in its financing and operations to the first bank. It also had a similar fate, its charter being allowed to lapse in 1836. The state banks again had the banking field to themselves until the National Banking Act of 1864. The act provided for a system of federally chartered banks to take over the note-issuing function of the state banks. Congress also intended these national banks to help finance government spending for the Civil War. It was not, however, until the establishment of the Federal Reserve System in 1913 that a true central bank was created.

For Further Study and Analysis

Study Questions

1. Have you ever transformed near money into money? How?
2. Are there any barter transactions that take place in today's economy? Why would anyone prefer barter to money transactions?
3. Using the criteria by which money is judged, how well would each of the following serve as a medium of exchange? (1) empty beer cans, (2) four-leaf clovers, (3) IOUs written on cards with the name and address of the writer, (4) fresh fish.
4. Which of the above items could serve one or both of the other two functions of money, even if it is not a good medium of exchange?
5. Because many people take vacations in the summer, there is an increased demand for currency. How is this additional demand satisfied? Does it increase the money supply? Why or why not?
6. Suppose that in one week the First National Bank made loans of $217,000. During that same week repayment on earlier loans amounted to $220,000. What happened to the money supply as a result?

7. Examine Table 2A. Show what the bank's balance sheet would look like if the Fed increased the required reserve ratio to 40%. What would it look like if the bank bought $30 million worth of bonds from the Fed? What would it look like if demand deposits increased from $100 million to $150 million?

8. If banks have no excess reserves, what happens when the Fed raises the required reserve ratio? What happens if the ratio is lowered?

9. Why doesn't the value of the public's assets change when the money supply is reduced through open market operations?

10. Since bank interest rates are always higher than the Fed discount rate, why does a rise in the discount rate discourage banks from making new loans?

11. Why does appointing members of the Federal Reserve Board of Governors for terms of 14 years make the board independent? Why was this provision put in when the Federal Reserve System was established?

Exercises in Analysis

1. Determine what Federal Reserve district you live in and write a short paper on the Federal Reserve bank that serves the district. Include such information as what states are served by the bank and the bank's capitalization, assets, and liabilities. This information can be obtained from the bank, the Federal Reserve Bulletin, or by visiting one of the many Federal Reserve Bank Web sites (A citation for the Chicago Fed that has links to all district banks is given below).

2. Assume the banking system is fully "loaned up" (no excess reserves) and the required reserve ratio is 20%. If the Fed then purchases $10 billion worth of U.S. Treasury securities from the banks, what is the effect on bank reserves? What is the total potential effect on the money supply?

3. Make a table showing current interest rates for different types of borrowing. Include interest rates on the following types of bank accounts, loans, and investments: deposit accounts; automobile loans; mortgage loans; 90-day certificates of deposit; money market funds; prime rate; Fed discount rate; Federal Funds rate; 26-week Treasury bills. (The first three rates can be obtained at local banking institutions and may vary from one to another; the remainder can be found in the *Wall Street Journal,* other financial publications, or at a Federal Reserve Web site.)

4. Look at a copy of the Nilson Report at your local library, and prepare a report on the trends in the use of check cards, ATMs, and credit cards.

Further Reading

An excellent Federal Reserve Web site is the one for the Chicago Fed at http://www.frbchi.org/. Click on the "map" option to find links to the other Fed branches and to find out just about anything you would like to know about the Federal Reserve System.

To learn about America's banking industry, check out the American Bankers Association at http://www.aba.com. Their site map will lead you to a world of information about money, banking, and our financial system.

Federal Reserve Bank of Chicago. "Money Matters: The American Experience With Money." *On Reserve #31,* April 1995. This presents the history of the banking system in the United States from colonial times until the present. Also available online at http://www.frbchi.org/pubs-speech/publications/BOOKLETS/money_matters/money_matters.html.

Federal Reserve Bank of Chicago. "Lesson Plan on Electronic Banking: The Check Is Not in the Mail." *On Reserve #34,* April 1996. This presents a description of banking in the electronic age and how technological innovations are changing the nature of the banking industry. Also available online at http://www.frbchi.org/ pubs-speech/publications/BOOKLETS/ electronic_money/electronic_money.html.

Galbraith, John Kenneth. *Money: Whence It Came, Where It Went*. Boston: Houghton Mifflin, 1975. An easy to read historical account of money, how it has been used, and how it affects economies.

Graziano, Loretta. *Interpreting the Money Supply*. New York: Quorum Books, 1987. The author takes the position that "the money supply is in the eye of the beholder." She discusses the pitfalls in interpreting data on the money supply. She draws conclusions regarding the relationships between the money supply and interest rates and the money supply and inflation.

Kurtzman, Joel. *The Death of Money: How the Electronic Economy Has Destabilized the World's Markets and Created Financial Chaos*. New York: Simon & Schuster, 1993. In the context of the twentieth-century history of money and of the financial services industry, the author examines how electronic funds transfers have changed the rules of the game. The resulting consequences for the economy have been negative, according to the author. Also looks at the effects on the securities market of program trading.

Miller, Roger Leroy, and David D. VanHoos. *Essentials of Money and Banking*. Reading, Mass.: Addison-Wesley, 1997. A little bit advanced, but a thorough explanation of the U.S. banking and financial systems.

Yablonsky, Lewis. *The Emotional Meaning of Money*. New York: Gardner Press, 1991. Money is more than just a means of exchange, a standard of value, and a store of wealth. According to the author, it has social and psychological aspects in addition to its traditional three functions.

chapter eleven

Economic Instability

Earning an income is necessary to get along in our economic system. The access to money is generally gained by means of having a job. Without a job, the ability to acquire the necessities of life, not to mention the luxuries that enhance life, is limited or nonexistent. The introductory article examines the changing nature of employment in the 1990s.

Movin' On Up!

What's going on in the U.S. economy? Since the recession of 1991, the economy has experienced a 7-year expansion, one of the longest in history. New jobs are being created at record numbers, and in April 1998 the unemployment rate dropped to 4.3%—its lowest level in almost 30 years. At the same time, inflation in consumer prices slowed to an annual rate of close to 1%, again one of the lowest levels in recent memory. Prices at the producer level were actually falling! Lyle Gramley, a former Fed official and now the chief economist for the Mortgage Bankers Association, says that this combination of strong growth in output, low unemployment, and low inflation is "virtually unprecedented" in our economic history.

This is all great news for most people, but it is puzzling news for the nation's economists who are having trouble explaining just why everything is going so well. At one time, and not too long ago, the conventional wisdom was that as an economy's output grew and unemployment fell, inflation would pick up and slow the economy back down. But after 7 years, unemployment and inflation are continuing to move in the same direction: down.

One idea as to why things are going so well is that the nation's workforce is getting older. Unemployment is always highest among the young and lowest among those in their forties and fifties, the current age range of those in the baby boom generation. Another is that lower federal budget deficits are freeing more of the nation's resources for capital investment, and the resulting improvements in technology and productivity are enabling the economy to produce more at lower costs. Lower oil prices are also helping. The world runs on energy, and as it gets cheaper, producing the nation's goods and services gets less expensive as well.

All this leads to good news on the job front for Generation X—those born between 1965 and 1979. Job openings for the college class of 1998 are expected to be up a record 27.5%, according to the annual survey done by Michigan State University. Starting salaries are up between 4 and 5 percent, the fifth straight year that they have increased, and they are up 15% for some graduates, especially those in information technology, engineering, and pharmacy. Part of these increases are due to the booming economy and business's demand for skilled employees, and part to the low number of graduates—a reduced supply.

The job market has become so tight that Congress, at the urging of the computer industry, is increasing the number of high-skilled foreign workers permitted to enter the country to work. The limit is currently 65,000 immigrants per year, but different plans in the House and Senate each propose raising the cap to 115,000.

It has not, however, been sweetness and light for all the country's workers. Consistent with the dual labor market in America (see chapter 9, p 233), the increase in the nation's jobs is split among those in the upper-income and lower-income professions. The number of new high-wage jobs increased by 18.8% between 1989 and 1997, and the number of low-wage jobs increased about 10%. During the same period there was essentially no growth in the number of "middle-wage" jobs. And while the earnings of college graduates continue to spiral upwards, the same does not hold true for others. After adjusting for inflation, real earnings for those in the lower and middle categories have either declined or stayed the same since the early to mid-1980s.

Increasing competition has forced many companies to look for ways to cut costs. Since wages and salaries make up about 70% of the average firm's total costs, reducing these numbers has been the first place that many employers have looked. The corporate downsizing movement of the 1980s and early 1990s has been followed by what is being called "downwaging," the cutting of pay and benefits for the blue-collar labor force.

Many of the new jobs being created are part-time jobs that have few, if any, benefits such as health insurance or employer-funded retirement programs. Nine out of ten workers with jobs of less than 35 hours per week do not have employer-paid health insurance, compared with only one in four workers with jobs of 35 hours per week or more. In 1997, there were 23 million Americans working in part-time jobs, or about 18% of all workers. This percentage has remained fairly constant throughout the 1990s, but it is up from 14% in 1968. Although many people, such as students, housewives, and the semiretired prefer part-time work, most surveys show that about 20% of those with part-time employment are actively seeking full-time work.

The employment problem faced by Generation X is not that there will be no jobs available. The economy will continue to create jobs, normally enough jobs to employ 94% to 95% of those in the labor force. The problem is that unless the members of Generation X and succeeding generations acquire the skills for highly productive occupations, their wages may be so low that they will not be able to maintain a satisfactory standard of living. We have already seen a substantial increase in the numbers of the working poor. If we do not find a way to bring the skill level of the workforce into line with the demands of the evolving new production system, the pessimistic expectations of Generation X, 75% of whom do not think they will have as high a standard of living as their parents, may be fulfilled.

The increased number of part-time workers and the lower wage rates being paid to them was one of the major reasons for the United Parcel Service (UPS) workers' strike in 1997. About 80% of all the workers hired by UPS since 1993 were part-time employees earning less than half the hourly rate earned by the company's full-time employees. As a result of the successful strike, UPS agreed to hire more full-time workers and to raise the hourly wage of part-timers.

If the result of the UPS strike becomes a trend, many economists think that rising wages throughout the economy will put upward pressure on prices and cause inflation to increase. Although this might not be good for the economy, at least economists will be able to rest easier knowing that their predicted trade-off between low unemployment and inflation really does exist, after all.

Chapter Preview

The experience of decreasing unemployment and inflation during an economic expansion is puzzling to many economists because the conventional wisdom is that when one increases the other decreases. This leads us to an investigation of the causes of economic instability. We want to know, What causes unemployment? What causes inflation? Is there a trade-off between unemployment and inflation? What are the consequences of unemployment and inflation?

Learning Objectives

After completing this chapter, you should be able to:

1. Describe the three major causes of unemployment.
2. Explain why some unemployment is hidden.
3. Define the natural rate of unemployment and explain what happens when it differs from the actual rate of unemployment.
4. Understand what inflation is and how it is measured by the CPI.
5. Describe the three major causes of inflation.
6. Use the quantity equation to explain the relationship between the money supply and the price level.
7. Use the Phillips curve to explain the relationship between unemployment and inflation.
8. Explain how changes in aggregate demand and aggregate supply affect the relationship between unemployment and inflation.
9. Explain the consequences of unemployment and inflation.

▶ What Causes Unemployment?

Economists agree on three reasons why people experience unwanted unemployment. They are between jobs, their skills are not in demand, or the economy is not growing rapidly enough to provide jobs for all who want them.

◼ Unemployment

The U.S. **civilian labor force** is defined as all people over 16 years of age who are working or looking for work. It does not include full-time students, retirees, or people who choose not to work. People in the civilian labor force are classified as either being employed if they have a job, even if it is a part-time job and they are actively seeking full-time work, or as being unemployed. People are classified as being unemployed only if they are actively seeking work but cannot find any. The **unemployment rate** is defined as the number unemployed and looking for work divided by the civilian labor force. In April 1998, there were 137,242,000 people in the civilian labor force, and 5,859,000 were unemployed, and the resulting unemployment rate was 4.3%.

Figure 1 shows the unemployment rate in the United States over the past 2 decades. As indicated in the opening article, the overall rate has declined steadily since 1992. White males over age 20 traditionally have the lowest rates of unemployment, and teenagers, blacks, and high school dropouts have the highest rates.

---

civilian labor force the number of persons age 16 or older who are either employed or are unemployed but actively looking for work.

unemployment rate the percentage of the civilian labor force that is actively looking for work but is unemployed.

Figure 1

Unemployment Rates for All Workers and Selected Groups, 1975–1997

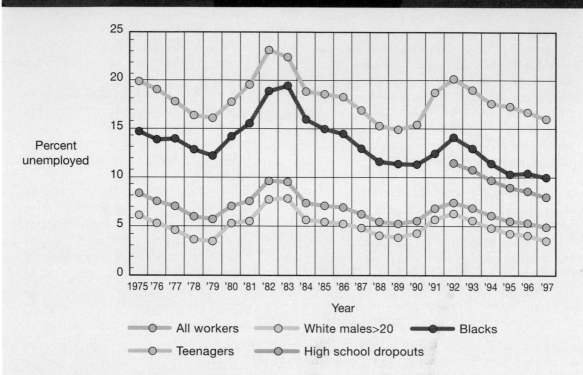

White males over 20 years of age traditionally experience the lowest unemployment rates and teenagers the highest. Unemployment rates increased during recessions in the early 1980s and 1990s, but have decreased steadily during the expansion of the mid-1990s.

Source: U.S. Department of Labor, Bureau of Labor Statistics.

Frictional Unemployment

It is expected that in a market economy a certain number of people will be changing jobs at any given time. They may have quit their jobs to find better ones or they may have lost their jobs because they were laid off. There are also people who are entering the labor force for the first time or reentering the labor force after taking time away from work to start a family or pursue other interests. In a dynamic economy there will always be some workers between jobs. This type of unemployment is called **frictional unemployment.** In a healthy economy, however, workers who are experiencing frictional unemployment should be able to find other jobs within a few weeks or months.

Frictional unemployment is a declining portion of the total number unemployed for two reasons. First, frictional unemployment results from a lack of perfect information on the part of employers and employees. Employers do not hire the first person who walks through their door, nor do those looking for work ac-

frictional unemployment unemployment that occurs when people change jobs, enter the job market, or reenter the job market.

cept the first job offered without looking around at their alternatives. The availability of better information (for example, via the Internet), job placement facilities, labor mobility, and, presumably, the efficiency of market clearing in labor markets should be better than in the past. It follows that frictional unemployment should be on the decline. Second, younger people tend to change jobs more often than older workers. As the baby boomers reached their 40s and 50s, they changed jobs less frequently, thus leading to a reduced amount of frictional unemployment.

Generous unemployment benefits can also contribute to frictional unemployment. The better the benefits and the longer they last, the less pressure there is on the unemployed to pound the pavement in pursuit of a job. This phenomenon has contributed to the high unemployment rates in Western Europe today (see Case Application El Desempleo on page 295).

Structural Unemployment

The skills needed to succeed in a dynamic economy are constantly changing. Workers who cannot adapt because their skills are obsolete or no longer needed will not be able to find meaningful jobs unless they can be retrained in the skills that are in demand. Likewise, workers who lose their jobs because employers move from one region to another may find themselves out of work with little hope of finding employment in their part of the country.

Structural unemployment occurs when the quantity demanded of particular kinds of labor falls short of the quantity offered in the job market at the going wage rate. When a large number of workers in an industry lose their jobs, it may be difficult or impossible to absorb them into other industries, even in the best of times. Skills and work experience in one line of work are not always easily transferred to another. The automobile and steel industries provide good examples of structural unemployment. The Detroit and Pittsburgh regions were hard hit by declines in these industries. The skilled auto or steel worker who is laid off is not automatically employable in the field of medical or information technology, even though there are numerous jobs in those fields in both cities.

These unemployed workers are looking for jobs. There are different types of unemployment and many reasons why those looking for work cannot always find it.

The same holds for people who make typewriters and vinyl record albums—products being replaced due to technology. Even if workers have transferable skills, they may not know about available jobs or may not be able to take them. Unemployed workers in Detroit may not be aware that they have the qualifications for job openings in Atlanta, Georgia. Even if they knew about a job in Atlanta, they might not be in a position to pull up stakes and move there.

There has always been a certain amount of structural unemployment. It goes with a technologically progressive market economy—some industries decline while others expand. Imagine what it must have been like in the early 1900s when automobiles replaced horse-drawn vehicles! Thousands of blacksmiths, grooms, and harness makers became structurally unemployed. They either learned the skills necessary to make cars and moved to Detroit, learned

structural unemployment the lack of work that occurs because of changes in the basic characteristics of a market, such as a new substitute product, a change in consumer tastes, or new technology in production.

some other skills, or remained unemployed. The older a worker is, the more difficult it is to make the transition to a new career. For this reason, structural unemployment is more of a problem among older Americans.

Unlike frictional unemployment, which has been declining because of technological progress and an older workforce, the amount of structural unemployment may have taken an upward shift for these same two reasons. In recent years the rate of technological change has speeded up, making more skills obsolete in a shorter span of time. And the older baby boomers who lose their jobs are less likely to be able to learn the new skills that can help them find meaningful employment in other professions.

Inadequate Aggregate (Total) Demand

Frictional and structural unemployment are distressing for the particular individuals and communities affected. But they are a fact of life in a market economy and are necessary for flexibility in the allocation of resources. Changing consumer tastes and the development of new products and production technologies require a continual reallocation of resources, including labor.

A more disturbing type of unemployment for the economy, one that can affect much larger numbers of workers, is **cyclical unemployment** associated with inadequate total de-

mand. When demand is down throughout the economy, there are simply not enough jobs to employ the labor force fully.

The total spending for all types of goods and services is called **aggregate demand.** When aggregate demand is below the full employment level, people will be out of work, some of them for long periods of time. **Full employment aggregate demand** is the level of demand necessary to put all an economy's resources to work in order to satisfy it. During a **recession,** such as the one in 1990–1991, aggregate demand is below the full employment level and the economy is operating far below its capacity. Resources, both human and nonhuman, are left idle.

Figure 2 illustrates the relationship between unemployment and aggregate demand. It shows a tank much like a water tank. The size of the tank represents the capacity of the economy to produce goods and services, and the purple represents the aggregate demand for those goods and services. When aggregate demand reaches the top of the tank, as shown on the left (Figure 2A), full employment results. When aggregate demand is not sufficient to employ all of the labor, capital, and other resources of the economy, a recession occurs; or, if the excess capacity is very large, a **depression.*** This situation is illustrated on the right, in Figure 2B. The white space between the purple and the top of the tank is unused capacity—unemployment.

---

cyclical unemployment the lack of work that occurs because the total effective demand for goods and services is insufficient to employ all workers in the labor force.

aggregate demand the total effective demand for the nation's output of goods and services.

full employment aggregate demand the level of total effective demand that is just sufficient to employ all workers in the labor force.

recession a decline for at least 2 successive quarters in the nation's total output of goods and services.

depression a severe and prolonged period of decline in the level of business activity.

What Causes Unemployment?

EconExplorer

In a recession there is too little buying to keep the economic wheels turning at a rate that will provide full use of the available resources, including labor. A recession tends to spread throughout the system and affect all parts of the nation's economy. It may be aggravated by structural problems, such as those in the auto

*There is another way to distinguish between a recession and a depression. A recession is when your neighbor loses his or her job; a depression is when you lose yours.

Figure 2

Production Capacity and Unemployment

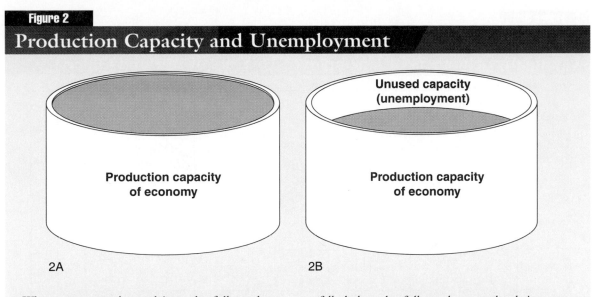

Unused capacity (unemployment)

Production capacity of economy

Production capacity of economy

2A

2B

When aggregate demand is at the full employment level, the production capacity is fully utilized (2A). However, when aggregate demand

falls below the full employment level, it causes unused production capacity, creating unemployment (2B).

industry, but the main problem is inadequate total spending. When workers are unemployed, they have less to spend and therefore reduce their purchases. This results in more workers being laid off and therefore spending less, and aggregate demand falling even further. A downward spiral is created that, if it isn't stopped, leads to a depression (Figure 3).

◢ Natural Rate of Unemployment

The combined unemployment arising from frictional and structural causes is referred to as the **natural rate of unemployment.** It is often also referred to as full employment. This might seem strange at first because we tend to think of full employment as a state where there is absolutely no unemployment. This, however, is unreasonable to expect since people will always be moving in and out of jobs and technology is constantly changing. Consequently, we say there is full employment when full employment aggregate demand exists and cyclical unemployment is equal to zero.

Economists and policymakers increasingly base their analyses of the economy on a comparison of the natural rate of unemployment to the actual measured rate. If the actual rate of unemployment is greater than the natural rate of unemployment

employment, it indicates that aggregate demand is too low, and policies might be considered that would stimulate the economy and provide more jobs. If the actual rate is below the natural rate, it indicates that the economy is expanding too quickly. The excess demand for workers (and other resources) will put upward pressure on wages, leading to increased inflation. Policymakers, especially the Fed, may then consider policies designed to slow the economy's rate of growth.

A wordy, but more precise, term used to define the natural rate of unemployment is the non-accelerating-inflation rate of unemployment (NAIRU). This definition implies that the natural rate is as low as unemployment can go without fueling an overall increase in the price level. It is the minimum sustainable level of unemployment consistent with stable prices.

There is disagreement over exactly what the natural rate of unemployment is in today's labor market. It changes over time, and will be affected

natural rate of unemployment the combined total of frictional and structural unemployment.

Figure 3

Unemployment by Origination 1979–1997
Cumulative Numbers of Unemployed 16 Years of Age and Older

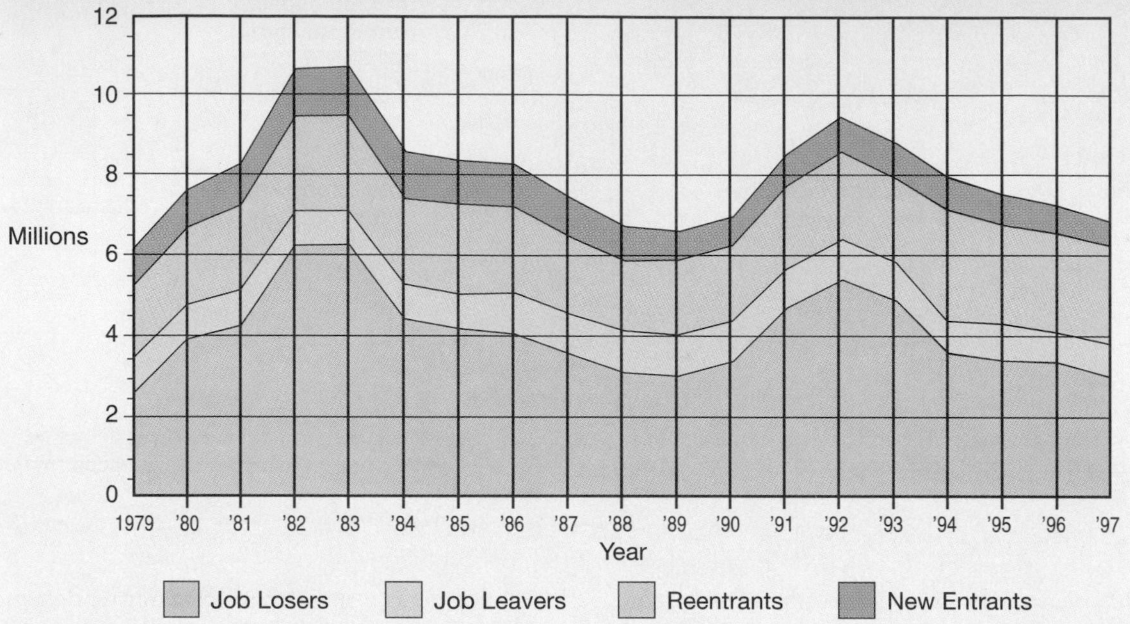

| Job Losers | Job Leavers | Reentrants | New Entrants |

Most of the unemployed have lost their jobs, but many are reentering the labor force or are new entrants.

Source: U.S. Department of Labor, Bureau of Labor Statistics.

by such things as minimum wage laws, labor mobility, the age of the population, retirement plans, unemployment benefits, the percentage of women entering the workforce, foreign competition, and so forth. The Congressional Budget Office uses the figure of 5.5% in its forecasts. Whatever it is, most economists believe that the unemployment rates of less than 5% recorded throughout 1998 and into 1999 are below the natural rate, and they are fearful that these cannot be sustained without increased wages and prices.

◣ Hidden Unemployment

The labor force is made up of persons who are either working or unemployed but actively looking for work. Someone who would like to have a job but is not actively looking for work is not counted as a part of the civilian labor force or among the unemployed. Such individuals are part of the hidden unemployment in the United States.

Some of those who have looked for a job for a long time without finding one become discouraged. They decide that it is useless to look for work and stop trying to find employment. In the employment statistics, they are then no longer counted as unemployed. The Bureau of Labor Statistics has put the number of these "discouraged" workers at about 1 million. Others, outside of government, have estimated the number to be almost 3 million.

Another form of hidden unemployment is represented by the workers who have had their work hours reduced involuntarily. If a factory cuts back from a 40-hour workweek to a 30-hour week as a result of slow sales, the official measure of unemployment is not affected. For the workers involved, however, this situation is the same as a 25% drop in their employment level, and a change from a full-time job to a part-time one. The term underemployed has been used to describe those workers who can find only part-time work or jobs that are beneath those for which they are qualified.

El Desempleo

El desempleo, le chomage involontaire, die Arbeitslosigkeit—whether you say it in Spanish, French, German, or English, unemployment is a bad word in Europe these days. The major European countries have not been accustomed to such mass unemployment since the Great Depression of the 1930s. For 3 decades following recovery from World War II, unemployment rates in the dominant economies of Europe were lower—generally much lower—than in the United States (Figure 4).

This is no longer the case. In the mid-1980s unemployment rates in Europe caught up with and surpassed the unemployment rate in the United States. In 1997, some 18 million workers in the European Union were unemployed and the unemployment rate in the 15 EU countries reached an average of over 10.6%, more than double the U.S. rate. Even worse, nearly half of those unemployed in Europe were without work for over a year. The percentage of long-term unemployed in the United States was small by comparison.

Those figures for Europe are the official rates. The real rates of joblessness, including discouraged workers and the underemployed, arc much worse. Also, in some European countries the numbers of individuals subtracted from the labor rolls because of being on disability are exceedingly large, forming another group of hidden unemployed. According to a 1992 study, fully one-quarter of the Dutch labor force over the age of 45 was on disability payments. A large fraction of those were actually able-bodied workers given disability pensions only as a means of removing them from the labor rolls. If they were counted among the unemployed, it is estimated that the official unemployment rate would have been double that reported.

European workers who lose their jobs can expect to be out of work for a long time. Only 5% find another job within a month. In the United States, on the other hand, about half of those out of work find employment within a month. The U.S. economy has proven much more prolific in creating new jobs than European economies.

The reasons for Europe's high unemployment rates are easy to understand. Overly generous unemployment benefits paid out over long periods of time provide little incentive for workers to actively pursue jobs. High employment taxes and legally mandated fringe benefits make it costly for firms to hire new employees. High minimum wage rates reduce job opportunities for teenagers and low-skilled workers. Government-imposed job protection laws make it difficult to fire workers, so few are hired. As result, many European firms are moving their operations to other countries. German firms, for example, have increased overseas employment by 50% since 1985 while creating hardly any new jobs at home.

The other side of the picture, however, is not so rosy for American workers. For one thing, it is also much easier to lose your job in America than in Europe. Labor turnover rates are much higher. Another difference is that in the United States many of the jobs available are so low-paying that they leave the worker in or

Figure 4

Unemployment Rates in the United States and Major European Countries, 1963–1997

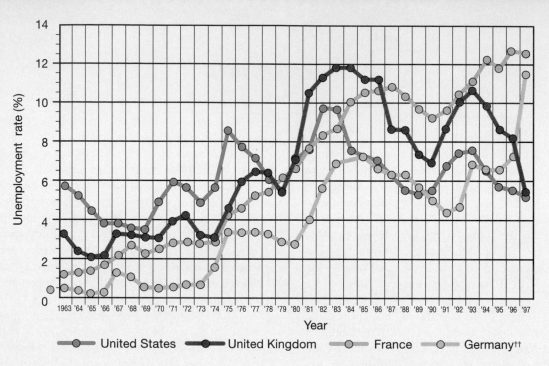

††Former West Germany area (before unification)

Unemployment rates were lower in major European countries than in the United States until the 1980s. Since then, unemployment in Europe has climbed well above that in the United States.

Source: Department of Labor, Bureau of Labor Statistics; *The Economist*, Economic Indicators.

just above poverty. In Europe, low-income workers in comparable deciles earn 44% more, based on the purchasing power of their wages, than in America. A European worker in the lowest 10% of wage earners earns 68% of the average European pay. The U.S. worker in the lowest decile earns only 38% of the average U.S. pay.

Economic Reasoning

1. What are some examples of hidden unemployment in Europe?
2. What kind of economic policies might work to reduce unemployment in Europe?
3. Which workers do you think are better off with respect to unemployment problems, American or European? Why?

▶ What Causes Inflation?

Unemployment is one of the twin devils of economic instability; the other is inflation. This section sheds some light on the forces that give rise to inflation, forces that can arise on the demand side of the economy or on the supply side. But first we will examine what inflation is and how it is measured.

◧ Measuring Inflation

Inflation is a period of generally rising prices in the economy as a whole. In a market economy, it is normal for the prices of some things to rise and others to fall because of changing demand and supply. But when the prices of nearly everything rise, inflation occurs. This increases the cost of living. Each dollar is worth less and buys fewer goods and services.

The **consumer price index (CPI)** is the most commonly used measure of changes in the general price level. This index is a statistic issued monthly by the Bureau of Labor Statistics of the U.S. Department of Labor. It is popularly known as the cost-of-living index, although it actually measures changes in a specific group of prices rather than people's living costs. Costs of living are affected by changes in buying habits as well as by price changes.

 ## What Causes Inflation?

EconExplorer

The CPI expresses the price of consumer goods in a given month as a percentage of the price prevailing in some earlier period, known as the **base period.** In computing the index, the total cost of a representative sample of 205 household purchases during the base period is calculated. The cost of that same "market basket" of goods and services is then computed in subsequent months. The base period price level is assigned an index number of 100. If the current cost of the market basket is 25% greater than in the base period, the CPI is 125. Figure 5 shows the CPI for the period 1960–1997,

with 1982–1984 as the base period. The index increased steadily throughout the 1970s, but it has leveled off in recent years. The rate of inflation is measured as the percentage change in the index from one period to another. The inflation rate as measured by the percentage change in the CPI from 1970 to 1997 is shown in Figure 5.

Many economists believe that the CPI overstates the actual inflation rate because it does not take into account the improvement in the quality of the goods and services that make up the market basket. In addition, it fails to incorporate the fact that as the prices of some goods rise, consumers will switch to less expensive substitutes. While the CPI might represent the price of goods, it does not necessarily mean that all of us will need to increase our expenditures by the same amount as it increases. A 1995 report by a presidential committee appointed to study the CPI concluded that it overstated the real rate of inflation by a little bit—about 1.5%.

◧ Demand-Pull Inflation

You will recall from chapter 4 that when the demand for a good or service increases, both the quantity exchanged of the product and its price increase. The relative increases in price and quantity depend on the slope of the supply curve. When supply is inelastic and the supply curve is relatively vertical, increases in demand lead to increases in price with little impact on quantity. When the supply curve is flatter, in-

---

consumer price index (CPI) a statistical measure of changes in the prices of a representative sample of urban family purchases relative to a previous period.

base period (base year) the reference period for comparison of subsequent changes in an index series; set equal to 100.

Figure 5

The Inflation Rate as Measured by the Percentage Change in the CPI, 1970–1997

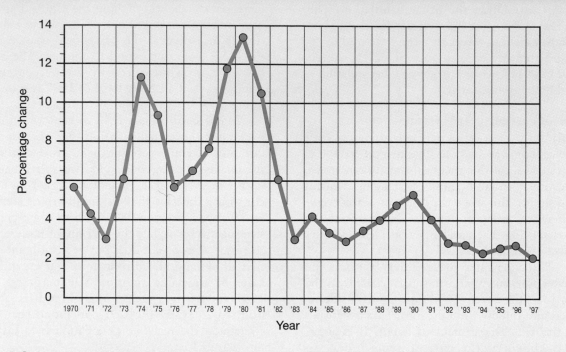

Inflation, measured by the Consumer Price Index (CPI), accelerated in the 1970s, plunged in the recession of the early 1980s, and slowed considerably during the 1990s.

Source: U.S. Department of Labor, Bureau of Labor Statistics.

creases in demand lead to more increases in output and smaller increases in price.

The same basic logic applies when we analyze the effects of increases in aggregate demand. When the economy is near full employment and it is difficult to squeeze more output from its resources, an increase in aggregate demand will result in increases in the overall price level with little impact on the economy's out-

demand-pull inflation a continuing rise in the general price level that occurs when aggregate demand exceeds the full-employment output capacity of the economy.

put of goods and services. When this happens, the demand for goods and services exceeds the production capacity of the economy, and we have **demand-pull inflation.** This is illustrated in Figure 6A, where we again have a tank representing the capacity output of the economy. The amount of purchasing power attempting to buy goods and services is shown in purple. When demand reaches the top of the tank, the economy is unable to produce additional goods and services in the short run. As a result, the purchasing power overflows the tank and is reflected in the economy as a general rise in prices, or inflation.

If the economy is not near full employment, and there are a significant number of unemployed resources—both human and non-human—then an increase in aggregate demand

Figure 6

Production Capacity and Inflation

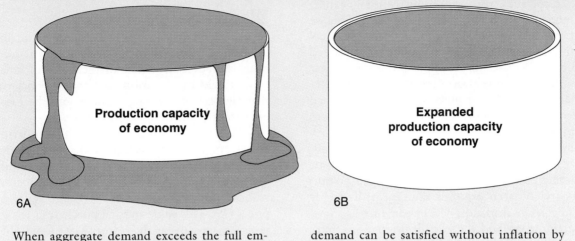

Production capacity of economy

6A

Expanded production capacity of economy

6B

When aggregate demand exceeds the full employment level, it causes inflation (6A). However, over a period of time, increased aggregate demand can be satisfied without inflation by increasing the production capacity of the economy (6B).

will result in a relatively greater increase in output and employment, and a smaller increase in the price level.

Even if the economy is near full employment, if the increase in aggregate demand is not too rapid, the economy can adjust. In the long run, producers can expand their capacity to produce more goods and services. If the increase in demand occurs gradually over a period of time, it can be matched by an enlargement of the output capacity of the economy without causing inflation. This is shown in Figure 6B. But when demand increases rapidly at or near full employment, as during a period of increased spending by households, businesses, and governments, the excess purchasing power overflows in the form of inflation, as in Figure 6A.

When inflation gets started, it is likely to be self-reinforcing. If people see that prices are going up, they may attempt to stock up on goods before prices rise even further. This boosts demand and accelerates the inflation. **Speculators** also contribute to inflation. With prices rising rapidly, it is profitable to buy something, hold it for a while, and then sell it. This fuels inflation, not only by adding specula-

tive demand to the market, but also by holding supplies of goods off the market.

◆ Cost-Push Inflation

Inflation can also result from reduced supplies of production inputs as well as from increased total demand. When inflation comes from the supply side, it is called **cost-push inflation.**

A major cause of high inflation in the late 1970s was the increase in energy costs brought on by the OPEC oil cartel. Because energy is an important factor input in the production of so many goods and services, the rise in energy prices increased production costs. Prices rose

---

speculators people who purchase goods or financial assets in anticipation that prices will rise and they can sell at a profit; speculators can also speculate on a fall in prices.

cost-push inflation a continuing rise in the general price level that results from increases in production costs.

throughout the economy. The increase in oil prices also raised the demand for oil substitutes, such as coke, a coal residue. Industries that use coke for fuel, the steel industry for instance, found that they had to pay more for it. Because of the increase in this production cost, steel prices went up. This price rise, in turn, resulted in price increases for all of the goods using steel.

There is often an interaction between demand-pull and cost-push inflation forces, each feeding the other. When the cost of living goes up, workers demand higher wages so that they can maintain their real incomes and living standards. The wage increases raise production costs, causing producers to increase prices again. Workers try to catch up with the cost of living by higher wage demands, which again increases production costs and the cost of living. Sometimes this wage inflation is built into labor union contracts with a **cost-of-living adjustment (COLA)** clause. The COLA clause calls for automatic wage increases when the consumer price index goes up a specified number of percentage points.

The government has been accused of contributing to cost-push inflation by its environmental controls and other regulations. Government-imposed emission controls and safety requirements for automobiles have increased car prices by several hundred dollars. Smokestack emission controls on industries have increased their production costs, which raises the price of products. Businesses complain that the

increase in paperwork required by government reports and regulations has raised their costs of doing business and the prices they must charge.

◢ Monetary Inflation

Demand-pull and cost-push inflation are attributed to changed demand and supply conditions. An alternative view of the cause of inflation is held by the **monetarists,** who believe that changes in the money supply are the most important factor in inflation.

This view is embodied in the **quantity equation.** The quantity equation states that the total value of goods and services purchased during a given period, say a year, is the number of transactions **(T)** times the average level of prices **(P).** This value of total purchases (T × P) must be the same as the quantity of money **(M)** times the average number of times that each dollar of the money supply changes hands, called the **velocity of money (V).** In other words, the quantity equation says that the total spending during a period (M × V) must be the same as the total value of goods and services bought and sold (T × P). Stated in shorthand equation form, it is M × V = T × P. If the volume of transactions (T) remains the same, as it would at full employment, and the velocity of money (V) is constant, an increase in the money supply (M) necessarily results in a rise in the price level (P). This relationship between the money supply and the price level is summarized in the quantity equation below.

$$M\uparrow \times V = T \times P\uparrow$$

money   velocity   transactions   prices
up   constant   constant   up

The quantity equation is a truism rather than a statement of economic analysis since the total amount spent (M × V) must always necessarily be the same as the total amount received (T × P). For some time, the quantity equation was out of fashion in economic theory because it was not considered important to solving economic problems. Economists noted that you could have full employment and stable prices with any given money supply,

(Continued on page 302)

---

cost-of-living adjustment (COLA) a frequently used provision of labor contracts that grants wage increases based on changes in the Consumer Price Index; often referred to in negotiations as the "escalator clause."

monetarists those who believe that changes in the money supply have a determining effect on economic conditions.

quantity equation (equation of exchange) the quantity of money **(M)** times the velocity of its circulation **(V)** equals the quantity of goods and services transacted **(T)** times their average price **(P)**; M × V = T × P.

velocity of money (V) the average rate at which money changes hands.

Case Application

The High Cost of Loving

The increase in the cost of living has slowed down recently, but the same isn't true for the cost of loving. Raymond F. DeVoe Jr., who writes a stock market newsletter, has been calculating a cost of loving (COL) index since 1955. (Please note that the COL index is not the same as COLA, the cost-of-living adjustment.) Since that time, the general price level of consumer goods and services has increased 6.1 times the level in 1955. In other words, if 1955 were the base period, the CPI would have risen from 100 to 610.

To figure the COL, we take a representative sample of goods and services involved in the mating game and compare their prices in 1955 with the prices today. A cost of loving index might be calculated as shown in Table 1. The 1998 COL index was 748.

The cost of loving has gone up much more than the CPI. The COL assumes that young men still court young women the same way they did in 1955. Today's courting practices may include fewer candlelight dinners and fewer birthday gifts of expensive perfume. The same type of problem affects the CPI. Changes in lifestyles and consumption habits make comparisons of the cost of living over a number of years difficult. For this reason, the base period and the contents of the market basket of goods for the CPI are periodically updated.

Table 1   Cost of Loving Index*

Item	Number Purchased (Q)	Price in 1955 (P_0)	$P_0 \times Q$	Price in 1998 (P_1)	$P_1 \times Q$
Bottle of wine	4	$1.55	$6.20	$9.95	$39.80
First-run movie	14	1.00	14.00	7.50	105.00
Candlelight dinner	6	2.75	16.50	80.00	480.00
Silver bracelet	2	1.29	2.58	26.00	52.00
Dozen roses	2	5.00	10.00	40.00	80.00
Perfume	1	35.00	35.00	95.00	95.00
Diamond ring	1	400.00	400.00	2,750.00	2,750.00
Blood test	1	7.00	7.00	45.00	45.00
Marriage license	1	2.00	2.00	45.00	45.00
			$493.28		$3,691.80

$$\text{COL (1998)} = \frac{P_1 \times Q}{P_0 \times Q} \times 100 = \frac{\$3,691.80}{\$493.28} \times 100 = 748$$

*This index is based on but is not identical to the one devised by Raymond F. DeVoe Jr.

Economic Reasoning

1. One of the most inflationary items in the COL was the candlelight dinner. The price of dining out increased because more women entered the labor force and, with two people working full time, they dined out more frequently. Would you call the inflation of dining out a demand-pull or a cost-push type of inflation? Why?

2. Which index is a better measure of our purchasing power, the CPI or the COL? Why?

3. Do you think that the high cost of loving has actually affected dating practices? How? Do price changes affect our buying habits in general? What implication does this have for the validity of the CPI?

(Continued from page 300)

whether it be large or small, because the monetary unit itself is arbitrary.

The quantity theory of money made a comeback in the 1980s, and the monetarists had a large influence on policy. First they noted that T grows over time—it is the growth rate of the economy. They argued that if the economy is at full employment and V is stable, then increasing the money supply annually by the same percentage as the annual growth rate of T would result in a stable price level over time. Although this works on paper, economists have found three problems with it. First, velocity might not be sta-

ble, so there is no way to know what effect an increase in M might have on T × P. Second, since financial markets have been deregulated, it is increasingly difficult to accurately control the growth rate of the money supply. Third, there has been a lack of correspondence between changes in the money supply and the rate of inflation in recent years. As we saw in chapter 1, regardless how good a theory may look on paper, if it doesn't work in the real world, it must be rejected. As a consequence, monetarism has been relegated to the back seat of economic analysis.

Is There a Trade-off between Unemployment and Inflation?

Unemployment and inflation have plagued economic systems since the beginning of market economies. But in earlier experience, they did not occur together. In this section, we will examine the question of whether we must necessarily have more of one when we have less of the other.

Phillips Curve

In 1958 an economist from New Zealand, A. W. "Bill" Phillips, published a paper demonstrating that for a century there had been a trade-off between unemployment and inflation—the more you had of one, the less you had of the other, and vice versa. Historically, economic booms resulted in full employment, and the high level of aggregate demand caused shortages of goods and services. As a consequence, prices rose. When the boom collapsed, demand fell off, sur-

pluses of goods appeared, and workers were laid off. Prices and unemployment generally moved in opposite directions. The graphic illustration of this trade-off was named the **Phillips curve** after its detector.

In the last 25 years, however, there has been a controversy over whether the historic relationship between inflation and unemployment still exists. Did Bill Phillips discover something that expired soon after it was discovered?

The Phillips curve trade-off was alive and healthy in the 1960s, as shown in Figure 7.

Phillips curve a statistical relationship between increases in the general price level and unemployment.

Figure 7

Inflation and Unemployment Rates, 1960–1968

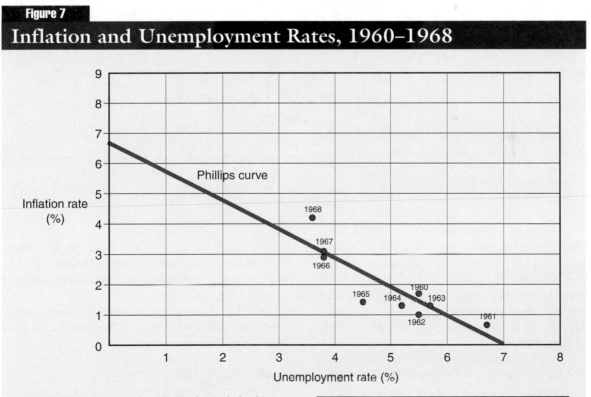

The Phillips curve in the 1960s showed the historic trade-off between inflation and unemployment.

Source: U.S. Department of Labor, Bureau of Labor Statistics.

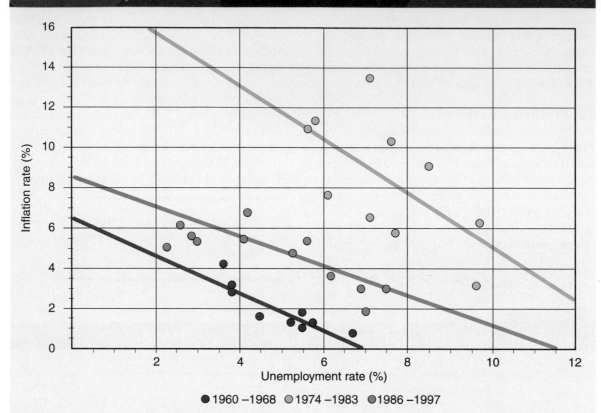

Figure 8

Inflation and Unemployment Rates, 1960–1968, 1974–1983, 1986–1997

● 1960 –1968 ○ 1974 –1983 ● 1986 –1997

The Phillips curve showing the trade-off between inflation and unemployment is not constant over time. It shifts according to economic expectations and other factors. But under any given conditions, the greater the amount of unemployment, the lower inflation is likely to be, and vice versa.

Source: Calculated from data from the U.S. Department of Labor, Bureau of Labor Statistics.

The unemployment rate is on the horizontal axis, and the inflation rate is on the vertical axis. The line through the inflation-unemployment points for 1960–1968 shows that the average change of one variable is clearly inversely related to a change in the other. It is the Phillips curve.

When the unemployment rate was over 4%, the inflation rate was less than 2%. The higher the unemployment rate, the lower the inflation. In 1961, when unemployment reached 6.7% of the workforce, the inflation rate was negligible, only 0.7%. On the other hand, when unemployment fell below 4%, the inflation rate rose sharply. In 1968, when unemployment was only 3.6%, the inflation rate reached 4.2%. This does not seem like a high inflation rate in view of what followed in the 1970s, but at that time it was considered quite high.

◤ Stagflation

In the 1970s the inflation-unemployment relation saw a dramatic change. Instead of having *either* high unemployment or high inflation rates as we had in the 1960s and earlier periods, we had *both* high unemployment and high inflation. When we have a combination of high unemployment and high inflation rates, the situation is called **stagflation,** a combination of stagnation and inflation.

This led some economists to say that there was no longer a Phillips curve trade-off. But the Phillips curve for 1974–1983, the blue line in Figure 8, shows that a trade-off between inflation and unemployment did exist, although at a higher level than in the 1960s. Both variables had shifted upward and the trade-off was not as definitive. Nevertheless, it appears that the Phillips curve still represented the relationship between inflation and unemployment, even under conditions of stagflation. The green line in Figure 8 shows that the trade-off still exists today, but at lower rates of both inflation and unemployment.

Stagflation is very unpleasant, both for the public suffering from it and for the economic policymakers trying to cure it. How did the economy get into that situation in the 1970s? Traditionally inflation was not supposed to become a problem until the economy was producing at full capacity. The situation represented in Figure 2B on page 293, where there is excess production capacity, provides no reason for prices to go up. Only when aggregate demand exceeded capacity was there expected to be a spillover into inflation, as in Figure 6A on page 299.

Why wasn't this true in the 1970s? Why did the Phillips curve shift upward? To help us with the answers to these questions, let us look at another set of diagrams that relate **aggregate supply** to aggregate demand. Figure 9A shows the same simplified conditions as the output tanks we saw earlier in Figures 2 and 6, but in a different way, by using aggregate demand and supply curves. The aggregate supply curve (AS) is assumed to be perfectly elastic (horizontal) at an existing price level as long as the economy is operating at much less than full capacity. Because output and employment are directly related, output levels such as Q_1 and Q_2 occur when the economy is operating far below full employ-

The 1970s oil crisis contributed not only to stagflation in the economy, but also to long lines at gas stations.

ment. When output increases and approaches the full employment level (Q_5), however, the aggregate supply curve begins to bend upwards, until, at the full employment level of output (Q_3), it becomes perfectly inelastic (vertical). This output level is the maximum that the economy can produce, increasing demand cannot lead to greater output, only higher prices.

When aggregate demand is on the elastic part of the supply curve, as it is with demand curves AD_1 and AD_2, demand can increase with no rise in the price level (P_1 and P_2 are the same). The increase in demand results in increased output only (Q_1 to Q_2). In the inelastic part, as with AD_3 and AD_4, increases in

stagflation a term created to describe the situation where high inflation and high unemployment occur simultaneously.

aggregate supply the total amount of goods and services available from all industries in the economy.

Figure 9

The Effect of Increases in Aggregate Demand on Prices

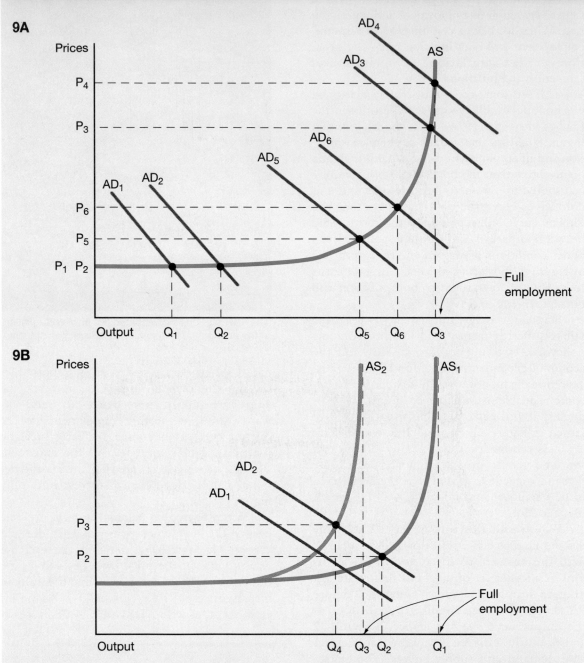

9A

9B

In Figure 9A aggregate supply (AS) is assumed to be perfectly elastic (horizontal) at the existing price level (P_1) when the economy is operating below its full production capacity. Aggregate demand can increase with no increases in prices (AD_1 to AD_2). When output approaches the full employment level (Q_5), however, the aggregate supply curve begins to bend upwards, indicating that demand increases (AD_5 to AD_6) will be accompanied by both price and output increases.

When the economy reaches full employment (Q_3), the aggregate supply curve becomes perfectly inelastic (vertical). Increases in demand (AD_3 to AD_4) will result in price increases with no increase in output.

In Figure 9B, the aggregate supply curve decreases from AS_1 to AS_2. As a consequence, output and employment will fall, regardless of whether the aggregate demand curve is AD_1 or AD_2. The result is stagflation.

demand lead only to increases in price (P_3 to P_4) because the economy is already operating at its maximum potential output. In between the two extreme cases, however, an increase in aggregate demand—AD_5 to AD_6—will lead to increases in both prices (from P_5 to P_6) and output (Q_5 to Q_6). As output expands, employment expands along with it and unemployment decreases. It is this curved portion of the aggregate supply curve that gives rise to the Phillips curve relationship between inflation and unemployment. The actual supply curve in the 1960s probably was like that shown in Figure 9A.

The Phillips curve in Figure 7 and the aggregate supply curve in Figure 9A show the normal relationship between unemployment and inflation prior to the 1970s. How, then, did we get into the stagflation situation? The stagflation problem of the 1970s originated in the second half of the 1960s, when the war in Vietnam escalated at the same time that major new domestic social programs got under way. Additional demand resulted from increased government expenditures for these activities. The increased government spending was not offset by higher taxes, thus generating an increase in aggregate demand from AD_1 to AD_2 in Figure 9B. If aggregate supply had remained the same, the economy might have experienced near full employment with a slight increase in prices (Q_2 and P_2).

The aggregate supply curve, however, did not remain the same. The surge in oil prices and the resulting energy shortage in the 1970s caused the aggregate supply curve to shift from AS_1 to AS_2. With fewer energy resources, the maximum possible output of the economy fell from Q_1 to Q_3. With aggregate demand at AD_2, instead of finding ourselves at a high output level with a small increase in the price level, the economy's output was reduced to Q_4 and prices increased all the way to P_3.

If the aggregate supply curve is at AS_2 instead of AS_1, changes in aggregate demand will result in the familiar trade-off between inflation and unemployment, but at a greater level of both. This explains why the Phillips curve in the 1970s moved up to the blue line in Figure 8. For example, had the aggregate demand decreased back to AD_1 along AS_2, output and prices still would have fallen, and unemployment would have increased.

But aggregate demand did not decrease. Instead, a succession of economic stabilization programs failed to stem the inflation. This failure created expectations in the minds of consumers, workers, and businesspeople that prices would continue to rise. Inflationary expectations probably played a large role in what happened during the decade. When the public loses faith in a stable price level, prices are bid up by people stocking up in anticipation of even higher prices to come. Attempts by labor unions to keep wages in step with, or ahead of, increases in the cost of living raised the cost of labor resources and resulted in more leftward shifts of the aggregate supply curve. Programs designed to increase aggregate demand in order to create jobs moved the aggregate demand curve to the right. Together they resulted in an ever-increasing upward spiral of prices.

It took the shock treatment of a severe recession in the early 1980s to break the inflationary psychology, and the Phillips curve shifted back to a lower level (green line, Figure 8). Although unemployment and inflation are not as low as they were during the 1960s, they are getting closer. The improved technology and increased productivity that are spurring the amazing expansion of the 1990s are apparently pushing the aggregate supply curve further and further to the right. The point in Figure 8 that shows our 1997 experience (2.3% inflation and 5.0% unemployment) could very well fit along the Phillips curve for the 1960s, and it might be signaling another downward shift in the curve.

Case Application

Going Down?

Although the steady decreases in the rates of both inflation and unemployment are surprising to a generation of economists that grew up believing in the trade-off between the two described by the Phillips curve, it is not the first time in American history that this has happened. In the 1870s, improvements in manufacturing technology (especially steel) and the rise of the large, modern business corporation led to strong growth and falling prices. The same occurred during the Roaring Twenties with the spread of mass production and the increased use of electricity in manufacturing. The root of increased growth with lower prices in the 1990s is the increased use of information technology—computers.

Low unemployment rates translate into a shortage of workers, so companies need to find ways to boost the productivity of their existing workers. The answer is in increased investment in new technologies and the training necessary to keep employees up to date. So far in 1998, investment in information technology is increasing at an annual rate of 26%, and as noted in chapter 7 (page 183), high technology training is booming.

What the three time periods (the 1870s, 1920s and 1990s) have in common is that they each represent a wave of innovation in the way that we produce our goods and services. In all three instances, we made major breakthroughs that allowed us to produce more and more output at lower and lower costs.

But it isn't just the improvements in American productivity that are leading prices down. The crisis in Southeast Asia is also contributing. In the late 1980s and early 1990s, the economies of East and Southeast Asia were the fastest growing in the world. In order to be able to provide the capital and consumer goods needed to fuel and sustain this growth, investment in the region soared, especially in automobile manufacturing facilities. Although the region's industrial production grew at nearly 9% per year from 1995 through 1997, consumer spending was growing at only around 7.5%. The difference led to an overcapacity of manufacturing capital and, ultimately, an oversupply of goods that put downward pressure on prices.

When the Asian boom ended and the financial crisis hit in late 1997, the oversupply problems became worse. Desperate to put their people back to work and keep their factories running, businesses in Thailand, Malaysia, and Indonesia cut prices even further and their governments allowed the value of their currencies to depreciate in order to increase their international sales. As we will explain in chapter 16, this made the prices of their exports even less expensive.

For generations of Americans raised on steady increases in the price level, the current climate of decreasing inflation has been a pleasant surprise. Not only are American-made goods getting cheaper because of productivity gains, but the flood of low-priced Asian imports is forcing domestic producers and producers in other parts of the world to keep their prices low in order to compete.

Is it all goods news, or can lower prices be harmful to an economy? Although we have been experiencing decreases in the rate that prices increase, inflation still does exist, albeit at very low rates. Deflation, an actual decrease in prices, has not occurred, at least not yet.

This can be dangerous to people who have borrowed heavily hoping that rising prices would enable them to pay back their debts with cheaper dollars (see page 310). If prices and incomes were to actually decrease, households with debt (which means most households) would find it increasingly difficult to meet the principal and interest payments on existing car loans, home mortgages, and consumer debt.

▶ What Are the Consequences of Unemployment and Inflation?

Having examined the nature and causes of unemployment and inflation and their relationship to each other, we will now take a look at their economic and social consequences.

◩ Income Effects of Unemployment

Unemployed people and their families must continue to pay living costs when their income is cut. Nondiscretionary expenditures such as insurance, housing payments, utility bills, and taxes take a large part of some unemployed people's savings, especially after their eligibility for unemployment compensation is exhausted. The loss of medical insurance coverage resulting from unemployment is a major financial problem for families in case of illness, accident, or pregnancy (see the introductory article for chapter 13, p. 349). The loss of income means a reduction in buying power and living standards for the unemployed and their dependents.

The drop in income of the unemployed also hurts others who are not unemployed. Reduced spending means lower receipts for retail merchants, manufacturers, workers, and others in the chain of production. As we have seen, each person's income generally depends on someone else's spending.

Unemployment reduces the revenues of federal, state, and local governments while adding to their outlays for unemployment compensation and welfare support. When unemployment increases 1%, the federal treasury alone loses $30 billion in tax revenue and increased welfare and unemployment compensation payments. Conversely, our current low unemployment is one of the major reasons that the federal budget deficit has all but disappeared.

◩ Real Output Effects of Unemployment

From the standpoint of the overall economy, a rise in unemployment means a decline in the nation's production. For each 1% of unemployment, the country loses over $100 billion in output. Goods and services not produced because of unemployment are gone forever. This means that the nation as a whole is poorer by $100 billion, not just the unemployed.

What Are the Consequences of Unemployment and Inflation?

EconExplorer

A Senior at Old Dominion University finds an unusual way of expressing the employment concerns of recent Generation X college graduates.

The real output effects of unemployment continue into the future. Some of the goods not produced during a period of high unemployment are capital goods. The result is reduced growth in the production capacity of the economy that will affect the amount of future output of goods and services. Although the economy resumes growing after a recession, it is on a lower growth path than it would have been. This reduces future production and standards of living.

Social Effects of Unemployment

Unemployment has social as well as economic costs. When people lose their jobs, especially when they cannot find another for an extended period, they tend to become depressed and their health suffers. Suicides increase, families break up, and there is more child abuse. A study by Harvey Brenner of the Johns Hopkins University School of Hygiene and Public Health shows that for every 1% increase in the unemployment rate, there is a 1.9% increase in deaths from stress-related diseases, a 4.1% increase in suicides, a 5.7% increase in homicides, and a 4% increase in commitments to state prisons.

Other studies have found that the mental and physical health of the spouses and children of unemployed workers are also affected. Children in families where one or both parents have lost their jobs are more likely to suffer from malnutrition, child abuse, and behavior problems than children of working parents.

Income Effects of Inflation

In the past 15 years, the purchasing power of the dollar has fallen by almost 40%. Taking the average of 1982–1984 as the base, when $1.00 would buy a dollar's worth of goods and services, that same dollar in 1997 would buy only $0.62 worth of goods and services. For people whose money income did not keep pace with the rise in prices, these inflated dollars meant a decline in real income.

The income effects of inflation are not the same for everyone. Those on a fixed money income are bound to suffer during periods of inflation. One of the great ironies of inflation is that it often penalizes thriftiness. Many people who have worked hard and lived frugally over a working lifetime and who planned to live off their savings in old age have found the purchasing power of their savings has declined substantially as a result of inflation.

But not everyone is hurt by inflation. Those whose dollar incomes rise faster than the general price level enjoy a rise in real income. Chief executives of major corporations and sports stars have been among the big winners in the inflation race, with their income from salaries and bonuses going up much faster than prices. Asset owners also do well in inflationary times. Property owners see the value of their properties rise. Owners of scarce resources and speculators receive windfall profits.

Debtors are another group benefiting substantially from inflation. When the time comes to pay off their loans, they pay them off with dollars that are worth less than the dollars that they borrowed. Because of this, the federal government, with its debt of about $5.5 trillion, is the biggest beneficiary of inflation. As people come to anticipate continuing inflation, and as these inflationary expectations are reflected in

(Continued on page 312)

Comparative Case Application

Inflation—How High Is Up?

America's experience with inflation in the 1970s was a problem. But here the inflation rate reached "only" 13.3% a year at its height in 1979. In other places inflation has fed on itself to such an extent that it exploded, a condition called hyperinflation. Extreme inflation can paralyze an economy. The bad effects—hoarding, uncertainty, loss of confidence in the value of money, production bottlenecks—may so greatly override the investment-stimulating and output-expanding effects that they virtually halt production.

A classic example of this was the hyperinflation experienced in Germany during the early 1920s. The acceleration in the rate of inflation became so great that firms had to pay workers by the day. If firms refused to pay their workers daily, they would refuse to work at all. Why should they put in a week's work for an agreed-upon wage of DM100,000, the workers argued, if prices were rising at such an unpredictable rate that by the end of the week they couldn't be sure DM100,000 would buy a kilogram of bratwurst and a loaf of bread? The rate of inflation became so extreme by 1923 that prices were literally rising by the hour and workers had to be paid twice a day. As soon as a worker received his morning's pay, he would rush out to the entrance and thrust the large bundle of marks into his wife's hands. She would rush off to spend them within the hour, for in a few hours perhaps that bundle of marks would buy only half as much. With the institution of money shattered, market-directed activity all but collapsed.

That was the most extreme case of inflation in this century, but in recent years there have been other countries that experienced hyperinflation. The former communist countries in Eastern and Central Europe and the countries that were once a part of the USSR experienced

In post–World War I Germany, hyperinflation made some paper money good only for lighting fires.

high inflation rates during their transition to market economies. But their experience (up to 577% in Bulgaria in 1997) has not been as bad as in other countries. In 1994 Zaire (now the Republic of the Congo) had an incredible annual inflation rate of 23,700%, and in 1984–85 Bolivia had hyperinflation that reached an annual rate of 11,750%. A number of other Latin American and African countries have experienced runaway inflation. They include Brazil (2,750%), Argentina (3,080%), and Peru (7,500%). In these countries, as in Germany in the 1920s, prices of some goods rose daily or even twice a day. This situation greatly complicates life for consumers and producers alike.

A number of studies have shown that inflation rates are highest in countries where the government has the most control over the money supply. As we saw in chapter 10, the money supply in the United States is controlled by the Fed, and the Fed is not under the control of the Congress or the president. When the U.S. government cannot pay its bills, it must either raise taxes or borrow through the sale of bonds. In many of the lesser developed countries where hyperinflation is a problem, the money supply is under the control of the government. This gives the government a third option when its bills come due—it can simply create new money and use it to pay its employees and creditors.

Economic Reasoning

1. Which effects of inflation does the case of hyperinflation in Germany during the 1920s illustrate?
2. The German government was unable to sell bonds, so it had to resort to "printing press" money. Why would no one buy German government bonds in the early 1920s?
3. Every year or so, a bill is introduced in Congress that would take control of the money supply away from the Fed and give it to Congress. The argument is that control of the money supply is so important that it should be in the hands of elected representatives who are responsible to their constituents. Do you think this is a good idea? Why or why not?

(Continued from page 310)

higher interest rates, for the individual the advantage of incurring new debt disappears.

◤ Real Output Effects of Inflation

The rise of aggregate demand associated with demand-pull inflation tends to increase the real output of the economy up to the full employment level. An increase in demand, given some slack or unused productive capacity, stimulates production. Idle resources are put to work, and idle plant capacity is utilized more fully. These developments may favorably affect business profit expectations and lead to increased investment spending on new plants, equipment, inventories of raw materials, and goods in process.

This is only part of the story, however. As inflation continues and as the system moves closer to full employment, cost-push inflation forces strengthen. Though on the average all prices are rising in a period of inflation, not all individual prices are rising at the same time. Firms that feel reasonably confident that the prices of the things they are selling will rise faster than the prices of

what they must buy will have an incentive to expand by investing. Others may find that their costs are rising faster than their selling prices, or they may fear that this will happen. This causes considerable differences in supply responses. The patterns of production change.

Inflation is tricky. It may stimulate production in some areas and simultaneously create bottlenecks, uncertainties, or other difficulties that can hold back production in other areas. Inflation may induce some producers to anticipate future needs for materials, to buy more heavily than they otherwise would, and to hoard the materials.

As inflationary expectations strengthen, interest rates rise well above normal levels, making business investment in plant and equipment too costly. This discourages further expansion of output and thus contributes to higher inflation by creating shortages. On balance, it appears that the higher the inflation rate and the longer the period of time the inflation goes on, the greater will be the negative effects on output.

▶ Putting It Together

Normal adjustments to changing demand and supply conditions for different products and services in a market economy result in the loss of jobs for some people. Not everyone in the civilian labor force can find a job. The percentage of those who cannot is the unemployment rate. Some workers quit their jobs because of dissatisfaction or for other personal reasons. In a healthy economy, these people should be able to find new jobs within a few weeks. While they are seeking employment, they constitute a *frictional unemployment* bloc in the labor force.

When a whole industry or region has less business because of changing consumer tastes or changing cost conditions, some workers lose their jobs. There may not be enough jobs immediately available in other industries to reemploy them, or they may not have the skills and training necessary to take jobs in other industries. This *structural unemployment* may result in extended periods without work for some people.

The most serious and widespread unemployment, however, is *cyclical unemployment*, which occurs when there is inadequate aggregate (total) demand for goods and services. If there is insufficient spending in the economy to purchase all of the goods and services that could be produced, workers will not be able to find jobs. Those workers without jobs are forced to cut back on their consumption, and this results in a further decline in output and a further increase in unemployment.

When unemployment is high for a prolonged period of time, some workers who have been unable to find jobs become discouraged and stop looking. Since they are not actively seeking employment, they are not included in the unemployment statistics. They constitute a segment of *hidden unemployment*. Other workers forced to work only part time are part of this segment as well.

Just as unemployment may be caused by insufficient demand, *inflation* may be the result of too much demand. If demand exceeds the

capacity of the economy to produce at full employment, prices will rise. Inflationary expectations and speculation tend to accelerate *demand-pull inflation* even more.

Another cause of inflation can be an increase in the costs of production. Shortages of raw materials, higher wages, or government regulations raise prices. The interaction between demand-pull and *cost-push inflation* can result in an inflationary spiral.

According to the *monetarists*, increases in the money supply are inflationary because of the relationship between the quantity of money and the price level. This is expressed by the quantity equation $M \times V = T \times P$, where M is the money supply, V is the velocity of money, T is the number of transactions during the period, and P is the average price level. If output (T) and the rate at which money turns over (V) are constant, there is a direct ratio between changes in the money supply and changes in the price level.

There has historically been a trade-off between the rate of unemployment and the rate of inflation. This relationship is shown by the

Phillips curve. Phillips curves based on data from earlier periods show that when unemployment was high the inflation rate was low, and vice versa. During the 1970s, however, the economy had simultaneously both high unemployment and high inflation. This situation is referred to as *stagflation*. From 1984 to 1993 stagflation abated, but the trade-off between unemployment and inflation was at a higher level than in the 1960s and before.

The *natural rate of unemployment* after adjustment of worker expectations, also called the *non-accelerating-inflation rate of unemployment (NAIRU)*, depends mainly on the amount of frictional and structural unemployment but is influenced by other labor market circumstances.

Unemployment has an effect upon income, real output, and social conditions. The *income effects* result in lower living standards for those who are unemployed, their families, and those who supply them with goods and services. The *real output effects* result in smaller production, investment, and growth for the whole economy. The *social effects* include health problems, family disintegration, and higher crime levels.

Inflation, too, has income effects and real output effects. The income effects vary for different groups. Some, especially those on fixed incomes, lose, while others, such as debtors, gain. When inflation rates are low, the real output effect of a small rise in prices may be to stimulate production. But when inflation rates are high, speculation takes precedence over production, and rising production costs discourage output. The high interest rates that accompany inflation deter new investment, and productivity and economic growth decline.

$ Perspective $

Black Thursday and the Great Crash

Crowds gathered on Wall Street on Black Thursday as stock prices declined. The Great Depression was soon to follow.

More on the crash and the Great Depression can be found in *The Great Myths of 1929 and the Lessons to Be Learned* by Harold Bierman (New York: Greenwood Press, 1991); *The Great Depression* by David A. Shannon, ed. (Englewood Cliffs, NJ: Prentice Hall, 1960); *The Great Crash* by John Kenneth Galbraith (Boston: Houghton Mifflin, 1988); *America's Great Depression* by Murray N. Rothbard (Oakland, CA: Liberty Tree Press, 1983); *The Great Slump* by Goronwy Rees (New York: Harper and Row, 1971); and *The World in Depression, 1929–1939* by C. P. Kindleberger (London: Allen Lane, 1973).

Black Thursday, as it is called, was Thursday, October 24, 1929. It was a truly black day for stock market investors, and for the nation as a whole. Stock prices declined rapidly during the morning hours in a panic of selling. The market volume was so large that the stock market ticker did not finish reporting the day's transactions until after midnight.

People's savings were wiped out and many stock speculators were bankrupted within a few hours. Among the many rumors that spread on Wall Street that day was the story that 11 stock speculators had committed suicide. According to a report in the next day's *New York Times*, "A peaceful workman atop a Wall Street building looked down and saw a big crowd watching him, for the rumor had spread that he was going to jump off." Humorist Will Rogers wrote in his newspaper column, "When Wall St. took that tail spin, you had to stand in line to get a window to jump out of." (Actually, the legend of suicide leaps by ruined Wall Street financiers is largely myth. There were only two such suicides from Black Thursday up until the end of the year, while a few other investors took their lives in alternate ways.)

Significant and dramatic as the events on Wall Street were, they were not "the" cause of the Great Depression that followed. The causes were in the fundamental weaknesses in the economy, not just in the excesses of speculation in the stock market. Although the decade of the 1920s was a period of prosperity and growth, not all sectors of the economy participated in the prosperity. The farmers, who constituted a large proportion of the population, were suffering from overproduction and low prices throughout the second half of the decade. The farm population and the low-paid unskilled workers had insufficient purchasing power to absorb all of the goods that were produced by the large investment in production facilities during the boom. Excessive financial speculation was founded on a weak banking structure. There was not yet a Federal Deposit Insurance Corporation, so when defaults by debtors created liquidity problems for some banks and forced them to close, panic withdrawal of deposits from other banks took place, forcing them to close too.

The significance of Black Thursday and the Great Crash was that the events in the stock market revealed the fallacy of faith in endless prosperity. This loss of faith did not happen all at once. For a time there were assurances from many "experts" that the setbacks were only temporary, that the economy was basically sound and would soon turn up again. Instead, it sank further and further into depression until universal pessimism in the 1930s replaced the unbounded optimism of the 1920s.

For Further Study and Analysis

Study Questions

1. Mr. Jones was disabled in an accident in 1990 and has not been able to work since. Is he included in the unemployment statistics? Why or why not?

2. If the average propensity to consume (see chapter 5) increased, how might aggregate demand and the price level be affected? Under what circumstances would such an increase be inflationary? Under what circumstances would it not necessarily be inflationary?

3. Is it possible that the number of people employed increases while the unemployment rate increases? Explain.

4. A reduction in space exploration programs has resulted in a loss of jobs in the aerospace industry. This situation is an example of what type of unemployment?

5. What is happening in the economy if the natural rate of unemployment is less than the actual rate of unemployment?

6. According to the quantity equation, could the money supply go down and prices go up at the same time? What would have to happen for this to come about?

7. The economy is currently in what phase of business conditions—recovery, boom, peak, bust, contraction, recession, trough, or stagflation? How can you tell?

8. How can the production capacity of the economy expand from the amount shown in Figure 6A to the amount shown in Figure 6B?

9. If an anticipation of price inflation leads business firms to build up inventories of raw materials and semifinished goods, what effect does this have on economic conditions? Why?

10. What are some things that could cause the aggregate supply curve to shift to the right? What effect would this have on prices, output, employment, and the unemployment rate? How are these effects different from the effect of an increase in aggregate demand?

11. If Mrs. Sawyer were living on a fixed pension of $500 a month, how would she fare if inflation increased by 10% per year for the next 5 years?

12. Why did homeowners who bought houses in the 1980s benefit from inflation?

Exercises in Analysis

1. The text indicated that increased environmental and safety regulations can contribute to cost-push inflation. Write a short paper that compares the benefits and costs of such government regulation.

2. Assume that inflation is taking place and that it appears that it will continue for the foreseeable future. You have a nest egg from an inheritance of $25,000. Write a short paper on what you would do with the money and why.

3. From the following data, calculate the student cost-of-living (SCOL) index for 1995 with 1983 as the base year.

Item	Number Purchased per Semester	1983 Price	1995 Price
Hamburgers	40	$ 1.50	$ 2.50
Blue Jeans	2	25.00	35.00
Books	6	20.00	30.00
Movie Tickets	10	2.00	7.50

4. From the statistical tables in the most recent Economic Report of the President or from an Internet source, find the unemployment and inflation rates for the past 4 years. Plot them on a diagram similar to the one in Figure 7 in this chapter and draw a conclusion about the existence of the Phillips curve. Can you use this data to draw any conclusions about changes in the economy's aggregate demand or aggregate supply?

5. Visit the United States Department of Labor, Bureau of Labor Statistics at http://stats. bls.gov/datahome.htm and use the "Selective Access" option to access the BLS data banks. Examine the historical unemployment rates for women, Hispanics, and other groups you might be interested in. Use the data to construct a figure like Figure 1 in the text.

Further Reading

Case, John. *Understanding Inflation*. New York: William Morrow, 1981. "This book is for people who want to know why prices keep going up. It is not—rest assured—an economics textbook. It contains no equations, one graph, and only a few statistics" (p. 7). Includes an appendix on how the inflation rate is calculated.

Economic Report of the President. Washington, DC: Superintendent of Documents, annual. A report by the president to Congress on the state of the nation's economy. Includes the annual report of the Council of Economic Advisers, which covers a number of macroeconomic subjects, such as inflation and unemployment. Also includes an appendix of statistical tables relating to income, employment, and production. The report is also online at http://www.access. gpo.gov/eop/index.html.

Gowland, David. *Money, Inflation, and Unemployment*. New York: St. Martin's Press, 1992. Covers the role of money in economic stability and the effect of inflation on unemployment.

Layard, Richard, Stephen Nickel, and Richard Jackman. *Unemployment: Macroeconomic Performance and the Labor Market*. New York: Oxford University Press, 1991. A study of the effect of changing aggregate output and inflation on the employment level.

Padoa-Schioppa, Fiorella, ed. *Mismatch and Labor Mobility*. New York: Cambridge University Press, 1991. The proceedings of an international conference on the relationship between labor mobility and unemployment.

Paarlberg, Don. *An Analysis and History of Inflation*. Westport, CT: Praeger, 1993. The causes and course of inflation in earlier periods of economic instability.

Rielhe, Kathlene A. *What Smart People Do When Losing Their Jobs*. New York: John Wiley and Sons, 1991. A practical guide to protecting yourself against the worst consequences of job loss, including the psychological consequences.

Skene, G. Leigh. *Cycles of Inflation and Deflation: Money, Debt, and the 1990s*. Westport, CT: Praeger, 1992. An examination of U.S. business cycles and the monetary policies effected to control price instability.

chapter twelve

The Economy's Output

In order to deal with economic instability, we need to understand where the economy is going and how it gets there. This introductory article captures the uncertainties in predicting the ups and downs of an economy, which are akin to going to a fortune-teller.

Forecasting or Fortune-Telling?

Forecasting is difficult, especially about the future.

—Anonymous

Citizens of ancient Greece could get a prophecy about a military campaign or a long, dangerous sea trip by going to the oracle at the temple of Apollo at Delphi. The oracle predicted future events by examining the intestines of a goat or by asking for a sign from Apollo. The prophecy was often so vague that no matter what happened the oracle could claim the prophecy had been fulfilled.

The demand for prophecies still flourishes. Businesses and governments go to present-day oracles for help in planning for the future. Increasingly, the oracles to which they go are those of economic model builders such as Chase Econometrics, Wharton Econometric Forecast Associates, Evans Economics, and Mc-Graw-Hill's Data Resources. Complex systems of equations, rather than mystical signs, are the sources of modern prophecy.

A great quantity of statistical data is cranked into their computer models. The data deal with economic variables whose interrelationships are shown by sets of mathematical equations. The more complex your economic view, the more equations you must use to forecast the results of changes in variables. For example, the Wharton Quarterly Model of the U.S. economy uses 1,100 equations to forecast hundreds of specific economic changes—in prices, interest rates, automobile sales, retail sales, tax collections, unemployment, and so on.

The track record of the leading forecasting establishments has been far from perfect. In October 1981 Evans Economics predicted that the economy would grow 3.3% in 1982, Wharton Associates predicted 2.2% growth, and Chase Econometrics forecast a 2% growth rate. In actuality, the economy shrank by 2.5% in 1982, measured in dollars of constant purchasing power. As a group, they greatly underestimated the strength and duration of the economic expansion following 1983. And none of them foresaw the high federal government bud-

get deficits, foreign trade deficits, and high real interest rates that marked the 1980s. Even when individual forecasters or forecasting companies have been right in a particular instance, they have not been able to repeat their success consistently.

Why have modern economic oracles not been more successful? One of the problems of the forecasters is caused by the accuracy—or lack of it—of the original data that go into the forecasting models. The figures published by the agencies responsible for gathering the data are almost never correct when they first appear. Sometimes they are off by a factor of 10. As more accurate data become available, the figures are revised; but it may be 2 years before the final figures are available. Even after revisions, the data may not be reliable.

And why are the economic data so unreliable? Collecting the raw data is not the job of the forecasting businesses. Their function is to determine what the data mean for the industries and firms who are their clients and for the economy as a whole. Only the federal government is in a position to collect and organize economic data on the huge scale needed. But, according to Courtney Slater, former chief economist of the Commerce Department, "Too many statistical series are outmoded, and there are too many data gaps. Information about new industries and rapidly growing economic sectors is often scanty and sometimes misleading." Cuts in the budget for data collection and reporting have made the problem worse.

The unreliability of data is just one problem in economic forecasting. Another problem is understanding what effects a change in one economic variable will have on other variables. Forecasting models are based on past relationships of the variables—for example, the Phillips curve, discussed in the last chapter. But, as we saw, those relationships may change over time, resulting in inaccurate predictions. The pace of

such shifts in relationships seems to be accelerating. Management consultant Peter Drucker describes this as an "age of discontinuity" in which old rules and relationships do not apply anymore.

It is possible to compensate somewhat for unreliable data and inexact models by putting predictions in the form of a range of possibilities rather than as an exact figure. This approach, however, may be too wimpy to impress potential clients and others. According to Herbert Stein, former chairman of the Council of Economic Advisers, "Certitude pays money. It pays in attention, influence. . . . There is no 'don't know' school to which you can belong."

A difficulty that has plagued forecasters from ancient Greece to modern days is the effect of external forces on developments. Wars, disasters, shifts in government policies, all types of unforeseen occurrences can play havoc with even the most astute predictions. For example, oil prices escalated in the 1970s as a result of OPEC manipulations of the petroleum market. That changed the economic picture so much that the forecasters were left with models that were no longer relevant.

Despite their fallibility, the forecasting companies are handsomely rewarded for their services. Not all forecasting involves computers and fat fees, however. The Delphic oracle of old has many contemporary imitators. A Chicago pawnbroker, for instance, indexes economic trends by the percentage of pawnshop items that are redeemed. A psychologist predicts economic ups and downs by the number of patients signing up for expensive therapy. A Los Angeles pet store operator believes that an important economic omen is the number of rhinestone-studded poodle collars the store sells. A shoe repair business predicts recessions based on how many people have their shoes resoled instead of buying new ones.

The newest twist in forecasting business cycles is the use of lyrics of current popular songs. Harold Zullow, a research fellow in social psychiatry at Columbia University, correctly predicted the recession of 1990–91 by analyzing the content of the lyrics on Billboard magazine's Hot 100 chart. Studying the hit songs of the past 40 years, Zullow found that when the lyrics of the songs turned from optimistic to pessimistic it signaled that an economic downturn was approaching in 1 to 2 years. What Zullow is unsure of is which is cause and which effect. Are the song lyrics merely a reflection of underlying currents in society? Or do they reinforce and spread pessimism and bring about the downturn?

Chapter Preview

The statistical models used in economic forecasting were originally developed as tools for understanding what happens in the economy. Only later did they become devices for predicting what may happen in the future. In this chapter we will use the most basic formulation of a national income model to explain the following: How much does the economy produce? What determines domestic output from the demand-side point of view? What determines domestic output from the supply-side point of view?

Learning Objectives

After completing this chapter you should be able to:

1. Define the GDP and explain the two ways of measuring it and why they give the same result.

2. List the four types of expenditures that make up the aggregate demand for goods and services.

3. Define constant dollar GDP and explain how it is related to current dollar GDP.

4. Explain why GDP is not a good measure of economic or social well-being.

5. Explain the Keynesian economic model and describe under what conditions it claims the output of the economy is at equilibrium.

6. Describe what happens to GDP when leakages exceed injections of purchasing power and what happens when injections of purchasing power exceed leakages.

7. Explain Say's Law.

8. Explain how supply-side economics differs from demand-side economics.

▶ How Much Does the Economy Produce?

There are two methods of measuring the total output of the economy. We can measure the sales value of the output of goods and services, or we can measure the incomes received by the workers and the owners of other factors used in production. These two measurements should give us the same figure because the value of what is sold ends up in the pockets of those who produced and distributed it. Income should be the same as the value of the output.

◪ Expenditure Categories

In 1997, the national output of the United States totaled $8,083.4 billion in goods and services, a 5.8% increase over 1996. This was the sum of four types of spending: consumer purchases, investment outlays for new capital goods, government spending, and net exports. The total of those expenditures was the **Gross Domestic Product (GDP)**. The 1997 GDP consisted of the outlays shown in Table 1 on page 322. The largest class of spending, shown in the left column of the chart, was **personal consumption expenditures (C).** They comprised all household outlays for durable goods, such as automobiles, nondurable goods, such as food and clothing, and services, such as medical care, repairs, and entertainment.

Gross private domestic investment (I) refers to outlays for capital goods. Such

---

Gross Domestic Product (GDP) the sum of the values of all goods and services produced within the country during the year.

personal consumption expenditures (C) spending by households on goods and services.

gross private domestic investment (I) private-sector spending on capital equipment, increased stocks of inventories, and new residential housing.

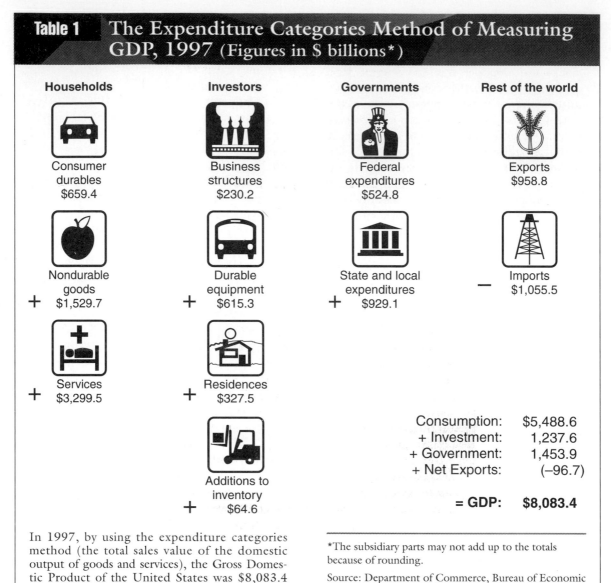

Table 1 — The Expenditure Categories Method of Measuring GDP, 1997 (Figures in $ billions*)

Households	Investors	Governments	Rest of the world
Consumer durables $659.4	Business structures $230.2	Federal expenditures $524.8	Exports $958.8
+ Nondurable goods $1,529.7	+ Durable equipment $615.3	+ State and local expenditures $929.1	− Imports $1,055.5
+ Services $3,299.5	+ Residences $327.5		
	+ Additions to inventory $64.6		

Consumption:	$5,488.6
+ Investment:	1,237.6
+ Government:	1,453.9
+ Net Exports:	(−96.7)
= GDP:	$8,083.4

In 1997, by using the expenditure categories method (the total sales value of the domestic output of goods and services), the Gross Domestic Product of the United States was $8,083.4 billion.

*The subsidiary parts may not add up to the totals because of rounding.

Source: Department of Commerce, Bureau of Economic Analysis.

---

inventories the value of finished and semifinished goods and raw materials in the hands of producers and distributors.

spending enables businesses to maintain and expand their production capacity. The two main types of investment spending are for fixed investment in buildings and for capital equipment, such as machinery. GDP measures the total value of goods and services produced in a year, even if they are not sold in that year. Increases in **inventories** of goods in the hands of producers or on the shelves of dealers must be included, and they are considered part of investment. If inventories were to fall during the year it would be disinvestment, a reduction in (I). In addition, in the U.S. system of accounts, new residences sold during the year are included in fixed investment.

The **government sector spending (G)** includes both purchases from the private sector (for example, purchase of military equipment) and the costs of government itself (for example, salaries paid to government workers). Government spending is a mixture of consumer-type purchases, such as school lunches, and investment-type purchases, such as highways and hydroelectric dams.

The GDP also includes the net value of U.S. international trade. Since GDP measures only what is produced domestically, we subtract imports (M) from exports (X). The difference is **net exports (X – M)** and is added into the GDP. As you can see in Table 1, net exports were negative in 1997, indicating that the United States imported more than it exported.

Because it was produced in an earlier year, the cost of producing a used car is not included in this year's GDP. The profit earned by the used car dealer is, however, included.

How Much Does the Economy Produce?

EconExplorer

Adding these various expenditure categories, the GDP measures the current output of our economy as the grand total of final spending (aggregate demand). It is the sum of spending by the nation's households (C), investors (I), governments (G), and the excess, if any, of the nation's exports over its imports (X – M). Thus, GDP = C + I + G + (X – M).

Before 1992 the measurement used for total output was not Gross Domestic Product but **Gross National Product (GNP).** The difference between the two is that GDP measures income generated by production within our borders. GNP, on the other hand, measures the income generated by U.S. companies anywhere in the world. It includes the interest and dividends received by U.S. residents on overseas investments and the earnings of foreign branches of U.S. corporations, while excluding such U.S. payments to foreigners. As an example, a Honda built in Ohio counts as part of GDP, but not GNP. A Ford built in Mexico counts as part of GNP, but not GDP. As international investments greatly increased in recent years, the GNP

became a less accurate measure of the actual amount of production activity within this country, and the decision was made to use GDP instead. Also, GDP is the figure generally used by other countries so adopting it in this country allows for better international comparisons.

Income Categories

The second method of measuring GDP is to add together all of the incomes earned in production: labor earnings, business profits, interest, and rent payments. This total of income

government sector spending (G) spending by the various levels of government on goods and services, including public investment.

net exports (X – M) the value of goods and services exported minus the amount spent on imported goods and services.

Gross National Product (GNP) the sum of the values of all goods and services produced by residents of the country during the year, including earnings on overseas investments and excluding foreign earnings on investments in this country.

Figure 1

The Income Categories Method of Measuring GDP
$ billions (1997)

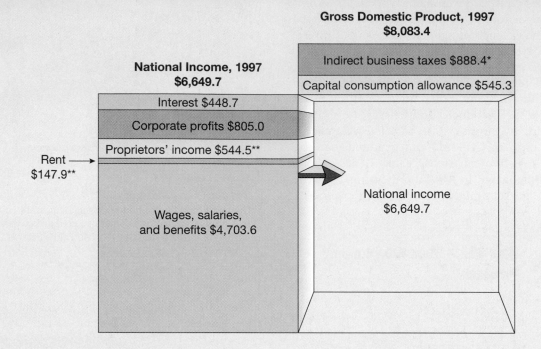

Gross Domestic Product, 1997
$8,083.4

Indirect business taxes $888.4*

Capital consumption allowance $545.3

National Income, 1997
$6,649.7

Interest $448.7

Corporate profits $805.0

Proprietors' income $544.5**

Rent → $147.9**

Wages, salaries, and benefits $4,703.6

National income $6,649.7

*Includes statistical discrepancies and business transfers.

** Proprietor's income and rental income have been adjusted for capital consumption (depreciation).

In 1997, by using the income categories method (the sum of all incomes earned plus capital consumption allowances [depreciation], indirect taxes, and business transfer payments), the Gross Domestic Product of the United States was $8,083.4 billion.

Source: Department of Commerce, Bureau of Economic Analysis.

National Income (NI) the total of all incomes earned in producing the GNP.

excise taxes a tax on a particular type of good or service; a sales tax.

business transfer payments outlay by business for which no good or service is exchanged, such as payouts under deferred compensation arrangements, gifts, and donations.

earnings is called **National Income (NI).** The GDP measurement by income categories is the sum of National Income earned from domestic production plus nonincome costs of production such as depreciation on capital goods, **excise taxes,** and **business transfer payments.** The components of NI and GDP using the income approach for 1997 are shown in Figure 1.

The largest part of National Income consists of the earnings of labor, including professional and managerial salaries. Other income components are proprietors' net income, corporate profits, interest, and rent. The National

Income in 1997 totaled $6,649.7 billion. This was a 6.3% increase over 1996, a slightly bigger increase than the overall increase in GDP. In addition to National Income, GDP also includes cost allocations to cover the depreciation of plant and equipment, listed in Figure 1 as **capital consumption allowances.** It further includes **indirect taxes** such as business excise taxes and other business transfer payments, which are not a part of earnings but do constitute a cost of production. The fact that National Income rose more than GDP from 1996 to 1997 implies that these costs grew faster than GDP. When we add these nonincome costs to National Income, we obtain the same GDP figure that we arrived at using the expenditures approach in Table 1, $8,083.4 billion.

◢ Value Added

The GDP is a measure of the total goods and services produced by a nation's economy in a given year. To avoid overstating the real output, the same good must not be counted more than once. For example, if we count the sale of iron ore used in making steel, then count the value of the steel sold, and finally count the selling price of an automobile in which the steel is used, we would be counting the value of the iron ore three times. To avoid double counting, only the **value added** at each stage of production is counted. The final sale price includes and is equal to all the individual values added at each intermediate stage of production. The worth of production that actually takes place in the industries making goods like automobiles is indicated by the sum of values added. It is not the total prices of intermediate and final sales.

Table 2 shows an example of value added by following the production of bread from a farmer to a retail grocery store.

The farmer sells wheat to a miller for $200, and the miller then grinds it into flour and sells it to a baker for $250. The baker bakes bread and sells her loaves to a grocer for $500, and the grocer, in turn, sells the bread to his customers for $600. How much value was added to GDP? We can find out by either looking at the $600 value of the final product, or we can add up the value added at each stage of production: $200 + $50 + $250 + $100 = $600. Notice that if we

Table 2	Calculating Value Added	
	Market Price	**Value Added**
Wheat sold by farmer to miller	$200	$200
Flour sold by miller to baker	$250	$50
Bread sold by baker to grocer	$500	$250
Bread sold by grocer to customers	$600	$100
Total Value Added		**$600**

We can find the value of goods and services added to GDP by either looking at the price of the final product or by adding the value added at each stage of the production process.

added the market value of the intermediate goods to the market value of the final good, we would come up with $1,550, a "gross" overstatement of the true addition to GDP.

When calculating GDP, we must also avoid double counting when dealing with the sale of used goods. The value of a 1994 Chevrolet that was sold at a used car lot in 1998 was already counted once when it was produced and originally sold new in 1994. However, the difference between what the car lot paid for the car and what it received for the car represents value added by the business and should be included in the 1998 GDP. Similarly, the sale of existing stocks and bonds from one person to another is simply a change in ownership of a financial asset. It does not

capital consumption allowances the costs of capital assets consumed in producing GDP, also known as depreciation.

indirect taxes taxes collected from businesses (other than income taxes) that do not directly become part of someone's income, such as sales, excise, and property taxes.

value added the difference between the value of a firm's sales and its purchases of materials and semifinished inputs.

Figure 2

Current and Constant (1992) Dollar GDP, 1975–1997

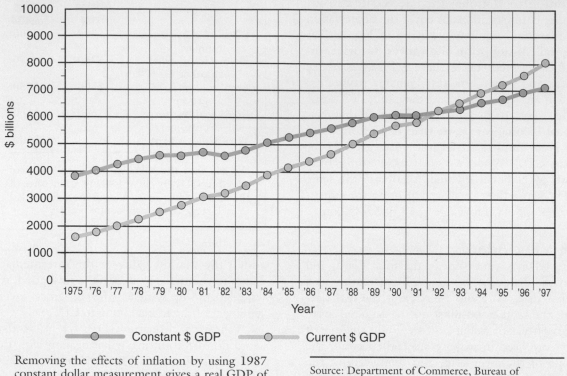

Constant $ GDP   Current $ GDP

Removing the effects of inflation by using 1987 constant dollar measurement gives a real GDP of $5,132.7 billion, as compared to the current 1997 dollar GDP of $8,083.4 billion.

Source: Department of Commerce, Bureau of Economic Analysis.

represent current economic output and should not be included in GDP.

Current and Constant Dollar GDP

In estimating GDP, an item's current worth is the price paid for it. A **current dollar GDP** reflects the current price level of goods and services. Current dollar GDP may increase over time because of increases in either output or inflation.

A real or **constant dollar GDP** is used to remove the effects of inflation in order to see the real change in output. This measure indicates what the GDP would be if the purchasing power of the dollar had not changed from what it was in the base year (see chapter 11, p. 297). The U.S. **national income accounts** now use 1992 as the base year. Figure 2 shows the real or constant dollar GDP for the years 1975–1997, measured in the value of 1992 dollars (green line), compared to the GDP measured in current year dollar values for those years (blue line). Because 1992 was the base year, current and constant dollar GDP are the same in that year. The figure shows that the real or constant dollar GDP for 1997 was only $7,191.4 billion, as compared to the

current dollar GDP the dollar value of GDP unadjusted for inflation.

constant dollar GDP (real GDP) the value of GDP adjusted for changes in the price level since a base period.

national income accounts the collective name for various macroeconomic measurements such as GDP and National Income.

(Continued on page 328)

The Roller-Coaster Ride

The historical course of economic activity has been similar to a roller-coaster ride, with its climbing, peaking, plunging downward, and bottoming out. Let us take a figurative ride on the business cycle.

We start at the bottom, as one does on roller coasters. The first part of the ride up is not steep. The economy is getting in gear, picking up speed. Factories have a great deal of unused capacity. As demand increases, output can be expanded easily without increasing average production costs. Interest rates are unusually low, making it easy for producers and merchants to obtain financial capital. This is the recovery phase of the business cycle.

The climb begins to get steeper. More jobs, larger incomes, increased spending, and higher profits create an enthusiastic atmosphere. A confident buying public goes into debt to acquire new cars, appliances, and other consumer durable goods. Would-be entrepreneurs see the profits being made by others and decide to undertake new business ventures. This is the expansion phase of the business cycle. In the rosy glow of prosperity, speculation replaces real investment and price increases accelerate, creating an economic "boom."

After a while the steep climb begins to level off. As labor and other resources become fully employed, production costs rise and cut profit margins. The banking system has become fully loaned up and interest rates increase, making credit hard to obtain. Consumers reach their debt limits and demand for durable goods decreases. This is the peak or downturn phase. Some firms fail, affecting the financial situation of their suppliers and creditors, which leads to more failures, resulting in an economic "bust."

As the economy starts its downward plunge, it rapidly gains momentum. Widespread bank-

ruptcies result in a collapse of the credit market. Worker layoffs and falling incomes result in declining sales in all industries. This is the contraction phase of the cycle, which leads to a recession or, if it is severe, a depression.

The ride down seems as if it will never stop, but it does. The economy bottoms out. The rate of business failures slows. Inventories are reduced. Consumer purchases begin to increase. Due to the small amount of lending in the slump, banks have an increased amount of liquidity and interest rates are lowered. The

Figure 3

The Phases of a Business Cycle

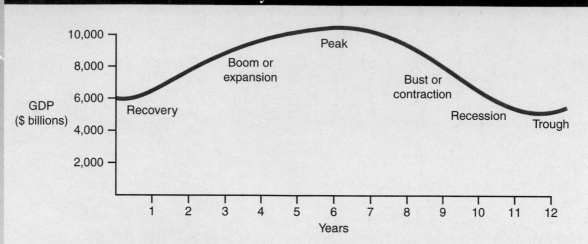

Throughout history, the United States has experienced a succession of swings in the level of economic activity, more or less following the phases of this typical business cycle.

stage is set for the trough or upturn, the last phase of our cyclical roller-coaster ride.

A theoretical picture of the business cycle is shown in Figure 3. Actual business cycle fluctuations are not so smooth or regular. The historic behavior of the business cycle in the U.S. since 1959 is shown in Figure 4. As you can see, we have been experiencing a prolonged expansion since 1992. However, whatever goes up must eventually come down. Sooner or later the economy will reach its peak and an economic contraction will occur.

(Continued from page 326)

1997 current dollar GDP of $8,083.4 billion. The difference reflects price increases since 1992.

How Much Does the Economy Produce?

EconExplorer

Economic Reasoning

1. At what phase of the business cycle would you expect GDP to be increasing the fastest? The slowest?
2. Identify changes in consumption and investment in this case application.
3. Do you think that the government should allow the economy to slip into its "natural" periods of booms and busts, or should it intervene to reduce business cycle swings? Why or why not?

▨ Shortcomings of GDP

GDP is a measure of an economy's output in a given period of time. It is not a measure of economic or social well-being. For example, it does not take into account the value of leisure time. An $8 trillion GDP is an $8 trillion GDP whether it takes us 30 hours or 40 hours a week to produce it. Nor does GDP take the environment into account. If we increase our output by fouling our air and water, the value of the extra output gets added into GDP while the

Figure 4

Historic Behavior of U.S. Business

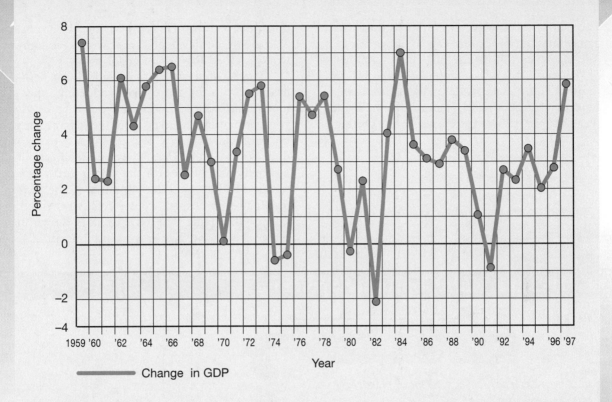

Despite its ups and downs, the U.S. economy has averaged GDP increases of 3.3% since 1959.

Source: U.S. Department of Commerce.

environmental losses are not subtracted out. If output is reduced because of strict environmental laws, the GDP decreases but the value of clean air and water are not added in. Nor does GDP account for the distribution of income. If one million people divide $7 trillion while the remaining 259 million split up the other $1 trillion, GDP is still $8 trillion. Finally, GDP does not take into account the production of things that we would rather not be producing. New prisons and home security systems are not things that we wish to have, but their production does add to the nation's output.

Measured GDP also misses nonmarket transactions such as barter and underground (illegal) activities. If a carpenter agrees to build a deck in exchange for a mechanic fixing his or her car, the value of the services does not become part of GDP. If a woman marries her gardener, whom she was paying $1,000 a year, and now the gardener works around the garden for nothing, GDP falls by $1,000. Although it has its pitfalls and problems, GDP does, however, give us a consistent measure of economic performance that can be tracked and monitored over time.

What Determines Domestic Output from the Demand-Side Point of View?

There are two principal interpretations of what determines total output. One emphasizes the role of demand in determining how much will be produced; the other emphasizes the role of supply. The demand-side analysis dominated economic thinking and planning from World War II to the 1980s. It stems from the writings of British economist John Maynard Keynes. The model he developed of how the economy works is called **Keynesian economics.**

The Keynesian economic model can be illustrated with the use of the production capacity tank introduced in the previous chapter. As you will recall, the size of the tank represents the maximum capacity of the economy to produce goods and services. Since the total output of goods and services for the year is Gross Domestic Product and the contents of the tank represent that output, we will refer to the tank as the GDP tank. The GDP tank is shown in Figure 5 with the flow of consumer spending.

Keynesian economics the body of macroeconomic theories and policies that stem from the model developed by John Maynard Keynes.

Figure 5

GDP Tank with Consumer Spending

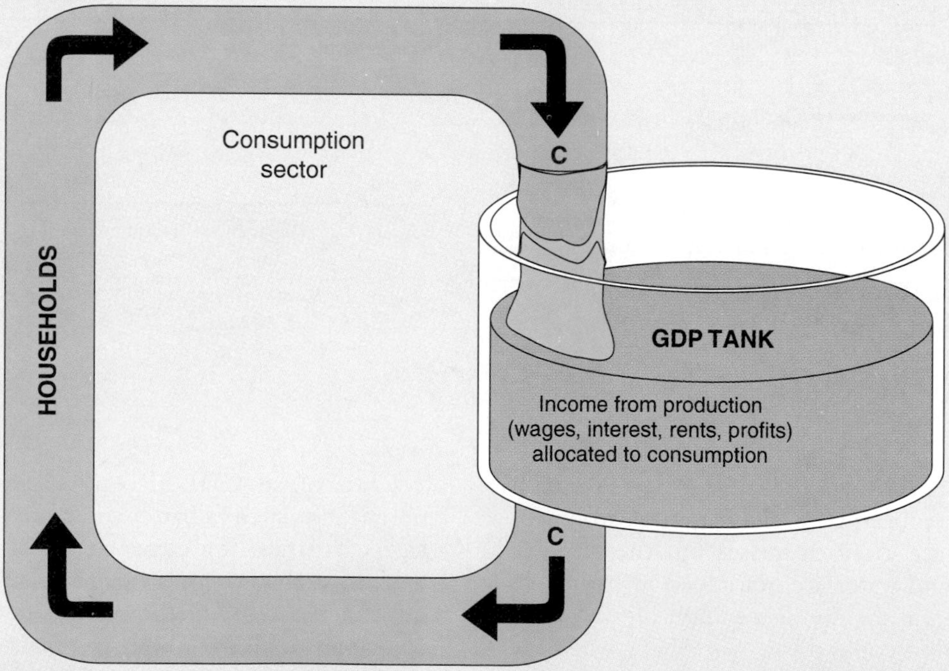

The GDP tank represents the nation's output of goods and services. Consumption demand by households takes the largest part of that output. Purchasing power flows into the top of the tank in the form of consumer spending. It becomes income to the households in payment for their productive services. The income that households allocate to purchase additional consumption goods and services flows out of the bottom of the tank and is returned in the form of new purchasing power.

◤ Consumption Demand

The GDP tank model with consumer spending is related to the circular flow model from chapter 3, shown in Figure 6. Most of the wage, rent, and interest payments that households receive from businesses are allocated to consumption purposes. These are shown in the GDP tank model by the outflow from the bottom of the tank to the consumption sector.

The outflow is marked "C." This is the amount of income generated by production that is allocated to purchase new consumer goods and services. It flows back into the tank where it again becomes income to the producers of those goods and services. The inflow, the amount spent, is also marked "C" because it is equal to the outflow, the amount of their income that households allocate to consumption.

The amount of consumer spending depends basically on people's **disposable income.** Disposable income is income received minus taxes. Most of this disposable income is spent on consumption. In 1997 disposable personal

---

disposable income the amount of after-tax income that households have available for consumption or saving.

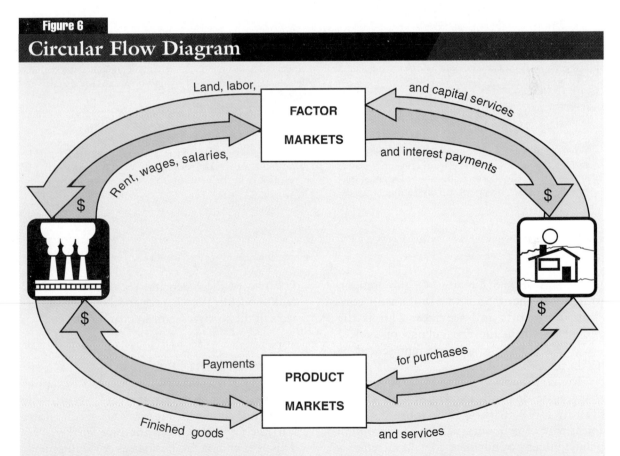

Figure 6

Circular Flow Diagram

The GDP tank diagram with consumer spending (Figure 5) shows the same flow of purchasing power through the economy as this circular flow diagram from chapter 3. Households use the income that they receive from the sale of their labor, land, and capital services in production to purchase the consumption goods and services produced by the firms. The GDP tank diagram, however, is better than the circular flow diagram for showing the effects of the other sectors of the economy, as will be shown later.

Figure 7

GDP Tank with Investment Spending

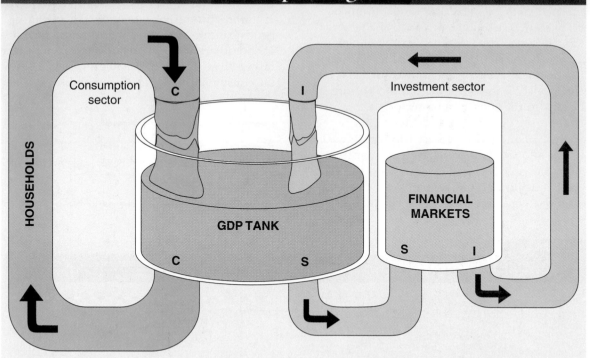

Whereas all of the income that households allocate to consumption is spent on consumer goods and services, the income allocated to savings may or may not all be spent on investment goods.

Savings go into financial markets; and that amount, or less, or more, may be returned to the economy in the form of investment spending.

income was $5,885.2 billion. Of this amount, households spent $5,488.6 billion on consumption goods and services. This is the amount shown in the first column of Table 1 (see p. 322) and the amount represented by "C" in the GDP tank model.

The consumption sector is the largest part of aggregate demand, making up over 70% of GDP in 1997. Although it represents the largest part of economic activity, consumption spending does not fluctuate a lot. It therefore is not responsible for much economic instability. The other sectors, although smaller, account for more instability. These other sources of demand are investment demand, government demand, and foreign demand. We will add the

first two of these demand sectors to the GDP tank model in this chapter and consider the effects of the foreign sector in chapter 16.

◪ Investment Demand

A second determinant of the amount of output is investment demand. Private investment spending, shown in Figure 7 in green, flows into the GDP tank from the pipe marked "I." This is spending by businesses for equipment, factories, office buildings, and inventories. It also includes spending on new residences. As shown in the second column of Table 1, investment demand in 1997 was $1,237.6 billion.

According to Keynes, Hoover Dam does more than control the river's flow. Government spending on such projects also adds to demand in the economy.

The money to finance investment spending comes principally from savings—disposable income that households divert from consumption. The amount of income generated in producing GDP that is allocated to savings is shown flowing out of the GDP tank from the pipe at the bottom marked "S." The savings outflow, however, is not directly connected to the investment inflow. Instead, most savings flow through the banking system or other parts of the financial marketplace, for example, the stock and bond markets. This financial marketplace is represented in Figure 7 by the investment sector holding tank to the right of the GDP tank. Savings flow into the financial markets and are then drawn out to be invested in capital equipment, structures, and inventories. (This does not apply to that part of business investment which is financed out of retained earnings. In that case the savings flow directly from the company's earnings into capital spending without passing through financial markets.)

EconExplorer

The amount of savings flowing into the financial markets through pipe "S" is not necessarily the same as the amount of investment spending flowing out of the financial markets through pipe "I." As we saw in chapter 10, the banking system can create money by making loans. In that way investment spending can be greater than intended savings. It would also be possible for the financial markets to absorb more savings than the amount of new investment spending. In that case, the amount of income flowing out of the GDP tank in the form of savings would be larger than the amount of purchasing power flowing into the tank in the form of investment.

Unlike the rate of consumption spending, which normally has a fairly consistent relationship to disposable income and tends to be rather stable, investment spending may be quite unstable. It depends a lot on expectations of future economic conditions, which may be influenced by all kinds of events and are likely to change frequently and violently. For lack of a better way to express it, Keynes wrote that investment is determined by the "animal spirits" of business people. Inventory investment is an especially unstable component of investment.

Government Demand

A third source of demand is federal, state, and local government purchases of goods and services. These purchases include armaments, highways, police and fire protection, and schools, among other things. Government spending is added to consumption and investment demand for GDP in Figure 8 on p. 334. It is shown by the red flow from the pipe at the top of the GDP tank marked "G." This

Figure 8

GDP Tank with Government Spending

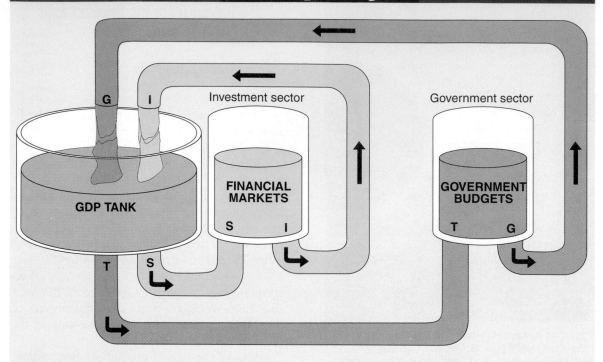

Government spending is funded by taxes: but, as with the investment sector, the amount drawn out of the economy in taxes is not necessarily the same as the amount returned to the economy in government spending. Generally, government spending, especially federal government spending, is greater than tax receipts. The government adds more to income than it withdraws, resulting in budget deficits.

amounted to $1,453.9 billion in 1997, as shown in the third column of Table 1.

At the bottom of the tank, income is drawn off by government in the form of taxes through the pipe labeled "T." As with the relation between savings and investment, the amount of income drawn off in taxes is not necessarily the same as the amount of government spending going back into the economy. If the government has a **deficit** in its budget

deficit a negative balance after expenditures are subtracted from revenues.

surplus a positive balance after expenditures are subtracted from revenues.

(spending more than it takes in), it is pumping more purchasing power into the economy than it is drawing off in taxes. If, on the other hand, the government has a **surplus** (spending less than it takes in), there is an accumulation in the pink government sector holding tank. The flow of purchasing power back into the economy is reduced. For the most part, state and local governments must keep their budgets in balance, except for spending on long-term capital projects. It is mainly federal government deficits or surpluses that affect changes in the income stream.

Equilibrium Output

Aggregate demand in the domestic sectors of the economy is the total of consumption (C), investment (I), and government (G) spending.

Savings that flow out of the GDP and into financial markets are used by businesses to invest in capital equipment, inventory, and other business needs.

The flow of purchasing power from these three sectors determines the quantity of goods and services that can be sold. (The foreign sector is excluded for the present. It will be incorporated in the model in chapter 16.)

The quantity of goods and services demanded in turn determines how much output firms will produce. If the flow of purchasing power from one or more of these sectors is reduced, output and employment will go down. When the expenditure flows are increased, output and employment go up, unless the economy is already at full-capacity production. In that case, as we saw in Figure 6A in chapter 11, on page 299, the increased demand results in demand-pull inflation rather than increased output.

Production will be at the **equilibrium output level,** whether at full employment or below it, when the additions to purchasing power from domestic consumption (C), investment (I), and government spending (G) are just equal to the leakages from the income tank. These leakages are the income generated in the tank and allocated to consumption (C), intended savings (S), and taxes (T). Since the amount of income allocated to consumption

of domestic goods (C) is always the same as the amount of purchasing power returned to the tank in consumer spending (C), only the other two sectors can get out of equilibrium. GDP will be constant when all of the income that is *drawn out* of GDP in the form of savings (S) and taxes (T) is *returned* to GDP in the form of investment (I) and government (G) spending. When I + G = S + T, domestic output is at an equilibrium level. Output, employment, and income will remain the same as long as there is no change in one of those variables.

If there is a change in one of the demand sectors, there will be a change in the level of GDP. For example, if there is a decrease in investment, purchasing power flowing into the GDP tank from investment and government demand will be less than the outflow into savings and taxes (I + G < S + T). This causes production to decline, as shown in Figure 9. (This figure is a schematic version of the GDP tank model in Figure 10.) The resulting fall in output and employment reduces people's income.

When their income is reduced, households save less and pay less taxes, as well as reduce their consumption of goods and services. Output, employment, and income will continue to fall until the reduction in investment spending is offset by a comparable decline in savings and taxes, so that inflows again equal outflows (I + G = S + T). A new equilibrium GDP results, with a lower level of output and income accompanied by higher unemployment and unused production capacity. This outcome is shown in Figure 10.

equilibrium output level excluding the foreign sector, it is the level of GDP at which aggregate demand (C + I + G) is just equal to aggregate supply (C + S + T); the level where income leakages (S + T) are exactly equal to income additions (I + G).

Effect of a Decrease in Investment Spending

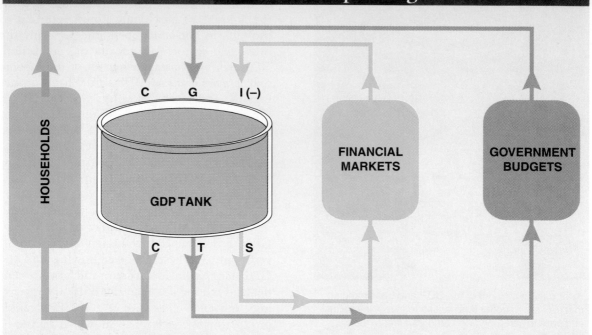

If there is a reduction in the amount of investment spending, as indicated by I(−), there will be a decline in aggregate demand. The amount of purchasing power flowing into the economy (C + G + I) will be less than the amount flowing out (C + T + S). This will lower the level of economic activity, as shown in Figure 10.

New Equilibrium Level of GDP

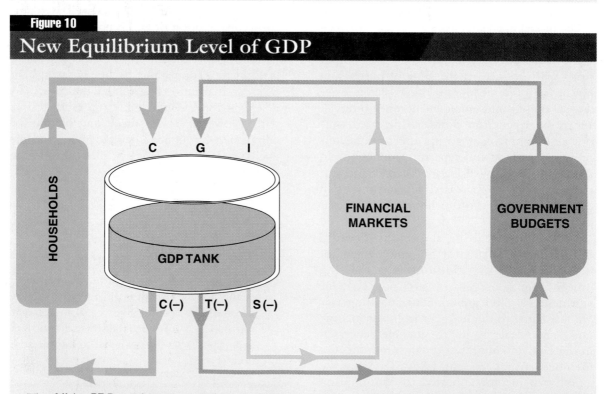

The fall in GDP resulting from reduced investment spending will decrease incomes. This will result in reduced consumption, taxes, and savings, as shown by C(−), T(−), and S(−). There will be a new lower equilibrium level GDP when the reduced T + S equals the reduced G + I.

Case Application

Squaring the Economic Circle

Art Buchwald

WASHINGTON—The recession hit so fast that nobody knows exactly how it happened. One day we were the land of milk and honey and the next day we were the land of sour cream and food stamps.

This is one explanation.

Hofberger, the Chevy salesman in Tomcat, Va., a suburb of Washington, called up Littleton, of Littleton Menswear & Haberdashery, and said, "Good news, the new Novas have just come in and I've put one aside for you and your wife."

Littleton said, "I can't, Hofberger, my wife and I are getting a divorce."

"I'm sorry," Littleton said, "but I can't afford a new car this year. After I settle with my wife, I'll be lucky to buy a bicycle."

Hofberger hung up. His phone rang a few minutes later.

"This is Bedcheck the painter," the voice on the other end said. "When do you want us to start painting your house?"

"I changed my mind," said Hofberger, "I'm not going to paint the house."

"But I ordered the paint," Bedcheck said. "Why did you change your mind?"

"Because Littleton is getting a divorce and he can't afford a new car."

That evening when Bedcheck came home his wife said, "The new color television set arrived from Gladstone's TV Shop."

"Take it back," Bedcheck told his wife.

"Why?" she demanded.

"Because Hofberger isn't going to have his house painted now that the Littletons are getting a divorce."

The next day Mrs. Bedcheck dragged the TV set in its carton back to Gladstone. "We don't want it."

Gladstone's face dropped. He immediately called his travel agent, Sandstorm. "You know that trip you had scheduled for me to the Virgin Islands?"

"Right, the tickets are all written up."

"Cancel it. I can't go. Bedcheck just sent back the color TV set because Hofberger didn't sell a car to Littleton because they're going to get a divorce and she wants all his money."

Sandstorm tore up the airline tickets and went over to see his banker, Gripsholm. "I can't pay back the loan this month because Gladstone isn't going to the Virgin Islands."

Gripsholm was furious. When Rudemaker came in to borrow money for a new kitchen he needed for his restaurant, Gripsholm turned him down cold.

"How can I loan you money when Sandstorm hasn't repaid the money he borrowed?"

Rudemaker called up the contractor, Eagleton, and said he couldn't put in a new kitchen. Eagleton laid off eight men.

Meanwhile, General Motors announced it was giving a rebate on its new models. Hofberger called up Littleton immediately. "Good

Art Buchwald, "Squaring the Economic Circle," *Cleveland Plain Dealer*, February 22, 1975. Reprinted with permission of the author.

news," he said, "even if you are getting a divorce, you can afford a new car."

"I'm not getting a divorce," Littleton said. "It was all a misunderstanding and we've made up."

"That's great," Hofberger said. "Now you can buy the Nova."

"No way," said Littleton. "My business has been so lousy I don't know why I keep the doors open."

"I didn't realize that," Hofberger said.

"Do you realize I haven't seen Bedcheck, Gladstone, Sandstorm, Gripsholm, Rudemaker or Eagleton for more than a month? How can I stay in business if they don't patronize my store?"

What Determines Domestic Output from the Supply-Side Point of View?

The demand-side national income model was developed by Keynes in the 1930s and refined after World War II by his intellectual heirs, the neo-Keynesians. It emphasized the importance of aggregate demand in determining the levels of output, employment, and prices. Government macroeconomic policies have been based largely on Keynesian economics. From the 1940s to the 1960s, those policies worked quite well. The economy was more stable than it had been during the 1930s and before.

However, the stagflation of the 1970s raised doubts about Keynesian economic policies. Some economists and politicians advocated a different approach based on **supply-side economics.** This approach was implemented in

supply-side economics an approach to macroeconomic problems that focuses on the importance of increasing the supply of goods and services.

Ronald W. Reagan, elected president in 1980, embraced supply-side economics so avidly that the theory became known as Reaganomics. This approach to policy formulation in the 1980s was in response to the stagflation of the 1970s, which had raised doubts about Keynesian economic policies.

the economic policies of the 1980s known as "Reaganomics." Supply-side economics is more an approach to policy formulation than it is a model of how the economy operates. In fact, supply-side proponents use the Keynesian model of how the economy works to analyze and explain the effects of their supply-side policies.

Say's Law

Supply-side economics is not entirely new. Its roots go back at least as far as the early nineteenth century, when a French economist by the name of J. B. Say formulated **Say's Law of Markets.** Say's Law states simply that "supply creates its own demand." In a money economy, this means that when an entrepreneur produces something, enough income is created in payments for wages, raw materials, capital, and other costs to purchase what was produced.

The prevailing idea prior to the **Keynesian revolution** in economic thinking was that overproduction or underproduction would not be a problem because, in the end, demand would always be equal to the amount supplied. If there were a temporary glut, prices would fall and permit the excess goods to be purchased. Full employment would automatically be restored.

The Keynesian model showed that this was not the case. A decrease in investment spending, for example, would mean that some goods that were produced would not be sold, as indicated in Figures 9 and 10 on page 336. There is a good deal of institutional resistance to reducing prices. There is especially resistance by labor unions to a reduction in the price of labor (wages). Demand therefore remains insufficient to achieve full employment. As a result, high unemployment could last for a long time. The experience of the 1930s depression, when the "underproduction" proved to be more than temporary, discredited Say's Law and led to the acceptance of Keynes's theories.

Incentives

The emphasis in modern supply-side economics is on the importance of incentives in determining output. Keynesian economics assumes that an increase in aggregate demand automatically results in more goods and services being produced, as long as there is excess capacity in the economy. Supply-side proponents, on the other hand, maintain that increased production will not take place if costs are too high. These high costs include high interest rates and high tax rates.

Today's supply-side economists believe that there is a basis of truth in Say's Law. They believe that a reduction of costs, especially taxes, increases the incentive to produce, and that this increased production will create jobs and income. Increasing the net returns to producers by reducing taxes and other costs provides an incentive for them to produce more. They believe that reducing taxes will also cause households to save more, thereby making additional funds available to businesses for investment in new capital equipment. This additional investment will increase aggregate supply from AS_1 to AS_2 as shown in Figure 11, and the economy's production capacity as shown in Figure 6B in Chapter 11. As a result, there will be a decrease in inflation and unemployment as the general price level falls from P_1 to P_2 and output increases from Q_1 to Q_2.

The advocates of supply-side economics believe that increased financial incentives can affect the supply of labor as well as the supply of capital. They maintain that reducing marginal tax rates will induce managers and workers to increase their labor input. Worker absenteeism will decline; workers will seek more overtime and second jobs; there will be less voluntary unemployment.

Say's Law of Markets A theory of the French economist J. B. Say, which holds that when goods or services are produced, enough income is generated to purchase what is produced, thereby eliminating the problem of overproduction.

Keynesian revolution the name given to the transformation in macroeconomic theory and policy that resulted from the ideas of Keynes.

Figure 11

Supply-Side View of the Effect of a Decrease in Taxes on Aggregate Supply

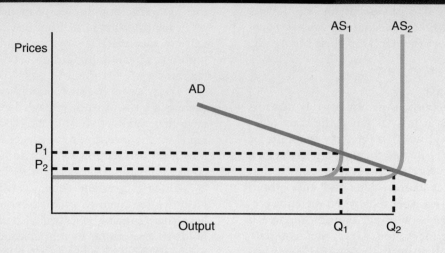

Supply-side economics believes a reduction in taxes on businesses will provide an incentive to expand production. This expansion will shift aggregate supply from AS_1 to AS_2 and prices will fall from P_1 to P_2 as output increases from Q_1 to Q_2.

It is true that a reduction in tax rates means an increase in real wages, and the Law of Supply states that an increase in the price of a good or service will increase the amount offered for sale. There is some question, however, as to whether this applies to the supply of labor, and under what conditions. If real wages increase, does this cause people to seek more work, or does it cause them to work less and take more leisure time? Studies show that the effect varies among different groups of workers. Many workers prefer more vacation time to higher wages, which suggests that greater real income might actually reduce the amount of labor that they supply.

The evidence of the effect of lower taxes on labor supply is mixed. The **labor force partici-** pation rate for all workers increased from 63.6% in 1981 when taxes were significantly reduced, to 67.2% at the end of 1997. This supports the supply-side view that lower taxes increase amount of labor supplied to the market. During the same period, however, the participation rate for men decreased from 76.6% to 75.0%, while the rate for women increased from 52.0% to 60.0%. As with many economic questions, it is difficult to ascertain what forces led to the overall increase—lower taxes or changing social attitudes that encouraged more women to enter the labor force.

labor force participation rate the percentage of the population over 16 years old that is in the civilian labor force.

What Determines Domestic Output from the Supply-Side Point of View?

EconExplorer

Figure 12

Effect of Government Borrowing Crowding Out Private Investors

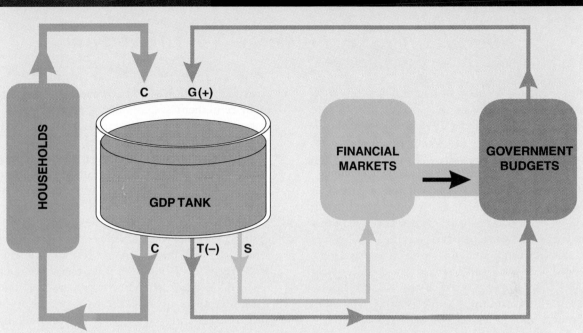

When an increase in government spending, G(+), or a decrease in taxes, T(−), is financed by government borrowing, investment sector funds may be diverted from private investment to the government sector. This is the "crowding out" effect shown by the connecting flow between the financial markets (green) and government budgets (pink). The effect is exaggerated in the diagram by completely eliminating the investment flow.

Government Deficits

Supply-side economics also differs from demand-side economics in another way. It emphasizes the effect of government deficits on the availability and cost of capital to investors in the private sector. When government spends more than it collects in taxes, it finances the difference by borrowing money in the financial markets. State and local governments sell tax-exempt **municipal bonds** to finance major projects, and the federal government sells Treasury bills and bonds to finance federal deficits. The sale of these government securities draws large quantities of financial capital out of the private capital market. The decreased supply of financial capital raises its price—it raises interest rates. This process is illustrated in Figure 12 above. It is the same as the previous GDP tank models except that government budgets are connected to the financial markets out of which governments siphon off investment capital.

municipal bond a debt incurred by a state or local government that uses either its tax revenues or the proceeds from a specific project to pay principal and interest to bondholders.

Case Application

Spending Like There Is No Tomorrow

Americans have not shown much interest in saving in recent years. The private savings rate fell from an average of 7%–8% of disposable income in the 1960s and 1970s to a low of 3.2% in 1987, and in the early 1990s it was less than 5%. At the close of 1997 it was down to 4.0%. This is a much lower personal savings rate than in other industrialized countries. Savings in other parts of our economy are also low. Total savings in the economy—savings by households, governments and businesses—was 15.9% of GDP in 1997. In comparison, the rates were 30.8% in Japan, 24.6% in the Netherlands, 21.4% in Germany, 20.5% in Italy, 19.7% in France, and 17.1% in Canada. Why is our savings rate so low? There are a number of possible reasons.

One of the explanations for a low savings rate is the income security provided by our Social Security system. The Japanese, for instance, must depend much more on lifetime savings to provide for retirement income. Western Euro-

pean citizens, however, have extensive government retirement systems like that in the U.S., but their savings are nonetheless higher than ours. Another factor is the ready availability of credit in this country, making it less necessary to save for a rainy day. (For example, people in most countries are not constantly solicited to sign up for new credit cards.)

Still another explanation lies in the demographics of different countries. Younger adults tend to be net borrowers as they finance cars and houses and begin their careers. As they reach middle age, they become net savers and they put away money for their retirement and/or their children's college education. The Japanese did not experience a baby boom in the 1950s like we did in the United States, and their population is on average older, and hence more inclined toward saving. Despite the fact that the baby boomers are well into middle age, however, our savings rates remain low. The baby boom generation has been

Figure 12 shows current GDP, the purple area in the GDP tank, at less than full employment. Some supply-siders argue that the reason

for the unemployment is that the government is **crowding out** private investment, depriving it of capital. (The crowding-out effect is exaggerated in Figure 12 by showing a complete elimination of private investment flow from the financial sector.)

If the private investors had access to this capital, supply-siders say, they would invest it in new plants and equipment, thereby creating jobs and increasing GDP. But the government returns some of its payments to the

crowding out the term given to the effect government has in reducing the amount of financial capital available for private investment.

saving 2% to 3% less during their prime saving years than did their parents at the same age. One view is that they are starting families at a later age than previous generations did, and that their savings rate will increase as they assume family responsibilities.

Supply-side economists believe that our tax structure provides disincentives to save. The interest paid on some borrowing, such as mortgages and home equity loans is tax-deductible, making borrowing less expensive. At the same time, households must pay income taxes on the interest and dividends that they earn from their savings, reducing the returns to savings. As a result, our tax structure tends to reward borrowing while penalizing saving.

The reasons for the especially low savings rate in the last decades, however, may be found in particular economic circumstances of the period. The rise in the values of real estate in the 1980s and of stock portfolios in the 1990s encouraged spending. Owners of those assets could spend more of their income and yet see an increase in the worth of their assets at the same time. This reduced the need to save for retirement and other things.

As for Generation X, the perceived weakness in the financial structure of the Social Security system (Chapter 9, p. 245) may cause them to save more for a secure retirement, despite recent increases in the stock market. Altering the Social Security system to allow households to establish their own private savings plans in lieu of Social Security contributions might change the type of saving that is done, but not the amount. If, however, the system is forced to reduce retirement benefits in order to remain solvent, savings will need to increase if Generation X expects to enjoy their golden years in financial comfort.

Economic Reasoning

1. Why are U.S. savings rates so low?

2. Why would supply-side proponents favor a reduction in Social Security benefits?

3. Should the government levy consumption taxes on goods and services to discourage consumption spending and raise revenue for the government, as European governments do? Why or why not?

economy in the form of income transfers, which are nonproductive and tend only to raise prices and not output. This is the rationale for reducing government spending and balancing the budget.

There has been a controversy among supply-siders between those who believe in the need for tax cuts to provide production incentives and those who fear that the resulting government deficits will crowd out private investment. Even with the record government deficits of the 1980s, however, this did not occur, in part because the demand by businesses for investment funds was moderate and in part because a large amount of funds was supplied to the U.S. capital market by foreigners, especially the Japanese. The reduction of the federal deficit in the late 1990s together with continued lending by foreigners have made financial capital plentiful and kept interest rates low. As a result, private investment has been able to increase substantially.

Putting It Together

The total output of the economy, *Gross Domestic Product (GDP)*, can be measured either by the sales value of the output of goods and services or by the total incomes received in producing these goods and services. In measuring sales, there are four sources of demand for goods and services: *consumption demand, investment demand, government demand,* and *net export demand.* The total expenditures by these four sectors constitute GDP.

In measuring GDP as the total of incomes, we first determine *National Income,* which is the sum of wages, rents, interest, and profits. To arrive at GDP, the amount of capital equipment used up during the year (depreciation) plus *indirect business taxes* and other *business transfer payments* are then added to National Income.

In measuring the value of GDP, we do not include the total sales for each industry. That is because the value of goods produced by finished goods industries already includes the value of the semifinished goods used to produce the finished products. To avoid double counting, only the *value added* by each industry in the production process is included. In order to compare changes in real output from year to year, the effects of inflation are removed from the figures. This is done by adjusting *current dollar GDP* to eliminate the effect of higher prices. Deflating current dollar GDP by the price index gives us *constant dollar GDP.* Although GDP provides a consistent measure of economic output, it does not necessarily provide a good measure of social or economic well-being.

The *Keynesian economic model* is the basis for demand-side economics. The model, including only the domestic sectors for the present, holds that consumption (C), investment (I), and government (G) spending determine an economy's total output. When purchasing power going into the economy from investment and government spending is exactly offset by the allocation (leakages) of income into savings (S) and taxes (T), an economy's output will be at its equilibrium level. On the other hand, if the income leakages into S and T are greater than the injections of purchasing power from I and G, then output, employment, and income will fall. Or if spending injec-

The measure of economic output of a country can be determined by using the supply side or the demand side—by the sales values of the output of goods and services, or by the total incomes received in producing these goods and services.

tions exceed leakages, output will rise, unless the economy is already at full employment.

Keynes's model demonstrated that the economy could be at equilibrium even though it was operating at less than full employment. This contradicted classical theories of economics, including *Say's Law of Markets,* which states that "supply creates its own demand."

Say's Law was an early formulation of *supply-side economics.* Modern supply-side economists claim that Keynesian economic policies are misguided because they ignore the effects of these policies on supply. In order to induce producers to risk their capital, it is necessary to provide adequate profit incentives. Adding to aggregate demand without providing incentives to producers only drives up prices. Supply-siders call for a reduction in tax rates, both on investment income to increase capital formation, and on labor services to increase the *labor force participation rate.* They also want to decrease the size of the government sector to reduce *crowding out,* cut back on government services and transfer payments, and reduce cost-increasing government regulations.

$ Perspective $

The Keynesian Revolution

John Maynard Keynes (1883–1946) Keynes was raised in the intellectual environment of Cambridge University where his father, a noted writer on political economy and logic, taught and where his mother was mayor of the city of Cambridge. Upon graduation from the university, he took the examinations for entry into the British Civil Service and received his lowest mark in the economics part of the examinations. His explanation for the low grade was that "the examiners presumably knew less than I did" about economics. His career alternated between government service, teaching, writing, editing, and business, including making a fortune in the commodities market. He was a patron of the arts and married a star ballerina of the Russian Imperial Ballet. In 1942 he was made a peer and became Lord Keynes. He died of a heart attack in 1946.

In addition to *The General Theory,* his other important publications include *The Economic Consequences of the Peace* (1919), in which he predicted the results of the heavy war reparations imposed on Germany that later contributed to the rise of Hitler; *A Treatise on Probability* (1921); and *A Treatise on Money* (1930).

In a 1935 letter to Irish playwright George Bernard Shaw, British economist John Maynard Keynes predicted that the book he was working on would revolutionize the way people thought about economic problems. That book, *The General Theory of Employment, Interest and Money,* was published in 1936. Keynes was prophetic. *The General Theory* did revolutionize economic thinking, and the transformation became known as the "Keynesian revolution," sometimes capitalized as "Keynesian Revolution" to dramatize its significance.

Prior to the publication of *The General Theory,* the working hypothesis of macroeconomics was that the economy had a natural tendency to full employment. Unemployment was assumed to be the result of a *temporary* malfunction. The depth and length of the Great Depression, however, appeared to belie this assumption. In the United States, output fell by almost one-half and prices dropped nearly as much. Unemployment reached as high as one out of every four in the working population. By the time *The General Theory* appeared, the Depression had been going on for over half a decade and it continued, only somewhat abated, until the outbreak of World War II.

The revolutionary model that Keynes presented in *The General Theory* showed how an economy can be stuck at an equilibrium output level far below full employment because of insufficient aggregate demand. The policy implication of the model was that government should take an active role in bringing the economy out of a depression by injecting government spending into the income stream. This increased spending by government at a time of declining tax revenues would, of course, result in large budget deficits. To those who were concerned about the long-run consequences of such policies, Keynes's response was, "In the long run we are all dead."

Keynes wrote in his letter to Shaw that the revolution in economic thinking would not take place overnight. Keynes's theory was elaborated on by a number of other economists, including Joan Robinson (see chapter 7 Perspective). Perhaps the final triumph of the Keynesian revolution was reached when conservative Republican president Richard Nixon said, "I am a Keynesian." Ironically, this triumph of the Keynesian revolution came at a time when the structure of the economy had changed so much that Keynesian economics no longer seemed to provide an adequate solution to our economic problems.

For Further Study and Analysis

Study Questions

1. If you tutored a classmate for 10 hours at $8 an hour, what would be the effect on the GDP?
2. If antitheft devices added $400 to the price of every new car sold in the United States, what impact would this have on GDP? Are we better off because of it?
3. Do current dollar GDP and constant dollar GDP become closer or further apart as inflation decreases?
4. On January 1, 1998, a grocery store had on hand an inventory valued at $240,000. During 1998 the store bought groceries worth $600,000. Sales for that year came to $800,000. How much did this firm contribute to the investment component of GDP for 1998?
5. If you had a $1,000,000 "dream house" built, what would be the effect on GDP? What component of aggregate demand would be affected?
6. You are working at a job with a take-home pay of $200 a week. You have been putting $15 into a savings account every week, but you want to build up your savings faster, so you increase it to $25. What effect would this have on GDP?
7. Assuming the economy is at an equilibrium level of output, what are three examples of changes that would cause output to fall?
8. If output were not at the full employment level, what are three examples of changes that would increase GDP?
9. According to Keynesian economics, what would happen to output, employment, and income if government spending were reduced by 50% and taxes by 25%?
10. According to supply-side economics, what would happen to equilibrium GDP if government spending and taxes were both reduced by 50%?

Exercises in Analysis

1. Use a Web source such as the Bureau of Economic Analysis (http://www.bea.doc.gov/) to find the changes in current dollar GDP for the most recent quarter reported compared to the same quarter in the preceding year. List the components of GDP (consumption, investment, government, net exports) and then write a short paper on which components of GDP were principally responsible for the changes in GDP during the year.

2. The following are GDP figures for a hypothetical country: Consumption—$2,000; Investment—$300; Government spending—$400; Exports—$150; Savings—$400; Taxes—$400; Imports—$100. From these figures calculate the aggregate demand in the economy. Does the total demand equal the value of current output? If not, what would you expect to happen to output? Why?

3. Write a short paper that explains why GDP is not a good measure of social and economic well-being. What things that are really important in life are not included in GDP?

4. Write a short paper on whether demand-side economics or supply-side economics is, in your opinion, a better explanation of how the economy behaves and why.

Further Reading

Annual Editions: Macroeconomics. Guilford, CT: Dushkin/McGraw-Hill, various years. These texts always contain interesting and easy-to-read articles that discuss different aspects of GDP and its measurement.

Anderson, Victor. *Alternative Economic Indicators.* New York: Routledge, 1991. Discusses National Income accounting, traditional economic indicators, and social economic indicators. Examines their usefulness for economic policy and development.

The Bureau of Economic Analysis home page at http://www.bea.doc.gov/ is a good starting point for finding many articles that can help you in doing research about the national income accounts. When you are at this site, click on "Articles."

Center for Popular Economics. *Economic Report of the People.* Boston: South End Press, 1986. An alternative view of the economy to that in the *Economic Report of the President.* (see Further Reading at the end of the last chapter). Discusses supply-side economics in the 1980s.

Hailstones, Thomas J. *A Guide to Supply-Side Economics.* New York: Prentice Hall, 1983. Compares the evolution and policies of Keynesian and supply-side economics.

Hall, Peter A. *The Political Power of Economic Ideas: Keynesianism across Nations.* Princeton, NJ: Princeton University Press, 1989. Explores the spread of the Keynesian Revolution from country to country and the effect it had on politics and policies.

Hillard, John, ed. *J. M. Keynes in Retrospect: The Legacy of the Keynesian Revolution.* Aldershot, U.K.: Edward Elgar, 1988. This book is a collection of articles on the Keynesian Revolution in the past and where it stands today.

Kotlikoff, Laurence J. *What Determines Savings?* Cambridge, MA: MIT Press, 1989. There are sections on the motives for savings, the relation of fiscal policy to savings, and how social security and demographics affect savings.

chapter thirteen

Public Finance

Government spending and taxing have a large effect on the economy. With the government sector accounting for a third of all economic activity and almost a fifth of all direct purchases, its impact cannot be overlooked. The following article examines the health care industry—an area where the role of government is being increasingly debated.

Rx Health Care Reform

The American health care system is sick and badly needs a cure. There is no lack of consensus about its problems, but there exists widespread disagreement over the proper treatment. President Clinton, among others, thought major surgery was required, and in 1993 he proposed a system of national health insurance in which all employers would be required to provide health insurance to their employees, and the unemployed would receive insurance through regional "health alliances." The 1,300 page piece of legislation was defeated in Congress because of opposition by the health care industry and others. Other legislation, amounting to little more than a few Band-Aids, has been passed, but the patient is still in serious to critical condition.

Drivers under 25 years old have a high probability of being in an auto accident, and their auto insurance premiums are consequently expensive. People in their 80s are more likely to die sooner than people in their 30s, and their life insurance premiums are consequently higher. People over age 65 use 2½ times more health services than people under 65, and the economics of insurance should require that they pay higher health insurance premiums. Our society, however, believes that, unlike automobile or life insurance, everyone is entitled to health care, just as everyone is entitled to food and shelter. Therefore, health insurance for those over 65 is heavily subsidized via taxpayers through the Medicare program. But the costs of health care and insurance premiums are skyrocketing, and the basic problem is how to provide affordable coverage for everyone.

One of the worst symptoms of the health care crisis is the large and growing number of people without health insurance, amounting to an estimated 42 million in 1996, or 15.6% of the population. That was up from 32.6 million, or 13.3% of the population in 1988. Ninety percent of the private health insurance in the United States is employment-related, and losing or changing jobs often results in the loss of access to health insurance. The increases in the numbers of the uninsured stem in large part from layoffs by major firms, and the increased use of part-time and temporary labor with no fringe benefits. In fact, a leading reason for the shift by companies to the use of more contingent workers is to escape the rising costs of health coverage for their labor force.

Health care costs the United States much more than it does other countries, despite the fact that most other industrialized countries have long had universal health care coverage. In 1995 Germany spent 10.4% of its gross domestic product (GDP) on health care, while France spent 9.8% and Canada 9.6%. Great Britain and Japan each spent much less, 6.9% and 7.2%, respectively. The U.S. health care bill translated into $3,701 for each man, woman, and child in 1995. In comparison, Germany spent about $2,134, France about $1,956, and Canada $2,049. As Figure 1 shows, governments in other countries play a much greater role in the provision of health care for their citizens. In the United States the government pays for about 46% of all health care (primarily through Medicare and Medicaid), while the governments of France, Germany and Japan each pay for about 80% of all health care.

The elevated health care costs in this country are to some extent due to the extensive use of high-tech medicine, especially in the final stages of a patient's life. In the United States we are more apt than other countries to spend hundreds of thousands of dollars to extend a person's life by a year or two. Heart and liver transplants, heart bypass surgery, and other miracles of modern medicine are enormously expensive. A liver transplant and follow-up treatment carry a price tag of $300,000 in the first year. Every year, some 400,000 Americans undergo heart bypass surgery at a total cost of about $12 billion. Angioplasty to unclog blocked arteries is now performed 300,000 times a year at a cost of approximately $10,000 per procedure, or $3 billion.

Figure 1

The Share of GDP Spent on Health Care
Public and Private Shares in 1995

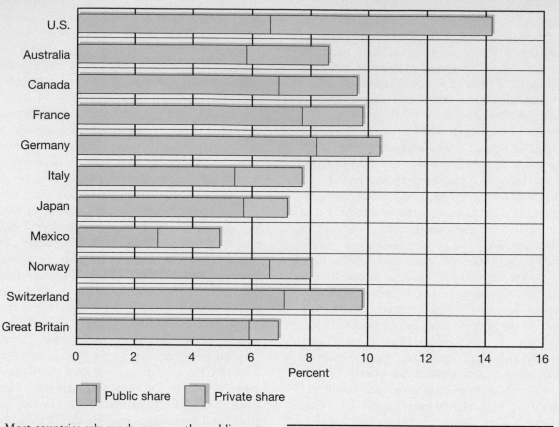

Public share   Private share

Most countries rely much more on the public sector to provide health care than does the United States.

Source: *Statistical Abstract of the United States.*

There has been a tendency to employ high-tech medical treatments excessively, even when they could not be shown to improve health outcomes. Like climbing a mountain, high tech is used because it is there. No longer will physicians settle for using a $40 dollar X-ray when instead they can use a $1,500 magnetic resonance imaging (MRI) scan. The use of angioplasty has risen despite a lack of evidence that it prevents heart attacks and in spite of the fact that drug treatment has been shown to yield similar results at a fraction of the cost. At half of all deliveries, obstetricians connect the fetus in the womb to an electronic monitor to check for signs of distress. The rising popularity of this procedure, at a collective cost of $1 billion a year, flies in the face of a number of studies that show no better outcomes than with the use of a stethoscope placed on the mother's abdomen, even in high-risk pregnancies.

The increased use of high-tech procedures has been accompanied by purchase of diagnostic scanners and other costly equipment by hospitals. Most hospitals in the United States have one or more MRI machines, while there are less than 20 in all of Canada. When every hospital in an area purchases the same equipment in order to stay competitive, it drives up hospital costs, and these costs are passed onto patients.

The use and overuse of high-tech medicine is only one of the causes of the larger medical costs in this country than in other advanced countries. Another explanation lies in the inflated cost of prescription drugs, among the most expensive in the industrialized world. A General Accounting Office survey done for the U.S. Senate found that for 121 prescription drugs, Canadians paid on the average only 62% as much as U.S. citizens. Residents of the United Kingdom, France, Italy, and Japan pay even less for the same drugs. Only in Germany are the prices of prescription medicines comparable to those in the United States.

Physicians' fees are also substantially higher in this country. Relative to average incomes in this country, incomes of physicians are much higher than in other industrialized countries; the mean income of a self-employed American physician is $170,000. But in this regard it should be noted that doctors in other countries do not leave medical school with debts of $50,000 and more, since the cost of their medical education is covered by the government. Also important in the greater cost of physician services in this country is the relative proportion of specialists, who are typically more expensive than generalists. Here nearly 80% of the doctors are specialists, while in other Western countries the proportion is half that.

Health care costs are also inflated by fraud. The first comprehensive audit of Medicare showed that overpayments to hospitals, doctors, and nursing homes accounted for 14% of total Medicare spending in 1996. Experts in the field estimate that fraud and abuse add between $50 billion and $80 billion to the nation's total medical bill each year. This ranges from such lesser abuses as the ordering of unnecessary tests and procedures to pad medical bills to outright scams, such as the false medical lab billings in an elaborate Southern California scheme run by the two Russian immigrant Smushkevich brothers. Government and private health care insurers paid out $50 million in claims before the racket was exposed. The hundreds of billions of dollars spent by governments for health care is just too big a pot of money to be ignored by people looking for a quick and illegal scam, and the system is too big and unwieldy to keep a close tab on where the money goes.

Another factor that contributes to the high cost of health care are the costs that drug, alcohol, and tobacco abuse impose on society. Emergency room treatment for drug overdoses is expensive, and hospitals cannot turn a person away because he or she has no means to pay a bill in the thousands of dollars. To recoup these costs, prices are raised for those who have insurance coverage. The same holds true for babies born with AIDS, or who are born addicted to crack cocaine or heroin. Keeping these infants alive may cost hundreds of thousands of dollars, but we have an ethical obligation to do so. Drunken drivers who cause accidents can pile up huge medical bills for themselves and their victims, and the rest of us end up bearing the cost.

Failure to cover millions of citizens and the high costs of care are merely the symptoms of what ails the U.S. health care system. The basic causes are to be found in the structure of the system itself. Unlike most markets in our free-enterprise economy, the market for medical treatment has not been subject to the discipline of price competition for the customers' business. Neither the employer-paid health care plans for workers nor the government Medicare and Medicaid programs for older people, people with disabilities, and the poor provide adequate incentives for patients to economize on their use of medical resources.

Because little or none of the extra cost of more expensive medical treatments comes out of the pockets of the patients, there is no incentive to economize on health care costs. Generally, insured patients do not even know what the costs of the treatments they receive will be. On the supply side of the market, doctors, hospitals, and labs have financial incentives to expand the amount and price of services, while on the demand side there is little motivation for the customer to shop for the less expensive service. The government and the private insurance companies try to hold down costs; but since they depend on the information supplied by the service providers, they are not in a position to be knowledgeable purchasers.

The result of this inefficient market system is that health care costs have escalated to levels that hamper the economy and threaten to drive the federal budget out of control. The demand for medical care is price inelastic and prices are going up. As a result, total spending on health care has increased from 6% of GDP in 1965 to over 15% in 1997. This was twice the amount spent on education. Unless changes are made in the system, it threatens to take 20% of GDP within another decade. Because of our belief that health care is a merit good that everybody should have, governments are bearing a huge part of these higher costs. Health care spending has been growing four times faster than any other component of the federal budget. The percentage of total federal government revenues going to health care increased from 9% in 1972 to 20% in 1997.

The rapid rise in the private and public costs of health care, along with the inadequacies of the system—lack of universal coverage,

exclusion by insurers of people with preexisting conditions, lack of portability of health care coverage for workers changing jobs, insurance that can be canceled in cases of catastrophic illness—have led to the demand for reform. The federal government and numerous state governments have responded by enacting "patients' bills of rights." Some of these rights require doctors to explain how they are paid by insurance companies and forbid them to make extra income by limiting treatment. Others are directed at health insurance companies and require them to pay for hospital stays of minimum length for different procedures, and limit their ability to deny coverage to people who have preexisting conditions or who change jobs.

The battle over the current reforms concerns the extent of changes in the system, how big a role the government will play, and how the changes would be paid for. No one can say for sure how the reforms will affect the government budget down the road; but, without a cure for the ailing health care system, the road of escalating health care costs is leading not only the government but individuals and businesses as well to the poorhouse.

Chapter Preview

The rapid rise in U.S. health care costs has been one of the factors in increasing government spending at all levels. But the American people have come to consider health care, like food and shelter, to be a basic human right. To the extent that the market does not provide adequate health care to everyone at an affordable price, the public looks to government to fill the need. People want the programs that government provides, but they do not want the country to go broke paying for them. In this chapter we will examine the issues of public finance by asking these questions: On what do governments spend money? Where do governments get the money to spend? Who pays for government programs?

Learning Objectives

After completing this chapter, you should be able to:

1. Discuss the relative size of the government in the U.S. economy.
2. Distinguish between the total amount of money spent by the government sector and the amount spent on direct purchases.
3. List the largest expenditures made by the federal government.
4. List the largest expenditures made by state and local governments.
5. List the most important sources of revenue for the federal, state, and local governments, respectively.
6. Explain the three criteria for equity in taxation.
7. Describe how "bad" taxes decrease economic efficiency.
8. Understand what is meant by the incidence of a tax.

On What Do Governments Spend Money?

In the United States, governments at each level have three basic responsibilities: to influence the allocation of resources through their spending patterns, to redistribute income from wealthier to poorer citizens, and stabilization—to deal with unemployment and inflation (the topic of chapter 14). The first role is carried out primarily by state (provincial) and local governments, and the latter two by the federal government.

Size of Government Spending

Just how big is "big government"? The tax burden for the typical American worker is equal to almost four months of total earnings. About one-third of all money flow in the U.S. economy (around $2.5 trillion) is channeled through governments. To get a better idea of just how much money this is, consider that the budgets of all levels of government (federal, state, and local) together equaled 32% of the GDP in 1997. (As we noted in chapter 9, this is less than the share of government spending in other advanced economies.)

That figure, however, overstates the impact of government spending on the economy because a large part of government payments, especially in the federal budget, are not purchases but rather income transfers. In 1997, only 28% of all federal spending was in the form of direct purchases. The rest was used for transfer payments to individuals (social insurance, public assistance, veterans' benefits, and so on), for grants to state and local governments, and for paying interest on the national debt.

Figure 2

Government (Federal, State, and Local) Spending as a Share of GDP, 1959–1997

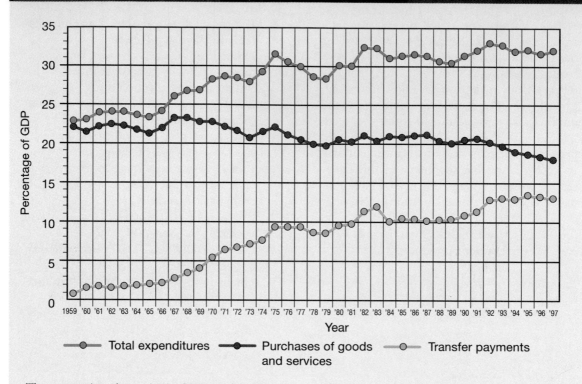

The proportion the nation's GDP used by government for the purchase of goods and services has been steadily declining over the past 40 years. In contrast, the proportion used for transfer payments has increased faster than direct spending has decreased. As a result, the total share of GDP that goes through the government sector increased from 23% in 1959 to 32% in 1997.

Source: *Economic Report of the President.*

In 1959 direct expenditures by all levels of government accounted for 22.1% of GDP. Although the absolute amount spent increased, it did not increase as fast as GDP. As a result, by 1997 direct expenditures accounted for only 18.0% of GDP (Figure 2). In contrast, transfer payments increased from less than 1% to about 14% of GDP. The biggest increases occurred because of recessions (1975, 1982, and 1992), and then they decreased or leveled off, but at an overall higher percentage than before. The consequence of increased transfer payments has been an increase in total government spending from 23% to 32% of GDP during the past 40 years.

The lion's share of direct government purchases are made by the country's 50 state and 85,000 local governments. Of the 18.0% of GDP spent by governments in 1997, their purchases accounted for 11.5% while the federal government's share was only 6.5%. A major portion of state and local government spending is for health care and public assistance. Much of this spending, however, is financed through transfers from the federal government. Federal grants to these governments for health care increased from less than $4 billion in 1970 to over $100 billion in 1997, and grants for public assistance increased from less than $6 billion to about $60 billion.

Figure 3

Federal Government Spending, 1997

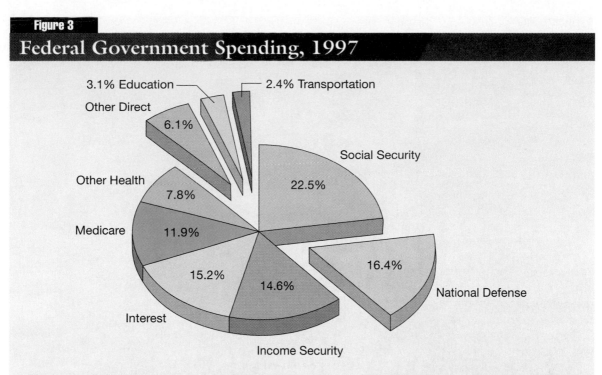

The largest direct expenditure item in the federal budget is for national defense. Altogether, direct spending, represented in the figure by the exploded (set off) sections, accounted for 28% of the budget. The other 72% consisted of transfer payments, of which Social Security was the largest. The federal government is therefore more important in redistributing income than in allocating resources.

Source: *Economic Report of the President.*

State- and local-level employment has increased along with the increased responsibility for delivering social services. About 17 million people worked for state and local governments in 1997, while federal employment was only around 3 million. These 20 million workers represent about 14.5% of the civilian labor force, or in other words, about one worker in 7 in the United States works for the government. The size of the federal workforce has been virtually constant for the last 2 decades and has actually declined as a percentage of the total labor force. Meanwhile, the number of employees in state and local governments has increased by about 25%.

◤ Federal Spending

Figure 3 shows the allocation of federal outlays in 1997. The federal budget is divided between purchases of goods and services and transfer payments. The largest single direct expenditure item in the 1997 budget was for national defense. With the end of the cold war, defense expenditures have fallen from over 20% of the budget to 16.4%. All other direct expenditures—for running the executive, legislative, and judicial branches of the government, natural resources and the environment, research and development (R&D), the space program, education, transportation, energy, and everything else—accounted for only 11.6% of the budget. It is this direct spending that makes up the government sector (G) in determining the level of national output (GDP) discussed in the last chapter.

Most of the income transfer programs are entitlements, which means that eligible recipients are legally entitled to payments or services from the government. These entitlements

The government allocates resources for public spending programs, such as health care, defense, foreign aid, and environmental protection. These decisions may often be influenced by lobbyists working for special interest groups.

include Social Security benefits, federal employee retirement benefits, Medicaid, Medicare, veterans' benefits, and unemployment assistance. More and more people have become eligible to receive these benefits in recent years. The total number of beneficiaries of these various entitlement programs is now over 75 million, or nearly three of every ten persons in the population. These recipients constitute a very large group in support of continuation of these programs. For example, most politicians consider Social Security to be "untouchable" because of the negative impacts changes might have on voters in their districts. As the age distribution of the population shifts toward older ages, more people become eligible for these programs, especially costly medical programs. These people will demand that more, rather than fewer, resources be transferred to them. This creates a

built-in pressure for continuing increases in transfer payments.

The largest of these income transfer programs in 1997 was Social Security pension and disability benefits, which accounted for 22.5% of total federal spending. (For a full discussion of Social Security, see the introductory article to chapter 9, p. 229). Next in size was interest on the national debt, which took up 15.2% of the budget. Interest on the debt was only 9% of the budget in 1980; as the debt grows, so does its interest cost. The next largest transfer was for income security—federal employee pension and disability payments, unemployment compensation, food stamps, and others—with 14.6% of spending. Other major transfers are for Medicare and other health programs. In 1980 Medicare accounted for 5% and other health care spending for 4% of the budget. By 1997 Medicare had grown to 11.9% and other health programs to 7.8%. In total, annual health care costs to the federal government were $322 billion in 1997.

Transfer payments are not limited to the lowest income segments of our economy. Agriculture price support payments go to some of the biggest and richest farms in the country, companies like Motorola and McDonald's are given government subsidies to promote their overseas business, and Social Security benefits are paid to everyone who paid into the system, regardless of their retirement income from other sources. Although they do not show up in the budget, **tax expenditures** that result from income tax deductions are also a form of transfer payments. For example, allowing households to deduct the interest paid on their mortgages from their taxable income costs the federal government billions in forgone tax revenue and represents a major subsidy for middle- and upper-income families. The same holds true for companies that are allowed to deduct employee health insurance premiums from their corporate income for tax purposes.

 ### On What Do Governments Spend Money?

EconExplorer

Since transfer payments account for almost three-quarters of the budget, the federal government is more important in redistributing income in the economy than it is in allocating resources through its purchases. Furthermore, it is obvious from these figures that reducing "waste and inefficiency in government," insofar as federal government civilian activities are concerned, cannot accomplish a great deal in cutting government spending. Eliminating all federal government direct spending other than defense would have a very small impact on the overall budget. Making government agencies more efficient rather than eliminating them can reduce government spending by only a negligible amount.

State and Local Expenditures

In contrast to the federal budget, most state and local expenditures are direct rather than transfer payments. As shown in Figure 4, state and local governments spend more on education than any other area. Education absorbs 28% of state and local budgets, and public welfare takes up another 14%. The interest costs on the debt of state and local governments amount to only 4% of their budgets, much less than for the federal government. This is because state and local governments in general are legally prevented from running deficits in their current spending. Except for capital expenditures such as construction projects that are funded by specific bond issues, state and local government budgets must be in annual balance.

Unable to run current budget deficits to cover shortfalls, burdened with federally mandated programs, limited in revenue collections by taxpayers' revolts and sluggish economies, state and local governments had been caught in a financial squeeze during the late 1980s and early 1990s. The result has been dilapidated school buildings and overcrowded classrooms; deteriorating highways, bridges, and public transit; and inadequate water and sewage systems. The robust economy of the late 1990s has filled state and local coffers, but much of the increased tax revenues have been diverted to increased spending on health care, prisons, and public assistance. Between 1980 and 1995, education spending increased 280%, health care 336%, public assistance 440%, and spending on corrections (jails and prisons) grew a whopping 586%.

---

tax expenditure tax revenue that the government forgoes because it allows certain expenses to be deducted from taxable income.

Case Application

Collective Choice

There are certain things that we cannot buy for ourselves although we want them: public safety, national defense, and flood control projects are examples of goods that we must provide and consume collectively if we are to have them. A problem arises, however, when we must choose what goods to provide for ourselves as a group instead of as individuals.

If Angie and Roberto go to a grocery store to shop, each can choose as much or as little of each good as they like. Angie might like a box of Cheerios, 1½ pounds of broccoli, and a six-pack of root beer. Roberto might like Frosted Mini-Wheats, a pound of carrots, and a gallon of skim milk. The same holds true when they go to a fast food restaurant or a mall. But when we must decide as a group (town, state, or nation), we often must decide on one and only one amount of a good. Angie cannot have $100 billion of national defense goods while Roberto has $80 billion. Likewise, Angie cannot have a small, 15-minute fireworks display on the 4th of July while Roberto has a big 45-minute display. As a result, whenever we choose collectively, some people end up with more of a good or service than they want while others end up with less.

In a democracy, the decisions about what and how much governments provide are made by elected representatives who are supposed to represent us and our wishes. But unfortunately, most of us do not know about even a tiny fraction of the things that our government is buying or the things that it does to influence the allocation of resources. How much information does the average person have about whether to buy one kind of weather satellite or another? Or how big a proposed dam should be? Or if we should be buying more jet fighters or more unmanned missiles? On the other hand, we do know which umbrella to buy, how many bathtubs we want in our house, and whether we want a motorcycle or a car.

Of course, businesses that build satellites, dams, and military equipment have a great deal at stake with such decisions; they spend a lot of money for lobbyists to "inform" our representatives about which public spending options should be chosen, and they back up the information with campaign contributions. These "special interests" have an incentive to persuade governments to buy their products or give them special tax or subsidy treatments. Because the rest of us are uninformed about these particular policies, and because each one costs each of us only a little, we do not make our voices heard. As a result, the government allocation of resources is strongly influenced by special interests.

When we vote for a representative, we have to accept the fact that he or she may agree with us on some issues, but not others. For example, we might agree with a representative's views on public health, national defense and cigarette taxes, but disagree with her views on education and public funding for stadiums. Instead of being free to roam the grocery aisles picking and choosing what we want, voting for one of two candidates for office is like being limited to a choice between two already filled grocery carts.

When people make a choice about whether or not to buy something, they spend their own money and get the benefits from the good being bought. Consequently, when making a major purchase like a car, people making individual choices want the best possible deal and are very careful about how they spend their money. When people working for the government make choices, they are spending someone else's (the taxpayers') money. Therefore they do not personally suffer the consequences of making a bad choice. If the chosen jet fighter is a lemon, the cost of the poor performance is spread over all voters.

When the government provides goods and services, it is lacking one of the most important things that makes private businesses efficient—the existence of profit or loss. Profits tell private businesses which goods and services people want and losses tell them the things that people do not want. The government has to make its decisions based on rare elections and referenda (when most of us don't vote anyway). Except in a few instances at the local level, governments also lack the competition that forces private firms to provide the best products at the lowest cost.

Governments are essentially monopolies that have the power to force people to pay taxes for goods they may or may not want. As monopolies, they do not need to worry about providing the best possible service. How long does it take to get a pothole in front of your house repaired, and how long does it take to get a plumber to your house to fix a leak? How many places and at what hours can you bank or go shopping for new clothes, and how many places and at what hours can you take a driver's license test or conduct any business with a government agency?

Despite these problems, we do need governments to provide us with things that we cannot provide for ourselves. Individuals cannot defend the country, help the poor and sick, provide public safety, protect the environment, or manage the country's water resources. And it is not that people who are working for the government are any more inefficient than those in the private sector. The problem lies with the institution of government and the fact that individual choice leads to a more efficient satisfaction of consumer wants than collective choice.

Economic Reasoning

1. What are some reasons that it is more difficult for a society to make collective decisions about what it wants than it is for individuals to make decisions about what they want?
2. How does the absence of profits in the government sector make it difficult for governments to satisfy citizens' wants in an efficient manner?
3. What changes do you think could be made to improve the collective choice process?

Collective Choice

The National Taxpayer Union is a private organization that monitors the nations' tax policy. Visit their Web site at www.ntu.org and check out their ratings of the members of Congress. What grades did they give your senators and representatives?

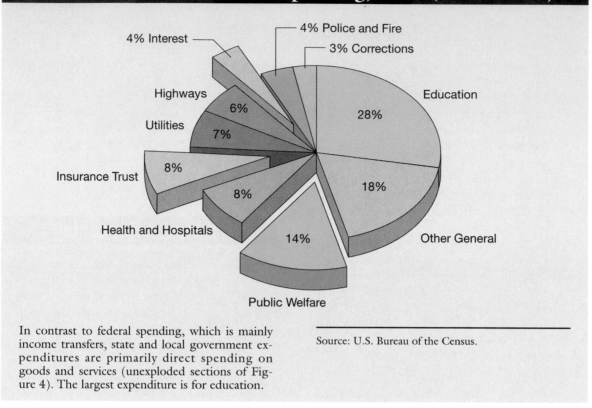

Figure 4

State and Local Government Spending, 1995 ($1.35 trillion)

- 4% Interest
- 4% Police and Fire
- 3% Corrections
- Highways 6%
- Utilities 7%
- Insurance Trust 8%
- Health and Hospitals 8%
- Education 28%
- Other General 18%
- Public Welfare 14%

In contrast to federal spending, which is mainly income transfers, state and local government expenditures are primarily direct spending on goods and services (unexploded sections of Figure 4). The largest expenditure is for education.

Source: U.S. Bureau of the Census.

▶ Where Do Governments Get the Money to Spend?

In the preceding section, we saw that there are major differences in what the federal government spends money on and what state and local governments spend money on. In this section we will see that there are also major differences in the sources of their funds.

payroll tax a tax on wages and salaries to finance Social Security and Medicare costs, with equal amounts paid by employee and employer; the 1997 tax rate on each was 7.65%.

◤ Federal Government Revenues

The largest source of revenue for the federal government is individual income taxes. As shown in Figure 5, the tax on personal incomes provided 46.7% of the federal government's revenue in 1997. The personal income tax component of federal receipts has changed little over the past 2 decades.

Next to income taxes, the largest revenue—over one-third—comes from Social Security **payroll taxes.** Social Security taxes have been steadily increasing and making up an ever larger part of federal government income. Over half of the nation's workers, those at the lower end of the income scale, pay more in Social Security contributions than in income taxes.

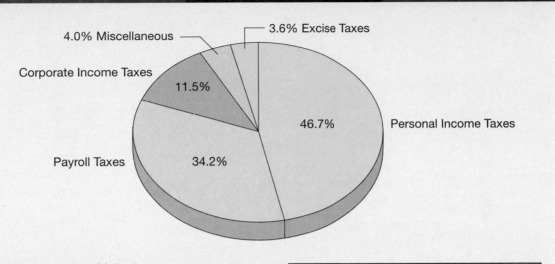

Federal Government Revenue, 1997

4.0% Miscellaneous

3.6% Excise Taxes

Corporate Income Taxes

11.5%

Personal Income Taxes

46.7%

Payroll Taxes

34.2%

The largest source of federal government revenue is personal income taxes. The second largest is payroll taxes from Social Security and federal pension contributions. The largest item in the miscellaneous category is earnings by the Federal Reserve System.

Source: Congressional Budget Office.

Corporate income taxes generated over 11% of federal revenues in 1997, down from 13% in 1980. Excise taxes—the federal taxes on gasoline, alcohol, cigarettes, and public utility services—customs duties on imports, and miscellaneous receipts such as user fees and earnings by the Federal Reserve System accounted for the balance.

◤ State and Local Government Revenues

As Figure 6 shows, the largest sources of state and local government revenues come from sales taxes, which the states principally depend on, property taxes, which local governments principally depend on, and federal transfers and user fees, which help finance both levels. User fees include such things as payments for garbage collection, licenses, auto registration, admission to parks, and the use of airports. A growing share of state and local revenues (2.5% in 1996) comes from state lotteries and other forms of legalized state run gambling.

🖱 Where Do Governments Get the Money to Spend?

EconExplorer

The system by which federal funds are transferred to lower branches of government is referred to as **fiscal federalism.** Much of the transfers arc to cover federally mandated programs, but in recent years the mandated costs have tended to exceed the amounts transferred, leaving the states to make up the difference. States such as Florida and California have sued

fiscal federalism tax collection and disbursement of funds by a higher level of government to lower jurisdictions.

Figure 6

State and Local Government Revenue, 1995 ($1.42 trillion)

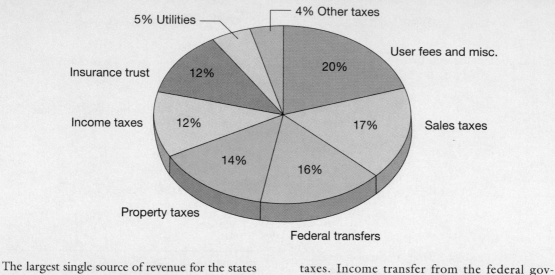

The largest single source of revenue for the states is sales taxes. The share of revenue from user fees has been increasing, while that of state income taxes has been decreasing. For local governments, the largest revenue source is property taxes. Income transfer from the federal government are important to both state and local governments.

Source: U. S. Bureau of the Census.

the federal government to recover the costs of educational and health services mandated for illegal immigrants. The amounts of federal transfers to each state in 1997 are shown in Table 1. As we saw in chapter 9, the method by which the nation's public assistance programs are funded has been changed to ease this burden on the states.

State and local governments face increasingly vocal demands from their citizens for improvements in highways, transportation, and other infrastructure; better schools; and pollution control. They are required by mandated federal programs to spend more on Medicaid, social services, and income maintenance. At the same time, federal aid to the states has been declining as a percentage of state revenues. Taxpayers resisted state efforts to raise taxes to fund these programs with what has come to be known as the "taxpayers' revolt" of the 1980s. In many states, voters initiated and passed referenda that limited the states' ability to raise taxes or tax revenue. The result has been a squeeze on state budgets, especially during downturns in the economy when tax receipts naturally decline.

There are some indications, however, that voters are willing to pay more to get the improved services that they want. In California, where the taxpayer revolt began, and a number of other states, including Florida, Massachusetts, Montana, Nevada, Oklahoma, Texas, and Vermont, either state voters or local governments have passed tax increases to fund specific programs. Voters are apparently willing to accept targeted taxes earmarked for specific purposes that they feel are needed.

Table 1 — Federal Income Transfers to States and the District of Columbia, 1997

State	Federal Aid Total (billions)	Per Capita
Alabama	24,563	806.45
Alaska	4,701	2,140.34
Arizona	22,108	736.65
Arkansas	12,668	905.05
California	160,874	837.16
Colorado	10,702	627.86
Connecticut	17,864	888.32
Delaware	3,452	856.69
District of Columbia	23,112	5,179.05
Florida	82,060	580.35
Georgia	35,778	730.50
Hawaii	8,266	997.84
Idaho	5,683	773.63
Illinois	52,818	781.44
Indiana	25,115	603.54
Iowa	13,557	603.06
Kansas	12,507	624.44
Kentucky	21,261	947.40
Louisiana	23,156	1,024.04
Maine	7,184	1,109.11
Maryland	39,137	775.37
Massachusetts	37,378	1,040.44
Michigan	40,652	740.46
Minnesota	20,088	843.35
Mississippi	15,026	961.42
Missouri	31,694	783.32
Montana	5,132	1,126.99
Nebraska	7,809	740.76
Nevada	7,085	586.31
New Hampshire	5,041	718.14
New Jersey	39,537	819.79
New Mexico	12,441	1,244.05
New York	95,622	1,344.41
North Carolina	34,731	846.33
North Dakota	4,331	1,675.93
Ohio	50,707	744.37
Oklahoma	17,317	756.71
Oregon	14,633	879.76
Pennsylvania	65,314	854.24
Rhode Island	5,879	1,158.71
South Carolina	18,815	794.46
South Dakota	4,149	1,330.42
Tennessee	28,558	848.54
Texas	88,332	678.21
Utah	8,436	658.04
Vermont	2,728	1,020.27
Virginia	52,908	522.40
Washington	30,321	801.34
West Virginia	10,409	1,156.55
Wisconsin	20,806	699.59
Wyoming	2,643	1,587.45
United States (total)	1,428,818	846.38

The federal government provides grants-in-aid and other income transfers to state and local governments under a system of fiscal federalism. Other than the District of Columbia, which is financed by the federal government, the largest federal aid per capita in 1997 went to Alaska ($2,140 per Alaskan). The smallest amount went to Virginia ($522 per Virginian).

Source: U.S. Bureau of the Census, *Federal Expenditures by State for Fiscal Year 1997.*

Case Application

The Numbers Game

During the Roaring 20s and into the 1930s, Dutch Schultz (whose real name was Arthur Flegenheimer) became one of the most notorious gangsters in American history. What was his business and how did he make his millions? Among other illegal enterprises, Dutch ran the numbers game in Harlem. People played by picking a 3-digit number between 000 and 999. At the end of each day, the winning 3-digit number was determined randomly by the order of finish of race horses at the Aqueduct Race Track. While the odds against winning were 1,000 to 1, Dutch and his organization would pay anyone with a winning number about 600 times the amount they bet. Most people would bet a penny or two each day with the hopes of hitting their number and winning $6 or $12. Although illegal, the game attracted hundreds of thousands of players a day and made Dutch a very rich man.

Dutch didn't invent the numbers game. It had been run for years by lots of individual "banks"—often there was one on each city block. Of course, with lots of competition, each bank had to keep its odds and payoffs high enough to ensure that local residents didn't play on other blocks. Dutch took care of that problem. He took over all the small banks and consolidated them into one big bank. With this monopoly power, he was able to lower the payoffs to winners.

As usually happened to people like Dutch Schultz, he was killed in a New Jersey restaurant by rival gangsters. But his legacy lives on in the 38 states that run state lotteries to raise state funds. With one major difference, the daily number game that these states allow and encourage their citizens play is no different than the numbers game that Dutch controlled in Harlem. The difference is that it is illegal when a private individual runs a numbers game, but it is legal if the government does it.

The lotteries are actually run by private companies hired by the states. One company, GTECH, runs 29 of the country's lotteries, while Automatic Wagering, Inc. runs the other 9. Each company takes about 4 cents of every dollar bet in return for their services—enough to earn GTECH $744 million in revenues in 1996. If the advertisements and the games offered by the states seem very similar, it is because these two companies also are responsible for developing the games and the ads.

To keep customers interested, the 38 states that have lotteries keep adding new games and have even formed a multistate association to promote the multistate Powerball, Wildcard, and Daily Millions lottery games. The states also advertise heavily to encourage residents to play—they spent over a billion dollars on advertising in 1997, making the lottery one of the most advertised goods in America. A concern of many is that these ads are often misleading and actually fraudulent in their claims of payouts and odds. For example, if you visit the Multi-State Lottery Association home page you might see a notice saying that the odds on winning a prize are 35 to 1. What they don't tell you is that the odds of winning a million-dollar prize are often several million to 1.

A more important concern of many is that the promotion of gambling is not what the American Dream is supposed to be about. While American children are being taught that the way to succeed is to stay in school, work hard, and save your money, the glamorous ads run by state governments are seducing the public into dreams of getting rich quick without having to work. They entice players to

State and multistate lottery games are popular all over the country, although private lotteries are illegal in most states. Many people are concerned about lottery ads that provide a deceptive picture of the odds of winning.

play games that offer infinitesimal odds of winning big and encourage people to make sure they "play" every day.

Beginning with New York in the 1960s, states began to run lotteries as a way of raising revenues without having to raise taxes. While they have been successful (the 38 states with lotteries earned about $35 billion in 1996), critics point out that the lottery constitutes a very regressive tax. Most people who play are from lower-income groups. Many state lottery ads are targeted at the poor and are actually timed to run during the time of the month that people receive their Social Security and public assistance checks. Both GTECH and AWI target their efforts in poor neighborhoods. In Chelsea, a low-income Boston suburb, the state set up one lottery ticket vendor per 363 residents. In Wellesley, an affluent suburb, there was one agent per 3,063 residents. The result? The average Chelsea resident spent $915 per year playing the lottery while the average Wellesley resident spent only $30.

Advocates of the lotteries argue that it is a fairer way to raise needed money than by increasing taxes. At least lottery players can choose whether to play or not—taxpayers have no choice. About 34 cents out of each dollar bet in lotteries ends up in state treasuries, and this money is often earmarked for special programs such as education, economic development, or helping older residents. Advocates also argue that people will play the numbers game whether the state offers it or not, and it is better for the state to earn the profits than some modern-day Dutch Schultz.

Economic Reasoning

1. How do states make money from lottery games?

2. Why is the lottery considered to be a regressive tax on the poor?

3. Do you think that running lotteries is a good way for states to raise money to pay for needed public programs?

The Numbers Game

Visit the Multi-State Lottery Association at www.powerball.com and write a short report on the ads that you find. Does the site tell you your chances of winning the jackpot along with the size of jackpots? (Be careful of the way things are worded. The probability of winning "a prize" is not the probability of winning the jackpot.)

▶ Who Pays for Government Spending?

The question of who should pay how much of the cost of government—how the burden should be shared—is a continuing subject of debate. Economics can help enlighten this debate by providing certain criteria that are presented in this analysis section.

◼ Equity

In a democracy, governments can tax the citizens only with their agreement, and people will agree to be taxed only if they perceive the tax system to be fair. One of the conditions of fairness is that people who are equally able to pay should bear the same tax burden. This is **horizontal equity.** An example of failure to fulfill

this condition was the so-called marriage penalty. Because their joint return put them in a higher bracket, a married couple typically paid more taxes on a given income than two people living in one household who were not married. The income tax rate structure was changed to reduce this marriage penalty, although it still exists. Another question of horizontal equity is the relationship between tax rates on **earned income,** such as wages and salaries, and tax rates on such **nonearned income** as capital gains, interest, and dividends.

The differential between the tax rates on earned income and on capital gains is smaller than it once was, but there is a move to increase it once again by reducing capital gains taxes to stimulate investment.

Another criterion of a fair tax structure is **vertical equity,** which is based on the concept that those with higher incomes are in a better position to pay taxes with less sacrifice and should therefore pay a larger percentage in taxes. This is often referred to as the "ability to pay" principle. It is felt that the larger the income, the smaller the sacrifice for each dollar paid in taxes. Those below a certain income level, where the sacrifice is greater, pay zero income taxes.

Just what constitutes vertical equity is one of the most heated questions in the subject of taxation. The maximum **marginal tax rate** on

horizontal equity equality of treatment for all individuals at the same income level.

earned income wages, salaries, and other employee compensation plus earnings from self-employment.

nonearned income dividends, interest, capital gains, and other nonlabor income.

vertical equity fair differentiations of treatment of individuals at different levels.

marginal tax rate the tax rate applied to the last or additional income received.

Table 2 — Average Tax Rates and Taxes by Income Class in 1994

Household Adjusted Gross Income (AGI)	Tax as a Percentage of AGI	Average Tax per Household
$11,000–$13,000	2.4%	$700
$22,000–$25,000	8.1%	$1,900
$40,000–$50,000	10.8%	$4,900
$75,000–$100,000	15.1%	$12,900
$200,000–$500,000	25.6%	$73,700
Greater than $1,000,000	31.2%	$810,000

Both the absolute amount paid in federal income tax taxes and the proportion of income paid increase as household income increases. As a consequence, many argue that the federal income tax is vertically equitable.

Source: *Statistical Abstract of the United States, 1997.*

high-income earners was reduced from 50% to 31% in the 1986 and 1991 tax bills, but the 1993 tax bill increased the maximum federal tax rate on the last dollar earned to 39.6%. The average tax rate is much lower than 39.6% because the first dollars earned are taxed at much lower rates. In 1994, the average federal income tax bill was equal to 14.3% of household income.

Many people believe that the federal personal income tax is vertically equitable. In 1994, only 4% of all taxpayers earned incomes greater than $100,000, yet they paid 44% of all federal income taxes. Only 0.06% of the population had incomes that year in excess of $1,000,000, yet they provided 10.6% of the nation's personal income tax receipts. As shown in Table 2, both the absolute amount of taxes paid and the percentage of income paid in taxes increase as household incomes increase. The average tax rate for households earning between $11,000 and $13,000 was 2.4% of income in 1994, while the average rate paid by those with incomes over $1,000,000 was 31.2%.

A different approach to tax equity is applied in some cases where the proceeds of a tax are directly allocated to a corresponding government service. An example of this is the highway trust fund, which is used to finance the construction and maintenance of our highway system and is financed by gasoline sales taxes and motor vehicle fees. This represents the **benefits principle** of equity in taxation.

Efficiency

Along with their effect on equity, taxes are also judged for their effect on economic efficiency. To be efficient, the tax should neither interfere with the way resources are allocated nor discourage production. An exception to this rule is made in the case of **sin taxes** such as those levied on tobacco and alcohol, in part to reduce their consumption in the public interest.

A higher tax on cigarettes to help pay for health care is part of an ongoing debate and numerous court cases. There is little dissent over this tax, except from smokers and the tobacco industry. Its appeal stems from a combination of advantages: it satisfies the benefits principle in the sense that smokers cause higher health care costs; and as a sin tax it accomplishes the public policy objective of discouraging smoking, especially among the young. There could be a contradiction in the two objectives in that if a tax reduces consumption too

benefits principle levy of a tax on an individual to pay the costs of government service in proportion to the individual's benefit from the service.

sin tax an excise tax levied on commodities that public policy deems undesirable, such as cigarettes and alcohol, in order to limit their consumption.

much, the revenue it produces declines. But according to estimates of the elasticity of demand for cigarettes (see chapter 5, p. 131), a tax of around $1 per pack maximizes the revenue produced by the tax.

It is, of course, impossible to levy taxes that are completely neutral in their effects on output, but taxes that produce inefficiency should be avoided. A classic example of a "bad" tax was one that was levied in medieval England on the window space of houses. Glass windows were considered a luxury at the time, and those who could afford large houses with lots of windows were assumed to be able to afford the taxes. The result of the tax, however, was that new houses were constructed without windows. This was not a sensible way to build houses. The window tax was inefficient. It was inefficient, not because it produced too little tax revenue, although that happened to be the case, but rather because of the adverse effect it had on the allocation of resources.

All taxes are to some extent inefficient, and there is frequently a conflict between the principles of equity and efficiency in taxation. Finding the right mix of taxes that best satisfies these criteria and also provides the necessary revenue for the functions of government is a perpetual problem.

◢ Incidence

One of the major obstacles to devising an equitable and efficient tax system lies in the difficulty of determining who ultimately pays the tax. The **incidence of a tax** is not necessarily determined by those on whom the tax is levied by the government. Frequently those who pay the tax to the government actually shift it to someone else. Personal income taxes cannot be shifted, and the incidence of the tax falls on the person who pays it. This, however, is not the case with most other taxes. Excise taxes and property taxes on rental and business property, for example, are shifted to consumers. Even employer payroll taxes are shifted—to consumers in the form of higher prices and to workers in the form of lower wages.

The incidence of general sales taxes and excise taxes depends on the elasticity of demand for the product being taxed. If demand is inelastic and consumers must have the product, the tax gets shifted to buyers. If demand is elastic, buyers can take the product or leave it, and sellers end up bearing the incidence of the tax by being forced to lower prices. Elasticity is also important in determining the total amount of sales taxes collected. If the demand for a taxed product is elastic and people stop buying it because of tax-induced price increases, total tax revenues will be small. In contrast, a tax on something with an inelastic demand will bring in increased amounts of tax receipts.

Who Pays for Government Spending?

EconExplorer

The federal personal income tax has historically been a **progressive tax** because the tax paid as a percentage of income increases as income rises. Most taxes other than income taxes are **regressive taxes** as a result of shifting the incidence of the tax to consumers. This is due to the fact that the lower a person's income, the larger a percentage of that income is spent on the goods and services whose prices include the taxes. As a result, low-income consumers pay a larger percentage of their income on sales taxes, gasoline taxes, utility taxes, and so forth. Even though they may not own property, property taxes take a higher percentage of their income as property owners shift the tax to renters in the form of higher rents.

The federal personal income tax is amazingly complex and difficult to understand—the

---

incidence of a tax the amount of a tax that ultimately falls on households, irrespective of who initially pays the tax.

progressive tax a tax rate that increases as the income on which the tax is based grows larger.

regressive tax a levy that takes a higher proportion from low incomes in taxes than it takes from high incomes.

Case Application

Reflections in the Tax Mirror: Which Is Fairest of Them All?

Taxes are not pretty. In fact, though always unpopular, taxes in recent years have become downright ugly in the eyes of taxpayers. Yet the government services and benefits they pay for are in increasing demand.

The problem faced by legislators and executives at all levels of government is how to extract the necessary revenue from the citizenry with the least amount of pain and squealing. A multiplicity of taxes, surcharges, user fees, and license fees have recently been imposed on such things as credit reports and debt collections (Pennsylvania), dog and cat kenneling (Minnesota), ski equipment rentals (Lakewood, Colorado), and a $30 fee imposed on ex-convicts in Michigan's Washtenaw County for each monthly visit to their probation officer.

Although such revenue sources raise less public opposition than general tax increases, the collection costs are often so great as to offset a large part of the revenue. Substantial revenue sources are needed to pay for government services and benefits, but which type of tax is least undesirable? The federal income tax is under attack, especially by supply-side adherents (see p. 339), as a disincentive to work and investment, and the flat tax movement is gaining increasing support. State sales taxes are criticized for their regressive effect on low-income earners. Local property taxes are both regressive and obstacles to home ownership.

The alternative revenue source most often proposed is the value-added tax (VAT). The United States is the only major industrialized nation that does not have some type of VAT. Its revenue-generating power is enormous. The Congressional Budget Office has estimated that a VAT of 5% would bring in more than $100 billion annually.

The VAT is related to the concept of value added discussed in relation to calculating GDP (p. 325). At each stage of producing a good, the producer adds an amount of value to the raw materials or semifinished goods purchased from suppliers. With VAT, the producer is required to send the designated percentage of that value added to the government and include it in the cost passed on to the next production or distribution stage. When the finished product is sold to the customer, the price includes the total of the value-added taxes paid at each stage of production and distribution.

Generally, in countries that use a VAT, the amount of the tax paid on an item is not indicated on the sales tag, only a statement that the price includes the VAT. The public, therefore, does not have a constant tax irritant to react to. There is likely to be less squealing than with the normal sales tax added to the price of a purchase at the time of sale. This despite the fact that the VAT rate is greater than 20% in 8 of the European Union member countries, including France, Ireland, and all the Scandinavian countries.

Economic Reasoning

1. What is the incidence of the value-added tax?

2. Is a VAT regressive, proportional, or progressive? Why?

3. Should the VAT be adopted in the United States? Why or why not?

tax code that details the tax law covers thousands of pages. For example, in an effort to reduce the burden of special circumstances, such as large medical bills, it allows people to deduct these expenses from their income before calculating their tax bill. It also encourages and helps people to own their own homes by allowing them to deduct mortgage interest. To please special interests that lobby for special benefits, however, the code also includes deductions and special tax treatments that amount to subsidies for thousands of other things that benefit specific industries and activities. It also treats earned and unearned income differently. The tax code is so complex that thousands of accountants and tax attorneys, and millions of hours, are required to fill out tax forms.

The complexity of the current tax system has led many to call for a simple **flat tax** that would set one tax rate for everyone and would remove all deductions and other special treatments. The flat tax is an example of a **proportional tax**—one that would take the same percentage of income from taxpayers at all income levels. Although this would reduce vertical equity, it would have the advantage of freeing up scarce resources (accountants, lawyers, and tax preparers), which could be used for increasing the nation's output of goods and services instead of being used to comply with an unnecessarily complex tax code. When the federal income tax was more progressive, the total of all types of taxes in the country—federal, state, and local—was considered roughly proportional.

flat tax a proposed income tax structure that removes all deductions from the federal tax code and levies the same tax rate on everyone.

proportional tax a levy that takes the same proportion in taxes from low and high incomes.

▶ Putting It Together

Total government spending—federal, state, and local—amounts to about one-third of GDP. A large part of this represents *transfer payments* of income to individuals rather than government purchases or salaries for government employees. If these transfer payments are subtracted, government spending at all levels accounts for less than one-fifth of the nation's economic activity.

The largest item of direct spending in the federal budget is national defense, which accounts for about 16% of the total budget. All other direct expenditures account for 11.6% of the budget. All of the rest of federal government spending consists of transfer payments, the largest of which is Social Security. Next largest in size are interest on the national debt and income security. For state and local governments, the major expense is education. Most state and local government spending is for direct purchases rather than transfer payments. Although they do not show up in budgets, *tax expenditures* cost governments billions of dollars every year in forgone tax collections.

The largest revenue source for the federal government is *personal income taxes*. After that comes Social Security *payroll taxes*. State and local governments obtain their revenues from *sales taxes*, the largest revenue producer for the states; *property taxes*, the largest for local governments; user fees; and grants from the federal government under a system of *fiscal federalism*.

To make the tax system work, the public must perceive it as being fair. One criterion for fairness is that people in similar economic situations should pay similar amounts in taxes. This is referred to as *horizontal equity*. Another criterion is that people with higher incomes should pay proportionally more taxes than people with lower incomes. This is referred to as *vertical equity*. To promote vertical equity, *marginal tax rates* increase as a household's income increases. Horizontal and vertical equity often suffer because earned income

and unearned income are treated differently by the tax laws. A third criterion, applied to certain government programs, is that those who benefit from a government service should pay directly for that service. This is the *benefits principle* of equity.

Taxes should be levied in a way that least affects the allocation of resources and least discourages economic activity. If a tax results in some goods not being produced that otherwise would be produced, it is a "bad" tax. Public policy makes an exception in the case of *sin taxes*, such as alcohol and tobacco excise taxes, which are levied in part to reduce the consumption of items that society wishes to discourage.

Taxes frequently are not borne by the person who initially pays the tax. Taxes other than income taxes are shifted to consumers in the form of higher prices or to workers in the form of lower wages. How the tax burden is allocated is the *incidence of the tax*. Taxes that take a larger percentage of higher incomes than lower incomes are *progressive*. Those that take the same percentage from all income levels (like the proposed *flat tax*) are *proportional*, and those that take a larger percentage from low incomes are *regressive*.

$ Perspective $

The Growth of Big Government

More information on the growth of government spending can be found in *Deficit Financing: Public Budgeting in Its Institutional and Historical Context* (1992) by Donald F. Kettl; *The Inevitability of Government Growth* (1990) by Harold B. Vetter and John F. Walker; and *Growth of Government in the West* (1978) by G. Warren Nutler.

At the end of the 1920s total expenditures for all levels of government amounted to less than 10% of GDP (Gross Domestic Product). For the past 27 years they have been 30% to 35%. How did government grow so much in the second half of this century? Where is the growth of government taking us?

These are just some of the questions raised by the debate over "big government."

The size of government relative to GDP (Gross Domestic Product) doubled in the early 1930s, due primarily to the decline in GDP during the Great Depression rather than to an increases in government spending. The ratio of government expenditures to total output doubled again during World War II but dropped back to less than 20% after the war. It rose above 25% during the Korean War and the "cold war" years of the early 1950s. It remained around 27–28% until 1968, when a combination of the Vietnam War expansion and increased domestic social spending on the "War on Poverty" raised government outlays above 30% of GDP. Since then government spending has

hovered around one-third of total spending in the economy.

These figures on total government spending, however, do not reveal the important changes that have been occurring in the types of government spending. One significant change has been in the proportions of total government spending accounted for by the three levels of government. In the 1920s local government spending accounted for about half of the total. It fell to below 10% in the 1940s and today is over 22%. State government spending is almost the same amount. Meanwhile, the federal government's share reached a peak during World War II and has gradually declined since. Although federal outlays are greater than the combined spending of state and local governments, part of that federal government spending goes for funding state and local government programs under fiscal federalism.

The picture is also affected by changes in the makeup of federal spending. In the 1920s only about 10% of federal expenditures were transfer payments. This has increased over the years until today transfer payments account for over half of the federal budget. As a result, state and local government spending plays a larger part in economic allocations than does federal spending. In terms of economic activity and the number of employees, the growth of "big government" is now personified not so much by the federal government as by the growth in state and local spending.

For Further Study and Analysis

Study Questions

1. What types of government spending are included in GDP? What types are most readily subject to cost cutting?
2. How many people in your family and how many friends or acquaintances of yours are receiving transfer payments? What type of transfer payments are they receiving?
3. Have there been any recent reductions in government services in your area? What were they? In which level of government did they occur?
4. If a candidate for national office promised, if elected, to double the efficiency of federal government operations and thereby reduce taxes by half, why might you question that promise? What promises might that candidate make about tax reduction that you would find feasible?
5. Approximately how much have you paid in excise taxes (taxes other than those on income) in the past 3 days? On what items?
6. What revenues do state (provincial) and local governments receive, other than taxes? What is the impact on various income groups of these revenue sources?
7. How do special interests affect the size of government spending and tax revenues?
8. Why is it assumed that wealthier people have a smaller marginal utility for money than people with lower incomes?
9. What are three things, other than cigarettes and liquor, whose price is affected by a tax? What is the effect of the tax? What is the incidence of the tax?
10. How does the elasticity of demand influence the incidence of sales and excise taxes? How does it influence the total amount of taxes collected?

Exercises in Analysis

1. Write a report on current efforts to reform the federal tax system. You can find information in your library or on the Web. If it is an election year, write an analysis of candidates' proposals to reform the tax system.
2. Write a report on the sources of funding for your state or provincial budget. From a taxpayer's guide, list five personal income tax deductions and five business tax deductions. Why do you think these deductions are allowed? Are any "special interests" involved?
3. Search your local newspaper and news magazines for articles about public funding for health care and/or health insurance. Write a report that presents arguments for and against increased government involvement in health care finance.

4. Write a report that describes the major expenditures made by either your state (province) or local government. Are your tax dollars being spent for things that you do not agree with?

Further Reading

Coddington, Dean C. *The Crisis in Health Care: Costs, Choices, and Strategies.* San Francisco: Jossey-Bass, 1990. Examines what has happened to health care costs in the United States and the results of U.S. medical policy.

Congressional Budget Office. The CBO provides a number of reports and a wealth of federal budget data at www.cbo.gov.

Danziger, Shelden, and Peter Gottschalk, eds. *Uneven Tides: Rising Inequality in the 1990s.* New York: Russell Sage Foundation, 1993. Covers the trend in inequality, the rising importance of skill in the labor market, the effect of deunionization on earnings inequality, and the effect of federal taxes and cash transfers on income distribution.

Federal Reserve Bank of Cleveland. "The Government's Role in the Health Care Industry: Past, Present, and Future." *Economic Commentary,* June 1994. A short paper that discusses the economics of government involvement in health care and health insurance.

Fullerton, Don, and Diane Lim Rogers. *Who Bears the Lifetime Tax Burden?* Washington, DC: Brookings Institution, 1993. A study of the incidence of taxes and how different taxes are shifted.

Johnson, David B. *Public Choice: An Introduction to the New Political Economy.* Mountain View, CA: Bristlecone Books, 1991. An overview of public choice theory, the application of economic principles to describe how government decisions are made.

Konner, Melvin. *Medicine at the Crossroads: The Crisis in Health Care.* New York: Pantheon Books, 1993. A critical view of U.S. medical care policy and the associated costs.

Marmor, Theodore R., Jerry L. Mashaw, and Phillip L. Harvey. *America's Misunderstood Welfare State: Persistent Myths, Enduring Realities.* New York: Basic Books, 1990. Evaluates U.S. social policy, its public welfare system, Social Security, and Medicare.

Peterson, Peter G., and Neil Howe. *On Borrowed Time: How the Growth in Entitlement Spending Threatens America's Future.* San Francisco: ICS Press, 1988. An alarmist view of where Social Security, federal pensions, and inflation of health care costs are leading the country.

U.S. Government Printing Office. *The Economic Report of the President* (current year). An excellent source of statistics and reports that cover just about every aspect of government policy, spending, and revenues. Also on line at http://www.access.gpo.gov/eop/index.html.

Weidenbaum, Murray L. *Business and Government in the Global Marketplace.* 5th ed. Englewood Cliffs, NJ: Prentice Hall, 1995. A textbook review of the role of government and the ways that government policy interacts with the private sector.

Weiss, Lawrence David. *No Benefit: Crisis in America's Health Insurance Industry.* Boulder, CO: Westview Press, 1992. Reviews the historical development and current profile of the commercial health insurance industry, including price fixing and conspiracy in the industry, employer cost-cutting strategies, and how the uninsured were created.

chapter fourteen

Policies for Economic Stability and Growth

For better or for worse, the government has a big impact on the economy. Despite recent reductions in the budget deficit, fear is widespread that federal debt is dangerously evil. This introductory article examines the debt issue.

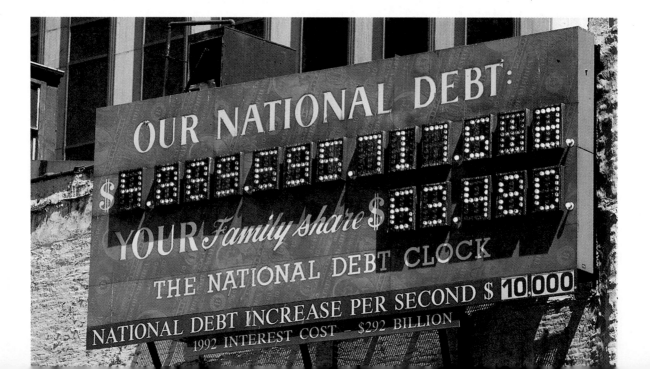

The Debt Bogeyman

Is it Jason? Is it Freddy? Or is it just a pretend spook in a white sheet? In the minds of some, budget deficits and the national debt are dangerous threats. To others, they are a minor nuisance. What are the budget deficit and the national debt, and should we be concerned about their size?

The national debt is the total amount that the U.S. government owes to its creditors. Every year that the government runs a budget deficit, that is, tax revenues are less than expenditures, it borrows to make up the difference and the extra borrowing adds to the national debt. Since the federal government has had a deficit every year since 1969, it has been steadily adding to its debt. During Ronald Reagan's terms as president, taxes were cut and military expenditures increased. As a result, the annual deficits grew and averaged $167 billion per year from 1981 to 1988. They grew even larger in the early 1990s, averaging $248 billion between 1990 and 1995.

In the 15 years between the time Ronald Reagan took office in 1981 and 1995, the national debt consequently ballooned from $994 billion to $4.9 trillion. How big is this? Comparing the debt to the country's total output is a more meaningful way to answer this question than by looking at the raw figures. Debt can only be considered large or small when it is compared to the debtor's income. For example, a $1 million debt might seem huge to you or me, but it is not a significant amount to Michael Jordan or Bill Gates. Relative to our nation's income, our debt has been growing—from 33% of GDP in 1981 to 68% in 1995. Whether debt equal to about two-thirds of the country's annual income is too much is subject to debate, but most agree that rapid growth of the debt can present problems for the economy.

Deficit reduction measures and the growth of the economy (which increases tax revenues) in recent years have resulted in a shrinking deficit of only $22 billion in 1997—the lowest deficit since 1974. The growth in the total debt has also slowed, reaching "only" $5.4 trillion in 1997. The slow growth in the debt and the increases in GDP have resulted in the debt/GDP ratio shrinking slightly to 67%. The latest projections by Congress show that deficits will be under $5 billion each year from 1998 to 2000, and that a surplus will occur in 2001. The president is more optimistic, projecting a budget surplus in 1999. If these forecasts are accurate and the economy continues to expand, the debt-to-GDP ratio will continue to shrink.

One word of caution should accompany the above figures that show a rapidly declining budget deficit. The reported figures include the positive surpluses that are piling up in the Social Security and other trust funds. These are referred to as "off-budget" items. If these are excluded, the 1997 deficit jumps from $22 billion to $103 billion, and budget surpluses are nowhere in sight (Figure 1). The real deficit of $103 billion is being made to look smaller through "loans" from the trust funds. At one time, the trust fund balances were not included when the size of the deficit was reported. But when the general revenue deficit—"on-budget" items—was increasing in the 1980s and the trust funds were showing increasing positive balances, it was politically appealing to combine the two into what has been termed the "unified budget." This will continue to make the deficit picture look rosy until the baby boom generation starts depleting all those Social Security "surpluses," when they begin to retire en masse, and the loans from trust funds need to be paid back.

Those are frightening numbers, all right. But before panic sets in, we might get a perspective by looking at earlier debt-to-GDP ratios (see Figure 2). In 1946, at the end of World War II, the debt was 127% of GDP. Ten years later it was still high at 71%, just a bit bigger than it was in 1997. In these postwar years the economy did not collapse as a result of the high debt. This was, in fact, a period of rising prosperity. Excluding 1946–1947, when the economy was converting from wartime to peacetime production and growth was negative,

Figure 1

The Federal Budget Deficit, 1970–1997

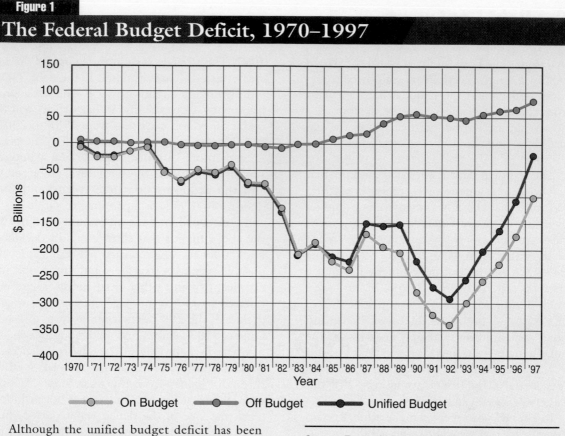

On Budget — Off Budget — Unified Budget

Although the unified budget deficit has been shrinking since 1992, a great deal of this deficit reduction has been due to the "surpluses" that have been accumulating in the Social Security and other "off-budget" trust funds.

Source: *Economic Report of the President.*

the average real growth rate in total output for 1948–1955 was 4.3%. The only comparable period of sustained growth that high for that length of time since then was 1962–1970, when real growth averaged 4.7%.

Judging by the historical data, the absolute size of the debt-to-GDP ratio does not seem to be a problem. Nor does it seem to matter whether the ratio is rising or falling. The expansions of 1948–1955 and 1962–1970 both occurred during periods when the ratio was falling, but periods of slow growth also occurred when the ratio was falling. The expansion from 1983 to 1989 occurred while the ratio was actually climbing steeply, and the debt-to-GDP ratio grew a little during the economic expansion from 1992–1997.

As we saw earlier, the federal government borrows by selling bonds—fancy IOUs. This means that at the end of 1997, there were $5.4 trillion worth of government bonds being held by the Fed (far and away the biggest bondholder), individuals, mutual funds, money market funds, insurance companies, banks, and people in other countries. The federal treasury is constantly selling new bonds and using the proceeds to fund deficits and pay the principal and interest due on existing bonds. As we saw in the last chapter, interest on the national debt was the third-largest expenditure item in the 1997 federal budget. Not surprising when it has to pay interest on $5.4 trillion in outstanding loans!

There are many factors affecting the economy besides the national debt, and high or low

Figure 2

National Debt and Debt as a Percentage of Gross Domestic Product, 1945–1998

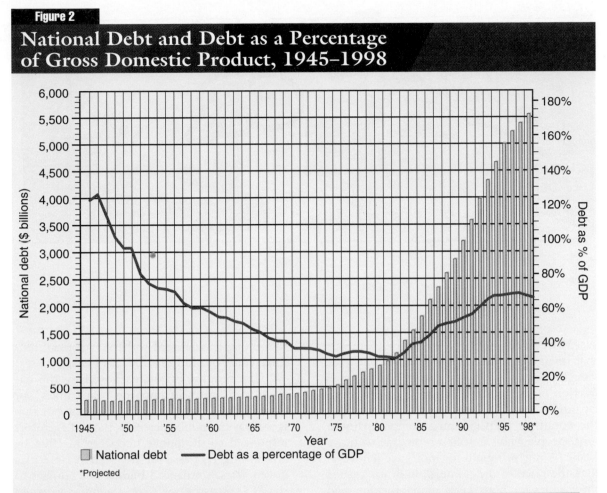

National debt ($ billions) — left axis
Debt as % of GDP — right axis

Year

☐ National debt　　━━━ Debt as a percentage of GDP

*Projected

The national debt rose gradually from the end of World War II until the 1970s, and then it began to rise rapidly. As a percentage of GDP, it fell to a low in 1981, accelerated through the mid-1990s, but decreased in 1997 for the first time since 1981.

Source: *Economic Report of the President.*

growth rates of GDP are not necessarily dependent on the size of the debt or whether it is increasing or decreasing. But a majority of the American public, many politicians, and some economists think it is critically important. Egged on by H. Ross Perot, who compared the federal deficits to a "crazy aunt" we keep locked in the basement, opinion polls in the early 1990s put the deficit and the size of the debt among the public's greatest worries, along with jobs and crime.

One unwarranted fear about the national debt is that it will bankrupt the country. For one thing, the federal debt cannot bankrupt the country in any literal sense. As we saw in chapter 10, the Fed can create as much money as the government needs. For another, we owe 78% of the federal debt to ourselves— 78% of the taxes collected to pay the debt are transferred to American bondholders. The remaining 22% of the debt is held by foreign individuals, banks, governments, and other foreign institutions. The amount of debt held by foreigners has increased rapidly in recent years, tripling between 1989 and 1997. As will be explained in later chapters, some of this is due to our foreign trade deficit, and some is due to the investors in the newly emerging democracies looking for a safe place to put their savings.

More fundamentally, bankruptcy means that one's debts exceed the value of one's assets. Large as the national debt is, it is a small fraction of the value of the assets of the country, and it is significantly less than one year of the country's total income. Compare this to most people who take out a mortgage to buy a home. A rule of thumb for mortgage lenders is that the price of the home should not exceed three times the borrower's annual income, and the vast majority of American homeowners have mortgages far in excess of their annual incomes. In comparison, the U.S. government looks positively prudent! National bankruptcy simply is one phrase used too loosely in discussions of the debt.

The allegation that a large national debt is a burden shifted onto the shoulders of future generations is also not true. Interest on the debt and repayments of the principal paid *by* future generations are paid *to* future generations. As noted in the discussion of Social Security in chapter 9 (p. 241), each generation consumes what it produces, except for net foreign trade. With that exception, each generation's consumption levels and living standards are determined by its own output, not by the deficits of earlier generations. Of course, a legitimate fear is that the growing share of our debt being held by foreigners means that a growing share of that future output will need to be sent abroad, thus threatening our future standard of living.

The biggest problems posed by the national debt are not simplistic "bankruptcy" or "shifting the debt burden" problems, but that is the way the public perceives them. Legislators responded to the public's concern in 1994 by attempting to pass, for the fourth time in a dozen years, a balanced budget amendment to the U.S. Constitution. The amendment would require that the federal budget be balanced every year. A 1994 CNN–USA Today poll showed that 66% of Americans support such a measure. Nonetheless, the amendment was narrowly defeated.

There was certainly good reason to be concerned about the escalation of the debt that occurred from 1981–1995. If the debt/GDP ratio continued to climb at that rate, it would have had a number of unfortunate consequences. For one, it would increase the share of the federal budget going to pay interest on debt. Second, the increased government demand to borrow money would push up interest rates, discouraging investment and growth. One of the reasons cited for the lower GDP growth rates during the current expansion compared to earlier ones is the crowding-out effect of government borrowing to cover its swollen debt (see chapter 12, p. 342).

Chapter Preview

According to the Employment Act of 1946 and the Full Employment and Balanced Growth Act of 1978, the federal government has a responsibility to maintain full employment, reasonably stable prices, and economic growth. This chapter examines the tools that the federal government has at its disposal for influencing economic activity by asking the following questions: What can the government do about unemployment and inflation? How can fiscal policy help stabilize the economy? How can monetary policy help stabilize the economy? How can economic growth be increased?

Learning Objectives

After completing this chapter, you should be able to:

1. Discuss the issues surrounding the budget deficit and the national debt.
2. Understand and explain how fiscal policy works.
3. Understand and explain how monetary policy works.
4. Differentiate among annually balanced budgets, cyclically balanced budgets, and functional finance.
5. Explain how discretionary fiscal policy works from the Keynesian and supply-side viewpoints.
6. Describe the multiplier and the multiplier effect.
7. Define and give examples of automatic stabilizers.
8. Explain how the Fed implements monetary policy.
9. Explain why recognition, decision, and impact lags make it difficult to properly time discretionary fiscal and monetary policies.
10. Explain the investment/GDP ratio and the capital/output ratio and explain why they are important.
11. Describe the effects on economic growth of the labor force participation rate and investment in human capital.

What Can the Government Do about Unemployment and Inflation?

The government's two principal instruments for **stabilizing** the economy are fiscal policy and monetary policy. Fiscal policy involves taxing and spending by the government, while monetary policy involves control of the money supply and interest rates by the Federal Reserve.

Fiscal Policy

In earlier periods, the national debt increased greatly during major wars and as a result of major depressions. The growth of the debt after 1981 was unprecedented, not only in size but because we neither fought a major war, excluding the cold war, nor were we following a Keynesian prescription to spend our way out of a major depression. We did, however, reduce taxes in 1981 to counter a recession.

The type of tax cut enacted in the 1981 tax bill represented a new direction in the government's **fiscal policy.** Previous major tax cuts to combat recession had been based on Keynesian

stabilization government policies designed to keep recessions from getting too deep and expansions from growing too fast. Stabilization policies are the government's tools for fighting unemployment and inflation.

fiscal policy the use of federal government spending, taxing, and debt management to influence general economic activity.

economic theory—they were aimed at stimulating demand by increasing disposable income. A tax reduction leaves people with more purchasing power and thus increases aggregate demand. This is especially true if the tax cut is directed toward households that will spend all or most of the extra after-tax income that they receive—those with a high propensity to consume. The 1981 tax bill, on the other hand, was intended to increase output by making production and investment more profitable, and by stimulating savings to finance that investment. It was a supply-side tax bill, designed to leave more money in the hands of those with a higher propensity to save (higher incomes) rather than those with a higher propensity to consume (lower incomes).

The difference between Keynesian and supply-side fiscal policy also shows up in the treatment of government expenditures. Supply-side economics calls for a reduction in government spending in order to reduce the government's competition with the private sector of the economy for labor, capital, and other resources. Reducing the growth of government spending during a time of high unemployment is the exact opposite of the Keynesian policies that the United States had pursued since World War II. According to demand-side economics, increased government spending should be used to offset a recession. Actually, despite the supply-side rhetoric of the 1980s, the huge military build-up during that period resulted in little, if any, reduction in government spending.

The policy of combining increased spending with reduced taxes to combat a recession results in government budget deficits. Before the experiences of the 1930s and before the writings of Keynes, it was traditionally held that the government should have an **annually balanced budget.** If the federal government took $25 million out of the spending stream in taxes in a given fiscal year, it should put $25 million into the spending stream through its purchases of goods and services. Such a budgetary policy, however, can be destabilizing. When an economy moves into a recession, tax receipts fall as production, employment, and income decline. If an annually balanced budget policy is followed, the government must then cut spending, or raise taxes, or do both. Such policies would make a recession worse by reducing aggregate demand.

On the other side of the business cycle, during a period of economic expansion, tax receipts automatically rise as increases in income generate more taxes. To balance the budget a tax cut or a spending increase would be necessary. Either action would tend to be inflationary by increasing aggregate demand.

Instead of an annually balanced budget, a **cyclically balanced budget** would allow active fiscal policy to stabilize the economy. Short-run budget deficits would be used to increase aggregate demand and offset recessions, and budget surpluses would be used to reduce demand and offset booms, but the deficits would offset the surpluses and the budget would balance over the course of the business cycle. There are problems, however, with this approach. Financially, recessions and booms may not cancel each other out, and the budget may not balance over the long run. Also, it is politically far more popular to reduce taxes and increase spending than to increase taxes or cut spending. Fiscal policy under these conditions thus might result in ongoing budget deficits.

A third budget philosophy, **functional finance,** sees noninflationary full employment as the most important economic goal; balancing the budget becomes a secondary objective. Under this philosophy, taxes and spending

annually balanced budget a budgetary principle calling for the revenue and expenditures of a government to be equal during the course of a year.

cyclically balanced budget a budgetary principle calling for the balancing of the budget over the course of a complete business cycle rather than in a particular fiscal or calendar year; over the course of the cycle, tax receipts and expenditures would balance.

functional finance the use of fiscal policy to stabilize the economy without regard to the policy's effect on a balanced government budget.

Figure 3

Economic Instability, 1970–1997

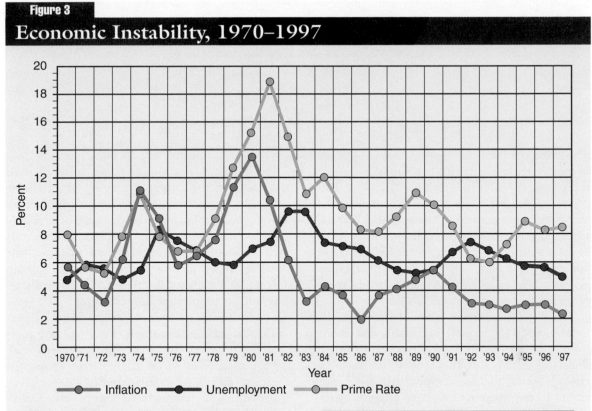

The magnitude of economic fluctuations in the 1980s, as measured by the swings in unemployment, inflation, and interest rates, was greater than any time during the last 40 years. In contrast, the 1990s have proved to be a period of relative economic stability.

Sources: Inflation and unemployment rates: U.S. Department of Labor, Bureau of Labor Statistics.
Prime interest rates: Federal Reserve System.

should be administered at whatever level is necessary to promote full employment without increasing prices. This policy might leave the budget permanently out of balance.

A fourth alternative has been proposed recently as a guide to budget management. It recognizes that there are two basic types of government spending—spending on current services and spending for capital investment. The rationale for the proposal is that revenues should cover spending for current consumption, but that capital spending on infrastructure can be financed by deficit spending since it increases future production (see the discussion of infrastructure investment later in this chapter, p. 399). This approach mirrors the business practice of borrowing to finance new private investment. Increased future GDP will generate tax revenues to pay the interest and principal costs on the resulting debt, just as increased future business profits can be used to pay off the debt-financed investment. This budget approach has been called the **golden rule** (Figure 3).

golden rule a budget approach that calls for current services to be covered by revenues while paying for capital expenditures with deficit financing.

Case Application

Who's at the Wheel?

The economy has been on a wild ride in the last 2 decades. It has had three recessions, including the worst recession (1982) since the Great Depression of the 1930s. It has experienced the second longest expansion since World War II. It has had record-breaking inflation, record-breaking interest rates, and record-breaking government deficits and national debt. Despite our efforts at predicting economic trends, most of these developments came as a surprise.

As the introductory article for chapter 12 showed (p. 319), predicting where the economy is going has always been more or less a guessing game. But these days, the pace of change seems to have speeded up, while our ability to anticipate and react to changes in direction has diminished. It is as if we are at the wheel of a runaway bus with the gas pedal pressed to the floor and the windshield painted black.

Just who *is* at the wheel in control of the economy? The Full Employment Act, passed in 1946 and amended in 1978 as the Humphrey-Hawkins Act, assigns to the federal government the legal responsibility to ensure maximum employment, output, and purchasing power. The agency charged with this task, the Council of Economic Advisers, advises the president on economic issues and submits an annual report to Congress on the state of the economy—The Economic Report of the President. In addition to the Council, the Federal Reserve Board has the responsibility for conducting monetary policy in a manner that avoids both recession and inflation. But the best-laid plans of the Council and the Fed are subject to two types of forces that may upset them: unforeseen, uncontrollable events and the behavior of you, me, and the rest of the country.

While external events—wars, fluctuating energy prices, economic crashes in other parts of the world—complicate the job of stabilizing the U.S. economy, an even bigger problem for policymakers is the unpredictable behavior of the public. If we decide to spend less, we may cause a recession or make an existing one worse. If we change the way we pay for our purchases, we may interfere with the Fed's attempts to control the money supply.

Although people often respond in predictable ways to economic incentives, attempts to make us behave in certain ways are not always successful. In an attempt to increase the saving rates of American families, tax-sheltered Individual Retirement Accounts were established in the 1980s. Instead of increasing the amount of savings, savings actually decreased to their lowest level in years. The tax cuts of 1981 that were supposed to encourage an increase in savings by the wealthiest segments of the economy instead led to increased purchases of major luxury goods like mink coats and yachts.

Individuals watch government policy for clues as to what actions they should take to protect or promote their personal well-being. For example, if the Fed increases the money supply to encourage more production and investment, people take this as an indicator that inflation is coming. The result of these "rational expectations" is a rise in long-term interest rates to compensate for the anticipated inflation, thereby discouraging new investment and frustrating the Fed's attempt. Because the actions of people reacting to policy initiatives can negate their effectiveness, some economists argue that stabilization policy is ineffective and should be ignored.

1. When income tax rates were cut in the 1980s in the hopes that people would increase their savings, was this an example of fiscal policy or monetary policy?
2. Why do people believe that an increase in the money supply will lead to inflation?
3. Should the government get around the problem of public behavior that negates stabilization policies by forcing people to act in certain ways, instead of providing incentives for them to do so? For example, forcing them to save more rather than reducing their taxes if they do?

Monetary Policy

Neither the president nor Congress has control over **monetary policy;** it is under the control of the Federal Reserve Board. The money supply is managed indirectly by the Fed, through its influence on financial institutions' required and excess reserves. By employing the control techniques described in chapter 10, the Fed can vary the volume of excess reserves. This action affects the ability of lending institutions to grant loans and thereby their ability to increase the money supply.

In a recession, the level of aggregate demand is below that necessary for full employment. In that situation, the Fed, through its monetary policy actions, brings about an increase in the volume of bank reserves. Bankers are then able to grant more loans. The loans stimulate higher total spending in the economy, and income and employment rise, along with the money supply. Conversely, to combat inflation, the Fed uses its controls to decrease the volume of bank reserves. Bankers grant fewer loans, the money supply falls, and there is less total spending in the economy.

How Can Fiscal Policy Help Stabilize the Economy?

The principal reason for government taxing and spending is not to stabilize the economy, but rather to provide the services that citizens require from the government. The fiscal activities of government can be managed, however, to counteract cyclical fluctuations.

Discretionary Fiscal Policy

Decisions about increasing or decreasing taxes and decreasing or increasing government spending with the deliberate intention of intervening in the economy and influencing economic activity are referred to as **discretionary fiscal policy.** It is sometimes referred to as activist or interventionist policy. Keynesian and supply-side economists differ on how discretionary fiscal policy should be implemented.

monetary policy actions of the Federal Reserve Board to produce changes in the money supply, the availability of loanable funds, or the level of interest rates in an attempt to influence general economic activity.

discretionary fiscal policy the use of fiscal policy with the deliberate intention of trying to slow economic growth during a boom (to fight inflation) or increase growth during an economic slowdown.

Figure 4

Keynesian Unemployment Policy

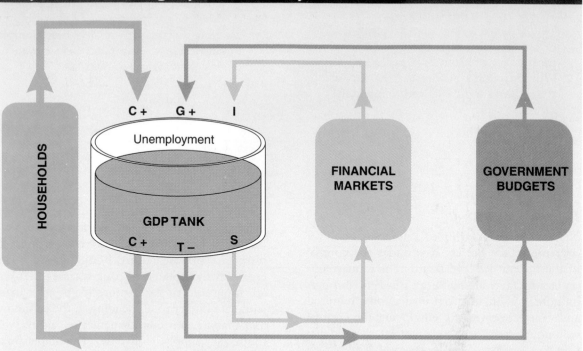

Keynesian fiscal policy to increase GDP and reduce unemployment is to lower taxes (T–) and increase spending (G+) in the government sector (pink). This results in an increase in purchasing power and demand (C+) in the consumption sector (blue). The increased demand raises the GDP level (purple) and reduces unemployment.

Keynesians focus on the use of fiscal policy to compensate for inadequate or excessive demand in the private sector. It is presumed that supply will increase or decrease to accommodate the changes in aggregate demand. How Keynesian fiscal policy is used to combat unemployment can be traced in the GDP tank diagram in Figure 4.

If the amount of purchasing power flowing into the economy from consumption (C), government (G), and investment (I) demand is not sufficient to provide full employment, as indicated by the level in the tank, the government can increase demand by larger expenditures, causing more purchasing power to flow from government (G+), and/or by reducing taxes (T–), taking less from the income stream. If the tax cuts are directed primarily at the lower-income groups, which have the

highest propensity to consume, nearly all of the tax savings will be allocated to increased consumption (C+), which stimulates production and employment.

Supply-side fiscal policy also calls for a reduction in taxes when aggregate demand is too low. But government spending is reduced rather than increased in order to reduce government competition with the private sector for productive resources and financial capital. The purpose of reducing the leakage into taxes (T–) in the supply-side approach is not to increase consumption (C), but rather to increase savings (S+) and investment (I+), as shown in Figure 5. Therefore, the tax cuts are directed toward businesses and toward individuals in high tax brackets, who save more, rather than toward consumers. Supply-side policy is consistent with Say's Law. It presumes that increases in productive

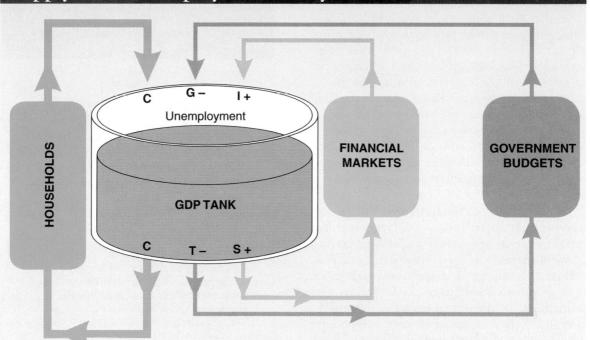

Figure 5

Supply-Side Unemployment Policy

Supply-side fiscal policy to reduce unemployment is to lower taxes (T–) and spending (G–) in the government sector (pink) in order to increase savings (S+) and investment (I+) in the investment sector (green). The reduction in taxes provides incentives and financial capital for increased investment. The added investment increases the level of GDP and reduces unemployment. At the same time, lower government spending reduces competition in the factor markets for real and financial resources, helping to hold down prices and interest rates.

capacity and output will not result in a surplus of unwanted goods and services.

The use of discretionary fiscal policy to combat recession at a time when the government is already running large deficits is difficult. When deficits are already large, as they were in the 1980s, increasing the deficit and debt further to combat a recession is not an attractive policy option. Interest rates would have to be raised to sell the government securities necessary to finance the deficit. Higher interest rates are the opposite of the monetary policy needed to overcome recession. This problem is one of the most troublesome aspects of the expanded debt. Among the advantages of a small deficit, or even a surplus, is that it gives the government the option of using discretionary fiscal policy to stimulate the economy if it chooses to do so.

◼ The Multiplier Effect

Fiscal policy can be used not only to combat unemployment caused by insufficient aggregate demand, but also to combat inflation caused by too much demand. In either case, fiscal policy is more effective as a result of the **multiplier effect.** The multiplier effect refers to the magnified impact on national income of an initial increase or decrease in spending. It is similar in principle to the money multiplier in chapter 10 (p. 276).

multiplier effect the process by which an initial increase in income results in a total income increase that is a multiple of the initial increase.

Suppose, for example, an outsider comes into your community and spends $100 on a single purchase. Someone's income would increase by $100 with that expenditure. The income receiver would probably not hold onto the $100 very long but would spend most of it, say four-fifths ($80), on increased consumption of goods and services. The rest would go to taxes and into savings. Those who receive the $80 that was spent would now spend four-fifths of that amount, or $64. The process, as shown in Table 1, would continue until the original injection of $100 had generated additional income to the community of another $400, for a total of $500.

The multiplier effect is based on the assumption that people, on the average, spend a certain fraction of any increase in after-tax income and put the rest into savings. The smaller the amount that leaks into savings in each round of spending, the larger will be the **multiplier.** In the above example, the multiplier was 5 since an initial increase in spending of $100 ultimately resulted in a total increase in spending of $500. The size of the multiplier is easy to calculate if you know the percentage of new income that goes into taxes and savings. The multiplier is found by dividing the savings rate plus the tax rate, expressed in decimal form, into 1. If savings plus taxes are 20% of new income, you divide 1 by .20, which gives a multiplier of 5.

$$\textbf{Multiplier} = \frac{1}{(\text{Savings rate} + \text{tax rate})} = \frac{1}{.20} = 5$$

If instead, the leakages to saving and taxes were 50%, the multiplier would only be equal

Table 1	The Multiplier Effect Initial Spending Increase $100	
Person 1	C $ 80.00	S + T $ 20.00
Person 2	C $ 64.00	S + T $ 16.00
Person 3	C $ 51.20	S + T $ 12.80
All others	C $204.80	S + T $ 51.20
Total (Including initial $100)	C $500.00	S + T $100.00

An initial increase in spending of $100 (when leakage to savings and taxes is 20%) will multiply through the community until it has generated an additional $400 in consumption spending (C) for a total of $500. Total leakages to savings and taxes (S + T) will be $100.

to 2; if leakages were 5%, the multiplier would be 20. The multiplier process takes time to work. It is usually a matter of a few months before the major part of the effect is completed.

How Can Fiscal Policy Help Stabilize the Economy?

EconExplorer

Automatic Stabilizers
In order to put discretionary fiscal policy to work, the government must do something—must take some action. But there is another type of stabilization that takes effect as a result of automatic changes in government spending and revenue collections. These **automatic stabilizers** help increase incomes in

(Continued on page 391)

multiplier the ratio of the ultimate increase in income, caused by an initial increase in spending, to that initial increase.
automatic stabilizers changes in government payments and tax receipts that automatically result from fluctuations in national income and act to aid in offsetting those fluctuations.

Comparative Case Application

The Sun Also Sets

The Japanese miracle looks to be over, at least for now. After recording years of economic growth rates that the rest of the world could only marvel at, since 1991 the economy of the Land of the Rising Sun has been limping along like an out-of-orbit asteroid. Now, for the first time since the oil crisis of 1974, the second biggest economy in the world has slid into an actual recession. The Japanese economy declined at an annual rate of 5.3% in the first quarter of 1998, the second consecutive quarter of negative growth in a row—the usual economic definition of a recession.

Aggregate demand in Japan had been slumping for years. A series of bad loans ($600 billion worth of debt that probably will not be repaid) weakened the Japanese banking system in the early 1990s and reduced the availability of credit. Consequently, capital investment has been low, and is expected to continue its decline. The number of business bankruptcies in May 1998 rose 37.5% over May of the previous year. Consumer spending, always relatively low in Japan because of government policies and a cultural ethic that favor saving over spending, has become even smaller. And exports, an important part of Japanese aggregate demand, have slumped because of the plummeting economies of Southeast Asia, long a region that has purchased a large share of Japan's output of goods and services.

After years of slow growth, the recession was triggered by a 1997 tax increase that was designed to reduce Japan's budget deficit. With aggregate demand already slumping, the tax increase—needed to prepare for the increasing number of Japanese who will be retiring in the next few years—was the straw that broke the camel's back. Now, the Japanese government is looking to reverse its course. It just undertook a $128 billion combination of Keynesian-style tax cuts and government spending designed to stimulate economic growth.

The government spending worth $92 billion—an amount equal to the entire GDP of Poland—will include projects for the environment, energy generation, research and development, social welfare and education. It is estimated that most of this spending will be felt by the economy in about one year. Such investment should not only provide an immediate stimulus to the economy, but should pay off in long-run productivity gains. There has been some controversy about the $36 billion tax cuts: should they be permanent or just a one-time "bonus" for the Japanese people? Most economists favor the former policy because households tend to save most of a one-time windfall, or use it to pay off old debts. Only if they are convinced that their disposable income will continue to be higher will they increase their spending and give the economy its much-needed boost.

The rest of the world is very interested in the outcome of Japan's fiscal policy efforts. Japan is the largest importer of products made in the collapsing economics of Thailand, Indonesia, and South Korea. These countries depend on exports to keep their aggregate demand strong, and like any country, Japan's imports decrease when its economy falters.

Consumer spending in Japan has traditionally been low. In order to stimulate the failing economy, the government is introducing government spending programs and cutting taxes to encourage consumer spending.

Many observers believe that a strong, importing Japan is necessary for the recovery of these developing countries. If the Japanese do not increase their imports, the only remaining possible markets are the United States and Western Europe. Since neither the United States nor the European Union wants to be flooded with South Asian imports, both have been very vocal in encouraging the Japanese to undertake their planned fiscal policy program.

Economic Reasoning

1. How will the Japanese program of tax cuts and government help stabilize their economy?

2. Why is a strong Japanese economy important for the economies of Thailand, Indonesia and South Korea?

3. Do you think that the United States and other countries should be making suggestions to Japan (or any other country) about how to manage their economy?

The Sun Also Sets

Use the Internet or any other source to track the most recent performance of the Japanese economy. Do you think their fiscal policy program will work?

Food stamps and other welfare programs are designed to redistribute income. They are based on income levels, so that they automatically kick in when incomes fall, providing additional spending to boost the economy when it is slow.

a depressed economy and decrease incomes in an inflationary economy.

Automatic stabilizers consist of taxes, which automatically rise and fall with changes in income, and some form of payments that are designed to redistribute income. Most types of welfare and other government transfer payments, such as Temporary Assistance to Needy Families, are based on the income of the recipient. When a person's income falls, as it does during a recession, government expenditures provide income supplements. These supplements add to the spending stream, keeping demand from falling too much. Unemployment compensation paid to workers who lose their jobs does the same thing. When GDP is increasing during periods of economic growth, income taxes increase and more money is put into the Unemployment Compensation Trust Fund. These leakages slow the rise in aggregate demand. By themselves, automatic stabilizers are not strong enough to reverse a trend, but they do cushion the economic shock until discretionary fiscal policy can be implemented or the economy rights itself on its own.

How Can Monetary Policy Help Stabilize the Economy?

The three measures available to the Federal Reserve for affecting bank reserves—changing legal reserve requirements, discounting, and open market operations—were discussed in chapter 10 on pages 000–000. Now we will look at the way these monetary controls are used in stabilization policy and examine what the targets of monetary policy are.

Monetary Policy Tools

Open market operations is the Fed's most flexible tool of monetary control and the tool most often utilized. If the Fed attempts to curb inflation, it offers U.S. government securities, which

How Can Monetary Policy Help Stabilize the Economy?

EconExplorer

it has in its possession as a result of earlier purchases, for sale at an attractive price. Financial institutions, other businesses, or individuals buy these securities. Regardless of who purchases them, reserves are transferred from commercial banks' reserve accounts to the Fed to pay for the securities. This reduces the ability of the banks to expand their lending activity and may even force them to contract credit. The resulting limitation on the money supply raises interest rates, thus reducing aggregate demand, especially for capital goods, new housing, and consumer credit purchases of durable goods such as new cars.

If the problem is too little aggregate demand rather than too much, the Fed purchases government securities from banks, other businesses, or individuals. This action by the Fed pumps more reserves into the banking system and has an expansionary effect on the economy.

As an alternative to or in addition to selling securities to combat inflation, the Fed can also raise the discount rate it charges on loans to financial institutions. A rise in the discount rate is contractionary because it limits the money supply and raises other interest rates, while a reduction in the discount rate is expansionary.

How Can Monetary Policy Help Stabilize the Economy?

EconExplorer

The most forceful monetary tool the Fed has is its power to change the required reserve ratio. Because this is also the least flexible tool, it is infrequently used. The changes in the money supply that would result from changing the ratio are too drastic for most Fed objectives. Raising the reserve ratio from, say, 10% to 12% of banks' deposit liabilities would wipe out a large portion of their excess reserves and force them to contract credit. That would have a deflationary effect on economic activity. Lowering the legal reserve requirement, on the other hand, would make it possible for banks to extend more credit on easier terms, thus increasing the money supply. This increase might or might not have an expansionary effect on economic activity, depending on economic conditions. If the economic outlook is very poor, businesses still might not borrow and invest—even at low interest rates. Consequently, although monetary policy is very effective when used to contract excessive aggregate demand in a

boom period, it may be powerless to stimulate demand to bring about a recovery at the bottom of the cycle. The effectiveness of monetary policy, therefore, is asymmetrical. Some economists refer to using monetary policy to increase aggregate demand during periods of negative expectations as trying to "push on a string."

Controlling Interest Rates

The traditional target of Federal Reserve monetary policy has been the control of interest rates. Specifically, the Fed attempts to control the Federal Funds rate, the interest rate banks charge each other on short-term lending of excess reserves. By controlling the Federal Funds rate, the Fed can influence the various other interest rates that are charged on loans. By causing interest rates to rise, the Fed would have a deflationary effect on economic activity and prices, and by causing interest rates to fall, it would have an expansionary effect.

A problem inherent in trying to target a specific interest rate is that it can lead to unwanted fluctuations in the money supply. In the late 1970s and early 1980s, interest rates were rising steeply, in part due to government borrowing to finance its growing debt. To keep interest rates stable, the Fed increased the supply of money. The result contributed to increases in inflation.

Control of the Money Supply

Rather than controlling interest rates directly, the Fed may aim at keeping the money supply growth at a predetermined level as it began to do in the early 1980s. According to the quantity theory of money, $M \times V = T \times P$, if the money supply (M) goes up at the same rate as the increase in transactions (T), the price level (P) will remain constant and we will not have inflation—that is, if the velocity of money (V) does not change (see chapter 11, p. 300).

Actually, the velocity has been on a long-term rising trend since the Great Depression. This in itself would not be a problem if the increase were predictable, since it could be taken into account in setting the growth rate of M. But problems arise when V jumps around unpredictably and when it moves in a destabilizing direction. Studies indicate that when we have inflation and high interest rates, V accelerates. This offsets the stabilizing effects of limiting M and thus makes it difficult for a monetarist approach to stability to achieve satisfactory results.

A strict monetarist approach, as advocated by its foremost proponent, Milton Friedman (see Perspective, p. 407), would have a "monetary rule" setting annual increases in the money supply equal to the average long-run increase in real GDP. If this could be accomplished, the price level would remain constant. Although this makes sense on paper, it is becoming increasingly difficult to accurately control the money supply, especially M1 (see chapter 10, page 263). Because of the deregulation of the banking industry in the 1980s and the increasing number of "near monies" that have been created, the line between M1 and M2 is becoming blurred, and the actual numerical link between $M \times V$ and $T \times P$ is more difficult to predict.

◆ The Timing of Discretionary Policy

A weakness of both discretionary fiscal and monetary policy is that it is often difficult to properly time such policies. To be effective, expansionary policies should impact the economy as it is entering a recession, and contractionary policies when inflation is about to set in. It takes several months, however, for the data that describe economic performance to be gathered and reported. A recession may have started months before policymakers are aware of it. Because of the **recognition lag,** the government and/or the Fed will be getting a late start in implementing policies to deal with the problem. Furthermore, one can't be sure that the problem is a permanent up- or downturn in the economy, and not just a temporary "glitch."

Even after it is acknowledged that a serious problem exists, there is a **decision lag** in the time it takes to formulate a policy. Congress and the president must agree on whether the appropriate antirecession fiscal policy is to cut taxes or increase spending, and then they must agree on how large and what kinds of spending or taxes should be used. The Open Market Committee of the Fed meets very regularly and, because of its small size, takes much less time to reach a decision about implementing monetary policy.

Finally, there is an **impact lag** in the time that it takes the policy to actually affect the economy. Once decided upon, the impact lag for fiscal policy is much shorter than the impact lag for monetary policy. These lags make it difficult to properly time any discretionary policies. Because of this, critics argue that the government and the Fed should not follow activist policies and that they should not intervene in the workings of the economy.

For example, a great deal of criticism has been directed at the Fed for mistakes in the timing of its actions. In the past, it often seemed to wait too long before putting on the brakes in a boom period, allowing the inflation rate to become exceedingly high before raising interest rates sufficiently to cool the economy. When it finally did act, the results of this action too often appeared after the turning point in the economy and resulted in emphasizing the severity of the downturn. Similarly, in upswings the Fed delayed too long raising interest rates, resulting in inflation.

As the economy recovered from the 1991 recession, the Fed appeared determined not to repeat previous mistakes of delay in implementing monetary stabilization measures. It initiated interest rate increases prior to any evidence of inflating prices. In doing so it was criticized in some quarters for raising rates prematurely and thereby weakening the recovery. The Fed aimed at a slow, steady expansion that would, it hoped, continue over a long period of time. As the history of the 1990s has shown, this policy has proved to be very effective. Although the growth rate of GDP is less than in other economic expansions, it has continued since 1992 with very little threat of inflation.

recognition lag the time that it takes policymakers to recognize that the economy is entering a recession or that inflation is increasing.

decision lag the time that it takes the government or the Fed to determine a course of discretionary action.

impact lag the time that it takes for monetary or fiscal policy to have an impact on the country's economic activity.

Comparative Case Application

Coming Together

The European Union, comprised of the 15 countries listed in Table 2, made history on January 1, 1999. On that date, the signers to the 1991 Maastricht Treaty began the process of discarding their 15 different currencies and replacing them by July 2002 with a common currency, the euro. While the different currencies will remain in use for most purposes until then, beginning in 1999, stocks and government debt will be denominated in euros. Such a conversion is tricky, as people will need to get used to their new currency.

But what can be even trickier is implementing common fiscal and monetary policies. In the past, Greece could expand its money supply to stimulate its economy while at the same time

Denmark could shrink its money supply in order to fight inflation. Now, all the countries will be moving in monetary unison. With only one currency, there can be only one central bank that controls the Union's money supply and interest rates. Instead of each country conducting its own monetary policies, beginning in 1999, the newly created European Central Bank (ECB) will be in charge of implementing monetary policy for all the participating countries. To do so, however, the countries that are involved must be starting from similar fiscal and monetary positions.

Suppose that at the formation of a monetary union, France has a much higher deficit- or debt-to-GDP ratio than Germany. The price and interest paid on existing and new French bonds

Table 2	Meeting the Maastricht Treaty Convergence Criteria			
	Deficit/Surplus as a Percentage of GDP	Debt as a Percentage of GDP	Relative Inflation Rate**	Long-Term Goverment Interest Rates
Target	3.0%	60%	2.7%	8.0%
Austria	2.5	66.1	1.2	5.7
Belgium	2.1	122.2	1.5	5.7
Denmark*	(0.7)	64.1	2.0	6.2
Finland	0.9	55.8	1.2	5.9
France	3.0	58.0	1.3	5.6
Germany	2.7	61.3	1.5	5.6
Greece*	4.0	108.7	5.5	9.7
Ireland	(0.9)	67.0	1.2	6.3
Italy	2.7	121.6	1.9	6.6
Luxembourg	(1.7)	6.7	1.4	5.6
Netherlands	2.0	76.8	2.0	5.6
Portugal	2.5	62.0	1.9	6.2
Spain	2.6	68.3	1.9	6.2
Sweden*	1.0	77.6	1.9	6.6
United Kingdom*	1.9	53.4	1.9	6.9

* Will not participate in the first round of monetary union.

** A special inflation index constructed for this purpose. It is not the actual inflation rate.

Source: Organization for Economic Cooperation and Development.

will be converted from francs to euros. Because the French government needs to borrow more of the limited supply of euros, it will create a shortage in other countries and a surplus in France. That would make it difficult to keep interest rates and inflation equal throughout Europe—one of the goals of monetary union.

Interest rates and inflation rates in the different countries are also a concern. Eventually, a common currency will lead to similar interest rates and inflation rates in the different countries. It will be difficult, however, for the ECB to conduct a monetary policy with interest rates targeted at 7%, if one country enters the union with 2% interest rates and another with rates around 17%. The impact of an overnight shift to 7% will upset financial markets in both countries. The same kind of shock will occur if inflation rates are far apart in the member countries.

To avoid severe economic shocks, the countries agreed that to qualify to become part of the monetary union, they would need to meet targets designed to "harmonize" their budgets and monetary situations. It was agreed that each country could have a budget deficit no greater than 3% of GDP and a total debt no greater than 60% of GDP. The inflation rate could be no more than 1½ percentage points greater than the three countries with the lowest inflation rates, and the interest rate on long-term government bonds could be no more than 2 percentage points higher than the three countries with the lowest rates.

Meeting these criteria was difficult for European countries where unemployment rates were averaging nearly 10% in 1998. Getting budget deficits down, and keeping them down, meant lower government spending or increased taxes, hardly the prescription for reducing unemployment. The same is true for monetary policy. Keeping inflation in check required monetary austerity, a policy that is also inconsistent with stimulating economic growth.

The target date for meeting the criteria was May 1998, and Table 2 shows the target rates and the values that existed in each of the countries as of that date. As you can see, many countries did not meet the debt-to-GDP ratio criterion, but they decided to proceed anyway. Only Greece failed to meet the other criteria, and it was excluded from the first round of monetary union.

The euro became the official currency of 11 European countries on January 1, 1999. It is currently used only for financial and business transactions. In 2002 euro notes and coins will appear for the first time and replace all the existing currencies.

Denmark, Sweden, and the United Kingdom met the criteria, but chose not to participate.

Economic Reasoning

1. Why will large budget deficits in one European country lead to an increase in the amount of euros it needs?

2. How would the borrowing plans of businesses and governments in other countries be affected if, at the time of monetary union, France had an enormous budget deficit?

3. Do you think that a common monetary policy for all European countries is a good idea? Suppose you were a retired German citizen whose central bank had always kept inflation low. Now, decisions at the central bank will be made by people from many different countries, including those with a history of very easy money and inflation. Why might you be worried about the actions of the ECB?

Coming Together

Visit the Organization for Economic Cooperation and Development at www.oecd.org. Is the monetary union going as planned?

How Can Economic Growth Be Increased?

The danger posed by a large national debt is not that it will bankrupt the country or shift the real cost of interest payments and repayment of principal from the present generation to future generations. The actual danger is that it will hamper economic growth, leaving future generations poorer than they would be otherwise.

Importance of Economic Growth

Our standard of living is determined largely by the rate of economic growth. At the 3% real growth rate that characterized the U.S. economy in the last 2 decades, our output of goods and services doubles in 24 years. An increase to 4% would cut the time to 18 years, a decrease to 2% would increase it to 36 years. A higher growth rate makes it easier to solve many economic problems, from balancing the budget to stabilizing the economy to overcoming poverty.

Figure 6 shows the inflation-adjusted GDP growth rate in the United States for 1959 to 1997. As can be seen from the graph, the economy grew at a higher rate in the 1960s and 1970s than it has since then. Even though growth has been at a slower rate than in the past, it is still positive, and it has occurred with a minimum of inflation. Since 1980, growth has been negative in only three years: the recessions of 1980, 1982, and 1991.

| Figure 6 |

Percentage Change in Real Gross Domestic Product, 1959–1997

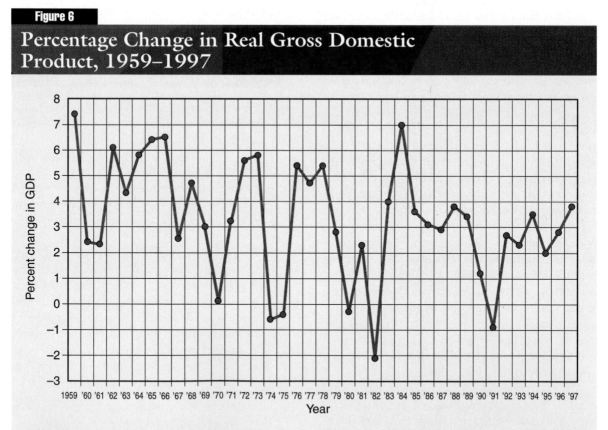

The growth of GDP is the main determinant of our material standard of living. In the decades of the 1960s and 1970s, when the national debt was relatively low and the debt/GDP ratio was falling, the U.S. economy grew at significantly higher rates than it has since.

Source: *Economic Report of the President.*

How Can Economic Growth Be Increased?

EconExplorer

Increasing Capital Investment

The proportion of a nation's output that goes into private capital formation in the form of fixed equipment and business structures is another important determinant of growth. The measure of that proportion is the **investment/GDP ratio,** the fraction of each year's GDP that is allocated to investment goods. As you will see, it is not just the total volume of productive capital that contributes to growth,

but also the quality of that capital. New capital embodies new technology. We talk a lot about how technology improves productivity, and that technology is usually introduced into the economy in the form of new capital.

Figure 7 shows the U.S. investment/GDP ratio for the years 1960–1997, expressed as a percentage. Prior to 1976, we were putting about 9–11% of our output into fixed, nonresidential investment (which excludes investment in inventories and housing). This was less than

investment/GDP ratio the proportion of GDP that is allocated to private investment.

Figure 7

Investment/GDP Ratio, 1960–1997*

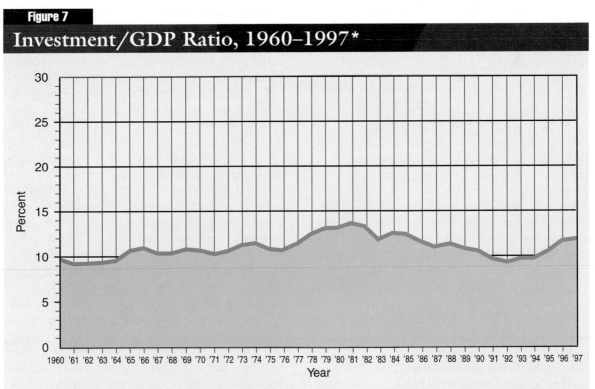

*Fixed nonresidential investment as a percentage of GDP

Investment in business equipment and structures as a percentage of GDP was high in the 1980s, and the economy experienced a prolonged economic expansion. It dipped during the recession of the early 1990s, but it has increased every year since 1992.

Source: Calculated from data from the *Economic Report of the President.*

the investment/GDP ratios in the countries of Western Europe, especially in what was West Germany, where it was almost 50% greater than here, and Japan, where it was twice as great. As a result those countries grew more rapidly than the United States.

In the United States, investment rates increased from 1976 to 1981, then trended downward until 1992. Since that time they have increased steadily to 11.77% in 1997. Much of this investment is in new information technology. Computer software is not considered an investment good when investment statistics are calculated. If it were, as many economists think it should be, then the ratio would be much, much higher.

How Can Economic Growth Be Increased?

EconExplorer

The growth rate of output, however, does not increase at the same time as the investment ratio. On the basis of historical experience, it is not surprising that we do not immediately see a productivity payoff from the new investment. There is a lag of some years between the introduction of new technology and the resulting growth that it generates. For example, productivity failed to grow much for 20 years after the introduction of the assembly line in 1901.

It takes companies time to assimilate the new technologies and make the best use of them. Some firms that have automated their operations have realized significant productivity gains, while others have not. For some reason, office automation has led to less of a reduction in white-collar staffing than factory automation has led to displacement of blue-collar labor. As a result, productivity gains (output per worker) have been much larger in manufacturing than in services. Because it is difficult to measure the output of service industries, however, our statistics may not reveal an accurate picture of the

actual productivity gains in this sector of the economy.

The effects of increasing the investment/GDP ratio are shown in Figures 8 and 9. In Figure 8 there is an initial reduction in consumption spending (C–) to finance the increased savings that are necessary for investment (S+ and I+). This results in increasing the production capacity of the economy, shown in Figure 9 by an expanded GDP tank. More production means more future consumption (C+) and higher levels of savings and tax receipts (S+ and T+), which make possible more investment and government services (I+ and G+).

The real cost (opportunity cost) of economic growth is the current consumption that must be given up in order to save for investment in new capital formation. Diverting resources to the production of investment goods may initially reduce consumption levels, but it increases the total production capacity of the economy. In the long run, more production means more real income. There will be multiplied effects on consumption spending, increased savings, and an increase in tax receipts for the government.

One of the controversial questions in public policy is, Whose consumption is going to be reduced in order to free the resources for increased investment? The market system allows individuals to make a choice. Those who reduce their current consumption and save earn interest and profits (stock dividends), and therefore increase their wealth and future consumption.

Proponents of activist policies believe that the government should pursue policies that make the solution to this problem easier by reducing the unemployment level, increasing the total resources engaged in production, and increasing the total output of the economy. More current output makes sacrifices easier. Supply-side economists argue that too much government involvement crowds out the private sector. They believe that the best way for government to encourage investment is by reducing its spending and freeing up financial capital for private investment. For example, anything that causes higher interest rates, such

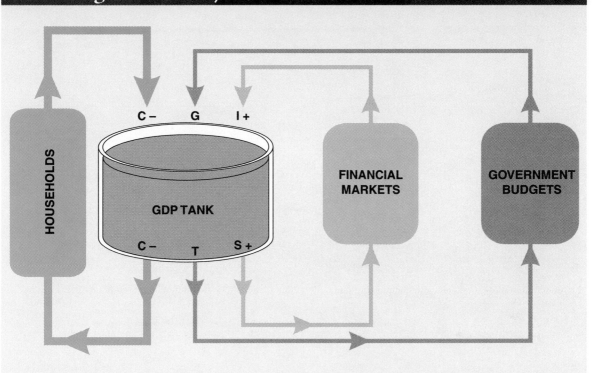

Figure 8

Increasing Investment/GDP Ratio

HOUSEHOLDS

C –   G   I+

GDP TANK

C –   T   S+

FINANCIAL MARKETS

GOVERNMENT BUDGETS

The investment/GDP ratio can be increased by shifting spending from the consumption (blue) sector to the investment (green) sector to finance the production of more investment goods (I+).

as borrowing to finance the large national debt, discourages private investment in increased production capacity.

Even supply-side and nonactivist economists agree on the importance of government investment in public infrastructure—highways, bridges, harbors, transportation, water supplies, and sewage treatment. A lack of such investment would result in discouraging private investment by making it less productive. Better highways speed delivery for businesses; deepwater harbors facilitate foreign trade; adequate water and sewage facilities encourage new plant construction. This type of government investment in improved infrastructure provides a long-run stimulus to private investment as well

as a short-run stimulus to employment in construction. The disadvantages are that, all other things being equal, it increases the deficit and national debt and competes with the private sector for resources.

Government tax policies have a big impact on investment. By using taxes and tax reductions to make capital goods relatively less expensive than consumption goods, the government can create incentives to save and invest. If, however, the interest and dividends earned on savings are taxed, the return to savers is lowered and saving is discouraged. The introduction of tax-sheltered individual retirement accounts and proposals to reduce taxes on capital gains are designed to induce people to save

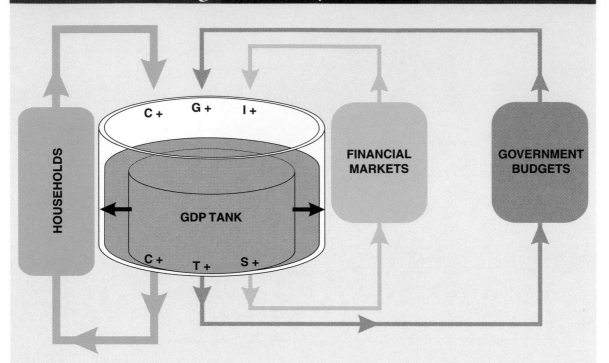

Figure 9

Results of Increasing Investment/GDP Ratio

HOUSEHOLDS

C +   G +   I +

GDP TANK

C +   T +   S +

FINANCIAL
MARKETS

GOVERNMENT
BUDGETS

As a result of increasing the investment/GDP ratio, the production capacity of the economy increases, as shown by the expansion of the GDP tank. This increases income, with a multiplied expansion of consumption spending (C+). More income also means more allocation to savings (S+) and taxes (T+). This provides the funds to finance further increases in investment (I+) and increased government services (G+).

more. One of the advantages of the value added tax (see the case application, Reflections in the Tax Mirror: Which Is Fairest of Them All? p. 369) is that it is a tax on consumption, and thus gives another incentive to save. Business tax credits for investment and special tax reductions for capital depreciation encourage businesses to spend more of their profits on new capital.

stock option the right to purchase a specific amount of a corporation's stock at a fixed price. Often part of the compensation package for a company's top executives.

Among the nontax proposals for promoting more real investment are measures to encourage a change in business focus from a fixation on short-term profits to a longer-term outlook. Presently, company executives with **stock options** are motivated to concentrate on short-term profits to produce rapid increases in the prices of their firms' securities. Providing tax incentives to reward performance over a long period of time might change this motivation.

◢ Increasing Capital Efficiency

The quantity of capital investment is not the only thing that affects growth. The quality of investment may be even more important. If new investment consists simply of more of the

The labor force participation rate of women in the United States is higher than in all other Western bloc countries, with the exception of Canada and Sweden.

same type of capital equipment without a change in technology, the growth of output will not be as large as if the new investment goods are more technologically advanced. In fact, increased capital efficiency from new technology has contributed more to growth than the actual amount of capital.

The new technologies made possible by the microprocessor are an important means of increasing productivity, the amount of output per hour of labor. The efficiency of capital is measured by the **capital/output ratio.** The capital/output ratio is the relationship of investment in capital equipment to the resulting increase in production output. The smaller the ratio, the more efficient the capital. The ratio varies from industry to industry, but an investment of $4 in new equipment may increase output by $1 a year. Another way to look at this is to say that the new capital "will pay for itself in 4 years." If the efficiency of

a new technology were to reduce the capital/output ratio in an industry from 4:1 to 3:1, economic growth stemming from new investment in the industry would increase by one-third, and the investment would pay for itself in only 3 years.

The government is engaged in an effort to help companies improve productivity from the new technologies. The Commerce Department's National Institute of Standards and Technology (NIST) provides instruction to workers in small firms to train them in computer-aided manufacturing, which involves

---

capital/output ratio the ratio of the cost of new investment goods to the value of the annual output produced by those investment goods.

programming machines to be controlled electronically rather than by hand, and using blueprints. This change can cut production times for many jobs by as much as 50%. NIST has established regional centers in Ohio, South Carolina, and New York. These centers are the technological equivalent of the agriculture extension agents that helped make American agriculture the world's most productive.

Increasing Labor Force Participation Rate

An increase in the percentage of the population that is in the labor force can increase output even without an increase in productivity. A sizable part of U.S. economic growth that has taken place in recent years has been the result of increased labor force participation rate.

This is partly due to the baby boom generation entering the labor force and partly because a much larger percentage of married women hold jobs than was the case in earlier years. This is especially true for younger couples between the ages of 25 and 35. In 1973 47% of the wives in such families worked; now over two-thirds do.

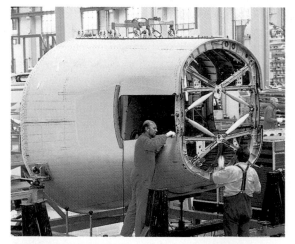

A competent labor force with the necessary skills and training is required to function in the emerging high-tech economy. On-the-job training is one way that businesses can make the investment in human capital keep pace with the investment in capital equipment.

The study by Edward F. Denison on U.S. economic growth from 1929 to 1982 (chapter 7, p. 189) shows that the increase in labor input was the largest single factor contributing to growth. Its contribution to growth has increased steadily since 1964. But with a baby bust generation following on the heels of the baby boom generation, a decrease in labor force participation rates by males, and indications that increases in women's participation in the labor force will not continue at the same level, economic growth in coming years will have to depend on factors other than increases in the labor force participation rate.

Increasing Investment in Human Capital

Investment in new types of capital equipment can substantially increase economic growth only if there is skilled labor available to implement the new technology. Investment in human capital involves investment in the public school system, university education, occupational skills training programs, and on-the-job training. The role that business firms can play in improving the quality of human capital was discussed in chapter 7, but basic education skills have been primarily the responsibility of government.

As noted previously, a competent labor force with the necessary skills and training is required to operate the emerging high-tech economy. The most basic competency requirement is literacy, and the rate of illiteracy in the United States is shocking. One in five adults lack the minimum reading and writing skills even to meet the demands of daily living. Another 20–30% of the population are only marginally capable of being productive workers. Some 13% of high school students graduate with the reading and writing skills of sixth graders, and another 1 million students drop out of school each year without graduating. Many of the students who graduate from high school and go on to college are so unprepared that an estimated two-thirds of the colleges and universities find it necessary to provide remedial reading and writing courses for them. The

Case Application

Investing in the Future

Policies to promote economic growth call for a longer time horizon than stabilization policies. Some growth measures may have a relatively quick payoff. For instance, increased investment in production plant and equipment can expand output in a matter of months. If, however, the investment does not raise productivity as well as production, the output may not be competitive.

Advances in technology that do raise productivity take time to yield results. Studies of the learning curve (chapter 7, p. 185) show that the harvest period for technological innovations in U.S. firms is longer than in some other countries. Particularly in the service industries, the increase in computer technology put in place in the 1980s showed little productivity improvement by 1990.

The growth instrument with the longest period for results is investment in human capital. But the fact that it has a long payoff interval does not mean that it should not be given high priority in national policy. Technological advances will not produce results without a workforce that has the skills to make use of sophisticated equipment. Automated equipment that is designed for very simple work tasks, referred to as "idiot-proof" machines, does not provide the high-productivity growth that raises living standards.

A 1990 study by the Commission on the Skills of the American Workforce compared the education-training systems in the United States, West Germany, Japan, Sweden, Denmark, Ireland, and Singapore. It found that all of the other countries except Ireland provide far better schooling and job training than the United States for those youth not going on to college.

It also found that the other countries have much more effective national systems for facilitating high school graduates' movement into industry. It characterizes the system in the United States—or virtual absence of any system—as "the worst of any industrialized country." When combined with the fact that the United States has the world's greatest system of higher education, it is no wonder that we have developed a dual labor market (see chapter 9, p. 233).

The commission study recommended a drastic overhaul in the way that the nation educates and trains that portion of its citizens who will not graduate from a 4-year college, some 70%. One proposal of the study was for a national fund to upgrade worker skills. The fund would be financed by a 1% tax on business payrolls. Employers could avoid the tax by spending an equivalent amount on their own company training programs.

There is some good news to report, however. As shown in chapter 7, productivity has been increasing. The output of firms that "downsized" their labor forces in the early-to-mid-1990s has been increasing while costs have been stable. The most probable explanation for this phenomenon is that previous investments are bearing fruit and the output per worker has been increasing.

Economic Reasoning

1. Of the factors that affect economic growth, which one produces results in the shortest period of time and which one takes the longest to increase the growth rate?

2. Why is the growth measure that takes effect most quickly not necessarily the one that public policy should concentrate on?

3. Should the recommendation of the Commission on the Skills of the American Workforce that employers be required to spend an amount equal to 1% of their payroll on in-house or national training programs be adopted into law? Why or why not?

Investing in the Future

Visit the Bureau of Labor Statistics Data Center at http://stats.bls.gov/datahome.htm. If you select "Selective Access" and scroll down, you will find a series called "Major Sector Productivity and Cost Index." You can use this to find the most recent quarterly productivity figures for manufacturing or for all nonfarm businesses. How has our productivity been doing over the past few years?

Tax cuts and hikes play an important role in determining consumer spending and saving. This is one way the government influences aggregate demand in the economy.

Japanese population, by comparison, has a literacy rate of 95%.

This decline in the educational quality of the workforce is yet another explanation for the slowing of labor productivity that the country has experienced since 1973. Up to then productivity had been growing at the rate of 2% a year from as far back as 1900. Since 1973, however, the productivity growth rate has been only a little more than half that, 1.2% per year. This has affected our ability to compete in the world and our standard of living.

If the United States is to take advantage of the second Industrial Revolution, it must invest not only in high-tech hardware but also in high-tech human capital. Many types of work can increasingly be done in cyberspace. For example, a firm can hire an accountant in India to keep accounts on an Excel spreadsheet, and then e-mail it to New York. If the Indian accountant can do the work as well as an American, and do it for less pay, the gap between the standard of living in the two countries will shrink as one grows and the other declines. A better workforce is the ultimate key to a better standard of living.

▶ Putting It Together

Since the 1930s, the federal government has used *fiscal policy* and *monetary policy* as the principal means to *stabilize* prices and maintain full employment. In implementing fiscal policy, the government adapts its spending and taxing activities in order to increase aggregate demand when there is unemployment and to decrease aggregate demand when there is inflation. Prior to the 1930s, government policy was an *annually balanced budget*. The Great Depression and the spread of the ideas of John Maynard Keynes led the government to adopt new policies that purposely created deficits in the budget to compensate for inadequate demand in the private sector and to provide for full employment.

It would be well for the government to have budget surpluses at times to counteract inflation. Over the whole business cycle, if the surpluses offset the deficits, we would have a *cyclically balanced budget*. Some economists argue that balancing the budget either annually or cyclically is not important. What is important is to do what is required for stabilization at any given time. This is *functional finance*.

The Keynesian method of solving unemployment by use of *discretionary fiscal policy* is to increase government spending on goods and services in order to expand aggregate demand, raise production, and thus stimulate employment. By increasing transfer payments, for example with cash subsidies to lower-income families, the government provides larger purchasing power to the private sector, which also increases aggregate demand. On the taxation side, the Keynesians would cut taxes to boost consumption spending, thus increasing production and stimulating employment.

The amount of increased government spending and/or decreased taxes necessary to bring about full employment depends on the *multiplier*. Any increase in sales provides purchasing power to those producing the goods and services, most of which they in turn use to purchase additional goods and services. The total increase in spending is a multiple of the original increase in sales. The smaller the propensity to save, the larger is the *multiplier effect*.

Supply-side economic policy also involves the use of tax cuts, but with a different purpose. The objective of supply-side tax cuts is to make production and investment more profitable and thereby provide incentives to businesses, workers, and other factor inputs to make more of these inputs available for production. The resulting increase in economic activity would create more jobs, and the rising output of goods and services would reduce or eliminate price increases by reducing scarcity.

The existence of *recognition, decision,* and *impact lags* makes it difficult to properly time discretionary policies. In addition to the discretionary fiscal policy tools used by the federal government, there are *automatic stabilizers* built into the economy. These are tax provisions and government expenditures, such as unemployment insurance payments, that help counteract cyclical fluctuations.

The principal tools of Federal Reserve monetary policy are open market operations, changes in the discount rate, and changes in the required reserve ratio. Prior to the 1980s, Fed policy was targeted on the control of interest rates. Since then, the target first changed to the control of the money supply itself, and then to the direct control of inflation.

The monetarist approach assumes that if the money supply is allowed to rise only at the rate of the average long-run increase in real output, the price level will be stabilized. Monetarist theory is based on a constant velocity of money circulation and the ability to accurately control the money supply, neither of which may be possible.

Economic growth is promoted by having a higher proportion of total output flow into new investment—raising the *investment/GDP ratio*. Another determinant of growth is the ratio between the amount of new capital spending in an industry and the increase in output resulting from that investment—the *capital/output ratio*. If the capital/output ratio is low, there is a larger increase in output for a given amount of capital spending, and the profit incentives for investment are greater.

Raising the *labor force participation rate*, while it may in the short run reduce labor pro-ductivity, increases total and per capita output and is a significant growth factor. In the United States in the last 2 decades, increased participation by women in the labor force has contributed to intensive growth and raised per capita income. Growth also results from upgrading human capital through additional education and occupational training.

The federal budget deficits of the 1980s and early 1990s led to a move for a balanced budget amendment to the Constitution. This was defeated in 1994, but the deficits have been reduced considerably since then.

$ Perspective $

Monetarism—Does Money Matter?

Milton Friedman (born 1912) Friedman was born in Brooklyn, New York, and attended the University of Chicago and Rutgers University. He received a Ph.D. from Columbia University in 1946. During his schooling Friedman worked on the research staff of the National Bureau for Economic Research and in the tax research division of the U.S. Treasury Department. He taught for 1 year at the University of Minnesota before returning to the University of Chicago, where he spent the rest of his teaching career, becoming the Paul Snowden Russell Distinguished Service Professor of Economics. In 1977 he became a senior Research Fellow at the Hoover Institution at Stanford University. Friedman served as the president of the American Economics Association in 1967 and was awarded the Nobel Prize in economics in 1976. He has repeatedly proven to be a formidable opponent in his numerous public debates with liberal economists because of the great amount of data he has developed from his prodigious research. He is not only the leading spokesman for monetarism but also for the conservative economic viewpoint associated with the Chicago School. Among his publications are *Essays in Positive Economics* (1953), *Inflation: Cause and Consequences* (1963), *A Theoretical Framework for Monetary Analysis* (1972), *There's No Such Thing as a Free Lunch* (1975), and *Price Theory* (1976).

In the early years of the Keynesian revolution, during the 1940s and early 1950s, the role of money in determining the level of economic activity was generally dismissed as having no relevance to economic stabilization policy. Keynes's discussion of the role of prices in *The General Theory* was interpreted by many of his followers to mean that wage rates were rigid, except at full employment when increasing demand would cause inflation of wages and other prices. Some latter-day Keynesian followers (neo-Keynesians) have noted that the assumption about fixed wages and prices was only a simplifying assumption that Keynes dropped in later chapters when he discussed the effects of price changes. Still others say that what he meant was that wages *should* be rigid to prevent even greater economic instability.

In any event, the role of prices and money was largely ignored in discussions of macroeconomic theory and economic stabilization policy. Everywhere, that is, except at the University of Chicago, where the quantity theory of money (M × V = T × P) was kept alive and nurtured by a group of economists that came to be known as "The Chicago School." The foremost member of the Chicago School of economists was Milton Friedman.

In his monumental study (with Anna Schwartz), *A Monetary History of the United States, 1867–1960,* Friedman demonstrated a close correlation between changes in the money supply on the one hand and inflation and the level of economic activity on the other. In his view, it was fiscal policy that was irrelevant. Promoted by Friedman and other Chicago School economists and reinforced by the persistent inflation of the 1970s, monetarism had a strong influence on both theory and policy in the early 1980s.

The rise of monetarism to the forefront of macroeconomics did not last long, however. In the area of theory, monetarism proved unable to explain what was happening any better than, or as well as, Keynesian economics. On the basis of monetarist analysis, Friedman predicted a recession in early 1984, followed by renewed inflation. Neither of these things happened, either then or for some years after.

On the policy side, the implementation of monetarist policies by the Fed did put a halt to inflation in 1981–1982 by contracting the money supply and bringing about the most severe recession since the depression of the 1930s, but that was no great trick. The real trick is to restrain inflation and at the same time provide full employment and a healthy growth rate. Monetarist policies were not any more successful in accomplishing this than previous approaches.

For Further Study and Analysis

Study Questions

1. If there had been such a thing at the time, would fiscal stabilization policy have been very effective in the early years of this century when the federal government was quite small? Why or why not?
2. Why would a Constitutional amendment that requires annually balanced budgets make discretionary fiscal policy impossible?
3. What advantage do automatic stabilizers have over discretionary fiscal policy?
4. How do the existence of recognition, decision, and impact lags make the proper timing of discretionary policy difficult?
5. What explains the difference in the effectiveness of monetary policy at opposite ends of the business cycle?
6. The investment/GDP ratio is based only on private investment. What are some examples of government spending that might increase economic growth?
7. Why does the capital/output ratio vary among different industries within a country? Which U.S. industries would you expect to have a high capital/output ratio? Which ones would you expect to have a low capital/output ratio?
8. Why has the U.S. labor force participation rate increased? What could be done to increase it further? What events might cause it to decrease?

9. What are some examples of technological improvements that do not require investment in new capital equipment?

Exercises in Analysis

1. Using the most recent Economic Report of the President or other sources, write a short paper on the government's recent fiscal and monetary policies.
2. From news accounts of current government stabilization measures, write a short paper on whether those measures represent Keynesian (demand-side) economic policies, supply-side economic policies, or monetarist economic policies.
3. Assume you are an economist on the staff of the Federal Reserve Board and the series of leading economic indicators suggests that the economy is headed into a severe recession. Write a report to the board recommending what actions it should take.
4. From news accounts or other sources, find articles that suggest that the government should be more active in controlling economic fluctuations, and find other articles that say that it should be less involved. Summarize their arguments and conclude with your opinion.

Further Reading

Biven, W. Carl. *Who Killed John Maynard Keynes?* Homewood, IL: Dow Jones–Irwin, 1989. Reviews basic Keynesian propositions and shows how they were replaced by monetarism, rational expectations, and Reaganomics. Concludes that the alternative formulations have not proved satisfactory and suggests a return to reworked Keynesian ideas.

Buiter, William H. *Principles of Budgetary and Financial Policy.* Cambridge, MA: MIT Press, 1990. Covers the question of the crowding out of private investment by government borrowing.

Burdekin, Richard C., and Farrokh K. Langdana. *Budget Deficits and Economic Performance.* New York: Routledge, 1992. An intercountry comparison of deficit financing, especially in the European Union.

Calleo, David P. *The Bankrupting of America: How the Federal Budget Is Impoverishing the Nation.* New York: William Morrow, 1992. An extremist outlook on the consequences of U.S. fiscal policy.

Friedman, Benjamin. *Day of Reckoning.* New York: Random House, 1988. "This book is about debt: debt and the material and moral impoverishment that inevitably follow, no less for a nation than for an individual or family, from continually borrowing for no purpose other than to live beyond one's means" (p. vii).

Friedman, Milton. *Monetarist Economics.* Cambridge, MA: Basil Blackwell, 1991. The leading proponent of monetarist economics explains the view on monetary policy supported by the Chicago School of economics.

Kotlikoff, Laurence. *Generational Accounting: Knowing Who Pays, and When, for What We Spend.* New York: Free Press, 1992. Explains how tax burdens affect different generations and the real impact of budget deficits and debt interest payments.

Lindsey, Lawrence. *The Growth Experiment: How the New Tax Policy Is Transforming the U.S. Economy.* New York: Basic Books, 1990. This is a justification for supply-side tax policy. It maintains that the tax cuts of the 1980s were not the cause of the federal deficits, although conceding that they contributed to making the deficits greater than they would otherwise have been.

Minarik, Joseph. *Making America's Budget Policy: From the 1980s to the 1990s.* Armonk, NY: M. E. Sharpe, 1990. A review of taxes, federal budgets, and budget deficits during the Reagan years.

Ortner, Robert. *Voodoo Deficits.* Homewood, IL: Dow Jones–Irwin, 1990. Supply-side economic policy and how budget deficits are not what they seem. The role of international competition and the U.S. balance of trade is examined.

Unit Four

World Economics

The economy of the United States is closely integrated into the world economy. Our economic policies have a major impact on other countries and vice versa.

chapter fifteen

International Trade

The basic logic of international trade does not differ from the basic logic of domestic trade—in both cases specialization and trade increase total output. However, domestic industries that cannot compete with foreign ones are often harmed by free trade, and the costs and benefits of trade restrictions remain hotly debated topics.

chapter sixteen

International Finance and the National Economy

International payments are made and the exchange rates of currencies are determined in the foreign exchange market. There are important links among currency values, imports, exports, trade balances, and the domestic economy.

chapter seventeen

Economies in Transition

The unraveling of the Soviet Union and the collapse of communism there and in East Europe are historic changes. The methods of converting an economy from communism to capitalism are many, but none have ever been attempted before. The consequences of transition have been painful for all, but not all transition economies have experienced successes worth the pain.

chapter eighteen

The Less Developed Countries

Two-thirds of the people in the world live in countries with low living standards and numerous obstacles to development. The prospects for overcoming poverty in less developed countries depend to a large extent on how they meet their population, debt, environmental, legal, and institutional problems.

chapter fifteen

International Trade

The motivations for international trade are basically no different from those for trade within a country, but in the past, nations imposed special regulations and restrictions on foreign trade. Now, nations are working to negotiate agreements to reduce the restrictions that limit trade. These agreements generate a great deal of controversy, as in the two instances discussed in the introductory article.

▶ Do You Hear a Giant Sucking Sound Yet?

The debate in Washington during 1993 over the North American Free Trade Agreement (NAFTA), establishing a free trade area among the United States, Canada, and Mexico, rose to an unusually frenzied pitch. Among the heated charges was businessman/politician H. Ross Perot's prediction that if trade barriers between the United States and Mexico were eliminated, there would be heard a "giant sucking sound" as American jobs were siphoned off to low-paying Mexico.

The opposition to NAFTA came from a strange coalition of organizations and individuals that are generally not on the same side of public policy questions. Besides Perot, the strongest opponents were the labor unions. Labor leaders exerted a great deal of pressure on their traditional allies in the Democratic Party. They threatened to cut off campaign contributions and to actively work to defeat in the next election any Democrat who voted for the NAFTA pact.

Environmental organizations were split over the issue, some opposing NAFTA and others supporting it. Ralph Nader, who came to national prominence as a consumer advocate, mounted a vigorous campaign in opposition to NAFTA. This seemed a strange position for a consumer advocate to take, since, whatever its effect on jobs, free trade is generally conceded to benefit consumers through lower prices. When questioned about his position, Nader held Japan up as a model of the benefits of protectionism, ignoring the heavy cost to Japanese consumers from their government's protection of sheltered industries.

But the main battle for the hearts and minds of voters over NAFTA centered on its effect on jobs. Perot claimed that as many as 5.9 million jobs would be lost to Mexico, asserting that even jobs in such high-technology industries as guided missiles and space vehicles were "at risk." A less exaggerated estimate came from Washington's Economic Policy Institute, projecting the possibility of a 490,000 job loss. On the other side, the International Economics Institute estimated a net gain of 171,000 American jobs.

The heat of the argument over NAFTA's effect on jobs was misplaced. Whether the effect turned out to be plus or minus, it would not be very significant relative to total domestic employment fluctuations. If the job change turned out to be some 200,000, whether in the positive or negative direction, it would be no more than the average number of jobs the U.S. economy creates and loses in one month, and less than 0.2% of the nation's labor force. Actually, the results are still in doubt. Many low-wage, unskilled jobs have been lost to Mexico, but at the same time, exports of high-wage products have increased. After 5 years, most estimates are that perhaps 100,000 to 200,000 jobs have been lost. On the other hand, nearly as many jobs have been created in high-wage industries as U.S. exports to Mexico increased along with our imports (Table 1).

Looked at in larger perspective, the NAFTA battle was really over what future direction the U.S. economy should take. Should the nation attempt to protect and retain relatively low-skill manufacturing jobs in the face of increasing competition from less developed countries in traditional industries? Or should it let those jobs go and shift its capital and labor resources into high-tech and service industries?

The opposition of the labor unions to the type of change represented by NAFTA is understandable. Their base of strength—already seriously eroded—is in the manufacturing industries that are threatened by such a change. The unions are fighting a rear-guard action to slow down further erosion. On a personal level, many of their members are too old or too ill-equipped educationally to retrain for more skilled jobs. If they lose their present jobs, they are unlikely ever to have another job that pays as well. Despite the formidable opposition to NAFTA, it passed Congress by a narrow margin and was signed into law.

Table 1 — U.S.–Mexico Trade since 1992 (Millions of dollars)

Year	U.S. Exports to Mexico	U.S. Imports from Mexico
1992	$40,592	$35,211
1993	41,581	35,917
1994	50,843	49,484
1995	46,292	62,101
1996	56,791	74,297
1997	71,378	85,830
1998*	78,360	90,393

*Estimate based on first 4 months

NAFTA resulted in increases in both U.S. exports to Mexico and U.S. imports of Mexican goods.

Source: U.S. Department of Commerce

NAFTA, the European Union, and Mercosur (Argentina, Brazil, Uruguay and Paraguay) are trading "blocs" designed to promote free trade within a select group of countries, while maintaining trade barriers with countries not in their group. At the same time that these groups were being formed, most of the world's countries, including the ones in these trading blocs, were involved in intense negotiations to reduce barriers to trade among all countries—the General Agreement on Tariffs and Trade (GATT). Since it was first established with negotiations among 23 countries in Geneva in 1947, GATT participants have met for eight rounds of talks and the number of participants has grown to 132.

The negotiations among the three countries over the terms of NAFTA were a breeze compared to the quarrelsome, drawn-out negotiations over the latest round of GATT talks. The discussions began in September 1986 at Punta del Este in Uruguay, giving the name "Uruguay Round" to the meetings, and continued off and on for 7 years in different locations over various continents.

The main sticking points were agricultural protection, a particularly French obstacle; protection against the piracy of intellectual property such as patents, copyrights, and trademarks, important to U.S. negotiators; and freedom from restrictions on foreign competition in the service sector, especially banking and financial services. Hard-fought compromises and an implicit agreement to continue the disagreement on some issues, such as opening markets to financial services, finally resulted in conclusion of the Uruguay Round in December 1993. A year later in December 1994, Congress approved the new GATT.

The agreement slashes tariffs on industrial goods by an average of about one-third; requires cuts in subsidies by European countries to their farmers; restricts piracy of intellectual property such as music, films, and software; and extends free trade rules to many services that were not covered in past agreements. The World Bank estimates that the Uruguay Round will result in an additional $274 billion to the world's GDP by the year 2002—a 1.3% increase.

It also sets up a new organization to continue the process of trade liberalization—the World Trade Organization (WTO). Among other things, the WTO enforces the provisions of the Uruguay Round and serves as an international referee to settle trade disputes among member-nations.

Chapter Preview

Foreign trade is the subject of much controversy, but in this chapter we will see that the basic logic of international trade does not differ from the basic logic of domestic trade. We shall examine international trade by dealing with the following questions: Why do we trade with other countries? Who benefits and who is hurt by foreign trade? How do we restrict foreign trade? Should foreign trade be restricted?

Learning Objectives

After completing this chapter, you should be able to:

1. Explain the difference between absolute and comparative advantage.

2. Explain why specialization is sometimes complete, but normally is limited.

3. Compare the types of goods exported by the United States to the types of goods imported.

4. Describe the effects of foreign trade on economies.

5. Specify who benefits and who loses as a result of foreign trade.

6. Compare the different types of restrictions imposed on foreign trade.

7. Discuss the different vehicles for trade negotiations and explain the meaning of "most-favored-nation status."

8. Critically evaluate the arguments in favor of trade restrictions.

▶ Why Do We Trade with Other Countries?

Trade between countries results from specialization of production. Figure 1 shows the regional breakdown of the world's $5.5 trillion in international trade. Although the U.S. economy is far and away the biggest in the world, most of our economic activity occurs within our borders, and our participation in international trade is very small compared to the size of our economy. If Western Europe were truly to unite into one large country (see the case application, Europe Calling), their trade would then also be within the borders of one country and the volume of international trade would fall.

◼ Absolute Advantage

The South American country of Ecuador has excellent climate and terrain for growing coffee, cocoa, and bananas. It has an absolute advantage over the United States in the production of these goods. The United States, on the other hand, has an absolute advantage over Ecuador in many manufactured goods such as computers, airplanes, and electric razors. Ecuador does not have the capital equipment, technology, or trained personnel to produce these things economically. Thus there is trade between the two that benefits each country based on their respective absolute advantages.

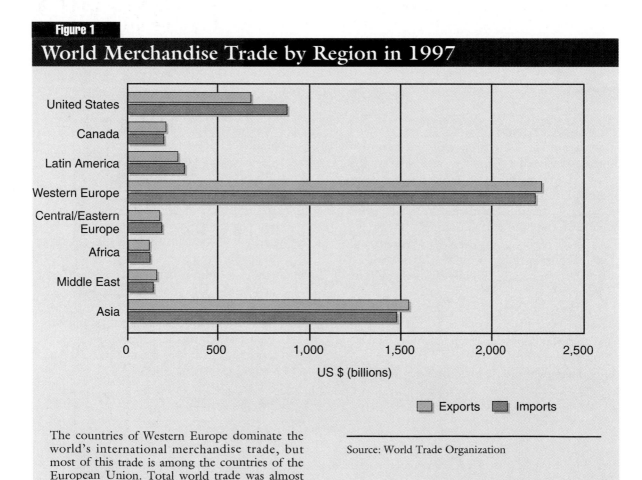

Figure 1

World Merchandise Trade by Region in 1997

US $ (billions)

☐ Exports ◼ Imports

The countries of Western Europe dominate the world's international merchandise trade, but most of this trade is among the countries of the European Union. Total world trade was almost $5.5 trillion in 1997.

Source: World Trade Organization

◾ Comparative Advantage

During the GATT negotiations, there was pressure on U.S. trade representatives from the textile industry to restrict imports. Textile imports from Malaysia, China, the Philippines, and other countries have eliminated a large part of the market for U.S. textiles. The United States is an efficient producer of textiles, but labor and capital in this country are more efficient in the production of other goods. As an example, let us assume that the United States has an absolute advantage over the Philippines in the production of both electric drills and bedspreads. The efficiency advantage of the United States, however, is greater in producing drills than in producing bedspreads. The United States has a comparative advantage in drills with respect to the Philippines, and the Philippines has a comparative advantage in making bedspreads with respect to the United States. The advantage of a cheaper labor supply in the Philippines is not sufficient to offset the technological superiority of the United States in manufacturing drills. It is sufficient, however, to offset the U.S. technical superiority in making bedspreads.

🕸 Why Do We Trade with Other Countries?

EconExplorer

The Philippines may not be able to produce bedspreads as efficiently as they could be produced in the United States, but the production of bedspreads is adaptable to different levels of technology. With lower wage rates, Philippine manufacturers can use a more labor-intensive method of producing bedspreads and can sell them more cheaply in the United States than can American producers. Therefore, the Philippines exports bedspreads to the United States on the basis of its comparative advantage in producing them.

Countries, like individuals, find it profitable to produce those goods that they are best suited to produce. One country may be very efficient in the production of both electric drills and bedspreads, but another country will have a comparative advantage in the production of bedspreads if its opportunity costs for that production are low. The drills and bedspreads in a neighborhood store were made in all parts of the world.

Even though the United States is absolutely more efficient in bedspread production than the Philippines, the opportunity costs of producing bedspreads there are lower than in the United States. Let us assume that when the Philippines produces one bedspread, it must give up the production of one drill. We'll assume that production of one bedspread in the United States, however, means that two drills will not be produced here. Thus, the opportunity cost, or real cost, of producing a bedspread in the United States is two drills, compared to an opportunity cost of only one drill in the Philippines. In effect, we must give up only one-half of a bedspread when a drill is produced in the United States, compared to the sacrifice of a whole bedspread when a drill is produced in the Philippines. Drills are therefore cheaper to produce in the United States (a cost of ½ bedspread versus 1 bedspread in the Philippines) and bedspreads are cheaper to produce in the Philippines (a cost of 1 drill versus 2 drills in the United States).

◤ Specialization

As was found in the case of individuals in chapter 3, countries find it profitable to produce those goods that they are best suited to produce. Countries like the Philippines, with a relative abundance of labor but not capital, tend to specialize in industries that are **labor-intensive,** such as textiles and clothing. Other countries with large amounts of capital per worker, such as the United States, tend to specialize in high-technology industries. By specializing in what they do best and trading their output to other nations for what *they* can do best, both nations can maximize the value of their output and maximize their standards of living. As a result, specialization of production requires that each nation must engage in trade to sell its surplus production and acquire what it does not produce.

◤ Increasing Costs

Sometimes specialization is complete. Between Ecuador and the United States, there is complete specialization in the cocoa and aircraft industries. Ecuador does not manufacture any airplanes and the United States does not grow cocoa commercially. For most products, however, specialization is only partial. The United States imports most of the bedspreads that are sold in this country, but it still produces a quantity of bedspreads. The Philippines imports most of the electrical equipment that it needs, including drills, but it does produce some electrical equipment itself. Instead of complete specialization, we more often have **limited specialization.**

The reason for this limited specialization is the existence of **increasing costs.** The Philippines can produce some electrical equipment that is competitive with that produced by the United States. Because of its limited supplies of skilled labor and capital equipment, however, it cannot increase the output of its electrical equipment industry sufficiently to satisfy all of its domestic needs without running into higher production costs. The concept of increasing costs was illustrated in Figure 3 of chapter 2 (p. 45) in connection with the trade-off between the production of steel and oranges.

---

labor-intensive refers to production processes that employ a large amount of labor relative to the amount of capital equipment.

limited specialization specialization in producing goods or services according to comparative advantage when the specialization is not complete due to increasing costs (decreasing returns).

increasing costs a rise in average production costs as the quantity of output of the good increases.

Comparative Case Application

Europe Calling

Former U.S. secretary of state Henry Kissinger once asked, "If I want to talk to Europe, whom do I call?" After years of functioning as independent countries, the nations of Europe have agreed to integrate their economies and nations into one combined economic powerhouse with headquarters—and a telephone—in Brussels, Belgium.

In 1952 Belgium, Holland, Luxembourg, Germany, France, and Italy created the European Coal and Steel Community, which was designed to help these two industries prosper by allowing tariff-free coal and steel trade among the six countries. In 1956, they signed the Treaty of Rome and created the European Economic Community (EEC). Denmark, Ireland, and the UK joined in 1973, Greece in 1981, Spain and Portugal in 1986, and Austria, Sweden, and Finland were admitted in 1995. The fledgling organization has grown into what is now known as the European Union (EU), a common market comprised of 15 countries with more than 300 million people and a combined 1997 GDP of $6.4 trillion. Waiting in the wings and anxious to join the Union as soon as they can are Poland, Hungary, the Czech Republic, and Turkey.

The EEC was originally a free-trade area, an arrangement whereby tariffs were eliminated among the member-countries, but each country could establish its own tariff levels with outside countries. It then evolved into a customs union, a free-trade area with common external tariffs, and finally, in the 1980s, into a common market, a customs union that allows the free movement of capital and labor among its member-states. The next step for Europe began in 1999 with the introduction of a common currency, common monetary and fiscal policies, and coordinated tax and social welfare policies. With this step, ratified by the signing of the Maastricht Treaty of 1992, Europe at last has become an economic union with a governing body in Brussels.

Among the advantages of being an economic union are the increase in trade and lower prices that accompany the removal of trade barriers. In the past, firms in each country were somewhat limited by the size of their domestic economy. Although a Dutch lightbulb maker could always sell bulbs in other European countries, tariffs raised their price, made them uncompetitive with domestic bulbs, and limited the size of Dutch exports. Because of this, manufacturers in Holland, and other countries, often produced at output levels that were too small to achieve economies of scale. With a market of 300 million people now open to them, producers of products from lightbulbs to banking services to books will be able to expand their output, lower their average costs, and provide more and less expensive goods and services to consumers throughout Europe.

The benefits of an economic union will not come without some pain. Just as there was opposition to NAFTA in the United States, many Europeans are not happy with the idea of an economic union. Steelmakers in France may find that they are losing markets to more efficient German steel companies, and German textile makers may find themselves losing ground to Spanish weavers. It is the old issue of comparative advantage all over again. Although free trade will not destroy jobs in a country, over time it will change the type of jobs being done. With time, however, the gains from specialization and trade will lead to an increased standard of living for European citizens.

Although it is not always easy to do, workers in different countries are now free to seek employment in any other member-country. The consequence of labor mobility will put downward pressure on wages and benefits in high-wage countries. Competition for industry will force high-tax governments to reduce their tax burdens and bring them into line with governments that impose lower taxes on businesses and households. As a result, many fear that the welfare states of Europe (see chapter 9 page 229) will need to reassess their role in the lives of their citizens. While consumer and capital goods will get cheaper and be more plentiful, citizens might be forced to give up some highly valued social goods.

Exporters in countries outside the EU will also suffer because while tariffs are being removed within Europe, they still remain very high for nonmember-countries that desire to sell their products in Europe. Before the formation of the EC, German tariffs were similar for products imported from France and from Chile. Suppose Chile is the world's most efficient producer of canned anchovies and used to sell lots of anchovies to the Germans. Now, with the removal of tariffs between the French and the Germans, Chile will lose its German market and the German people will be forced to eat higher-priced French anchovies on their pizza.

Economic Reasoning

1. What are the differences among a free trade area, a customs union, a common market, and an economic union?
2. How does the formation of the economic union result in increased consumer satisfaction?
3. Do you think that the gains from freer trade are worth the price the Europeans might have to pay in reduced government benefits?

Figure 2

The European Union

Member Countries (year of entry)

France (1967)	Ireland (1973)
West Germany (1967)	Greece (1981)
Netherlands (1967)	Spain (1986)
Belgium (1967)	Portugal (1986)
Luxembourg (1967)	Austria (1995)
Italy (1967)	Finland (1995)
Denmark (1973)	Sweden (1995)
Great Britain (1973)	

■ Original EU members (6)

■ Other EU countries

□ Countries that have rejected membership

Who Benefits and Who Is Hurt by Foreign Trade?

Specialization according to absolute or comparative advantage results in a net gain to both of the trading partners in foreign trade, but not everyone within a country benefits equally. Some individuals or firms may even suffer economic losses as a result.

Consumer Benefits

Without foreign trade, there are some things that we would be unable to enjoy. Chocolate lovers would probably not appreciate cocoa grown in greenhouses in this country as a substitute for the beans grown in Ecuador. Even if they were willing to drink it, they wouldn't be able to afford much domestically grown cocoa because it would be very expensive.

Most imports, however, unlike cocoa, are items that we can and do produce domestically. This is a direct consequence of increasing costs.

Those items that are produced by domestic firms and are also imported are called **import-competing.** Consumers benefit from the availability of imported goods because they have a greater selection, foreign products are very often less expensive or of better quality, and the import competition helps keep down the price of domestically produced goods.

The consumer benefits that derive from foreign trade can be demonstrated with the use of the hypothetical data in Figure 3,

import-competing industry a domestic industry that produces the same or a close substitute good that competes in the domestic market with imports.

Figure 3

The Effects of Free Trade in the Production of Raspberries

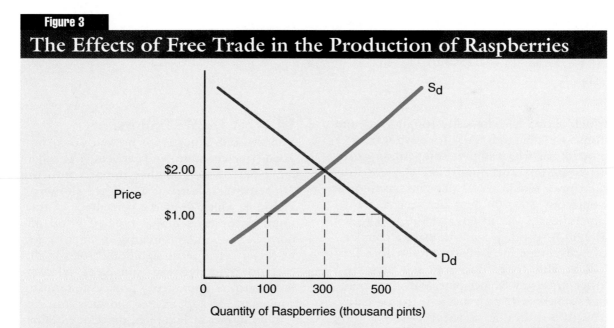

In the absence of free international trade, the price and quantity of raspberries bought and sold would be determined by domestic supply (Sd) and domestic demand (Dd). The price would be $2.00 per pint and 300,000 pints would be consumed. With free trade at a global price of $1.00 per pint, consumers would be able to consume 500,000 pints, of which 100,000 pints would be produced domestically and 400,000 pints would be imported.

Figure 4

U.S. Imports by Type, 1997

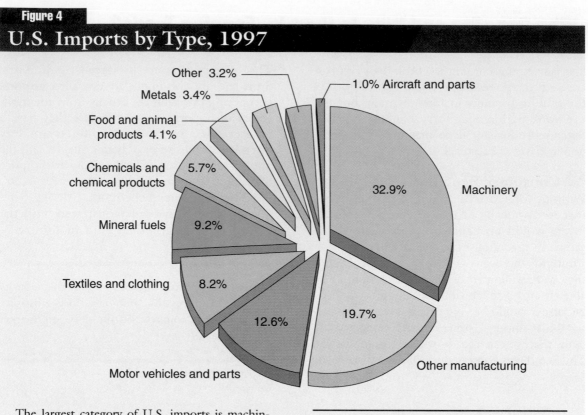

The largest category of U.S. imports is machinery. This includes such things as consumer electronics, telecommunications equipment, and other specialized equipment.

Source: U.S. Bureau of the Census, *Highlights of U.S. Export and Import Trade.*

which shows the domestic supply (Sd) and domestic demand (Dd) for raspberries, a product for which import competition exists. Without any foreign trade, the equilibrium price would be $2 per pint, consumers would buy 300,000 pints per year, and total expenditures would equal $600,000 ($2 × 300,000). If other countries have a comparative advantage in raspberry production, they will be able to produce and sell them at a lower price, say $1 per pint. With free trade, consumers will now be able to consume 500,000 pints at a total cost of only $500,000. At a price of $1, domestic demand exceeds domestic supply because only 100,000 pints will be produced domestically. The balance, 400,000 pints, will be imported.

⚔ What Do We Import?

Imports and exports are broken down into goods (merchandise) and services. The different types of merchandise imports into the United States during 1997 are shown in Figure 4, which gives the percentage of total imports for each major type of good imported. The largest category of imports was machinery. The most significant items in this category were electrical equipment, telecommunications apparatus, power-generating equipment, and specialized industrial machinery. As shown in Figure 5, the United States is also an exporter of these types of products. This illustrates how integrated the world economy has become. By far the largest part of U.S. trade is with other industrialized

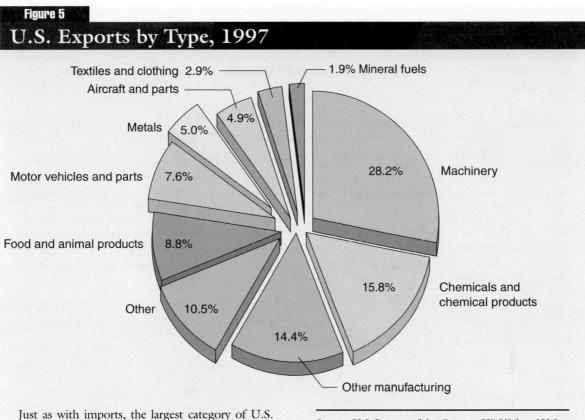

Figure 5

U.S. Exports by Type, 1997

- Textiles and clothing 2.9%
- Aircraft and parts
- 1.9% Mineral fuels
- Metals 5.0%
- 4.9%
- Motor vehicles and parts 7.6%
- Machinery 28.2%
- Food and animal products 8.8%
- Chemicals and chemical products 15.8%
- Other 10.5%
- Other manufacturing 14.4%

Just as with imports, the largest category of U.S. exports is machinery, followed by chemicals and chemical products. The data are highly aggregated and hide the fact that the types of machinery we export are sometimes different than the types we import.

Source: U.S. Bureau of the Census, *Highlights of U.S. Export and Import Trade*.

countries that have similar production systems. Worldwide, three-quarters of exports go from developed countries to other developed countries. Comparative advantage now rests largely on very specific products within broad categories. For example, 70% of worldwide exports of friction bearings go to countries that also export bearings.

Trade in services is a growing part of the world economy. The money that Americans spend when traveling in other countries and for tickets on foreign airlines counts as imported services. The spending of U.S. businesses and tourists when they travel abroad is our largest category of imported services, accounting for over 40% of the total.

In 1997, the U.S. imported $882 billion worth of goods and $174 billion worth of services, for a total of $1,056 billion in imports. About $1 out of every $8 that we spent in 1997 was spent on imports of goods and services. This is not a particularly large import ratio compared to most other countries, because our economy is so large that it can produce most of the things that we want or need. For example, Germany and Great Britain spend $1 out of every $4 on imports, and the Netherlands, a much smaller country, spends over half its income on imports. For the United States, however, this amount of import spending is much higher than it has been historically. In 1992, our ratio was only $1 in every $10 being spent on imports.

Table 2	United States Export, Import-Competing, and Domestic Industries		

Export Industries	**Import-Competing Industries**	**Domestic Industries**
Computers	Textiles and clothing	Construction
Aircraft	Steel and other metals	Health services
Chemicals	Autos and parts	K–12 education
Instruments	Furniture	Personal services
Lumber and paper products	Consumer electronics	Wholesale
Financial services	Agriculture	Domestic transport
Films and other media	Shoes and luggage	Printing and publishing
Higher education	Toys and jewelry	Rubber and plastic products

The export sector creates jobs and raises wages for workers in the exporting industries. Workers in the import-competing industries suffer job losses and lower wages. Jobs in the domestic sector industries are not affected by trade, but the workers in those industries, along with workers in the other sectors, benefit from greater availability, lower prices, and improved quality of goods and services in the import-competing sector.

Sources: U.S. Bureau of the Census, *U.S. Merchandise Trade: Exports, General Imports, and Imports for Consumption;* U.S. Department of Commerce, Bureau of Economic Analysis, *Survey of Current Business.*

◢ Producer and Worker Benefits

Many industries and workers also benefit in various ways from foreign trade. Some American industries depend on raw materials that can only be acquired abroad. Other firms purchase semifinished components for their products from foreign sources, including both independent producers and subsidiaries of American firms abroad. Still others import the machinery they use in their domestic production.

Perhaps the most important benefit of foreign trade to producers and workers, however, is providing markets for our export industries. During 1997 we exported $679 billion worth of goods and $280 billion worth of services, a total of $937 billion worth of exports. As shown in Figure 5, machinery, including computers, accounts for more than a quarter of all merchandise exports. While most of us are aware that our exports create jobs for American workers, we sometimes overlook the fact that imports also create jobs and income for all those who transport, deliver, distribute, and sell them.

Just as American foreign travel is our biggest service import, foreign business and tourist travel in the United States is our largest service export, accounting for over 25% of the total. Other major categories of exported services include higher education (foreign students studying in the United States), and the rapidly growing export of American financial services such as banking, insurance, and investment services. The U.S. industries that benefit from sizable exports are shown in the first column of Table 2. As you can see, two of our top exports are services—financial services and higher education.

Although we exported $106 billion more services than we imported in 1997, we imported $203 billion more goods than we exported. As we will discuss at length in the next chapter, the net excess of imports over exports leaves us with a current trade deficit of $97 billion. This figure would be entered as a negative $97 billion when calculating our GDP as we did in Table 1 of chapter 12.

Import-Competing Firms' and Workers' Losses

In Figure 3, the hypothetical importing of raspberries resulted in the sale of domestically grown raspberries falling from 300,000 to 100,000 pints per year, and total revenues for domestic producers falling from $600,000 to $100,000. In the real world, the heavy pressure exerted by some industries on Congress for protection from imports is a good indication of which groups are actually hurt by foreign trade. Pressure from the automobile industry and the United Auto Workers Union resulted in restrictions on automobile imports. The textile, steel, furniture, agriculture, and other import-competing industries plead for more protection. The closing of plants and loss of jobs in these industries have caused hardships.

Who Benefits and Who Is Hurt by Foreign Trade?

EconExplorer

Free trade can be costly to workers and owners in import-competing industries. But these costs are no different from the costs resulting from domestic competition. For example, the once-thriving U.S. railroad industry was devastated by competition from the automobile and trucking industries. And think about how the harness, blacksmith, horse breeding, and stable industries were crushed by the advent of the automobile! The market mechanism allocates resources to their most efficient employment in accordance with costs and consumer demand, whether it is inside or outside the domestic economy.

Mobility of Capital and Labor

If sales of the U.S. textile industry are reduced because of imports, while sales of drills are in-creased because of export demand, capital and labor should move from the textile industry to the drill industry. The difficulty is that these factors of production are not perfect substitutes for one another, and the transfer of some factors from one employment activity to another can cause hardships. Workers in southern textile mills may not want or be able to move to drill factories in the Midwest or they may not have the necessary skills. Fixed capital has even less mobility: textile industry machinery, for example, cannot be used to produce drills. Industrial transition will eventually occur, but it can be a slow, painful process. Accordingly, the U.S. government provides special **trade adjustment assistance** to workers who lose their jobs because of foreign competition.

Domestic Consumers of Export Industries

International trade equalizes the prices of products. Before trade, the price of electric drills was relatively low in the United States and relatively high in the Philippines. With trade, the price of drills tends to rise in the United States because of the increase in the total global demand for drills, and the price falls in the Philippines because imported drills increase their total supply. At the same time, bedspread prices will increase in the Philippines and fall in the United States. Eventually this adjustment process leads to equal prices in both countries, except for transportation costs and import taxes.

free trade international trade that is unrestricted by government protectionist measures.

trade adjustment assistance supplementary unemployment payments to workers who have lost their jobs because of import competition, and assistance to firms in shifting to other types of production.

Comparative Case Application

Flying Carpets and Grounded Computers

Economists are always claiming that there is no such thing as a free lunch, and they make the same claim when it comes to protecting domestic industry. On the surface, it might appear that erecting trade barriers to protect our domestic industries could only help American workers. If we dig a little deeper, however, we'll find that the bill for such a lunch can be very expensive.

Suppose that the United States has a comparative advantage in producing computers and Turkey has a comparative advantage in producing handwoven carpets. With free trade, the United States specializes in producing computers and ships 1,000 PCs to Turkey in exchange for 4,000 carpets—an exchange ratio of 4 carpets per PC. Now suppose that American carpet makers are losing business because of the competition from the cheaper Turkish carpets, and successfully lobby Congress to restrict the number of imported Turkish carpets to only 2,000 (a quota). By doing so, they argue, we'll be protecting the jobs of American weavers from cheap foreign imports—and they are right!

So far so good, and this lunch seems very appetizing and very free. But let's look at the bill.

If the exchange ratio (the terms of trade) does not change, and there is no reason to think it should, limiting the number of Turkish carpets to 2,000 means that Turkey will only be able to import 500 PCs. Our reduced output of PCs will be felt in the computer industry, where profits and employment will both be lower. Even if other export markets are found today, our computer industry will not grow as fast as it would have without the trade restriction, and there will be a smaller number of job openings for computer engineers, systems analysts, and chip designers.

What then is the price of protecting our domestic carpet industry? The cost of increased employment for carpet weavers is fewer jobs in the computer industry! By limiting the imports in an import-competing industry, we wind up increasing output and employment in one of our relatively inefficient industries while decreasing output and employment in one of our most efficient industries.

When all the costs of this lunch are added up—the lost jobs and income in the computer industry, the lost benefits of not being able to have a Turkish carpet, the resulting higher prices for domestic and imported carpets—it comes to a staggering figure. Estimates of the cost of protecting domestic jobs in various industries range from a few hundred to thousands of dollars per job. Some studies even show that the number of jobs (and potential jobs) lost is 2 to 3 times greater than the number of jobs saved.

and able to make their views known and felt on Capitol Hill. Because the losses in the computer industry are less apparent and because potential computer industry employees are not organized, the computer industry has much less influence on trade restriction legislation.

Economic Reasoning

1. What is the purpose behind import restrictions on Turkish carpets? Who wins?

2. What is the opportunity cost of protecting domestic carpet makers from foreign competition? Who loses?

3. Selecting which industries to protect from foreign competition is a very difficult decision. Who do you think should make it?

The issue of free trade versus protectionism is a controversial one. Free trade proponents argue that by allowing items such as Turkish carpets to be imported into the United States, U.S. exports will be boosted because Turkey will have the ability to buy U.S. products.

How does such a thing happen? Aren't members of Congress and the Senate aware of what is happening? Yes and no. They may be aware of the overall impact of a carpet quota, but the job gains in the carpet industry are much more apparent to them and the public than the losses and potential losses in the computer industry. Carpet manufacturers and textile worker unions are organized

Flying Carpets and Grounded Computers

Visit the U.S. Trade and Tariff Web site at http://205.197.120.17/scripts/tariff.asp and type in the word "carpets" in the search box. How many types of carpets are listed as being subject to import tariffs? Select one category and find the ad valorem (percent of value) duty for countries with most-favored-nation (MFN) status and those without it.

▶ How Do We Restrict Foreign Trade?

International trade would be larger than it is if it were not for the restrictions countries put on it. These restrictions take various forms.

◥ Tariffs

Tariffs are a tax on imports either on the value of the imports or on the per unit of quantity imported. Tariffs could be used for revenue purposes, but in recent times their principal purpose has been to shelter domestic firms from foreign competition. U.S. tariffs have historically been imposed on selective goods and at one time were relatively high.

The economic effect of a tariff is shown in Figure 6, which replicates Figure 3 but adds a

---

tariff a tax placed on an imported good; also, the whole schedule of a country's import duties.

---

tariff on raspberries equal to 50 cents per pint. Now the equilibrium price for raspberries rises to $1.50 per pint, and the equilibrium quantity demanded falls from 500,000 pints per year to 400,000. The higher price induces an expansion of domestic production from 100,000 to 200,000 pints. The difference between total purchases and domestic production is made up by imports, which fall from 400,000 to 200,000 pints. Domestic revenues will increase from $100,000 to $300,000 ($1.50 × 200,000). The government also gains tariff revenue equal to $100,000—50 cents per pint times 200,000 imported pints. This is shown by the shaded rectangle in the figure.

The gains to producers and the government are offset by the losses to domestic consumers. Instead of eating 500,000 pints of berries at only $1.00 per pint, they must now be content with only 400,000 pints at $1.50 per pint. Expenditures by raspberry lovers will

---

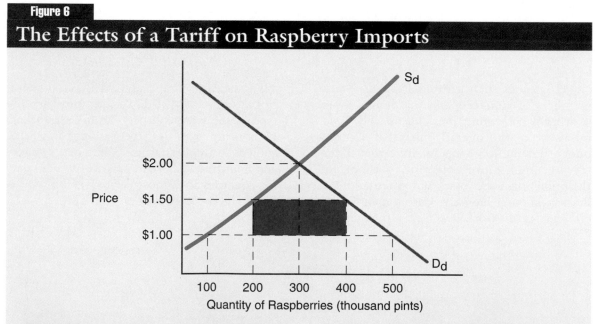

Figure 6

The Effects of a Tariff on Raspberry Imports

The imposition of a 50¢ tariff on raspberry imports raises the price from $1.00 to $1.50 per pint. At the higher price, domestic production increases from 100,000 to 200,000 pints, but the total quantity demanded falls to 400,000 pints. The shaded area shows the government's tariff revenues of $100,000—50¢ per pint times 200,000 pints of imported raspberries.

increase from $500,000 to $600,000—they will be paying $100,000 more for 100,000 fewer pints of raspberries! Consumers unwilling or unable to pay the higher price will be forced to switch to a less satisfactory substitute, perhaps blackberries. If producers could eliminate all foreign competition, consumers would wind up paying the same $600,000 ($2.00 × 300,000) for only 300,000 pints of raspberries! Although the analysis is too complicated to be shown here, economists agree that the total losses to consumers are greater than the gains to producers and the government.

Empowered by the Reciprocal Trade Agreement Act of 1934 and its extensions, U.S. presidents have steadily reduced tariffs through **bilateral trade negotiations.** These negotiated reductions depended upon the willingness of other countries to lower tariffs imposed on U.S. exports. Because bilateral negotiations can create confusing multiple tariff rates for different nations, **most-favored-nation (MFN) clauses** in trade agreements extend the benefits of tariff reductions negotiated with one country to all other countries that accord the United States similar treatment. Most countries with which the United States trades have MFN status, therefore it is now more commonly known simply as "normal trade status." Because of copyright and patent infringement, and perceived human rights abuses, extending the benefits of most-favored-nation treatment to some countries, notably China, has been a politically charged issue. Unlike other countries, China's MFN status is subject to annual review and approval by Congress.

How Do We Restrict Foreign Trade?

EconExplorer

The original 1947 General Agreement on Tariffs and Trade provided for nondiscrimination among the cooperating nations. It set a pattern for **multilateral trade negotiations** as a substitute for bilateral trade negotiations. When all of the participating countries negotiate simultaneously, the possibilities for making deals for tariff reductions are greatly expanded. Through a succession of GATT agreements, tariffs have been markedly reduced. Although some significant exceptions exist, trade between the United States and the rest of the world is much freer today than ever before.

Quotas

Restrictions on the quantity of a good that may be imported or exported during a given time period are called **quotas.** They are established either in physical terms—a set number of tons of a commodity, for example—or in value terms—a set number of dollars' worth of a commodity. Quotas may be directed toward one or a number of specific countries, or they can be established without regard to the country of origin. The quota may be stated in absolute terms; that is, a fixed quantity or value of a commodity may be allowed to enter a

Appealing to pride in domestic manufacture has become an important sales strategy for firms in import-competing industries.

bilateral trade negotiations trade negotiations between two countries only.

most-favored-nation clause (MFN) a provision in trade agreements that extends lower tariff concessions granted to one country to all other countries that are accorded most-favored-nation treatment.

multilateral trade negotiations simultaneous trade negotiations among a number of countries.

quota a limit on the quantity or value of a good that can be imported in a given time period.

country. Alternatively, the quota may be stated as a tariff quota, which allows a given quantity or value of commodity to enter a country duty free or at a low tariff, with larger quantities or values entering at a higher rate of duty.

Quotas have been largely responsible for limiting Japanese auto penetration in European markets. France has restricted Japanese cars to 3% of total sales, and tough quotas in Italy and Spain have held Japan's share of their markets to less than 1%. The main difference in the effect of a tariff and a quota—at least an absolute quota—is that the tariff still allows the price system in the importing country to allocate goods and resources. Quotas, on the other hand, set an absolute limit and, no matter how high the domestic price is above the price abroad, no more can be imported. The Uruguay Round of GATT succeeded in further reducing the use of quotas as a protectionist device.

The photo shows the U.S. Customs House Tower in Boston. Custom duties (import tariffs) are one of the ways that domestic producers are protected from foreign competition.

◢ Nontariff Barriers

Besides tariffs and quotas, there are a number of other ways of restricting imports. These are termed **nontariff barriers.** If industries lobbying for protection are unable to get high tariffs or import quotas imposed, they still have other weapons. For example, a requirement may be imposed that all goods that have foreign components must have labels affixed. This labeling can serve to encourage nationalistic sentiments. In addition, labeling adds to the costs of the foreign producer. Some industries are even more creative. In Germany, for instance, the old definition of beer required that it be made with German water. Processed foods imported into Japan must show the date of production instead of the ex-

piration date, thus making them appear older and less appetizing.

An informal type of barrier to foreign imports is to make the clearing of foreign goods through customs difficult and slow, and therefore expensive. Imported goods can be subjected to a series of tests and inspections for reasons of safety, health, and general public welfare. These nontariff barriers, when applied and enforced, can be very effective in discouraging imports.

◢ Export Embargoes

Export embargoes are prohibitions on the export of commodities, capital, or technology. They are sometimes imposed for political reasons, such as the 1980 embargo on exports of U.S. grain to the Soviet Union because of the Soviet invasion of Afghanistan, the 1990 embargo on Iraq arising from Iraq's invasion of Kuwait, and the current embargo on Cuba to force a restoration of democratic government.

Export embargoes might instead be used to prevent other countries from having access to valuable new technologies. They could also be imposed to block the outflow of important raw materials and thus keep down their prices to domestic producers.

nontariff barriers restrictions on imports resulting from requirements for special marking, test, or standards enforced on imported goods or the time delays in clearing them for importation.

export embargo a prohibition of the export of a commodity, capital, or technology.

Comparative Case Application

Protection, Japanese-Style

American producers regularly complain that the Japanese market is particularly tough to crack. Public officials in the United States insist that the enormous trade deficit with Japan—$26 billion in the first four months of 1998—must be reduced.

The Japanese, for their part, claim that they have greatly reduced their tariffs in recent years; the average tariff level of Japan is in fact below that of the United States. If Japanese tariffs are not especially high, why is it so difficult for U.S. businesses to penetrate the Japanese market?

One area in which Japan does have stiff import restrictions is on agricultural products. Quotas on imports of meat and fruit create large price differences between the Japanese market and the American market—$20 a pound for steak and $35 for melons in Tokyo, for example. Overall, food is three times more expensive and clothes two times more expensive than in the United States.

The main obstacles to selling more American products in Japan, however, are not formal trade barriers; one of them is Japanese government red tape. For instance, documentation and testing of American cars sold in Japan add as much as $500 to the price of each car. Testing for the safety of U.S. health care products is required in Japan, even if similar tests have already been performed for the same products marketed in the United States.

To protect the way of life of small retailers, the Japanese also have "big store laws" that make it very difficult to build large department stores. Not only does this keep prices high because of the inability to take advantage of the great economies of scale in

America's love affair with the automobile is becoming a lasting romance with imported Japanese cars.

high-volume retailing, but it also imposes difficulties on foreign manufacturers of consumer goods. Sony and Canon can sell thousands of televisions and cameras in the United States through one or two massive sales agreements with Wal-Mart or Sears. Foreign producers cannot do this in Japan because they need to reach agreements with thousands of independent retailers.

Still another problem for foreigners in penetrating the Japanese market is the existence of tightly linked organizations of Japanese firms—the *keiretzu*—that produce a final product and most of the intermediate products needed to produce it. The biggest *keiretzu* are those that produce motor vehicles (for example, Toyota, Honda, and Nissan) and consumer electronics (for example, Sony, Hitachi, and Sanyo). Member firms of an automobile *keiretzu* produce steel, glass, tires, paint, and upholstery. The *keiretzu* will include a bank to provide financing and a shipping company to carry the cars overseas. Foreign suppliers of intermediate products have no chance of selling them to the tightly integrated Japanese firms. Even the smaller Japanese producers are frozen out of their own domestic markets in this way. As a result, some of them are now entering into joint production and marketing arrangements with American and other foreign firms—taking advantage of trade liberalization pressures on the Japanese government—in order to gain an entry into their *own country's* markets!

Other Japanese policies are directly focused on helping their industries at the expense of their consumers. For example, the *shaken* (pronounced "shah-khan") system is a policy designed to impose extremely tough automobile inspections on all cars in Japan. Once a car becomes 5 or 6 years old, it can cost a car owner hundreds of dollars to pass the annual safety inspection. While it does lead to marginally safer cars on Japan's roads, it also provides an incentive for car owners to buy new cars more frequently, thus helping the Japanese auto industry.

All these policies and practices contradict the notion that the purpose of trade is to enhance consumer well-being. This is because while an improved standard of living is the accepted basis for free trade in the United States, it is not so in all countries. In Japan (and South Korea), for example, people believe that the purpose of trade is to improve the nation's economic strength and its share of world markets. Consumption and consumer well-being do not have the importance that they do in the United States. Increased consumption also subtracts from saving, and saving is necessary to finance the capital investment necessary for industrial growth. (This is another reason for our trade deficit with Japan: Americans like to spend and Japanese like to save. As a result they put money into U.S. bonds and stocks and we use the money to buy Japanese imports.)

From the Japanese perspective, the world does not remember the great consumers, it remembers the great producers. Japanese trade policies reflect their ideology. Consumers may suffer in terms of higher prices and less consumption, but this is consistent with their national economic goals. American businesses complain that Japanese policies make for an "uneven playing field." The Japanese response is that theirs is simply a policy decision designed to strengthen domestic industries at the expense of their consumers.

Economic Reasoning

1. What types of nontariff barriers, other than quotas, restrict imports into Japan? Can you think of any similar barriers that restrict imports into the United States?
2. Would U.S. farmers and ranchers be able to export more to Japan if the Japanese applied tariffs rather than quotas to imports of agricultural products? What are the assumptions underlying your answer?
3. Do you think that the United States should adopt Japanese-style policies that are designed to promote production at the expense of consumers' well-being? Could the average American household do with fewer consumer goods?

Protection, Japanese-Style

The data in the table below were found at the U.S. Bureau of the Census Web site at http://www.census.gov/foreign-trade/www/javabal.html. Visit the site and update the table. (Given what you know about NAFTA, do you think that trade barriers are the only cause of trade deficits?)

Table 3	The Top Ten Countries with Which the United States Has a Trade Deficit	
Country	**May 1998 Deficit US$ Millions**	**Year To Date (1998) Deficit US$ Millions**
Japan	–4,952.75	–25,768.47
China	–4,633.98	–20,412.24
Federal Republic of Germany	–1,842.01	–9,043.37
Mexico	–1,523.40	–5,534.05
Canada	–1,457.99	–7,006.26
Taiwan	–1,150.35	–5,175.96
Italy	–955.71	–4,583.49
Malaysia	–667.25	–2,889.90
Thailand	–612.86	–2,888.62
Korea, Republic of	–608.76	–3,233.08

▶ Should Foreign Trade Be Restricted?

As can be seen in Figure 7 the level of protectionist sentiment in this country has fluctuated widely, though over the years **protectionism** has generally been high. Since the GATT agreement in 1947, trade barriers have been greatly reduced. But the fierce opposition to NAFTA showed that protectionism is still alive and well in the United States. Why does the protectionist movement keep reappearing? This analysis section examines some of the arguments over free trade versus protectionism.

Traditional Protectionist Arguments

The most common justification given for protectionism is that it is supposed to increase domestic employment by protecting the U.S. worker from the unfair competition of cheap foreign labor. But as we explain in the case application, Flying Carpets and Grounded Computers, the cost of this increased employment is greater un-

employment in our exporting industries. Trade is based on comparative, not absolute, advantage. Low foreign wages do not necessarily create comparative advantage for those countries.

The wage issue, in essence, ignores the productivity of workers. Wages of American workers are high because of their high productivity. The low wages of foreign workers are due to their low productivity. When their productivity increases, so do their wages. Imports, as a result of specialization according to comparative advantage, increase the living standard of American workers.

Furthermore, competition from foreign producers increases productivity in an industry. A

---

protectionism measures taken by the government in order to limit or exclude imports that compete with domestic production.

Figure 7

U.S. Tariff History

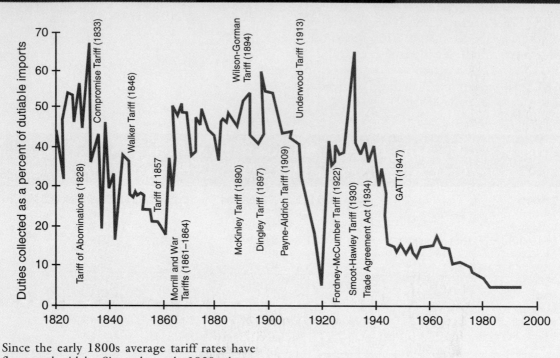

Since the early 1800s average tariff rates have fluctuated widely. Since the early 1930s, however, the trend has been downward.

1993 study by William Lewis of McKinsey & Company and others examined productivity in nine manufacturing industries in Japan, Germany, and the United States. They examined the reasons for productivity differences in each of the industries among the three countries. They concluded that it was not differences in capital equipment, labor education, or managerial techniques that accounted most for differing productivity, but the degree of foreign and domestic competition in the industry. In Japan, the auto, auto parts, consumer electronics, metal working, and steel industries—all of which are subjected to vigorous foreign and domestic competition—have high productivity rates. In the processed foods, soap and detergent, and beer industries, on the other hand—which are sheltered in Japan—the U.S. firms have productivity rates as much as 70% higher than the Japanese firms.

A second argument for protectionism is that imports represent a leakage of spending from the economic system and that a reduction in spending for imports would increase domestic aggregate demand. This argument is true as far as it goes, but one country's imports are another's exports. If we reduce our imports, foreign countries will not be able to afford to buy our exports. The imposition of tariffs also generally causes retaliation, further reducing employment in U.S. export industries as much or more than the increased employment in import-competing industries (again, see the case application, Flying Carpets and Grounded Computers).

One situation in which protection can be justified for a period of time is where a *new industry* could be efficient and competitive if it had a chance to mature and achieve economies of scale. This argument holds that newly established industries need to be protected until they reach levels of production that allow them to be competitive in the world market. The costs of temporary trade restrictions might be worth

Neomercantilists contend that exporting high technology can cause a country to lose its competitive advantage.

paying in order to gain a long-run benefit. This **infant industry argument** may have limited validity for underdeveloped countries, but it generally has little applicability in the United States or other mature economies.

Terms of Trade

The average price of exports relative to the price of imports is called the **terms of trade.** It shows how many units of imports can be purchased with a given amount of exports.

Countries may desire to improve the terms of trade in order to increase their purchasing power in the international marketplace. They want the value of the goods they export to increase relative to the value of the goods they import. They would then be able to buy more imports for the same quantity of exports, thus raising their standard of living.

The terms of trade can be altered either by a reduced price for imports or an increased price of exports. For example, when the Organization of Petroleum Exporting Countries (OPEC) raised the price of oil from $2.50 to $14.00 per barrel in 1974–75, they improved the terms of trade in their favor. Because the demand for oil is inelastic, importing countries could not reduce their purchases very much. Consequently, they needed to exchange increased amounts of drills, wheat, cars, and textiles for each barrel of oil they imported. In contrast, the expanded use of fiber optic cables has reduced the world demand for copper. Less developed countries that rely heavily on copper exports have found that their terms of trade have deteriorated.

Neomercantilist Arguments

The **mercantilists** around the time of Queen Elizabeth I of England believed that the strength of a nation lay in how much gold and other precious metals it held. They believed a country must export more than it imported. For if there is an excess of exports over imports, goods and services will flow out of the country; and in payment, gold will flow into the country. An exception to their export drive was an embargo on the export of machinery. England prohibited the export of textile machinery, or even the plans for constructing it, because that would have enabled France and other rivals to compete with English textiles.

The **neomercantilists** of today are reviving the ideas of the seventeenth-century mercantilists. They argue that, whereas in the past comparative advantage came in large part from the basic resources of a country, comparative advantage for a modern industrialized economy is primarily a function of technology. Thus, a country will retain a comparative advantage only as long as it retains a technological lead over other countries. When technology is being rapidly

infant industry argument the contention that it is economically justified to provide trade protection to a new industry in a country to enable it to grow to a size that would result in production costs that are competitive with those of foreign producers.

terms of trade the ratio of average export prices to average import prices.

mercantilists those who advocated mercantilism, a doctrine that dominated policies in many countries from the sixteenth to the eighteenth centuries. It held that exports should be maximized and imports minimized to generate an inflow of gold, and that exports of machinery and technology should be prohibited to prevent competition from foreign producers.

neomercantilists contemporary advocates of mercantilist trade policies to restrict imports, maximize exports of consumer products, and restrict exports of capital equipment and technology to prevent competition from foreign producers.

exported, as it is now, a domestic industry has less time to capitalize on any comparative advantage that it might have due to superior technology. If the industry loses this comparative advantage, it is faced with resource dislocation and the accompanying structural unemployment.

No one can deny that technology is more mobile today than it has ever been. A country can lose its comparative advantage if it does not remain technologically superior. A major strength of the U.S. economy has been its ability to generate technology. Many claim that to be its fundamental comparative advantage. The question is should it—or can it—prevent the export of its technology to China and other countries? Or, failing that, should it restrict the importation of the products of that technology?

Protectionist arguments fail to take into account the basic rationale for trade—to raise standards of living by maximizing the efficiency of resource allocation through comparative advantage. Furthermore, the matter of technology transfer is becoming a two-way street as Japan and Western Europe devote more resources to research and development.

Since the nation as a whole benefits from the advantages of foreign competition and new technology, however, it must be prepared to compensate those who are injured in the process. This provides an economic reason for the trade adjustment assistance the United States government gives to workers in industries injured by foreign competition to help capital and labor shift to new products.

The Power of Special Interests

Another important reason that governments restrict trade is to help import-competing firms in exchange for their help in financing election campaigns. Firms have discovered that very often the return on a few thousand dollars "invested" in a politician who can restrict the imports of the firm's foreign competitors is greater than the same dollars invested in new capital.

Import-competing producers are able to convince Congress to impose tariffs because they are usually well organized and are able to communicate their side of the issue to their representatives. Because of the large benefits that producers can receive from the tariff, it is

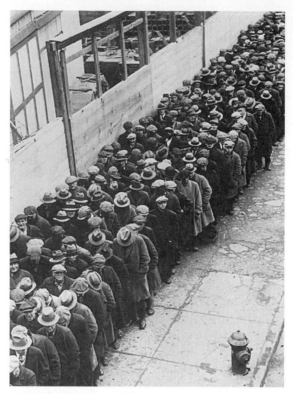

Unemployed men stand in a breadline at the New York Municipal Lodging House during the Depression in 1930. The effects of the Depression were made worse by the strongly protectionist Smoot-Hawley Tariff of 1930, the subject of the Perspective on page 439.

in their interest to lobby Congress with both their time and financial support (see the discussion of special interests on page 356). For example, it is estimated that everyone in the United States pays an extra dollar per year for sugar and products that contain sugar because of tariffs on imports from Latin America and the Caribbean. It simply is not worth the effort for each of us to write and lobby our representatives in order to save $1 per year. But $1 times 260 million people means $260 million to the country's few hundred sugar farmers, and it certainly pays them to mount an organized campaign in support of sugar tariffs!

Should Foreign Trade Be Restricted?

EconExplorer

Case Application

Bastiat's Petition

The controversy between protectionists and free traders has remained very much alive, as the current pressure for increased protection from foreign competition shows. The most extreme protectionist position was neatly satirized in the nineteenth century by French economist Frederic Bastiat (1801–1850) in his famous "Petition of the Manufacturers of Candles, Waxlights, Lamps, Candlesticks, Strut Lamps, Snuffers, Extinguishers, and the Producers of Oil, Tallow, Resin, Alcohol, and Generally Everything Connected with Lighting," which was addressed to the French parliament.

Gentlemen:
We are suffering from the intolerable competition of a foreign rival, placed, it would seem, in a condition so far superior to our own for the production of light, that he absolutely *inundates* our *national market* with it at a price fabulously reduced. . . . This rival . . . is no other than the sun.

What we pray for is . . . a law ordering the shutting up of all windows, skylights . . . in a word of all openings, holes, chinks, and fissures. . . . If you shut up as much as possible all access to natural light and create a demand for artificial light, which of our French manufacturers will not benefit by it?

Make your choice, but be logical; for as long as you exclude, as you do, iron, corn, foreign fabrics, *in proportion* as their prices approximate to zero, what inconsistency it would be to admit the light of the sun, the price of which is already at zero during the entire day!

Economic Reasoning

1. What type of protectionist argument was Bastiat satirizing?
2. If the French parliament had adopted Bastiat's petition, what effect would this have had on the manufacturers of candles, wax lights, lamps, and candlesticks? What would have been the effect on the French economy?
3. Do you think that the U.S. industries that are suffering from import competition should be accorded protection? Why or why not? Is there a difference between the argument for restricting the imports of textiles, steel, or Japanese automobiles and Bastiat's petition to restrict the competition from the sun?

▶ Putting It Together

Specialization according to absolute or comparative advantage means that resources are employed efficiently and total world output increases. Specialization may be complete, especially in smaller countries with a limited variety of resources. But most often specialization is *limited*. Countries both produce and import a specific item. The reason they do not produce enough for their needs, even though they are capable of producing the item, is because of *increasing costs*. Increasing the output of the industry would raise costs due to a limited supply of factor inputs. It is resource availability and technology that determine the nature and extent of specialization.

Consumers are the greatest beneficiaries of foreign trade. Because goods are made where they can be produced most inexpensively, consumers' real purchasing power is maximized. Production firms that use imported machinery, raw materials, and components are also beneficiaries of trade. Export industries and their workers also benefit. Firms that must compete with imports sustain losses. These losses are more lasting and severe when the mobility of capital and labor between different industries is limited. Domestic consumers of the products of export industries will also suffer to the extent that the export demand raises the prices of the products.

Tariffs and *quotas* are methods of restricting imports. *Nontariff barriers,* such as regulations on labeling, packaging, and testing, also restrict imports. On rare occasions, exports may be taxed or prohibited *(export embargoes)* when the authorities believe that it is in the best interest of the country to do so.

In order to reduce trade barriers, nations negotiate mutual concessions in *bilateral* or *multilateral trade negotiations*. When a nation grants a tariff reduction or other trade concession on imports of a good from one country through these negotiations, it automatically extends the concession to all other countries to which it extends *most-favored-nation* treatment.

Among the older *protectionist* arguments is the "cheap foreign labor" argument, which maintains that the wages of American workers

are held down by competition from low-wage workers abroad, notwithstanding that the foreign wages are low because the foreign labor is not very productive. Other current justifications for protection, such as to stimulate domestic employment or improve the terms of trade, usually ignore the cost to exporting firms or the likelihood of retaliation.

The only protectionist argument that has received limited approval by most economists is the *infant industry* argument. This argument holds that a country that has the resource endowment for a particular industry to be efficient can justifiably protect that industry from foreign competition during the industry's early growth period. The assumption is that import restrictions will be removed when the industry matures. This argument may have validity for underdeveloped nations but generally has little application to developed economies.

Neomercantilist arguments for restricting exports of American capital and technology contradict the principle of comparative advantage. Because firms in import-competing industries are often organized and have a lot to gain from import restrictions, they are likely to lobby Congress to help their cause. On the other hand, consumers who only spend a dollar or two more per year because of import restrictions are less likely to be aware of or involved in tariff issues.

$ Perspective $

Smoot-Hawley Revisited

For additional information on Smoot-Hawley and U.S. tariff history, see John M. Dobson, *Two Centuries of Tariffs* (Washington, D.C.: United States Trade Commission, 1976); David A. Lake, *Power, Protection, and Free Trade* (Ithaca, NY: Cornell University Press, 1988); Stefanie Ann Lenway, *The Politics of U.S. International Trade* (Boston: Pitman, 1985); and F. W. Taussig, *The Tariff History of the United States* (New York: Augustus M. Kelley, 1967).

In 1930 a thousand members of the American Economics Association begged Congress to defeat the Smoot-Hawley Tariff Bill. However, their petitions fell on deaf ears. Unemployment was rising, and Congress reasoned that if workers were displaced because of cheap foreign imports, then why not curtail the imports and protect the United States worker? It proceeded to enact the most restrictive set of import duties ever adopted in the United States.

Passage of this legislation turned some economists' worst fears into reality. It set in motion massive, worldwide trade restrictions. The powerful and not-so-powerful nations of the world responded to the Smoot-Hawley Tariff of 1930 out of self-protection and self-interest. They did not have enough dollars or gold to continue to pay for U.S. goods if the United States bought less from them. And they reasoned that if it was advantageous for the United States to protect its industries from foreign competition, then it was equally advantageous for them to protect their industries from American competition. The result was a marked reduction in world trade—a reduction that left the export industries of most countries in shambles. Incomes fell. Unemployment grew. The intensity of the Great Depression increased.

The loss of export markets was especially hard on farmers. The farm economy had been in a depression since the mid-1920s, years before the crash hit industry and commerce. Exports were an outlet for excess American farm production prior to Smoot-Hawley.

The irony of Smoot-Hawley was that all during the preceding decade the United States had an excess of exports over imports. In 1928 the export surplus was over $1 billion, more than $9 billion in today's dollars. During the years leading up to Smoot-Hawley, the United States on balance gained, not lost, jobs from foreign trade.

Raising the barriers against the import of goods from abroad made it impossible for other countries to pay their accumulated debts to American banks and other lenders. The consequent defaults added more pressure on the crumbling U.S. financial structure.

Once the international trading system was virtually destroyed by the protectionist policies of the early 1930s, it was slow to recover. The lessons learned as a result of Smoot-Hawley and its aftermath conditioned the international approach to trade following World War II. Led by the United States, the Western countries adopted GATT and other agreements intended to liberalize trade and avoid in the future the havoc that followed Smoot-Hawley.

For Further Study and Analysis

Study Questions

1. If the United States has an absolute advantage in the production of rubber boots, does it necessarily follow that it will also have a comparative advantage in producing rubber boots? Explain.

2. How could a country have a comparative advantage in the production of a certain quantity of a good but a comparative disadvantage in producing larger quantities of that same good?

3. If all countries followed their comparative advantage and world output increased, who would get this increased output?

4. Explain how free trade causes the prices of exported products to increase in the country in which they are produced.

5. Some people benefit from an increase in foreign trade while others lose. Despite the fact that the total benefits exceed the total losses, we still impose restrictions and tariffs on many imports. Why?

6. Explain how trade barriers imposed to protect import-competing industries can result in reduced output and employment in export industries.

7. Many people believe that the United States needs to use tariffs or quotas to protect our workers from "cheap foreign labor." Why is this a fallacious argument?

8. Which parts of the U.S. economy are harmed by import restrictions?

9. Why is foreign trade such a big part of Holland's economy and such a small part of the U.S. economy?

10. How does the economic philosophy of Japan and South Korea differ from that of the United States? How do the results of their economic policies reflect this philosophy?

Exercises in Analysis

1. Locate five imported items in stores in your area. List the items, where they were produced, what materials were used in their manufacture, and whether competing products manufactured in the United States were also available. For those items in which foreign-made and U.S. goods competed, compare the prices. If the prices differed, explain why. If the prices were identical or nearly the same, explain why.

2. Write a short paper on the impact of foreign trade on your area. Include such information as: what local businesses export all or part of their production; what local businesses are in direct competition with imported products; what local businesses use imported raw materials; and whether any local businesses provide tourist services to foreigners. You can find a list of imports into your town or a nearby port at http://govinfo.kerr.orst.edu/cgi-bin/imp-all-country. You can find a list of exports at http://govinfo.kerr.orst.edu/cgi-bin/exp-all-country.

3. In the *Readers' Guide to Periodical Literature* in the library, or another source, find a recent article on the results of NAFTA. Write a short paper summarizing the article and explaining who has benefited and who has lost.

4. Write a brief paper arguing for or against increased protection for U.S. industries.

Further Reading

Anderson, Terry L., ed. *NAFTA and the Environment*. San Francisco: Pacific Research Institute for Public Policy, 1993. Evaluates the environmental impacts stemming from the agreement and its effect on trade and resources.

Batra, Ravi. *The Myth of Free Trade: A Plan for America's Economic Revival*. New York: C. Scribner's Sons, 1993. Batra takes a contrarian view of the effects of free trade on the U.S. economy. In his opinion, "Few realize that the cause of America's unprecedented economic debacle is the policy of free trade." He advocates an increase in average tariffs from 5% to 40%.

Bhagwati, Jagdish N. *Political Economy and International Economics.* Cambridge, MA: MIT Press, 1991. Written by perhaps the most prolific economist in the field of international economics, this book covers the theory and policy of free trade versus protectionism.

European Union. "Market Access Database." http://mkaccdb.eu.int/. The Sectoral and Trade Barriers Database at this Web site contains exhaustive up-to-date reports and foreign trade data for a large group of countries.

Friman, H. Richard. *Patchwork Protectionism: Textile Trade Policy in the United States, Japan, and West Germany.* Ithaca, New York: Cornell University Press, 1990. A case study of the use of government trade policies in three countries to shelter and promote a particular industry.

Jackson, Tim. *Japan, America, and the New European Market.* Boston: Houghton Mifflin, 1993. Focuses on the success of Japanese industrial/trade policy. Contrasts the pitfalls of European industrial policy.

Khosrow, Fatemi, ed. *North American Free Trade Agreement: Opportunities and Challenges.* New York: St. Martin's Press, 1993. Evaluates the prospective consequences of NAFTA, depending on how commercial policies are implemented.

Lawrence, Robert Z., and Charles L. Schultze, eds. *An American Trade Strategy: Options for the 1990s.* Washington, DC: Brookings Institution, 1990. The arguments for free trade versus protectionism in contemporary U.S. trade policy are examined in this scholarly work.

Leuenberger, Theodor, and Martin E. Weinstein, eds. *Europe, Japan, and America in the 1990s: Cooperation and Competition.* New York: Springer-Verlag, 1992. A look at economic relations among the three centers of world economic power, viewed from a number of different perspectives.

Lincoln, Edward J. *Japan's Unequal Trade.* Washington, DC: Brookings Institution, 1990. How Japan maintains a favorable trade balance with the United States through a variety of nontariff barriers to trade.

Low, Patrick. *Trading Free: The GATT and U.S. Trade Policy.* New York: Twentieth Century Fund Press, 1993. An examination of the trade policy disputes in the Uruguay Round and the goals of U.S. commercial policy.

Saborio, Sylvia, ed. *The Premise and the Promise: Free Trade in the Americas.* New Brunswick, NJ: Transaction Publishers, 1992. How the liberalizing of trade measures in an American trading bloc will affect the economies of Latin America and United States.

Thurow, Lester C. *Head to Head: The Coming Economic Battle among Japan, Europe, and America.* New York: William Morrow, 1992. One of the best-known contemporary economists examines the changing nature of international economic relations and how the nation should respond.

U.S. National Commission for Employment Policy. *The Employment Effects of the North American Free Trade Agreement: Recommendations and Background Studies.* Washington, DC: National Commission for Employment Policy, 1992. These studies concern the impacts of North American economic integration on jobs.

University of Michigan Documents Center. *"Statistical Resources on the Web: Foreign and International Economics."* http://www.lib.umich.edu/libhome/Documents.center/stecfor.html. This site provides many sources of data and reports about the foreign trade of the United States and most other countries in the world. It can also be accessed by going to their comprehensive data center at http://www.lib.umich.edu/libhome/Documents.center/stecon.html and clicking on Foreign Trade.

Yoffie, David B., ed. *Beyond Free Trade: Firms, Governments, and Global Competition.* Boston, MA: Harvard Business School Press, 1993. This study finds that patterns of international trade result from five factors: traditional production advantages in an industry, the international structure of the industry, specific characteristics of multinational firms, government policy, and the inertia of history.

chapter sixteen

International Finance and the National Economy

International transactions impact the domestic economy in a variety of ways. The effects can be positive or negative—or both, depending on your viewpoint. The following article takes a satirical look at the contradictions posed by international transactions, with the help of Lewis Carroll's familiar characters.

Alice in the Wonderland of International Finance

According to the *Economist*, a British journal of political economy, there are only some 600 people in the world who really understand how the international monetary system works. The editors of the *Economist* believe that it is unfortunate that the rest of us don't take more interest in the subject because it "affects everybody's everyday lives. What happens to exchange rates, trade, interest rates, and debt translates into jobs, the safety of a nest egg, the cost of a foreign holiday. For millions, it can mean the difference between tolerable and intolerable poverty" (*Economist*, October 5, 1985, p. 5).

What the magazine does not reveal is that, in addition to the 600 academic economists, government officials, and commercial moneymen, there is another "expert" on the workings of the international monetary system—a little girl by the name of Alice who learned the secrets of international finance while on a visit to Wonderland, one of the few places where it is understood.

The subject first came to Alice's attention when the Queen of Hearts announced that her land would make war on the Land of the Rising Sun. The reason for the war, it seemed, was that the Land of the Rising Sun was sending them too many things.

"Are these things it is sending you things that you don't want?" asked Alice.

"Don't ask impudent questions, little girl," said the Queen.

The helpful White Rabbit pulled on Alice's sleeve and whispered in her ear, "Oh, no, we like the things they send us very much. They are better than the things we have here, but they are sending too many things and won't take enough from us in return."

Alice thought this a peculiar reason for starting a war, but before she could ask any more questions, the Dormouse came running up, all out of breath, exclaiming, "The dollar is sinking. The dollar is sinking."

Upon hearing this news, some of those in attendance cheered and others moaned. The March Hare scampered off to see his broker.

"Why is the dollar sinking?" inquired Alice.

"Don't ask stupid questions," said the Queen. "The dollar is sinking because of the floating exchange rate system."

"Oh, dear," said Alice, "I hope no one is hurt when the dollar sinks."

"Lots of people will be hurt," replied the King, gleefully. "The importers will get killed. So much the worse for them. Consumers will have to pay more for all of those things from the Land of the Rising Sun and won't be able to afford them. So much the worse for them. Producers will have to pay more for imported raw materials and will have to raise their selling prices. So much the worse for them."

"But that is terrible," Alice said. "What caused the dollar to sink? Can't we rescue it?"

"Get that ninny of a girl out of my sight," screamed the Queen, "or I'll have her head."

The White Rabbit took Alice aside where he could explain to her the facts of international exchange rate policy. "We purposely caused the dollar to sink so that we would have to pay more for the things we get from the Land of the Rising Sun and other lands," he said. "The other lands will, of course, pay less for what we send them. They weren't very happy about it, but we threatened them with a trade war if they didn't go along. So the finance ministers of the other six lands in the Group of Seven agreed to cooperate with us in sinking the dollar."

"How do you sink the dollar?" asked Alice.

"The Queen was right. You are a ninny," said the Rabbit. "You sink the dollar by floating more of them. The more dollars you float, the lower the dollar sinks."

"This all gets curiouser and curiouser," thought Alice. "Everything in the World of International Finance seems to be upside-down."

Just then she heard a commotion and went to see what caused it. There was the Queen, purple with rage, shouting, "Cut off their heads! Cut off their heads!"

"Oh, my, whose head does she want to cut off now?" asked Alice.

"She has proof that the foreign exporters of hats are being subsidized by their governments to sell us hats below their costs of production," responded the Gryphon. "It has made the Queen furious and the Mad Hatter even madder."

"But if they are selling us hats below the costs of producing them, aren't they giving us something for nothing?" puzzled Alice. "Shouldn't we thank them instead of cutting off their heads?"

"You might at first think so," replied the Gryphon, "but if we took their low-priced hats, what would the Mad Hatter do?"

"Couldn't he make something else that no one wants to give us?" asked Alice.

The Gryphon, normally quite polite, looked at her with visible disdain. "But then he wouldn't be the Mad Hatter anymore, would he?"

"Oh, my," sighed Alice. "I don't think that I will ever understand international finance. The more you have to pay for something, the better. If people outside your land want to give you something, they should have their heads cut off. If they send you too much of what you want, you declare war on them. If your currency floats too high, you try to sink it. It seems to me that in the World of International Finance nothing is the way it's supposed to be."

At this, she heard a chuckle. Turning in the direction from which it came, Alice saw the Cheshire cat grinning at her from the bough of a tree. "When you understand that, you understand everything there is to know about international finance," said the cat. Having pronounced that bit of wisdom, the cat grinned even wider and gradually began to disappear, from its tail forward, until all that was left behind was its smile.

Chapter Preview

The Cheshire cat was smiling at the contradictions in our attitudes and policies with regard to international trade and finance. These contradictions are partly inherent in the problems posed by the foreign sector of the economy. But they are also in part the result of a lack of understanding of how the international financial system works and how it impacts the national economy. This chapter will make it more understandable by answering the following questions: How do we pay for imports? What happens when exports and imports do not balance? What is the relationship between international finance and the domestic economy?

Learning Objectives

After completing this chapter, you should be able to:

1. Explain how payments are made for imports.
2. Distinguish among fixed, freely floating, and pegged exchange rates and explain how the rate of exchange is determined under each system.
3. Differentiate among currency depreciation, appreciation, devaluation, and revaluation.
4. Define exchange rate risk and understand how it can lead to smaller or larger returns on foreign investments.
5. Define the balance of payments and distinguish among the different accounts in the balance of payments.
6. Understand how the basic deficit is determined and the role that foreign currency reserves play in balancing the balance of payments.
7. Explain how freely floating exchange rates cause currencies to appreciate to eliminate basic surpluses and depreciate to eliminate basic deficits.
8. Understand the concept of national economic equilibrium in an open economy.
9. Understand how an import surplus allows an economy to consume more than it produces.
10. Describe the role of foreign investment in compensating for insufficient domestic saving and taxes.

▶ How Do We Pay for Imports?

One answer to the question, How do we pay for imports? is that we pay for imports with exports. But, although bartering is more common in international trade than in domestic trade, most imports are paid for with a medium of exchange—money. The problem is that different kinds of money, or currencies, are used in different countries: dollars in the United States, pounds in the United Kingdom, marks or euros in Germany, and yen in Japan. How can importers pay in their currency and exporters receive payment at the same time in theirs?

◪ Foreign Exchange Market

The conversion of U.S. dollars into foreign currency occurs in the **foreign exchange market.** Here the price of any one money in terms of

---

foreign exchange market a set of institutions, including large banks in the world's financial centers, private brokers, and government central banks and other agencies, that deal in the exchange of one country's money for another's.

Figure 1

Exchange Rates of Selected Foreign Currencies
Values in U.S. Dollars: Selected Years, 1980–1998*

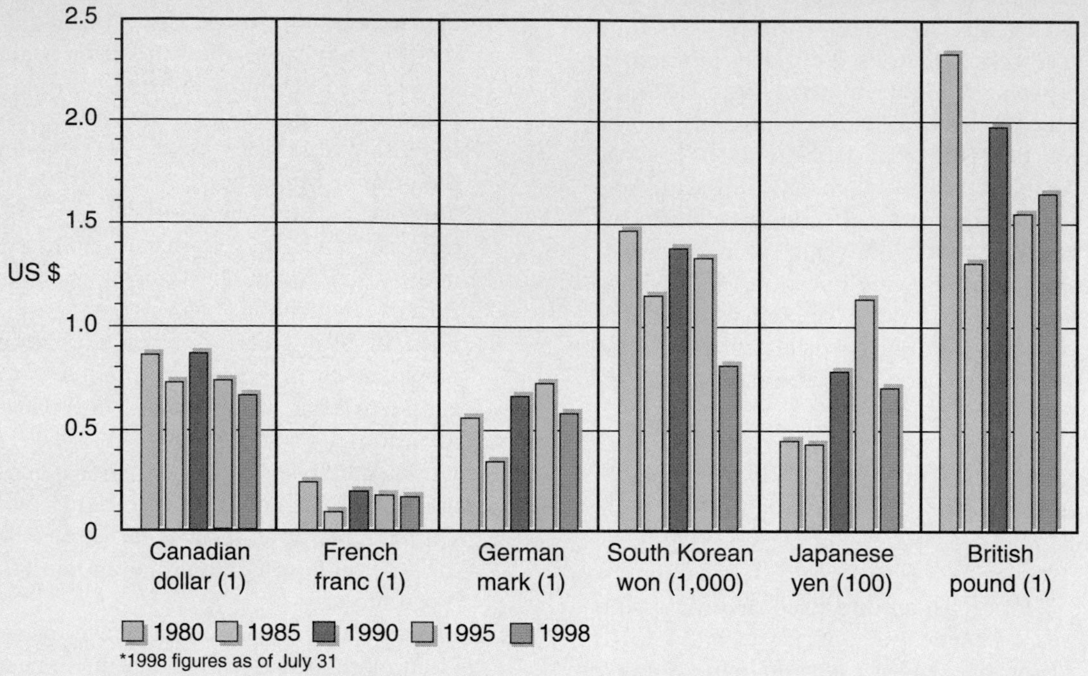

Legend: ☐ 1980 ☐ 1985 ■ 1990 ☐ 1995 ■ 1998
*1998 figures as of July 31

Since the system of fixed exchange rates was abandoned in the early 1970s, currency exchange rates have fluctuated widely. Because the graph shows how many dollars it takes to buy foreign currencies, when the bar gets shorter the dollar is appreciating and when it gets taller the dollar is depreciating.

Source: Board of Governors of the Federal Reserve System, *Federal Reserve Bulletin*.

another is set either by market forces of demand and supply, or by government price-fixing, or by a combination of both. Once the price has been set, a foreign currency can be bought very easily through a bank.

Local banks obtain foreign money from centrally located **correspondent banks** that deal in the foreign exchange market. These are generally the larger banks in principal trading centers such as New York, London, Frankfurt, and Tokyo. Such banks supply their customers

correspondent bank a bank in another city or country that a bank has an arrangement with to provide deposit transfer or other services.

and other banks with foreign money from balances they hold abroad. For example, the Chase Manhattan Bank may have an account with Deutsche Bank in Frankfurt. If an American auto importer needs German marks (or euros) to pay for a shipment of BMWs, the Chase Manhattan Bank will sell the importer some marks in its Frankfurt account. The American importer can use these marks to pay the German exporter. The account balance held in Germany by the Chase bank was created by payments made by Germans for U.S. goods or in settlement of accounts owed to American citizens from other transactions.

◥ Exchange Rates
The price of an imported good is made up of two parts: the price of the good in its home

The exchange rates of currencies on the international market change daily in response to the forces of demand and supply. This newspaper clipping shows one day's values of various currencies in relation to the U.S. dollar.

currency and the price of that currency in the foreign exchange market—the foreign exchange rate. The foreign exchange rate expresses the price of one currency in terms of another (see Figure 1). To find the price of an imported good in dollars, multiply the price of the good in its own currency by the foreign exchange rate. For example, suppose a French sweater costs 120 French francs and the exchange rate is 6 French francs = $1. The price of the sweater in dollars would be 120 French francs × $1/6 French francs = $20. When converting foreign prices to dollars, the dollar value always goes in the numerator of the second part of the formula. When converting dollar prices to a foreign currency price, the dollar value always goes in the denominator. For example, a CD that costs $16 in the United States would cost $16 × 6 French francs/$1 = 96 French francs in France.

Like any price, an exchange rate may vary in the free play of market forces. For example, the British pound was priced at $2.40 in 1970. It declined to $1.30 in 1985, and in July 1998 it was worth approximately $1.64.

Exchange rates were not always allowed to fluctuate with market conditions. From the end of World War II to the early 1970s, the major Western countries maintained a system of **fixed exchange rates.** For the system to work, each country had to accept or supply money at the fixed rate. If a nation ran short of a particular foreign money, it could obtain that currency by trading for it with gold or other foreign currencies it might have in its possession. If it had enough of neither, it could resort to short-term loans from the **International Monetary Fund (IMF)** to maintain the fixed price. But because of chronic imbalances in the demand and supply of various countries' currencies (especially the U.S. dollar), the system of fixed rates was abandoned.

How Do We Pay for Imports?

EconExplorer

Under a fixed exchange rate system, with exchange rates set by the government, a lowering of the exchange rate by government regulation is called a **devaluation.** If the government raises the exchange rate of its currency under a fixed exchange rate system, that is termed **revaluation.**

fixed exchange rates exchange rates between currencies that are legally set by the respective countries.

International Monetary Fund (IMF) an organization established in 1946 to assist in operation of the world monetary system by regulating the exchange practices of countries and providing liquidity to member countries that have payment problems.

devaluation a decrease in the value of a country's currency relative to other currencies due to an official government reduction in the exchange rate under a fixed-rate system.

Although there were internationally agreed upon rules that limited the practice, a country would sometimes want to devalue its currency because this would make its exports cheaper, increase its aggregate demand, and increase domestic employment. Other countries would often retaliate, however, by devaluing their currencies, and the devaluations would cancel each other out.

The opposite of a fixed-rate system is one of **freely fluctuating (flexible) exchange rates** that vary daily in response to demand and supply. With such rates, increased demand for a foreign money results in a rise in its price in terms of domestic currency. Conversely, increased supplies of a particular national currency depress its price. If the supply of a country's currency in the foreign exchange market is greater than the demand for that currency, the currency will depreciate. **Currency depreciation** means that a unit of the country's currency will buy less of other currencies than it did previously. Stated differently, depreciation means that it takes more of a country's currency to buy a unit of another currency. The opposite of depreciation is **currency appreciation,** an increase in the foreign value of a nation's currency. By definition, if Country A's currency appreciates relative to Country B's, then Country B's currency is depreciating relative to Country A's.

revaluation an increase in the value of a country's currency relative to other currencies due to an official government increase in the exchange rate under a fixed-rate system.

freely fluctuating (flexible) exchange rates an exchange-rate system by which the relative values of different currencies are determined by demand and supply rather than by government fiat.

currency depreciation a decline in the value of a country's currency relative to other currencies as a result of an increase in its supply relative to the demand for it.

currency appreciation an increase in the value of a country's currency relative to other currencies as a result of a decrease in its supply relative to the demand for it.

Flexible exchange rates tend to roughly equalize the prices of internationally traded goods. For example, if the price of the French sweater in the previous example increases from 120 French francs to 240 French francs because of French inflation, it would now cost 240 French francs × $1/6 French francs = $40. The sweater will only be competitively priced in the United States if the franc depreciates to 12 French francs = $1: 240 French francs × $1/12 French francs = $20.

The Causes of Fluctuations in Exchange Rates

The value of a country's currency is influenced by the demand for its exports, its interest rates, its political stability, its domestic inflation, and government intervention.

In order to purchase a country's exports, an importer must first purchase that country's currency. All else the same, an increase in the demand for a country's exports will increase the demand for its currency and increase its price. The same holds true if someone wants to buy financial assets in another country. They must first convert their currency into the other country's, and then use that currency to purchase its stocks and bonds. If interest rates and stock returns are higher in one country than in another, investors will increase their demand for that country's currency in order to buy its financial assets. High interest rates are one of the most important reasons that a country's currency will appreciate.

Political instability in the world will also affect exchange rates. If a country is threatened with civil war, invasion, or any other factor that might make its currency worth less, people will exchange their currency for one that will keep its value, like the U.S. dollar, the German mark or the euro, or the Japanese yen. The result is an appreciation in the value of these currencies, and a depreciation of the threatened country's currency.

A common reason for currency depreciation is domestic inflation. If the general level of prices is going up faster in one country than in others, that country will find it difficult to export goods, while at the same time it will be importing more. This results in a surplus of the country's currency on the foreign exchange market, which lowers its exchange rate value. Another way to look at this is to remember that inflation is usually caused by a country increasing its money supply too rapidly (chapter 11). By doing so, it increases its supply relative to the supplies of other currencies, and its value will therefore decrease. If a country decreases its money supply, its currency will become relatively scarce, and its value will increase. This also results in higher interest rates, and, as noted above, this is a major cause of exchange rate swings.

Even under a freely fluctuating exchange rate system, government central banks may attempt to control exchange rate movements within limits or otherwise manipulate the rate. For example, if a country wants to increase the value of its currency, the central bank may use foreign currencies that it owns to buy its own currency on the foreign exchange market. Alternatively, if a country's currency is exchanging at such a high rate that it hurts exports, as was the case with the U.S. dollar in the mid-1980s, the central bank may lower the rate by selling its own currency on the foreign exchange market. As the White Rabbit explained to Alice in the chapter introduction, the added supply floated on the market results in lowering the currency's exchange rate.

Alice isn't the only person who is confused about whether an appreciating ("strong") dollar is better or worse than a depreciating ("weak") dollar. Like many things in economics, it depends on whom you ask. Exporting industries prefer a weaker dollar because it makes their products cheaper to foreigners and enables them to sell more goods overseas. Consumers prefer a strong dollar because it makes imports less expensive and puts downward pressure on the prices of competing domestic products.

◤ Exchange Rate Risk

Fluctuations in currency values increase the uncertainty and risk of international transactions. When a person or business invests their money in a foreign country, they usually earn profits and interest in the local currency. When they are ready to spend their profits or interest at home, or reinvest them in another country, they must exchange the local currency to the one they need. This exposes the investor to **exchange rate risk**—if the local currency has depreciated, they may lose money. Suppose an American buys a one-year 10,000 French franc bond from the French government when the annual interest rate is 10% and the exchange rate is $1 = 5 French francs. The bond costs $2,000 and the expected return is 1,000 French francs, or $200. Now suppose that after one year French inflation results in the franc depreciating (the dollar appreciating) to $1 = 10 French francs. When the investor cashes in her bond, she receives 11,000 French francs in principal and interest. When she converts this back to dollars at the new exchange rate, she only has $1,100—a $900 loss despite her 10% interest! Of course, had the franc appreciated during the year, she would have earned more than a 10% return.

To insure foreign investors against exchange rate risk, the governments of smaller countries will sometimes link the value of their currency to the value of a larger country's currency, usually the U.S. dollar. For example, in the 1980s, Mexico set the exchange rate of its peso at about 3.5 pesos = $1. **Pegging** the value of the peso to the dollar in this manner essentially establishes a fixed exchange rate between the two currencies. As with other fixed exchange rate systems, the Mexican central bank needed to have enough dollars to guarantee that anyone who walked in its doors with 3.5 pesos could exchange them for $1. Pegging the peso to the dollar assured foreign investors that if they invested their money in Mexico and earned pesos, they could always convert them to dollars at a known rate (see case application, Going South).

---

exchange rate risk the chance that an investor in a foreign country may earn more or less than anticipated due to unanticipated changes in exchange rates.

currency peg a fixed exchange rate between two currencies, usually done by smaller countries pegging their currency's value to that of a bigger country.

Comparative Case Application

Good as Gold

In chapter 11 we saw that not everybody loses from inflation. Those who win are those people who hold their wealth in the form of real assets, such as real estate. At one time, people protected themselves from inflation by buying gold, because the price of gold would always go up with inflation. In today's world this strategy doesn't work as well. Gold must be weighed; it does not normally come in perfectly divisible units; and it cannot be put into a savings account to earn interest. In addition, unscrupulous dealers might mix the gold with another metal so that the gold one buys may not be 100% pure or 24-carat.

Turkey is a country that has experienced high levels of inflation for many years. The annual average inflation rate in Turkey from 1980 through 1998 was 61%. If a Turkish price index had a base year in 1980 with a value of 100, it would have equaled 318,634 by the end of 1998. That means that something that cost 1 Turkish lire in 1980 would have been 3,186.34 Turkish lire in December 1998.

Exchange rate theory predicts that inflation will lead to the depreciation of a country's currency. Has this happened in Turkey? Figure 2 shows the annual inflation rate and annual depreciation of the Turkish lire from 1980 through 1998. The lire depreciated an average of 37% a year for each of these years. In 1980, it took 78 Turkish lire to buy US$1. At the end of July 1998, it took 270,700 Turkish lire to buy that dollar. You can see that one line in the figure is almost the mirror image of the other—as one increases the other decreases, and vice versa.

Such inflation is difficult for people, especially if they get paid once a month like most Turks do. If you are paid on the first of the month, by the time the end of the month rolls around prices will have gone up by 5 or 6 percent. But necessity is the mother of invention, and people have learned that one way to deal with the problem is to spend the lire they need to get by for a week or so, and convert the rest into dollars. During the remaining weeks of the month, they convert their dollars back to lire as they need them to buy groceries, go to the movies, and pay their usual bills.

On July 1, 1998, the official exchange rate was about 255,500 Turkish lire = $1, and on July 29 it was 270,700 Turkish lire = $1. By buying dollars on the 1st and selling them back on the 29th, an individual could earn 15,200 Turkish lire, a 5.6% return—enough to keep up with inflation and more than could be earned in a regular savings account.

But like any other service, there is a fee that one must pay to convert money from one currency to another. For example, suppose the "official" international exchange rate is 1.82 German marks = US$1. If you go to a local bank or airport, you will find that they may offer you only 1.75 German marks for your dollar. And, if you show up with marks, they may charge 1.89 German marks for $1. The difference, or the spread, of 0.14 German marks per dollar, is profit for the money-changer. Such a high spread, about 7.7% of the official rate, is not unusual in Western Europe or the United States.

Turkish households would not be able to convert their money from lire to dollars and back to lire if there was a 7.7% fee on each transaction. But because of the large number of people wishing to make such transactions, the Turkish moneychangers—döviz—are able to charge a

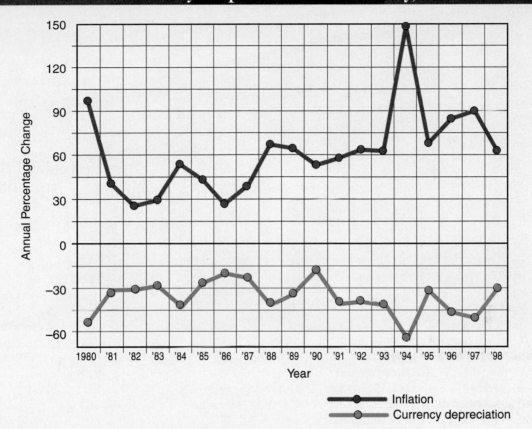

Figure 2

Inflation and Currency Depreciation in Turkey, 1980–1998

The value of a country's currency in foreign exchange markets is inversely related to its domestic rate of inflation.

Source: Turkish Central Bank

very small fee per transaction and make a good profit on the volume of transactions. For example, if the official exchange rate is 270,000 Turkish lire equals $1, the döviz may sell dollars for 270,500 Turkish lire and buy them for 269,500 Turkish lire—a spread of only 0.37%.

There is also the "shoe leather" cost involved with going to the döviz 3 or 4 times a month. Time is money, and if one has to go all the way across town to change money, it makes the transaction less inviting for the public. Luckily for the locals, döviz are as common in most Turkish cities as convenience stores are in the United States.

Although the practice of living with inflation by holding dollars makes sense for the Turkish people, it poses problems for the economy. In the United States, most people keep their money in checking accounts, and banks can use these funds to make loans. In Turkey, the practice of holding dollars instead of bank accounts reduces the amount of money going into new investment.

And how does all this affect the United States? Dollars represent claims against U.S. goods and services. If someone shows up in the United States with a wallet full of these dollars, we owe them whatever goods they choose to buy. But as long as they are being used for other purposes, U.S. prices stay lower and Americans have to send fewer of our goods abroad.

Turkey has an extremely high rate of inflation. For stability, the Turks convert their salaries from Turkish lire into U.S. dollars at a döviz (money changer). In Turkey, the döviz is as familiar as a convenience store is in the United States.

Economic Reasoning

1. How does changing money into dollars protect a Turkish consumer from inflation? Why is the dollar as "good as gold" in Turkey?

2. Suppose the Turkish government pegged the lire to the dollar at the July 1998 exchange rate of 270,000 Turkish lire = $1, but inflation continued at its current pace. If the government forbade the döviz from operating, what do you think the Turkish people would do? Do you think under such circumstances it is morally acceptable for people to buy and sell currency in illegal black markets?

Good as Gold

Check the current value of the German mark, Japanese yen, or some other widely traded currency in a daily newspaper or at http://quote.yahoo.com/ (click on Currency Exchange Rates). Contact a local bank or airport, see what exchange rates you are offered to buy and sell that currency, and calculate the percentage spread. Why do you think it is so much higher than in Turkey? (Hint: how many places did you find with foreign currency for sale and what does this tell you about sales volume and market structure?)

What Happens When Exports and Imports Do Not Balance?

Under a system of freely fluctuating exchange rates, the demand for and supply of that currency in the foreign exchange market determine its price—its exchange rate. If a country's international transactions are out of balance, the exchange rate for the country's currency will be unstable.

Balance of Payments

The accounting record of all international transactions between the residents of one country and the residents of the rest of the world is the country's **balance of payments.** When a country imports something, the cost shows up in its balance of payments. Similarly, when a country exports something, the receipts from the sale are recorded in the balance of payments (see Table 1).

The balance of payments is divided into different types of transactions. The imports and exports of goods (merchandise) and services are recorded in the **current account** section of the

balance of payments. Take, for example, the importation of an Armani suit from Italy. This is a merchandise import in the current account section. The difference between merchandise imports and merchandise exports is the **balance of trade.** If merchandise exports during the year are greater than merchandise imports, the

---

balance of payments an annual summary of all economic transactions between a country and the rest of the world during the year.

current account those transactions in the balance of payments consisting of merchandise and service imports and exports and unilateral transfers (gifts).

balance of trade the net deficit or surplus in a country's merchandise trade; the difference between merchandise imports and exports.

Table 1	**Simplified Hypothetical Balance of Payments for Country A for a Given Year (Billions of dollars)**		
Credit Items **(Foreign earnings by Country A)**		**Debit Items** **(Liabilities of Country A to Foreigners)**	
Current Account	$321	Current Account	$429
Exports of merchandise	224	Imports of merchandise	349
Exports of services	75	Imports of services	30
Earnings from investments abroad	22	Earnings by foreign investments in Country A	33
Foreign aid from abroad	0	Foreign aid to other countries	17
Capital Account		Capital Account	
New foreign investments in Country A	120	New investments by Country A in foreign countries	45
Basic Balance Total	$441	Basic Balance Total	$474
Basic Deficit ($474 – $441) = $33			
Residual Account			
Reserves transferred to foreigners	$30		
International Monetary Fund loan	3		
Balance Items Total	$33		
Balance of Payments Total	$474	Balance of Payments Total	$474

---

balance of trade is said to be **favorable.** If imports are greater than exports, the balance of trade is said to be **unfavorable.**

But the current account includes more than just merchandise trade. It also includes services. One major type of service "import" is foreign travel. If an American tourist in a Milan boutique had bought the Armani suit, the effect on the U.S. balance of payments would have been the same as if it had been imported. The purchase of the suit required that the tourist first changed dollars to lire, both of which would have remained in Italy while the suit returned to America.

Military assistance, foreign aid, government remittances, and private gifts are special types of current account transactions for which there may be no actual material import. The "import" may be national security or goodwill. But note the basic rule: if it results in a money outflow, it is an import-type transaction. Profits, dividends, and interest earned by Americans on foreign assets result in a money inflow, therefore they are export-type transactions. What is exported is the use of American capital.

Country A in Table 1 is experiencing a merchandise trade deficit of $125 billion ($349 billion – $224 billion)—it has an unfavorable balance of trade. It does, however, have a trade surplus in services of $45 billion, and when the other parts of the current accounts are added in, its total current account deficit is $429 billion – $321 billion = $108 billion.

Italy's exports include high fashions, such as Armani suits. Whether you purchased one in the United States or in Italy, the transaction would have the same economic effects: U.S. dollars would flow into the Italian economy.

International Capital Flows

If a country exports less goods and services than it imports, one way to make up the difference is by giving up capital assets in return for the imports. These can take the form of portfolio assets, such as stocks and bonds, or real physical assets, such as real estate, stores, and factories.

At the time when capital is transferred abroad, it appears in the balance of payments in the **long-term** or **short-term capital accounts.** The long-term capital account summarizes the flow of public and private investment into and out of the country. This includes only those new investments undertaken during the year. If an American firm builds a plant abroad or if an individual buys stock in a foreign company, these are capital import-type transactions. The short-term capital account consists of liquid funds transferred from one country to another, such as transfers of bank deposits.

favorable balance of trade the surplus in a country's merchandise trade when exports during the year are greater than imports.

unfavorable balance of trade the deficit in a country's merchandise trade when imports during the year are greater than exports.

long-term capital direct investment in plant and equipment or portfolio investments in stocks and bonds.

short-term capital transfers of demand deposits or liquid investments such as money market funds, CDs, or Treasury bills.

In the sense that for every transaction there is an import or export on one side of the balance of payments and an offsetting transfer of the payment on the other side, the balance of payments always balances. What, then, is meant by a deficit or a surplus in the balance of payments? If a country's total import-type payments are greater than its total export-type receipts for these transactions, the difference is the country's **basic deficit.** Table 1 shows that Country A exported $75 billion more capital than it imported ($120 billion – $45 billion), it had a capital account surplus that almost offset its current account deficit. This, however, still left it with a basic deficit of $33 billion owed to its foreign trade partners.

The balance-of-payments system has two means to offset a basic deficit and bring the accounts into balance. Either foreigners can, in effect, extend credit to the deficit country by holding larger amounts of the debtor country's currency, which are in the nature of IOUs, or the deficit can be covered with **foreign currency reserves** of the country's currency. Movements of foreign currency reserves, and other minor adjustments, constitute the **residual accounts** that bring the balance of payments into balance. If the deficit country does not have sufficient reserves and foreigners are not willing to accept more of its money, it can turn to the International Monetary Fund for a loan to temporarily solve its balance-of-payments problem while it attempts to eliminate its basic deficit.

What Happens When Exports and Imports Do Not Balance?

EconExplorer

Under a freely fluctuating exchange rate system, the existence of a basic deficit results in a depreciation of the country's currency. An excess of imports over exports results in more of the country's currency going into the foreign exchange market than is demanded. As a result of the excess supply, the exchange rate falls. The lower exchange rate helps to eliminate the

Before a shopper can buy a foreign product, he or she must first buy some foreign currency.

basic deficit by increasing exports and decreasing imports. Conversely, a country with a basic surplus will see its currency appreciate. Its excess of exports over imports means that it is supplying relatively little of its currency to the foreign exchange market, and the shortage will cause its price to rise. The higher exchange rate helps eliminate the basic surplus by decreasing exports and increasing imports.

basic deficit the excess of import-type transactions over export-type transactions in a country's current and capital accounts in the balance of payments.

foreign currency reserves amounts of foreign currencies held by the central bank of a country.

residual accounts the short-term capital transfers and foreign currency reserve transactions that compensate for the imbalance in a country's basic balance of international payments.

Case Application

Going South

In early 1994, Mexico's economic future seemed bright. It had plentiful petroleum reserves to export, it had opened its economy to foreign investment and trade, it had been admitted to the Organization for Economic Cooperation and Development (OECD), and it had just entered into a free trade agreement (NAFTA) with its two big, rich neighbors to the North. Along with Poland, Turkey, Brazil, and some Southeast Asian nations, Mexico had rightfully earned the designation as one of the world's "big emerging markets."

As a big emerging market, Mexico attracted a lot of foreign investment in the early 1990s, about three-quarters of which was portfolio investment—investment in Mexican corporate stocks and Mexican government bonds. Foreign investors would be nervous about investing in securities in a developing country if they feared that its currency might depreciate. To assure investors that exchange rate risk would not be a problem, the Mexican government pegged the peso to the U.S. dollar, allowing its value to vary only slightly. Between November 1993 and November 1994, the exchange rate for the peso varied between 3.15 pesos to 3.44 pesos to the dollar.

To peg the peso, however, the Mexican Central Bank had to be willing and able to do two things: First, it had to guarantee the exchange rate at the pegged rate. Anyone walking through the doors of the Central Bank with 3.44 pesos in their pocket in November 1994 could use them to buy US$1. Knowing that the Central Bank would exchange at this rate was an assurance that the rate would be good anywhere else in Mexico.

Second, it had to keep enough dollars in reserve to back up its promise. Basically, if the peso is pegged to the dollar, then the supply of pesos is tied to the Central Bank's supply of dollars. For example, if the bank has $1 billion (or other currencies that it can use to buy dollars), then it should only supply 3.44 billion pesos to the Mexican economy. If it issues too many pesos, there won't be enough dollars in reserve to buy them at the guaranteed exchange rate.

Everything was going well in Mexico until fall 1994 when things began to unravel. First, the inflow of foreign capital was offset by a growing current account deficit and a growing basic trade deficit. This put downward pressure on the value of the peso because if it depreciated exports would increase, imports would decrease, and the deficit would disappear (see p. 447). Nonetheless, the government stood firm in its guarantee of the pegged exchange rate. There was a presidential election coming up, and allowing the peso to depreciate would cause import prices to increase—which would not sit well with the voters.

Then a series of political events occurred that shook the faith of investors in the Mexican economy. First, long-simmering disputes in the southern state of Chiapas reached a boiling point and the Zapista revolutionary movement erupted into a civil war. Second, a number of foreign business executives were kidnapped and held for ransom. The government's inability to stop the kidnappers made foreigners think twice about the safety of their investments. Finally, one of the leading candidates for the Mexican presidency was assassinated.

The Mexican peso was pegged to the dollar prior to 1994. Economic and political crises in that year led to a change in policy, and the peso became freely fluctuating, losing about 50% of its value against the U.S. dollar.

at the guaranteed rate of about 3.44 pesos to $1. Just as it does in the United States, the mass sales of government bonds increased their supply, pushed down their prices, and increased interest rates. Not wanting the higher interest rates to slow down the economy (remember, this was an election year), the Central Bank purchased many of the bonds, keeping their price high and interest rates low.

Again, as would happen anywhere, the purchase of bonds by the Central Bank caused the money supply to increase, putting further downward pressure on the peso. There were pesos everywhere, and everyone was trying to exchange them for dollars, but the Central Bank had only a limited supply. Ordinarily, the price of dollars would have increased as the value of the peso declined—but the Mexican government kept trying to keep the price of the peso where it was.

Eventually, something had to give. On December 22, 1994, the Mexican government made the decision to allow the peso to float freely and find its market price. One month later, on January 30, 1995, it took 6.50 pesos to buy $1—a depreciation of nearly 50%.

With all the political turmoil and instability, investors decided to put their money somewhere else. Conveniently, the interest rates on U.S. Treasury bonds were rising at this time, so some investors began to sell their Mexican bonds with the intention of converting the pesos they earned into U.S. dollars—

Economic Reasoning

1. What did the Mexican government need to do in order to keep its peso pegged to the dollar?
2. What caused the peso's value to depreciate?
3. Do you think it is a good idea for a developing economy to peg its currency to the dollar? Why or why not?

What Is the Relationship between International Finance and the Domestic Economy?

In chapter 12 we examined the conditions of national economic equilibrium when we considered the domestic sectors of the economy. In this analysis section, we will see how the foreign sector affects macroeconomic equilibrium in an open economy.

The Foreign Sector in the National Economy

In discussing gross domestic product (chapter 12, p. 321), we noted that aggregate demand was the sum of consumer demand (C), investment demand (I), government demand (G), and net foreign demand (X – M). The first three sectors were included in the GDP tank model in chapter 12 showing domestic equilibrium. Figure 3 adds the foreign sector (pictured in gold) to the three domestic sectors of the economy in the GDP tank diagram. Economists use the term "closed economy" when describing a model of the economy that does not include the foreign sector and "open economy" when describing one that does.

The amount of income that consumers and businesses allocate to imports, indicated by M, flows out of the tank into the foreign sector. The expenditures by foreigners on U.S. exports flow from the foreign sector into the GDP tank as demand for goods and services, shown by X. As was the case with the investment and government

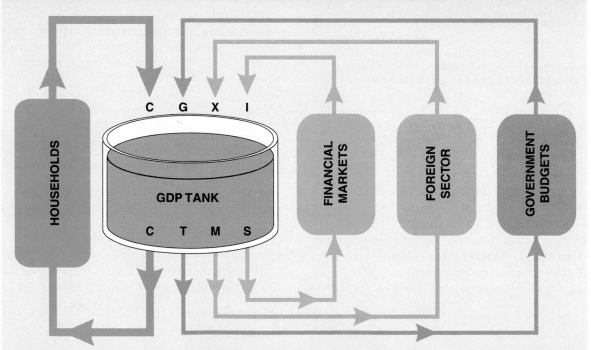

Figure 3

GDP Tank National Income Model Including the Foreign Sector

C G X I

HOUSEHOLDS

GDP TANK

C T M S

FINANCIAL MARKETS

FOREIGN SECTOR

GOVERNMENT BUDGETS

Economic equilibrium requires that the allocations of GDP income to savings (S), taxes (T), and imports (M) be equal to the purchasing power flowing back into the economy from investment (I), government spending (G), and exports (X). In the United States in recent years, the amount of savings and taxes has been less than investment and government spending (S + T < I + G). The difference has been compensated by an excess of imports over exports (M > X), so that savings, taxes, and imports together equal the total of investment, government spending, and exports (S + T + M = I + G + X).

sectors, the amount of purchasing power flowing out of the economy for imports is not necessarily the same as the amount of purchasing power flowing into the economy for export purchases.

What Is the Relationship between International Finance and the Domestic Economy?

EconExplorer

If the balance of trade is unfavorable, as it has been for the United States in recent years, there are more dollars flowing out of the economy into the foreign sector in payment for imports than there are flowing into the economy from the foreign sector in payment for exports. The excess dollars accumulated by foreigners could be held as deposit balances in U.S. or foreign banks, but most of the excess dollars from the foreign sector have been used for capital investment in the United States. They have been used to buy securities, both government and private, and to purchase or create real assets such as office buildings, chemical plants, and automobile factories.

The Foreign Sector and National Economic Equilibrium

The economy is in equilibrium when aggregate demand equals aggregate supply (review the discussion of equilibrium output in chapter 12, (pp. 334–336). Considering only the domestic sectors, the U.S. economy has not been in equilibrium for some time. Saving has been less than investment, and taxes have been less than government spending. As a result, the amount of funds flowing into the investment and government sectors has been less than the amounts flowing from those sectors into the demand for goods and services.

The difference between the amounts allocated to savings and taxes and the total of investment and government spending $(S + T < I + G)$ has been made up by an excess of imports over exports $(M > X)$. In other words, the U.S. import surplus has compensated for the deficiency in our savings and taxes. This results in savings, taxes, and imports equaling investment, government spending, and exports $(S + T + M = I + G + X)$. Since aggregate demand $(I + G + X)$ equals aggregate supply $(S + T + M)$, the national economy is in equilibrium.

There is no such thing as a free lunch. If American exporters do not send Germans enough goods in return for the sports cars they send us, the Germans will accept investments in American assets (stocks, bonds, real estate) instead.

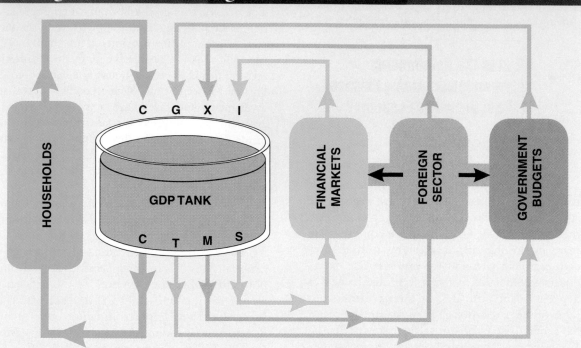

Figure 4

Foreign Sector Financing of U.S. Domestic Deficits

There is more income going to the foreign sector from imports (M) than is being returned to the economy in export demand (X). The excess dollars in the foreign section (gold) are invested in U.S. private financial markets (green) and U.S. Treasury securities (pink). The import surplus has permitted the economy to consume (including I and G) more than it produces. It also has been the source of foreign capital to finance domestic deficits.

The United States has been living beyond its means, consuming and investing more than it has been producing. But the foreign sector has balanced the domestic sectors. Foreigners made it possible for aggregate demand to exceed aggregate supply in the domestic sectors by sending us more goods and services than we send them and lending the accumulated dollars back to us to finance our deficits.

This process is shown in Figure 4. A portion of the funds flowing out of the economy in payments for imports (the M outflow from the bottom of the tank) are channeled from the foreign sector into U.S. financial markets (the green sector) and into financing government deficits (pink). The flow to the private sector consists of both portfolio investments in corporate stocks and bonds and direct investments in new plant and equipment, as well as the acquisition of existing companies and other real assets. The flow into the government sector consists principally of the purchase of U.S. Treasury securities.

These investments compensated for the imbalance in aggregate demand and supply in the domestic sectors of the economy. The import surpluses gave rise to dollar balances in the hands of foreigners. When those dollars were invested, they paid for our excess domestic spending. The American banking system can create money to finance investments and fund government deficits, as we discovered in chapter 10 (p. 272). But the banking system cannot provide the economy with additional resources and products that allow us to consume (including

(Continued on page 464)

Case Application

Selling America

Rockefeller Center in New York City bears the name of one of the most powerful financial dynasties in American history. But during the 1980s there was a different name on the ownership papers—Mitsubishi Estate Company. Mitsubishi owned the controlling interest in Rockefeller Center. Mamma Leone's restaurant, a well-known New York tourist spot, now belongs to Kyotaru Company, a Japanese restaurant firm.

These, along with such purchases as Columbia Pictures, San Francisco's Mark Hopkins Hotel, and exclusive Beverly Hills real estate, are all Japanese acquisitions. Less newsworthy but also important are sizable foreign investments in such basic industries as chemicals; glass, stone, and clay; primary metals; printing and publishing; and electrical machinery. Foreign auto companies are making Hondas in Ohio, BMWs in South Carolina, and Mercedes in Alabama. As of 1997, foreigners owned almost $5.5 trillion of U.S. assets while the U.S. owned "only" about $4.2 trillion in foreign assets (Figure 5).

What is happening and why are America's assets being sold out from under our noses? Why did we become a net seller of assets after 1988, for the first time since 1914? Surprisingly, the answer is that Americans simply do not save enough of their incomes. Recall that investment is financed out of forgone consumption—savings. During the 1980s, there were very attractive investment opportunities in the United States, but domestic savings fell short and foreign investors closed the gap by pouring billions of dollars into all kinds of U.S. assets—corporate stocks and bonds, factories and real estate, and U.S. Treasury securities.

The United States has long been a desirable place for foreigners to invest their funds because of its political stability. When U.S.

Rockefeller Center, in which Mitsubishi once had a controlling interest, was considered to be the epitome of foreign investment in the United States—the result of negative merchandise trade balances. Although Mitsubishi no longer owns this famous symbol of New York, the increasing sale of American assets to foreigners is one of the ways we pay for our merchandise trade deficit.

firms needed capital injections in the 1980s and American savings were insufficient to fund all the desired investment projects, they received the funds through corporate stock and bond sales to foreign investors. The money has continued to flow into the stock market in the 1990s, and many analysts believe that the foreign demand for U.S. stocks has contributed to the great bull market of the 1990s.

Figure 5

U.S. International Investment Position, 1984–1997

$ Billions (y-axis: 0, 1000, 2000, 3000, 4000, 5000, 6000)

Year (x-axis: 1984 1985 1986 1987 1988 1989 1990 1991 1992 1993 1994 1995 1996 1997)

— U.S. assets abroad   — Foreign assets in the United States

Between 1914 and 1988 the United States was a net creditor with respect of the rest of the world (green shaded area). Since then, its net obligation to foreign investors has grown rapidly (blue shaded area).

Source: U.S. Department of Commerce, Bureau of Economic Analysis.

Foreign manufacturers increased their foreign direct investment (FDI) in the United States, which has a market of over 260 million people and the world's largest national income, in order to have better access to U.S. customers and to avoid paying import tariffs. With the passage of NAFTA, U.S. manufacturing and distribution sites also give foreign companies tariff-free access to the Canadian and Mexican markets. The current investment boom increased U.S. employment in foreign-owned businesses from about 2 million in 1980 to over 5 million in 1996. Although many people incorrectly believe that the foreign investment strategy of most American firms is to move to low-wage areas, the fact is that American strategy is similar to that of other developed nations. Most U.S. FDI is in Europe and other developed countries that have high external tar-

iffs and large, wealthy markets. Likewise, most European FDI occurs in the United States.

Although the focus of attention has been on Japanese acquisition of American companies and property, Japan is only in second place as a foreign owner of U.S. assets. Its investments trail those of the United Kingdom, with the Dutch third, and Germany fourth. It might at first seem strange that the Dutch hold so many U.S. assets, but when the U.S. was founded and was growing during the early 1800s, the Dutch and British were two of the world's richest countries, and they had a lot of money to invest throughout the world. Many U.S. railroads and Old West cattle ranches were financed and owned by the Dutch and British.

The low domestic savings rate and large government budget deficits also meant high interest rates, which made U.S. securities attractive to foreign investors. The rising interest rates signaled the rest of the world that financial capital was in short supply in the United States. Foreign investors were willing to buy U.S. bonds, unlike those of other countries that experience high interest rates, because the stability of the dollar meant that there was little exchange rate risk. Foreigners increased their holdings of U.S. Treasury securities from $261 billion in 1987 to $614 billion in 1996, helping to finance our federal budget deficits in those years.

In terms of the balance of payments, the sale of real and financial assets led to a large capital account surplus for the United States. Foreign individuals and businesses paid for these assets with consumer goods. Our saving rates have been low because we prefer current consumption, so we used the income we received from selling assets to buy imported consumer goods—hence our current account deficit. Essentially, the United States has been swapping its assets in return for current consumption. This is reflected in our balance of payments accounts where, in order to balance, the capital account surplus must be offset by a current account deficit.

In a sense, then, the increasing foreign debt of the United States was due in part to the strength of its economy rather than its weakness— foreigners wanted to invest here because returns were greater and more secure. For the United States, the inflow of foreign capital was very useful in helping to finance domestic investment and its record federal budget deficits, compensating for the low savings rate of the U.S. population. Nevertheless, it created an uneasy situation because foreign funds can be withdrawn very rapidly if the outlook changes. If there were a flight of foreign capital from the country, the shortage of domestic savings would make it difficult for the government and businesses to raise money, driving interest rates higher.

The rising foreign ownership of U.S. assets has alarmed many Americans. Do foreigners have too much power over our economy? Can they use their ownership of American business to injure the country? Are we losing control of our destiny? For the most part, these fears are groundless. Foreign-owned businesses contribute only around 5 to 6% of our GDP, and the government can always intervene if there is any hostile intent.

The meaning for the United States is that our excess consumption now may result in lower levels of consumption in the future. But the foreign capital inflow compensates for our low savings rate by enabling the United States to invest more than our level of savings permits. The current investment financed by capital inflow means more production and consumption in the future. Part of that production, however, will be transferred to foreign investors in the form of interest and dividend payments. If the investments were financed domestically, there would be no such transfers.

Economic Reasoning

1. Why does the low savings rate in the United States contribute to the foreign ownership of U.S. assets?

2. How do foreign investments in the United States affect the U.S. current account balance?

3. Should the United States restrict foreigners from acquiring assets, such as businesses, real estate, and financial securities, in this country? Why or why not?

Selling America

Visit the Bureau of Economic Analysis at http://www.bea.doc.gov/bea/ai1.htm. Click on International Investment Position and Direct Investment Positions for 1997: Country and Industry Detail of the United States. Has the difference between U.S. assets held abroad and foreign assets held in the United States increased or decreased? Has the ranking of the top four foreign investors in the United States changed?

I and G) more than we produce. Only the foreign sector can do that.

Although the Queen of Hearts in the introductory story wanted to make war on the Land of the Rising Sun for not buying as much from us as it sold to us, the fact is that it was only by means of our import surplus that we managed to have the level of consumption, investment, and government spending that we have had in recent years. Of course, we will have to pay the piper for our excess consumption dance in the form of future interest and dividends on the foreign debt. We cannot continue increasing our foreign debt indefinitely; the rest of the world will not permit this. To reverse the trend, in the future we will have to consume less than we produce.

▶ Putting It Together

Payments for international transactions are made through the *foreign exchange market,* which consists mainly of major banks in the financial capitals of the world, plus some other foreign exchange dealers and brokers. *Correspondent banks,* which possess deposit accounts in banks overseas, facilitate the purchase of foreign exchange.

Under the *freely fluctuating exchange rate system* currently in existence, the demand for and supply of the country's currency in the foreign exchange market determine the exchange rate for a country's currency. An increase in the supply of a country's currency on the exchange market will cause the currency to depreciate in value. An increase in the value of a country's currency is called *appreciation;* a decrease is called *depreciation.* Under a system of *fixed exchange rates,* governments set the rates of exchange for their currencies. If the government lowers the international value of its currency, it is *devaluation;* raising the value is *revaluation.* Although exchange rates generally are freely fluctuating, sometimes a developing country will *peg* its currency to the dollar to shelter foreign investors from *exchange rate risk.*

The summation of foreign transactions of a country is its *balance of payments.* The net of merchandise imports and exports is the *balance of trade.* If exports are larger than imports, the balance of trade is said to be *favorable;* if imports are larger, it is *unfavorable.*

In addition to merchandise exports and imports, the balance of payments includes service exports and imports in the *current account,* foreign investments in the *long-term capital account,* and *short-term capital* movements and *foreign currency reserves* in the *residual accounts.* When receipts from abroad in the current and long-term capital accounts are less than foreign spending,

The Chestire Cat was smiling at the contradictions in our attitudes and policies with regard to international trade and finance. These contradictions partly are inherent in the problems posed by the foreign sector of the economy. But they are also in part the result of a lack of understanding of how the international financial system works and how it impacts the national economy.

there is a *basic deficit.* This basic deficit is covered by a short-term capital inflow or the use of reserves so that the balance of payments balances.

Export demand added to consumption, investment, and government demand makes up aggregate demand for the nation's output. If imports exceed exports, the excess dollars in the foreign sector are used to finance foreign investments in the United States.

The economy is in equilibrium when aggregate demand equals aggregate supply. Since demand in U.S. domestic sectors has been greater than supply, the foreign sector made up the difference. Imports have been greater than exports, offsetting the deficiency in savings and taxes and making $S + T + M$ equal to $I + G + X$. The foreign sector has provided the additional resources and products that have allowed the United States to consume more than it produced. The excess dollars in the foreign sector have been channeled into investments and the purchase of U.S. Treasury securities.

$ Perspective $

Bring Back Gold?

For additional information on the gold standard, see *The International Gold Standard Re-interpreted* (1940) by W. A. Brown Jr.; *The Downfall of the Gold Standard* (1936) by C. G. Cassel; *Gold or Credit* (1965) by Francis Cassel; *The Gold Standard in Theory and Practice* (1947) by R. G. Hautrey; *Gold and the Gold Standard* (1944) by E. W. Kemmerer; *Gold and the Dollar Crisis* (1961) by Robert Triffin; *The Rise and Fall of the Gold Standard* (1934) by C. M. Webb; and *A Tool of Power: The Political History of Money* (1977) by W. Wiseley.

The extreme fluctuations of currency values under the system of freely fluctuating exchange rates (see Figure 1, p. 446) have given rise to calls for a return to the gold standard. Under the gold standard, which was in effect from the 1830s to the 1930s and in a modified form in the United States up to 1971, the value of a currency was defined by how much gold it was worth. The U.S. government specified the value of the dollar at $35 per ounce of gold. It maintained this value of the dollar by offering to both buy and sell gold at that price, thereby ensuring that the value of the dollar would be stable with respect to gold and other gold standard currencies.

Those advocating a return to the gold standard believe that it would stabilize exchange rates and prevent a return of inflation by imposing a monetary discipline on our government that the current paper money standard does not. If a country were to permit inflation, its imports would exceed its exports and the surplus of its currency on the foreign exchange market would be used by foreigners to buy its gold. The resulting drain on its gold reserves would force the government to reduce the domestic money supply and stop the inflation.

The problem with the gold standard when it was in effect was that it made the domestic economy a slave to what happened abroad. If, for example, other countries were in a recession, exports to those countries would fall. This resulted in an outflow of gold to cover the difference between export earnings and import spending. Following the "rules of the game" for the gold standard, the government would permit the outflow of gold to deflate the domestic economy. In this way, recessions would be "imported." That is basically why the worldwide depression in the 1930s put an end to the international gold standard. Governments refused to follow the rules because doing so would increase unemployment.

After the Depression, the United States continued to value its currency in gold but restricted its sales of gold only to official transactions, not to private gold dealers. Other countries valued their currencies either in terms of the dollar or the British pound. In 1971, with the foreign trade deficit threatening to deplete its gold supply, the United States first devalued the dollar and later abandoned any ties to gold, setting the U.S. dollar free to fluctuate according to demand and supply in the foreign exchange market.

For those who today advocate a return to the gold standard, it should be noted that during the time that the gold standard was in effect there were periods that were highly inflationary as well as periods of severe depression.

For Further Study and Analysis

Study Questions

1. Assuming that the price of the Swiss franc is $1.50, if there is a large increase in the demand for Swiss watches in this country, what would you expect to happen to the franc-dollar exchange rate under a system of freely fluctuating exchange rates?

2. How does inflation affect the international value of a country's currency? Does it cause the currency to appreciate or depreciate?

3. Why does a rise in U.S. interest rates affect the foreign exchange rate of the dollar? Would it cause the dollar to appreciate or depreciate?

4. In what sense is an export surplus favorable to the exporting country? In what way might an export surplus not be favorable?

5. How do flexible exchange rates correct a country's basic deficit? How do they correct for a basic surplus?

6. Can a country have a surplus in its balance of trade and at the same time have a basic deficit in its balance of payments? How?

7. What determines the amount of income that consumers allocate to imports? What determines the level of exports?

8. If foreigners reduced their investments in the United States, how would this be shown in the GDP tank diagram? What effect would it have on exports and/or imports? Why?

9. How do the dollars earned by foreign exporters return to the United States? Why do some dollars fail to return?

10. Suppose you buy a one-year, 120,000 peso Mexican government bond that pays 20% interest. When you buy the bond, the exchange rate is $1 = 8 pesos, so the bond costs $15,000. When you redeem the bond in one year, the peso has depreciated to $1 = 10 pesos. When you convert your earnings back to dollars, how much money will you have?

Exercises in Analysis

1. The following table shows some of the international prices of a copy of the *Economist* that were printed on the cover of the July 11, 1998, international edition of the magazine, and the currency exchange rates that appeared on pages 105 and 106:

Country	Price		Exchange Rate per U.S. Dollar
Belgium	160	francs	37.5
Czech Republic	95	krones	32.5
France	28	francs	6.1
Germany	7.9	marks	1.8
Nigeria	280	nairas	85.4
Poland	11	zlotys	3.5
Turkey	700,000	lires	269,000.0

In U.S. dollars, how much does the *Economist* cost in each country? Write a report that explains why you think the prices might be different in the different countries, and what you think prevents people from buying the magazine in Turkey and reselling it in France. (The magazine is written in English in all countries.)

2. Write a report on what has happened to the foreign exchange rate of the dollar against each of the currencies in Figure 1 since 1998. If the exchange rate has gone up or down since then, explain why. You can find the current rates in the *Wall Street Journal*, most daily newspapers, or use the currency converter at http://quote.yahoo.com/ (click on Currency Exchange Rates). The Federal Reserve publishes historical exchange rate data at http://www.bog.frb.fed.us/releases/H10/hist/.

3. From the most recent *Economic Report of the President* or other sources, find the U.S. balance of payments for the last year reported. Write a brief analysis of the balance-of-trade position and the balance-of-payments position of the United States. You can also find the most current trade statistics at http://www.bea.doc.gov/bea/di/trans1.htm or go to the Bureau of Economic Analysis home page at http://www.bea.doc.gov/ and click on International Data.

4. Make a report on the current equilibrium position of the U.S. economy. Show what has happened to the investment, government, and foreign sectors. Illustrate with a schematic GDP tank diagram.

Further Reading

Atlas, Peter. "Currency Conversion Lessons." http://staff.feldberg.brandeis.edu/~petera/cchs/currency/MainPage.html. Provides games and lessons on converting one currency to another, how to use currency conversion tables, and an interesting exercise involving changing money on a trip to more than one foreign country.

Cole, Don, ed. *Annual Editions: Economics,* and *Annual Editions: Macroeconomics.* Guilford, CT: Dushkin/McGraw-Hill, various years. These annual publications always include a number of articles (with commentary) on international finance.

Cleaver, Tony. *Understanding the World Economy: Global Issues Shaping the Future.* London: Routledge, 1997. Chapters 7, 8, and 10 focus on international finance and exchange rate issues.

Daniels, Joseph, and David VanHoose. *International Monetary and Financial Economics.* New York: South-Western College Publishing, 1999. A little more advanced, but an up-to-date reference that might be useful for researching specific topics.

Epping, Randy Charles. *A Beginner's Guide to the World Economy: Seventy-Seven Basic Economic Concepts that Will Change the Way You See the World.* New York: Vintage Books, 1995. The book has been described as presenting information about the world economy ". . . simply but never simplistically—and without a single graph." It is a very useful, easy to read volume that covers foreign trade as well as a number of other economic topics.

Federal Reserve Bank of Kansas City. *Maintaining Financial Stability in a Global Economy.* Kansas City: The Federal Reserve Bank of Kansas City, 1997. This volume contains copies of papers presented at a symposium that took place in 1997. Participants from a number of different countries present their views on international financial policy.

Kenen, Peter B. *The International Economy.* Cambridge: Cambridge University Press, 1994. A basic textbook for someone looking to learn more about some specific issues involving international financial transactions.

King, Philip, ed. *International Economics and International Economic Policy: A Reader.* New York: McGraw-Hill, 1995. Section 7 contains some essays that directly address the issues of exchange rate determination.

Krugman, Paul. *Pop Internationalism.* Cambridge: MIT Press, 1997. One of the leading authorities on global economics in the world today presents a critique of orthodox theory and widely accepted views in a readable and entertaining way.

Panic, M. *European Monetary Union: Lessons from the Classical Gold Standard.* New York: St. Martin's Press, 1992. The gold standard, although it has not been around for decades, still maintains a place in the discussions of international monetary policy in Europe. The French, in particular, are still preoccupied with gold standard considerations.

University of Michigan Documents Center. *Statistical Resources on the Web: Foreign Trade* has links to a number of excellent information sources, including the International Trade Administration, a great source for international trade statistics. (http://www.lib.umich.edu/libhome/Documents.center/stectrad.html).

U.S. Department of State, Country Reports on Economic Policy and Trade. http://www.state.gov/www/issues/economic/trade_reports/index.html. State Department annual reports on economic policies of individual countries beginning 1993, including basic trade data for the past 3 years.

chapter seventeen

Economies in Transition

The collapse of the Berlin Wall in 1989 and the dissolution of the Soviet Union in 1991 were the most significant economic events of the last 50 years. Just as the formation of the world's first communist country in 1922 was difficult to evaluate because of its uniqueness, the world is now trying to learn the best way to restructure communist economies into capitalist ones. It is turning out to be more difficult than anyone ever imagined.

State Socialism, Soviet-Style

The Union of Soviet Socialist Republics, or simply the USSR or Soviet Union, was established in 1922 as the world's first communist nation. It dissolved in late 1991 into 15 separate republics, each of which made a decision to abandon communism in favor of free-market capitalism.

How did the Soviet economy function? The most important aspect was that the government owned virtually all of the country's land, natural resources, transportation and communication facilities, and industries. The idea of a private citizen owning productive property and using it in its most advantageous employment did not exist. Prices were set and controlled by the government, with energy, food, and housing being priced well below market levels. As one would expect, the results were severe shortages and long lines of consumers trying to buy whatever happened to be available.

Another crucial aspect of the Soviet economy was the system of central planning that determined what was to be produced, how it was going to be produced, and how the output was to be distributed. The Soviet economic system was built around 5-year production plans. Instead of choices being made through a constantly adjusting market system, they were made by an enormous bureaucracy headquartered in Moscow. It was as if the Soviet economy was one big firm, with all the economic decisions for 300 million people being made by a handful of politicians.

The planning process was a hierarchy, and at the top were the leaders of the Communist Party, the Politburo, who set the general national priorities: for example (hypothetically), 30% of GDP should go for investment, industrial output needed to increase by 15%, oil exploration and refining should be expanded, and so on. These priorities were sent to the government's central planning agency, Gosplan, which then made more specific plans, such as, how many tons of steel and bread to produce, how many apartments to construct, how many trac-

tors and cars to build, how many oil wells to drill, and so on. These targets were then passed down the hierarchy to about 40 different ministries (housing, military, steel, for example), which in turn assigned specific output quotas to the managers of individual state-owned firms.

Firm managers would examine the output targets they were given, determine the needed inputs of labor and resources, and pass resource requests back up thorough the ministries to Gosplan, which sent the final, adjusted targets and resource provisions back on down to the ministries and firms. The managers of each firm had specific instructions about the inputs they were permitted to buy (and at what prices), which firms to get their inputs from, and which firms to sell their output to (also at set prices). If their quota was met or exceeded, managers could look forward to financial bonuses and other rewards.

For a number of reasons, the hierarchical system never worked very well. First, even the best planners with the best information at their disposal could not accurately plan for business and consumer needs on such a massive scale. This was increasingly evident as the goods and services produced became more and more complex over time. It might be feasible to plan on the inputs and outputs of a simple steel factory, but trying to coordinate all the parts that go into something as complex as a car or television became a bureaucratic nightmare.

Second, firm managers were not permitted to negotiate with one another. A construction company charged with building apartments, for example, could not coordinate with a woodworking firm about door or window sizes or styles; nor could the woodworking firm negotiate with a hardware firm about hinges, doorknobs, and nails. Is it any wonder that doors would not hang properly or that windows would not keep out drafts?

Third, the system left the Soviet people out in the cold as to what products they did or did not want. Consumer sovereignty did not exist—the people had to choose from whatever products the Politburo and ministries thought they should have. And the truth is consumer goods, houses, and cars were not high on the Politburo's list. Most resources were directed toward heavy industry and the military. Even agriculture was largely ignored. The peasants worked on state-owned collective farms, and few resources were allocated to produce tractors, to build barns to store equipment and shelter livestock, or to construct silos for grain storage. The Soviet diet was pretty basic, not just because the farmers were not productive, but because crops could not be efficiently harvested and often rotted in the fields. Even today (1998) Russia imports about three-quarters of its food from other countries.

Fourth, the system of bonuses for managers who met or exceeded their quotas backfired in an unforeseen way. Managers were rewarded for meeting quantity quotas, and quality or usability were not a consideration. If the quota called for a million nails, small nails were produced; if it called for 100 tons of nails, big nails were produced. The nail sizes needed by the users did not matter—they were required to buy so many nails from the supplier, regardless of size. Ten tons of brittle steel would be manufactured instead of 8 tons of high quality steel; clothes would be sewn with big, loose stitches instead of small, tight ones; 1,000 meters of shallow furrows would be plowed instead of

500 meters of appropriately deep ones; appliances would be held together with a minimum number of nuts and bolts; and so on. Spare parts were scarce because given the choice between supplying more tractors or spare parts for tractors, for example, managers would naturally opt for more tractors to enhance their bonuses.

The bonus system also led to problems on the input side of the ledger. Because delivery dates were rarely more specific than on a quarterly basis, important inputs were often unavailable when needed. Even then, they were often unusable. One remedy was to produce inputs internally, and this led to the creation of giant manufacturing facilities that employed thousands and thousands of workers. Additionally, to ensure their bonuses, it was common for managers to overstate their input needs and understate their capacity. A firm might have been capable of producing 1,000 loaves of bread an hour with 10 workers and 1,000 pounds of flour, but the manager would be inclined to state that his or her capacity was only 850 loaves, and he or she needed 20 workers and 1,100 pounds of flour to produce that quantity!

On the positive side, there was no official unemployment in the USSR; all citizens were guaranteed employment. Much of this employment, however, took place at firms like the hypothetical bakery described above. There were often far more workers than were needed, and

the lack of a need to be efficient and productive took its toll on worker morale. There was little incentive to work hard or advance, and there was a great deal of truth in the Soviet workers' saying, "We pretended to work and they pretended to pay us."

The government also made sure that food, housing, and medical care were affordable. But what was produced was usually in short supply and of very poor quality. It sometimes took years and substantial bribes to get a government-owned apartment, owning a car was a luxury reserved for only the lucky few and usually required "connections," and the average citizen spent literally hours in line every week to buy whatever grocery items happened to be available. Years of dependence on the government, guaranteed jobs, a shortage of even poor quality consumer goods, and constant mismanagement of the economy led to a general inertia and unhappiness throughout the country.

By the late 1980s, alcoholism had reached epidemic proportions, illnesses resulting from environmental degradation contributed to declining life expectancies, and the economy was getting worse, not better. In an attempt to keep up with the U.S. militarily, over half of Soviet industry was involved with manufacturing armaments, leaving little capacity to produce basic consumer goods. The Soviet people had had enough. They weren't real sure where they were going, but anything had to be better than where they were. One after another, in late 1991, the republics seceded from the Soviet Union and the USSR ceased to exist. The Baltic States (Latvia, Lithuania, and Estonia) and Georgia opted for complete independence and the remaining republics formed a loose confederation called the Commonwealth of Independent States (CIS).

Chapter Preview

In 1989 more than a third of the world's population lived in communist countries. Today just about all of them are experiencing economic changes as their countries are moving more and more toward free-market capitalism. This chapter will examine the transformation by asking the following questions: How is the former Soviet Union's economy being restructured? How are the economies of East Europe being restructured? How is the Chinese economy being restructured?

Learning Objectives

After completing this chapter you should be able to:

1. Explain why prices for most goods increased after the collapse of the former communist countries.
2. Explain the reasons why privatization has proved to be so difficult to implement in Russia.
3. Explain why financial markets have been slow to develop in Russia.
4. Explain how the role of government in Russia is changing and the difficulties involved in making these changes.
5. Contrast crony capitalism as practiced in some countries with the rule of law, and understand why the latter is necessary for capitalism to work.
6. Explain how the privatization policies followed in Poland and Hungary were different.
7. Understand why economic restructuring has been more successful in Central and Eastern Europe than it has been in the former USSR.
8. Understand what the Council for Mutual Economic Assistance was and why its demise presents a hardship for former communist countries.
9. Know about Mao Zedong and his vision of China.
10. Explain how the Chinese experience with restructuring has been different than that in the former Soviet Union and the CEE countries.

How Is the Former Soviet Union's Economy Being Restructured?

After the collapse of their **communist** (also referred to as **socialist**) economies, the newly independent countries of the former Soviet Union, especially Russia, followed the advice of Harvard University economist Jeffrey Sachs and attempted to **restructure** their economic systems through **shock therapy:** the immediate establishment of political and economic freedom (Figure 1). So far the program has not proved successful. From 1991 through 1996, the countries of the former USSR averaged GDP declines of over 10% per year. After achieving positive economic growth for the first time in 1997, by mid-1998 the Russian economy had sunk

communism (or socialism) an economic system in which all nonhuman productive assets are owned by the government in the name of the people, and in which the government decides what is produced, how it is produced, and how the output is distributed.

restructuring changing the laws, institutions, and the overall economy from communism to free enterprise.

shock therapy the immediate imposition of free-market rules and institutions, such as market-determined prices, private property, free trade, and so on, in a former communist economy.

Figure 1

Map of the Countries of the Former USSR

back into recession and teetered on the brink of total economic collapse. Incomes in Russia and the other former Soviet republics not only are far below those in the West, but also far below those in their former satellites in Central and Eastern Europe (Figure 2).

Although Russia was only 1 of 15 Soviet republics, it was the biggest and most influential. The following discussion focuses on Russia, but the issues and problems can be generalized to the other 14 former Soviet republics.

Getting Prices Right

Under the Soviet regime, prices of all goods were set by the government. The prices of some goods, particularly energy, basic foods, housing, and transportation were kept artificially low. As indicated in the opening article, this resulted in long lines at grocery stores and long waits for available apartments. As it is often stated, allowing the market to set prices instead of the government **gets prices right** and results in an efficient allocation of resources.

When Russian prices were freed, they increased dramatically, causing rising inflation and imposing severe hardships on the Russian people. It was hoped that the high prices would spur production, increase supplies, and bring prices down. Unfortunately, firms were not efficient or experienced enough to increase the output of consumer goods, so prices stayed high. The situation was aggravated by the large amounts of rubles in savings accounts. Prior to

getting prices right a phrase that refers to allowing prices to be set by market forces instead of by government agencies.

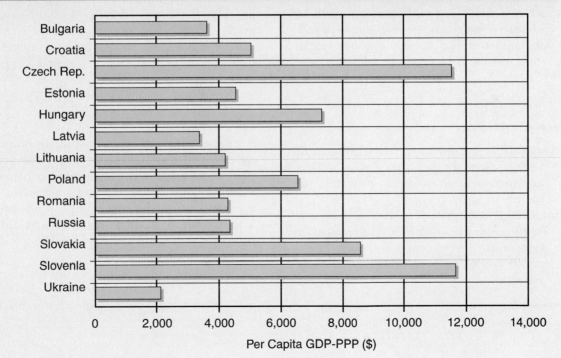

Figure 2

Per Capita GDP in Selected Former Communist Countries, 1997

Per Capita GDP-PPP ($)

The members of the former Soviet Union have not fared as well as their former Eastern European satellites during their transitions to market economies.

State socialism was built around bureaucracy, symbolized in the ceremonial May Day parade. On an everyday level, centralized planning of production led to massive inefficiency, and lines for daily necessities were a way of life for Soviet citizens.

the collapse, there were few consumer goods available at any price; with nothing much to spend their money on, people simply saved. When imported and domestic goods began showing up on shelves, saving accounts were emptied as the Russian people went on a buying spree that increased the upward pressure on prices. Those who did not spend their rubles experienced considerable losses as galloping inflation reduced the value of their savings to next to nothing.

privatization the process of selling government enterprises to private buyers and/or turning government services over to private-sector operation.

state-owned enterprises (SOEs) the thousands of businesses formerly owned and operated by communist governments; in the new, free-market economies these enterprises are being privatized.

◣ Privatization

A market economy requires private property rights in order to function properly. The **privatization** of government-held property has been a daunting task for all former communist countries, but it turned into a nightmare in Russia. The basic idea was that **state-owned enterprises (SOEs)** should be sold, but the question was, Sold to who?

In Russia, for example, all means of production technically were owned by the "people." Ideally, the new governments wanted to make this ownership a reality by transferring control of state-owned businesses to Russian citizens. The vast majority of Russians, however, did not have the financial means to purchase them. Many did have the resources to open small new retail shops and kiosks, and privatization in this part of the economy did flourish. Sadly, the government's inability to guarantee private property rights meant that to stay in business these fledgling entrepreneurs had to pay for "protection" and make other payoffs to organized crime and even to government bureaucrats in order to stay in business.

In 1992 and 1993, the government distributed vouchers to citizens that could be used to buy shares in Russian companies—like buying corporate stock. Most firms accepted a plan whereby their managers and workers could retain 51% of the voting equity in the firm, 29% was made available for sale to voucher holders, and the other 20% was retained by the government. But the typical Russian citizen knew nothing about investing, stock markets, or all the other institutions that most of us take for granted. After three generations of being taken care of by the Soviet government, and many more prior generations of being virtual slaves to landed aristocrats, most Russian people had little understanding of profits, self-interest, and how markets work. Many people sold their vouchers at bargain basement prices to the few who understood how capital markets operate, and many of these people became rich overnight.

In 1994 the Russian government expanded their privatization program to allow for the outright sale of SOEs for cash. Foreign buyers were an attractive alternative because they had the financial capital necessary to modernize existing plants and the expertise to make them globally competitive. In addition, the Russian government needed foreign currency with which to buy imports, and this would be a good way to obtain it. Unfortunately, there proved to be very little foreign interest in investing in Russia. This was in part due to the political instability and rampant crime that frightened potential investors, partly due to inflation and a devalued currency that made exchange-rate risk a real concern, and partly due to the fact that without standard Western accounting practices, it was difficult to assess the true value of firms being offered for sale.

An even greater problem was that no one—foreign or domestic—was interested in buying the huge, outdated, inefficient firms that dominated the Russian economy, the so-called **dinosaurs.** The only big firms that foreign investors were interested in were those that controlled Russia's vast natural resources, its telecommunications, and its energy. Like most countries, Russia balked at ceding control of these vital industries to foreign interests.

Through connections, bribes, and outright theft, the **nomenklatura**—the old communist insiders—gained control of most of the valuable resources that were transferred from government to private hands. Those in charge of representing the Russian people in the sales sold the most valuable assets to cronies at prices far below their real worth. For example, the VAZ automobile manufacturer was purchased for $45 million in vouchers in 1995, although Fiat

dinosaurs the massive heavy industry manufacturing plants common throughout the former communist world.

nomenklatura former communist party members and government officials who gained control of privatized businesses in the postcommunist era, often through illegal means.

had offered $2 billion for the company in 1991 and had been turned down. According to the Harvard Institute for International Development, the total voucher sales price of all Russia's industry, including some of the world's richest oil and natural gas sources, was equal to about $12 billion, less than the value of Anheuser-Busch. On average, Russian firms and assets were sold to insiders at less than one-fortieth of their true market value. The nomenklatura essentially stole the Russian people's assets from them.

Although statistics show that anywhere from 60 to 90 percent of Russian assets had been privatized as of 1998, the numbers hide the fact that many of these "private" firms still rely heavily on the state for subsidies and special favors. The same people who were able to steal Russia's assets gained enough political influence to pressure the government to continue this special treatment. Although some firms may technically be bankrupt and should be out of business, because of political influence the government continues to provide them with funds to keep operating. This **crony capitalism** is crippling Russia's attempts to establish a true free-market economy.

The huge state-owned dinosaurs that no one wants to buy continue to be owned by the government. With thousands of employees, it just is not politically feasible to shut these firms down, despite the fact that they are not capable of efficiently producing anything that anybody wants. After 1995, the government stopped subsidizing these firms and stopped paying wages to employees who often go months at a time without being paid. Managers frequently pay their employees with the firms' output, which the employees must sell on the street to earn whatever they can.

◤ Financial Markets

For free-market capitalism to work, there need to be efficient capital markets that can transfer financial resources from savers to borrowers. The most fundamental capital market is a sound banking system. In Russia, private banks are a new concept, and many that opened were poorly managed, unregulated, and subject to corruption. Many have failed due to bad loans and people's savings have been lost. Instead of putting their money in banks that often fail or will not return their deposits when needed, Russians convert their savings into U.S. dollars (and euros) as a hedge against inflation and depreciation of the ruble (see the case application, Good as Gold in chapter 16). These dollars are hidden under mattresses, or in other such places, and therefore are not available to the banking system for making business and consumer loans. The practice is so widespread that Russians possess the largest volume of U.S. currency outside of the United States.

Stock markets are another capital market whereby finances are transferred from savers to the business sector. Beginning in the early 1990s, a number of stock exchanges sprang up all over Russia. They are not linked by computers, however, and trading of stocks in different markets is difficult. An efficient stock market requires that potential stock buyers have information about the companies they are investing in, and this information is often nonexistent or withheld by managers. On top of all these problems, the markets are not well regulated, and fraud is rampant. Finally, as noted above, Russians have little knowledge of stock markets and are reluctant to invest in domestic firms.

Bond markets, the final important capital market, are most heavily used for government borrowing. The Russian government has issued billions of dollars worth of bonds in both ruble and dollar denominations but is now

crony capitalism a slang expression referring to an economic system based on the allocation of resources and goods according to favoritism and "who you know" rather than according to who can make the most productive use of the resources.

having a difficult time paying its debt. In August 1998 the government announced it was delaying payment on outstanding debts to foreign and domestic bondholders; in other words, it defaulted. As a result of its difficulties in honoring its debts, the interest rate it must pay is extremely high in order to attract risk-taking investors. The high interest rates paid by the government spill over to the private sector, where firms must pay equally high, or higher, interest rates if they wish to compete with the government for funds.

◤ The New Role of Government

The role of the government in a market economy is much different than under communism. Rather than owning the country's industries, the government must now establish legal guidelines and regulations under which the nation's firms must operate. One reason for the poor performance of the Soviet economy was that state controlled monopolies had no competition. The Russian economy must now avoid replacing state-owned monopolies with private monopolies. This requires establishing antitrust laws and a legal system to enforce them, institutions that never existed in the past. It also requires setting policies on imported goods. As happens everywhere, Russian firms want tariffs to protect them from foreign competition, while Russian consumers want low tariffs to keep imports inexpensive. It is a new and difficult balancing act because free trade did not exist in the USSR, but presents a problem that the government must address.

The government must also deal with its responsibilities to provide public goods and services to the Russian people. In the past, pensions, health care, day care, recreational facilities, and other social services were provided to workers by the firms where they worked. Such expenses were part of the budget that managers considered when establishing their annual input and output plans. Privatized firms, however, do not provide these services and the dinosaurs cannot afford to. As in other market economies, the role of providing such

services falls on the shoulders of the government. In addition, the government must continue to fund such government goods as public safety and national defense. Despite the end of the **cold war** and the reduction in military spending, a country cannot simply cease funding for its army, navy, and air force.

The old Soviet government was able to generate funds through the profits earned by government-owned companies, but privatization has removed this source of revenue. To provide social services, as well as resources to fund the military, police, and fire departments, the subsidies necessary to keep the dinosaurs afloat, and everything else, the government needs to collect taxes. This has proved to be extremely difficult. First of all, tax collecting requires the establishment of an entirely new national agency from nothing. Tax collectors and accountants need to be trained in how to determine tax liabilities, and the legal system needs to enforce the new tax laws. The system also needs to learn how to catch tax evaders, one practice at which Russian businesses have proved to be quite adept. Again, the nomenklatura have used their political influence to protect the few profitable businesses in the economy from their fair share of the tax burden. The tax-collection problem proved to be so severe that the IMF, which had been helping the Russians with billions of dollars in loans to ease their transition, refused to make agreed-upon loan installments until the government dealt with its tax-collecting problem.

The government in any country must also establish stabilization policies to combat unemployment and inflation. Again, such policies are

---

cold war the political, and threatened military, conflict between communism (the Soviet Union) and capitalism (the United States and Western Europe) for world domination and influence between the 1950s and 1991.

new to Russia and the other former communist countries. Under the Soviet regime, inflation was controlled by controlling prices and unemployment did not officially exist because everyone was guaranteed a job. Now, however, the government needs to establish some way to deal with these problems. An independent central bank was established to control inflation through regulating the money supply, and it was able to reduce inflation from over 1500% a year in 1992 to 11% in 1997. Keeping inflation down is difficult, however, because, given the problems in collecting taxes, the only way for the government to meet its financial obligations is by creating more money. Following this path led to the Russian hyperinflation of 1992–93, which threatens to reappear.

How Is the Former Soviet Union's Economy Being Restructured?

EconExplorer

There are literally hundreds of other areas where the Russian government must establish and enforce new laws and regulations that have never before existed. Laws regarding bankruptcy, for example, that protect credi-

rule of law the principle that all people and businesses have equal protection under the law, and the rejection of favoritism and special favors for the privileged few.

tors; contract law that sets the rules of trade among firms and individuals; security regulations that govern the new private banking system and the fledgling stock market. Think about all the agencies and laws in the United States that protect businesses and consumers (see chapters 8 and 9), and think of establishing them overnight in a country where they never existed before. People must also be trained in the professions needed to administer the laws and regulations, professions that never before existed. The process could be overwhelming, and indeed, it has overwhelmed the Russian economy.

Even in the private sector of the new economy people are facing situations that they never faced before. Managers who were always guaranteed markets in the past must now learn how to find customers and market their products. Businesses that had always been told what inputs to buy and where to buy them must now learn the art of purchasing. Customers used to waiting in lines for hours for whatever goods were available must learn the power of consumer sovereignty.

But perhaps the biggest failure of the Russian government has been its inability to establish and enforce a **rule of law** whereby all people and businesses are treated fairly and equally. This inability has allowed organized crime to run rampant and terrorize and extort protection money from businesses trying to succeed in a market environment. It has allowed a "good old boy" network of connected nomenklatura to rob the country blind. And, what could be even more damaging, it has presented an image of capitalism that suggests that one gets ahead by corruption and having contacts, not by being productive. The Russian people, many of whom are much worse off than they were before the collapse of communism, given the chance, might choose to return to it.

Case Application

An Accident Waiting to Happen

During the cold war, the United States and the Soviet Union built and stockpiled enough nuclear weapons to destroy the entire earth many times over. Although the threat of a nuclear war has abated with the breakup of the Soviet Union, a new, and perhaps even more dangerous, nuclear threat is unfolding: the threat of radiation poisoning from poorly contained nuclear wastes and from accidents at nuclear power plants.

Most of us are aware of the Soviet Union's nuclear military arsenal, but few are aware of how the Soviets disposed of their nuclear waste. Much of it was simply dumped into the Kara Sea off the coast of Siberia, and some was dumped into the Sea of Japan. Farther west, and not too far from Scandinavia, dozens of decommissioned nuclear-powered warships have been sunk with their reactors on board, or the reactors have been removed and are being stored on rusting freighters.

Since the breakup of the Soviet Union, most nuclear weapons have been transferred from the other republics to Russia (only Belarus has refused to transfer weapons that were originally installed in its territory). Maintaining these weapons safely is a difficult job that requires skilled personnel and highly specialized equipment. With the current economic crisis in Russia, however, soldiers at military installations have not been paid in months, and there are no funds to maintain or improve the facilities where the weapons are stored. Many fear that unpaid physicists and engineers who have the skills to build nuclear warheads and the missiles to carry them, may be forced to leave Russia and move to less friendly countries that are eager to develop a nuclear weapons capability.

An even more dangerous threat comes from the poorly built and aging nuclear power plants scattered throughout the country. Most

of us have heard of the 1986 explosion at the nuclear reactor at Chernobyl (in Ukraine) but are unaware that there are 15 reactors similar to the one at Chernobyl still operating in Russia, and many more in the other republics. Nor are most people aware that between 1992 and 1994 there were over 250 reported accidents at Russian nuclear facilities, many of them major incidents that released significant amounts of radiation over miles and miles of Russian countryside and hundreds of cities. Once in the atmosphere, the radiated particles are free to drift over Russia's neighbors, reaching as far as Western Europe.

Since the collapse of the Soviet Union, the Russians have been more forthright and open about their record of nuclear safety. Prior to 1991, however, the Soviet government was extremely secretive about these matters, and we can only imagine the extent of the nuclear contamination that occurred during that period. One thing that is apparent, though, is that the Soviet Union's reputation for producing poor quality goods carried over into its design and production of nuclear power plants. Despite these problems, the Russians are considering a 50% expansion in their nuclear capacity—a situation that is raising concern throughout the rest of the world.

Nuclear waste and the threat of nuclear accidents are not the only environmental problems facing the Russian people. The central planners in the Soviet Union forgot to include one very important item in the instructions passed down to the managers of the country's factories—taking care to protect their environment. The former Soviet republics, especially Russia, contain perhaps the most polluted environments in the world. The air, the water, and the land have all been polluted to an extent that no one could have imagined. Half the Russian

Nuclear contamination was obviously not a concern in the Soviet Union. The accident at the nuclear power plant in Chernobyl is well known, but, as this picture shows, power plant wastes are often dumped irresponsibly, and contamination is widespread.

people drink unsafe water, and almost three-quarters breathe unsafe air.

The poor quality of Soviet manufactured goods is also evident in the quality of their oil pipelines. In 1994 a section of the trans-Siberian oil pipeline ruptured and spilled an estimated 200,000 tons of crude oil. This followed a 1989 spill of 500,000 tons that spread out over the land and remained there because the region was too cold and snow-covered to clean it up. The Russian response to the disaster was similar to that of the old USSR. It first denied that the spill had ever occurred, and then it reported that the size of the spill at only 10,000 to 20,000 tons.

Efforts to meet quotas led Soviet managers to expand production regardless of the environmental outcomes. The waste generated by a giant nickel smelter near the Arctic city of Nikel has destroyed every living thing within an 18-mile diameter. No grass, no trees, no wildlife. In Monchegorsk, a few miles south, nuclear blasts were used to assist in the nickel mining, without regard for the radiation poisoning that resulted. This area, too, has a basically dead environment. The average life span for Russians in such industrialized portions of the country has declined from 62 in 1965 to less than 50 today.

Russia's vast lakes and inland seas have not escaped the degradation. Lake Baikal in Siberia holds more fresh water than any other lake in the world. It is 40 miles long, 50 miles wide, 1 mile deep, and is so filled with the discharge from pulp mills and covered with acid rain from coal fired-power plants that it is practically dead. The wholesale dumping of industrial wastes and the runoff of fertilizers and pesticides have just about killed the freshwater Aral Sea in southern Russia. Water from the sea was diverted to irrigate regional cotton plantations, severely reducing the amount of water that remained, and even further concentrating the poisons in it. Rivers and streams fed by the sea carried its toxic water throughout the region. It was and still is used for drinking water, washing clothes, and watering crops.

The environmental legacy of the Soviet Union is now left to the Russian Republic, which simply does not have the funds to clean up the mess. Estimates of the cleanup costs of the nuclear wastes alone are in the hundreds of billions of dollars, and Russia's total GDP was only about $465 billion in 1997, and if anything, it is shrinking rather than growing. How can a country that cannot even feed its people or pay its workers and pensioners find the money for pollution control equipment or toxic waste cleanup?

Economic Reasoning

1. Why is pollution so severe in Russia today? Review the case application, A Common Problem, in chapter 8 and evaluate the pollution problem in terms of common property resources.

2. What is the connection between the quality of manufactured goods in the Soviet Union and current environmental problems in the country?

3. Russia is a nuclear accident waiting to happen, but the Russians cannot afford to fix their nuclear power plants or properly dispose of their nuclear waste. Do you think that it is the responsibility of the developed countries to pay to clean up Russia's environment?

An Accident Waiting to Happen

Visit http://www.webdirectory.com or a similar Web site and see if you can find some up-to-date information on the Russian environmental crisis.

How Are the Economies of Central and Eastern Europe Being Restructured?

The former communist countries of Central and Eastern Europe (Bulgaria, Romania, Hungary, Poland, the Czech Republic, Slovakia, and East Germany) broke away from Soviet economic and political domination in 1989 and 1990 (Figure 3). Since that time these Central and Eastern European (CEE) countries have struggled to restructure themselves into market economies with varying degrees of success. The entire region fell into an economic collapse as bad as our Great Depression from 1990 through 1992, with regional GDP falling 6.5%, 11.6%, and 6.9% in these 3 years. Since that time, however, most countries have turned the corner, and overall economic growth has been positive

(Table 1, p. 483). This section focuses on two success stories in the region: Poland and Hungary, and then presents a very brief summary of what is occurring in the other CEE countries.

Restructuring the Polish Economy

Although the Hungarians and Czechs had rebelled unsuccessfully against Soviet domination in the 1950s and 1960s, the Polish people were the first to challenge Soviet dominance in the 1980s. Led by Lech Walesa, in 1980 the workers at the Gdansk Shipyards in northern Poland forced the government to accept the formation

Figure 3

The Eastern and Central European Countries

of their noncommunist labor union, Solidarity, and to give the workers increased rights and freedoms. This was the beginning of the unraveling of Soviet domination in the CEE countries and led to the end of Communist Party rule in Poland and Walesa's election as president in 1990. After a shaky start, Poland's economy has become one of the fastest growing in Europe and the world. As of 1998, alone among all the former communist countries, it had generated a per-capita GDP greater than its 1989 GDP.

Like the Russians, the Poles opted for a crash program of free markets and privatization. Beginning in 1990, prices were decontrolled and set free to be determined in markets by supply and demand. Inflation soared at first—585% in 1990—but then steadily decreased to about 13% in 1997 (Table 2).

For a number of reasons, the Polish transition to market capitalism has been much more successful than in Russia. Unlike the Russians, the Poles are familiar with capitalism, having adopted a market economy in the 1800s and

Table 1 · GDP Growth in Selected Former Communist Countries, 1990–1997

GDP (% change)	1990	1991	1992	1993	1994	1995	1996	1997
Bulgaria	−9.1	−11.7	−7.3	−1.5	1.8	2.9	−10.1	−6.9
Croatia	−7.1	−20.6	−11.7	−0.9	0.6	6.8	6.0	6.5
Czech Republic	−1.2	−11.5	−3.3	0.6	3.2	6.4	3.9	1.0
Estonia	−8.1	−7.9	−14.2	−8.5	−1.8	4.3	4.0	11.4
Hungary	−3.5	−11.9	−3.1	−0.6	2.9	1.5	1.3	4.4
Latvia	−3.5	−10.4	−34.9	−14.9	0.6	−0.8	3.3	6.5
Lithuania	−6.9	−13.4	−37.7	−17.1	−11.3	3.3	4.7	5.7
Poland	−11.6	−7.0	2.6	3.8	5.2	7.0	6.1	6.9
Romania	−5.6	−12.9	−8.7	1.5	3.9	7.1	3.9	−6.6
Russia	−3.0	−5.0	−14.5	−8.7	−12.6	−4.1	−3.5	0.8
Slovakia	−2.5	−14.6	−6.5	−3.7	4.9	6.9	6.6	6.5
Slovenia	−4.7	−8.9	−5.5	2.8	5.3	4.1	3.1	3.8
Ukraine	−2.6	−11.6	−13.7	−14.2	−23.0	−12.2	−10.0	−3.0

The transition to capitalism proved difficult for all the former communist countries. After a rough start, however, most CEE countries have experienced solid growth. Unfortunately, the members of the former Soviet Union are still struggling.

Source: Business Central Europe (www.bcemag.com/_bcedb/stat_main.htm). Primary sources include Reuters and the European Bank for Reconstruction and Development.

Table 2 · Inflation in Selected Former Communist Countries, 1990–1997

Inflation (%)	1990	1991	1992	1993	1994	1995	1996	1997
Bulgaria	23.8	333.5	82.0	73.0	96.3	33.0	311.1	578.7
Croatia	609.5	123.0	666.0	1518.0	97.6	3.7	3.5	4.0
Czech Republic	9.7	56.6	11.1	20.8	10.0	7.9	8.7	9.9
Estonia	17.2	210.5	1076.0	89.8	48.0	28.8	15.0	12.3
Hungary	28.9	35.0	23.0	22.5	18.8	28.5	20.0	18.4
Latvia	10.5	172.0	951.2	108.0	35.9	23.3	13.2	7.0
Lithuania	8.4	224.7	1020.5	410.4	72.1	35.5	13.1	8.5
Poland	585.8	70.3	43.0	35.3	32.2	22.0	18.7	13.2
Romania	5.1	161.1	210.4	256.1	136.7	27.7	56.8	151.7
Russia	5.3	92.6	1526.5	874.3	307.2	131.4	21.8	11.0
Slovakia	10.6	61.2	10.1	23.2	13.4	7.4	5.5	6.5
Slovenia	549.7	117.7	201.3	32.3	19.8	9.0	9.0	8.8
Ukraine	4.8	91.0	1210.0	4700.0	891.0	181.7	39.7	10.1

Most of the former communist countries experienced bouts of hyperinflation during their transition to capitalism and a few are still struggling to bring it under control.

Source: Business Central Europe (www.bcemag.com/_bcedb/stat_main.htm). Primary sources include Reuters and the European Bank for Reconstruction and Development.

maintained it until World War II. The Poles also had much more freedom to travel than their Soviet counterparts, and many were allowed to travel to the West and came into contact with market economies and could see how well they worked in comparison to communism. Additionally, many Polish emigrants sent money back to the "old country," and these funds were used to start many small businesses. Finally, foreign investors have been much more willing to invest in Poland than they are in the former Soviet Union. The government is more stable, the rule of law is better established, and employees are well educated and highly motivated.

Privatization in Poland occurred through the use of vouchers, which were distributed in 1996. The vouchers could be used to buy shares in 1 or more of 15 National Investment Funds (NIFs) that in turn bought stock in different companies. The NIFs operate like stock mutual funds in the United States, and an investor's share can be freely bought and sold.

Stock markets are nothing new in Poland. The Warsaw Stock Exchange had existed from 1817 until 1945, and it reopened in 1991. In addition to the NIF funds, domestic and foreign investors are free to buy and sell stocks in Polish companies. The market has been very successful, increasing in value by 89% in 1996. As of mid-1998, it was up about 9% for the year. This may not seem like a lot, but keep in mind that the stock markets of many emerging countries took a huge battering during this period.

Like other former communist countries, Poland has had difficulty with its dinosaurs. Investors have no interest in buying them and there is little demand for their products. Unlike Russia, which subsidized its dinosaurs to keep them operating until 1995, Poland make the difficult decision to let them fail right away. This was a painful transition, and GDP fell by almost 12% in 1990 and another 7% in 1991. Since that time, the Polish economy has grown more rapidly than most other countries in the world in each successive year.

Despite its successes, Poland still faces several hurdles on its road to economic pros-

Luxury items were a low priority in communist countries, but that does not mean that people in those countries would not have liked to have them.

perity. During the communist era, international trade among CEE countries was controlled by the **Council for Mutual Economic Assistance (CMEA)**. CMEA determined which countries would produce which goods and to which countries these goods would be exported. Most such trade involved the Eastern European countries selling manufactured goods to the Soviet Union in return for natural resources and energy (oil and natural gas), which was sold at well below market prices. Trade with Western countries was severely limited.

With the collapse of communism came the collapse of the CMEA and the old trade patterns. On the input side, the Poles and the other CEE countries now had to pay the much higher world prices for energy and other resources. On the output side, the Poles needed to develop new markets for their goods in

Council for Mutual Economic Assistance (CMEA) the formal international trade agreement that outlined and set the international trade patterns among the USSR and the communist countries of CEE.

Unemployment (%)	1990	1991	1992	1993	1994	1995	1996	1997
Bulgaria	1.7	11.1	15.3	16.4	12.8	11.1	12.5	13.7
Croatia	11.4	13.2	13.2	14.8	14.5	17.6	15.9	17.6
Czech Republic	0.8	4.1	2.6	3.5	3.2	2.9	3.5	5.2
Estonia	na	na	na	5.0	5.1	5.0	5.6	4.6
Hungary	1.9	7.5	12.3	12.1	10.4	10.4	10.5	10.4
Latvia	na	na	2.3	5.8	6.5	6.6	7.2	6.7
Lithuania	na	0.3	1.3	4.4	3.8	7.3	6.2	6.7
Poland	6.3	11.8	13.6	16.4	16.0	14.9	13.2	10.5
Romania	0.4	3.0	6.2	9.5	9.5	9.5	6.6	8.8
Russia	na	0.0	4.8	5.7	7.5	8.9	9.3	9.0
Slovakia	0.8	4.1	10.4	12.2	13.7	13.1	12.8	12.5
Slovenia	4.7	8.2	11.5	14.4	14.4	14.5	14.4	14.8
Ukraine	na	0.0	0.3	0.4	0.4	0.6	1.5	2.8

Table 3 Unemployment in Selected Former Communist Countries, 1990–1997

Despite their economic troubles, most former communist countries have been moderately successful at getting unemployment down to manageable levels.

Source: Business Central Europe (www.bcemag.com/_bcedb/stat_main.htm). Primary sources include Reuters and the European Bank for Reconstruction and Development.

countries that had the money to buy them. Overall they have been quite successful in these endeavors. The quality of their products has improved to Western standards and they have been able to keep prices low. As a result, they have been very successful in increasing their exports to Western European countries.

The transition to a market economy is not being made without hardship for many. Large collective farms are being closed and private Polish farms are too small to be efficient. They need to acquire modern farm equipment, although such modernization will probably reduce the number of Polish farmers by half. Coal and steel workers are also suffering. During the communist era government subsidies ensured that they were among the highest paid of all Polish workers, earning more than doctors, lawyers, and, heaven forbid, economics professors. With the loss of subsidies and an outdated capital stock, these industries cannot compete in global markets, and workers are losing their jobs. As a consequence, unemployment is also high at about 10.5% of the labor force (Table 3).

Retirees and others on government assistance have seen their transfer payments reduced and their incomes have not kept pace with inflation. On the other hand, those people who are educated, entrepreneurial, or are well-connected through old communist party ties (the nomenklatura) are doing well in the new Poland.

Hungary

The Hungarians and the Czechs had the highest standards of living during the communist era. Like the Poles, Hungarians had a long history of free-market capitalism prior to the communist takeover at the end of World War II. Never happy with the communist system, the Hungarians implemented many economic reforms even while under Soviet domination. These reforms allowed managers to set wages and product prices, to procure inputs from foreign suppliers, and to make decisions about replacement capital. Efficiency and profitability rather than quotas were used as criteria for economic success, and unprofitable firms were closed. Because the Hungarian economy was so far along in its transition to a full-fledged market economy, shock therapy was unnecessary.

Despite their reliance on market-like processes, the government retained ownership of most productive resources while the communists were in power. Unlike the Poles, Russians, and Czechs who relied heavily on a voucher system to privatize their industries and put their ownership into private hands, the Hungarians put their industries up for sale to anyone, including foreign companies. Legal changes in 1989 allowed domestic companies to issue stock and permitted the establishment of firms with 100% foreign ownership. To encourage foreign investment, the government enacted laws that gave foreign investors tax reductions, provided them with legal protection, and, in general, did everything possible to make it easy for foreign investors. The results were spectacular, and as of 1998 Hungary had received over 40% of all the direct foreign investment in CEE, and the government was left owning only a small handful of firms. Looked at in another way, foreign direct investment in Hungary averaged about $200 per person in 1997 while it averaged only about $75 per person in Poland and $20 per person in Russia.

Two-thirds of Hungarian exports are manufactured in factories owned by foreign companies, and foreign banks have opened branches throughout the country. Even the Hungarian telephone system was sold to foreign (German and American) companies. Although putting such a vital industry into foreign hands might be unpopular, the number of Hungarians waiting for phone service dropped from 800,000 in 1993 to 20,000 in 1998. In Poland, where the government maintained control of its telecommunications firms, 2 million people were still waiting.

It is not just foreign businesses that are doing well. The Budapest Stock Exchange has been booming. Raising financial capital through issuing stock is a pretty sophisticated undertaking. Many CEE firms are reluctant to cede control to stockholders who demand accountability and profits, and prefer to finance expansion through borrowing, though it might not be the most economically efficient alternative. Hungarian firms, however, have easily adopted the use of equity markets, and they have introduced 60 new stock offerings in the last 6 years compared to only 1 in the Czech Republic.

Similar to all the former communist countries, transition has not been easy. With it came a widening gap between rich and poor, and extreme hardship for almost 20% of the population who were on pensions. Although pensions subsequently have been indexed to inflation to ease the financial hardship of the elderly, the poorer segments of Hungarian society continue to be unhappy with the transition. GDP growth in Hungary was negative from 1990 through 1993, and was positive but slow through 1997 (Table 1). Inflation has hovered around 20% or more per year since the transition began, and unemployment has been stuck around 10 to 12% (Tables 2 and 3). Despite the recent gains, the per capita income in Hungary is still slightly below what it was in 1989.

With the ouster of the communist government in 1989, many Hungarians expected to see a rapid rise in their living standards. As it became apparent that incomes as high as those in the West would not happen overnight, they became increasingly disillusioned and elected a socialist government made up of former communist leaders in 1994. Even as late as 1997, the per capita income in Hungary was only 32% of that in Western Europe. The socialists, however, stayed the course toward capitalism and continued to cut government spending and interference in the economy. As noted, the results have been positive and Hungary's economy is growing steadily stronger. If and when the European Union expands, many expect Hungary (along with Poland) to be the among the first former communist countries to gain admittance.

◥ The Other CEE Countries

The other CEE countries have had the same difficulties in restructuring their economies as did Poland and Hungary: initial drops in GDP, high inflation, and increased unemployment, although all have experienced improved economic performance after the transition period.

How Are the Economies of Central and Eastern Europe Being Restructed?

EconExplorer

Czechoslovakia was the most industrialized and richest CEE country prior to the communist takeover after World War II. It had a well-educated labor force and a long history of free enterprise. On December 31, 1992, the country split into two independent countries, the Czech Republic and Slovakia. The Czechs are more industrialized and richer than their Slovak counterparts, and have proceeded much faster toward privatization (using vouchers) and installing the institutions necessary in a modern free-market economy.

Romania and Bulgaria have been much slower than the countries discussed above in restructuring their economies. Both economies are primarily agricultural, and had little experience with industrialization or market economics prior to their conversion to communism. Former communists have been elected and held power through most of the 1990s in each country, and the governments have been slow to privatize their economies. Bulgaria has yet to seriously undertake a restructuring program and the Romanian government was late in doing so—it did not aggressively pursue privatization and free-market policies until 1997. As has been the case elsewhere, the adoption of such policies initially led to an economic downturn.

East Germany's experience differs markedly from those of other CEE countries. Formed through a partition of Germany after World War II, it adopted one of the most strictly communist economic systems in CEE until it was reunited with free-market West Germany in 1990. It is now a part of the Federal Republic of Germany, or simply, Germany. At the time of reunification, the East was far behind the West in just about every measure of economic performance. The West Germans poured massive amounts of aid into the eastern part of the new country to modernize businesses, build a new infrastructure, improve public services, and raise the incomes of their eastern counterparts. This imposed a heavy financial burden on the West, but the investment has paid off handsomely, and the eastern part of the country is closing the gap with the West.

Albania and the former Yugoslavia have had different experiences than the other CEE countries. Both adopted communist economic systems, but neither accepted Soviet domination. Albania was and continues to be a totalitarian country ruled according to strict communist ideology and isolated from the rest of the world. It has not given up its belief in communism and it has made no move to restructure its economy. It is also by far the poorest country in Europe.

Unlike the other CEE countries (except for Albania), the Yugoslavs drove the Germans out of their country at the end of World War II without the aid of the Soviet Union, and ended the war without Soviet soldiers in their country. As a consequence of this and the strength of their independent-minded leader Marshall Josip Tito, the Yugoslavs adopted their own form of communism that proved to be more successful than the state socialism practiced in the Soviet bloc (see the case application, A Different Shade of Red). Unfortunately for the Yugoslav people, the 1990s brought a lengthy and destructive civil war that saw the country break apart into 5 independent republics (as of 1998). Except for Slovenia, which avoided being dragged into the war and is prospering, issues of economic restructuring have taken a backseat to putting the war-torn countries back together again.

Comparative Case Application

A Different Shade of Red

The country of Yugoslavia was created after World War I from pieces of the defeated Austro-Hungarian and Ottoman Empires. The new country contained a variety of people from different ethnic and religious backgrounds and was made up of six semiautonomous republics. Slovenia, Serbia, and Croatia were industrialized and affluent. Bosnia-Herzegovina, Montenegro, and Macedonia were agricultural and much poorer.

The country was invaded by the Italians and Germans in World War II, but under the leadership of Josip Broz who united the people from the different republics, a rag-tag but dedicated group of communist partisans managed to expel both forces from the country by the end of the war. Broz adopted the name Tito, and unified the country under a strong central communist government with himself as "president for life." Unlike the other communist states in Central and Eastern Europe, Tito refused to accept Soviet domination or Soviet-style state socialism. Instead, he established a communist economy where economic decisions were made by the workers rather than central planners in Belgrade.

Under Tito, small businesses (five or fewer employees) were allowed to own their enterprise and operate according to market principles. Bigger firms, however, were all owned by the government, which established the firms and then turned control over to the workers. In an effort to reduce income differences throughout the country, Tito spread the new industrial enterprises throughout the country. He also encouraged people to migrate to the new jobs in different republics.

The workers at the government-owned firms elected workers' councils, which in turn elected a management board, which in turn appointed the firm's manager. Through their elected representatives, the workers decided on what to produce, how much to pay for inputs, how much to charge for outputs, what production techniques to use, and how much to borrow for investment. In short, through their managers, the workers made the same decisions that managers in Western businesses make.

Although the manager actually made the decisions, a key difference was that Western managers are responsible to shareowners and Yugoslav managers were responsible to the workers at the firm. Stockholders are happy and support management when they make profits. Workers are happy and support management when they get to do as little as possible for the most money. The result was a less than highly motivated workforce and managers that could do little about it. Another significant difference was that the firm's capital could not be sold. It belonged to the workers as long as they worked there. If they changed jobs, which they were free to do, they became "owners" of their new firm. There was no such thing as corporate stock that employees could buy or sell, in their firm or in any other firm.

The workers determined how the firm's profits were to be used. One option was to reinvest them in the firm. This was not a popular option because once the new capital was put into place, it only belonged to them as long as they stayed with the firm. Once they quit or retired, any increased profits stemming from the investment were lost to them. A second option was to use the profits to build facilities such as employee gyms, playgrounds, or recreation centers. This also proved to be an unpopular option because, for example, younger workers may prefer gyms, middle-aged workers may want playgrounds for their children, and older workers may want neither. The obvious choice of most workers was to devote most profits to increasing their salaries. As a consequence, private investment was low, and most investment programs had to be carried out by the central government.

The lack of a stock market where equity capital could be bought and sold reduced the economic efficiency of the Yugoslav economy. Suppose a car factory was earning a 15% annual rate of return while a furniture company was earning 5%. If the companies were owned by stockholders, the owners of furniture company stock would sell their shares and use the proceeds to buy shares in the auto company. This essentially moves capital resources from the lesser to the more efficient enterprise. Such movement could not happen in Tito's Yugoslavia—the furniture company employees could only shift resources to the car industry by moving their labor.

Would the car company workers vote to hire new workers from the furniture factory? Not often. If an auto worker retired or quit, the remaining workers had a choice of dividing the worker's salary among themselves or hiring someone new. Despite the fact that a new worker might actually increase the firm's profits, the existing workers could often increase their individual salaries by not replacing the departed employee. As a result, unemployment in Yugoslavia was much higher than in might otherwise have been.

The lack of a stock market also meant that the most common way to raise investment funds was through borrowing from the government-owned banking system. Firms not only borrowed to buy new capital, but if there was not enough profit to ensure a government–set minimum wage, they were permitted to borrow to meet their payroll and other expenses. With such a guarantee in place, there was little incentive to operate efficiently. Another consequence was increasing volumes of bank loans, an increased money supply, and ongoing inflation.

Under Tito's strong leadership, the country held together as Serbs, Bosnians, Croats, Macedonians, Slovenes and Albanians all learned to work and live with each other. After his death in 1980, the country fell apart into separate independent republics. Sadly, his legacy of integrating the population turned into a tragedy. Members of ethnic groups living outside the republic with which they identified (for example, Serbs living in the new Croatia) engaged in a terrible civil war during the 1990s that crippled the region's economies. With the exception of the Slovenes who avoided being embroiled in the war and have made a successful transition to a market economy, the remaining countries are currently more concerned with recovering from the war than with restructuring their economies.

Economic Reasoning

1. How was communism in Yugoslavia different than the communist economic system in the Soviet Union?

2. How did the lack of a capital (stock) market lead to economic efficiency in Yugoslavia?

3. Do you think that workers should be allowed to make business decisions (such as wages, prices, and so on) for a firm? Why or why not?

A Different Shade of Red

You can review current events (economic and otherwise) in Macedonia, Slovenia and Croatia at http://www.kenpubs.co.uk/investguide/. Use this resource to prepare an analysis of the economic progress being made in these countries. A little less up-to-date analysis of all the former countries of Yugoslavia can be found in the CIA World Fact Book at http://www.odci.gov/cia/publications/factbook/.

▶ How Is the Chinese Economy Being Restructured?

An old Chinese proverb says that "one crosses the river by touching the stones." What it means is that you don't decide which rock you are actually going to step on until you are ready to take the step. The Chinese leaders are following this philosophy as a guide to restructuring their economy. Rather than making long-range plans or plunging into economic shock therapy, they are seeing what works and what doesn't work before they take another step.

◨ China under Mao

Mao Zedong established the world's most populous communist nation when he proclaimed the establishment of the People's Republic of China in 1949. The country was among the poorest in the world, and the vast majority of the Chinese people were illiterate peasants who lived in rural villages and had never come into contact with the industrialized world. Mao's vision was to create a Utopian society where the idea of self-interest would be eliminated and replaced with a desire to work for the good of society.

Under Mao, nearly all agricultural, industrial, and commercial property was nationalized (taken over) by the government, which established Soviet-style central planning to direct the economic activity of the country. From 1949 through the mid-1950s, Mao and the communist leadership did a great deal to modernize Chinese industry, educate the populace, and improve health care and sanitary conditions.

In 1957, wanting even faster growth, Mao instigated the **Great Leap Forward,** a 5-year plan designed to double China's GDP in the first year and continue to increase it in the fu-

---

Great Leap Forward Mao Zedong's ambitious 5-year plan (1957) that was to achieve accelerated economic growth through the abolition of self-interest and financial incentives, making the people's sole motivation the desire to improve Chinese society.

---

ture. Growth was to be achieved by getting rid of all remaining financial incentives and expecting people to work night and day for the good of China. In the early days of Chinese communism, farmers had been allowed to use small "family plots" to grow produce for local farmers' markets, but during the Great Leap Forward these were abolished. Individual family units were also abolished, and men and women were forced to live in barracks and eat in mess halls, while their children were raised in government nurseries. Millions of people were moved from their homes and forced to work digging irrigation canals and reservoirs with shovels and hauling away the dirt in buckets. Lacking capital, the Chinese leadership exploited the huge population and built their infrastructure by forcing workers to work around the clock under extremely harsh conditions.

The same principles were applied to industry. In addition to the traditional Soviet-style pattern of erecting giant industrial complexes, 60 million Chinese were conscripted into making pig iron and other industrial products in inefficient backyard furnaces and workshops. Mao and the other leaders believed that this was a good way to utilize surplus rural labor and was preferable to shipping light industrial products from the giant SOEs in the cities.

The Great Leap Forward failed miserably. Although output did increase by 15% in the first year, the strain of the hard work and the limits of even China's huge population had been reached. Inefficient production methods and poor weather combined to generate a famine that killed millions of Chinese. By 1962 output was back at its 1957 level—in 5 years the Great Leap Forward had not increased GDP at all! Instead of blaming the program, its failure was blamed on landlords, rich peasants, and others accused of looking out for themselves instead of the Chinese people. Mao's response, in 1966, was to become even more extreme. All wage differences were abolished in an attempt to form a completely classless society. Young people known as the Red Guards traveled throughout China enforcing Mao's dictates that everyone should labor equally for equal pay. Teachers, doctors, physicists, engineers—it did not matter. All were forced to work in the fields as peasants or in factories as industrial workers.

The abolition of incentives and the failure to utilize comparative advantages among the Chinese people led to another economic disaster. Finally, in the mid-1970s, China's leaders began to relent and backed away from strict **communist ideology** in favor of a more pragmatic approach to creating prosperity in China.

◤ Pragmatism

When Mao died in 1976, about 80% of China's population still lived in agricultural communes; the country had made little progress in industrialization and living standards had not improved for years. The heavy manufacturing industries that did exist were owned by the national government and light industry and other businesses were owned by cooperatives or local governments. Unlike Mao, who was a believer in following strict communist ideology, his successor, Deng Xiaoping's approach to the economy was rooted in **pragmatism:** he was willing to try whatever worked, regardless of whether it was consistent with communist ideology or not, in order to increase Chinese incomes. Instead of shock therapy, however, Deng opted for small-scale experimentation at first. Only if something worked on a small scale would it be adopted throughout the economy.

Deng began to reform the Chinese economy in a number of areas as early as the late 1970s, much earlier than the parallel reforms in the USSR and CEE countries. First, although the government retained ownership of the land, peasants were allowed to lease land and use it to grow produce for local markets and to sell much of it at market-determined prices. Prices were also gradually freed in other sectors of the economy. The government set production quotas for most goods, agricultural and industrial, and set the prices for this required output. Output beyond the quota, however, could be sold at higher market prices. Although the government retained ownership of most industrial firms, less reliance was placed on central planning at the national level, and the ownership of many businesses was transferred to local governments and to different government agencies.

In place of the national government, the management and control of most rural businesses have been turned over to **town and village enterprises (TVEs)** or government ministries. The TVEs are industrial firms in interior China, and they provide jobs for the agricultural workers who are being replaced by the newly purchased tractors and other capital that is being used to increase agricultural productivity. Most TVEs are owned and managed by local governments. Well aware of the problems of urban migration and growing slums that characterize most developing countries (see chapter 18), the Chinese leaders want to ensure that peasants who lose employment on the farms have an alternative source of work. Consistent with the pragmatic approach, Deng acknowledged that this Maoist strategy was a good idea and incorporated it into his policies.

In an effort to reduce the financial burdens on the central government, Deng required many government agencies to earn their own keep. This was another step in unleashing Chinese business from the control of central planners in Beijing. One of the most successful at

---

communist ideology Mao's belief that the principles of communism must be followed regardless of whether or not they proved to be economic successes.

pragmatism Deng's belief that economic policies and programs that proved to be successful should be adopted, whether they were consistent with strict communist ideology or not.

town and village enterprises (TVEs) community-owned industrial and commercial firms that have been established in the rural parts of China.

doing so was the Chinese Army. By 1997, it owned and operated 15,000 different businesses, including hotels, shoe repair shops, clothing manufacturers, airlines, and munitions manufacturers. Another successful agency was the Railroad Ministry which also operated a wide variety of businesses. In many ways the Chinese economy was operating very much as a free-market economy by 1998, with one major exception: private property was still the exception and not the rule.

Although Mao had initially opened China to international trade in the early 1970s, Deng put increased emphasis on its importance. Foreign direct investment was invited and encouraged, although it was restricted to certain coastal regions called **special economic zones (SEZs),** and the Chinese government insisted on partial ownership of all firms in the country. Billions of dollars of investment poured into China in the 1990s, and it grew to become one of the largest trading partners of the United States. Exports from the SEZs boomed, increasing from $5 billion in 1980 to $181 billion in 1997. Adding to China's newfound success in foreign trade is the return of Hong Kong, one of the world's richest and most free-market cities, to its control in 1997 (see case application, The Odd Couple).

How Is the Chinese Economy Being Restructured?

EconExplorer

---

special economic zones (SEZs) geographic areas near the Chinese coast where foreign firms are allowed to operate and are given special economic subsidies.

The Chinese method of dealing with their dinosaurs—and there are thousands of them left in China—has been to encourage private firms to compete with them by producing the same or substitute products. On the one hand, the competition should improve efficiency, and on the other, as the private firms flourish they will gradually absorb the workers who are let go by the dinosaurs. Managers of the SOEs have been given increased leeway to make their own decisions about what inputs to use, what wages and prices to pay, and what products to produce. Perhaps most important, Deng directed the managers of the SOEs to operate according to market principles—to produce goods that satisfied consumer demand and attempt to earn a profit. This was in sharp contrast to the old Maoist notion of production based on what the communist leadership decided was best for society—social goods and employment security.

◆ The Chinese Future

A joke making the rounds these days is that the world's greatest computer was built and programmed to answer the world's most important questions. The honor of asking the first question went to the president of the United States, who asked, "What is the future of the human race?" The computer whirred, buzzed, rang, and then ejected a piece of paper that the president took and examined with a puzzled look on his face. Asked what it said, he finally answered, "I don't know, it's written in Chinese."

It may be less of a joke than we think. With a population of 1.2 billion people, it would only take a per capita GDP of about $6,700 per person for the size of the Chinese economy to replace that of the United States as the world's largest. Increases in the Chinese GDP have averaged around 9% since the 1980s, making it the world's fastest growing economy over the past 2 decades (Figure 4). If growth at this rate continues, China will have the world's largest economy by 2020. Because of the extremely low incomes in China 20 years ago, the per capita GDP was still less than $1,000 in 1998

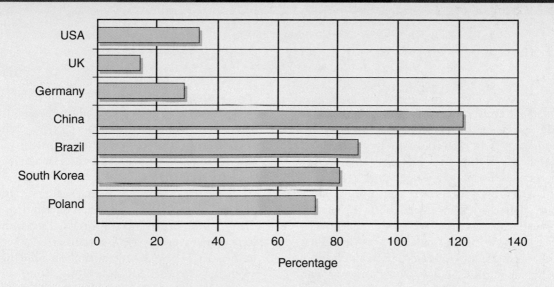

Figure 4

GDP Growth Rate in Selected Countries 1991–1997

Percentage

The size of the Chinese economy, the fastest growing in the world, more than doubled between 1991 and 1997. During the period the U.S. economy expanded by about one-third.

Source: World Bank, *World Development Report,* 1997

despite the recent growth. This figure understates the true buying power of the average Chinese. In terms of **purchasing power parity,** the average Chinese income is probably closer to $3,500.

Jiang Zemin assumed the leadership of China in 1997 after the death of Deng Xiaoping. He has continued to liberalize the Chinese economy, and one of his first efforts has been to move towards the privatization of the means of production. In mid-1998, Jiang issued a decree requiring the Chinese Army and other government institutions to turn over their assets to the private sector. The problem is that Western-style corruption has accompanied Western-style markets, and the government agencies have been giving preferences to their own businesses when making "official" government purchases.

Despite the freeing up of China's economy, the Communist Party remains very much in charge of the country's political system. It still sets the overall economic policy of the country and refuses to allow opposition political parties. In spring 1989, thousands of students went to Tiananmen Square in Beijing and staged a pro-democracy rally, demanding free elections, an end to Communist Party rule and the adoption of free-market economics.

---

purchasing power parity the value of an income measured in U.S. dollars, but reflecting the buying power of the dollar in countries where prices are much lower or higher than the United States.

(Continued on page 495)

Case Application

The Odd Couple

According to the Heritage Foundation's *1998 Index of Economic Freedom*, Hong Kong is once again the world champion of free enterprise. This makes 4 years in a row that this bustling Asian economy has topped the charts. What are the characteristics that make for a winner in the realm of free markets? Well, there are virtually no tariffs on international trade, the government owns no businesses and takes only 5% of GDP, taxes are low, there are no restrictions on foreign investment, prices are free to vary with market conditions, private property is fully protected, and the only regulations on business are to protect the environment.

The Hong Kong economy is one of the most successful in the world, with a GDP per capita (purchasing power parity) of around $26,000. In addition to producing a wide variety of manufactured goods, it is one of Asia's leading financial centers. Lying off the southern coast of China, it is essentially a city-state of about 6½ million people with a land area about six times larger than Washington, D.C. The area was annexed by the British following wars with China in 1842 and 1860, and remained a British colony until July 1, 1997, when it was returned to the Chinese. Although China will control Hong Kong's defense and foreign policy, the residents of Hong Kong have been guaranteed that they will retain control of their economic system. For the next several years, there will be one country with two sets of rules.

Talk about your "odd couples!" China, a communist nation with one of the least free economies in the world (ranking 120 out of 156) is essentially now in control on the world's freest free-market economy. How is it going to work? Actually, little has changed so far and little is expected to change in the future. The Hong Kong and Chinese economies have been pretty tightly connected for several years, and Hong Kong has served three major functions for the Chinese.

First, Hong Kong is China's largest trading partner. Even if the ultimate destination of many Chinese products is Brazil, England, or Kenya, many goods are first transferred to companies in Hong Kong and then reshipped around the globe. Second, Hong Kong serves as China's financial center. Despite the growth of stock markets in Beijing and Shanghai, the stocks of many of China's new corporations are most actively traded on the Hong Kong stock exchange.

Finally, for years Hong Kong has served as a middleman between China and the rest of the world. When the Chinese established their special economic zones and opened their economy to foreign investors, few businesses in the world had the connections in the country that Hong Kong businesses did. Even during the most stringent periods of communism under Mao, the two countries were major trading partners. Western companies looking to get into China found that the best way to do so was via Hong Kong, where the local merchants and traders had established personal relationships, and distribution networks.

Economic Reasoning

1. What characteristics of the Hong Kong economy contribute to its being considered the most economically free country in the world?

2. How are the Chinese and Hong Kong economies different?
3. Do you think it is fair to have different sets of rules for different people? Is China's policy toward Hong Kong an example of the pragmatism that is being practiced by Chinese leaders? Why or why not?

The Odd Couple

Check the latest Heritage Foundation's *Index of Economic Freedom* at http://www.heritage.org:80/index/execsum.html. Is Hong Kong still number one?

(Continued from page 493)

The government's response was to call out the army. The troops opened fire with machine guns and tanks, and hundreds of students were massacred. Despite outrage throughout the world, the Communist Party has continued to resist granting political freedom to the Chinese people along with increased economic freedom.

Unlike the former communist countries in CEE and the former Soviet Union, China is moving very slowly toward establishing a free-enterprise economy. Table 4 shows the Heritage Foundation's 1997 rankings of 156 countries, which placed China 120th in the world in terms of economic freedom (the lowest-ranking countries were the communist nations North Korea, Cuba, and Laos). Also unlike most of those other countries, however, the Chinese economy is growing rapidly, unemployment is low, and inflation is under control. There might be no political freedom, but there is political stability, and the Chinese economic philosophy is that the latter is more important than the former in promoting economic growth. The evidence supports their point of view.

Table 4 1997 Economic Freedom Index Rankings for Selected Countries

Country	Rank	Country	Rank
Hong Kong	1	Czech Republic	20
Singapore	2	South Korea	24
Bahrain	3	Hungary	66
New Zealand	4	Poland	69
Switzerland	5	Russia	104
United States	5	China	120
Luxembourg	7	Ukraine	125
Taiwan	7	Iraq	153
United Kingdom	7	Cuba	154
Japan	12	North Korea	154

Source: The Heritage Foundation, *1998 Index of Economic Freedom.*

▶ Putting It Together

After what proved to be a failed economic experiment that lasted almost 70 years, *communism* collapsed in Central and Eastern Europe in 1989 and in the former Soviet Union in 1991. The collapse marked the end of the Soviet Union, the end of the cold war, and a desire by the people in these countries to *restructure* their economies into capitalist free-market systems. Poland and most of the countries of the former Soviet Union opted for an overnight restructuring through a program of *shock therapy*, while other countries took a more moderate approach.

The transition from communism to capitalism has not been easy, and most countries have experienced difficult economic times. Attempts to *get prices right* and unwise increases in money supplies have resulted in galloping inflation. *Privatization* has proved difficult, especially for the countries' *dinosaurs*, for a number of reasons. Many of the *SOEs* are outdated and inefficient, and no one is interested in buying them. Even when they are viable businesses, foreigners have been scared away by the political instability in Russia, and the local populace often has neither the financial resources nor the managerial experience to buy or operate them. As a consequence, many of the potentially most profitable businesses have fallen into the hands of the *nomenklatura*. Their practice of *crony capitalism* instead of true free enterprise under a *rule of law* has contributed to economic turmoil and local mistrust in millions of people's first experience with capitalism.

The former communist countries of Central and Eastern Europe have been more successful than the countries of the former USSR in restructuring their economies. Overall they have experienced lower inflation, lower unemployment, and greater growth in incomes and living standards. One problem faced by these countries has been the demise of the *Council for Mutual Economic Assistance*, which has forced them to adjust to market prices for energy and to find new international markets for their products.

Under Mao Zedong, China was one of the world's most strictly communist countries. His 5-year plans, including the disastrous *Great Leap Forward*, were patterned after the same

types of plans that failed in the Soviet Union. The Chinese have been slowly restructuring their economy since Mao's death in 1976, but China has taken a very gradual approach to the transition. Under first Deng and now Jiang, the Chinese have abandoned Mao's strict adherence to *communist ideology* above all, and have adopted a more *pragmatic* approach that stresses adopting whatever works. Most prices have been freed, property is increasingly in private hands, and foreign investment in the country's *special economic zones* has been booming. Many of the new government-owned businesses are rural *town and village enterprises* that are owned by local governments. Despite the increased economic freedom, the Chinese Communist Party still controls the government and has refused to allow free elections or opposition political parties. Although there is little political freedom, there is political stability and the result has been the fastest-growing economy in the world over the past 2 decades.

$ Perspective $

The Legacy of Marx

Karl Marx (1818–1883) Marx was born in Germany, the son of a lawyer. Entering Bonn University at the age of 17, he intended to be a lawyer, too. However, after being arrested for public intoxication, he was transferred by his father to Berlin University, which was a more academic institution. There he became a brilliant student and developed a passionate interest in philosophy. After receiving a doctorate from the University of Jena in 1841, he turned to journalism. In 1843 he married the daughter of an aristocratic family from his hometown and moved to Paris. It was there that his interest in communism began. There also he began a collaboration with Frederick Engels that would continue for a lifetime. Together they wrote the *Manifesto of the Communist Party* in 1848. They went to Cologne, Germany, to edit a liberal paper backing the German revolution. The revolution failed and Marx, having been banished from Germany and then expelled from Paris, moved to London. He spent the remainder of his life in London, most of it without funds and in poor health, studying, writing, and organizing the Communist International. The first volume of his major work, *Capital (Das Kapital)*, was published in 1867. The second and third volumes were compiled and published by Engels from Marx's unfinished manuscripts after his death in 1883.

The father of communism, Karl Marx, lived in the early era of capitalism when children labored long hours in unsafe factories, capitalists made huge fortunes, and ordinary working people were exploited, hungry, and totally confused about this new economic system. If you ever read about Oliver Twist and Fagan, you've read about the kind of world that Marx was observing.

According to Marx, and his collaborator, Frederick Engels, all historical changes come about through conflict between opposing social forces, one an existing *thesis* and the other an opposing *antithesis*. The outcome is a *synthesis* that becomes the next thesis. No matter how society is organized, however, it will always contain internal conflicts in search of a new synthesis. In Marx's view, the conflict contained in capitalism was the conflict between the owners of capital (the capitalists or *bourgeoisie*) and the

workers (the *proletariat*) who needed to sell their labor to survive.

Marx's view was that capitalism, like all other social arrangements, contained the seeds of its own destruction. His theory of capitalism was based on the belief that all profits come from the exploitation of labor—paying workers less than they earn for the firm. In attempting to increase profits, however, capitalists would employ more and more capital while hiring fewer and fewer workers. With fewer workers to exploit, profits would fall until the capitalists would simply go out of business and the factories would be taken over by the workers who would establish the new synthesis, a "dictatorship of the proletariat" in which the workers would be in charge. In Marx's view, capitalism would not end with a bang, but with a whimper.

Government by the workers was only the first step to the new socialist (or communist) society that would replace capitalism. In the second phase, government would actually disappear as people arranged themselves into a totally classless society where they enjoyed a communal way of life and an economy based on the principle that each should contribute to production according to their abilities and each should receive the output of goods and services according to their needs. Marx believed that people's basic values are shaped by the economic setting in which they live. Under capitalism, people were guided by self-interest, but under socialism, people would evolve to a higher plane and they would put society's needs ahead of individual needs. The final synthesis would represent the ultimate social evolution of humankind, and conflicts between competing forces would be replaced by universal harmony.

Communism didn't develop the way Marx predicted, nor did it ever lead to the idyllic communal society that he envisioned. In the USSR and China, the world's two greatest communist experiments, communism did not evolve out of a capitalist conflict between the bourgeoisie and the proletariat because neither country ever had a capitalist economy from which a communist economy could evolve. In each case communist leaders seized power and forced the economic system on an agricultural population. Nor did the state ever wither away and give rise to the beautiful communal society that he envisioned. Instead, if anything, a strong central government controlled by a new class of "politburo bourgeoisie" repressed the working class more than capitalism ever did.

Despite the failure of communism in the twentieth century, Marx did awaken people to the importance of social justice in modern economies. His grand vision is indeed an admirable one—people living in harmony with more concern for each other than for base self-interest. Before we dismiss him as simply another murky figure or failed philosopher from the past, remember that at one time his ideas ruled the lives of nearly 2 billion people, and that he changed the world in a way that very few people throughout history ever have.

For Further Study and Analysis

Study Questions

1. Explain why the Soviet system of giving bonuses to managers who met their quotas resulted in less than desirable results.

2. Why has it been so difficult for Russia to privatize its government-owned businesses?

3. Why do the people in Russia have so many U.S. dollars?

4. Why is Russia having such a difficult time collecting taxes? What is one consequence of the government's inability to collect taxes?

5. Why is it important for countries to impose a rule of law if they are to successfully transform their economies from communism to capitalism?

6. What were the differences in the Hungarian and Polish privatization strategies?

7. Why has the dissolution of the Council for Mutual Economic Assistance (CMEA) caused economic hardships in many of the formerly communist CEE countries?

8. How do the economic philosophies of Deng Xiaoping and Jiang Zemin differ from those of Mao Zedong?

9. In what ways is the Chinese economy similar to a capitalist economy and in what ways is it different?

10. Why was economic restructuring more successful (at least initially) in the CEE countries than it was in the countries of the former Soviet Union?

Exercises in Analysis

1. Use both the annual and the monthly data provided by Business in Central Europe to update Tables 1, 2, and 3. Write a report that summarizes the progress being made in each of the countries. (You do not need to select a country, only an "indicator"). The URL address is http://www.bcemag.com/_bcedb/stat_main.htm.

2. This is being written in September 1998, when the Russian economy was in turmoil and near collapse. Write a paper that describes what has happened in the Russian economy since its positive economic growth in 1997.

3. Prepare a paper that evaluates the success of privatization in a former communist country. Two good places to begin your research are at the Investment Guide to Central and Eastern Europe http://www.kenpubs.co.uk/investguide/ and Asia Week, which is available online at http://www.pathfinder.com/asiaweek/.·

4. Write a report that describes the recent economic performance of the Chinese economy. Has it continued its rapid growth, or did the 1997 financial crisis in Southeast Asia cause it to slow down?

Further Reading

Angresano, James. *Comparative Economics.* 2nd ed. Upper Saddle River, NJ: Prentice Hall, 1996. Chapter 15 provides a good, if somewhat advanced, explanation of the philosophical basis for a communist command economy. Chapters 16 through 18 present a discussion of transformation issues.

Cole, Don. ed. *Annual Editions: Macroeconomics* and *Annual Editions: Economics.* Guilford, CT: Dushkin/McGraw-Hill, various years. These readers always contain interesting and easy-to-read articles that discuss different aspects of the transition from communism to capitalism.

AsiaWeek. A good magazine for keeping up with current events in all the former communist countries in Asia, from China to Russia. Available free online at http://www.pathfinder.com/asiaweek/.

Business in Central Europe. This Web site provides very current economic statistics for a select number of former Soviet Republics and Central/East European countries. http://www.bcemag.com/_bcedb/stat_main.htm.

Goldman, Minton F. *Russia, The Eurasian Republics, and Central/Eastern Europe.* 7th ed. Guilford, CT: Dushkin/McGraw-Hill, 1996. This title in the Global Studies series contains textbook-style summaries of economic restructuring and a number of articles about each of the countries.

Gregory, Paul R., and Robert C. Stuart. *Soviet Economic Structure and Performance.* 4th ed. New York: Harper Collins, 1990. One of the great things about being out of date is that this book provides a good account of how the Soviet economy operated without being biased by the changes that occurred shortly after its publication.

Heilbroner, Robert L. *The Worldly Philosophers.* 6th ed. New York: Touchstone Books, 1997. This economic classic contains a wonderful chapter on "The Inexorable System of Karl Marx," a great summary of Marx's visions and ideas about communism.

Investment Guide to Central and Eastern Europe. Contains data and links to a number of current articles and news releases dealing with the former communist countries at http://www.kenpubs.co.uk/investguide/.

Kohler, Heinz. *Economic Systems and Human Welfare: A Global Survey.* Cincinnati, Ohio: South-Western, 1997. Chapters 8 and 9 provide a good review of communism in the Soviet Union and Yugoslavia, Chapter 15 does the same for Maoist China, and Chapter 11 provides a description of the transition in all three.

Johnson, Bryan T., Kim Holmes, and Melanie Kirkpatrick. *1998 Index of Economic Freedom.* New York: The Heritage Foundation, 1998. In addition to the rankings, the index includes summaries of each country's scoring as well as a few excellent articles detailing the links between economic freedom and economic growth. The rankings and an executive summary are available at http://www.heritage.org:80/index/execsum.html.

Ralston, Richard E. *Communism: It's Rise and Fall in the Twentieth Century*. Boston: Christian Science Publications Society, 1991. A historical study of communism in Europe. Deals primarily with the political and governmental aspects of communism.

Rosser, J. Barkley, and Marina Rosser. *Comparative Economics in a Transforming World Economy*. Chicago: Irwin, 1995. An advanced but extensive discussion of transformation and restructuring issues is presented in Part III, chapters 10 through 15.

Schumpeter, Joseph. *Ten Great Economists*. New York: Oxford University Press, 1951. Schumpeter was one of the greatest economists of the twentieth century. Like Heilbroner, he presents a good summary of Marxist philosophy and the reasons that over a billion people adopted his proposed economic system.

Wright, Anthony. *Socialism: Theories and Practices*. Oxford: Oxford University Press, 1986. Covers the evolution of socialism, its arguments, doctrines, and methods.

chapter eighteen

The Less Developed Countries

Despite all the optimism in the world (literally), the miraculous and amazing economic growth in East and Southeast Asia has come to a screeching halt. Is it a temporary setback, such as occurs regularly throughout the developed world, or does it signal the onset of a global depression?

The Asian Flu

At the end of World War II, people in India, China, sub-Saharan Africa, and Southeast Asia were equally poor, with per capita incomes averaging less than $500 per year. The Chinese economy has improved some, and not much has changed in Africa and India. But somehow, the economies in East Asia began to grow much faster than the others. South Korea, Taiwan, Hong Kong, and Singapore became known as the Asian tigers, the fastest-growing and most dynamic economies in the world. Singapore and Hong Kong attained living standards higher than those in most of Europe, South Korea moved from utter poverty to become the world's 11th-largest economy by 1997, and Taiwan became the center of East Asian chips and computer assembly. Moving up fast in the 1980s and 1990s were the tiger cubs: Indonesia, Malaysia, and Thailand. Though not as developed as the tigers, growth was taking off, incomes were up, and confidence in their economies spread throughout the globe (Figure 1). The exuberance is exemplified by the fact that the world's tallest buildings, the Petronas Towers, are in Kuala Lumpur, Malaysia.

Then, in late summer 1997, the economies began to get sick. What began as a seemingly routine case of the currency sniffles in Thailand became a full-blown financial flu. As with any other contagious disease, the "Asian contagion" did not limit itself to Thailand, but soon spread to Indonesia, Malaysia, South Korea, and Hong Kong. Taiwan has been immune so far, and Singapore has managed to avoid a severe case, but the other five countries saw their GDPs decrease for the first time in years, and there does not seem to be any end in sight. To make matters worse, the regional entity with the money and power to help cure the illness, Japan, was still struggling to overcome a debilitating bout of a serious financial illness of its own. With a stagnant economy being dragged down by a near-bankrupt financial system, Japan could not figure out how to cure its own illness, much less how to help anybody else.

After decades of hard work and sacrifice that raised millions of people out of poverty and gave them hope for their future and the future of their children, the economic collapse has thrown millions of people back into poverty. Frustrated and angry, hungry mobs of Indonesians rioted and forced President Suharto out of office after 30 years in power. The arrest of Anwar Ibrahim, the popular former deputy prime minister of Malaysia, by Prime Minister Mahathir Mohamad in late 1998, while the economy spiraled downward, may be the straw that brings down his multidecade rule of the country. Voters in Japan, South Korea, and Thailand threw out ruling political parties that had been in power for years.

To understand what went wrong, it is first necessary to understand what went right. Although each country had its own unique experience, there are some things that they did have in common that contributed to their rapid growth. Most important, the tigers and tiger cubs opened their borders to foreign trade and foreign direct investment. With three of the world's four most populous countries in the world (China, India, and Indonesia), the Asian market was simply enormous. Despite some small uprisings, the tigers and tiger cubs have all experienced decades of peace and political stability—factors necessary to induce foreign firms to build factories within their borders.

Each country also opened their markets to foreign portfolio investment and allowed their currencies to be freely traded. Billions of dollars flowed into mutual funds that specialized in buying stock in Southeast Asian companies. Japanese, European, and American banks poured billions into local banks who loaned the funds to finance real estate developments, new business start-ups, and the other business ventures that seemed to be springing up everywhere.

Unlike the United States, where risk, returns, and markets dictate which business ventures get financed and which do not, East and Southeast Asian cultures have always had a preference for central control of the allocation of

Figure 1

Growth Rates for the Asian Tiger and Tiger Cub Economies

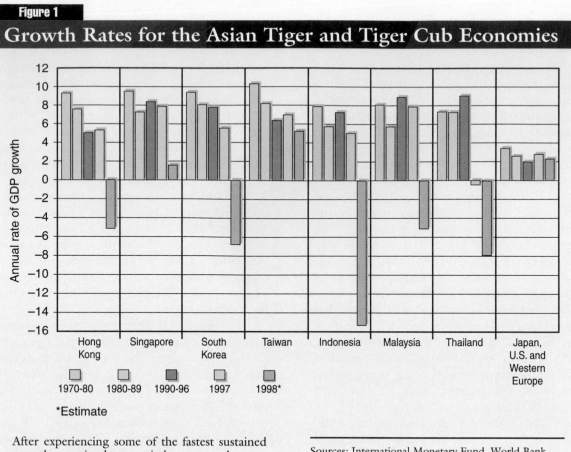

1970-80   1980-89   1990-96   1997   1998*

*Estimate

After experiencing some of the fastest sustained growth rates in the twentieth century, the economic miracle in East and Southeast Asia collapsed in late 1997.

Sources: International Monetary Fund, World Bank, *The Economist*.

resources. Rather than letting the highest investment returns and profits determine which businesses receive investment funds and which goods get produced, the Asian view is that national priorities should also be considered in the allocation of scarce financial capital. Consistent with this view, governments and government-controlled banks followed a policy of "relationship banking"—a practice whereby governments were very active in determining which industries and projects received both domestic and foreign investment funds.

In South Korea, government controlled banks lent the *choebels*—huge conglomerates—money to develop steel and auto industries at low interest rates in an effort to rapidly industrialize the economy. In Indonesia, Malaysia, and Thailand money was funneled into those firms and industries that the government determined were most important to rapid development. Even in Japan, the world's second largest economy, a close relationship among banks, government leaders, and businesses helped guide financial capital to where they collectively felt it would do the economy the most good.

Relationship banking seemed to work, and it was touted as one of the keys to the Asian economic miracle. Although the allocation of credit through the market system might work in the United States, the region's leaders proudly pointed to their new way of making an economy work. Socially guided market capitalism was the underlying essence of their amazing

success. Seeing is believing, and with investment returns much higher than in the rest of the world and a desire to globalize their investments, banks, investment houses, and individuals continued to pour money into the region to get their share of the profits.

So what went wrong? The main problem was that there simply were not the institutions in place to efficiently handle the amount of money that was pouring into these countries. They lacked strong central banks that monitored and enforced sound lending practices, agencies to oversee and ensure legitimacy in stock and bond markets, bankruptcy courts to force deadbeat borrowers to pay their loans, and a rule of law that could stop greedy political leaders from lining their pockets and passing laws to help their own financial interests.

Perhaps a most telling result is that the term "relationship banking" has been replaced in our vocabulary by the term "crony capitalism." While it was easy for governments to pick the first few winners in a developing economy, as time went on and more money flowed in, investment projects that could yield the same high level of returns became scarcer and scarcer. In an open market economy, the result would be lower returns to investors who would then take their money elsewhere. But that didn't happen. Rather than allowing investors to see where their money was going and what returns it was earning, local banks, investment firms, and political leaders hid problems and continued to direct foreign funds to favored businesses at low interest rates, hoping that earnings would improve and the problems would disappear. In an effort to post the higher returns necessary to offset their increasing debt burden, these businesses undertook riskier and riskier projects.

The issue is often referred to as "transparency." In the developed parts of the world, investors have access to a company's annual report that details its debt levels, sales, profits, and other pertinent information. Investors can then make informed decisions about whether or not to invest in a firm because the financial condition of the firm is transparent. Such transparency did not exist in the Asian economies, and unwary investors did not know that their money was going into unwise investments.

And there was corruption. The billions of dollars pouring into the area were just too tempting for many in power, and a significant amount of the funds were diverted into payoffs, bribes, or put under the control of politicians' friends and relatives. For example, foreign money was used to build aircraft and auto factories in Indonesia that were controlled by Suharto's friends and family.

The problems first showed up in Thailand where some investments, especially speculative real estate investments in office buildings, apartment houses, retail space, and recreational resorts began to go sour. When growth began to slow, developers could not pay back their banks and other lenders, who in turn could not repay their depositors and investors, which included a large number of foreign interests who were to be paid back in U.S. dollars. Investors began to sell their Thai assets and convert their Thai bahts into dollars and other currencies on a huge scale. This pushed down the value of the baht and made it even more difficult for Thais to pay their foreign debts. It also caused other investors to become scared of the exchange rate risk that could drag their profits down. The portfolio investment—the "hot money"—that had poured into Thailand began to pour back out.

Investors seeing what was happening in Thailand figured that Indonesia and Malaysia might be next, and they pulled their cash out of these countries. Like a self-fulfilling prophecy, as the foreign capital pulled out, credit dried up and businesses began to fall like dominoes. As of the end of 1998, only about half of the space in the Petronas Towers is leased. And the disease spread. Although Russia's problems were unrelated, investors seeing what had happened there and in Southeast Asia withdrew their funds from other emerging markets, especially those in South America. This led to a credit crunch throughout the developing world. The profits were nice while they lasted, but once things began to sour, American and European investors decided there's no place like home to invest their dollars and euros.

Chapter Preview

As part of the economically developed world, it is difficult for us to appreciate fully the vast gap between our way of life and the way of life that exists in the less developed countries (LDCs) comprising four-fifths of the world. Even in the countries of East and Southeast Asia that came so far so fast, the average worker earns a bare subsistence wage and can only dream of someday owning a home or a car. This chapter will address the problem of economic development by examining three basic questions: What are the characteristics of the less developed countries? What makes countries poor? What are the prospects for the economic development of the LDCs?

Learning Objectives

After completing this chapter, you should be able to:

1. Explain what economic development means.

2. Discuss the characteristics that set apart the developed and less developed countries of the world.

3. Identify those regions in the world where poverty is most prevalent.

4. Explain why per capita GDP alone is not always an accurate measure of world poverty.

5. Explain the difference between environmental and cultural determination as causes of economic development.

6. Describe the necessary preconditions for industrialization and economic development.

7. Understand the differences between import-substitution and export-promotion and their consequences.

8. Explain why external indebtedness is a problem for less developed countries.

9. Describe the connection between overpopulation and the economic development in the less developed countries.

What Are the Characteristics of Less Developed Countries?

The defining characteristic of the world's **less developed countries (LDCs)** is their poverty. The characteristics of poor countries, however, go beyond simple measures of income and include a number of socioeconomic factors that are also associated with **economic development.**

Income

The most common measure used to define the LDCs is their income. While the overall size of an economy (its GDP) is important for some analyses, the issue of economic development is more appropriately addressed by examining the level of **per capita income** or per capita GDP. Figure 2 shows the geographic distribution of countries by per capita GDP in 1997 measured in U.S. dollars. This is done by taking the average income in the local currency and converting it to dollars at the existing rate of exchange. Measured this way, the 50 poorest countries in the world had an average annual income of $350 and the richest an average of $25,700.

---

less developed countries (LDCs) nonindustrialized countries generally characterized by low incomes, primarily agricultural labor forces, low standards of living, overpopulation, and widespread illiteracy.

economic development the process of increasing a country's income and improving the standard of living of its people.

per capita income the total national income (or GDP) divided by the size of the population.

Maybe a lot of high-tech, high-priced gadgets and gizmos aren't the most important thing in defining "quality of life."

Figure 2

The Global Distribution of Income, 1997

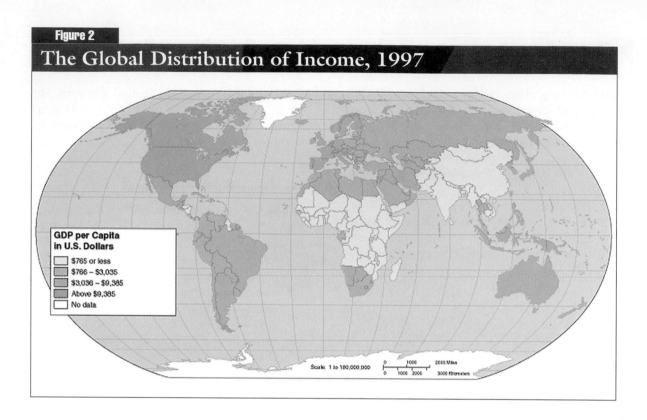

GDP per Capita in U.S. Dollars

- $765 or less
- $766 – $3,035
- $3,036 – $9,385
- Above $9,385
- No data

Scale: 1 to 180,000,000

According to the **World Bank,** the average income in the world was $5,130 in 1997. This is somewhat deceptive because the distribution of income in the world's countries is skewed, with only a handful of countries having incomes greater than $20,000 per person (Figure 3). As you can see in Table 1, the vast majority of the world's population (over 80%) have incomes less than $2,000 per year.

What Are the Characteristics of Less Developed Countries?

EconExplorer

World Bank (The International Bank for Reconstruction and Development) a specialized agency of the United Nations whose major role is to help finance development of the world's LDCs.

Table 1 and Figure 2 clearly show that the low-income countries of the world are concentrated in sub-Saharan Africa and South Asia. Of the ten poorest countries in the world, only one (Nepal) lies outside of Africa. Approximately 614 million people, or a little over 10% of the world's population, live in sub-Saharan Africa, and 350 million of these people live in poverty. The average income of the 1.2 billion people living in China was $860, making it 81st out of the 133 countries that the World Bank ranked. India, with nearly a billion people ranked 102nd, with an average income of $390, and the other large countries of South Asia, Pakistan and Bangladesh, ranked 97th ($490) and 116th ($270) respectively. Together, these four countries alone have a population in excess of 3.6 billion people, or over 60% of world's people. An obvious characteristic of world poverty, then, is that it is concentrated in China, South Asia, and sub-Saharan Africa.

Despite their huge oil reserves, the countries of the Middle East and North Africa have incomes that just barely place them in

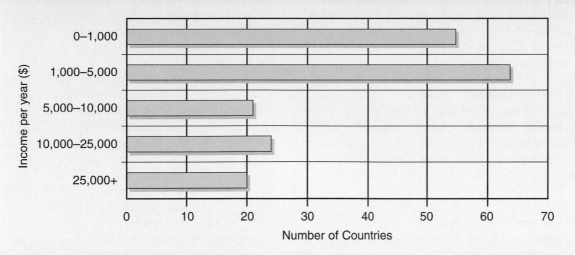

Figure 3

Per Capita GDP in the World

Income per year ($):
- 0–1,000
- 1,000–5,000
- 5,000–10,000
- 10,000–25,000
- 25,000+

Number of Countries (x-axis: 0, 10, 20, 30, 40, 50, 60, 70)

Only a handful of countries have average incomes in excess of $25,000 per person.

Table 1   Selected World Per Capita Incomes, 1997

	Population (millions)	Per Capita GDP (US$)	Purchasing Power Parity (US$)
World	5,829	$5,130	$6,330
By Income			
Low Income	2,048	350	1,400
Middle Income	2,855	1,890	4,550
High Income	926	25,700	22,770
By Region			
East Asia & Pacific	1,753	970	3,560
Latin America	494	3,880	6,660
Middle East & N. Africa	283	2,060	4,580
South Asia	1,289	390	1,580
Sub-Saharan Africa	614	500	1,470

The countries in the world with the lowest per capita incomes are generally also those with the largest populations. The disparity between rich and poor countries is not so great when purchasing power is accounted for.

Source: World Bank, *World Development Report*, 1998/99.

the middle-income category. The countries of Latin America (the Western Hemisphere south of the United States) are the upper middle-class of the world's economy. The average incomes in Thailand ($2,800) and Malaysia ($4,680) place them in the middle-income category, while Indonesia ($1,110) has not quite reached this plateau.

Simply looking at per capita GDP in dollars can be misleading. The buying power of a dollar varies from country to country. To adjust for the differences in buying power, economists have developed the concept of purchasing power parity. Because the cost of living is so much lower in the LDCs, the purchasing power of their incomes is much higher than it might at first appear. For example, while the average income in China was $860 per person in 1997, its purchasing power parity was equal to $3,570. When purchasing power is accounted for, the discrepancy in world incomes is not so large. In terms of per capita GDP, the average incomes in the world's richest countries are 73 times larger than those in the poorest countries. With adjustments for purchasing power, the ratio falls to 16 to 1.

Income Distribution

A second drawback of simply examining per capita GDP is that it does not accurately show the actual extent of poverty in less developed countries. Many LDCs have highly skewed income distributions, with a large percentage of total income going to a small percentage of the population. In Sierra Leone, for example, the highest 20% receive 63.4% of the total income, while the poorest 20% must exist on only 1.1%. In the Western Hemisphere, a similar pattern exists among many of the middle-income countries such as Brazil, Guatemala, Colombia, Chile, Mexico, and Panama. Although the average income may indicate that a country has reached a middle-income status, it has little impact on national poverty if only a fraction of that income reaches the majority of the people.

Most LDCs have very large agricultural sectors. In such economies, the distribution of income will be determined by the distribution of land. Very often most land is held by a small elite class and the result is a very unequal income distribution. This type of inequality differs from the inequality in income distribution that results from development activities. The former perpetuates poverty, while the latter results in increasing demand for labor, thereby raising incomes down the line. Through land reform programs, industrialization, and social programs such as universal education and health care, the **Asian tigers** made a more equitable distribution of income a central focus of their economic policies. The **tiger cubs,** although not yet as far along, incorporated this idea in their government policies, primarily because they understood that a wide range in incomes can lead to political unrest and social upheavals—a most dangerous threat to economic growth and prosperity.

Asian tigers a nickname used to describe Hong Kong, Singapore, Taiwan, and South Korea—four Asian economies that achieved almost miraculous rates of growth from the 1960s to the mid-1990s.

tiger cubs a nickname used to describe Indonesia, Thailand, and Malaysia—the three Southeast Asian countries that experienced rapid development in the 1980s through the mid-1990s and then experienced an economic collapse beginning in 1997.

social indicators noneconomic characteristics that reflect the societal aspects of a country's standard of living.

Social Indicators

Per capita income and income distribution are the most direct measures of economic development. A low income, however, is not necessarily such a bad thing as long as people are well fed, healthy and safe. The ultimate purpose of economic development is to improve people's lives and their standard of living. Table 2 shows some basic **social indicators** for each income class of countries and data for five of the larger countries in each group. The table lists their rates of child malnutrition, life expectancy at birth, child mortality rate, and adult illiteracy rate. It shows a clear positive relationship between per capita incomes and improvements in living standards. The relationship holds not only for the social indicators listed in the table, but also for a host of other indicators such as

Living standards in less developed countries often lack even the minimums—food, shelter, and clothing—that are taken for granted in economically developed countries.

access to safe drinking water, electricity, paved roads, telephones, and sanitation facilities.

The nutrition level, especially during the early years of childhood, is an important social indicator of the standard of living in a country. It has an effect on child development, on the ability to learn in school, and on future productivity as an adult. The prevalence of malnutrition among children under 5 averaged 66% in India in 1997, and has actually increased during the last decade. Although information is not available for all low-income countries, among those for which estimates are available, India is exceeded only by Bangladesh in the level of malnutrition among children (68%).

Life expectancy and infant mortality rates reflect a country's overall health standards, diet patterns, and available medical care. Compared to the developed countries, LDCs have poorer diets, far fewer doctors, shortages of basic drugs, and poorly equipped hospitals. Diseases that have all but been eradicated in the richer countries still kill thousands of people per year in these countries, and the very young and the very old are more likely to die from them. Illiteracy is still widespread in the LDCs and for a number of cultural reasons progress in obtaining equal rights for women has been very slow. One consequence is a large disparity in the educational opportunities available to girls, which results in higher rates of female illiteracy. A 1998 study by the group Population Action International, however, shows that women are closing the literacy gap in sub-Saharan Africa and the Middle East, although much progress is still needed in South Asia.

One reason for China's good performance in the socioeconomic categories is its rapidly rising per capita income. The Chinese purchasing power parity of $3,570 per person in 1997 might not seem like much, but it is a remarkable improvement over the 1993 figure of $1,838. With increased income comes an increased ability for a country to provide

Table 2   Basic Social Indicators in Selected Countries, 1996

Country	Child Malnutrition*	Life Expectancy Male	Life Expectancy Female	Under 5 Mortality Rate**	Adult Illiteracy Male	Adult Illiteracy Female
Low Income	N/A	58	60	113	35	59
China	16	68	71	39	10	27
India	66	62	63	85	35	62
Pakistan	40	62	65	123	50	76
Ethiopia	48	48	51	177	55	75
Indonesia	40	63	67	60	22	37
Middle Income	N/A	66	71	43	12	25
Mexico	14	69	75	36	8	13
Malaysia	23	70	74	14	11	22
Thailand	13	67	72	38	17	21
Turkey	10	66	71	47	8	28
Brazil	7	63	71	7	17	17
High Income	<1	74	81	7	<1	<1
United States	<1	74	80	8	<1	<1
Japan	3	77	83	6	<1	<1
South Korea	<1	69	76	11	1	3
Great Britain	<1	74	80	7	<1	<1
Singapore	14	74	79	5	4	14
World	N/A	65	69	73	21	38

Although income by itself may not be the only indicator of a good quality of life, there is a very strong correlation between it and just about all social indicators.

*Percentage of children under 5 years suffering malnutrition

**Mortality rates per 1,000 children under 5 years old

Source: World Bank, *World Development Report 1998/99*.

---

schools, better medical care, better sanitation, and a better diet. These in turn lead to even greater productivity, more economic growth, higher incomes, and an even better standard of living.

◼ Consumer Goods

An improvement in the standard of living enhances people's ability to obtain desired consumer goods. One might say that the world got along just fine for thousands of years without things like televisions and telephones, and therefore they are not necessary now. Al-

though "crass materialism" is often sneered at, being able to have modern conveniences and luxuries is a very real part of an improved standard of living. People everywhere like nice clothes, cars, movies, and comfortable houses. Table 3 (p. 514) shows the number of televisions, personal computers, telephone lines and Internet hosts for a sampling of regions and developing countries. (Figures for the United States and Japan are included to provide a point of reference.)

(Continued on page 514)

Case Application

The Dark Continent

Africa is the world's poorest continent—the only one where the people are poorer now than they were in 1980. In 1997, even in terms of purchasing power parity, incomes in sub-Saharan Africa were less than $1,500 per year. Prospects for the future do not look good. Except for South Africa, the countries in the region cannot look forward to regaining their 1970s standard of living any time in the near future.

How did they get into such a situation? It resulted from the legacy of colonialism, corruption, war, disease, and explosive population growth. After achieving independence, most of these countries found themselves ruled by military dictatorships that imposed highly regulated economic systems. The rulers were not averse to lining their pockets generously by stealing foreign aid and controlling any profitable industries. It is estimated that almost 10% of Nigeria's GDP was siphoned out of government accounts by unscrupulous leaders. Former prime minister Mobuto of Zaire (now the Democratic Republic of Congo) socked away billions in Swiss bank accounts and built lavish palaces at home and abroad while his people suffered from blinding poverty. Mobuto was overthrown by Laurent Kabila, but hopes for reform and honesty were dashed as Kabila is turning out to be almost as bad as Mobuto.

Even more debilitating is the constant warfare. Since independence, African countries have had a long history of civil wars—the result of European colonists' drawing of boundaries that did not coincide with the ethnic distributions of the local populations. Millions have died in civil wars in the Congo, Nigeria, Ethiopia, Angola, and Sudan as different tribes have attempted to seize control of or secede from an existing country. Recently, however, wars have been spilling over international borders as more and more countries are sending their troops into other countries to restore order, reinstate ousted leaders, or install a leader whom they prefer.

A common military tactic is to deny food and other resources to the opposing side, and no one seems to care if civilians are also denied the basics of life. Towns are burned, the young men drafted into different armies, women and children are forced to serve as porters and cooks, and local roads are mined. The millions fleeing the fighting are living in refugee camps, waiting for peace so that they can go home. But it might be a long time. In the meantime, no one is left to work the farms or in the factories, and output continues to decline.

Disease is another factor in Africa's impoverishment. Of the approximately 31 million people worldwide whose blood is HIV positive, 21 million live in Africa. Even more widespread is malaria. Spread by mosquitoes, it afflicts most of the sub-Saharan population, who have recurring bouts of the disease, which saps their energies, throughout their lives. Then there are other diseases—yellow fever, the fatal Ebola virus, and dysentery and cholera that are caused by unclean water and a lack of sanitary facilities. Even those who can avoid the fighting long enough to try go to work often find themselves too sick and weak to be productive.

Crime is also rampant and spreading especially in western Africa. Without stable governments, anarchy reigns and people are constantly robbed, beaten, and killed because the police and courts are either powerless to do anything or simply do not care. The government armies also get into the act, often holding up foreign travelers on their way from the airport to their hotels for payments before they are allowed to proceed. Even relatively stable South Africa is reeling from gang warfare and violence, causing many to flee their country for safer places to live.

Another reason that Africa is doomed to poverty is overpopulation. At nearly 3% per year since 1980, sub-Saharan Africa has the fastest-growing population in the world. The production of food and other necessities is not growing as fast, and as a result, perhaps only one child in five receives nutrition adequate to lead a healthy and productive life.

Africa, a basket case of LDCs, needs a great deal of help from the outside world, both public and private. But the rich countries of the world and international organizations are tired of pouring their money down a sinkhole of corruption, warfare, and disorganization. For years, Africa has received more economic aid than any other part of the world, but the results strongly discourage a continuation. And as for foreign direct investment, despite the low labor costs, most businesses are put off by the bribes demanded for every permit, the difficulty of enforcing contracts, the lack of infrastructure, and the lack of safety for their workers and their capital.

Economic Reasoning

1. What characteristics does sub-Saharan Africa have that mark it as a less developed region?
2. How does the vicious cycle of poverty help explain Africa's declining economies?
3. Should the richer countries of the world do more to help countries in this part of the world? Why or why not?

(Continued from page 512)

Table 3   Consumer Electronics and Telecommunications Infrastructure in Selected Countries, 1996

	Televisions*	Personal Computers*	Telephone Main Lines*	Internet Hosts**
South Asia	53	1.5	14	0.06
India	64	1.5	15	0.05
Pakistan	24	1.2	18	0.07
Bangladesh	7	<0.1	3	0.00
East Asia and the Pacific	228	4.5	41	0.57
Indonesia	232	4.8	21	0.54
Malaysia	228	42.8	183	19.30
Thailand	167	16.7	70	2.11
China	252	3.0	45	0.21
Sub-Saharan Africa	43	N/A	14	2.03
Nigeria	55	4.1	4	0.00
Dem. Republic of the Congo	41	<0.1	1	0.00
Ethiopia	4	<0.1	3	0.00
Latin America	217	23.2	102	3.48
Brazil	289	18.4	96	0.69
Colombia	188	23.3	118	1.81
Mexico	193	29.0	162	3.72
Argentina	347	24.6	174	5.32
Japan	700	128.0	489	75.80
United States	806	362.4	640	442.11

Although televisions, PCs, telephones, and the Internet represent some of the "better things in life" for most people, they are also an essential part of a country's telecommunications infrastructure.

*per 1,000 persons

**per 10,000 persons, July 1997

Source: World Bank, *World Development Report 1998/99*.

▶ What Makes Countries Poor?

Why is it that 80% of the world's population lives on per capita incomes of less than $2,000 per year? Why, despite years of foreign aid from the World Bank and individual countries, are so many countries still economically underdeveloped? Although there are numerous theories of development, no one theory can satisfactorily provide an answer to these questions. But there are certain basic development lessons that are clear.

◪ Theories of Economic Development

The earliest theories of economic development examined the relationship between a country's development and its physical attributes. The theory of **environmental determination** hypothesizes that there is a connection between a country's natural resources and its level of development. For example, a country with an abundance of resources should be able to develop faster and attain higher incomes and living standards than a country that does not.

At first blush this seems to make sense, as countries such as the United States and Germany have plentiful resources and are very advanced, while countries such as Greece and Tunisia that are resource-poor are also economically poor. But there are simply too many contradictions—such as economically rich but resource-poor Japan and Switzerland, and poor but resource-rich Russia and Nigeria—for the theory to be an acceptable major explanation for economic development. Even among the tigers and the cubs there are contradictions: Singapore and South Korea have far fewer natural resources than Indonesia or Malaysia, yet they are far wealthier. The key to wealth in today's world is industrialization, not natural resources.

An alternative theory is that of **cultural determination,** which seeks to explain a country's level of development through an analysis of its cultural values. For example, in a country such as the United States, where the pursuit of material wealth permeates the cul-ture, we will naturally be inclined to attempt to increase our standard of living. It has been argued that Western, Protestant cultures may have prospered because of their emphasis on hard work and thriftiness as the means to that material wealth—the Protestant work ethic. Similar values are a part of the East Asian culture. On the other hand, many people throughout the world have much less interest in material things, and therefore concentrate their efforts on more spiritual endeavors. People in some cultures often adopt a **capricious universe view,** the idea that there is no connection between what you do and what you get, so why bother?

Both theories can contribute to an explanation of why Northern countries are on average much more developed than Southern countries (see Figure 2). Very early on, people in cold climates had to learn to save and store their harvest in order to survive long winters. Over time, this environmental factor generated a cultural bias toward saving, a necessary condition for capital formation in modern economies.

◪ Lack of Physical and Human Capital

In order to grow and develop, a low-income country must surmount a number of severe problems. Perhaps the most difficult of these is

---

environmental determination a theory of economic development that emphasizes the importance of natural resources and the physical environment of a country.

cultural determination a theory of economic development that emphasizes the importance of the cultural attitudes and values of a country.

capricious universe view the belief that there is no connection between the work and effort that one puts forward and the rewards that one receives.

Less developed countries lack the sophisticated capital equipment and infrastructure of the economically developed countries. In the 1990s, this Indian farmer uses a centuries-old method of drawing water from a well to irrigate his fields.

breaking the **vicious circle of poverty.** Per capita output in LDCs is close to the subsistence level. There is no **economic surplus** to allocate to capital accumulation. As a result, productivity remains low and the subsistence standard of living is perpetuated.

Without a sufficient surplus to fund capital investment, many developing countries have turned to foreign sources to finance their investment needs. As we noted in the opening article, the tigers and tiger cubs of East Asia opened their economies to foreign portfolio and direct investment, and the billions of dollars that poured in contributed to their growing capital stock. To an even larger extent, the same is true of the Latin American economies. Portfolio investment in Latin America averaged almost $200 per person in 1996 and foreign direct investment in real capital averaged $77 per person (Table 4). Of course, the outflow of portfolio investment that sent the tiger cubs

vicious circle of poverty the self-reinforcing pattern of economic stagnation that arises from an initial lack of productivity and/or income.

economic surplus a margin of output over and above consumption needs that can be allocated to capital investment.

into an economic tailspin could also occur in Latin America, and that possibility made a lot of foreign investors quite jittery in 1998.

What Makes Countries Poor?

EconExplorer

Other parts of the developing world have not been as fortunate in attracting foreign investment. Although it has recently opened up its economy to foreign trade and investment, for many years India refused to do so and instead funded most of its investment needs from a very high level of savings. To a lesser extent, China has done the same. Civil wars and political turmoil have made sub-Saharan Africa a less than desirable place for foreign investors who, above all, look at political stability as a prerequisite to investing their money in a foreign country. Some countries, like Ethiopia, experienced net outflows of desperately needed funds, and the region as a whole only averaged $1.40 per person in foreign direct investment.

Other than internal saving or private foreign investment funds, the only sources of foreign aid for the LDCs are organizations like the World Bank or individual countries. Sub-Saharan Africa has long been one of the largest recipients of foreign aid, but nonetheless remains the poorest region in the world. Until the area becomes more stable, aid will be needed to help house and feed the refugees from the region's continuing wars and disputes instead of being used to build a solid capital base as a foundation for future growth.

Investment in human capital is perhaps even more essential than investment in physical capital. One of the major obstacles to economic development in most LDCs is the lack of healthy, literate, skilled labor. Poor diets and poor education lead to a lack of productivity, which perpetuates and reinforces the vicious cycle of poverty in the developing world. One of the first things done by the Asian tigers was to require universal education, at least through

Table 4	Sources of Foreign Funds in Selected Countries, 1996			
	Net Portfolio Investment ($ per capita)	Foreign Direct Investment ($ per capita)	Official Foreign Aid ($ per capita)	Foreign Debt as a percentage of GDP
South Asia	**6.8**	**2.7**	**4.0**	
India	6.7	2.7	2.0	22%
Pakistan	14.1	5.0	7.0	39
Bangladesh	0.7	0.1	10.0	30
East Asia and the Pacific	**57.7**	**33.4**	**5.0**	
Indonesia	90.5	5.5	6.0	64
Malaysia	576.0	214.3	0.0	52
Thailand	221.6	38.3	14.0	56
China	40.8	32.7	2.0	17
Sub-Saharan Africa	**7.1**	**1.4**	**26.0**	
Nigeria	6.0	11.8	2.0	114
Dem. Republic of the Congo	0.1	0.1	4.0	127
Ethiopia	−3.4	0.1	42.0	149
Latin America	**193.5**	**77.0**	**17.0**	
Brazil	173.1	60.3	3.0	26
Colombia	203.6	87.4	7.0	40
Mexico	248.9	80.2	3.0	44
Argentina	400.5	119.0	8.0	31

Although foreign investment has helped economic development efforts in many LDCs, it has also resulted in dangerously high levels of foreign debt.

Source: World Bank, *World Development Report 1998/99.*

the primary grades where the basic essentials of literacy—reading, writing, and arithmetic—would be mastered by just about the entire population. As you can see in Table 2 (p. 514), the tiger cubs have a long way to go.

The opportunity cost of a basic education is much higher in the LDCs than it is in the developed countries. Not only are there fewer schools because of a lack of money, but in the world's poorer countries children often have to work on the family farm or in factories to help support their families. The use of child labor in many LDCs has been the focus of human rights organizations, such as Amnesty International and others. Parents throughout the world would prefer to send their children to school rather than off to work in a factory, but the sad truth is that sometimes there are no schools, and sometimes the families need the child's earnings to survive.

Exploitation

Another barrier that underdeveloped countries must overcome is external and internal **exploitation.** Many of the LDCs were previously colonies of other countries. The intended purpose of the colonies was to provide the mother country with a supply of raw materials and a captive market for its processed goods. Other nations, such as China, although not formally colonies, were frequently used by more powerful states for similar purposes.

exploitation obtaining labor services, raw materials, or finished products for a price less than their true value. Alternatively, forcing people to purchase one's products at a price above their true value.

Economic exploitation was not the worst legacy of colonialism in Africa. The African countries as they exist today are artificial creations of the occupying colonial countries of Europe. Between 1870 and 1914, France, Britain, and Germany colonized 8,600,000 square miles of African territory with a population of 72 million. Those countries, along with Belgium, Portugal, and Italy, subjugated virtually the whole continent. They carved out countries for administrative purposes, and their borders bore no relation to tribal boundaries or the natural flow of commerce.

Members of the same tribe who shared a common language, heritage and culture found themselves divided among different countries, often ruled by a majority from a different tribe. When the countries were liberated from colonial rule after World War II, the natural inclination was for members of the same tribe to reunite in their own country, without regard for the artificial borders established by the Europeans. During the cold war, both the United States and the Soviet Union made the situation even worse as they fought for domination of the continent by supplying opposing sides with modern weapons. The result has been incessant (and well-armed) civil war and political strife.

Another obstacle to development is the internal exploitation of one class by another. As mentioned above, most LDCs are predominantly agricultural, with ownership of the land usually concentrated in the hands of a wealthy elite class who also controls the government. The landless peasants are kept at a subsistence level. Corruption is another form of exploitation. Political leaders and their allies often siphon significant amounts of foreign aid and investment funds to their own pockets, depriving the poorer segments of society of needed help. Bribery, kickbacks, improper subsidies, and special import licenses issued to only a favored few also enrich the elite class at the expense of the poor.

import substitution a policy that encourages the replacement of imported goods with domestically produced ones.

Economic Policies

Misguided government policies frequently contribute to the difficulties of LDCs. One common strategy, particularly among African countries, has been the exploitation of agriculture to provide cheap food for the growing urban populations. Holding down agricultural prices is popular with the politically powerful urban areas but has often resulted in a decrease in agricultural output so that countries that historically were self-sufficient have had to begin importing food. Ironically, much of the free food sent to this part of the world to help combat famine and starvation also put downward pressure on agricultural prices and drove many local farmers out of business.

Another policy frequently adopted by LDCs, including many in Latin America, has been a concentration on developing **import-substitution** industries that will domestically produce certain goods that were traditionally imported. Sometimes referred to as an "inward-looking" strategy, such a policy usually requires that protectionist measures be enacted to keep out imported manufactured goods. This leaves the market to high-cost, low-quality domestic producers. This policy, obviously, is popular both with the producers and with labor unions, but it results in inflation and inefficient production.

Many LDCs also spend an excessive amount on the military. Military expenditures in the LDCs have increased from $24 billion in 1960 to over $200 billion today. In Angola, Chad, Pakistan, Oman, Nicaragua, Syria, Uganda, and Zaire, for example, spending on arms is at least double the amount spent on health and education. In Iraq and Somalia, the amount spent on the military is five times greater than the amount spent on health and education.

Successful government development strategies in LDCs are not policies that are popular with the politically powerful segments of the economy in the short run. They call for government budget restraint in avoiding grandiose projects and large military spending in favor of strengthening the country's basic infrastructure, improving education and health care, establishing legal and financial institutions, and maintaining a stable environment for investment.

Case Application

The Sick Man of Asia

About one-sixth of the world's population lives in India, one of the world's poorest countries. In 1997, the per capita GDP was only $390 per year, and even when adjusted for purchasing power, the average income was only $1,650. India's economic growth has been much slower than that of most other Asian nations. In 1950, its per capita income was about the same as that in South Korea and Hong Kong. In 1997, the per capita incomes in those countries were $10,550 and $25,200, respectively. It is not just in terms of income that India has lagged behind the rest of the world. In 1997 it ranked 139th out of 174 countries in the United Nation's Human Development Index, which ranks countries according to a number of factors, including literacy, mortality rates, and other social indicators. India's growth has lagged for a number of reasons, one of the most important being that it adopted an inward, rather than outward, development strategy.

When India achieved its independence from Great Britain in 1947, it was primarily an agricultural country with land ownership concentrated in the hands of a small, elite class of society. The father of Indian independence, Mohandas Gandhi, disapproved of industrialization and the pursuit of wealth. Instead, he glorified the traditional village lifestyle with its emphasis on traditional handicrafts, and considered it to be the optimal form of economic organization for India. In contrast, India's first prime minister, Jawaharlal Nehru, saw industrialization as providing the brightest future for the Indian people. Nehru's opinions ruled the day. After first undertaking land reform in a not-so-successful attempt to redistribute land more equitably, he turned his attention to developing a manufacturing base.

Despite its democratic form of government and its policy of nonalignment during the cold war, India patterned its economy after the Soviet Union. Like the USSR, India attempted to industrialize its economy by following a series of 5-year plans designed to promote heavy industry at the expense of consumer goods. It also nationalized a number of industries, including energy generation, iron and steel, shipbuilding, and coal mining. For the firms in the private sector, strict government control of the economy was enforced through regulations, trade restrictions, and the government control of banks and credit. Businesses were required to obtain licenses to expand output, build new facilities, hire and fire employees, change product lines, install telephones and electric hook-ups, sell off parts of their firms or merge with other firms. The administration was sarcastically referred to as the "license raj" (kingdom), and the only way for businesses to get many of the licenses was through bribing public officials, a practice that became so widespread that bribes became a normal part of doing business.

The government also pursued a Soviet-style policy of autarky, or self-sufficiency, designed to limit economic trade with the rest of the world. Instead of relying upon comparative advantage and trade like the Asian tigers did, India sought to develop import-substitution industries, encouraging the production and consumption of domestic goods in place of imports. To import most manufactured products, an Indian company needed to obtain a special license that was only issued if the firm could demonstrate that a substitute product was either not made in India or could not be made in a "reasonably" short time. While great for domestic producers, it was a disaster for consumers who were forced to get by with high-priced, poor-quality, domestically produced goods.

Between 1965 and 1990, India's GDP grew at an average annual rate of about 4.0%. Its population was also growing rapidly, however, and as a result, the growth in per capita income was only 1.9%. Slow growth, continued poverty, and the collapse of the Soviet Union caused India to rethink its economic strategy. Beginning in 1991, it liberalized its trading policies, reduced tariffs significantly, and opened its doors to foreign investment. Within a few years, foreign investment and consumer goods began rolling in. GDP growth accelerated to 4.6% per year from 1990 to 1995, and, coupled with a slowing rate of population growth, led to solid increases in the standard of living.

Since 1995, however, India has made few improvements in its open trade policy. According to the Index of Economic Freedom published by the Heritage Foundation, its reforms have stalled and its level of openness has remained basically unchanged from 1995 to 1997. It is currently ranked 117th in the world, behind such relatively unfree economies such as Nigeria, Romania, Bulgaria, and Algeria. Despite its poverty and lack of economic development, India has developed the technology to build and test nuclear weapons. It exploded its first nuclear devices in 1998, and shortly after, Pakistan, its traditional enemy, tested nuclear weapons of its own to keep up in the arms race.

The Sick Man of Asia

The 1998 United Nations Human Development Report is available in most libraries, and online at http://www.undp. org/hdro/ 98.htm. The last column of the table shows the real per capita GDP rank minus HDI rank. How would you interpret positive and negative values for these data? As a hint, find the value for Kuwait or other Persian Gulf countries, and then find the values for New Zealand and Belgium. (Remember that lower HDI rankings imply "better" economies).

What Are the Prospects for the Economic Development of the LDCs?

The economic development of the world's poorest countries is not easy to achieve. If it were, these countries would have been developed by now. Whether their desire is for material goods or social improvements, the key to obtaining their goals lies in increasing their people's incomes.

Industrial Development

Economic development requires that LDCs make the structural transition from being an agrarian economy to being a manufacturing or industrial economy. Because industrialization requires an urban labor force, this means a shift of the population from rural to urban areas. Seventy-eight percent of the population in high-income countries lives in urbanized areas compared to only 28% in low-income countries.

To support an urban workforce, a country must first have an agricultural sector that is productive enough to free a significant portion of the population from the land. Urban workers must eat, and unless or until manufactured exports can be traded for imported food, the domestic agriculture workers must be able to feed themselves and everybody else. Once established, the value of the output generated by manufacturing industries is much higher than that in agriculture. This allows for higher wages, higher incomes, and a higher standard of living. One reason for South Korea's remarkable growth was a rapid movement of people from farm jobs to city jobs. Korean urbanization increased from 57% in 1980 to 83% in 1997.

In contrast to policies favoring import substitution, the Asian tigers adopted a policy of **export promotion,** an "outward-looking" policy that encouraged the development of export industries based on comparative advantage. Rather than imposing trade barriers, they relied on free trade to sell their exports throughout the world and used a large part of their earnings to increase their capital base. This policy succeeded for the tigers, and the cubs have been following a similar strategy. Such programs have created a lively debate among development economists. Some claim that the successes were due to sound government intervention to subsidize and help export industries. Others point to the free international trade as the key to economic development.

Another characteristic of the LDC economies is a dependence on mining and other extractive industries. Not only are the prices of such outputs low relative to the prices of manufactured goods, but their prices can and do fluctuate much more during global economic cycles, causing these countries to experience wide fluctuations in their export earnings. The oil-rich countries of the Persian Gulf provide good examples. Despite their massive reserves of petroleum, the average 1997 incomes in Iraq and Iran were $2,000 and $5,200, respectively. Even the supposedly super-rich Saudi Arabians had an average income of less than $7,000 per person. Countries that get truly rich in the oil business are those that have the industrial base and advanced technology necessary for a petroleum refining industry that produces gasoline, synthetic fibers, plastics, and so on.

Infrastructure

Industrialization cannot occur in a vacuum. Factories require electricity and/or natural gas to power machines. They need paved roads, reliable railroads, and modern airport facilities to ship supplies in and finished products out. Even with a willing and educated labor force, a country cannot improve itself economically without the prerequisite physical infrastructure.

Businesses also need modern telecommunications systems to stay in contact with customers and suppliers. The goods listed in Table 3 (p. 514)—televisions, telephones, PCs, and the Internet—are not merely consumer goods; they are the basics for communications in the modern world. It is difficult for businesses to develop and prosper in the absence of a strong communications infrastructure. Thailand and Malaysia are well ahead of most middle-income countries in using PCs and developing Internet networks, and Indonesia is well out in front of most low-income countries. Again we see an upward-spinning cycle: income growth allowed these countries to purchase advanced telecommunications, and the presence of the technology permitted even greater growth.

Overpopulation

Educated and trained human capital is an asset to economic growth. Increased numbers of mouths to feed are not. A nation's standard of living is determined by the amount of food, housing, and other goods and services available to each person. The number of people and the rate of population increase are important factors

export promotion a policy that encourages the production and export of goods based on comparative advantage.

Figure 4

Projected World Population Growth by Geographic Area, 1950–2150 (Population in millions)

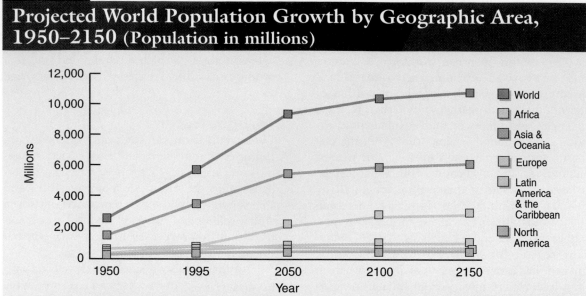

This graph shows the breakdown of total world population and population growth by geographic area, based on United Nations medium growth assumptions. The population of Africa is expected to almost quadruple by 2150, while the population of Europe is expected to steadily decrease.

Source: United Nations, Department of Economic and Social Affairs, 1998

in this measure. Economic growth must increase faster than the growth rate in the population for per capita incomes and living standards to improve. For many developing nations, overpopulation can be a major obstacle to improving living standards. In many LDCs, especially those in Africa, virtually all economic gains from development efforts are canceled out by population growth.

The world's population, which stands at over 6 billion people, grew at an average annual rate of 1.5% a year from 1990 to 1997. While this is a decrease from the prior decade, most of this growth is still occurring in the already overpopulated and poor regions of the world. Sub-Saharan African nations grew at a 2.7% annual rate and those in South Asia at a 1.9% rate. Through an aggressive birth control program, China has slowed its population growth to an average rate of 1.1%.

A number of factors contribute to the population explosion in the LDCs. Being primarily agrarian, new babies mean new hands to help work the land. In the absence of stable and secure retirement programs, the more children a family has the better the parents' chances of being well taken care of when they can no longer work. Finally, many people in the LDCs either are unaware of birth control options, have no access to birth control products, or follow religious and/or cultural beliefs that discourage their use. Until population growth slows, the prospects for economic development are not bright.

◤ The Debt Crisis

Of more immediate concern to many LDCs than the overpopulation problem is their debt crisis. The two problems are not unrelated. In order to provide for the food and other needs of their growing populations and at the same time invest to expand and modernize their production capacity, developing countries have borrowed to the hilt from foreign banks and international lending institutions. Indonesia's external debt in 1996 amounted to $129 billion, Malaysia's to

$40 billion, and Thailand's to $91 billion. Among the industrializing countries of the upper-middle-income group, Brazil had an external debt of $179 billion, Mexico $157 billion, and Argentina $94 billion. To put these numbers into perspective, Indonesia's foreign debt was equal to 62% of its entire GDP, Thailand's equal to 56%, and Malaysia's equal to 52%.

Most external debt is denominated in U.S. dollars or other major international currencies. When the value of the Southeast Asian currencies fell, it raised their cost of obtaining the dollars they needed to repay their debts. For example, in September 1997, it took Rp 3,000 (Indonesian rupiahs) to buy US$1. One year later that same dollar cost Rp 11,000, and consequently Indonesians spent almost four times as much to repay debts owed in dollars. Even a much smaller drop, like the Thai baht falling from 35 Bht (bahts) = US$1 to 40 Bht = US$1 increased the cost of servicing Thailand's foreign debt by over 14%. Should this kind of currency collapse strike the debt-laden countries of Latin America, the result could be devastating.

The International Monetary Fund (IMF) has stepped in to help alleviate the current crisis faced by the tiger cubs and South Korea (whose currency lost almost half its value from 1997 to 1998). The IMF has raised billions of dollars from the world's richer countries, and made billions of dollars in emergency loans to Korea, Indonesia, Thailand, and Malaysia (not to mention additional billions to Russia). The intent is to use the IMF funds to pay private creditors, and then to repay the IMF over a longer period of time at lower interest rates.

These loans do not come cheap. If an individual finds him- or herself in so much debt that they need to go to a credit counselor, the advice they receive will not be pleasant. Until their bills are paid, there will likely be no movies, no meals in restaurants, no new clothes, no Sunday roasts, and so on. The IMF policies towards debtor countries are very similar. They are being forced by the IMF to pursue politically unpopular austerity measures. These include curbing government spending on public works projects, reducing inflation, freeing up markets, and disposing of money-losing nationalized industries.

Sometimes, much of an LDC's limited output is siphoned off to support the opulent lifestyles of its leaders.

The conditions imposed on the debtor countries have meant cutbacks in social programs, higher unemployment, and shortages of imported goods. Any dollars coming into the country as export earnings cannot be used to buy medicines, spare parts, new capital, or fertilizers. They must be used to repay debts. Realizing that most of these payments are going to affluent Western countries raises a great deal of local resentment toward the foreign creditor nations.

These austerity measures have also caused internal social unrest that threatens to topple the governments in some countries. Their leaders are walking a tightrope between defaulting on the loans—thereby alienating the creditors and cutting off future financial assistance, foreign investment, and even essential imports—and economically squeezing their populations to the point of revolution. Some 40 impoverished countries in sub-Saharan Africa collectively pay about $1 billion a month in interest on their external debt. According to the former president of Nigeria, "Indebtedness is the single major obstacle to development of the continent. The debt is crippling. We cannot continue this way."

Until existing debts are paid, forgiven, or at least brought under control, it will be difficult for the LDCs to raise the additional funds that are needed to industrialize and grow. The IMF programs have not yet been in place long enough in Southeast Asia to offer an evaluation of their effectiveness.

Environmental Threats

Less developed countries attempting to industrialize rapidly are running into severe environmental problems. Their skies are choked with soot and fumes, their waterways are poisoned with chemical wastes. Additionally, due to the increase in mineral fuel prices (oil, kerosene, coal) in the 1970s, millions of people in the underdeveloped nations resorted to the use of wood as their principal fuel for cooking and heating. The result was a massive denuding of trees, which in turn caused erosion of the topsoil, reducing agricultural output.

The external costs of industrialization in the LDCs are enormous. When the prices of mineral fuels fell, people in the LDCs turned to them once again, and burned them with little regard for the environmental damage they caused. Like people everywhere, once incomes began to rise, one of the first things people in the LDCs purchased was an automobile that burns gasoline and pollutes the air. Few efforts have been made to internalize those external costs because of the economic burden of doing so. With insufficient capital for normal investment purposes, the LDCs have been unwilling to divert resources into environmental protection. Furthermore, they lack the technology needed to cure such environmental problems as smokestack emissions.

The growing concern over ozone depletion and global warming in the industrialized countries leaves the developing world indifferent. After all, they argue, the high-income nations became wealthy exploiting the environment. Is it fair now to ask the LDCs to sacrifice their own growth to satisfy world environmental concerns? In view of the consequences of global warming for everyone on spaceship Earth, it may be in the interest of the wealthy countries to subsidize such measures as pollution control and the preservation of tropical rain forests in the LDCs.

Institutions

One of the lessons the world learned from the economic crisis in East and Southeast Asia is that inflows of foreign investment capital can help accelerate the economic development of an LDC. An even more important lesson was that managing these flows is a sophisticated undertaking that requires a more advanced legal and institutional setting than most LDCs have in place. **Transparency** is necessary for investors to make informed decisions. Strict banking regulations are necessary to assure that customer deposits are safe and that loans are being made on sound economic grounds. Laws governing contracts, stock issues, debt obligations, and bankruptcy are necessary to ensure that business transactions can be undertaken with a minimum of risk.

What Are the Prospects for the Economic Development of the LDCs?

EconExplorer

Perhaps the most important institutional reform necessary to generate sustained growth in the less developed parts of our world is the institution of peace. Essentially it boils down to a question of opportunity costs. The opportunity costs of war include the reduced investment and actual destruction of physical capital and human capital, the use of scarce resources to produce weapons of war instead of PCs, schools, and hospitals, and the security of knowing that what you are working for will be there when you wake up tomorrow morning.

---

transparency the ability of investors to easily obtain financial information about firms and companies that they are investing in.

Case Application

Back to the Future

Economists have wrestled for years to understand just what factors are responsible for economic growth. Advocates of the New Growth Theory (NGT) are looking to the past to find an answer. In *The Wealth of Nations*, Adam Smith proposed that economic growth occurs when business people have the freedom to pursue their self-interest within the confines of rules and laws laid down by the people through their governments. In contrast, a lack of growth and poverty result when governments restrict that freedom and attempt to direct the allocation of resources through political decisions.

Following Smith, albeit 200 plus years later, NGT economists contend that the keys to economic growth for both developed and less developed economies include accumulating physical capital, investing in human capital, keeping governments small, minimizing government regulations and controls, opening economies to free internal and international trade, and respecting property rights and the rule of law. These keys have two things in common. First, they generally describe the institutional setting or environment in which economic activity takes place, rather than placing an emphasis on a specific type of economic activity or policy. Second, they emphasize the importance of economic freedom for members of a society. Following Smith's ideas, the role of government is to create and maintain an environment where people are free to pursue whatever business they feel is best and not to interfere and attempt to plan economic activity.

The test of any theory is in its ability to explain the real world. So, do countries that follow the NGT prescription achieve faster economic growth? To test the theory, William Beach and Gareth Davis used the Heritage Foundation's Index of Economic Freedom as a measure of economic freedom. The index is constructed by rating countries according to the following factors: trade barriers, tax levels, government intervention, inflation rates, freedom of foreign investment, bank regulations, wage and price controls, protection of property rights, the ease of obtaining business licenses, and the size of the black market. Lower values of the index imply more freedom. If the NGT theory is correct, those countries with the lowest scores in the index should experience the greatest economic growth.

The graph on page 526 shows the results of the test using the index values for 1997 and the annual average growth of per capita GDP (in terms of purchasing power parity) for 1980 through 1993 (Figure 5). The results clearly confirm the NGT proposition: the more freedom a country allows its populace, the greater the amount of economic growth and development it will experience.

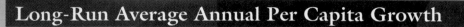

Long-Run Average Annual Per Capita Growth

Figure 5

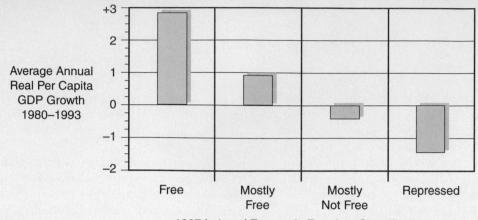

Average Annual Real Per Capita GDP Growth 1980–1993

1997 Index of Economic Freedom Classification

(bars labeled: Free, Mostly Free, Mostly Not Free, Repressed)

Note: Per capita GDP growth is expressed in terms of Purchasing Power Parities.

There is a strong correlation between economic freedom and economic growth.

Source: Adapted from William W. Beach and Gareth Davis, *The Institutional Setting of Economic Growth;* data source: Heritage Foundation, *1998 Index of Economic Freedom.*

Economic Reasoning

1. What is meant by economic freedom?

2. What is the connection between economic freedom and economic growth?

3. The NGT does not say much about the distribution of income. Which do you think is more important for a developing economy, achieving economic growth or economic equity?

Back to the Future

Obtain the latest copy of the Index of Economic Freedom from your library (or at http://www.heritage.org:80/index/execsum.html). Select about 20 countries at random, and draw a scatterplot that shows the country's index value on the horizontal axis and its GDP growth rate (available from the World Bank World Development Report) on the vertical axis. If the NGT is correct, your graph should show an inverse relationship between the two variables. Does it?

▶ Putting It Together

Two-thirds of the world's people live in poverty in the *less developed countries (LDCs)* of Asia, Africa, and Latin America. These countries are largely agricultural with small, inefficient manufacturing sectors and *per capita incomes* of only a few hundred dollars a year. Because of variations in costs of living, income comparisons across countries are more accurately expressed in terms of *purchasing power parity.*

Income distribution in the LDCs is generally skewed so that a small percentage of income receivers have most of the income. This is often the result of the unequal distribution of land that is common in most agrarian societies. Various *social indicators* such as illiteracy, life expectancy at birth, and infant mortality, along with the economic indicators, reveal a country's standard of living. The quality of life, as measured by these social indicators tend to increase with a country's income.

However measured, increasing incomes and living standards are the primary purposes of economic development. Some of the world's greatest progress in economic development occurred in the *Asian tiger* and *tiger cub* countries of East and Southeast Asia. The current economic crisis in that part of the world, however, threatens to take back many of the hard won gains of the past 30 years.

The poverty in developing countries stems from a number of factors. Theories based on *environmental determination* contend that development depends upon a country's natural resources and physical environment. Cultural determination theories instead put more emphasis on cultural values and attitudes, such as the *capricious universe view* of the world. Regardless of the initial causes, the *vicious circle of poverty* perpetuates low productivity because a lack of capital and the resulting low incomes do not provide an *economic surplus* with which to create new capital. The lack of capital, modern technology, and productive human capital re-

The image of this young man, who seems to favor Marlboros and uses a cell phone, suggests that he and his family have seen better days. After struggling to attain middle-class income, many Asian families have been cruelly thrown back into poverty.

sult in low per capita GDP, and the cycle perpetuates itself.

Rapid population growth compounds the problem of insufficient capital by consuming virtually all production. This prevents the accumulation of an economic surplus and a sufficient quantity of capital upon which growth and development can build.

Colonialism left a legacy of economic and social effects in many developing countries. Though some things left by colonial powers are beneficial, colonialism has had many negative effects. The world economic system prior to World War II was based on taking raw materials from the colonies to use in the industries of Western countries. This did not give Third World countries a chance to develop industries on their own. The European powers also carved up Africa into the countries that exist today for their own convenience and with no regard for natural borders and tribal divisions. Today, the resulting civil wars and political instability severely retard development.

Misguided government policies and *exploitation* have also interfered with growth. Many LDCs have embarked on ambitious industrialization programs, neglecting agriculture or attempting to develop *import-substituting* industries. The results of these programs too often were high-cost, poor-quality manufactured goods, food shortages, and serious balance-of-payments problems. Protectionist trade policies have frequently resulted in high-cost production and inflation with falling real income. The Asian tigers and their cubs proved to be more successful by following outward-looking *export promotion* policies.

There is a race between world population growth and increased food production. The long-run specter of food shortages, resource depletion, and environmental pollution is a threat not only to LDCs, but to the industrialized countries as well. The world's resources may be insufficient to satisfy demand if the developing countries begin to use them up at the same per capita rate as the industrialized countries do now.

A pressing problem for many LDCs is meeting the payments on their large external debt. If they default they will lose international credit and foreign investment, and perhaps have their imports cut off. But if the governments tighten their domestic economic belts in order to avoid defaulting, their citizens may revolt.

The economic development of the world's poorer countries will not be easy. It requires the replacement of an agricultural society with an urbanized workforce, the infrastructure necessary to support industrialization, and the legal framework and government institutions necessary to provide transparency and trust among both lenders and borrowers.

$ Perspective $

The Malthusian Dilemma

Thomas Robert Malthus (1766–1834) Robert Malthus was born in Surrey, England. He studied for the ministry at Cambridge, from which was derived the deprecatory reference to him by some of his later critics as "Parson Malthus." He was appointed professor of modern history and political economy at the Haileybury College of the East India Company, where he remained until his death. He was a friend and frequent correspondent of David Ricardo, who occasionally passed on to him tips on good investments in the commodities markets. Malthus did not act on the advice given by his successful friend and lived a life of genteel penury. In addition to six editions of the *Essay on Population,* Malthus wrote a text on the *Principles of Political Economy* (1820) and a number of pamphlets on such topics as prices, money, gold, rent, and foreign trade policy.

In his *Essay on Population* (1798), Thomas Robert Malthus predicted that the growth of population was bound to outrun the world's food supply. According to his calculations, population grew at a geometric ratio (1, 2, 4, 8, 16, etc.), while food production at most grew at an arithmetic ratio (1, 2, 3, 4, 5, etc.).

As a result, population would always push against the limit of food supplies and would be held in check by famine, as well as war and disease. Under these circumstances, there could be no improvement in living standards.

In the second edition of the *Essay on Population,* Malthus suggested that there might be a way to avoid mass starvation. He recognized that "moral restraint" might serve as a preventive check on population growth. He defined moral restraint as postponing marriage and also strict sexual continence prior to marriage. He was not, however, very hopeful that sufficient moral restraint would be practiced by the British working class to alleviate the population problem.

It was Malthus's very gloomy prediction of worldwide mass starvation that gave economics the designation of "the dismal science." So far, Malthus's expectations have not been fulfilled. On the whole, the world's population is better fed now than it has ever been in history. Malthus did not foresee the vast new areas that would be brought under cultivation in the New World and elsewhere, nor could he foresee the dramatic improvements in transportation that would make the New World's produce available throughout the world. Even less could he foresee the improvements in agricultural productivity that were to result from the agricultural revolution of the late nineteenth and early twentieth centuries and the green revolution that has resulted in more productive seed hybrids and improved irrigation and fertilization in the last 3 decades.

However, there are many today who believe that Malthus was basically right and only his timing was mistaken. These "neo-Malthusians" maintain that at the present rates of reproduction in many countries throughout the world, the population is bound to outrun the food-producing capacity of the earth, perhaps early in the next century. Even today the balance between food and population is precarious, with no reserves of staples in storage that could sustain the world over a series of shortfall production years resulting from drought or other production interruptions in major growing areas.

For Further Study and Analysis

Study Questions

1. What led to the collapse of the Southeast Asian tiger cub economies of Thailand, Indonesia, and Malaysia?

2. How can the LDCs increase the amount of capital available for investment in development projects to increase their rate of economic growth?

3. Why are educational and health programs important to economic growth?

4. What would it mean for a country if its population growth rate was higher than the growth rate of its GDP?

5. Explain the difference between import substitution and export promotion as economic development strategies.

6. What has changed in the world that makes the environmental determination theory of economic development less valid than it might have been 200 years ago?

7. How does income distribution in the LDCs compare with the income distribution figures given for the United States in chapter 9 (p. 232)?

8. What are the prerequisites for the economic development of the LDCs?

9. Why do LDCs accumulate so much international debt?

10. Why does environmental pollution get worse as a country begins to develop?

Exercises in Analysis

1. Compare East Asia and the Pacific region with Latin America and the Caribbean region with respect to per capita GDP and growth in per capita GDP. Write a short paper on the differences and what might account for them. A good source of data is the World Bank World Development Report, either in your library or online at http://www.worldbank.org.

2. Track the economic progress in Thailand, Malaysia, or Indonesia from 1990 through the present. Has the Asian flu proved to be fatal, or is the country you selected getting back on its feet? A good place to find current information is the *Economist* magazine or *Asia Week* magazine (available online at http://www.pathfinder.com/asiaweek/. More detailed analyses are available at the Asian Financial Crisis Web site given in the Further Reading section below.

3. Write a paper on world population growth, the problems it poses, the possible solutions to those problems, and the prospects for the future. The population Web sites given in the Further Reading section can provide a good starting point for your research.

4. Write an essay on one or all of the international problems hindering economic development. Can you recommend any solutions?

Further Reading

Cooper, Frederick, ed. *Confronting Historical Paradigms: Peasants, Labor, and the Capitalist World System in Africa and Latin America.* Madison, WI: University of Wisconsin Press, 1993. An examination of the economic and social conditions in the LDCs of Africa and Latin America. Evaluates the effect of capitalism on the agrarian societies of these countries.

Ghosh, Arun, *Planning in India: The Challenge for the Nineties.* New Delhi: Sage Publications, 1992. Examines the program of decentralization in government control over the Indian economy.

Gooptu, Sudarshan. *Debt Reduction and Development: The Case of Mexico.* New York: Praeger, 1993. Explains the means by which Mexico has handled its large foreign debt through a program of austerity and governmental fiscal restraint.

Gregory, Paul R., and Robert C. Stuart. *Comparative Economic Systems.* New York: Houghton Mifflin, 1999. Chapter 12, "The Asian Model," provides a good synopsis of the different development philosophies followed by the Asian tigers and India.

Grossman, Gene M. *Pollution and Growth: What Do We Know?* London: Center for Economic Policy Research, 1993. Reviews recent empirical studies on the relationship between pollution and per-capita income in both developed and developing countries. Findings show that, although some local pollution problems, such as urban water and air pollution, decrease as incomes increase, more large-scale environmental problems such as acid rain and carbon dioxide in the atmosphere steadily get worse.

Harrison, Paul. *The Third Revolution: Environment, Population and a Sustainable World*. New York: I. B. Tauris, 1992. Focuses on the relationship between population and the environment. The previous two revolutions implied by the title were the agricultural revolution and the industrial revolution. Both "were the response to pressures of population growth on the environment." The current revolution, according to Harrison, is brought on by waste.

International Investment Corporation Economics Department. *Internal and External Investments in Developing Countries: Financing Corporate Growth in the Developing World*. Washington, DC: World Bank Publications, 1991. Discusses corporate capital structures in industrial and developing countries, identifying similarities and differences. Compares the capital structures in fast-growing countries to those in slower-growing countries.

Mander, Jerry, and Edward Goldsmith, eds. *The Case against the Global Economy*. San Francisco: Sierra Club Books, 1996. A collection of essays contending that globalization brings more ills to developing economies than benefits.

Mann, Jim. *Beijing Jeep: The Short, Unhappy Romance of American Business in China*. New York: Simon & Schuster, 1989. A newspaper reporter's account of trials and tribulations accompanying the attempts of American Motors and, after its takeover of American Motors, Chrysler to produce Cherokee Jeeps in China prior to the Tiananmen Square massacre.

Negative Population Growth, Inc. at http://www.npg.org/index.htm. This organization provides a wealth of information about the problems of overpopulation. It also provides links to other such sites at http://www.npg.org/othrorgs.htm.

Office of Population Research, Princeton University. This organization publishes Population Index, a research report that is available on the Web at http://popindex.princeton.edu/.

Overholt, William. *The Rise of China*. New York: W. W. Norton, 1993. The author presents a very optimistic view of the economic prospects of China, predicting that it will be the next economic superpower. He sees difficulties to be faced in the conflicts between rich and poor regions and possible succession struggles, but he believes that pragmatism will overcome these difficulties.

Rosen, George. *Contrasting Styles of Industrial Reform: China and India in the 1980s*. Chicago: University of Chicago Press, 1992. A comparison of economic policies in India and China and the results of their differing paths to economic development.

Roubini, Nouriel. What Caused Asia's Economic and Currency Crisis and Its Global Contagion? This Web site at http://www.stern.nyu.edu/~nroubini/asia/AsiaHomepage.html contains a lifetime's worth of reading material on the Asian financial crisis, from current events to critiques to debates about what went wrong. If you have more than a lifetime to devote, there are also plenty of links. A number of papers by Paul Krugman, one of the world's leading authorities on the topic can be found here. (also accessible via a link from the University of Michigan's international economics and statistical resources site at http://www.lib.umich.edu/libhome/Documents.center/stecfor.html).

United Nations Population Information Network (POPIN), UN Population Division. This site at http://www.undp.org/popin/popin.htm provides links to the latest UN data on current population and population projections far out in to the future.

White, James C., ed. *Global Climate Change: Linking Energy, Environment, Economy, and Equity*. New York: Plenum Press, 1992. The author writes that "the nations of the world are not facing up to the global environmental needs. We are failing to recognize the potential severity of approaching problems and are not investing enough in prevention and amelioration to stem the deterioration of our environment."

glossary

This glossary has been prepared to provide you with a convenient and ready reference as you encounter terms in *The Study of Economics* that you wish to review. It includes the definition of each of the economic concepts contained in the in-text glossary.

Altogether there are a total of 397 items contained here. The number following the definition is the page number on which the item is first discussed in the text. For other references to each term in the text you should consult the index, which begins on page 549.

A

absolute advantage   a producer has an absolute advantage relative to another producer if he or she can produce more of a good or service than the other with the same amount of resources.   69

affirmative action program   a program devised by employers to increase their hiring of women and minorities; frequently mandated by government regulations.   236

aggregate concentration   a measure of the proportion of the total sales of all industries accounted for by the largest firms in the country. There is no common standard for measuring the aggregate concentration ratio.   192

aggregate demand   the total effective demand for the nation's output of goods and services.   292

aggregate supply   the total amount of goods and services available from all industries in the economy.   305

allocation   the different uses to which resources are put in order to produce different goods and services. The manner in which a society allocates its scarce resources determines what it produces.   44

annually balanced budget   a budgetary principle calling for the revenue and expenditures of a government to be equal during the course of a year.   382

antitrust legislation   laws that prohibit or limit monopolies or monopolistic practices.   206

Asian tigers   a nickname used to describe Hong Kong, Singapore, Taiwan, and South Korea—four Asian economies that achieved almost miraculous rates of growth from the 1960s to the mid-1990s.   510

automatic stabilizers   changes in government payments and tax receipts that automatically result from fluctuations in national income and act to aid in offsetting those fluctuations.   388

automatic transfer services (ATS)   a type of account that provides for the depository institution to automatically transfer funds from the depositor's savings account to her or his checking account when it has been drawn down.   264

automation   production techniques that adjust automatically to the needs of the processing operation by the use of control devices.   183

average costs   total costs divided by the number of units produced.   156

average propensity to consume   the percentage of after-tax income that, on the average, consumers spend on goods and services.   133

average propensity to save   the percentage of after-tax income that, on the average, consumers save.   133

B

balance of payments   an annual summary of all economic transactions between a country and the rest of the world during the year.   453

balance of trade   the net deficit or surplus in a country's merchandise trade; the difference between merchandise imports and exports.   453

barriers to entry or exit   legal or institutional factors that prevent a firm from entering or leaving an industry. For example, licenses, patents, or one firm's control of a necessary input.   160

barter   direct exchange of goods and services without the use of money.   267

base period (base year)   the reference period for comparison of subsequent changes in an index series; set equal to 100.   297

basic deficit   the excess of import-type transactions over export-type transactions in a country's current and capital accounts in the balance of payments.   455

benefits principle   levy of a tax on an individual to pay the costs of government service in proportion to the individual's benefit from the service.   367

bilateral trade negotiations   trade negotiations between two countries only.   429

bond   a long-term, interest-bearing certificate issued by a business firm or government that promises to pay the bondholder a specified sum of money on a specified date.   272

boycott   refusal by consumers to buy the products or services of a firm.   179

business process reengineering (BPR)   a reorganization of a company to make use of just-in-time methods, and multidisciplinary teams of workers aimed at production in the least time with no defects.   188

business transfer payments   outlay by business for which no good or service is exchanged, such as payouts under deferred compensation arrangements, gifts, and donations.   324

C

capital   the means of production, including computers, buildings, machinery, and tools; alternatively, it can mean financial capital, the money used to acquire the factors of production.   8

capital consumption allowances   the costs of capital assets consumed in producing GDP, also known as depreciation.   325

capital equipment   the machinery and tools used to produce goods and services.   182

capital gains   net income realized from an increase in the market value of a real or financial asset when it is sold.   233

capital/output ratio   the ratio of the cost of new investment goods to the value of the annual output produced by those investment goods.   401

capricious universe view   the belief that there is no connection between the work and effort that one puts forward and the rewards that one receives.   515

cartel   an industry in which the firms have an agreement to set prices and/or divide the market among members of the cartel.   163

central bank   an institution that controls the issuance of currency, provides banking services to the government and to the other banks, and implements the nation's monetary policy; in the United States the Federal Reserve is the central bank.   272

centrally directed (command) economy   an economic system in which the basic questions of what, how, and for whom to produce are resolved primarily by governmental authority.   74

certificate of deposit (CD)   a deposit of a specified sum of money for a specified period of time that cannot be redeemed prior to the date specified (without penalties for early withdrawal).   263

chart   a graphical representation of statistical data or other information.   21

check   a written order to a depository institution to pay a person or institution named on it a specified sum of money.   262

check (debit) cards   cards that can be used like Visa, MasterCard, Discover, or American Express credit cards, but instead of a loan being made to make the purchase, the purchase price is deducted from the card user's checking account balance.   262

circular flow diagram   an analytical diagram showing the economic relationships between the major sectors of an economic system.   81

civilian labor force   the number of persons age 16 or older who are either employed or are unemployed but actively looking for work.   289

cold war   the political, and threatened military, conflict between communism (the Soviet Union) and capitalism (the United States and Western Europe) for world domination and influence between the 1950s and 1991.   477

collective good (public good)   a good or service that can be used by many at the same time without diminishing any one person's consumption; it is difficult to exclude someone from using the good.   213

command-and-control regulations   a system of administrative or statutory rules that requires the meeting of certain standards of performance.   219

commodity   any economic good, but usually used to refer to basic raw materials such as oil or metals.   267

communism (or socialism)   an economic system in which all nonhuman productive assets are owned by the government in the name of the people, and in which the government decides what is produced, how it is produced, and how the output is distributed.   472

communist ideology   Mao's belief that the principles of communism must be followed regardless of whether or not they proved to be economic successes.   491

community demand schedule   the sum of all the individual demand schedules in a particular market showing the total quantities demanded by the buyers in the market at each of the various possible prices.   95

comparative advantage   a producer has a comparative advantage relative to another producer if he or she can produce a good or service at a lower opportunity cost than the other.   69

complement   a product that is employed jointly in conjunction with another product.   102

concentration ratio   the percentage of total sales of an industry accounted for by the largest four firms. An alternative measure is the percentage of sales accounted for by the largest eight firms.   192

constant dollar GDP (real GDP)   the value of GDP adjusted for changes in the price level since a base period.   326

consumer price index (CPI)   a statistical measure of changes in the prices of a representative sample of urban family purchases relative to a previous period.   297

consumer sovereignty   the condition in a market economy by which consumer decisions about which goods and services to purchase determine what is produced.   132

consumer tastes and preferences   individual liking or partiality for specific goods or services.   101

consumption   the use of income to buy consumer goods and services instead of saving. According to economic jargon, after-tax income can be used for only two things—consumption or saving.   129

cooperatives   producer and worker cooperatives are associations in which the members join in production and marketing and share the profits. Consumer cooperatives are associations of consumers engaged in retail trade, sharing the profits as a dividend among the members.   148

coordination problem   the problem of how we make sure that all the specialized activities of people will be brought together by an economic system to answer the basic economic questions.   70

corporation   a business enterprise that is owned by stockholders and is chartered by the state or federal government to do business as a legal entity.   148

correspondent bank   a bank in another city or country that a bank has an arrangement with to provide deposit transfer or other services.   446

cost-of-living adjustment (COLA)   a frequently used provision of labor contracts that grants wage increases based on changes in the Consumer Price Index; often referred to in negotiations as the "escalator clause."   300

cost-push inflation   a continuing rise in the general price level that results from increases in production costs.   299

Council for Mutual Economic Assistance (CMEA)   the formal international trade agreement that outlined and set the international trade patterns among the USSR and the communist countries of CEE.   484

crony capitalism   a slang expression referring to an economic system based on the allocation of resources and goods according to favoritism and "who you know" rather than according to who can make the most productive use of the resources.   476

cross-training   giving workers training in performing more than one task.   186

crowding out   the term given to the effect government has in reducing the amount of financial capital available for private investment.   342

cultural determination   a theory of economic development that emphasizes the importance of the cultural attitudes and values of a country.   515

currency appreciation   an increase in the value of a country's currency relative to other currencies as a result of a decrease in its supply relative to the demand for it.   448

currency depreciation   a decline in the value of a country's currency relative to other currencies as a result of an increase in its supply relative to the demand for it.   448

currency peg   a fixed exchange rate between two currencies, usually done by smaller countries pegging their currency's value to that of a bigger country.   449

currency   that part of the money supply consisting of coins and paper bills.   261

current account   those transactions in the balance of payments consisting of merchandise and service imports and exports and unilateral transfers (gifts).   453

current dollar GDP   the dollar value of GDP unadjusted for inflation.   326

cyclical unemployment   the lack of work that occurs because the total effective demand for goods and services is insufficient to employ all workers in the labor force.   292

cyclically balanced budget   a budgetary principle calling for the balancing of the budget over the course of a complete business cycle rather than in a particular fiscal or calendar year; over the course of the cycle, tax receipts and expenditures would balance.   382

D

decision lag   the time that it takes the government or the Fed to determine a course of discretionary action.   393

deficit   a negative balance after expenditures are subtracted from revenues.   334

defined benefits retirement plan   a pension plan that guarantees participants a specified level of income when they retire, regardless of how much they contributed to the plan.   244

defined contributions retirement plan   a retirement plan that requires participants to contribute a specific amount of income, with retirement benefits to be determined by the amount contributed plus earnings on the contributions.   244

demand   the relationship between the quantities of a good or service that consumers desire to purchase at any particular time and the various prices that can exist for the good or service.   93

demand curve   a graphic representation of the relationship between price and quantity demanded.   94

demand deposits (checking accounts) liabilities of depository institutions to their customers that are payable on demand.   262

demand-pull inflation   a continuing rise in the general price level that occurs when aggregate demand exceeds the full-employment output capacity of the economy.   298

demand schedule   a table recording the number of units of a good or service demanded at various possible prices.   93

deposit liabilities   the amount that a depository institution is obligated to pay out to its depositors, for example, the amount deposited in its checking and savings accounts.   275

depository institutions   financial institutions that maintain deposit account obligations to their customers; includes commercial banks, savings banks, savings and loan associations, and credit unions.   273

depreciation   the costs of buildings, machinery, tools, and equipment that are allocated to output during a given production period.   155

depression   a severe and prolonged period of decline in the level of business activity.   292

deregulation   the process of eliminating government regulations and reducing the scope and power of regulatory bodies.   209

derived demand   the demand for a factor of production that comes from the demand for the goods or services that the factor produces.   124

devaluation   a decrease in the value of a country's currency relative to other currencies due to an official government reduction in the exchange rate under a fixed-rate system.   447

diagram   a graph that shows the relationship between two or more variables that may or may not have values that can actually be measured; a graphical model.   23

differentiated competition   an industry without entry barriers in which there are a large number of firms producing similar but not identical products; sometimes called monopolistic competition.   161

differentiated products   similar but not identical products produced by different firms.   161

diminishing returns   the common condition in which additional inputs produce successively smaller increments of output.   156

dinosaurs   the massive heavy industry manufacturing plants common throughout the former communist world.   475

direct relationship   a relationship between two variables in which their values increase and decrease together.   24

discount rate   the interest rate charged by the Federal Reserve on loans to depository institutions.   274

discounting   the Fed's practice of making loans to depository institutions at below-market interest rates.   277

discretionary fiscal policy   the use of fiscal policy with the deliberate intention of trying to slow economic growth during a boom (to fight inflation) or increase growth during an economic slowdown.   385

disposable income   the amount of after-tax income that households have available for consumption or saving.   331

dual labor market   a labor force that is increasingly divided between high-skilled and low-skilled workers and jobs, with fewer and fewer workers or jobs in the middle.   233

E

earned income   wages, salaries, and other employee compensation plus earnings from self-employment.   366

earned income tax credit (EITC) a federal tax credit for poor families with earnings that offsets their tax liabilities and, for the poorest, provides an income subsidy.   238

eco-tax a fee levied by the government on each unit of environmental pollutant emitted.   220

economic concept a word or phrase that conveys an economic idea.   17

economic development the process of increasing a country's income and improving the standard of living of its people.   507

economic good any good or service that sells for a price; that is, a good that is not free.   12

economic growth an increase in the production capacity of the economy.   54

economic model a simplified representation of the cause-and-effect relationships in a particular situation. Models may be in verbal, graphic, or equation form.   18

economic profits earnings on invested capital that are in excess of the normal rate of return.   158

economic reasoning the application of theoretical and factual tools of economic analysis to explaining economic developments or solving economic problems.   11

economic surplus a margin of output over and above consumption needs that can be allocated to capital investment.   516

economies of scale decreasing costs per unit as plant size increases.   193

efficiency maximizing the amount of output obtained from a given amount of resources or minimizing the amount of resources used for a given amount of output.   55

elastic a demand condition in which the relative size of the change in quantity demanded is greater than the size of the price change.   130

elasticity ratio a measurement of the degree of the response of a change in quantity demanded to a change in price.   130

employee empowerment giving workers the ability and responsibility to make decisions about how their work should best be done.   187

employee involvement (EI) various programs for incorporating hourly-wage workers in decision making; may involve decisions on production methods, work scheduling, and purchase of capital equipment.   187

entitlement program government benefits that qualified recipients are entitled to by law, such as Social Security old-age benefits.   237

entrepreneur a business innovator who sees the opportunity to make a profit from a new product, new process, or unexploited raw material and then brings together the land, labor, and capital to exploit the opportunity.   9

environmental determination a theory of economic development that emphasizes the importance of natural resources and the physical environment of a country.   515

equilibrium output level excluding the foreign sector, it is the level of GDP at which aggregate demand (C + I + G) is just equal to aggregate supply (C + S + T); the level where income leakages (S + T) are exactly equal to income additions (I + G).   335

equilibrium price the price at which the quantity of a good or service offered by suppliers is exactly equal to the quantity that is demanded by purchasers in a particular period of time.   98

equity the owner's share of the value of property or other assets, net of mortgages or other liabilities.   133

excess reserves reserves of depository institutions that are in excess of those required by the Federal Reserve.   274

exchange rate risk the chance that an investor in a foreign country may earn more or less than anticipated due to unanticipated changes in exchange rates.   449

excise taxes a tax on a particular type of good or service; a sales tax.   324

exploitation obtaining labor services, raw materials, or finished products for a price less than their true value. Alternatively, forcing people to purchase one's products at a price above their true value.   517

export embargo   a prohibition of the export of a commodity, capital, or technology.   430

export promotion   a policy that encourages the production and export of goods based on comparative advantage.   521

external costs   costs of the production process that are not borne by the producer or by the purchaser of the product and are therefore not taken into consideration in production and consumption decisions.   218

external economies   benefits that accrue to parties other than the producer and purchaser of the good or service; benefits for which payment is not collected.   214

externalities   external economies or external dis-economies (external costs).   215

F

factor incomes   the return to factors of production as a reward for productive activity.   80

factor market   a market in which resources and semifinished products are exchanged.   80

factors of production   another name for the productive resources of land, labor, and capital.   8

favorable balance of trade   the surplus in a country's merchandise trade when exports during the year are greater than imports.   454

Fed Board of Governors   the governing body of the Federal Reserve System, consisting of seven members appointed by the president for 14-year terms.   272

Federal Funds market   the market among depository institutions for temporary transfer of excess reserves from one institution to another.   277

Federal Funds rate   the interest rate paid on Federal Funds borrowed.   277

Federal Open Market Committee   a committee consisting of the Federal Reserve Board and the

presidents of five regional Federal Reserve banks that decides on the purchase or sale of government securities by the Federal Reserve to implement monetary policy.   277

Federal Reserve System (Fed)   the central bank of the United States; a system established by the Federal Reserve Act of 1913 to issue paper currency, supervise the nation's banking system, and implement monetary policy.   261

financial capital   the money to acquire the factors of production.   9

fiscal federalism   tax collection and disbursement of funds by a higher level of government to lower jurisdictions.   361

fiscal policy   the use of federal government spending, taxing, and debt management to influence general economic activity.   381

fixed costs   production costs that do not change with changes in the quantity of output.   155

fixed exchange rates   exchange rates between currencies that are legally set by the respective countries.   447

flat tax   a proposed income tax structure that removes all deductions from the federal tax code and levies the same tax rate on everyone.   370

food stamps   certificates that can be used in place of money to purchase food items.   238

foreign currency reserves   amounts of foreign currencies held by the central bank of a country.   455

foreign exchange market   a set of institutions, including large banks in the world's financial centers, private brokers, and government central banks and other agencies, that deal in the exchange of one country's money for another's.   445

"for whom" question   the question concerning the decisions made by an economy about income distribution—who gets how much of the goods and services produced.   51

free good   a production or consumption good that does not have a direct cost.   12

free trade international trade that is unrestricted by government protectionist measures. 425

freely fluctuating (flexible) exchange rates an exchange-rate system by which the relative values of different currencies are determined by demand and supply rather than by government fiat. 448

frictional unemployment unemployment that occurs when people change jobs, enter the job market, or reenter the job market. 290

full employment employment of nearly everyone who desires to work. In practice, an unemployment level of not more than 4-5% is considered full employment. 56

full employment aggregate demand the level of total effective demand that is just sufficient to employ all workers in the labor force. 292

functional finance the use of fiscal policy to stabilize the economy without regard to the policy's effect on a balanced government budget. 382

functional income distribution the shares of total income distributed according to the type of factor service for which they are paid, that is, rent as a payment for land, wages for labor, and interest for capital. 123

G

getting prices right a phrase that refers to allowing prices to be set by market forces instead of by government agencies. 473

gold standard a method of controlling a country's money supply by tying the amount of money in circulation to the amount of gold held by the banking system. 261

golden rule a budget approach that calls for current services to be covered by revenues while paying for capital expenditures with deficit financing. 383

government regulation government control of the prices charged and services provided by firms that produce goods that are vital to the public's well-being. 207

government sector spending (G) spending by the various levels of government on goods and services, including public investment. 323

Great Leap Forward Mao Zedong's ambitious 5-year plan (1957) that was to achieve accelerated economic growth through the abolition of self-interest and financial incentives, making the people's sole motivation the desire to improve Chinese society. 490

Gross Domestic Product (GDP) the sum of the values of all goods and services produced within the country during the year. 321

Gross National Product (GNP) the sum of the values of all goods and services produced by residents of the country during the year, including earnings on overseas investments and excluding foreign earnings on investments in this country. 323

gross private domestic investment (I) private-sector spending on capital equipment, increased stocks of inventories, and new residential housing. 321

H

horizontal equity equality of treatment for all individuals at the same income level. 366

household an economic unit consisting of an individual or a family. 80

"how" question the question concerning the decisions made by an economy about the technology used to produce goods and services. 49

human capital labor that is literate, skilled, trained, healthy, and economically motivated. 185

hypothesis a tentative explanation of an event; used as a basis for further research. 10

I

impact lag the time that it takes for monetary or fiscal policy to have an impact on the country's economic activity. 393

implicit costs the opportunity costs of using one's own labor and/or capital resources in a business. Although there are no direct monetary payments associated with implicit costs, they are real costs of doing business. 157

import-competing industry a domestic industry that produces the same or a close substitute good that competes in the domestic market with imports. 421

import substitution a policy that encourages the replacement of imported goods with domestically produced ones. 518

incentive a motivation to undertake an action or to refrain from undertaking an action; in a market economy profits are the incentive to produce. 80

incidence of a tax the amount of a tax that ultimately falls on households, irrespective of who initially pays the tax. 368

income effect the effect of a change in the price of a good or service on the amount purchased that results from a change in purchasing power of the consumer's income due to the price change. 93

increasing costs a rise in average production costs as the quantity of output of the good increases. 418

indirect taxes taxes collected from businesses (other than income taxes) that do not directly become part of someone's income, such as sales, excise, and property taxes. 325

individual retirement account (IRA) a private savings account that is given special tax treatment as long as funds are not withdrawn before retirement. 244

industry consortium a combination of firms in an industry to carry out a common purpose. 207

industry market structure a classification system that describes industries according to the number of firms in the industry, the ease of entry, and the standardization of industry products. The four usual classifications are pure competition, differentiated competition, oligopoly, and monopoly. 160

inelastic a demand condition in which the relative size of the change in the quantity demanded is less than the size of the price change. 130

infant industry argument the contention that it is economically justified to provide trade protection to a new industry in a country to enable it to grow to a size that would result in production costs that are competitive with those of foreign producers. 435

inflation a continuously rising general price level, resulting in a reduction in the purchasing power of money. 57

infrastructure an economy's stock of capital—much of it publicly owned—that provides basic services to producers and consumers. Includes such facilities as highways, electric power, water supplies, educational institutions, and health services. 50

institutions decision-making units, established practices, or laws. 15

interdependence the relationships between individuals and institutions in a country or between countries that arises because of specialization of production. 70

interest a factor payment for the use of financial capital. 80

internalize external costs the process of transforming external costs into internal costs so that the producer and consumer of a good pay the full cost of its production. 218

International Monetary Fund (IMF) an organization established in 1946 to assist in operation of the world monetary system by regulating the exchange practices of countries and providing liquidity to member countries that have payment problems. 447

inventories the value of finished and semifinished goods and raw materials in the hands of producers and distributors. 322

inverse relationship a relationship between two variables in which the value of one decreases as the value of the other increases. 25

investment/GDP ratio the proportion of GDP that is allocated to private investment. 397

J

junk bonds bonds that pay higher than normal interest rates because they have a greater risk of default. 184

just-in-time a system that provides for raw materials and subassemblies to be delivered by suppliers to the location where they will be processed at the time they are needed rather than being stored in inventories. 184

K

Keynesian economics the body of macroeconomic theories and policies that stem from the model developed by John Maynard Keynes. 330

Keynesian revolution the name given to the transformation in macroeconomic theory and policy that resulted from the ideas of Keynes. 339

kickback the return of a portion of a payment or commission in accordance with a secret agreement. 193

L

L a measure of the money supply that includes M3 plus commercial paper, savings bonds, and government securities with maturities of 18 months or less. 263

labor all human resources, including manual, clerical, technical, professional, and managerial labor. 8

labor force participation rate the percentage of the population over 16 years old that is in the civilian labor force. 340

labor-intensive refers to production processes that employ a large amount of labor relative to the amount of capital equipment 418

land all natural resources, including fields, forests, mineral deposits, the sea, and other gifts of nature. 8

law of demand the quantity demanded of a good or service varies inversely with its price; the lower the price the larger the quantity demanded, and the higher the price the smaller the quantity demanded. 93

law of supply the quantity supplied of a good or service varies directly with its price; the lower the price the smaller the quantity supplied, and the higher the price the larger the quantity supplied. 97

learning curve a diagram showing how labor productivity increases as the total number of units produced by a new plant (or with new technology) increases over time. 185

legal reserve requirement (required reserves) the minimum amount of money that a depository institution must have in its vault or on deposit with the Fed. The amount is a set percentage of the bank's deposits. 274

less developed countries (LDCs) nonindustrialized countries generally characterized by low incomes, primarily agricultural labor forces, low standards of living, overpopulation, and widespread illiteracy. 507

limited liability a legal provision that protects individual stockholders of a corporation from being sued by creditors of the corporation to collect unpaid debts of the firm. 149

limited specialization specialization in producing goods or services according to comparative advantage when the specialization is not complete due to increasing costs (decreasing returns). 418

liquidity the degree of ease with which an asset can be converted into money without a significant loss in value. 263

long run a period of time sufficiently long that the amount of all factor inputs can be varied. 107

long-term capital direct investment in plant and equipment or portfolio investments in stocks and bonds. 454

luxury a good or service that increases satisfaction but is not considered essential to well-being. 132

M

M1 a measure of the money supply that includes currency in circulation, demand deposit accounts, negotiable order of withdrawal (NOW) accounts, automatic transfer savings (ATS) accounts, traveler's checks, and checkable money market accounts. 263

M2 a measure of the money supply that includes M1 plus savings deposits, small time deposits (CDs), and certain money market mutual funds. 263

M3 a measure of the money supply that includes M2 plus large time deposits (CDs). 263

marginal tax rate the tax rate applied to the last or additional income received. 366

market concentration a measure of the number of firms in an industry. 192

market economy an economic system in which the basic questions of what, how, and for whom to produce are resolved primarily by buyers and sellers interacting in markets. 72

marketplace (market) a network of dealings between buyers and sellers of a resource or product (good or service); the dealings may take place at a particular location, or they may take place by communication at a distance with no face-to-face contact between buyers and sellers. 79

Medicaid a federally subsidized, state-administered program to pay for medical and hospital costs of low-income families. 238

Medicare the health and medical care program for older Americans that is funded through one of the Social Security Trust Funds. 242

medium of exchange a commodity accepted by common consent in payment for goods and services and as settlement of debts and contracts. 267

mercantilists those who advocated mercantilism, a doctrine that dominated policies in many countries from the sixteenth to the eighteenth centuries. It held that exports should be maximized and imports minimized to generate an inflow of gold, and that exports of machinery and technology should be prohibited to prevent competition from foreign producers. 435

merger a contractual joining of the assets of one formerly independent company with those of another; may be a horizontal merger of companies producing the same product, a vertical merger of companies producing different stages of a product in the same industry, or a conglomerate merger of companies producing in different industries. 193

merit goods goods (including services) that have a social value over and above their utility for the individual consumer. 215

misallocation of resources not producing the mix of products and services that would maximize consumer satisfaction. 193

mixed economy an economic system in which the basic questions of what, how, and for whom to produce are resolved by a mixture of market forces with governmental direction and/or custom and tradition. 76

monetarists those who believe that changes in the money supply have a determining effect on economic conditions. 300

monetary policy actions of the Federal Reserve Board to produce changes in the money supply, the availability of loanable funds, or the level of interest rates in an attempt to influence general economic activity. 385

money market mutual fund an investment fund that pools the assets of investors and puts the assets into debt securities that mature in less than 1 year: short-term bank CDs, corporate bonds, and 6-month Treasury bills. 263

money multiplier the ratio of the maximum increase in the money supply to an increase in bank reserves. Determined by the required reserve ratio. 276

monopolistic pricing setting a price above the level necessary to bring a product to market by restricting the supply of the product. 193

most-favored-nation clause (MFN) a provision in trade agreements that extends lower tariff concessions granted to one country to all other countries that are accorded most-favored-nation treatment. 429

multilateral trade negotiations simultaneous trade negotiations among a number of countries. 429

multiplier the ratio of the ultimate increase in income, caused by an initial increase in spending, to that initial increase. 388

multiplier effect the process by which an initial increase in income results in a total income increase that is a multiple of the initial increase.   387

municipal bond   a debt incurred by a state or local government that uses either its tax revenues or the proceeds from a specific project to pay principal and interest to bondholders.   341

N

National Income (NI)   the total of all incomes earned in producing the GNP.   324

national income accounts   the collective name for various macroeconomic measurements such as GDP and National Income.   326

natural monopoly   an industry in which the economies of scale are so extensive that a single firm can supply the whole market more efficiently than two or more firms could; natural monopolies are generally public utilities.   208

natural rate of unemployment   the combined total of frictional and structural unemployment.   293

near money (monies)   assets with a specified monetary value that are readily redeemable as money; savings accounts, certificates of deposit, and shares in money market mutual funds.   263

necessity   a good or service which is considered essential to a person's well-being.   132

negotiable order of withdrawal (NOW) accounts   savings and loan bank customer accounts on which checks can be drawn.   263

neomercantilists   contemporary advocates of mercantilist trade policies to restrict imports, maximize exports of consumer products, and restrict exports of capital equipment and technology to prevent competition from foreign producers.   435

net exports (X – M)   the value of goods and services exported minus the amount spent on imported goods and services.   323

nomenklatura   former communist party members and government officials who gained control of privatized businesses in the postcommunist era, often through illegal means.   475

nonearned income   dividends, interest, capital gains, and other nonlabor income.   366

nontariff barriers   restrictions on imports resulting from requirements for special marking, test, or standards enforced on imported goods or the time delays in clearing them for importation.   430

normal rate of return (normal profit)   the rate of earnings on invested capital that is normal for a given degree of risk.   158

O

oligopoly   a shared monopoly in which there is no explicit agreement among the firms.   163

open market operations   the purchase or sale of government securities by the Federal Reserve to implement monetary policy.   274

opportunity cost   real economic cost of a good or service produced measured by the value of the sacrificed alternative.   44

other checkable deposits   accounts, other than demand deposit accounts in commercial banks, on which checks can be drawn, principally negotiable order of withdrawal (NOW) accounts in savings and loan banks.   262

P

partnership   a nonincorporated business enterprise with two or more owners.   148

payroll tax   a tax levied on wages and salary but not on other forms of income, such as interest, dividends, or capital gains; a tax on wages and salaries to finance Social Security and Medicare costs, with equal amounts paid by employee and employer; the 1997 tax rate on each was 7.65%.   242, 360

per capita income   the total national income (or GDP) divided by the size of the population.   507

perfectly elastic   a demand condition in which the quantity demanded varies from zero to infinity when there is a change in the price.   132

perfectly inelastic a demand condition in which there is no change in the quantity demanded when price changes. 132

personal consumption expenditures (C) spending by households on goods and services. 321

personal income distribution the pattern of income distribution according to the relative size of people's income. 232

Phillips curve a statistical relationship between increases in the general price level and unemployment. 303

poverty line the family income level below which people are officially classified as poor. 232

pragmatism Deng's belief that economic policies and programs that proved to be successful should be adopted, whether they were consistent with strict communist ideology or not. 491

predatory business practice any action on the part of a firm carried out solely to interfere with a competitor. 193

price discrimination selling a product to two different buyers at different prices where all other conditions are the same. 193

price elasticity of demand the relative size of the change in the quantity demanded of a good or service as a result of a small change in its price. 129

price leadership a common practice in shared monopoly industries by which one of the firms in the industry, normally one of the largest, changes its prices, and the other firms follow its lead. 165

price stability a constant average level of prices for all goods and services. 57

private property rights the exclusive right of someone to use a scarce resource or good in whatever manner they think best. 72

privatization allowing the private sector to produce goods and services that once were provided by the government; the process of selling government enterprises to private buyers and/or turning government services over to private-sector operation. 214, 474

product differentiation a device used by business firms to distinguish their product from the products of other firms in the same industry. 194

product market a market in which finished goods and services are exchanged. 80

production possibility frontier (PPF) the line on a graph showing the different maximum output combinations of goods or services that can be obtained from a fixed amount of resources. 44

productivity a ratio of the amount of output per unit of input; it denotes the efficiency with which resources (people, tools, knowledge, and energy) are used to produce goods and services; usually measured as output per hour of labor. 176

profits the net return after subtracting total costs from total revenue. If costs are greater than revenue, profits are negative. 157

progressive tax a tax rate that increases as the income on which the tax is based grows larger. 368

promissory note (IOU) a written obligation to pay a specified amount at a specified time. 270

proportional tax a levy that takes the same proportion in taxes from low and high incomes. 370

proprietorship a business enterprise with a single private owner. 148

protectionism measures taken by the government in order to limit or exclude imports that compete with domestic production. 433

public assistance government aid to needy families. 237

public utility an industry that produces an essential public service such as electricity, gas, water, and telephone service; normally, a single firm is granted a local monopoly to provide the service. 162

public utility commission a regulatory body whose members are appointed by government to set rates and services provided by public utility firms. 208

purchasing power parity the value of an income measured in U.S. dollars, but reflecting the buying power of the dollar in countries where prices are much lower or higher than the United States.   493

pure competition   a condition prevailing in an industry in which there are such a large number of firms producing a standardized product that no single firm can noticeably affect the market price by changing its output; also an industry in which firms can easily enter or leave.   160

pure monopoly   an industry in which there is only one firm.   162

Q

quantity demanded   the amount of a good or service that consumers would purchase at a particular price.   93

quantity equation (equation of exchange)   the quantity of money (**M**) times the velocity of its circulation (**V**) equals the quantity of goods and services transacted (**T**) times their average price (**P**); $M \times V = T \times P$.   300

quota   a limit on the quantity or value of a good that can be imported in a given time period.   429

R

rate discrimination (price discrimination) charging different customers different rates for services of equal production cost.   206

real capital   the buildings, machinery, tools, and equipment used in production.   154

real investment   the purchase of business structures and capital equipment; measured in dollars of constant value to adjust for inflation.   182

recession   a decline for at least 2 successive quarters in the nation's total output of goods and services.   292

recognition lag   the time that it takes policymakers to recognize that the economy is entering a recession or that inflation is increasing.   393

regressive tax   a levy that takes a higher proportion from low incomes in taxes than it takes from high incomes.   368

rent   a factor payment for the use of land.   80

required reserves   see legal reserve requirement.   274

residual accounts   the short-term capital transfers and foreign currency reserve transactions that compensate for the imbalance in a country's basic balance of international payments.   455

resources   the inputs that are used in production. They include natural resources (minerals, timber, rivers), labor (blue collar, white collar), and capital (machinery, buildings).   8

restructuring   changing the laws, institutions, and the overall economy from communism to free enterprise.   472

revaluation   an increase in the value of a country's currency relative to other currencies due to an official government increase in the exchange rate under a fixed-rate system.   448

rule of law   the principle that all people and businesses have equal protection under the law, and the rejection of favoritism and special favors for the privileged few.   478

S

savings deposits   liabilities of depository institutions to their customers that are not transferable by check and for which the institution may require advance notice before withdrawal.   263

Say's Law of Markets   A theory of the French economist J. B. Say, which holds that when goods or services are produced, enough income is generated to purchase what is produced, thereby eliminating the problem of overproduction.   339

scarcity   the limited resources for production relative to the demand for goods and services.   8

scientific method   a procedure used by scientists to develop explanations for events and test the validity of those explanations.   10

shared monopoly an industry in which there are only a few firms; more specifically, an industry in which four or fewer firms account for more than 50% of industry sales.   163

shift in demand a change in the quantity of a good or service that would be purchased at each possible price.   108

shift in supply a change in the quantity of a good or service that would be offered for sale at each possible price.   109

shock therapy the immediate imposition of free-market rules and institutions, such as market-determined prices, private property, free trade, and so on, in a former communist economy.   472

short run a period of time so short that the amount of some factor inputs cannot be varied.   106

short-term capital transfers of demand deposits or liquid investments such as money market funds, CDs, or Treasury bills.   454

shortage an excess of quantity demanded over quantity supplied that occurs when a price is below the equilibrium price. Shortages cause prices to increase.   98

sin tax an excise tax levied on commodities that public policy deems undesirable, such as cigarettes and alcohol, in order to limit their consumption.   367

social indicators noneconomic characteristics that reflect the societal aspects of a country's standard of living.   510

social insurance government programs designed to maintain people's incomes so that they do not fall into poverty.   241

Social Security The Old Age, Survivors, Disability and Health Insurance (OASDHI) program established by the Social Security Act of 1935. Its purpose is to provide retirement and health benefits to the elderly, and public assistance to the aged, blind, and disabled poor.   241

Social Security Trust Funds the Social Security funds that are by law reserved for specific uses.   242

socioeconomic goal the type of social goal that has important economic dimensions.   59

special economic zones (SEZs) geographic areas near the Chinese coast where foreign firms are allowed to operate and are given special economic subsidies.   492

specialization concentrating the activity of a unit of a production resource-especially labor-on a single task or production operation. Also applies to the specialization of nations in producing those goods and services that their resources are best suited to produce.   68

speculators people who purchase goods or financial assets in anticipation that prices will rise and they can sell at a profit; speculators can also speculate on a fall in prices.   299

stabilization government policies designed to keep recessions from getting too deep and expansions from growing too fast. Stabilization policies are the government's tools for fighting unemployment and inflation.   381

stagflation a term created to describe the situation where high inflation and high unemployment occur simultaneously.   305

state-owned enterprises (SOEs) the thousands of businesses formerly owned and operated by communist governments; in the new, free-market economies these enterprises are being privatized.   474

statistics the data that describe economic variables; also the techniques of analyzing, interpreting, and presenting data.   15

stock option the right to purchase a specific amount of a corporation's stock at a fixed price. Often part of the compensation package for a company's top executives.   400

store of value a means of conserving purchasing power for a future time.   267

structural unemployment the lack of work that occurs because of changes in the basic characteristics of a market, such as a new substitute product, a change in consumer tastes, or new technology in production.   291

substitute a product that is interchangeable in use with another product.   102

substitution effect the effect of a change in the price of a good or service on the amount purchased that results from the consumer substituting a relatively less expensive alternative.   93

Supplementary Security Income (SSI)   a federal government transfer program designed especially to help poor people who are aged, blind, or otherwise disabled.   237

supply   the relationship between the quantities of a good or service that sellers wish to market at any particular time and the various prices that can exist for the good or service.   96

supply curve   a graphic representation of the relationship between price and quantity supplied.   96

supply schedule   a table recording the number of units of a good or service supplied at various possible prices.   96

supply-side economics   an approach to macro-economic problems that focuses on the importance of increasing the supply of goods and services.   338

surplus   an excess of quantity supplied over quantity demanded that occurs when a price is above the equilibrium price. Surpluses cause prices to decrease; a positive balance after expenditures are subtracted from revenues.   99, 334

T

tariff   a tax placed on an imported good; also, the whole schedule of a country's import duties.   428

tax expenditure   tax revenue that the government forgoes because it allows certain expenses to be deducted from taxable income.   357

technology   the body of skills and knowledge that comprises the processes used in production.   9

Temporary Assistance for Needy Families (TANF)   a federally subsidized public assistance program that provides income to needy families for a limited period of eligibility.   237

terms of trade   the ratio of average export prices to average import prices.   435

tiger cubs   a nickname used to describe Indonesia, Thailand, and Malaysia—the three Southeast Asian countries that experienced rapid development in the 1980s through the mid-1990s and then experienced an economic collapse beginning in 1997.   510

time series   the changes in the values of a variable over time; a chart in which time—generally years—is one of the variables.   21

total costs   the sum of fixed costs and variable costs.   156

total quality management (TQM)   a way of managing a firm that puts an emphasis on satisfying customer needs by continuous improvement in product quality, employee training, employee involvement, and the use of statistical tools to monitor the quality of output.   188

total revenue   the sum of receipts from all of the units sold; price × quantity.   157

town and village enterprises (TVEs)   community-owned industrial and commercial firms that have been established in the rural parts of China.   491

trade adjustment assistance   supplementary unemployment payments to workers who have lost their jobs because of import competition, and assistance to firms in shifting to other types of production.   425

trade-off   the choice between alternative uses for a given quantity of a resource.   43

traditional economy   an economic system in which the basic questions of what, how, and for whom to produce are resolved primarily by custom and tradition.   75

transfer payments   expenditures for which no goods or services are exchanged. Welfare, Social Security, and unemployment compensation are government transfer payments.   236

transparency   the ability of investors to easily obtain financial information about firms and companies that they are investing in.   524

Treasury bill   a short-term, marketable federal government security with a maturity of 1 year or less.   272

trust   a combination of producers in the same industry under joint direction for the purpose of exerting monopoly power.   205

U

underemployed resources   resources that are not used to their fullest potential.   49

unemployment rate   the percentage of the civilian labor force that is actively looking for work but is unemployed.   289

unfavorable balance of trade   the deficit in a country's merchandise trade when imports during the year are greater than exports.   454

unit of measurement (standard of value or unit of account)   a common denominator of value in which prices are stated and accounts recorded.   267

unitary elasticity   a demand condition in which the relative change in the quantity demanded is the same as the size of the price change.   130

utility   the amount of satisfaction a consumer derives from consumption of a good or service.   135

V

value added   the difference between the value of a firm's sales and its purchases of materials and semifinished inputs.   325

variable   a quantity—such as number of workers, amount of carbon dioxide, or interest rate—whose value changes in relationship to changes in the values of other associated items.   18

variable costs   production costs that change with changes in the quantity of output.   156

velocity of money (V)   the average rate at which money changes hands.   300

vertical equity   fair differentiations of treatment of individuals at different levels.   366

vertical integration   separate divisions of one company producing the different stages of a product and marketing their output to one another.   194

vicious circle of poverty   the self-reinforcing pattern of economic stagnation that arises from an initial lack of productivity and/or income.   516

W

wage or salary   a factor payment for labor service.   80

"what" question   the question concerning the decisions made by an economy about what (and how much of) particular goods and services to produce with its limited resources.   49

workfare   originally a program that required nonexempt welfare recipients to work at public service jobs for a given number of hours a month; now it may also include job training and wage subsidies.   237

World Bank (The International Bank for Reconstruction and Development)   a specialized agency of the United Nations whose major role is to help finance development of the world's LDCs.   508

index

This index has been prepared to help you easily find important information contained in *The Study of Economics*. It includes names, literary references, and subject entries.

The index is alphabetically arranged by *principal entry*. Each principal entry is immediately followed by the page number or numbers of the text on which it appears or by a *subentry* or series of subentries with page references to enable you to find the discussion of a particular aspect of the principal entry. **Boldface** page numbers are references to in-text glossary items. These items can also be found in the general glossary. Italic page numbers are references to information in figures or tables.

T

Taiwan, U.S. trade deficit with, *433*
Tariffs, **428,** 438; elimination in EU, 419; functions of, 428–29; history in U.S., *434, 439*
Tastes and preferences, **101**
Tax code, 368–70
Tax cuts, 381–82
Tax expenditures, **357**
Taxes: on cigarettes, 122; and economic efficiency, 367–68; equity in, 366–67, 369; in former Soviet Union, 477; impact on investment, 399–400; impact on real interest rates, *279,* 280; incidence of, 368–70; as percentage of earnings, 353; for pollution, 220; reductions as incentives, 339–40; role in Japan's recession, 389
Taxpayers' revolts, 362
Teams, and productivity, 187–88
Technology, **9;** and economic growth, 398; and efficiency, 55; in health care, 349–52; and the "how" question, 50–51; impact on farming, 145; impact on guitar makers, 65; impact on natural monopolies, 209; impact on oil supplies, 111–12; impact on steel industry, 40–41; impact on supply, 105; and income distribution, 233; and neomercantilism, 435–36; personal computers, 58–59, 164–65; and productivity, 183–84, 189, 190–91, 308, 401–2; and U.S. competitiveness, 173–74
Telecommunications industry, 203–4
Telecommunications Reform Act, 204
Telephone industry, 203–4
Television, 134
Temporary Assistance for Needy Families (TANF), **237,** 252
Terms of trade, **435**
Textiles, 251, *422*
Thailand: basic social indicators in, *512;* beginnings of Asian crisis in, 506; infrastructure in, *514;* U.S. trade deficit with, *433*
Theoretical tools of economics, 17–18
The Theory of the Leisure Class, 140
Tiananmen Square massacre, 493–95
Tiger cubs, **510**
Time, opportunity costs of, 44

Time-distance graphs, 32–37
Time period, effect on supply, 105–7
Time series, **21,** 28
Timing, of fiscal policy, 393
Tito, Josip Broz, 488
Tobacco. *See* Cigarettes
Tools of economics, 15–18
Total costs, **156,** 167. *See also* Costs of production
Total production. *See* Gross domestic product (GDP)
Total quality management, **188**
Total revenue, **157,** 167
Tourism, 14
Town and village enterprises (TVEs), **491**
Toyota, 180
Trade adjustment assistance, **425,** 436
Trade agreements: GATT, 138, 146, 414, 429; MFN clauses in, 429, 438; NAFTA, 5, 146, 413–14
Trade deficits: causes and effects of, 453–55; of United States, 424, *432,* 459–64
Trade-offs, **43**–44, 60, 218
Trade restrictions, 438; costs of, 426–27; types of, 428–33
Trademarks, 137, 138
Trading blocs, 414. *See also* European Union; North American Free Trade Agreement (NAFTA)
Traditional economies, **75**–76, 85
Training, 185. *See also* Human capital
Trans-Siberian pipeline accident, 480
Transfer payments, **236,** 252, 371; as automatic stabilizers, 391; criticisms of, 241; extent in U.S., 353–57; growth of, 72–73
Transparency, 505, **524**
Traveler's checks, *263*
Treasury bills, **272;** Fed purchase of, 277–78, 391–92; foreign investment in, 463
Treaty of Rome, 419
Trustmarks, 251
Trusts, **205**
Tuna fishing, 179
Turkey: basic social indicators in, *512;* inflation in, 450–51

U

Ucar International, 207
Ukraine: inflation and GDP growth in, *483;* unemployment in, *485*

Underemployed resources, **49**
Underemployed workers, 294
Underground activities, 329
Unemployment: causes of, 289–94, 313; consequences of, 309–10, 314; and economic growth, 56; in Europe, 229, 295–96; in former communist countries, *485;* government efforts to reduce, 381–85; versus inflation, 287, 303–7; Keynesian policies for, *386*
Unemployment compensation, 229, 295
Unemployment rates, **289,** *290*
Unfavorable balance of trade, **454**
Unified budget, 377
Union of Soviet Socialist Republics (USSR). *See* Soviet Union
Unions: competition with employers, 199; impact of deregulation on, 210; opposition to employee involvement programs, 188; opposition to NAFTA, 413
Unitary elasticity, **130**
United Nations environmental site, 15
United Nations Human Development Report Web site, 520
United Parcel Service (UPS) strike, 288
United States: basic social indicators in, *512;* foreign ownership in, 461–63; GDP growth in, *493;* infrastructure in, *514;* steel production in, *41*
Units of measurement, **267.** *See also* Measurement
Universal cards, 265
Universal health care, 349
Urbanization, 520–21
Uruguay Round, 414
U.S. Bureau of the Census Web site, 236, 240, 433
U.S. dollar. *See* Dollar (U.S.)
U.S. Energy Information Administration Web site, 27
U.S. Trade and Tariff Web site, 427
User fees, 361, *362*
USSR. *See* Soviet Union
Utilities, 162, 207–9
Utility, **135,** 140–41

V

Value added, **325**–26, 344
Value-added tax, 369, 400

photo credits

All cartoons by Jay Bensen/Bensen Studios.

Chapter 1
4: Diaf; 10: Pamela Carley; 12: Ian Osborn/Tony Stone Images; 13: © Plowden 1989/Greenpeace; 14: © Great Vaughn/Tom Stack & Associates; 17: Connecticut Department of Economic Development; 18: Steve Delaney/EPA; 19: Grant Heilman Photography; 28: Diaf; 29: Marnie Crawford Samuelson.

Chapter 2
38: Paul Souders/Tony Stone Images; 44 (top): Chad Ehlers/Tony Stone Images; 44 (bottom): © Catherine Ursillo/Photo Researchers, Inc.; 45 (top): UPI/Corbis—Bettmann; 45 (bottom); Jon Riley/Tony Stone Images; 52: courtesy Stuart L. Shalat; 53: Reuters/Bettmann; 54: Andrew Sacks/Tony Stone Images; 57: © Mark Richards/PhotoEdit; 58: © Jon Riley/Tony Stone Images; 60: Paul Souders/Tony Stone Images; 61: John Kenneth Galbraith.

Chapter 3
64: Phyllis Lattner/Corbis—Bettmann; 66: © David R. Frazier Photolibrary; 69: © Clyde H. Smith/Tony Stone Images; 73 (top): Tom Pantages; 73 (bottom): © 1992 Terry Wold Studio; 74: © Jeff Greenberg/PhotoEdit; 75: TVA Washington Office and Tom Sweeten; 77: © David R. Frazier Photolibrary; 81: © Michael Newman; 83: © David R. Frazier Photolibrary; 84: © Tony Freeman/Photo Edit; 85: Corbis—Bettmann; 86: The Bettmann Archive, Inc.

Chapter 4
90: Pamela Carley; 91: Grant Heilman Photography; 98: © Spencer Grant/PhotoEdit; 100: Richard Kaylin/Tony Stone Images; 102: © Charles D. Winters/Photo Researchers, Inc.; 103 © Scott Markewitz/FPG International; 105: © Will & Deni McIntyre/Photo Researchers, Inc.; 106: Line drawing by Lucretia Brazeale Hamilton/University of Arizona Press; 109: © David R. Frazier Photolibrary; 112: Arnulf Husmo/Tony Stone Images; 114: Pamela Carley; 115: Corbis—Bettmann.

Chapter 5
120: © A. Ramey/PhotoEdit; 127: © Superstock; 129: © Tony Stone Images/Don Smetzer; 130: © D. YoungWolff/PhotoEdit; 133: © 1998 Terry Wilde Studio; 134: Peter Cade © Tony Stone Images; 136: © Mark Richards/PhotoEdit; 139: © A. Ramey/Photo Edit;

139: © D. YoungWolff/PhotoEdit; 140: Corbis—Bettmann.

Chapter 6
144: UPI/Corbis—Bettmann; 150: courtesy Chrysler Corporation; 155: USDA; 161: James L. Shaffer/© Dushkin/McGraw-Hill; 166: UPI/Corbis—Bettmann; 168: Corbis—Bettmann.

Chapter 7
172: © Stephen Simpson/FPG International; 179: courtesy StarKist Seafood Company; 185: © Tom Hollyman/Photo Researchers, Inc.; 187: Rosenfeld Images Ltd./Science Photo Library/Photo Researchers, Inc.; 197: © Stephen Simpson/FPG International; 199: New York Times Pictures.

Chapter 8
202: © Steve Grohe/The Picture Cube, Inc.; 206: The Bettmann Archive; 208: courtesy General Electric; 210: Pamela Carley; 211: © Kevin Horan/Picture Group; 223: © Steve Grohe/The Picture Cube, Inc.; 224: UPI/CorbisBettmann.

Chapter 9
228: Agence France Presse/Corbis—Bettmann; 237: Pamela Carley; 247: courtesy General Motors; 252: Agence France Presse/Corbis—Bettmann; 253: © Tom McHugh/Photo Researchers, Inc.

Chapter 10
258: © Tony Stone Images/Robert Gardner; 262: Pamela Carley; 266: UPI/Bettmann; 269: courtesy American Red Cross; 270: UN photo by Nagata; 281: © Tony Stone Images/Robert Gardner; 282: North Wind Picture Archives.

Chapter 11
286: Robert Neubecker; 291: © Tony Stone Images/Andy Sacks; 301: © Tony Stone Images/Ken Fisher; 305: Corbis; 310: Bob Firek/Old Dominion University, Office of Public Information; 311: UPI/Bettmann; 313: Robert Neubecker; 314: UPI/Bettmann.

Chapter 12
318: Cyberimage © Tony Stone Images; 323: © Dana White/PhotoEdit; 327: courtesy Busch Gardens; 333: Jeff Greenberg © David R. Frazier Photolibrary; 335: Corbis; 338: AP/Wide World; 344: Cyberimage © Tony Stone Images; 345: UPI/Bettmann.

Chapter 13
348: Margot Thompson/Three in a Box © J. Sohm/The Image Works; 356: Reuters/Corbis—Bettmann; 365: Monkmeyer/Greenberg; 371: Margot Thompson/Three in a Box © J. Sohm/The Image Works; 372: © Art Stein/Photo Researchers, Inc.

Chapter 14
376: © Michael A. Dwyer/Stock Boston; 382: © Mitch Kezar/Tony Stone Images, Inc.; 390: © David Ladd Nelson; 391: Kevin Horan © Tony Stone Images; 395: © Tony Stone Images/Peter Weber; 401: © Tony Stone Images/Jon Riley; 402: Rosenfeld Images Ltd./Science Photo Library/Photo Researchers, Inc.; 404: Troy Maben © David R. Frazier Photolibrary; 406: © Michael A. Dwyer/Stock Boston; 407: UPI/Bettmann.

Chapter 15
412: Derek Berwin/Image Bank; 417 (left): © David R. Frazier Photolibrary; 417 (right): © Bill Aron/PhotoEdit; 427: © Tony Stone Images/Glen Allizon; 429: Tony Stone Worldwide/Chicago Ltd. © Robert E. Daemmrich; 430: © Lee Snider/The Image Works; 431: © David R. Frazier Photolibrary; 435: © Superstock; 436: EPA/Documerica; 437: © Bill Bachman/Photo Researchers, Inc.; 438: Derek Berwin/Image Bank; 439: Library of Congress.

Chapter 16
442: Mike Eagle; 447: Joel Gordon; 452: Matthew Marlin; 454: Lee Page © Tony Stone Images; 455: © Mark C. Burnett/Photo Researchers, Inc.; 457: © Wesley Bocxe/Photo Researchers, Inc.; 459: © Rollin Geppert; 461: © Mark E. Gibson/Visuals Unlimited; 464: © Mike Eagle; 465: © Monkmeyer/LeDuc.

Chapter 17
468: © Bob Stern/The Image Works; 474 (left): P. Picardi/Stock Boston; 474 (right): © Adam Tanner/The Image Works; 480: © Tamas Revesz/Peter Arnold, Inc.; 484: © Patrick Ward/Stock Boston; 496: © Bob Stern/The Image Works; 497: North Wind Picture Archives.

Chapter 18
502: © Fritz Hoffmann/The Image Works; 507: © Still Pictures/Peter Arnold, Inc.; 511: © L. Dematteis/The Image Works; 516: © G. Schiff Zirinsky/Photo Researchers, Inc.; 523: © Jeff Greenberg/Visuals Unlimited; 527: © Fritz Hoffmann/The Image Works; 529: Corbis/Bettmann.